1 & 2 KINGS

THE NIV APPLICATION COMMENTARY

From biblical text . . . to contemporary life

1 & 2 KINGS

THE NIV
APPLICATION
COMMENTARY

From biblical text . . . to contemporary life

AUGUST H. KONKEL

ZONDERVAN.com/
AUTHORTRACKER
follow your favorite authors

We want to hear from you. Please send your comments about this book to us in care of zreview@zondervan.com. Thank you.

 ZONDERVAN®

The NIV Application Commentary: 1 & 2 Kings
Copyright © 2006 by August H. Konkel

Requests for information should be addressed to:

Zondervan, *Grand Rapids, Michigan 49530*

Library of Congress Cataloging-in-Publication Data

Konkel, August H.
    1 & 2 Kings / August H. Konkel.
        p. cm.—(NIV application commentary)
    Includes bibliographical references and indexes.
    ISBN-13: 978-0-310-21129-7
    ISBN-10: 0-310-21129-8
    1. Bible. O.T. 1 & 2 Kings—Commentaries. I. Title. II. Series.
  BS1335.53.K66 2006
                                        2006032090
                                                  CIP

This edition printed on acid-free paper.

The website addresses recommended throughout this book are offered as a resource to you. These websites are not intended in any way to be or imply an endorsement on the part of Zondervan, nor do we vouch for their content for the life of this book.

Printed in the United States of America

06 07 08 09 10 11 12 • 10 9 8 7 6 5 4 3 2 1

To Esther

כִּי אֵשֶׁה חַיִל אָתְּ

The NIV Application Commentary Series

When complete, the NIV Application Commentary
will include the following volumes:

Old Testament Volumes

Genesis, John H. Walton
Exodus, Peter Enns
Leviticus/Numbers, Roy Gane
Deuteronomy, Daniel I. Block
Joshua, Robert L. Hubbard Jr.
Judges/Ruth, K. Lawson Younger
1-2 Samuel, Bill T. Arnold
1-2 Kings, August H. Konkel
1-2 Chronicles, Andrew E. Hill
Ezra/Nehemiah, Douglas J. Green
Esther, Karen H. Jobes
Job, Dennis R. Magary
Psalms Volume 1, Gerald H. Wilson
Psalms Volume 2, Jamie A. Grant
Proverbs, Paul Koptak
Ecclesiastes/Song of Songs, Iain Provan
Isaiah, John N. Oswalt
Jeremiah/Lamentations, J. Andrew Dearman
Ezekiel, Iain M. Duguid
Daniel, Tremper Longman III
Hosea/Amos/Micah, Gary V. Smith
Jonah/Nahum/Habakkuk/Zephaniah,
  James Bruckner
Joel/Obadiah/Malachi, David W. Baker
Haggai/Zechariah, Mark J. Boda

New Testament Volumes

Matthew, Michael J. Wilkins
Mark, David E. Garland
Luke, Darrell L. Bock
John, Gary M. Burge
Acts, Ajith Fernando
Romans, Douglas J. Moo
1 Corinthians, Craig Blomberg
2 Corinthians, Scott Hafemann
Galatians, Scot McKnight
Ephesians, Klyne Snodgrass
Philippians, Frank Thielman
Colossians/Philemon, David E. Garland
1-2 Thessalonians, Michael W. Holmes
1-2 Timothy/Titus, Walter L. Liefeld
Hebrews, George H. Guthrie
James, David P. Nystrom
1 Peter, Scot McKnight
2 Peter/Jude, Douglas J. Moo
Letters of John, Gary M. Burge
Revelation, Craig S. Keener

To see which titles are available,
visit our web site at www.zondervan.com

Table of Contents

NIV Application Commentary
Series Introduction

THE NIV APPLICATION COMMENTARY SERIES is unique. Most commentaries help us make the journey from our world back to the world of the Bible. They enable us to cross the barriers of time, culture, language, and geography that separate us from the biblical world. Yet they only offer a one-way ticket to the past and assume that we can somehow make the return journey on our own. Once they have explained the *original meaning* of a book or passage, these commentaries give us little or no help in exploring its *contemporary significance*. The information they offer is valuable, but the job is only half done.

Recently, a few commentaries have included some contemporary application as *one* of their goals. Yet that application is often sketchy or moralistic, and some volumes sound more like printed sermons than commentaries.

The primary goal of the NIV Application Commentary Series is to help you with the difficult but vital task of bringing an ancient message into a modern context. The series not only focuses on application as a finished product but also helps you think through the *process* of moving from the original meaning of a passage to its contemporary significance. These are commentaries, not popular expositions. They are works of reference, not devotional literature.

The format of the series is designed to achieve the goals of the series. Each passage is treated in three sections: *Original Meaning, Bridging Contexts,* and *Contemporary Significance.*

THIS SECTION HELPS you understand the meaning of the biblical text in its original context. All of the elements of traditional exegesis—in concise form—are discussed here. These include the historical, literary, and cultural context of the passage. The authors discuss matters related to grammar and syntax and the meaning of biblical words.[1] They also seek to explore the main ideas of the passage and how the biblical author develops those ideas.

---

1. Please note that in general, when the authors discuss words in the original biblical languages, the series uses a general rather than a scholarly method of transliteration.

After reading this section, you will understand the problems, questions, and concerns of the *original audience* and how the biblical author addressed those issues. This understanding is foundational to any legitimate application of the text today.

THIS SECTION BUILDS a bridge between the world of the Bible and the world of today, between the original context and the contemporary context, by focusing on both the timely and timeless aspects of the text.

God's Word is *timely*. The authors of Scripture spoke to specific situations, problems, and questions. The author of Joshua encouraged the faith of his original readers by narrating the destruction of Jericho, a seemingly impregnable city, at the hands of an angry warrior God (Josh. 6). Paul warned the Galatians about the consequences of circumcision and the dangers of trying to be justified by law (Gal. 5:2–5). The author of Hebrews tried to convince his readers that Christ is superior to Moses, the Aaronic priests, and the Old Testament sacrifices. John urged his readers to "test the spirits" of those who taught a form of incipient Gnosticism (1 John 4:1–6). In each of these cases, the timely nature of Scripture enables us to hear God's Word in situations that were *concrete* rather than abstract.

Yet the timely nature of Scripture also creates problems. Our situations, difficulties, and questions are not always directly related to those faced by the people in the Bible. Therefore, God's word to them does not always seem relevant to us. For example, when was the last time someone urged you to be circumcised, claiming that it was a necessary part of justification? How many people today care whether Christ is superior to the Aaronic priests? And how can a "test" designed to expose incipient Gnosticism be of any value in a modern culture?

Fortunately, Scripture is not only timely but *timeless*. Just as God spoke to the original audience, so he still speaks to us through the pages of Scripture. Because we share a common humanity with the people of the Bible, we discover a *universal dimension* in the problems they faced and the solutions God gave them. The timeless nature of Scripture enables it to speak with power in every time and in every culture.

Those who fail to recognize that Scripture is both timely and timeless run into a host of problems. For example, those who are intimidated by timely books such as Hebrews, Galatians, or Deuteronomy might avoid reading them because they seem meaningless today. At the other extreme, those who are convinced of the timeless nature of Scripture, but who fail to discern its timely element, may "wax eloquent" about the Melchizedekian priest-hood to a sleeping congregation, or worse still, try to apply the holy wars of the Old Testament in a physical way to God's enemies today.

The purpose of this section, therefore, is to help you discern what is timeless in the timely pages of the Bible—and what is not. For example, how do the holy wars of the Old Testament relate to the spiritual warfare of the New? If Paul's primary concern is not circumcision (as he tells us in Gal. 5:6), what *is* he concerned about? If discussions about the Aaronic priesthood or Melchizedek seem irrelevant today, what is of abiding value in these passages? If people try to "test the spirits" today with a test designed for a specific first-century heresy, what other biblical test might be more appropriate?

Yet this section does not merely uncover that which is timeless in a passage but also helps you to see *how* it is uncovered. The authors of the commentaries seek to take what is implicit in the text and make it explicit, to take a process that normally is intuitive and explain it in a logical, orderly fashion. How do we know that circumcision is not Paul's primary concern? What clues in the text or its context help us realize that Paul's real concern is at a deeper level?

Of course, those passages in which the historical distance between us and the original readers is greatest require a longer treatment. Conversely, those passages in which the historical distance is smaller or seemingly nonexistent require less attention.

One final clarification. Because this section prepares the way for discussing the contemporary significance of the passage, there is not always a sharp distinction or a clear break between this section and the one that follows. Yet when both sections are read together, you should have a strong sense of moving from the world of the Bible to the world of today.

THIS SECTION ALLOWS the biblical message to speak with as much power today as it did when it was first written. How can you apply what you learned about Jerusalem, Ephesus, or Corinth to our present-day needs in Chicago, Los Angeles, or London? How can you take a message originally spoken in Greek, Hebrew, and Aramaic and communicate it clearly in our own language? How can you take the eternal truths originally spoken in a different time and culture and apply them to the similar-yet-different needs of our culture?

In order to achieve these goals, this section gives you help in several key areas.

(1) It helps you identify contemporary situations, problems, or questions that are truly comparable to those faced by the original audience. Because contemporary situations are seldom identical to those faced by the original audience, you must seek situations that are analogous if your applications are to be relevant.

(2) This section explores a variety of contexts in which the passage might be applied today. You will look at personal applications, but you will also be encouraged to think beyond private concerns to the society and culture at large.

(3) This section will alert you to any problems or difficulties you might encounter in seeking to apply the passage. And if there are several legitimate ways to apply a passage (areas in which Christians disagree), the author will bring these to your attention and help you think through the issues involved.

In seeking to achieve these goals, the contributors to this series attempt to avoid two extremes. They avoid making such specific applications that the commentary might quickly become dated. They also avoid discussing the significance of the passage in such a general way that it fails to engage contemporary life and culture.

Above all, contributors to this series have made a diligent effort not to sound moralistic or preachy. The NIV Application Commentary Series does not seek to provide ready-made sermon materials but rather tools, ideas, and insights that will help you communicate God's Word with power. If we help you to achieve that goal, then we have fulfilled the purpose for this series.

The Editors

General Editor's Preface

THE SEPARATION OF CHURCH AND STATE, a cornerstone of modern, religiously plural democracies, leaves unclear the relationship between prophet and king. The two books of Kings are crystal clear on the issue—the prophet has authority over the king.

To be sure, some present-day commentators are sure that modern Western democracies are clear on the relationship between prophet and king. The king (or president or prime minister or whatever the political ruler is called) rules. No ambiguity there, they say. Others demur.

Some of the confusion has to do with what is understood by the three terms in the phrase, "the prophet has authority over the king." What is a prophet? What is a king? What is authority? Some of the confusion can be traced to the different ways the biblical writer of 1 and 2 Kings understood these three terms and the way those of us in modern democratic pluralisms understand them.

The writer of Kings thought of a "prophet" as a charismatic person given a special message from God to present to a backsliding king of Israel. He considered a "king" a person anointed by God to politically rule over Israel. "Authority" was a kind of moral commitment and example on the part of either the prophet or king. The prophet, for example, demonstrated his "authority" by delivering his unpopular message from God to the king regardless of the danger or personal cost. The king, by contrast, demonstrated his authority by personal model—the people's character was represented by the king's character. When the king sinned, the people sinned; when the king was faithful and just, the people were considered faithful and just.

Part of the challenge facing Gus Konkel as he wrote this excellent commentary on these two biblical books is that none of these three terms is understood this way in modern (particularly Western), religiously plural democracies. We are faced with the classic commentator's challenge—how to bridge the difference in meaning between biblical times and contemporary times.

Who is a "prophet" today? Whereas biblical prophets were specially called individuals, the prophetic function today rests largely with the voice of the church. We sometimes still play with the idea of identifying individual prophets such as Martin Luther King and Billy Graham and Desmond Tutu—but our egalitarian leanings urge us toward the prophetic role of the entire church rather than special individuals.

Who is a "king" today? Whereas biblical kings ruled by law and God's anointing, political leaders in representative governments "rule" not by God's anointing but by making decisions based largely on the majority will of the people who elected them. Today's "kings" do occasionally exert "leadership" at odds with the so-called will of the people, but they tend not to stay in office long if they do.

What is "authority" today? The authority of political leaders does not rest in their personal willingness to and faithfulness in living a sanctified Christian life. I can feel all of you recoiling at the thought of having your character represented by Bill Clinton or George Bush. Yet we would be naïve to claim that the personal life and commitment of elected leaders has no "authority" in our lives. They have some constitutional authority and a great deal of what we might call "moral suasion," a platform from which their personal behavior and commitments influence countless young people looking for models.

And what of the authority of prophets? Of the rare individuals on whom we confer the title, too often they find themselves having to seek political power to change things, becoming politicians themselves in the process. More pertinent is the question of what is the authority of the church, today's prophetic voice. Unfortunately, we find a double standard operating. Officially we deny they have a role in a system dedicated to the separation of church and state. Unofficially, we play a role of moral suasion every bit as important as that exercised by our "kings."

People believe in and desire this unofficial relationship, much more than they do the official separation laws. Perhaps this implicit double standard is the way forward to make sure that the prophet always has a say in the work of the king. Perhaps making it more explicit would run us into dangers we have faced before of having the church overly involved in the politics of the world. But the message of 1–2 Kings is that no matter how we do it, the "prophet" must have a voice. God rules and we must tell the world of that fact.

Terry C. Muck

Author's Preface

A FREQUENT RESPONSIBILITY FOR ME as a minister was speaking at church retreats. On one such occasion the topic was faithfulness; a passage that intrigued me in this regard was the description of Hezekiah in 2 Kings 18:5–8. Hezekiah's faithfulness was uncompromising, even though the end of the story depicted his failure of faith (20:14–19). The story resonated as a genuine experience of the pilgrimage in learning to trust God, and it has continued to captivate my attention.

Many aspects of the Hezekiah story were difficult to unravel. Could Hezekiah really have been born when his father was just eleven years old (cf. 2 Kings 16:2; 17:1; 18:1–2)? How could Hezekiah have begun to reign in the time of King Hoshea of Israel if the siege of Sennacherib was fourteen years after Hezekiah began to reign (18:13), seven years after Hoshea's reign ended? Eventually I came to do a doctoral dissertation examining the Hezekiah story in all the biblical and Assyrian records.

My doctoral studies have led to a lifetime of study of the work of Kings, alongside Isaiah and Chronicles. I felt therefore particularly privileged when Tremper Longman III asked me to participate in this NIV Application Commentary series. In that regard, I am indebted to my lifelong mentor not only for the opportunity to participate in this project, but also for continuous progress in research, which involved numerous other publishing projects.

This commentary has been significantly enhanced through the review of John Walton, with his extensive knowledge of Ancient Near Eastern history and culture, and the editorial work of Verlyn Verbrugge, particularly in the Contemporary Significance sections. It was my desire to know more of the history and culture of biblical times that drove me to doctoral studies during my days as a pastor. By the grace of God, my doctoral studies were the beginning of a life-changing journey in understanding Scripture. I have always wanted to make the Bible a living Word to those who read it; they need to understand the social and historical contexts of its origins and to grasp how those issues might relate to contemporary times. The editors of this commentary have taught me much in that regard.

Students are one of the greatest contributors to growth in biblical knowledge. I wish to thank the students in my classes at Providence Theological Seminary in Manitoba who have stimulated, challenged, and informed my thinking over the last twenty years. Of particular note are those students who undertook the discipline of a thesis in which they researched topics of interest and importance.

The freedom to do biblical research can only happen with the support of family. In that regard, this book is dedicated to my wife, Esther, a tribute that love desires and is far less than debt requires. She has always been patient and understanding especially when what was needed was a great sacrifice of time and financial resources. She has not only been a constant encouragement, but has cheerfully and competently borne the task of caring for our four beautiful children. Melanie, Blythe, Theodore, and Tessa have been a joy and inspiration, a profound insight into God's design of creating us in his image. My family has not only provided much happiness, but also much significance in my work. God's story in this world is that of his name being glorified from generation to generation. Our two grandchildren, Liesl and Charis, have made that an existential truth for me, and it is profoundly gratifying.

In spite of its shortcomings, for which I alone remain responsible, it is my prayer this study may serve as a resource for pastors and teachers in years to come. May it be one of the ways in which the majesty of the name of God is proclaimed to all the earth.

August H. Konkel
July 2006

Abbreviations

AB	Anchor Bible
ABS	Archaeology and Biblical Studies
ABRL	Anchor Bible Reference Library
AOAT	Alter Orient und Altes Testament
ATD	Das Alte Testament Deutsch
AUSS	*Andrews University Seminary Studies*
BAR	*Biblical Archaeology Review*
BASOR	*Bulletin of the American School of Oriental Research*
BBR	*Bulletin for Biblical Research*
BHS	*Biblia Hebraica Stuttgartensia*
Bib	*Biblica*
BSac	*Bibliotheca Sacra*
BT	*The Bible Translator*
BWANT	Beiträge zur Wissenschaft vom Alten und Neuen Testament
CBOT	Coniectanea Biblica Old Testament Series
CC	Continental Commentary
DJD	Discoveries in the Judean Desert
DSD	*Dead Sea Discoveries*
EA	El Amarna tablets
ErIsr	*Eretz Israel*
ETL	*Ephermerides theologicae lovanienses*
FOTL	Forms of Old Testament Literature
GKC	Gesenius-Kautzsch-Cowley, *Gesenius' Hebrew Grammar*
HALAT	*Hebräisches und aramäisches Lexikon zum alten Testament*
HSM	Harvard Semitic Monographs
ICC	International Critical Commentary
IDB	*Interpreter's Dictionary of the Bible*
IDBSup	*Interpreter's Dictionary of the Bible, Supplement*
IEJ	*Israel Exploration Journal*
Int	*Interpretation*
ISBE	*International Standard Bible Encyclopedia*
JBL	*Journal of Biblical Literature*
JCS	*Journal of Cuneiform Studies*
JETS	*Journal of the Evangelical Theological Society*
JNES	*Journal of Near Eastern Studies*

Abbreviations

JNSL	*Journal of Northwest Semitic Languages*
JSOT	*Journal for the Study of the Old Testament*
JSOTSup	Journal for the Study of the Old Testament Supplements
KTU	*The Cuneiform Alphabetic Texts from Ugarit*
KJV	King James Version
LXX	Septuagint
NASB	New American Standard Bible
NCBC	New Century Bible Commentary
NEB	New English Bible
NIBC	New International Biblical Commentary
NIDOTTE	*New International Dictionary of Old Testament Theology and Exegesis*
NIV	New International Version
NIVAC	NIV Application Commentary
NLT	New Living Translation
NRSV	New Revised Standard Version
NSBT	New Studies in Biblical Theology
OBO	Orbis biblicus et orientalis
OTL	Old Testament Library
OtSt	*Oudtestamentische Studiën*
PEQ	*Palestine Exploration Quarterly*
RevExp	*Review and Expositor*
RIMA	The Royal Inscriptions of Mesopotamia, Assyrian Periods
RSV	Revised Standard Version
SBT	Studies in Biblical Theology
ScrHier	*Scripta Hierosolymitana*
SJOT	*Scandinavian Journal of the Old Testament*
SJT	*Scottish Journal of Theology*
TDOT	*Theological Dictionary of the Testament*
THAT	*Theologishes Handwörterbuch zum Alten Testament*
TOTC	Tyndale Old Testament Commentary
TrinJ	*Trinity Journal*
TS	*Theological Studies*
UF	*Ugarit-Forschungen*
VE	*Vox Evangelica*
VTSup	Vetus Testamentum Supplements
WBC	Word Biblical Commentary
ZAW	*Zeitschrift für die alttestamentliche Wissenschaft*

Introduction

THE HISTORY OF 1 AND 2 KINGS is a direct continuation of the account of the kingdom of David told in Samuel. The division between Samuel and Kings is somewhat artificial, as is evident in ancient editions of the books of Kings. The Greek translators of the books of Kings found the end of the book of Samuel at 1 Kings 2:11 in our Bibles.[1] This was a sensible division in the narrative, because that verse gives a summary of the reign of David from the time he was made king in Hebron (cf. 2 Sam. 5:1–5) until the time he died. This is comparable to the regular notations in the books of Kings, which provide summaries of the reign of a king at his death and then begin a new section with the introduction of the next king. The accession of Solomon was regarded as a continuation of the story of David's reign and introduced the narrative divisions in the manner typical of Kings. A break after 1 Kings 2:11 divides the long history of the kingdom, which began with Samuel and Saul, into two equal parts at a point where there is a natural division in the narrative. David has died, after a reign of forty years, seven in Hebron and thirty-three in Jerusalem.

It is also important to know that the Hebrew Bible adopts a different order of books than that familiar in the English Bible. The order of books in the English Bible has been largely influenced by early church tradition, which had the Old Testament in Greek and Latin translations. Complete Greek Bibles in book form (called a codex as opposed to a scroll) are known as early as the fourth century. The codex required that books be bound in a certain order. The Hebrews resisted the binding of their sacred scrolls in book form for centuries. The oldest Hebrew codices come from approximately A.D. 900, but as early as the first century the order of the Hebrew canon is partially known from the writings of Josephus.[2] His threefold division of the Hebrew Scriptures as the

---

1. See Appendix A on the Greek text of Kings.

2. In an apologetic work to the Gentiles, Josephus provides an identification of the Jewish Scriptures. "From the death of Moses until the time of Artaxerxes, the king of Persia succeeding Xerxes, the prophets after Moses recorded the events of their own times in thirteen books. The remaining four books contain hymns to God and precepts for human life" (*Against Apion*, 1.37–43). The exact number of books intended by Josephus and their order must be inferred. In his *Antiquities*, Josephus indicates that seven prophetical books were Joshua, Kings, Isaiah, Jeremiah, Ezekiel, the Minor Prophets, and Daniel; the succession of prophetic books after Moses would require Judges and Samuel to follow Joshua. Further detail is provided by Roger Beckwith, *The Old Testament Canon of the New Testament Church and its Background in Early Judaism* (Grand Rapids: Eerdmans, 1985), 79.

writings of Moses, the prophets after Moses, and the hymns is also found in the New Testament (see Luke 24:44). The standard order of the Hebrew Scriptures came to be Joshua, Judges, Samuel, and Kings as "the Former Prophets."

The church largely ignored the Hebrew Scriptures until the time of the Reformation. Origen in the third century did an elaborate comparison of the Greek Bible with the Hebrew (the Hexapla), and Jerome in the fourth century consciously used the Hebrew to assist in his revision of the Latin. However, influence on the Greek and Latin Scriptures was minimal, as is evident from the text of the Old Testament and the continuous use of the Apocrypha as part of the Scriptures—writings that were never used as part of the canonical books by the Hebrews. The Reformers went back to the Hebrew Scriptures for their translations and commentaries and regarded the Apocrypha as outside the canon. Their work gave new shape to the Scriptures, which came to be much more widely distributed because of the advancement of printing, but they never went back to the order of the Hebrew Scriptures in their publications of the Bible.

The result is that most contemporary readers of the English Bible read Kings more in association with Chronicles and Ezra-Nehemiah-Esther than they do with Joshua, Judges, and Samuel. The continuous narrative of Deuteronomy through Kings tends to be somewhat compromised and the many literary associations minimized. Kings also tends to be read as history in a more modern sense of the term rather than as prophecy, which was the way it was regarded in Hebrew. The books of the Former Prophets have much in common with the Latter Prophets. Both are concerned with the preaching of the prophets to the people bound to God by their covenant at Mount Sinai. The Former Prophets begin with the entrance to the Promised Land and end with the Exile, while the Latter Prophets begin with the demise of the kingdom of Israel (Amos, Hosea, Isaiah, and Micah) and end with the restoration during the time of Ezra-Nehemiah (Haggai, Zechariah, and Malachi).

There is a chronological overlap of about two hundred years as well as an overlap in content. The account of Hezekiah (2 Kings 18:17–20:19) is found almost word for word in Isaiah (Isa. 36:1–39:8), which is a prominent example of the influence of the prophet Isaiah in Jerusalem. The Latter Prophets are a prophetic analysis of the way God was at work in the history of the people, just as the Former Prophets. The basic difference is that the Former Prophets are more chronological in their presentation, while the Latter Prophets are anthologies.

Historical Progression in the Former Prophets

THE FORMER PROPHETS must not be read as straightforward chronological progression relating God's judgment on political events from Conquest to Exile.

The book of Joshua shows how God gave the land to the Israelites, a process that took much longer than the lifetime of Joshua (cf. Josh. 13:1). The book of Judges repeats events from Joshua in showing how the Israelites became Canaanite once they were in the land. The main point is that there was initial covenant faithfulness while Joshua was alive (Josh. 24:28–31), but that apostasy began once the leader had died (Judg. 2:6–10). The repetition of the death of Joshua distinguishes the purposes of the writings, which overlap in events they report. Samuel tells of David's rise to the throne after the death of Saul (2 Sam. 2:1–5:5) and gives a summary of David's reign (8:1–18). The narrative then returns to the earlier part of David's reign and the sin with Bathsheba, which led to continual conflict in David's household (11:1–12:12). That struggle did not end until David's death; Kings begins with the conflict for the throne between Solomon and Adonijah. This is the conclusion of the succession of David, a narrative that followed the description of David's reign.

The book of Kings follows the same pattern of emphasizing those events that were critical in the destiny of the nation. One of the most powerful and influential kings in ancient Israel was Omri, whose reign is related in a mere six verses (1 Kings 16:23–28). The achievements of Omri are known through various Assyrian records,[3] which also provide a reference for an absolute chronology of the kings of Israel. Omri established a dynasty in Israel that was continued by Ahab (1 Kings 16:29), Ahaziah (22:52), and Joram (2 Kings 3:1). The dynasty came to a violent end with the revolt of Jehu, who killed all the seventy sons of Ahab in Samaria and every last survivor of the house of Omri (10:1–17). Ahab is named in the Aramean coalition against the Assyrians in the battle of Qarqar in 853 B.C.[4] The beginning of the reign of Jehu is known from the reference to him on the Assyrian Black Obelisk, which can be dated to 841.[5]

The account of the dynasty of Omri, which lasted about forty years, occupies fifteen chapters in Kings, or about one third of the total narrative,

---

3. References may be readily consulted in James B. Pritchard, ed., *An Anthology of Texts and Pictures* (vol. 1 of *The Ancient Near East* [Princeton: Princeton Univ. Press, 1958]). Shalmaneser III (858–824 B.C.) refers to Jehu as a son of Omri in a fragmentary annalistic text of his eighteenth year (p. 191); also on the Black Obelisk Jehu is shown prostrate before the Assyrian king presenting tribute.

4. Pritchard, *An Anthology of Texts and Pictures*, 190. The battle at Qarqar is regarded as one of the few absolute dates in the history of Israel; see Gösta W. Ahlström, *The History of Ancient Palestine* (Minneapolis: Fortress, 1993), 577; J. A. Brinkman, "A Further Note on the Date of the Battle of Qarqar and the Neo-Assyrian Chronology," *JCS* 30 (1978): 173–75.

5. The Aramean coalition took place in the sixth year of Shalmaneser III according to the "Monolith Inscriptions" (Pritchard, *An Anthology of Texts and Pictures*, 189–90), and tribute was received from Jehu in the eighteenth year of the Assyrian king (ibid., 191–92).

which covers four hundred years. This disproportion is understandable in a prophetic work like Kings. The burden of Kings is to show the reason for the Exile, which was the violation of the covenant of Mount Sinai, through alliances and the worship of the Canaanite god Baal. The reign of Ahab was characterized by his alliance with the Phoenicians through his marriage to Jezebel. It was the most prominent example of the proliferation of the evils of the Baal cult, and the efforts of the prophets to counter such an influence were at peril to their own lives. This short period of time characterized the dangers of a foreign religion, a central concern of the prophetic writing of Kings.

It must further be observed that within this period of two generations the events do not appear to be arranged in chronological succession. Kings tells us of the ascension of Elijah (2 Kings 2:1) before the alliance of Joram king of Israel, Jehoshaphat king of Judah, and the king of Edom against the Moabite king (3:1–27). Chronicles tells us of the death of Jehoshaphat, the accession of his son Jehoram (2 Chron. 21:1), and the revolt of the king of Edom (21:8–10a). After this Elijah sends wicked Jehoram a severe letter (21:12–15), warning him of an awful death because he assassinated his brothers and followed in the ways of Ahab. If we accept the chronology of Edom offered within Kings, the Elijah–Elisha stories are not placed in chronological order.[6] Rather this cycle of stories serves as examples of prophetic activity in the midst of apostasy. As a prophetic work, the narrative of Kings shows the faithfulness of God and the disaster of the failure to keep the covenant.

Prophetic Character of Kings

THE STUDY IN HISTORICAL TRADITIONS by Martin Noth drew attention to the continuous narrative that extends from Deuteronomy through Kings.[7] Noth believed that this lengthy account of the whole history of Israel was originally the creation of a single writer who was both author and editor, bringing together material from highly varied traditions and arranging it according to a carefully conceived plan. He assumed that this author lived in the Exile, since that is the end point of the books of Kings. The novelty of Noth's model was not in the perception of the continuity of these books or in the observation of their being edited in a style conforming to Deuteronomy.

---

6. Various approaches to this chronological discrepancy will be taken up in the commentary.

7. M. Noth, *Überlieferungsgeschichtliche Studien: Die sammelnden und bearbeitenden Geschichtswerke im Alten testament*, 3rd ed. (Tübingen: J. C. B. Mohr, 1967); this work is translated as *The Deuteronomistic History* (JSOTSup 15; Sheffield: Sheffield Academic Press, 1981).

Rather, Noth believed that the original work of Deuteronomy through Kings was a continuous whole that was only later divided into books.

The influential study of Noth dramatically altered the scholarly conception of the earliest histories of the nation Israel. Joshua, Judges, Samuel, and Kings came to be recognized as continuous by design; they were not a patchwork created from two or more previous histories (sources) going back to Mosaic times. It became common to speak of a Deuteronomistic History in reference to the Former Prophets and to speak of the writers as the Deuteronomistic Historians. It should be noted that what Noth called the Deuteronomic History is not the present form of the Former Prophets, but an original composition found within these writings.[8] Noth found numerous later additions to the original work, some of them quite large (e.g., Joshua 13–22), but he made no attempt to relate them to each other or to the systematic revisions of later editors. Since Noth a great deal of study has been devoted to authorship and date of the composition process; it is usually assumed that there were at least two stages in the Deuteronomistic History: one at the time of Josiah, and one during the Exile.

Prophetic Speeches

NOTH CORRECTLY OBSERVED the important role that speeches play in the narrative of Israel. In the course of the history a leading person is introduced with a speech, long or short, which looks forward and backward in an attempt to interpret the course of events and draws the relevant practical conclusions.[9] At the beginning of the book of Joshua, after the introductory challenge of God, Joshua addresses the tribes east of the Jordan, outlining their responsibility in the task of occupation until Yahweh gives rest to all the rest of the tribes (1:12–15). Rest becomes a theological term for the fulfillment of the promise of inheritance of the land (cf. Deut. 3:20; 12:9–10; Josh. 21:44; 22:4; 23:1; 2 Sam. 7:1, 11; 1 Kings 5:18). Joshua gives a long solemn speech formulating critical instructions for conduct in the land they have come to possess (Josh. 23). This speech initiates the transition to the time period of the judges of Israel.

The books of Joshua and Judges are conscious contrasts of faithfulness to the covenant. Joshua tells of how the land of Canaan became the land of Israel under the leadership of Joshua because the people were faithful (Josh. 24:28–31). Judges is the account of how the land of Israel became Canaanite because

---

8. The term *Deuteronomistic* has come to be used of all those writings related to the Deuteronomic History. It is not the objective of this commentary to distinguish such stages of composition. In this work the term *Deuteronomistic History* will be used consistently to refer to all the writings of the Former Prophets.

9. Noth, *The Deuteronomistic History*, 5–6.

of the failure of the people to keep the covenant (Judg. 2:6–10). The failure of the judges was a failure of leadership; there was no king in Israel (17:6; 18:1; 19:1; 21:25). The transition to kings is introduced by a lengthy speech by the prophet Samuel (1 Sam. 12). The people are gathered to learn the lessons of past history and are admonished to be faithful in this new opportunity (12:20–25). Finally, after the completion of the temple in Jerusalem, Solomon gives a long speech in the form of a prayer (1 Kings 8:14–53), expounding the significance of the temple and emphasizing the importance of prayer and forgiveness for their failures. These speeches are prophetic admonitions and instructions to the three major periods of the history of Israel.

There are other summarizing reflections on the history presented as part of the narrative. Joshua provides a summary of the occupation of the land (Josh. 12); the cyclical and degenerative cycles of the judges are introduced with a description of covenant violation and judgment in spite of repeated divine intervention in mercy (Judg. 2:11–19). In the introduction of the well-known story of Gideon and the Midianites, an unnamed prophet provides the explanation for the devastation of their land (6:7–10); in the typical vocabulary and style of Deuteronomy this prophet rehearses the basic message of God's redemption and Israel's rebellion. This is an example of the retrospective reflection given for the grim outcome of the monarchic period in Israel and Judah (2 Kings 17:7–23). Yahweh had warned Israel and Judah through all his prophets (v. 13) to turn from their evil ways; their refusal to do so had led to their Exile, just as the prophets had said (v. 23).

The emphasis in this prophetic history is the voice of God, which manifests itself in the covenant requirements of integrity in relationships, with both God and people. As Noth pointed out, it is remarkable that there is no concern for the actual practice of the temple rituals, even after the dedication of the temple by Solomon.[10] There is, of course, an acknowledgment that sacrifices were a part of the customary form of worship, but the focus of the whole is on the practice of covenant requirements.

Covenant Obligation

THE ESSENTIALS OF COVENANT instruction are found in what Deuteronomy refers to as "this law." This expression is found eighteen times in Deuteronomy, most of them in the concluding chapters on maintaining the covenant (Deut. 27–32). The introduction to Deuteronomy makes clear that "this law" is the content of the book itself (1:5; 4:44–45), the teaching of Moses in Moab just before the entrance of Israel into the Promised Land. "This law" stands as the envy of all the nations (4:8), who may observe the wisdom of

---

10. Ibid., 6, 93.

the ways of the people that follow it. It is further described as "the covenant written in the book of this law" (29:21). The renewal of the covenant at Shechem (between Mount Ebal and Mount Gerizim) is a solemn oath to observe the teaching of the law written out before them (27:3, 8). Grievous curses rest on all those who fail to maintain this law (7:26; 28:58, 61).

The essence of the covenant is to reverence Yahweh exclusively. The covenant is the voice of God written in "the book of this law" (Deut. 30:10); their God demands uncompromising devotion of their mind and desire (cf. 6:1–6). The words of the covenant are to be kept with the ark (31:25–26) as a permanent testimony to their oath of commitment. The priests as the custodians of this book of the law are responsible to renew the covenant every seven years (31:9–13); they review its teaching to all the assembly (women, children, and the sojourners are included), gathered at the Feast of Booths.

According to Deuteronomy, the book of this law is the particular responsibility of the king, whom Yahweh will choose. When they come to the land, they are to install their king in accordance with the divine choice (Deut. 17:15). The king is required to make a copy of "this law" from the book, which is in the charge of the priests (v. 18), and the king must read it regularly, so he will learn to reverence Yahweh and learn to observe its requirements (v. 19). The king is one with his brothers in the requirement of subservience to the covenant, but the king is responsible to ensure that the practice of the covenant is carried out in the regulations of the kingdom. This becomes the sole criterion of evaluation applied to each of the kings of Israel and Judah in the history written about them.

Deuteronomistic Theology

IN A DETAILED AND COMPREHENSIVE STUDY, Moshe Weinfeld has identified nine theological tenets found in the Deuteronomistic presentation of history:[11] (1) the struggle against idolatry; (2) the centralization of the place of worship; (3) exodus, covenant, and election; (4) the monotheistic creed; (5) observance of the law and loyalty to the covenant; (6) inheritance of the land; (7) retribution and material motivation; (8) fulfillment of prophecy; (9) the election of the Davidic dynasty. All of these tenets are articulated in jargon that is distinctly Deuteronomistic.[12]

---

11. M. Weinfeld, *Deuteronomy and the Deuteronomic School* (Oxford: Clarendon, 1972), 1.

12. In a lengthy appendix (ibid., 320–55), Weinfeld lists subordinate themes to these nine tenets and the phraseology distinct to each of them. This is not to suggest these are new idioms and expressions, for language grows in an organic and natural manner and cannot be created artificially. The novelty of Deuteronomistic phraseology is its use in articulating a specific view of the religious upheavals of the time.

The kings of Israel and Judah are the chosen heirs of the covenant and the land. Their loyalty to the covenant is measured in terms of absolute allegiance to Yahweh; this exclusivity is unlike that of all the other religions, and it is a standard that is impossible to achieve (Josh. 24:16–20). The Israelites will constantly adopt the level of loyalty required by Canaanite gods, they will compromise their worship of Yahweh, and they will suffer the consequent judgment. The judgment passed on kings is not an evaluation of achievements and failures. The prophets are not concerned with good and evil actions, but with the one fundamental decision on which salvation and judgment depend. In the end the nation will fall, but the work of God will not fail.

The catastrophes of the exile of Israel (722 B.C.) and of Judah (586 B.C.) are of the most profound theological significance. The theological interpretation of these events is that Israel has cumulated an ever-increasing burden of guilt and faithlessness until at last Yahweh leaves his people to the ultimate judgment. This results in a considerable perplexity about the future of saving history. David was promised that the kingdom of God would be realized through an eternal dynasty of his descendants (2 Sam. 7:12–17). The grace of God was a mitigating factor for covenant failures, but there were limits. The fate of the kingdom of Israel was determined by the abomination of Jeroboam in setting up the calves at Dan and Bethel (1 Kings 14:16). In spite of this the kingdom continued for another two centuries. Even so wicked a king as Ahab humbled himself at the word of judgment (21:29), so the judgment on his house was not fulfilled in his lifetime.

During the times of severe oppression by the Arameans, Yahweh showed mercy and granted reprieve for the sake of his covenant (2 Kings 13:23; 14:25–26). The one enduring hope was the promise to David, a promise passed on to Solomon by David (1 Kings 2:4). In his prayer at the consecration of the temple, Solomon declared this promise to have been realized (8:20), though it was followed with a prayer acknowledging the condition of covenant obedience (vv. 25–26). Solomon himself followed the ways of the Sidonians (11:5–6), so the kingdom was taken from him, though for the sake of David one tribe remained (11:11–13, 32, 36). This promise was repeated to Abijah (15:4), the faithless successor to Rehoboam.

David is the model of covenant loyalty and integrity in the history of Kings,[13] the one who is worthy to receive the promise of the eternal dynasty. The dynasty of David survives in Judah, but in the end Judah does not survive. The survival of the nation has been conditional to keeping the covenant. The future of an eternal dynasty is left in tension with the demise of the temporal kingdom.

---

13. 1 Kings 9:4; 11:4, 6, 33, 38; 14:8; 15:5, 11; 2 Kings 14:3; 16:2; 18:3; 21:7; 22:2.

The promise of the eternal dynasty had its roots in the covenant of Sinai and in the promise to the patriarchs.[14] David was the servant of God (2 Sam. 7:5), in the manner of Moses (cf. Josh. 1:2, 7), and received rest (2 Sam. 7:1, 11), just as Moses had led the people into rest (Josh. 1:13, 15; 23:1). The divine obligation of the promise is not dependent on the human obligation to keep the covenant.[15] The demise of the nations of Israel and Judah is the consequence of covenant violation, but this does not annul the promise, which will be realized in a new covenant. The new covenant (Jer. 31:31–34) needs to be of a different order; it cannot simply be the nation being given another opportunity to fulfill the covenant responsibility.[16] In the dying days of the city of Jerusalem the prophet Jeremiah holds out the hope that God will supply the fundamental change required in the hearts of the people.

The transformation of the people will be entirely an act of divine grace; it will be the means of the divine promise coming to fruition. This hope is not explicit in the story of the nation as related in Kings; essentially it falls outside the scope of the history of the nation, since its realization will not be in nationalistic terms. At the same time the eternal promise to David is prominent in the account of the history of the nation and is one of the important tenets of the intellectual form in which the nation understands its significance and its corporate identity.

Prophetic Activity

IN THE CHRONICLES OF THE KINGS, the prophets are responsible to hold the kings accountable to maintain the covenant. They appear chiefly as opponents of the kings, to confront the rulers who are apostates, or inclined to become apostate, with an unambiguous statement of the word and will of God. The narratives of the prophets account for a considerable amount of the material in Kings; most notable are the stories of Elijah and Elisha (1 Kings 17–2 Kings 8) and the prophecy of Isaiah in the Assyrian crisis (2 Kings 18–21). Though other prophets are not as prominent, their role is no less significant.

The division of the kingdom begins with Jeroboam the son of Nebat, who becomes the prototype for the covenant failure of the kings of Israel (1 Kings 16:26, 31, etc.), but the division of the kingdom takes place under the direction of the prophet Ahijah of Shiloh (11:29). Jeroboam is enlisted

---

14. D. J. McCarthy, "II Samuel 7 and the Structure of the Deuteronomic History," *JBL* 84 (1965): 131–38.

15. D. N. Freedman, "Divine Commitment and Human Obligation," *Int* 18 (1964): 419–31.

16. A. H. Konkel, "Hezekiah in Biblical Tradition" (Ph.D. diss.; Philadelphia: Westminster Theological Seminary, 1987), 138–40.

in the service of Solomon as responsible for transportation of goods (v. 28). He revolts against Solomon and is forced to flee to Egypt (11:26; 12:2), but it is likely that he is encouraged in his rebellion by the prophet Ahijah. Ahijah declares that ten tribes will be given to Jeroboam (11:30–33) because of the failure of Israel to keep the covenant. The refusal of Rehoboam to conciliate the people and the successful coup of Jeroboam is part of the divine purpose (12:15), as spoken by the prophet. But Jeroboam leads the ten tribes into apostasy with the establishment of the calves at Dan and Bethel (12:26–31). The message of the prophet Ahijah to him is not only that his sick son will die, but also that the rule of his house will come to an end (14:10–11).

Another prophet, Micaiah son of Imlah (1 Kings 22:8), is summoned at the request of Jehoshaphat when Ahab is seeking his help to recapture Ramoth Gilead from the Syrians. Micaiah prophesies that Ahab has been lured into his own death by lying prophets (22:19–23). Ahab has him thrown into prison (v. 26), but the word of the prophet is fulfilled in that the king is killed in battle in spite of his efforts to disguise himself (vv. 37–38).

Prophetic Fulfillment

THE FULFILLMENT OF PROPHECY is thus one of the central themes of the books of Kings. The word of Yahweh concerning the requirement of the covenant is clear, although at times the summary judgment is given in general terms, simply saying that the king did not comply with the covenant requirement completely (1 Kings 11:4; 15:3, 14). With this determinative principle there is the certain efficacy of the word of God, which does not fail but is invariably fulfilled.[17] Ahijah tells Jeroboam that his family will be terminated (14:10–11), an event that is noted as fulfilled when the usurper Baasha destroys the royal house (15:29). The judgment against Jeroboam finds its ultimate fulfillment in the end of the nation of Israel (14:15–16).[18] An unknown prophet at Bethel specifically tells the idolatrous Jeroboam that a descendant of David named Josiah will kill the priests of his altar and burn human bones on it (13:1–3); this is fulfilled when Josiah purges the cultic places (2 Kings 23:16–18).

---

17. This point was developed by Gerhard von Rad in *Deuteronium Studien* (Göttingen: Vandenhoek & Ruprecht, 1948), translated as *Studies in Deuteronomy* (London: SCM, 1953), 78–82.

18. For developments in the promise-fulfillment motif see Helga Weippert, "Geschichten und Geschichte: Verheissung und Erfüllung im deuteronomistischen Geschichtswerk," in *Congress Volume: Leuven, 1989,* ed. J. A. Emerton (VTSup 43; Leiden: Brill, 1991), 116–31. Promise-fulfillment is present in all genres, in different periods, and spans greater and lesser stretches of text.

Some of the fulfillments are in reference to prophetic words antecedent to Kings. Joshua placed a curse upon Jericho, saying that anyone who rebuilt it would do so at the cost of an eldest and youngest son (Josh. 6:26); in disregard of this, Ahab incites an individual named Hiel of Bethel to rebuild it, with the result that he suffers precisely the penalty prescribed (1 Kings 16:34). On the positive side, Yahweh has determined the temple will be built by a son of David (2 Sam. 7:13), an achievement brought about by Solomon (1 Kings 8:20). Deuteronomistic theology views history as a fulfillment of the will of the Lord and therefore can be announced by the prophetic word. This prophetic word is not so much predictive as declarative of the requirement of the covenant and the consequences of failing to observe it.

Kings as Ancient History Writing

THE HISTORY OF THE BIBLE embodies a variety of incidental detail, but its central issues are the larger questions of life and destiny. As Speiser points out, the Bible is not so much a chronicle of events worth recording, or thought to be worth recording, as it is an interpretation of significant happenings. Thus it is essentially a "philosophy of history,"[19] with the purpose demonstrating a divinely ordained way of life. Its central theme is the quest of a life worth living, and if need be, worth dying for. The Scriptures are never intended to be a mere history of events or the biography of a nation.[20] The reader interested in such things is told where to find them, such as the "Book of the Wars of the LORD" (Num. 21:14), the "Book of Jashar" (Josh. 10:13), the "book of the annals of the kings of Israel" (1 Kings 14:19), and the "book of the annals of the kings of Judah" (2 Kings 23:28). The purpose of the Deuteronomistic History is to tell the story of a society in search of an enduring way of life, a life of universal validity.

It is important to define the concept of history. A concept of history is not an effort to set up scientific criteria by which writing may qualify as history, and not all literary forms dealing with the past can be classified as histories. The noted Dutch historian Johan Huizinga has defined history as "the intellectual form in which a civilization renders account to itself of its past."[21] The "intellectual form" of writing about the past may be referred to as history

---

19. E. A. Speiser, "The Biblical Idea of History in Its Common Near Eastern Setting," in *The Jewish Expression*, ed. Judah Goldin (New York: Bantam, 1970), 2.

20. Ibid., 7.

21. Johan Huizinga, "A Definition of the Concept of History," in *Philosophy and History: Essays Presented to Ernst Cassirer*, ed. R. Klibansky and H. J. Paton (Oxford: Clarendon, 1936), 9.

writing.[22] Rendering an account of the past requires an assessment of responsibility for past actions, passing judgment on them and showing their consequences for the present state of affairs. A civilization rendering an account of its past provides a corporate identity. It expresses what a nation is and what it stands for; it shows the essential character of the people and evaluates their actions.

This definition of history distinguishes it from other forms of writing about the past. Historiography is a more inclusive category for all writings about the past, which may be incorporated in the task of history writing.[23] History writing is corporate in character, considers the reasons for recalling the past and the significance given to past events, and plays a significant role in the tradition of the people.

The history of Kings, in which the respective histories of the kingdoms of Israel and Judah are portrayed in a synchronistic patchwork, may have been influenced by Babylonian historiography.[24] Mazar is surely correct in contending that this biblical history "has no peer for concise and persuasive expression, for the presentation of a clear picture of historical evolution, and for the evaluation of those personalities who have appeared on the stage of history."[25] The authors of Joshua through 2 Kings gathered material from stories, records, and royal chronicles to produce a work with structure and unity.

The history of Kings is presented in the form of a narrative. Since narrative is a literary creation, the credibility of the Scriptures as representing the events of the past has come under severe attack. Skeptical of narrative histories in general, various scholars have argued that little relation can exist between "biblical Israel" and "the Israel of the Iron Age."[26] While not all history writing is narrative, and certainly not all narrative is historiography, narrative is an important means of portraying history. Literature and history cannot be regarded as unrelated or mutually exclusive categories.[27] Historical narrative is not the mere statement of discrete facts but is the creation of a sequence of events to depict past reality. Such history writing is not mere invention, since it is not possible to construct the past in just any way at all.

22. John van Seters, *In Search of History: Historiography in the Ancient World and the Origins of Biblical History* (Winona Lake, Ind.: Eisenbrauns, 1997), 1.
23. Ibid., 2.
24. B. Maisler (= B. Mazar), "Ancient Israelite Historiography," *IEJ* 2 (1952): 84.
25. Ibid., 82.
26. N. P. Lemche, *The Israelites in History and Tradition* (Library of Ancient Israel; Louisville: Westminster John Knox, 1998), 166. The same skepticism is shared by P. R. Davies, *In Search of Ancient Israel* (JSOTSup 148; Sheffield: Sheffield Academic Press, 1992).
27. See especially I. W. Provan, "Ideologies, Literary and Critical: Reflections on Recent Writing on the History of Israel," *JBL* 114 (1995): 585–606.

Biblical historiography is in its own way as sophisticated as early modern history writing.[28] It distinguishes between individuals, groups, and nationalities; it understands actions as motivated by greed, jealousy, and power; it attempts to present conjunctions of events by indicating simultaneous sequences.[29] Events of the past are presented out of a sense that significant lessons can be learned from the past and applied to the time of writing. The partially accessible past of human interactions is broken down into causes and effects. The repetitive patterns of major events are explained in terms of divine causality.

Literary creation and religious imagination are joined in history in biblical narrative such as that of Kings, because it purports to be accounts of things that happened in historical time.[30] It becomes obvious that *"literary understanding is a necessary condition of historical understanding, and both literary and historical understanding are necessary conditions of competent biblical interpretation."*[31] The questions historians should ask, in understanding a narrative such as Kings, are similar to the questions that literary readers should ask.[32] The task includes the identification of the hero and his quest, observing the role of the narrator and the dialogues, and following the plot and the development of the narrative structure. Attending to the literary elements of historical narrative is necessary to understanding the medium through which the lessons of history are given.

The Process of History Writing

UNLIKE THE FIFTH-CENTURY historian Herodotus, whose writings to explain the Persian wars earned him the reputation among later Greek historians as the "father of history," the writings of the Former Prophets were left anonymous. Any knowledge of the time and circumstances of the writings must be inferred by literary analysis. Van Seters has proposed that the

> analogue to Herodotus in the Old Testament would be the Deuteronomistic Historian of Joshua to 2 Kings, seen not simply as a redactor of previously compiled blocks of material—the end of a long and complex tradio-historical process—but rather as a historian who

---

28. Ziony Zevit, *The Religions of Ancient Israel: A Synthesis of Parallactic Approaches* (New York: Continuum, 2001), 80.

29. S. Talmon, "The Presentation of Synchroneity and Simultaneity in Biblical Narrative," *ScrHier* 27 (1978): 9–26.

30. Robert Alter in "Introduction to the Old Testament," ed. R. Alter and F. Kermode, *The Literary Guide to the Bible* (Cambridge, Mass.: Belknap Press of Harvard Univ., 1987), 17.

31. Ian Provan, V. Philips Long, and Tremper Longman III, *A Biblical History of Israel* (Louisville: Westminster John Knox, 2003), 81 (italics theirs).

32. Ibid., 88–91.

gathered his own material, much of it in the form of disparate oral stories, but some from records and from the royal chronicles.[33]

Like Herodotus, the prose narrative within Joshua through Kings is made up of larger and smaller units in a loosely connected chain with little subordination of major and minor themes. Similar episodes are associated by analogy with interpretive introductions and summary statements rather than arranged in temporal or logical sequence.[34] Like Noth, van Seters believes that the original Deuteronomistic History was the creation of a single individual, but since it was anonymous, it has suffered the ignomiy of being fractured into canonical books and, worse yet, of being hopelessly dissected into collections and redactions by modern scholars.

Van Seters regards the Deuteronomistic History as the first Hebrew example of "history writing," that is, the conscious development of a national history with the purpose of providing a self-identity. There were various historiographic writings before this time, that is, other writings about past events that were a resource for this history writing. These would have included chronologies of events developed from king lists, royal inscriptions such as dedications or memorial texts, and chronicles that portrayed particular historical events. He disputes the presence of early historiographic works such as the "Story of Saul," the "Story of David's Rise," and the "Court History" or "Succession Story" (2 Sam. 9–20; 1 Kings 1:1–2:46)[35] during the early period of the kingdom of David and Solomon.

Joshua through Kings does not make a claim to being the work of one individual and has not been preserved in a form in which it is the work of one individual. Van Seters believes that a history was produced in the exilic period to provide a national identity for Israel by developing an ideology in which kings and people needed to be obedient to the covenant of Moses. It must be asked why such a history would first be produced in the Exile.[36] Most notable

---

33. Van Seters, *In Search of History*, 17.

34. Ibid., 35–39.

35. Since the study of L. Rost, *Die Überlieferung von der Thronnachfolge Davids* (BWANT 3/6; Stuttgart: Kohlhammer, 1926), this has been regarded as one of the most cohesive sources or previously written histories. The note on the establishment of the kingdom in the hands of Solomon (2 Kings 2:46) appears to be the conclusion of a self-contained tradition about the successor to David's throne. R. N. Whybray, *The Succession Narrative: A Study of II Samuel 9–20; I Kings 1 and 2* (SBT 2/9; Naperville-London: Allenson, 1968) offers additional evidence for such a history. However its role as a separate literary unit is rightly disputed by other notable historians; see Ahlström, *The History of Ancient Palestine*, 490–91; Mordechai Cogan, *1 Kings: A New Translation with Introduction and Commentary* (AB 10; New York: Doubleday, 2001), 166.

36. This is an improvement over Noth's proposal, that the writing was to show the word of God fulfilled in the Exile as a just judgment on the nation. H. W. Wolff, in "Das Kerygma

---

is the prominence of preexilic perspectives and themes, especially the hope of the dynasty of David. Much can be learned from Herodotus about the method and purpose of ancient historians, which may help us to understand the Former Prophets, but the parallels that can be observed are not sufficient to establish more than a general similarity between the two works. It is too bold to identify these as being a common genre of writing. The writing of Herodotus never functioned as a prophetic proclamation, while the Hebrew composition is known only as a prophetic word canonized as Scripture.

In the Hebrew canon the entire narrative from Genesis to Kings is presented as a continuous history.[37] A Deuteronomistic History seeking to develop a national identity on the basis of covenant loyalty has been incorporated in a much longer narrative. What other such sources were available in the exilic period to compose a history that concluded with the thirty-seventh year of the exile of Jehoiachin (2 Kings 25:27)? Brian Peckham maintains that the sources of the continuous history of Genesis to Kings were complete written works; these works were earlier versions of the Pentateuch and the Deuteronomistic History.[38] In his view the entire historical work from Genesis through Kings was formed in a series of revisions of a continuous historical tradition.

Junctures of previous compositions are still evident in the present form of the Former Prophets. There are notable repetitions of material with transitional statements to indicate a thematic presentation of past events. In Joshua the boundary list of Judah (Josh. 15:1–63) includes the account of Caleb receiving the city of Hebron (15:13–14; cf. 14:13–15) and of Othniel conquering Debir (15:15–19), with the notation that Jerusalem was not taken from the Jebusites (v. 63). Judges places the capture of the territory of Judah after the death of Joshua (Judg. 1:1–21), repeating the story of Caleb and Othniel (vv. 8–15, 20), with the notation that the Jebusites stayed in Jerusalem (v. 21), even though the summary introduction said Jerusalem was captured by Judah (v. 8). Later we are told of how David captured Jerusalem (2 Sam. 5:6–9). The statement that the Jebusites continued to live with the Benjamites "until this day" (Judg. 1:21; cf. Josh. 15:63) indicates the importance of understanding the past in the present. It marks one of those histories, complete at the time of "this day," written to explain how God was at work in the events that had taken place.

des deuteronomischen Geschichtswerk," *ZAW* 73 (1961): 173, rightly queries whether one would take pen in hand only to show that the end of Israel's history was justified.

37. D. N. Freedman calls this the "Primary History;" see "The Deuteronomic History," in *IDBSup*, ed. Keith Crim et al. (Nashville: Abingdon, 1976), 226–28.

38. Brian Peckham, *The Composition of the Deuteronomistic History* (HSM 35; Atlanta: Scholar's Press, 1985), 1–2. Noth "impugned his theory of a Dtr history by confining historicity to the aetiologies, sources and traditions that it quoted verbatim."

This Day and the Last Days

THE PHRASE "UNTIL THIS DAY" occurs fifty-five times in Deuteronomy and the Former Prophets, beginning with Deuteronomy 2:22 and ending with Manasseh (2 Kings 21:15); in the majority of cases it is a commentary added to a tradition to testify that the situation in question continued to the time of writing.[39] It is comparable to the phrase "as it is this day" (1 Kings 3:6; 8:24, 61) to indicate significance and application to the present reality.

The phrase "until this day" appears to have been used to validate some aspect of the tradition that could be verified at the time of writing. It could have belonged to the sources of the Deuteronomistic History rather than to the history itself,[40] or it could belong to a stage of the history. The detail about the district that Solomon annexed to Hiram of Tyre "called Cabul until this day" (1 Kings 9:13) may have belonged to the "book of the annals of Solomon" (1 Kings 11:41), which served as a source for the reign of Solomon. In a number of instances the phrase may have been part of the Deuteronomistic History, as the claim of Caleb to the city of Hebron (Josh. 14:14), since this could have still been true in the exilic period.

In two instances the phrase "until this day" is not part of a historical source and cannot have been true in the exilic period. The first is the reference to the poles for carrying the ark (1 Kings 8:8), and the second the details of the slave corvée of the surviving native populations (9:21). Even these have not been regarded as convincing evidence of a written form of the history in the preexilic period.[41] The first is textually uncertain, as it is missing in the Old Greek versions. Burney, however, argues that it was deliberately omitted by the Greek translator because it was no longer true in his day.[42] The second has the appearance of being a revision from the book of the annals of Solomon.

The phrase "until this day" appears in virtually all the sources that can be identified in the Deuteronomistic History, whether northern or southern, annalistic or literary. The majority of objects said to exist "until this day" are found in the area of Judah (Josh. 4:9; 7:26; 8:28–29; 10:27; 1 Sam. 6:18),

---

39. Brevard S. Childs, "A Study of the Formula 'Until This Day,'" *JBL* 82 (1963): 279–92; cf. Weinfeld, *Deuteronomy and the Deuteronomic School*, 174–75.

40. Richard D. Nelson, *The Double Redaction of the Deuteronomistic History* (JSOTSup 18; Sheffield: Sheffield Academic Press, 1981), 24; Childs, "A Study of the Formula 'Until This Day,'" 290–92.

41. Nelson, *The Double Redaction of the Deuteronomistic History*, 25.

42. C. F. Burney, "Notes on the Hebrew Text of the Books of Kings," in *The Book of Judges and Notes on the Hebrew Text of the Books of Kings with an Introduction and Appendix* (The Library of Biblical Studies; New York: KTAV, 1970), 107.

reflecting a distinctive southern familiarity. The phrase "until this day" is consistently used to speak of specific Deuteronomistic interests in the pre-exilic period: the use of non-Israelite forced labor (1 Kings 9:21), the destruction of altars of false worship (2 Kings 10:27–29), the ark (1 Kings 8:8), and the rebellion of Edom (2 Kings 8:22, 14:7, 16:6). A thorough study by Geoghegan leads him to the conclusion that the phrase "until this day" was adopted from sources used by a preexilic composer in the days "when the temple still stood, the poles of the ark still protruded beyond the curtain of the holy of holies, and the nation itself was undergoing unprecedented cultic reforms and territorial expansions under Josiah."[43] This composition included a great diversity of material with diverse perspectives, written in support of the Davidic throne and the cultic reforms of Josiah in the centralization of worship at Jerusalem.

The treatment of themes in the books of Kings is additional convincing evidence for a version of the Deuteronomistic History at the time of Josiah.[44] Obedience to the Mosaic covenant as expressed in "the book of this law" is central to the history of Kings, but this emphasis should not compromise the importance of the promise to David. David would always have a lamp (1 Kings 11:36; 15:4; 2 Kings 8:19) in Jerusalem. The apostasy of the house of Ahab and his alliance with the kings of Jerusalem almost extinguished that lamp when Athaliah, daughter of Ahab (2 Kings 8:18), attempted to destroy the entire royal family (11:1–3), but the dynasty was spared through Joash, grandson of Athaliah.

These two themes of covenant obedience and the promise to David reach their climax in the reign of Josiah. Josiah led the nation of Judah in covenant renewal (2 Kings 23:3), in the renewal of temple worship, in the removal of all the places of false worship (vv. 4–20), and in the renewal of the Passover (vv. 21–23). A sharp contrast begins with the death of Josiah. Manasseh receives the blame for the Exile (2 Kings 23:26–25:26), whose evil influence could not be removed by the reforms of Josiah. Judah had survived previous evil kings because of David's faithfulness. The renewal of Josiah

---

43. Jeffrey C. Geoghegan, "'Until This Day' and the Preexilic Redaction of the Deuteronomistic History," *JBL* 122 (2003): 224.

44. The analysis of F. M. Cross, "The Themes of the Book of Kings and the Structure of the Deuteronomistic History," in *Canaanite Myth and Hebrew Epic: Essays in the History of the Religion of Israel* (Cambridge, Mass.: Harvard Univ. Press, 1973), 274–89, shows that the themes and structure of Kings can best be understood if a preexilic version was revised by a more pessimistic exilic writer. The idea that the book of Kings originated in preexilic times goes back as far as the nineteenth-century literary critic Abraham Kuenen. Nelson (*Double Redaction of the Deuteronomistic History*, 14–22) reviews a number of proposals for a preexilic version of Kings leading up to the thesis of Cross.

was the high point of hope, because he had corrected all the false worship that had been brought by Manasseh. If the reform of Josiah had been ineffective or if the people had reverted to their sinful ways, the theme of judgment for covenant failure would have followed through more consistently. These striking features of the success of Josiah and the condemnation of Manasseh give the impression that a history celebrating the covenant at the time of Josiah was complemented by an explanation of the destruction of Jerusalem in the time of the Exile.

The Composition of Kings

OTHER EVIDENCES HAVE BEEN EXAMINED for earlier stages in the development of the books of Kings. The regnal formulas exhibit patterns of variation, especially in the valuations of judgment. An examination of these patterns led Weippert to the conclusion that an edition of the history was completed in the time of Hezekiah, a second in the time of Josiah, and a third in the Exile.[45] The first edition evaluated the kings of Judah from Jehoshaphat to Ahaz and the kings of Israel from Joram to Hoshea. The second edition evaluated the kings of Israel from Jeroboam I to Ahaziah and the kings of Judah from Rehoboam to Asa, then from Hezekiah to Josiah. The third edition brought a negative evaluation to bear on the four last kings of Jerusalem. Lemaire extended the study of Weippert to propose an earlier composition at the time of Jehoshaphat in the ninth century.[46] This ninth-century edition continued an earlier history of David and a work on the wisdom of Solomon. These were possibly part of the instructions of priests and prophets associated with the royal court at Jerusalem, serving as an encouragement for reform or correction.

Provan has complemented these studies with an examination of attitudes toward the high places.[47] He concludes that two different themes may be found. The first of these in 1 Kings 3–2 Kings 18 viewed these as shrines belonging to Yahweh. A later view, found also in additions to the sections containing the first view, regarded these as idolatrous places of worship. This evidence suggests that a preexilic edition of the history ended with Hezekiah, corroborating evidence from the judgment formulas. Provan thinks that an edition of Kings was written at the time of Josiah, but it did not include any material on Manasseh, Amon, or Josiah himself. He suggests that this edition

---

45. Helga Weippert, "Die 'deuteronomistischen' Beurteilungen der Könige von Israel und Juda und das Problem der Redaktion der Königsbücher," *Bib* 53 (1972): 301–39.

46. André Lemaire, "Vers l'histoire de la redaction des Livres des Rois," *ZAW* 98 (1986): 221–36.

47. Ian Provan, *Hezekiah and the Books of Kings* (Berlin: de Gruyter, 1988), 57–90.

must have included the books of Samuel in much their present form and may have included the last chapters of Judges (Judg. 17–21). He regards the "antimonarchial" sections of 1 Samuel 7–12, the book of Judges, and the ending of Kings as part of an exilic revision of the history. The addition of Judges would have provided the literary structure for the addition of Joshua and Deuteronomy. Such observations are scanty indications of the stages of a complete history, but it is evident that a prophetic history of Israel began long before the exile, and it was complemented by the prophets as time went on.

A study of themes and formulas is critical to understanding Kings. Reflection on the significance of historical events for understanding the covenant relationship with God was necessary at critical times. The days of Josiah were a high point in achieving the purity of covenant worship. The present form of Kings retains much of the optimism of the blessing of covenant obedience celebrated at that time. The tragic end of Josiah and the rapid demise of Judah within a generation brought about sober reflection on the covenant relationship. The history of Kings completed in the Exile juxtaposed the elements of obedience and judgment, blessing and curse.

The basic thesis of Noth, that a single writer was both author and editor of a large composition called the Deuteronomic History, must acknowledge the presence of earlier versions of such a history.[48] The ending of Kings, with its sharp contrast between the positive reforms of Josiah correcting all the wrongs of Manasseh and the blame for the exile assigned to Manasseh, is difficult to explain as the unified work of an exilic author. The portrayal of Josiah in Kings makes sense only as a version of the Deuteronomistic History before the Exile.

It is important to recognize a form of history writing in which a nation gives account to itself of its traditions. This history does not begin at the time of Josiah, but the optimistic outlook for the kingdom during the reign of Josiah is unmistakable. The catastrophe of the Exile then requires a revision of the history. The severity of covenant disobedience takes on tragic reality for the nation, but the Exile does not remove the hope of the promise. Whatever the future of the kingdom of Israel, the kingdom of God as promised to David will prevail.

---

48. See Steven L. McKenzie, *The Trouble with Kings: The Composition of the Book of Kings in the Deuteronomistic History* (Leiden: Brill, 1991), 147–48.

Outline

1. **Succession to David (1 Kings 1:1–2:46)**
   a. Advancing Debilitation of David (1:1–4)
   b. Enthronement of Solomon (1:5–53)
   c. Solomon Consolidates His Rule (2:1–46)
2. **God Confirms Solomon's Rule (3:1–28)**
   a. The Divine Gift of Wisdom (3:1–15)
   b. Justice of a Wise King (3:16–28)
3. **Administration of Solomon (4:1–34)**
   a. The Chief Officials (4:1–6)
   b. The District Governors (4:7–20)
   c. Provisions for the Kingdom (4:21–28)
   d. The Wisdom of Solomon (4:29–34)
4. **Royal Building Projects (5:1–7:51a)**
   a. Preparation of Materials (5:1–18)
   b. The Construction of the Temple (6:1–7:1)
   c. The Construction of the Palace Complex (7:2–12)
   d. Artifacts for the Temple (7:13–51a)
5. **Dedication of the Temple (7:51b–9:9)**
   a. Installation of the Ark (7:51b–8:13)
   b. Patronage of David (8:14–21)
   c. Dedication Prayer (8:22–53)
   d. Dedication Exhortation (8:54–61)
   e. Dedication Sacrifices (8:62–66)
   f. Covenant Confirmation (9:1–9)
6. **Solomon's Wealth and Wisdom (9:10–10:29)**
   a. Labor Provisions for Building Projects (9:10–25)
   b. International Fame and Fortune (9:26–10:25)
   c. Prosperity and Security in Jerusalem (10:26–29)
7. **Demise of the Kingdom (11:1–43)**
   a. Prophetic Judgment of Solomon (11:1–13)
   b. Enemies of Solomon (11:14–25)
   c. Revolt of Jeroboam (11:26–43)
8. **Division of the Kingdom (12:1–14:31)**
   a. Jeroboam Made King over Israel (12:1–24)
   b. Innovations in the Northern Kingdom (12:25–32)
   c. Prophetic Condemnation of Jeroboam (12:33–13:34)

30. **Last Days of Judah (23:31–24:17)**
    a. Egyptian Intervention (23:31–35)
    b. Babylonian Control (23:36–24:17)
31. **Fall of Jerusalem (24:18–25:30)**
    a. Breach and Plunder of Jerusalem (24:18–25:21)
    b. Reign of Gedaliah (25:22–26)
    c. Release of Jehoiachin (25:27–30)

Selected Bibliography

Commentaries

Brueggemann, Walter. *1 & 2 Kings*. Macon, Ga.: Smith & Helwys, 2000.

Burney, C. F. "Notes on the Hebrew Text of the Books of Kings." In *The Book of Judges and Notes on the Hebrew Text of the Books of Kings with an Introduction and Appendix*. The Library of Biblical Studies. Reprint edition. New York: KTAV, 1970.

Cogan, Mordechai. *I Kings: A New Translation with Introduction and Commentary*. AB 10. New York: Doubleday, 2000.

Cogan, Mordechai, and Hayim Tadmor. *II Kings: A New Translation with Introduction and Commentary*. AB 11. New York: Doubleday, 1988.

Cohn, Robert L. *2 Kings*. Berit Olam: Studies in Hebrew Narrative and Poetry. Collegeville, Minn.: Liturgical Press/Michael Glazier, 2000.

DeVries, Simon J. *I Kings*. WBC 12. 2nd ed. Nashville: Nelson, 2003.

Fritz, Volkmar. *1 & 2 Kings: A Continental Commentary*. Minneapolis: Fortress, 2003.

Gray, John. *I & II Kings*. 3rd ed. OTL. Philadelphia: Westminster, 1979.

Hobbs, Thomas R. *2 Kings*. WBC 13. Waco, Tex.: Word, 1985.

Jones, G. H. *1 & 2 Kings*. NCBC. 2 vols. Grand Rapids: Eerdmans, 1984.

Long, Burke O. *1 Kings with an Introduction to Historical Literature*. FOTL 9. Grand Rapids: Eerdmans, 1984.

_____. *2 Kings*. FOTL 10. Grand Rapids: Eerdmans, 1991.

Montgomery, James A., and H. S. Gehman. *A Critical and Exegetical Commentary on the Books of Kings*. ICC. Edinburgh: T. & T. Clark, 1951.

Nelson, Richard D. *First and Second Kings*. Interpretation. Louisville: John Knox, 1987.

Provan, Ian. W. *1 & 2 Kings*. NIBC. Peabody, Mass.: Hendrikson, 1995.

Wiseman, Donald J. *1 & 2 Kings: An Introduction and Commentary*. TOTC. Downers Grove, Ill.: InterVarsity Press, 1993.

Würtwein, E. *Das Erste Buch der Könige, Kapitel 1–16*. ATD. Göttingen: Vandenhoeck & Ruprecht, 1977.

_____. *Die Bücher der Könige, 1. Kön. 17–2. Kön. 25*. ATD. Göttingen: Vandenhoeck & Ruprecht, 1984.

Monographs

Ahlström, Gösta W. *The History of Ancient Palestine*. Philadelphia: Fortress, 1993.

Bright, John, and W. P. Brown. *A History of Israel*. 4th ed. Philadelphia: Westminster John Knox, 2000.

Davies, P. R. *In Search of Ancient Israel*. JSOTSup 148. Sheffield: Sheffield Academic Press, 1992.

Knoppers, Gary N. *Two Nations under God: The Deuteronomistic History of Solomon and the Dual Monarchies*. 2 vols. HSM 52. Atlanta: Scholars Press, 1993.

Lemche, N. P. *The Israelites in History and Tradition*. Library of Ancient Israel. Louisville: Westminster John Knox, 1998.

McKenzie, Steven L. *The Trouble with Kings*. VTSup 42. Leiden: Brill, 1991.

Nelson, Richard D. *The Double Redaction of the Deuteronomistic History*. JSOTSup 18. Sheffield: Sheffield Academic Press, 1981.

Noth, M. *Überlieferungsgeschichtliche Studien: Die sammelnden und bearbeitenden Geschichtswerke im Alten Testament*. 3rd ed. Tübingen: J. C. B Mohr, 1967. Translated as *The Deuteronomistic History*. JSOTSup 15. Sheffield: Sheffield Academic Press, 1981.

Peckham, Brian. *The Composition of the Deuteronomistic History*. HSM 35. Atlanta: Scholars Press, 1985.

Provan, Ian. *Hezekiah and the Books of Kings*. Berlin: de Gruyter, 1988.

Provan, Ian, V. Philips Long, and Tremper Longman III. *A Biblical History of Israel*. Louisville: Westminster John Knox, 2003.

Van Seters, John. *In Search of History: Historiography in the Ancient World and the Origins of Biblical History*. Winona Lake, Ind.: Eisenbrauns, 1997.

Vaughn, Andrew G. *Theology, History, and Archaeology in the Chronicler's Account of Hezekiah*. ABS 4. Atlanta: Scholars Press, 1999.

Von Rad, Gerhard. *Deuteronium Studien*. Göttingen: Vandenhoek & Ruprecht, 1948. Translated as *Studies in Deuteronomy*. London: SCM, 1953.

Weinfeld, M. *Deuteronomy and the Deuteronomic School*. Oxford: Clarendon, 1972.

Zevit, Ziony. *The Religions of Ancient Israel: A Synthesis of Parallactic Approaches*. New York: Continuum, 2001.

1 Kings 1:1–2:46

❦

WHEN KING DAVID was old and well advanced in years, he could not keep warm even when they put covers over him. ²So his servants said to him, "Let us look for a young virgin to attend the king and take care of him. She can lie beside him so that our lord the king may keep warm."

³Then they searched throughout Israel for a beautiful girl and found Abishag, a Shunammite, and brought her to the king. ⁴The girl was very beautiful; she took care of the king and waited on him, but the king had no intimate relations with her.

⁵Now Adonijah, whose mother was Haggith, put himself forward and said, "I will be king." So he got chariots and horses ready, with fifty men to run ahead of him. ⁶(His father had never interfered with him by asking, "Why do you behave as you do?" He was also very handsome and was born next after Absalom.)

⁷Adonijah conferred with Joab son of Zeruiah and with Abiathar the priest, and they gave him their support. ⁸But Zadok the priest, Benaiah son of Jehoiada, Nathan the prophet, Shimei and Rei and David's special guard did not join Adonijah.

⁹Adonijah then sacrificed sheep, cattle and fattened calves at the Stone of Zoheleth near En Rogel. He invited all his brothers, the king's sons, and all the men of Judah who were royal officials, ¹⁰but he did not invite Nathan the prophet or Benaiah or the special guard or his brother Solomon.

¹¹Then Nathan asked Bathsheba, Solomon's mother, "Have you not heard that Adonijah, the son of Haggith, has become king without our lord David's knowing it? ¹²Now then, let me advise you how you can save your own life and the life of your son Solomon. ¹³Go in to King David and say to him, 'My lord the king, did you not swear to me your servant: "Surely Solomon your son shall be king after me, and he will sit on my throne"? Why then has Adonijah become king?' ¹⁴While you are still there talking to the king, I will come in and confirm what you have said."

¹⁵So Bathsheba went to see the aged king in his room, where Abishag the Shunammite was attending him. ¹⁶Bathsheba bowed low and knelt before the king.

"What is it you want?" the king asked.

¹⁷She said to him, "My lord, you yourself swore to me your servant by the LORD your God: 'Solomon your son shall be king after me, and he will sit on my throne.' ¹⁸But now Adonijah has become king, and you, my lord the king, do not know about it. ¹⁹He has sacrificed great numbers of cattle, fattened calves, and sheep, and has invited all the king's sons, Abiathar the priest and Joab the commander of the army, but he has not invited Solomon your servant. ²⁰My lord the king, the eyes of all Israel are on you, to learn from you who will sit on the throne of my lord the king after him. ²¹Otherwise, as soon as my lord the king is laid to rest with his fathers, I and my son Solomon will be treated as criminals."

²²While she was still speaking with the king, Nathan the prophet arrived. ²³And they told the king, "Nathan the prophet is here." So he went before the king and bowed with his face to the ground.

²⁴Nathan said, "Have you, my lord the king, declared that Adonijah shall be king after you, and that he will sit on your throne? ²⁵Today he has gone down and sacrificed great numbers of cattle, fattened calves, and sheep. He has invited all the king's sons, the commanders of the army and Abiathar the priest. Right now they are eating and drinking with him and saying, 'Long live King Adonijah!' ²⁶But me your servant, and Zadok the priest, and Benaiah son of Jehoiada, and your servant Solomon he did not invite. ²⁷Is this something my lord the king has done without letting his servants know who should sit on the throne of my lord the king after him?"

²⁸Then King David said, "Call in Bathsheba." So she came into the king's presence and stood before him.

²⁹The king then took an oath: "As surely as the LORD lives, who has delivered me out of every trouble, ³⁰I will surely carry out today what I swore to you by the LORD, the God of Israel: Solomon your son shall be king after me, and he will sit on my throne in my place."

³¹Then Bathsheba bowed low with her face to the ground and, kneeling before the king, said, "May my lord King David live forever!"

³²King David said, "Call in Zadok the priest, Nathan the prophet and Benaiah son of Jehoiada." When they came before the king, ³³he said to them: "Take your lord's servants with you and set Solomon my son on my own mule and take him down to Gihon. ³⁴There have Zadok the priest and Nathan the prophet anoint him king over Israel. Blow the trumpet and shout, 'Long live King Solomon!' ³⁵Then you are to go up with him, and he is to come and sit on my throne and reign in my place. I have appointed him ruler over Israel and Judah."

³⁶Benaiah son of Jehoiada answered the king, "Amen! May the LORD, the God of my lord the king, so declare it. ³⁷As the LORD was with my lord the king, so may he be with Solomon to make his throne even greater than the throne of my lord King David!"

³⁸So Zadok the priest, Nathan the prophet, Benaiah son of Jehoiada, the Kerethites and the Pelethites went down and put Solomon on King David's mule and escorted him to Gihon. ³⁹Zadok the priest took the horn of oil from the sacred tent and anointed Solomon. Then they sounded the trumpet and all the people shouted, "Long live King Solomon!" ⁴⁰And all the people went up after him, playing flutes and rejoicing greatly, so that the ground shook with the sound.

⁴¹Adonijah and all the guests who were with him heard it as they were finishing their feast. On hearing the sound of the trumpet, Joab asked, "What's the meaning of all the noise in the city?"

⁴²Even as he was speaking, Jonathan son of Abiathar the priest arrived. Adonijah said, "Come in. A worthy man like you must be bringing good news."

⁴³"Not at all!" Jonathan answered. "Our lord King David has made Solomon king. ⁴⁴The king has sent with him Zadok the priest, Nathan the prophet, Benaiah son of Jehoiada, the Kerethites and the Pelethites, and they have put him on the king's mule, ⁴⁵and Zadok the priest and Nathan the prophet have anointed him king at Gihon. From there they have gone up cheering, and the city resounds with it. That's the noise you hear. ⁴⁶Moreover, Solomon has taken his seat on the royal throne. ⁴⁷Also, the royal officials have come to congratulate our lord King David, saying, 'May your God make Solomon's name more famous than yours and his throne greater than

yours!' And the king bowed in worship on his bed ⁴⁸and said,
'Praise be to the LORD, the God of Israel, who has allowed my
eyes to see a successor on my throne today.'"

⁴⁹At this, all Adonijah's guests rose in alarm and dispersed.
⁵⁰But Adonijah, in fear of Solomon, went and took hold of the
horns of the altar. ⁵¹Then Solomon was told, "Adonijah is
afraid of King Solomon and is clinging to the horns of the
altar. He says, 'Let King Solomon swear to me today that he
will not put his servant to death with the sword.'"

⁵²Solomon replied, "If he shows himself to be a worthy
man, not a hair of his head will fall to the ground; but if evil is
found in him, he will die." ⁵³Then King Solomon sent men,
and they brought him down from the altar. And Adonijah
came and bowed down to King Solomon, and Solomon said,
"Go to your home."

²:¹When the time drew near for David to die, he gave a
charge to Solomon his son.

²"I am about to go the way of all the earth," he said. "So be
strong, show yourself a man, ³and observe what the LORD
your God requires: Walk in his ways, and keep his decrees
and commands, his laws and requirements, as written in the
Law of Moses, so that you may prosper in all you do and
wherever you go, ⁴and that the LORD may keep his promise to
me: 'If your descendants watch how they live, and if they walk
faithfully before me with all their heart and soul, you will
never fail to have a man on the throne of Israel.'

⁵"Now you yourself know what Joab son of Zeruiah did to
me—what he did to the two commanders of Israel's armies,
Abner son of Ner and Amasa son of Jether. He killed them,
shedding their blood in peacetime as if in battle, and with that
blood stained the belt around his waist and the sandals on his
feet. ⁶Deal with him according to your wisdom, but do not let
his gray head go down to the grave in peace.

⁷"But show kindness to the sons of Barzillai of Gilead and
let them be among those who eat at your table. They stood
by me when I fled from your brother Absalom.

⁸"And remember, you have with you Shimei son of Gera,
the Benjamite from Bahurim, who called down bitter curses on
me the day I went to Mahanaim. When he came down to meet
me at the Jordan, I swore to him by the LORD: 'I will not put
you to death by the sword.' ⁹But now, do not consider him

innocent. You are a man of wisdom; you will know what to do to him. Bring his gray head down to the grave in blood."

[10]Then David rested with his fathers and was buried in the City of David. [11]He had reigned forty years over Israel— seven years in Hebron and thirty-three in Jerusalem. [12]So Solomon sat on the throne of his father David, and his rule was firmly established.

[13]Now Adonijah, the son of Haggith, went to Bathsheba, Solomon's mother. Bathsheba asked him, "Do you come peacefully?"

He answered, "Yes, peacefully." [14]Then he added, "I have something to say to you."

"You may say it," she replied.

[15]"As you know," he said, "the kingdom was mine. All Israel looked to me as their king. But things changed, and the kingdom has gone to my brother; for it has come to him from the LORD. [16]Now I have one request to make of you. Do not refuse me."

"You may make it," she said.

[17]So he continued, "Please ask King Solomon—he will not refuse you—to give me Abishag the Shunammite as my wife."

[18]"Very well," Bathsheba replied, "I will speak to the king for you."

[19]When Bathsheba went to King Solomon to speak to him for Adonijah, the king stood up to meet her, bowed down to her and sat down on his throne. He had a throne brought for the king's mother, and she sat down at his right hand.

[20]"I have one small request to make of you," she said. "Do not refuse me."

The king replied, "Make it, my mother; I will not refuse you."

[21]So she said, "Let Abishag the Shunammite be given in marriage to your brother Adonijah."

[22]King Solomon answered his mother, "Why do you request Abishag the Shunammite for Adonijah? You might as well request the kingdom for him—after all, he is my older brother—yes, for him and for Abiathar the priest and Joab son of Zeruiah!"

[23]Then King Solomon swore by the LORD: "May God deal with me, be it ever so severely, if Adonijah does not pay with his life for this request! [24]And now, as surely as the LORD

lives—he who has established me securely on the throne of my father David and has founded a dynasty for me as he promised—Adonijah shall be put to death today!" ²⁵So King Solomon gave orders to Benaiah son of Jehoiada, and he struck down Adonijah and he died.

²⁶To Abiathar the priest the king said, "Go back to your fields in Anathoth. You deserve to die, but I will not put you to death now, because you carried the ark of the Sovereign LORD before my father David and shared all my father's hardships." ²⁷So Solomon removed Abiathar from the priesthood of the LORD, fulfilling the word the LORD had spoken at Shiloh about the house of Eli.

²⁸When the news reached Joab, who had conspired with Adonijah though not with Absalom, he fled to the tent of the LORD and took hold of the horns of the altar. ²⁹King Solomon was told that Joab had fled to the tent of the LORD and was beside the altar. Then Solomon ordered Benaiah son of Jehoiada, "Go, strike him down!"

³⁰So Benaiah entered the tent of the LORD and said to Joab, "The king says, 'Come out!'"

But he answered, "No, I will die here."

Benaiah reported to the king, "This is how Joab answered me."

³¹Then the king commanded Benaiah, "Do as he says. Strike him down and bury him, and so clear me and my father's house of the guilt of the innocent blood that Joab shed. ³²The LORD will repay him for the blood he shed, because without the knowledge of my father David he attacked two men and killed them with the sword. Both of them—Abner son of Ner, commander of Israel's army, and Amasa son of Jether, commander of Judah's army—were better men and more upright than he. ³³May the guilt of their blood rest on the head of Joab and his descendants forever. But on David and his descendants, his house and his throne, may there be the LORD's peace forever."

³⁴So Benaiah son of Jehoiada went up and struck down Joab and killed him, and he was buried on his own land in the desert. ³⁵The king put Benaiah son of Jehoiada over the army in Joab's position and replaced Abiathar with Zadok the priest.

³⁶Then the king sent for Shimei and said to him, "Build yourself a house in Jerusalem and live there, but do not go

anywhere else. [37]The day you leave and cross the Kidron Valley, you can be sure you will die; your blood will be on your own head."

[38]Shimei answered the king, "What you say is good. Your servant will do as my lord the king has said." And Shimei stayed in Jerusalem for a long time.

[39]But three years later, two of Shimei's slaves ran off to Achish son of Maacah, king of Gath, and Shimei was told, "Your slaves are in Gath." [40]At this, he saddled his donkey and went to Achish at Gath in search of his slaves. So Shimei went away and brought the slaves back from Gath.

[41]When Solomon was told that Shimei had gone from Jerusalem to Gath and had returned, [42]the king summoned Shimei and said to him, "Did I not make you swear by the LORD and warn you, 'On the day you leave to go anywhere else, you can be sure you will die'? At that time you said to me, 'What you say is good. I will obey.' [43]Why then did you not keep your oath to the LORD and obey the command I gave you?"

[44]The king also said to Shimei, "You know in your heart all the wrong you did to my father David. Now the LORD will repay you for your wrongdoing. [45]But King Solomon will be blessed, and David's throne will remain secure before the LORD forever."

[46]Then the king gave the order to Benaiah son of Jehoiada, and he went out and struck Shimei down and killed him.

The kingdom was now firmly established in Solomon's hands.

THE KINGS NARRATIVE proceeds on the assumption that the account of the rise of David is familiar to the reader. The conspiracy depicted here for the throne is a new development in the story of David. The question of succession is first raised by Bathsheba (1:20).[1] The main protagonists, Solomon and Adonijah, have had no role in the previous

---

1. These chapters are not the continuation of a "Succession Narrative" (see "Process of History Writing" in the introduction). The question of succession has not been raised in the previous court history. Furthermore, references to the early history of David, such as the help of Abiathar (2:26–27; cf. 1 Sam. 3:11–14) and the murder of Abner by Joab (1 Kings 2:5, 32; cf. 2 Sam. 3) are outside the bounds of a Succession Narrative.

events of David's household. After the birth of Solomon, Bathsheba vanishes from the scene. This struggle for the throne provides the transition from the story of David's reign to Solomon as the new king.

In the early monarchy of Israel, the right of the firstborn to succeed on the throne (primogeniture) seems to have been recognized (cf. 1 Sam. 20:31; 1 Kings 2:22). Adonijah, the oldest surviving brother, has rallied to his side the leaders who have been with David from the days of his flight from Saul. These include Abiathar the priest and Joab, one of David's leading military generals. This right of succession, if it existed, is not uncontested. Supporting Solomon are Benaiah the military leader, Zadok the priest, and Nathan the prophet. The rivalry between these two parties has the appearance of the traditional leadership of the "men of Judah" (1:9) protecting their interests against a younger generation of rivals. David appears as a weak and vacillating king. His failure to declare a successor continues the conflict that has plagued his household from the days when Solomon was born.

Advancing Debilitation of David (1:1–4)

THE INABILITY OF David to function as king creates a crisis in the young kingdom. His inability to stay warm when provided an abundance of coverings is a sign of impending death. David's political advisers and protectors attempt to assist him by seeking out a beautiful young woman to provide him with personal care. In a society that accepted concubines as the right of a king, it is her duty to be his bedmate as well.[2] None of this would be shocking or even unusual in a society that expected kings to have the services of a large harem. Their provision of a young woman for David does not suggest they believed a king could not function when lacking sexual potency, or that by primitive rite of contractual magic they could convey health and heat of a young body to the old king.[3] The narrative provides no indication that Abishag is sought for the purpose of restoring virility. David's failure to respond is an indication that the vigor for which he was renowned has left him.

The position of Abishag is left ambiguous, since she is not fully inducted into his harem. Her intimacy with David and her extraordinary beauty gives her a special status. Solomon no doubt intends to make her a part of his own harem. When Adonijah requests her as a wife, Solomon interprets it a plot for the throne (2:21–22). She becomes the occasion for Solomon to rid himself of Adonijah in taking charge of the kingdom as the rightful successor to David.

---

2. The expression *škb bḥq* is used for intimacy (cf. Gen. 16:5).
3. Contra John Gray, *I & II Kings* (OTL; Philadelphia: Westminster, 1979), 77; cf. J. A. Montgomery and H. S. Gehman, *The Books of Kings* (ICC; Edinburgh: T. & T. Clark, 1951), 71–72.

Enthronement of Solomon (1:5–53)

THE SUCCESSION OF Solomon to the throne of David follows a pattern all too typical of ancient kingdoms. Rivalry for the throne often led to violence and death among family members and their associated supporters. The attempted coup by Adonijah and the counter-coup of Solomon are the outcome of moral compromises of David's reign. Adonijah is David's fourth son (2 Sam. 3:4), and apparently the oldest surviving son. Amnon, the oldest son of David, was killed by Absalom because of the rape of his sister Tamar (13:28–29). Absalom, the third oldest son, died in his revolt against David (18:14–15).

Adonijah believes he is entitled to be heir and attempts to take over the throne; David is either negligent in the matter of not fulfilling his earlier oath to Bathsheba (1 Kings 1:13, 17, 30), or he secretly sympathizes with the ambitions of Adonijah. Nathan the prophet intervenes for the safety of Bathsheba and her son; he devises a scheme to call the king to account for his earlier promise that Solomon will reign. David has not been in control of his own household (1:6), a pattern seen during his reign. After Solomon is installed as king by the authority of David, the group supporting Adonijah disbands, and Adonijah is offered conciliation. This is not God's design for the succession to the throne he established forever (2 Sam. 7:13–14). The brutal employment of military force leads to violence and guilt on all sides. Manipulative tactics and ruthless quest for political power are a drastic departure from Israel's political ideals.

Adonijah is aggressive in seizing the throne (1:5, 7, 9). He employs a personal chariot force and guard of honor to give him the status of king and to prepare for his coup. Though David has made limited use of chariotry (2 Sam. 8:4), Adonijah is well aware of its power. Joab, the powerful military leader of David's army, joins in the revolt, along with Abiathar, a leading priest.

Joab is a relative of David (1 Chron. 2:15–16) and the ruthless leader of David's army (2 Sam. 3:27; 18:15; 20:10). With Joab at the head of the conspirators, Adonijah has access to the entire army (2 Sam. 20:23), a far greater force than the palace guard of Benaiah. Abiathar the priest has served David from the beginning of his struggles (1 Sam. 22:20–23); he escaped from the slaughter of the priests at Nob, took refuge with David, and became a priest in the kingdom along with Zadok (2 Sam. 20:25). Adonijah calls together the royal family and all the men of Judah (1 Kings 1:9), his own clansmen, who under Joab constitute the striking force of the national army.

The location of the celebration of investiture is at the "Serpent Stone," or more probably the "Rock Slide."[4] It is outside Jerusalem, but close enough that

---

4. The word *zaḥal* primarily means to slide, and only secondarily is applied to a worm or snake (L. Koehler and W. Baumgartner, *Hebräisches und aramäisches Lexikon zum alten Testament,*

the counter-celebrations within the city can be heard (v. 41). It is located near En Rogel, at the present time a shaft tapping a subterranean stream just below the confluence of the Hinnom and Kidron valleys,[5] on the southeast corner of the city.

The counter forces consist of Zadok the priest, Benaiah the general of the standing army, Nathan the prophet, and Shimei, who had the status of friend of the king (v. 8).[6] Zadok appeared after David's occupation of Jerusalem (2 Sam. 8:17) and functioned as a leading priest along with the representative of the line of Eli (20:25). Benaiah also took office after David's conquest of Jerusalem (8:18); he was the commander of the royal army, those soldiers employed by the king and detached from their home communities. Nathan the prophet emerged after David took office in Jerusalem as well (7:2). He was always associated with the king and had sufficient influence he could confront and correct the king, as in the Bathsheba affair (12:1−15). Adonijah underestimated the resistance of those loyal to Solomon. His deliberate exclusion of them indicated that he did not intend to function with a peaceful coalition (1 Kings 1:10), and he overestimated the power of his forces to overcome them (v. 12).

Nathan the prophet previously served as the conscience to the king in the matter of temple building (2 Sam. 7:1−11). Knowing the oath of succession, Nathan is committed to ensuring the promise is fulfilled. Previous weakness of David in dealing with his children included the rape of Tamar, which merely roused his ineffective anger against Amnon (2 Sam. 13:21), and his lenience toward Absalom, which nearly cost him the loyalty of his troops (19:1−7). David may have had similar sympathies with Adonijah, and the results would have been similarly disastrous. This time Nathan brings his rebuke through the influence of Bathsheba. David would feel a sense of obligation to her, especially since the oath was initially made to her (1 Kings 1:17). Nathan does not trust David to live up to his obligations and is determined to be present to ensure the oath is fulfilled, though he makes no reference to it in speaking with David. Instead, he arrives as a messenger to report to David that the investiture of Adonijah is in progress. As on previous occasions, Nathan directly addresses the fail-

---

3rd. ed. [Leiden: Brill, 1995], 1:256−57). The "Stone of Zoheleth" may have been the name of a slide triggered by an earthquake.

5. En Rogel was on the boundary between Benjamin and Judah (Josh. 15:7; 18:16) and was part of David's espionage system in the revolt of Absalom (2 Sam. 17:17).

6. Translators often interpret "friend" as the name of another individual (Rei). This seems unlikely, as the name is unknown, and Shimei is the only individual not designated by function. "Friend of the king" was an officer of state (1 Kings 4:5), probably a privy counselor.

ure of the king without violating royal prerogative or rousing the anger of the king.

When confronted with his failures, David accepts responsibility for his wrong. His oath assures Nathan and Bathsheba that he will keep the vow made earlier (vv. 29–30). Prophet, priest, and general (Nathan, Zadok, and Benaiah) are to commence the coronation of Solomon immediately. Solomon mounts David's private mule, dramatic and visual evidence that royal authority has been turned over to the rightful heir. The Gihon Spring is the famous water source of Jerusalem in the Kidron Valley not far from the temple, about a quarter mile up the valley from the spring where the celebrations of Adonijah are taking place.

Zadok the priest anoints Solomon as king with the authority of Nathan the prophet. The trumpet blast announces the installation of the new king. With this prophet, priest, and general set out with the royal guard described as Kerethi and Pelethi (v. 38).[7] Zadok the priest anoints Solomon in a distinguished ceremony. A joyful procession follows with the playing of flutes or dancing.[8] The celebrations "split the land" as if an earthquake has taken place (v. 40),[9] marking this as a most significant occasion.

The tumult of the coronation attracts the attention of Adonijah's party just down the valley. Jonathan, the son of Abiathar the priest and a man of status, is apparently present at the proceedings of the anointing of Solomon and reports everything that has transpired. The last word, spoken by David himself, is a thanksgiving prayer that the dynasty will continue (v. 48). The party of Adonijah quickly disperses, unwilling to challenge the will of David and the forces who are with Solomon. Adonijah himself seeks refuge in the sanctuary, the place where the innocent can be protected from summary execution. He fears the fate of death at the hands of Solomon, since no doubt this is what he planned for Solomon had he been successful. The sanctuary protects the innocent, but it is of no help to the guilty. Adonijah seems to think he is in a position to bargain for mercy. Solomon grants him security on the condition that he conduct himself with loyalty and honor.

---

7. The two names are likely to be associated with Crete and Philistia, both a reference to the Sea Peoples from the west. David had taken up feudal service with Achish of Gath and had received Ziklag in perpetuity (1 Sam. 27:6). Apparently the warriors associated with David at that time became his standing army under the command of Benaiah (2 Sam. 8:18; 20:23). See J. C. Greenfield, "Cherethites and Pelethites," *IDB*, 1:557.

8. The Greek interprets the word used here as dancing, a variant vocalization of the Hebrew. As a spontaneous expression of joy this would more readily describe the people, especially since the immediacy of the ceremony did not allow for a lot of preparation.

9. The Old Greek says that the land resounds, reading *tqʿ* rather than *bqʿ*. In this commentary, Old Greek will be used for a distinctly earlier translation of Kings preserved within the manuscript tradition.

Solomon Consolidates His Rule (2:1–46)

CHAPTER 2 HAS a sharp disjunction between two distinct sections: the last words of David (vv. 1–9) and the consolidation of the kingdom under Solomon (vv. 12b–46). The report of David's death and the statement of Solomon's taking the throne serve as a transition to the topic of Solomon establishing his kingdom (vv. 10–12a).

David's charge to Solomon and his death (2:1–11). This chapter is a sequel to the enthronement of Solomon. The charge of David to deal with Joab and Shimei serve as a prolepsis for the task Solomon will have in securing his throne. The problem of Abiathar and Adonijah has already been established in the anointing of Solomon. Joab had a role in those events (2:28), though he was not mentioned, and Shimei humiliated David when he fled from Absalom (2 Sam. 16:5–14). The previous episode of Solomon gaining the throne is continued by introducing the role David had in securing the throne in the midst of various rivalries that carried over from his time.

The charge of David to Solomon (2:2–4) is typical Deuteronomistic theology, expressing the ideology of the kingdom. The fundamental obligation of the king is to rigorously observe the divine mandate (v. 3a), which is "written in the Law of Moses"—that is, Deuteronomy and its requirement of covenant faithfulness (cf. Deut. 30:10; 31:9–13).[10] Faithfulness to the covenant is the single discriminating factor in determining whether kings are good or bad. These final words of David are the fundamental first words for every succeeding king. They express the need for uncompromising faithfulness if the dynastic succession is to continue as God has promised (v. 4). Before David comes to the specifics of Solomon securing his own rule, he reminds Solomon of the one indispensable condition for the continuity of the kingdom.

As is the case in any transition of power, some matters need immediate attention to prevent continuation of the kind of conflict experienced with Adonijah. During David's reign there had been rivalry for power within the military. Joab and his brothers Abishai and Asahel (the three sons of Zeruiah) were a central force in David's wars against the house of Saul (2 Sam. 2:17–18). Abner was the chief of the military for the Benjamites, but he eventually defected to David in an agreement to unite the two political powers (3:12–21). This was a possible threat to Joab as the head of the military, but Joab also had a personal matter to settle. Abner in self-defense had earlier killed the fleet-footed Asahel, who refused to give up pursuit in battle (2:18–

---

10. For a discussion of this term in Deuteronomy, see "Covenant Obligation" in the introduction.

23). When Abner made peace with David, Joab lured him back into the gate of Hebron, where he killed him (3:24−27). This was a serious setback for David, since the people of Israel held him responsible for the death of their military leader.

Worse still was the murder of Amasa, a kinsman of David who replaced Joab at the head of the military (2 Sam. 19:13−14). David commissioned Amasa to raise a military force to quell the rebellion of Sheba, but he took too much time (20:1−6). Joab, under the command of Abishai, pursued the rebels, but in a fit of jealousy treacherously killed Amasa when he came to meet them at Gibeon (20:7−10). Joab regained his status as head of the army (20:23), through the death of those better than himself (see 1 Kings 2:32).[11] Solomon must now use his political savvy[12] to accomplish what David failed to do in bringing stability to the military.

David owes a favor to Barzillai, a Gileadite of Rogelim, who brought food and supplies to him and his followers at Mahanaim during Absalom's rebellion (2 Sam. 17:27−29). David offered Barzillai a permanent residence in Jerusalem as a member of the royal court, but he declined the offer because of his advanced age and asked that his son Kimham be rewarded instead (19:31−38). David now insists that this son be rewarded for this deed of loyalty. "Eating at the king's table" may have been an idiom for receiving a pension (cf. 9:7; 19:28), a phrase that had a long history of usage from Egypt to Mesopotamia.[13]

The name Barzillai is Aramaic, an indication of his residence in the northern part of the Transjordan in the border region between Israel and Syria. One of the purposes of retaining these men in the royal court may have been to help retain allegiance in a border area. Barzillai means "man of iron" and may refer to the profession of metalworker, since he came from the area of Succoth, famous for smelting.[14] Since smiths did not have land of their own, they might more readily settle in Jerusalem.

David was never able to overcome the hostility between Benjamin and Judah. The most dangerous rebellion was that instigated by Sheba, a threat

---

11. The reference to blood on the belt and shoes of the victorious warrior (2:5) may be a symbolic act to demonstrate superiority in power and mobility. The Baal myths provide gory detail of the victorious warrior goddess wallowing in the blood of her victims: *KTU* 1.3 ii 5−35; for translation, see Johannes C. de Moor, *An Anthology of Religious Texts from Ugarit* (Leiden: Brill, 1987), 5−7. Old Greek makes this a question of David's honor: "He put the blood of war on my girdle on my loins, and my sandals on my feet."

12. "Wisdom" in this context (2:6, 9) has the specific sense of acting with prudence and political expediency. The word has a wide range of meaning.

13. Montgomery and Gehman, *The Books of Kings*, 90.

14. Gray, *I & II Kings*, 102.

greater than that of Absalom (2 Sam. 20:6). The rift of north and south was evident during the rebellion of Absalom when Shimei, a Benjamite relative of Saul in Haburim, publicly cursed David and accused him of bloodguilt in supplanting the house of Saul (6:5–13). When the rebellion was quelled, Shimei petitioned David for his life, and David granted him an oath of clemency (19:16–23). David found it prudent on that occasion not to risk further rebellion by sanctioning revenge against Shimei, as the Benjamites were a large force. Solomon cannot allow such resistance to go unchecked, and David instructs him to find occasion to deal with it coercively.

David then dies and is buried in the "City of David," the walled fortress of the Jebusites that was first conquered by David and his personal striking force (2 Sam. 5:6–9). It remained crown property of David and his successors within the states of Israel and Judah. Burial within the palace precincts was common in ancient times; Ezekiel refers to the defilement of the temple by the bodies of the kings of Judah (Ezek. 43:7–9). Though Peter makes reference to the tomb of David as known in his time (Acts 2:29), it is no longer possible to authenticate that place. The tombs of Judahite kings have been identified on the south slope of Ophel, and it is more likely David is buried there than on the traditional site on the southern extremity of the western hill.

The summary of David's reign repeats the information given earlier (cf. 2 Sam. 5:4). The two periods of David's reign constituted an average adult life. David was thirty years old when he began to reign in Hebron. His rule in Hebron of seven years and six months is here rounded off to the typological seven years. Forty years was considered to be a generation (e.g., the Israelites wandered for forty years in the desert). Seventy years was by no means old for a person of David's vigor, but it was recognized as the average life span (Ps. 90:10).[15] The regnal résumé in customary fashion summarizes several key events in the life of David.

The consolidation of Solomon's reign (2:12–46). The consolidation of Solomon's reign is marked with a repetition of the introduction in its closure: "The kingdom was now firmly established in Solomon's hands" (vv. 12b, 46b).[16] The Old Greek versions insert the title of a new book before verse 12, interpreting the introduction to Solomon's reign as a new beginning.[17]

---

15. For discussion, see Ahlström, *The History of Ancient Palestine,* 501. Solomon similarly reigns for forty years (1 Kings 11:42).

16. A break following verse 12 is marked by a disjunctive in the text called setûmâ. These divisions generally followed divisions already seen in Qumran manuscripts; see Emmanuel Tov, *Textual Criticism of the Hebrew Bible* (Philadelphia: Fortress, 1992), 50–51.

17. See the introduction and Appendix A for more details on the Greek divisions of this continuous history.

The different textual divisions are indicative of the dual function of this verse and the use of the regnal summary as a transition in the narrative.

The investiture of Solomon does not settle the question of succession. Adonijah uses the influence of Bathsheba to rally support for his right to rule as the older brother. Solomon recognizes the popular support that Adonijah would have as the older brother (v. 22), and that he also has the support of a leading priest (Abiathar) and military leader (Joab). Adonijah's request for Abishag becomes the occasion for Solomon to rid himself of the adversary he has reluctantly spared (cf. 1:52).[18] Solomon takes a double oath (vv. 23–24) to express the certainty that Adonijah must die. He ordered his death through the agency of Benaiah (v. 25), who is responsible for the royal guard.

The role of Bathsheba in the proceedings is left somewhat enigmatic in the narrative. She has complied with Adonijah's request, though he is a rival and feels that his right of kingdom has been taken away (v. 15). Bathsheba is well aware of Solomon's claim to the throne because of the promise to David (v. 24). It is possible that in delivering the request she knows Solomon will have sufficient reason to bring closure to the question of succession through eliminating her rival.

Solomon bans Abiathar to Anathoth, where he is to make a living from his own estate and never again receive support from the sanctuary (vv. 26–27).[19] Abiathar had been David's faithful priest from the years before he reigned in Hebron and Jerusalem, but he was never able to supersede Zadok. Both Abiathar and Joab were newcomers in the city that David made capital, and as always in such circumstances, the old *garde* was in conflict with the new arrivals. Adonijah chose to ally himself with the priest of David's pre-Jerusalem days, as he would more truly represent both Israelites and Judahites. The sentence given to Abiathar as a man marked for death (v. 26) is commuted; this may be the regular form for an accession amnesty.[20] Abiathar can no longer function as a priest; according to the judgment of Deuteronomistic theology, this is a consequence of the sins of the house of Eli in Shiloh (1 Sam. 3:12–14). The genealogy from Eli to Ahimelech, priest of Nob, Abiathar's father, is never given explicitly (22:20), but there may have been independent tradition to confirm it.

The banishment of Abiathar signals to Joab that his time is up (vv. 28–35). Even the most fierce and fearless warrior will die by the sword as he lived by

---

18. For the status of Abishag, see comments on 1:1–4.

19. Anathoth was three and a half miles northeast of Jerusalem, the home of the prophet Jeremiah (Jer. 1:1). Some have suggested Jeremiah may have been a descendant of Abiathar. The location has not been identified conclusively.

20. S. J. DeVries, *1 Kings*, rev. ed (Nashville: Nelson, 200), 38.

the sword. Joab seeks refuge at the altar and determines to die there if necessary.[21] He may have hoped that Solomon will not resort to execution, at least not in the temple, but Solomon's resolve is undeterred. Joab has acted outside of his authority and for personal reasons in killing Asahel and Amasa; David has already recognized this as tantamount to anarchy, and the only resolution is the death of the anarchist.

Solomon gives amnesty to Shimei (vv. 36–38), but at a considerable cost. He is confined to Jerusalem, which prevents him from again rallying support against the Davidic dynasty in the Benjamite countryside. It also prevents him from managing his own lands in Bahurim, which he places under the care of servants. In the forced absence of their master, the servants are free to act on their own initiative and in their own interests. Two of them run away to Achish son of Maacah king of Gath (v. 39), evidently the same Philistine potentate who had been David's feudal lord (1 Sam. 27:2).

Shimei knows he is in danger of losing his property. According to the social conventions of Israel, land was safeguarded by kinship relations. By being confined to crown property in Jerusalem, Shimei has lost the protection of traditional residency. He obviously knows the risks of pursuing his servants in seeking to protect his economic interests. Solomon has forbidden him to cross the Kidron (v. 37), a valley just to the east of ancient Jerusalem that separated it from Shimei's territory in Bahurim. Shimei goes south and west to Gath, perhaps taking literally the prohibition of not crossing the Kidron, in the hope that this will not violate his oath. He returns with his servants before Solomon finds out about his departure, but this does not spare him. Solomon executes the oath according to its intent, if not the exact letter of the law.

THE CRUELTY OF HUMAN POLITICS **and the promise of God.** The execution of Shimei fulfills the last of David's injunctions to his successor, assuring the blessing of the kingdom of Solomon and the continuity of the kingdom of David (2:45). For the Deuteronomistic Historian, this is the accomplishment of the purpose of God. The violence of these events demonstrates spiritual failure and the cruelty of human politics. The failure of the narrator to condemn the brutality perpetrated in the struggle for power should not be taken as evidence that these are condoned or regarded as necessary. The focus of the account is to show how the promise of David is fulfilled (1:13, 36–37, 47–48) and the kingdom made secure to

---

21. The right of sanctuary was regulated in Mosaic law: Ex. 21:13; Num. 35:9–15.

Solomon (2:12b, 46b). In spite of arrogance and vengeance within the house of David, the promise of God is realized. There is a condition to the success of the kingdom, as expressed by David in his last words (2:4). The ultimate failure of the Davidic house is a consequence of the failure to meet the one fundamental requirement.

The prophetic account of the succession to David follows the course of history, but the occurrences reported do not have equal significance and value. The narrator understands these events as a dynamic between human volition and divine purpose. The accession of Solomon is a revelation of God seen in the outcome of the struggle with Adonijah. The technique of the narrator is to reveal the divine purpose through the key characters in the story.

The inability of David to "know" Abishag (1:4) indicates his inability to perform his duties as king. The reader hears echoes of the word after Adonijah has proclaimed himself to be king; Nathan tells Bathsheba that David does not know this (v. 11), and Bathsheba informs David what he does not know (v. 18). The legitimate heir to the throne is never in question according to the narrative. Solomon had been declared successor in an oath David had sworn to Bathsheba (1:13). This is the first mention of such a declaration. Adonijah is depicted as presumptuous and manipulative in his quest for the throne; he invites his supporters to a coronation ceremony, deliberately excluding those who may have contested his claims. David's words to Solomon at the time of his death (2:2—4) make him the heir of the kingdom promised to David in perpetuity.

The investiture of Solomon is recounted in the instructions of David (1:32—35), in the narration of the events themselves (vv. 36—40), and in the report of Jonathan to Adonijah and his guests (vv. 42—48). The divine purpose is revealed in the mouths of various speakers. When David tells Bathsheba he will fulfill his oath, she exclaims: "May my lord king David live forever" (v. 31). Benaiah replies to David's order to anoint Solomon with "Amen! May my lord the king confirm it" (v. 36).[22] Benaiah expands his petition to ask that the throne of Solomon be even greater than that of David (v. 37). In the report of Jonathan, the people repeat this petition, asking that God make Solomon's fame greater than that of David and his throne more exalted (v. 47). King David himself blesses God for providing one to sit on his throne while he can see it with his own eyes (v. 48).

Even Adonijah acknowledges that his quest for the throne has been in defiance of the divine will (2:15). By the will of the people, the right to the

---

22. The Greek provides an alternate and more suitable reading in this verse. Rather than the Masoretic text "declare it" (NIV), the Greek translates "confirm it" (a verbal form of the Hebrew word *'āmēn*).

throne was his as the eldest son; the events that transpire to give the throne to Solomon are divinely ordained. Bathsheba declares that the reign of David lives on in his descendants (1:31).[23] The prayer of Benaiah declares that God must confirm the rule of Solomon or it will have no effect (v. 36). The frustration of the ambitions of Adonijah is not the sociopolitical outcome of a struggle for succession, but a testimony that God is accomplishing his purpose in spite of the schemes of mortals.

The oath of David repeated by Nathan (1:13), Bathsheba (v. 17), and David himself (v. 30) is critical in the strategy of the narrative. The oath moves David from his lassitude (vv. 1—4) to appropriate action (vv. 28—40). David had earlier been declared to be the man after God's own heart (1 Sam. 13:14). This idiom has nothing to do with God's fondness for David or with any quality of David in his obedience to God.[24] Rather, it emphasizes the free divine selection of the heir to the throne as the alternative to the endurance of Saul's dynasty. Individual will as a desire of the heart is expressed in the petition of Psalm 20:4: "May he give you according to your heart and make all your plans succeed." The sovereign choice of David was rewarded by his determination to do what was right before God (1 Kings 14:8); David became the model of the resolve to follow in God's ways with all his heart. The sovereign choice of David as the heir to the throne is continued in the choice of Solomon as the successor in the house that God is building for David (2 Sam. 7:11b—12).

Repetition of elements is a technique used to convey critical items in the sequence of transference of power. As is the case in rivals for the throne, either Solomon or Adonijah will be executed. Nathan urges immediate action to ensure that Solomon and Bathsheba are the ones to escape (1 Kings 1:12); Bathsheba in turn informs David that if he does not take immediate action regarding Adonijah's declaration of rule, both she and Solomon will be held guilty (v. 21). There is but one question that is repeated by Bathsheba (v. 20) and by Nathan (vv. 24, 27): Who will be next king? The answer is that Solomon will be king; the oath must be made effective in the anointing (vv. 34—35, 39). Jonathan brings the news that is anathema to Adonijah: David has made Solomon king (vv. 43, 45, 46). Failure to anoint Solomon would have been disaster, but such an outcome is never actually possible.

God is at work. An enigma not addressed in the narrative is how the violence of succession is to be reconciled with God's foreordained will. The

---

23. "May my lord the king live forever" is a counter to the end of his life implied in the previous verse (Cogan, *1 Kings*, 160); it is a desire that David's life power should continue in his posterity (DeVries, *1 Kings*, 16).

24. P. Kyle McCarter, *I Samuel: A New Translation with Introduction, Notes & Commentary* (AB; Garden City, N.Y.: Doubleday, 1980), 229.

---

deathbed speech of David concerning Joab, Barzillai, and Shimei bring matters of the past in the former regime to the present. Joab had done much good for David; Barzillai had long ago renounced his offer to be David's guest, and Shimei had been among the first to abet David on his return. Time has changed nothing. DeVries describes this as a dangerous "dynamistic fatalism, so endemic in that and many other cultures."[25] The wisdom with which David counsels Solomon could be regarded as petty and vengeful schemes (2:6, 9). The haughtiness of Adonijah and the despotism of Solomon in dealing with him all appear equally lamentable. Joab surely deserves better than an ignominious burial; Abiathar deserves more than summary dismissal. Both have been loyal to David, repeatedly risking their own lives in the days when he was a fugitive fleeing from paranoid king Saul or David's own rebellious son Absalom. Solomon's arbitrary treatment of Shimei is motivated by a fear of unrest among the northern tribes. Solomon's investiture of power appears to be achieved by a ruthless tyranny.

Nothing in the narrative manifests a conviction that God is on the side of the clever or that might makes right. No comment is made on the motives of the players of this drama, their attitude toward God, or the role they think God has in their decisions. Commentators have never been able to agree on whether the story of the succession to David is pro-Solomon or anti-Solomon. Sufficient arguments can be established for either claim; there are no heroes in this all-too-typical account of transference of political power. The concern of the authors is to show that God is at work accomplishing the purposes of his kingdom in spite of personal aspirations and vendettas of the individuals concerned. The purposes of the kingdom of God are not achieved through violence and greed but in spite of them. The narrative appears to be ambivalent toward government as a kind of necessary monster.

The paradox of virtue and villainy excels in the household of David. David holds the highest possible good as his goal (2:4); he understands that God has fulfilled his word, and it is now the obligation of his successors to follow God as single purpose of their "heart" (*lēbāb*) and their sole desire (*nepeš*). Neither Solomon nor Adonijah demonstrate a commitment to God in their quest for the throne. The story of David's household is all too familiar in the world of politics. Assassinations and political revolts are the way of virtually every nondemocratic nation, and often the enmity is directed against family members. In this respect the story of David is like those of all others. There is one distinct dimension to the succession of David in prophetic teaching; the throne of David represents the kingdom of God, which will be forever. For this reason the succession to David is not just a

---

25. DeVries, *1 Kings*, 42.

matter of resolving family, priestly, and military rivalries; this is another case of the prophetic word being realized and of David following his commitment as a man seeking God with his whole heart.

After Solomon, succession to the throne is regarded as the right of the firstborn. Solomon understands very well that he has received the throne by countering those loyal to David from his earliest days (Abiathar and Joab), who chose to ally with the son who had the rightful claim to the throne (2:15). David received the throne through the superiority of his charismatic leadership after many wars in his struggle with Saul (2 Sam. 3:1). This was the outcome of a divine choice announced to David through the anointing of Samuel (1 Sam. 16:13).

The divine choice of Solomon was similarly known previously through the oath of David (1 Kings 1:30). David and Solomon alone of the kings of Judah share the distinctive of coming to rule through divine choice apart from the right of primogeniture. Divine choice did not preempt the political process; for the prophetic writers of the Deuteronomistic History, it served to interpret those events. The proper prophetic task is to show how God is at work in his world in the midst of the turmoil of human events.

The divine choice of David and Solomon as the founders of the kingdom is a point developed extensively in Chronicles. Though the Chronicler relies extensively on the history of Samuel and Kings, he has no parallel for the account of the Davidic succession. The word of Yahweh had come to David saying that a son would be born who would be a man of peace (1 Chron. 22:9–10); even his name (*š'lōmōh*) means peace (*šālôm*). The temple would be built in a time of peace. When David became old, he appointed Solomon to be king (1 Chron. 23:1). Out of all of David's many sons, God had declared that Solomon would succeed him and build the temple (28:5–7). In David's final prayer and blessing he asks that Solomon (*š'lōmōh*) have a whole heart (*šālēm*) to observe the regulations of the covenant and to build the great citadel, which he had prepared (29:19–20). The conflict by which Solomon came to be king has no significance in the version of Chronicles. In this respect the Chronicler interprets the Kings story correctly. The divine plan and purpose are the only matters of importance; it is important to discern them in the melee of human events.

Human government. Civilized societies exist by the order of human government. This is a central point of the Genesis flood story. Being made in the image of God was the power for humans to represent the rule of God in this world. God made his image as male and female (Gen. 1:26–27); they were to be fruitful and multiply because only collectively, as a human society, could they fulfill the mandate of representation, exercising dominion in God's world on his behalf (v. 28). The human choice to be godlike themselves and determine in their own estimate right and wrong (3:5) led to the disintegration of an orderly society. This disintegration began with the inability of humans to live as a family. Life would continue through childbirth, but the birth of children would bring distress.[26]

Cain's killing Abel reached a climax in the horrible statement of Lamech expressing his perverse idea of justice: "I have killed a man for wounding me, a young man for injuring me. If Cain is avenged seven times, then Lamech seventy-seven times" (Gen. 4:23b–24). This philosophy led to a human wickedness in which "every inclination of the thoughts of his heart was only evil all the time" (6:5b). The only possibility was a new beginning, which came about with the earth going back to water and with one family again representing the grace of God. God again provided for human society, requiring this family to also be fruitful, multiply, and fill the earth (9:1, 7). This time there was a provision for the inevitable violence stemming from the ethics of revenge: "Whoever sheds the blood of man, by man shall his blood be shed; for in the image of God has God made man" (v. 6). This is a mandate for order; it means that humans who violate the sanctity of the image representing God by killing a person will themselves come under the authority of those who represent the order of God's will. The enforcement of this order extends to the very right of life itself; human governments under certain conditions may need to exercise an ultimate authority over life.

The Scriptures never suggest that human government is a solution to the power of evil. They recognize that often it is government itself that is the worst perpetrator of violence and evil. There is good reason why the books of Daniel and Revelation describe human governments as horrible beasts trampling, devouring, and killing. Habakkuk complained about the injustice and disorder of human government, even within divine providence.

> Why then do you tolerate the treacherous?
>> Why are you silent while the wicked
>>> swallow up those more righteous than themselves?
> You have made men like fish in the sea,
>> like sea creatures that have no ruler.
> The wicked foe pulls all of them up with hooks,
>> he catches them in his net,

---

26. The pain (*ʿiṣṣābōn*) in Gen. 3:16 associated with bearing children is emotional. In 5:29 the name Noah (meaning "rest") was to express comfort from painful toil. See John H. Walton, *Genesis* (NIVAC; Grand Rapids: Zondervan, 2001), 227. The name *yaʿbēṣ* in 1 Chronicles 4:10 is a play on the word "pain" in Genesis; S. Japhet, *I & II Chronicles* (Louisville: Westminster John Knox, 1993), 109.

he gathers them in his dragnet;
    and so he rejoices and is glad.
Therefore he sacrifices to his net
    and burns incense to his dragnet,
for by his net he lives in luxury
    and enjoys the choicest food. (Hab. 1:13b–16)

The rule of human government has often seemed out of control, left to the devices of the most wicked, a situation no different than that of Lamech. Even in the best of human governments there is violence and there are victims. The chaos at the transfer of the reign of David was a judgment brought on by David's own failures and sins, as explained by Nathan the prophet (2 Sam. 12:11–12). Those of his own household would repeat the murder and adultery of David in the Uriah affair. The whole account of David's succession was a demonstration of the fulfillment of the prophetic word: the rape of Tamar by her brother Amnon, the revolt of Absalom, the revolt of Sheba, and finally the attempted coup of Adonijah. It was the conviction of the prophetic authors of Kings that David was the man "after the heart of God;"[27] their point was that God had chosen both David and his successor. That was never meant to suggest that in his life and in his kingdom he was always able to represent the rule and the will of God. Human government is necessary to order, but human government is not the solution to the violent disruption of order, as governments fail and create victims of their own.

A better kingdom. The succession of Solomon was an affirmation of the divine promise to David and a hope cherished by David. It was the search for a better order, the hope of a better kingdom. This hope is implicit in the Deuteronomistic History, as it continues the story of the promise to Abraham (Gen. 12:1–3) and the promise of Nathan (2 Sam. 7:11b–17). The hope of the kingdom lived on after the Exile, though an independent kingdom of David never again became a reality. The New Testament begins with this hope: "A record of the genealogy of Jesus Christ the son of David, the son of Abraham" (Matt. 1:1). The message of Jesus and of the Gospels was that the hope of the kingdom had become a reality. Immediately after the death of John the Baptist Jesus went throughout Galilee "proclaiming the good news of God. 'The time has come,' he said. 'The kingdom of God is near'" (Mark 1:14b–15a).

Like David, those who follow Christ and choose the kingdom often do not have a good record of living up to their ideals. This does not deny the

---

27. The genitive in this expression acts as the subject of the verbal idea; "heart" is a metaphor for decision or resolve. The meaning is that God had chosen David (1 Sam. 13:14), not that David had chosen God (an objective genitive).

reality of the kingdom of God. It is near—near to the extent that it is found in our midst insofar as God's will is done on earth as it is in heaven. Like David, those who pursue this hope may have to be called to account for their failures and may suffer the consequences of their sins. Like David, those who pursue this hope must not lose faith in its reality, even in the midst of the ugliness of human politics.

Contemporary Christians find themselves in a more compromised situation than the Deuteronomistic Historians in evaluating right of governance. Since Israel was deemed the chosen nation, there could be no doubt that the enthronement of Solomon was a demonstration of God's will. Yet the political responsibility of the faithful is comparable. The failure of nationalistic Israel will soon enough make her the object of divine wrath, unworthy of the loyalty of its citizens. Isaiah declares that God will avenge himself of his enemy, the formerly faithful city of Zion, for she has become a harlot in her failure to provide justice (Isa. 1:21—26).

Though Solomon was God's king and uncompromising allegiance belonged to him, by the end of his reign quite a different assessment is rendered. The verdict is that Solomon has done what was wrong in the Lord's opinion (1 Kings 11:6). That did not diminish his right to rule or the initial necessity of supporting that rule. The strategy of the whole narrative of Solomon is to show that Israel's brief moment of greatness is lost by the perverse actions of passionate and headstrong individuals.[28] Unqualified and enthusiastic loyalty is obligatory when Solomon comes to the throne.

Christians serve the kingdom of God, a kingdom that can never be identified with any of the kingdoms of human rule. This was true even in the time of David; though David represented the promise of the kingdom, his kingdom did not in itself constitute the kingdom of God. A nationalist state proved unable to serve as the true bearer of the will of God on earth. Though its succession of leaders will be orderly, especially in comparison to the kingdom of Israel in the north, the despotic nature of its dominion is not different in substance. Judah will share in the tyrannies of Israel, often as an ally as long as the state of Israel exists. Though Judah will endure more than a century longer than Israel, her temple and city are similarly doomed. The promise to David, so hopefully anticipated in the accession of Solomon, is not doomed. With the demise of Hebrew nationalism the promise to the son of Jesse comes to be reinterpreted as a kingdom of another order under a king who will truly represent the justice of God (Isa. 11:1—10). In the person of Jesus Christ the promise is realized, the announcement of the kingdom is made.

---

28. James S. Ackerman, "Knowing Good and Evil: A Literary Analysis of the Court History in 2 Samuel 9—20 and 1 Kings 1—2," *JBL* 109 (1990): 59.

THE DYNAMIC BETWEEN **human volition and divine purpose**. The account of Solomon securing his throne remains "a fairly sordid story of power politics disguised as a morality tale."[29] In removing all opposition to his rule, Solomon is depicted as acting in accordance with "wisdom" (2:6, 9); his acquisition of the throne is described according to the defining characteristic of his reign (3:12, 28; 4:29, 30, 34; 5:7, 12; 10:4, 6, 8; 11:41). Though the "wisdom of Solomon" is proverbial, his acquisition of the throne is not remembered as the prototypical example of wise conduct. It was the goal of the biblical authors to show that Solomon was the divine choice in the history of the kingdom. He was granted opportunity to become the greatest of all kings in fulfillment of the promise to David. His enthronement was an example of grace in a long account of missed opportunity and ultimate failure.

The enthusiastic statements about the celebration of Solomon's rule, with the wish that the fame of Solomon might exceed that of his father, leave no doubt about the conviction of the Deuteronomistic Historians (1 Kings 1:47–48). For the sake of the kingdom of God, it is important that the throne be made secure under Solomon's dominion, and to that end it is necessary and good that all opposition to his rule be quelled. The skeptical reader will find this to be an indictment of the low spiritual ideals of the time, demonstrating an attitude that the end justified the means. A desire to find God's will in these events inevitably lends legitimacy to the charge that implicit approval is given to the methods of Solomon. The contemporary Christian faces a similar cynicism when attempting to discern God's will in current events.

A high theology in this narrative may be discerned in the blunt presentations of the flawed actions of each of the characters. There is no flattering portrayal of a champion; the deeds of each individual are frankly described, even though this may diminish the reader's estimation of all of the characters. The prophetic authors present a realistic and believable portrait of the succession to David's throne. They hold God in highest esteem; God alone is allowed to be the hero in an otherwise sordid tale. Understanding the dynamic between human volition and divine purpose becomes particularly difficult in dealing with the depraved behavior of human conflict.

Christians in a more free and democratic society must be grateful for the possibility of succession of power more orderly than that of the succession of David. A more merciful understanding of personal interaction does not

29. Ian Provan, *1 & 2 Kings* (NIBC; Peabody, Mass.: Hendrickson, 1995), 40.

require that old animosities need to be settled with liquidation of former opponents. Christians have faith in divine guidance, but they have many different opinions about correct political decisions. No one country or leader can be identified as representing the rule of God, so Christians can never have an exclusive loyalty to one political power. Christians often disagree with political positions of other Christians, and sometimes favor the leadership of a non-Christian to that of someone professing to follow Christ.

In a democratic society, Christians are asked to be a part of the process by which leaders come into power. Admittedly the procedures are often not fair and equitable, and sometimes the leaders are flawed. Nevertheless, these procedures are regarded as a means ordained by God to accomplish his purpose in the world in which his people live. As with Solomon, God carries out his purposes through imperfect people using imperfect methods of achieving their goals.

Though no one nation or leader can be identified with God's rule in the same way, there is no doubt about the obligation of the Christian to support human government as an institution ordained by God for the good of people. The words of the apostle Paul are rightly cited in this regard: "Let every person be subject to the governing authorities. For no authority exists as such except by God's appointment, and the authorities which are have been ordained by God" (Rom. 13:1).[30] Paul's view is that the state serves the good of its citizens (v. 4), so support for the authority of the state can be regarded as part of one's debt of love to one's neighbor (v. 8). When the apostle says that all authorities have been ordained by God, he expresses a truth that is the main point of the succession of Solomon: God accomplishes his purposes for the establishment of his kingdom amidst the foul politics of nations. Those who actually achieve political authority may be deemed to represent the divine purpose in that time and circumstance.

Being subject to authority. Being subject to the governing authorities must not be understood as obedience. Being subject indicates the proper attitude of a Christian to the leaders of the church (Rom. 8:7), to civil authorities (1 Peter 2:13), and to God (James 4:7). It describes the mind of Christian wives to their husbands (Eph. 5:22), servants to their masters (1 Peter 2:18), the young to their elders (5:5), and the church to Christ (Eph. 5:24). Particularly noteworthy is the reciprocal obligation of Christians to each other (5:21). Calvin's comment on being "subject to one another" provides the clue to Christian responsibility:

---

30. Translation of C. E. B. Cranfield, *A Critical and Exegetical Commentary on the Epistle to the Romans* (ICC; Edinburgh: T. & T. Clark, 1979), 2:656.

God has so bound us to each other that no man ought to avoid subjection. And where love reigns, there is a mutual servitude. I do not except even kings and governors, for they rule that they may serve. Therefore it is very right that he should exhort all to be subject to each other.[31]

The obligation of being mutually subject to one another becomes clear when compared with other injunctions to believers.[32] Paul asks that believers "prefer one another in honor" (Rom. 12:10) and "in humility give consideration to others rather than themselves" (Phil. 2:3). Submission denotes the recognition that the other person has a greater claim upon oneself and the conduct that must be rendered in such a claim. Persons in authority, as Christians, must regard all subordinates as having a greater claim on them than they have on themselves. All other Christians must be regarded as a representative of Christ.

When used of civil authority, submission is a debt assumed under the authority of God. As God's servant and an instrument of Christ's kingly rule, a leader must exercise that debt of love to one's neighbor insofar as the authority of the state is for the good of one's neighbor. Since Christ himself is mysteriously present in the neighbor of the Christian, the neighbor has a claim greater than that owed to oneself. Such responsibility is not a blind uncritical obedience to every obligation the civil authority might require, because the final arbiter of the obligatory duty is not the state but God. Support of the state is necessary unless its requirements demonstrably violate the obligation of love to one's neighbor.

Christians may still find themselves in an authoritarian state like that of the nation of Israel, in which they are required to respect their masters and comply with their requirements, insofar as they do not conflict with Christian morality. They must pay their taxes willingly, since no government can function without such resources. The state authority is to be regarded as the agent of good as the appointed minister of God (Rom. 13:3–4).

This does not seem to take into account the possibility of an evil government that punishes good work and gives praise to the evil. It is impossible that Paul, who suffered so much at the hands of civil authority, did not consider this possibility, or that he limited his thought to only those governments that properly carry out their civil authority. The promise appears to be absolute: Christians, when in obedience to God, may be sure that the power of the state will honor them.[33] It may indeed punish them for good

---

31. John Calvin, *The Epistles of Paul the Apostle to the Galatians, Ephesians, Philippians, and Colossians*, trans. T. H. L. Parker (Grand Rapids: Eerdmans, 1965), 204.

32. Cranfield, *Epistle to the Romans*, 2:661–62.

33. Ibid., 665.

deeds, but its intended punishment will turn out to be praise. Christians may die under the power of the state, but in so doing will receive a crown of glory. If, however, Christians do wrong, it is the obligation of the state to punish them as the authority ordained of God for this purpose. The reason for this absolute promise is because the state authority is the minister of God (13:4), whether recognized or not.

The principles of Jesus' kingdom. The Christian lays claim to belonging to the kingdom that was the fulfillment of the promise to David. The desire of the authors who found in Solomon the one anointed of God is realized in the One proclaimed to be the King of all kings. The attitude of citizens of such a kingdom is expressed in the Beatitudes, in which Jesus taught the principles of his kingdom (Matt. 5:3–11). The reward of these Beatitudes is not only divine beneficence but divine approval, as expressed in Psalm 1:1–2. This approval comes on those who recognize their own weakness and poverty before God and accept their utter dependence on God's grace because of their own sins (Matt. 5:3). Such recognition leads to sorrow, but it is a sadness to which God will provide consolation (v. 4). These are the meek who will inherit the earth (v. 5), as God had said in the promise to David and Solomon.

The citizens of this kingdom desire the justice and mercy of God, and in this quest they will find satisfaction (Matt. 5:6). Having experienced God fulfilling what is right, they will be the ones to show mercy and in turn receive mercy (v. 7). Their motivation is none other than the kingdom of God; the singular focus of their minds will be rewarded with seeing God (v. 8). These are the peacemakers. Peacemakers most often arouse the wrath of all and may suffer the most, even at the hands of civil authority. This, however, will be the mark that they are the children of God (v. 9); when persecuted for reasons of justice, they will be assured that they are citizens of God's kingdom (v. 10). Such persecution may well come from those who regard themselves as the guardians of justice; such suffering is a cause of joy to the extent that it identifies the citizens of the kingdom with the prophets, who suffered for God in the same way (vv. 11–12).

Working for political influence. It has not been easy for Christians to find their proper place among the political forces of this world. Christians have sometimes had the role of an Adonijah and suffered at the hands of a Solomon, the political power indeed ordained of God. During the time of the Reformation Thomas Müntzer organized an armed insurrection against the state in a resistance known as the Peasant's Revolt (1524–25). Müntzer was an accomplished scholar of Latin, Greek, and Hebrew, one of the most learned in the writings of the Old and New Testaments. He was attracted to Martin Luther, but soon went his own way with his ideas of the Reformation as a revolution. He organized the working classes into a group called the "Eternal Covenant of God."

Out of egoistical, material, and provincial motives, Müntzer dismissed resistance to his movement as a revolt against God.[34] He attempted to relate his struggles for the immediate concerns of peasants, tradesmen, and commoners with the liberation of all Christendom. The common people briefly triumphed over the religious and civil authorities, but they were defeated by the strength of the princes in the Battle of Frankenhausen in 1525. Müntzer regarded the collapse of the revolt as the judgment of God on the as yet unpurified people, but not as the defeat of the creation of a new society. His revolution became the symbol for revolutionary movements in which there would be a free people, who themselves wielded the sword and who tolerated no governmental authority.

Violent resistance against the state also occurred among the early Anabaptists. Anabaptists were radical reformers in their rejection of the state church and their denial of the validity of infant baptism administered under state authority. A zealot by the name of John of Leiden (originally Jan Beuckelson) attempted to establish their "kingdom of a thousand years" in the city of Münster in 1534. The lawlessness of his theocratic rule seriously discredited the entire Anabaptist movement. In 1535 the local prince-bishop regained control of the city in a violent and bloody struggle. The iron cages in which the bodies of John and his followers were exhibited still hang in the Gothic tower of St. Lambert's Church.

In contrast to John of Leiden, Balthasar Hubmaier was an Anabaptist whose death at the hands of the state turned to his praise. Hubmaier was a doctor of theology, appointed cathedral preacher at Regensburg. In 1521 he arrived in Switzerland, where he became a leader of the fledging Anabaptist movement. Even the liberal Zwinglians persecuted him for his radical beliefs. Undeterred, he resumed his proselytizing in Augsburg and later in Moravia (modern Czech Republic). Constantly hunted by imperial authorities, Hubmaier was captured and burned at the stake as a heretic at Vienna. His example of living a life of peace and nonresistance against a violent state is vividly portrayed in the film *The Radicals* (1990). The film brilliantly shows how state leaders in their execution of Hubmaier gave praise to his courage and virtue, even as they believed they were fulfilling their God-given duties of enforcing law and order.

Hubmaier towers as an example of a citizen of the kingdom of God against the millenarian anarchism of Thomas Müntzer and John of Leiden.

---

34. Manfred Bensing, "Müntzer, Thomas," *Encyclopedia Britannica Macropaedia*, 15th ed., 12:620.

Regarding the "authority ordained by God" as illegitimate only brought about a great carnage of many victims. Like Adonijah, they regarded their claims as legitimate, oblivious to their own greedy ambitions. The church leaders of state power similarly regarded Hubmaier as a dangerous enemy, but in their brutal actions they unwittingly honored his good work. Fulfilling the will of God in doing good, he put to silence the ignorance of foolish men (1 Peter 2:15). Hubmaier was instrumental in a movement that attempted to live in peace in the midst of violence.

Politics is a subject that is taboo at many family gatherings. Families can agree on basic matters of faith, share similar values and ideals, but be hopelessly in conflict on matters of political policy. This is often true whether the issues concern community, state, national, or international matters. This conflict has been particularly evident at protests against summits dealing with global economic policy. The protesters often have little in common, other than that they oppose what they perceive will be the policies set at such summits by democratically elected governments. These summits are viewed as a collective collusion against the poor. But rather than voice their opinions through their representatives, the compulsion to personally express a different point of view drives them to alternate attempts at exercising political coercion, even some that are illegal. The irony is that often those inside the political process and those protesting against it are seeking to achieve the same goals. They simply differ on the means by which these may be achieved. These differences of opinion often divide those who are most closely bonded in other ways.

Citizens of the modern world must be grateful for the possibility of non-violent political influence. Christians in such societies have opportunity to exercise their debt of love to their neighbors, because the authority of the state takes seriously its responsibility to rule for the good of their neighbors. In a political climate less violent and confrontational than that of the Reformation or the succession of David, there is greater opportunity for Christians to live out the ideals of the kingdom as taught by Christ. This opportunity is both a great responsibility and a difficult challenge.

Politics is almost never truly altruistic. Invariably those who hold strong opinions on political points of view for good order in society have a great deal of personal ego and ambition for power invested in their efforts. Many cases of political conflict are almost purely a matter of individual aggression, but almost never are they solely a matter of self-sacrificing service for the well-being of others. The drive for personal prominence has the power to violate the most sacred of relationships, including those between spouses, siblings, and children. The drive for personal success, combined with personally held values about right and good in human society, becomes a formidable force.

Virtually every relationship can be sacrificed for the sake of political power. Charles Colson, the man who went to prison for his activities on behalf of a president of the United States, publicly confessed that at one time he would have sacrificed his own grandmother to achieve his political objectives.

The ideal of democracies is that we live by the will of the majority and protect the rights of the minority. This ideal is rarely, if ever, reached; in spite of ingenious schemes of representation, most of the time a powerful minority rules the majority. At times rights of the minority are in conflict with the rights or values of the majority. The merit of democracies is not that their rule is necessarily better, that they represent the will of the majority, or the rights of all. The merit of democracies is their provision for regular and orderly transfer of power. In human society transfer of power is often desirable for political reasons, but inevitable as leaders pass on.

In this age human government is God's provision for order, and that must include the means by which governments come into power. In the consummation of God's promise of the kingdom, the prophets looked for a descendant of David quite different than Solomon:

> For to us a child is born,
>   to us a son is given,
>   and the government will be on his shoulders.
> And he will be will be called
>   Wonderful Counselor, Mighty God,
>   Everlasting Father, Prince of Peace.
> Of the increase of his government and peace
>   there will be no end.
> He will reign on David's throne,
>   and over his kingdom,
> establishing it and upholding it,
>   with justice and righteousness,
>   from that time on and forever.
> The zeal of the LORD Almighty
>   will accomplish this. (Isa. 9:6–7)

1 Kings 3:1–28

SOLOMON MADE AN alliance with Pharaoh king of Egypt and married his daughter. He brought her to the City of David until he finished building his palace and the temple of the LORD, and the wall around Jerusalem. ²The people, however, were still sacrificing at the high places, because a temple had not yet been built for the Name of the LORD. ³Solomon showed his love for the LORD by walking according to the statutes of his father David, except that he offered sacrifices and burned incense on the high places.

⁴The king went to Gibeon to offer sacrifices, for that was the most important high place, and Solomon offered a thousand burnt offerings on that altar. ⁵At Gibeon the LORD appeared to Solomon during the night in a dream, and God said, "Ask for whatever you want me to give you."

⁶Solomon answered, "You have shown great kindness to your servant, my father David, because he was faithful to you and righteous and upright in heart. You have continued this great kindness to him and have given him a son to sit on his throne this very day.

⁷"Now, O LORD my God, you have made your servant king in place of my father David. But I am only a little child and do not know how to carry out my duties. ⁸Your servant is here among the people you have chosen, a great people, too numerous to count or number. ⁹So give your servant a discerning heart to govern your people and to distinguish between right and wrong. For who is able to govern this great people of yours?"

¹⁰The Lord was pleased that Solomon had asked for this. ¹¹So God said to him, "Since you have asked for this and not for long life or wealth for yourself, nor have asked for the death of your enemies but for discernment in administering justice, ¹²I will do what you have asked. I will give you a wise and discerning heart, so that there will never have been anyone like you, nor will there ever be. ¹³Moreover, I will give you what you have not asked for—both riches and honor— so that in your lifetime you will have no equal among kings. ¹⁴And if you walk in my ways and obey my statutes and

commands as David your father did, I will give you a long life." ¹⁵Then Solomon awoke—and he realized it had been a dream.

He returned to Jerusalem, stood before the ark of the Lord's covenant and sacrificed burnt offerings and fellowship offerings. Then he gave a feast for all his court.

¹⁶Now two prostitutes came to the king and stood before him. ¹⁷One of them said, "My lord, this woman and I live in the same house. I had a baby while she was there with me. ¹⁸The third day after my child was born, this woman also had a baby. We were alone; there was no one in the house but the two of us.

¹⁹"During the night this woman's son died because she lay on him. ²⁰So she got up in the middle of the night and took my son from my side while I your servant was asleep. She put him by her breast and put her dead son by my breast. ²¹The next morning, I got up to nurse my son—and he was dead! But when I looked at him closely in the morning light, I saw that it wasn't the son I had borne."

²²The other woman said, "No! The living one is my son; the dead one is yours."

But the first one insisted, "No! The dead one is yours; the living one is mine." And so they argued before the king.

²³The king said, "This one says, 'My son is alive and your son is dead,' while that one says, 'No! Your son is dead and mine is alive.'"

²⁴Then the king said, "Bring me a sword." So they brought a sword for the king. ²⁵He then gave an order: "Cut the living child in two and give half to one and half to the other."

²⁶The woman whose son was alive was filled with compassion for her son and said to the king, "Please, my lord, give her the living baby! Don't kill him!"

But the other said, "Neither I nor you shall have him. Cut him in two!"

²⁷Then the king gave his ruling: "Give the living baby to the first woman. Do not kill him; she is his mother."

²⁸When all Israel heard the verdict the king had given, they held the king in awe, because they saw that he had wisdom from God to administer justice.

WHEN SOLOMON WAS born, the prophet Nathan received a message from the Lord declaring his name to be Jedidiah, meaning "the beloved one of Yahweh" (2 Sam. 12:25). The new king ascended by royal and divine sanction, as did the kings of other nations.[1] The divine choice of Solomon is confirmed in a dream epiphany in which God grants to him the wisdom he will need to be a successful ruler (3:1–15). The judgment of Solomon in settling the quarrel of the two prostitutes over whose child has survived (3:16–28) serves to exemplify the legendary "wisdom of Solomon."

The renowned wisdom of Solomon is exemplified in two special collections in the Septuagint (LXX).[2] The first collection consists of ten verses after 1 Kings 2:35, the second an additional ten verses after 2:46.[3] Both miscellanies are carefully crafted to demonstrate Solomon's wisdom in his building projects and administrative policies.[4] For the ancient translators, these were two primary examples of Solomon exercising wisdom in his rule. Domestic and foreign policies are the fundamental elements of good rule, the way in which justice and peace may be brought to the people. In the Greek Bible this additional commentary serves to introduce the divine legitimation of Solomon.

The Divine Gift of Wisdom (1 Kings 3:1–15)

SOLOMON IS AN eminently successful king renowned for his wisdom and wealth. His success is the result of a superior administration, enabling him to raise revenues far beyond anything previous to that time. The introductory note about Solomon's marriage to the daughter of Pharaoh (3:1) is significant in relation to his worship at Gibeon and the building of the temple.

---

1. The accession of Solomon can be compared to that of Esarhaddon or Ashurbanipal (Ahlström, *The History of Ancient Palestine,* 501). Both were ritually chosen and installed as crown princes instead of their older brothers. Esarhaddon was militarily opposed, but when the armies met the soldiers of the rebels, they defected to Esarahaddon as the rightful king.

2. The appendix on the Greek text of Kings provides a brief description of these additions. The term Septuagint is used for the printed editions of the great Christian codices (Sinaiticus, Vaticanus, Alexandrinus) of the fourth and fifth centuries. These manuscripts contain a variety of translations and revisions. As noted earlier, Old Greek will be used for a distinctly earlier translation of Kings preserved within the manuscript tradition.

3. The first collection is followed by four verses that repeat David's orders concerning Shimei (2:8–9). The collections are placed before and after the account of Solomon dealing with Shimei (1 Kings 2:36–46).

4. This has been established by D. W. Gooding, *Relics of Ancient Exegesis: A Study of the Miscellanies in 3 Reigns 2* (Cambridge: Cambridge Univ. Press, 1976), 7–17.

Solomon has become allied to Pharaoh, likely in connection with Egyptian campaigns into Philistine country (9:16). The daughter of Pharaoh lives in the City of David (the royal fortress on the southeastern hill) until the completion of the royal building projects (9:24). The building of the temple begins in the fourth year of Solomon's reign (6:1); the death of Shimei takes place at the end of his third year (2:39). The vision at Gibeon takes place in the midst of these complicated political maneuvers. The mention of Pharaoh's daughter calls attention to Solomon's prominent international position early in his reign.

It is often suggested that the Greek translators deliberately omit mention of Pharaoh's daughter (3:1) because they are offended by the thought of a foreign woman in the precincts of the holy city.[5] The Greek text does include Pharaoh's daughter in the first miscellany on wisdom noted above (LXX 2:35–36); the Greek has a completely different arrangement of text rather than a difference in content. The many different details about Solomon's wisdom, polity, and administration, his visit to Gibeon, and his diplomatic relations with other kings all emphasize the different aspects of Solomon's wisdom and reign.[6] The first part of Solomon's reign is most magnificent.

Solomon's choice to worship outside of Jerusalem (3:4) is normal before the completion of the temple (3:2), but the choice of Gibeon is politically expedient.[7] Gibeonite territory was one of the first areas to become a part of Saul's kingdom, and a new king would need to renew the connection with the Gibeonites, possibly through a treaty, in order to become recognized as their ruler.

Gibeon is situated on the western edge of a large and level plateau just over five miles to the west of Jerusalem.[8] From Gibeon the roads turns north to Bethel and south to Jerusalem. It guards the roads leading east from the coastal plain through the Aijalon Valley via Beth Horon. Gibeon is the natural hub of conflict between Israel and Judah. It is also home to the largest "high place" (*bāmâ*) in the country, a prominent location for the worship of Yahweh before worship at the temple in Jerusalem is established.

The *bāmâ* is a place of worship, but it is not necessarily a "high place." This

---

5. DeVries, *1 Kings*, 50.

6. Gary N. Knoppers, *The Reign of Solomon and the Rise of Jeroboam*. Vol. 1 of *Two Nations under God: The Deuteronomistic History of Solomon and the Dual Monarchies* (HSM 52; Atlanta: Scholars Press, 1993), 77–80.

7. Ahlström, *The History of Ancient Palestine*, 504.

8. The city is identified with the ruin of Tell el-Jib by jar handles inscribed with the name. For the location see Barry Beitzel, *The Moody Atlas of Bible Lands* (Chicago: Moody Press, 1985), #15, 17. Gibeon is to be distinguished from the famous hill called Gibeah of Saul, usually identified with Tell el-Fûl, about a mile and a half to the southeast of Gibeon.

English translation is derived from Jerome's fourth-century Latin, which rendered *bāmâ* as *excelsus* ("high, eminent, illustrious"). The term appears over one hundred times in the Bible, primarily for a cultic site of some sort. A comparison of the social context of biblical texts with archaeological evidence of cultic sites indicates that there was a considerable development of worship at such shrines.[9]

Up until the time of David and Solomon these places of worship are found at locations within Israelite territory as legitimate places of Yahweh worship. They are found within settlements or in the countryside; their architecture ranges from a built-up pilgrimage site (Shiloh) to open-air sanctuaries (Mount Ebal). Sanctuaries excavated from the time of David and Solomon indicate that the *bāmâ* was usually within a building inside a village or town (Megiddo, Lachish, Beth Shean), often in peripheral locations where ethnically divergent populations may have required special attention to draw them into the Israelite nation. They often include limestone altars and limestone or ceramic stands. These places of worship seem to have become an institution for forging national unification of disparate elements through social and religious control.

This same policy is carried on during the divided monarchy; Dan and Bethel especially are constructed as sites to retain control over northern Israel. But once worship at the temple in Jerusalem is established, these other centers are not regarded as legitimate places for worship of Yahweh. Some of these shrines are not for the worship of Yahweh. Solomon, for example, builds alternate places of worship in Jerusalem for his non-Israelite wives and for the gods of Sidon, Ammon, and Moab (11:7—8). Centuries later, during the times of Hezekiah and Josiah, local places of worship to Yahweh are still in existence, providing certain regional autonomy for disenfranchised priestly groups to conduct worship outside of Jerusalem.

It is not evident that all these shrines can be called a "high place." Zevit limits the *bāmâ* to those public places of worship with standing stone pillars called *maṣṣēbôt*.[10] The *bāmâ* is to be distinguished from an altar, as both are said to be present at the same shrine and the former may be found inside a building (2 Chron. 14:2; 31:1; 34:3—4). Sacrifices and offerings are made at or near the high place (1 Kings 3:3; 12:31—32; 22:44), but they are not altars; rather, they only share certain features with altars (cf. 2 Kings 18:22; 21:3). It is a type of platform that could be taken apart stone by stone. It could serve as the base for images and was the location for rituals involving offerings to various deities.

---

9. Beth Alpert Nakhai, "What's a Bamah? How Sacred Space Functioned in Ancient Israel," *BAR* 20/3 (1994): 19—29, 77—78.

10. Zevit, *The Religions of Ancient Israel*, 262—63. The *maṣṣēbôt* are "aniconic representations of the deity whose function is to guarantee its presence when addressed" (261).

The worship of Solomon at Gibeon may have included a ceremony to achieve political union with a northern territory, but Solomon is also seeking guidance and blessing from Yahweh. Kings were the means of divine blessing, and like other similar royal ceremonies in the ancient Near East, Solomon may have offered his sacrifices in order to receive revelation.

A considerable variety of Assyrian and Babylonian royal inscriptions testify to the experience of a king receiving a message from his god.[11] It has been proposed that the entrance of the god into the dream of the king was facilitated by the presence of a statue of the divinity in the temple and particular ritual preparations.[12] In the case of Solomon, the presence of the sanctuary, the sacrifices, the night sleep, and a dream are features that have the closest resemblance in Scripture to institutionalized practices designed to receive a divine message.

In Greek practice, rituals referred to as incubation served to facilitate the reception of a divine message (usually for healing). These took place in temples of deceased heroes; purification took place through sacrifice, often accompanied by fasting, special diets, and sexual abstinence. The incubants went to sleep in a special part of the temple that seems to have been an arcade open to the elements on one side. There is little evidence, however, of such practices elsewhere in the ancient Near East; most incidents describe unsolicited dreams with no formal link between any ritual and the dream.[13] The sacrifices of Solomon at Gibeon fit this pattern; however, no questions are posed as part of the ceremony, nor is there reference to where he sleeps. From the beginning the divine word determines the structure of the dialogue (v. 5b). Solomon makes his request (vv. 6–9), and God grants the gift (vv. 11–14).

When Yahweh appears in the dream, Solomon makes his request in terms of the covenant relationship established with David his father (v. 6). "Great kindness" is an expression of covenant loyalty, describing integrity in a relationship. David had shown this kind of faithfulness, living before God with equity and justice, so God in turn had been faithful with David in providing a successor to the throne. As a new king Solomon is inexperienced; he is not really a "little child" (v. 7), since he already has a son when he begins his reign. Solomon rules forty years (11:42), and his son Rehoboam is forty-one when he begins to reign (14:21).

---

11. Jean-Marie Husser provides a number of examples in *Dreams and Dream Narratives in the Biblical World* (Sheffield: Sheffield Academic Press, 1999), 38–44.

12. Ibid., 46.

13. S. A. L. Butler provides a review of texts that may suggest incubation rituals in *Mesopotamian Conceptions of Dreams and Dream Rituals* (Münster: Ugarit-Verlag, 1998), 218–39. These provide no overall pattern to confirm the actual practice of such rituals.

As king, Solomon has the well-being of the people at heart; his request is to be able to rule with justice, having the wisdom to hear both sides of every story with a discerning mind (v. 9). As a king whose first concern is the well-being of the people, Solomon is also granted that which he does not request: wealth, honor, and a long life. Though any wise king would receive wealth and honor as a consequence of his good rule, these are given by God in abundant measure, so that Solomon is renowned for the greatness of his kingdom.

After the dream Solomon returns to Jerusalem, where he worships before the ark and has a great feast. Having been assured at Gibeon that his rule is secure, it is only appropriate that he bring offerings before the ark, which contains the words of the covenant with God, and holds a feast with his servants, who will share in his new empire.

Justice of a Wise King (1 Kings 3:16–28)

THE EXCEPTIONAL WISDOM granted to Solomon is next demonstrated in a difficult judicial case. Ancient Mesopotamian kings kept records of exceptional legal cases presented to their deity as a report that they had acted wisely as a just king.[14] This report of Solomon's judicial activity follows a similar practice. The evidence of both parties is presented as given orally before the king (vv. 16–22), and the king sums up the argument (v. 23). It is his responsibility to render a decision when there are no independent witnesses and where there is a great deal of bitterness between the two litigants.

The story has worldwide parallels that have been collocated for comparison.[15] It is commonly regarded as a familiar tale that has been linked to Solomon.[16] This event is a distinguished example in royal records that demonstrate the fulfillment of the divine promise. The purpose of the prophetic authors in the Bible is not to provide a review of various judicial activities of the king, critical as these are, but merely to illustrate his concern and competence for justice in the exercise of extraordinary wisdom that he has just divinely received.

Several features in the story about Solomon settling the dispute between the two women call attention to his insightful and sympathetic rule. Prostitutes

---

14. See D. J. Wiseman, "Law and Order in OT Times," *VE* 8 (1973): 9–10.

15. Montgomery (*The Books of Kings*, 108–9) documents a number of different studies and sources; one study by H. Gressmann entitled "Das Salomonische Urteil" (*Deutsche Rundschau* 103 [1907], 212) cites twenty-two similar cases in folktale and literature.

16. DeVries says, "If this anecdote actually were about Solomon, we would receive a charmingly favorable glimpse of his character" (*1 Kings*, 58). The temporal adverb "then" (ʾāz, v. 16) and the conclusion (v. 28) are regarded as providing a secondary application to Israel.

were tolerated as a part of Israelite society, though prostitution was disdained and condemned.[17] Ancient prostitutes were generally slaves, often daughters who had been sold by their own parents. Or they were poor women who had never had an opportunity to marry or who had lost their husbands and were not supported by their own families. A levirate marriage (Deut. 25:5–10) required that a widow become the wife of a surviving brother to provide for normal inheritance and to allow the widow to have economic security and the social status of marriage and children. It was possible for a brother to refuse this responsibility.

Prostitutes were most to be pitied as the victims of a society that failed to care for the helpless and the poor.[18] Kings were the highest recourse for justice, expected to be in a place of public access to take up the case of the widow, the orphan, and the oppressed. Note how Solomon has time for the most vulnerable of his subjects, not only in terms of their poverty but also in terms of their vices. These victims are not without faults of their own, and in this case at least one woman is prepared to sacrifice the life of a child to spite her housemate and satisfy her own feelings of grief and rage. The story demonstrates not only Solomon's wisdom, but also a genuine concern for the well-being of all citizens of his kingdom.

The judgment of Solomon shows both mercy and justice—in principle both mutually exclusive, but in practice both indispensably necessary. The Hebrew text makes the circumstances of the death explicit. The two women are together with no "stranger" (*zār*) present (v. 18); the women have no family, so anyone else in the house would have been a stranger, namely, one of their clients. Since none was present, the death of the infant can only be the responsibility of its mother. The mother of the dead child is charged with being careless, suffocating her child during the night by lying on it (v. 19); this fact can hardly have been known, since the death occurred while the other was asleep. This is a case of the word of one against the word of the other, and there are no witnesses.

There is obviously a lot of animosity between the two women, not surprising in the circumstances in which they live. Solomon's judgment does not deal with the circumstances of the death of the child or with the various accusations being made. His concern is with the bonding relationship of a mother and her child, which he presumes to be present by virtue of the fact that the case has come before him. The living child has no father, but the true mother is determined to care for her child and to give it hope in this world.

---

17. See Elaine Adler Goodfriend, "Prostitution," *ABD*, 5:505–10.

18. Prostitution could also have a religious dimension, such as a woman seeking a means to pay her vows (Prov. 7:14); see Karel van der Toorn, "Female Prostitution in Payment of Vows in Ancient Israel," *JBL* 108 (1989): 193–205.

Faced with the horror of watching her child die, the emotions of the true mother compel her to acquiesce to the demands of her wicked partner (v. 26). Once Solomon knows the identity of the true mother, he does not engage in further punishments, either to deal with the cause of the first death or the subsequent criminal actions in switching the children.[19] The circumstances of prostitution and the death of the child are regarded as punishment. Justice is best served when tempered with mercy; the life of a child is preserved and the bond of motherhood restored, and there is renewed opportunity to make the best of a bad situation.

The judgment of the new king causes the people to be filled with awe. The response is that of respect due to a king, but there is recognition that this king possesses wisdom beyond that of other mortals. Solomon has received a divine gift that is at work in enabling him to resolve an otherwise impossible case.

Bridging Contexts

WISDOM FOR A KING. The prayer for the heir to the throne, the descendant in the dynasty of David, is that God will grant him the gift of making decisions so the people may live in peace.

> Give the king your justice, O God,
>   and your righteousness to a king's son.
> May he judge your people in righteousness,
>   and your poor with justice.
> May the mountains yield prosperity for the people,
>   and the hills, in righteousness. (Ps. 72:1–3, NRSV)

Prosperity and peace are possible only when there is justice. It is the responsibility of the king to ensure that justice prevails, particularly for the vulnerable such as orphans and widows. Solomon is fully aware of the difficulty of this great task, and so he prays for wisdom to be able to fulfill his responsibility (3:9). Solomon's humility in not asking for wealth or the power of vengeance over his enemies becomes the basis for receiving the gift of wisdom (v. 11).

Wealth and honor are benefits for following the ways of wisdom. Wisdom is a tree of life to those who will receive her (Prov. 3:13–18). She is worth more than gold, silver, or pearls, but at the same time she dispenses them; long life is in her right hand, in her left hand wealth and honor (v. 16).

---

19. It is possible other legal actions were taken; the author may have limited himself to that aspect of the story that demonstrated the compassion and justice of the king.

Her ways lead to favor, her paths are the way to "prosperity" (*šālôm;* cf. Ps. 72:3; Prov. 3:17). The person who finds wisdom is called "blessed" (Prov. 3:13; *ʾešer*). This word needs to be distinguished from declarations of praise or receiving of benefits (*bārûk*).

This blessedness describes the character and distinction of a person; all nations recognize the stature of a wise king (Ps. 72:17; cf. 1 Kings 10:8).[20] The ruler who acts with insight to the poor is so blessed (Ps. 41:1); Yahweh will protect him, preserve him, and declare him fortunate (1:2). The person who does not follow in the paths of the ungodly but who delights in the instruction of Yahweh finds such favor (Ps. 1:1–2).

Proverbs warns against trusting our own wisdom (Prov. 3:7). Those who fear Yahweh will know how to honor him with their wealth (3:9) and will in turn find that God delights in enabling them to be prosperous. Wisdom means first to trust Yahweh in all our ways, not trusting in our own understanding, so that God may direct our paths (3:3–4). The humility of Solomon in asking for wisdom is evidence of his fear of Yahweh.

The ancient Near Eastern kings did not divide their world into the sacred and the profane. The most "profane" experience was religious, for the divine order was always present.[21] Wisdom was the expression of trust in God, conduct that would bring honor to God. The fear of Yahweh was the instinctive and intuitive recognition of the total claim of God, which was felt in religious and moral issues.[22] Solomon, in his request, is an example of the fear of Yahweh as the beginning of wisdom (Job 28:28; Prov. 1:7; Eccl. 12:13).

Lady Wisdom describes herself as the firstborn of creation; she is the essence of good order (Prov. 8:22–31). Her origin before creation is repeated in relation to various aspects of creation, providing a description of the cosmos, above and below. Lady Wisdom concludes with a statement of her own place in creation:

I was beside him as an *ʾmwn,*
I was delight day by day,
playing before him all the time,
playing on the surface of his earth,
and my delight (was) with humankind. (Prov. 8:30–31)[23]

---

20. M. Saebo, "אשר," *THAT,* 1:260; M. Brown, "אשר," *NIDOTTE,* 1:570–71.

21. Philip Nel, "A Proposed Method for Determining the Context of the Wisdom Admonitions," *JNSL* 6 (1978): 34.

22. U. Skladny, *Die ältesten Spruchsammlungen in Israel* (Berlin: de Gruyter, 1961), 15.

23. Translation by Roland E. Murphy, *The Tree of Life: An Exploration of Biblical Wisdom Literature,* 2nd ed. (Grand Rapids: Eerdmans, 1990), 136.

The ʾmwn is either a craftswoman playing a role in the activity of creation or a child delighting in God's presence. Von Rad viewed Lady Wisdom as a personification of the world order central to sapiential thinking. The most interesting feature "is that this world order turns, as a person, towards men, wooing them and encouraging them in direct address. What is objectified here, then, is not an attribute of God but an attribute of the world, namely that mysterious attribute, by virtue of which she turns towards men to give order to their lives."[24] Wisdom, however, is somehow identified with Yahweh; the call of Lady Wisdom is the call of Yahweh. She is the revelation of God, not merely the self-revelation of creation. In asking for wisdom, Solomon is seeking the will of Yahweh in governing the people.

As von Rad had said earlier, wisdom is the form in which the will of Yahweh and his salvation approaches humankind.

> Wisdom is the essence of what man needs for a proper life, and of what God grants him . . . wisdom is truly the form in which Jahweh makes himself present and in which he wishes to be sought by man. "Whoso finds me, finds life" (Prov viii. 35). Only Jahweh can speak in this way. And yet, wisdom is not Jahweh himself; it is something separate from him: indeed, it once designates itself as Jahweh's creature, albeit the firstborn of all creatures (Prov viii. 22), and identifies itself with the thoughts which God cherished in creating the world (Prov iii.19).[25]

To make a distinction between God and creation in Lady Wisdom is not necessary.[26] Ultimately the revelation of creation is the revelation of God. God speaks to humans through his works in creation.

Wisdom may be described as that which is found (Prov. 3:13), but it is received through instruction and teaching, particularly from parents (1:8). The divine gift of wisdom that Solomon receives must be distinguished from the acquisition of wisdom as it is described in Proverbs, but it is not different in kind. It is a special dispensation, granted on the basis of a divine offer as evidence that God has truly ordained Solomon to rule as king. When it comes to the exercise of wisdom, Solomon follows the principles of order and justice. In the case of the two prostitutes, it is evident to Solomon that the love of the true mother for her child is the impetus for this case coming before him. In appealing to those instincts, he is able to restore the child to its true parent without undue harsh punishment on the other angry and grieving mother.

---

24. Gerhard von Rad, *Wisdom in Israel* (Nashville: Abingdon, 1972), 156.
25. Gerhard von Rad, *Old Testament Theology* (New York: Harper & Row, 1962), 1:444.
26. Murphy, *The Tree of Life*, 139.

David instructed Solomon to act in wisdom in order to consolidate his reign. Wisdom in that instance was to act prudently in removing rivals such as Joab, who might threaten the stability of the military (1 Kings 2:6), and Shimei, who still had the potential to stir up an insurrection against the throne (2:9). Wisdom to rule as a competent and effective king consisted of much more than acting expeditiously in securing power and control. Control established by coercive force cannot bring about justice and deliverance that characterize the rule of a good king. They might be justified in consolidating rule, but they can never be the means to the goals of good rule. Wisdom adequate for the ideals of kingship must be divinely bestowed and humbly accepted. It is the skill necessary to maintain justice in contentious situations. The legitimation of the reign of Solomon as a wise king is established in a vision that assures him of the wisdom necessary to judge a great and sometimes difficult nation (3:9).[27] The challenge of his task and his readiness for it is illustrated in the story of the two prostitutes.

The choice of wisdom is not as obvious as it might appear. Lady Wisdom has prepared a great banquet and sent her maidens asking all to benefit from her feast (Prov. 9:1—6). Lady Folly also stations herself in the marketplace of life, making tantalizing and tempting offers to all who pass by minding their own affairs (9:13—18). She calls from the streets and the door of her house, luring the naïve with promises of pleasure; they follow her enticements without any suspicion that they are on the path of death.

Contrasting David and Solomon. The account of Solomon and the two prostitutes can be contrasted with David and the folly of his actions with Bathsheba (2 Sam. 11—12).[28] David and Solomon each make a choice, live with the consequences of their choice, and are scrutinized by the effect their choice has on others. The choice of wisdom or folly involves an act, its consequence, and an evaluation.

David's folly began with the Ammonite war (2 Sam. 10—12) and resulted in the death of a child and in continual conflict within his family, until it was finally resolved with the execution of Adonijah. The curse of conflict in the house of David was only resolved with the enthronement of Solomon, whose kingship was validated by the giving of wisdom at Gibeon and the celebration before the ark in Jerusalem. In contrast to David's adultery, Solomon is then confronted with two prostitutes, who are functionally widows, since

---

27. The Hebrew word *kabed* simply means "heavy" and can be used to mean "great, honorable, weighty" in other ways. DeVries (*1 Kings*, 48—49) takes it to mean difficult in the context of needing skills to deal with difficult situations.

28. See Carole Fontaine, "The Bearing of Wisdom on the Shape of 2 Samuel 11—12 and 1 Kings 3," *JSOT* 34 (1986): 62. Fontaine uses narrative structural analysis to link the portrayal of a wide range of events.

they have no male to protect them or provide for them. His intervention results in saving the life of a child as well as the unqualified support of all the people for his function as king.

The pattern of act, consequence, and evaluation is totally different for Solomon. Solomon, in seeking divine favor, leaves his capital to offer sacrifices at Gibeon, where wisdom comes to him in a dream. David sleeps by day in his capital and desires what is abhorrent to God. David seeks satisfaction for himself, while Solomon is concerned about duty to the people. The wise king can judge between two prostitutes; the immoral king commits adultery and brings a curse upon his house. The wicked king lives with deceit, trickery, and murder; the wise king receives riches, honor, and a long life. The judgment on the wicked king is brought before "all Israel" (2 Sam. 12:10–12), while "all Israel" holds the wise king in reverence (1 Kings 3:28). These two stories show us that the ways of wisdom lead to life and peace, while the ways of folly lead to destruction and death.

This contrast of folly and wisdom in the birth and accession of Solomon does not determine the final valuation of the lives of David and Solomon. David is the servant king who becomes the standard by which all later kings are measured (1 Kings 15:11; 2 Kings 18:3; 22:2). David's confession of his sin (2 Sam. 12:13) and his choice of Solomon as king (1 Kings 1:30), who loves the Lord and asks for wisdom, redeems him from the folly of his ways. Solomon, by contrast, does not escape the ways of folly. The verdict on his reign is that he does what is wrong in Yahweh's opinion (11:6).

The three tasks of a king are saving, ruling, and judging. This is readily seen in the scriptural songs about kingship. In the Song of the Sea (Ex. 15:1–18), the Israelites celebrated the kingship of Yahweh ("the LORD") over Pharaoh. The song first praises Yahweh as the "man of war" (v. 3), who casts Pharaoh and his armies into the sea. The song goes on to praise Yahweh for the redemption of his people, leading them to his holy place (v. 13); finally the song praises the rule of Yahweh as the eternal king (v. 18).

The same pattern is found in the Psalms. Psalm 98 first praises "the LORD" (Yahweh) as the one who delivers his people and makes known his salvation (98:1–3); it then praises Yahweh as king (vv. 4–6) and finally as the judge who brings justice to all the earth (vv. 7–9).

Psalm 96 has an identical pattern, but the same motifs may be found in all the psalms that praise God as king.[29] Saving, ruling, and judging are interrelated functions; the king who exercises judgment over evil and brings justice to the people brings about peace or deliverance. Apart from the coercion

---

29. For an analysis of these psalms see Tremper Longman III, "Psalm 98: A Divine Warrior Victory Song," *JETS* 27 (1984): 267–74.

of governance there is no control over evil, and there can be no justice or peace. Solomon is introduced as a king endowed with wisdom so these functions can be exercised to the ideal.

PRAYING FOR THOSE **in authority.** Prayer for those in authority in governance has dimensions in the New Testament that go beyond that of Solomon. Solomon makes his appeal on the basis of covenant fidelity, which Yahweh had shown to his father David in making him king (1 Kings 3:6). Under the new covenant no one government represents the kingdom of God, but government makes possible the advancement of the kingdom.

This is true even when a government is hostile to Christians and restricts or persecutes expression of faith in Christ. The apostle Paul was able to spread the gospel across Asia Minor and as far as Rome because of the security and order provided by *pax Romana*. The apostle therefore urges prayer and petition, making intercession, and giving of thanks for all persons. This specifically includes kings and all those in a place of preeminence, in order that Christians may lead a quiet and peaceful life with respect and dignity (1 Tim. 2:1–2).

Prayer for government is important not only to provide for good order, but is necessary because it is God's will that all should be saved and come to knowledge of the truth (1 Tim. 2:3–4). Solomon can assume the loyalty of his people, since all are to be "circumcised in mind" to love (be loyal to) God with all their will and emotion (Deut. 30:6). They shared in the covenant that requires a renewed commitment every seven years (31:9–13).

Such political conditions are never true for the church. The followers of Christ find themselves in a world where their values are often hated, since they do not belong to this world (John 17:14). The place of the Christian is in this world, but Christians must learn to live apart of this world's values and will need divine protection from evil forces in the world (17:15–18). The Christian is sent into the world to bear witness to the truth revealed in Christ. This includes testimony to those in authority, sometimes charged with the responsibility of opposing what Christians represent, since God desires their salvation as well. The prayers of the Christian are for the kingdom to come to the hearts of those with political power.

Christians are obligated to pray for the kind of order that Solomon desires. Even governments with an ideological antipathy to Christian values have a responsibility to protect the freedom of all citizens of their domain. These governments are God's provision for life in his world as long as they are there. Prayers and thanksgiving must be made on behalf of all who are in authority (1 Tim. 2:1-2). If God ordains prayer for those leaders hostile to Christian values, it is surely a privilege and responsibility to pray for those leaders who pray themselves. Though the policies of such a leader may be hated, even as there are those who hated Solomon and attempted to displace him, it is important to pray that divine wisdom be granted.

For over half a century now in the United States, the National Prayer Breakfast has been a symbol of the vital place of faith in the life of the nation. It has been a call to leaders of a purpose and power greater than their own. In times of calm and in times of crisis it has called the nation to pray for its leaders. The Office of the Press Secretary posted the following remarks by President George W. Bush at the National Prayer Breakfast of 2002:

> In this time of testing for our nation, my family and I have been blessed by the prayers of countless Americans. We have felt their sustaining power and we're incredibly grateful. Tremendous challenges await this nation, and there will be hardships ahead. Faith will not make our path easy, but it will give us strength for the journey.[30]

In that same speech the president said the following about the significance of prayer for the presidency and the nation:

> Since we met last year, millions of Americans have been led to prayer. They have prayed for comfort in time of grief; for understanding in a time of anger; for protection in a time of uncertainty. Many, including me, have been on bended knee. The prayers of this nation are a part of the good that has come from the evil of September the 11th, more good than we could ever have predicted. Tragedy has brought forth the courage and the generosity of our people.
>
> None of us would ever wish on anyone what happened on that day. Yet, as with each life, sorrows we would not choose can bring wisdom and strength gained in no other way. This insight is central to many faiths, and certainly to faith that finds hope and comfort in a cross.[31]

No amount of wisdom can protect a nation against the horrors of war and terror, a point that no doubt is well understood by Solomon. At such times the administration of a nation can be most difficult, the issues can be extremely divisive. Solomon's prayer is at a time when his own nation has considerable internal conflict. His prayer for wisdom is a particular reminder of the importance of recognizing God's sovereign direction.

---

30. Accessed from the National Prayer Breakfast website, May 20, 2004: http://www.whitehouse.gov/news/releases/2002/02/20020207-1.html.

31. Ibid.

Wisdom for daily life. As is demonstrated in Solomon's prayer, wisdom begins with a choice for God: "The fear of the LORD is the beginning of wisdom, knowledge of the Holy One is understanding" (Prov. 9:10). Such wisdom is called a "tree of life" (Prov. 3:18). The tree of life in the Garden of Eden is forever in the past; in this world we will always be mortals dealing with conflict and death. We look forward to the tree of life in the future, described by John as granting us eternal healing for all that ails (Rev. 22:1–2). There is, however, a tree of life for us now in the present. Wisdom is not simply ability to make right decisions or intelligence to know all the right things. Wisdom begins with the choice of learning to trust God; God in turn makes provision for peace and prosperity.

Wisdom to live this good life has eluded every society of every civilization. Every society has those individuals who have been coerced into a base way of life such as prostitution, or who have found it as the least evil of available choices. Others voluntarily have chosen violence and the violation of others as a way of life. Not all receive much from the tree of life called wisdom. The failure to provide for a good life within societies is also the responsibility of government. Government must make possible conditions in which each person has opportunity to make responsible choices for economic independence. Government must also provide a form of justice in which the grievances of individuals for unjust treatment can be addressed. The reign of Solomon demonstrates both the significant role that good government can have and the limitations every government faces in the complexity of dealing with diverse societies.

Solomon was able to deal with the grievances of two prostitutes, but he was never able to address the evil of prostitution itself. Poor social conditions led to economic prostitution; the presence of the high places and foreign religions led to cultic prostitution. Government, however wise, has its limitations. It is possible, though, for good governors to see the good in people who are otherwise regarded as outside the pale of a good life.

The prostitute in Israel was designated a "strange woman" (*zônâ*), designating her status as one outside the normal function of society, an outcast though not an outlaw. She was desired and despised, sought after and shunned. The story of the two prostitutes assumes these attitudes towards prostitution. Solomon in his wisdom is able to see individuals, their emotions, and their needs, rather than just another representative of a pitiful class of people. A woman might be a prostitute, but that does not make her less of a caring mother.[32] Society as a whole has little ability to make these distinc-

---

32. Phyllis A. Bird, "The Harlot as Heroine: Narrative Art and Social Presupposition in Three Old Testament Texts," in *Narrative Research on the Hebrew Bible* (Semeia 46; Macon, Ga.: Scholars Press, 1989), 133.

tions, to see the good in the ugly, to distinguish that which must be affirmed from that which is destructive.

Prejudice is a problem that plagues every society within the human race. Prejudice is a problem of generalization. It is the problem of assuming that every individual within a class of people share all the characteristics of that class. Prejudice grows out of a belief in proverbial sayings like "birds of a feather flock together." It is true that people develop associations with those that share their outlook on life and that individuals within a group reinforce their world view on all the individual members. But it is an error to assume that certain classes of people have somehow abandoned all knowledge of common human values. It takes wisdom to know how to deal with particular individuals in problematic situations. Solomon demonstrates the kind of insight that enables us to respect other individuals no matter what class associations they may happen to have.

It is the dream of all mortals that wisdom will simply come as a divine gift in a dream and enable them to make all the right decisions all of the time. The experience of Solomon is unusual, just as his position is unusual. Wisdom is a choice to follow God, with the knowledge that good choices will be made because of that choice.

This does not make sense to everyone. Christians choose the way of the cross as the wisdom that saves (1 Cor. 1:18–31). This is foolishness to those who seek signs, some miraculous revelation that will bring about knowledge of how to live in this world. This is foolishness to the philosophers who think that human thought will bring about the wisdom required for life in this world. Paul preached Christ crucified, foolishness to the wise of this world, but the power and wisdom of God to those who follow him. Wisdom in the time of Christ is to make a choice to become his disciple in all our other decisions. It may not always be possible to make decisions that are self-evidently the best, but it is possible to know that our values are those that bring about right relationships with God and others.

1 Kings 4:1–34

S O KING SOLOMON ruled over all Israel. ²And these were his chief officials:

Azariah son of Zadok—the priest;
³ Elihoreph and Ahijah, sons of Shisha—secretaries;
Jehoshaphat son of Ahilud—recorder;
⁴ Benaiah son of Jehoiada—commander in chief;
Zadok and Abiathar—priests;
⁵ Azariah son of Nathan—in charge of the district officers;
Zabud son of Nathan—a priest and personal adviser to the king;
⁶ Ahishar—in charge of the palace;
Adoniram son of Abda—in charge of forced labor.

⁷Solomon also had twelve district governors over all Israel, who supplied provisions for the king and the royal household. Each one had to provide supplies for one month in the year. ⁸These are their names:

Ben-Hur—in the hill country of Ephraim;
⁹ Ben-Deker—in Makaz, Shaalbim, Beth Shemesh and Elon Bethhanan;
¹⁰ Ben-Hesed—in Arubboth (Socoh and all the land of Hepher were his);
¹¹ Ben-Abinadab—in Naphoth Dor (he was married to Taphath daughter of Solomon);
¹² Baana son of Ahilud—in Taanach and Megiddo, and in all of Beth Shan next to Zarethan below Jezreel, from Beth Shan to Abel Meholah across to Jokmeam;
¹³ Ben-Geber—in Ramoth Gilead (the settlements of Jair son of Manasseh in Gilead were his, as well as the district of Argob in Bashan and its sixty large walled cities with bronze gate bars);
¹⁴ Ahinadab son of Iddo—in Mahanaim;
¹⁵ Ahimaaz—in Naphtali (he had married Basemath daughter of Solomon);
¹⁶ Baana son of Hushai—in Asher and in Aloth;
¹⁷ Jehoshaphat son of Paruah—in Issachar;
¹⁸ Shimei son of Ela—in Benjamin;

¹⁹Geber son of Uri—in Gilead (the country of Sihon king of the Amorites and the country of Og king of Bashan). He was the only governor over the district.

²⁰The people of Judah and Israel were as numerous as the sand on the seashore; they ate, they drank and they were happy. ²¹And Solomon ruled over all the kingdoms from the River to the land of the Philistines, as far as the border of Egypt. These countries brought tribute and were Solomon's subjects all his life.

²²Solomon's daily provisions were thirty cors of fine flour and sixty cors of meal, ²³ten head of stall-fed cattle, twenty of pasture-fed cattle and a hundred sheep and goats, as well as deer, gazelles, roebucks and choice fowl. ²⁴For he ruled over all the kingdoms west of the River, from Tiphsah to Gaza, and had peace on all sides. ²⁵During Solomon's lifetime Judah and Israel, from Dan to Beersheba, lived in safety, each man under his own vine and fig tree.

²⁶Solomon had four thousand stalls for chariot horses, and twelve thousand horses.

²⁷The district officers, each in his month, supplied provisions for King Solomon and all who came to the king's table. They saw to it that nothing was lacking. ²⁸They also brought to the proper place their quotas of barley and straw for the chariot horses and the other horses.

²⁹God gave Solomon wisdom and very great insight, and a breadth of understanding as measureless as the sand on the seashore. ³⁰Solomon's wisdom was greater than the wisdom of all the men of the East, and greater than all the wisdom of Egypt. ³¹He was wiser than any other man, including Ethan the Ezrahite—wiser than Heman, Calcol and Darda, the sons of Mahol. And his fame spread to all the surrounding nations. ³²He spoke three thousand proverbs and his songs numbered a thousand and five. ³³He described plant life, from the cedar of Lebanon to the hyssop that grows out of walls. He also taught about animals and birds, reptiles and fish. ³⁴Men of all nations came to listen to Solomon's wisdom, sent by all the kings of the world, who had heard of his wisdom.

Original Meaning

IN HIS VISION at Gibeon, Solomon asked Yahweh to grant him an understanding mind that he might govern justly (3:9), since a great challenge lay before him. This chapter shows the scope of that request. It gives us a list of his chief officials (4:1–6) responsible for the different offices of the kingdom and a list of governors to administer the different regions of the kingdom (4:7–20). This is followed by the extent of Solomon's kingdom, the daily requirements for the palace, and his fiscal administration (4:21–28). The section concludes with a review of the knowledge for which Solomon was famous (4:29–34), giving him a reputation for wisdom that drew leaders from distant nations. God has abundantly answered Solomon's prayer.

This chapter draws its information from "the book of the annals of Solomon" (11:41), an official archive of his reign. The opening of this chapter, with its reference to the reign of Solomon over all Israel (4:1), indicates that the author is referring to an archivist who began his record with this notation.[1] This opening line does not advance the narrative, but it does provide an introduction to a summary report on Solomon's reign. The regular reference to these records in Kings is evidence that the authors have a concept of history writing in which the interpretation of people and events is based on accessible and reliable information. The authors are not interested in merely chronicling these data, but they find it necessary to incorporate official material that will establish the perspective critical to their history.

The records show the sophistication of Solomon's reign in contrast to the earlier stages of the kingdom and stress that his wisdom focuses on the urgent practicalities of providing an administration where the people will have prosperity and contentment (4:20).[2] Though Solomon is famous for his thousands of proverbs on everything from a giant cedar of Lebanon to the hyssop growing out of the wall (4:33), the wisdom given to him by God that legitimizes his reign is an understanding of how to provide peace and prosperity for the people. The official records serve as a testimony to this gift of wisdom.

---

1. DeVries, *1 Kings*, 67.

2. A thorough examination of the administration of Solomon is provided by Tryggve N. D. Mettinger in *Solomonic State Officials: A Study of the Civil Government Officials of the Israelite Monarchy* (CBOT 5; Lund: Gleerup, 1971). Mettinger especially relies on Egyptian prototypes to elucidate administrative functions; Egypt had close connections to the monarchies of David and Solomon (cf. 11:14–22, 40) and was a center of cultural prestige. Knowledge of Aramean administration is minimal, and Canaanites had limited independent political power by the time of the Israelite state.

The Chief Officials (4:1–6)

THE ROSTER OF chief officials mentions eight distinct offices as compared with five in 2 Samuel 8:16–18 and six in 20:23–25. The priest heads the list (1 Kings 4:2) as the most influential of the officials. The secretaries (v. 3a) keep records and prepare correspondence. The recorder (v. 3b, NIV) is an officer who makes the king's name heard, either giving official notices to the people or bringing public affairs to the king's notice. He is the protocol officer who regulates the ceremonies of the palace, introduces people to royal audiences, and serves as master of ceremonies on an official tour.

The commander of the army (4:4a) may have also served in administrative responsibility as a kind of secretary of war. The officer over the district governors (v. 5a) is responsible for the provisioning system for the palace. The personal advisor to the king (v. 5b) is the king's most intimate confidant and perhaps a chief officer of government administration.[3] The officer in charge of the palace (v. 6a) is responsible for all the royal property, including lands and buildings. The officer in charge of conscripted service for the king (v. 6b) is responsible to provide the necessary labor for the king's projects.

The name Elihoreph (v. 3a) appears to be Egyptian in origin, corrupted in pronunciation to conceal its pagan origins; in Greek it is pronounced Eliaph, a reference to the Egyptian god Apis. Shisha (v. 3b) is a Hebrew way of saying the Egyptian word for scribe; Elihoreph and Ahijah belong to the scribal office; they are members of a guild. The Egyptian influence indicates that Solomon is reaching out to his Egyptian father-in-law for assistance in administering his realm.

The list has been transmitted with variations, the result of historical and textual developments.[4] The LXX does not make mention of Benaiah as head of the army in verse 4, but the Old Greek translation has Eliab son of Joab over the army in verse 6. Benaiah takes control of the army after executing Joab; it is unlikely that Solomon has enlisted a son of Joab as military commander.[5]

---

3. The "friend of the king" was an office held by someone who was regarded as part of the royal family; in the Sumerian Code of Lipit-Ishtar and the Code of Hammurabi, the "friend of the bridegroom" was his best man. Van Selms proposes that this individual is more than ceremonial but comes to hold official office; see "The Origin of the Title 'The King's Friend,'" *JNES* 16 (1957): 119. However, the office and its title in Israel may be of Egyptian derivation, as suggested by evidence from the Amarna tablets (Mettinger, *Solomonic State Officials*, 67–69).

4. Cogan, *1 Kings*, 202; Mettinger, *Solomonic State Officials*, 10.

5. New Jerusalem Bible, following the Old Greek, says "Eliab son of Joab, commander of the army" (v. 6), but this is unlikely to be original from a textual point of view. The Greek has a difficult textual history, part of which lacks a reference to the commander of the army. See D. Barthélemy, *Critique textuelle de l'ancien testament* (OBO 50/1; Göttingen: Vandenhoeck & Ruprecht, 1982), 338–39; Mettinger, *Solomonic State Officials*, 10–11.

The office of priest is mentioned twice: Azariah (v. 2) and Zadok and Abiathar (v. 4). Azariah succeeded his father Zadok as high priest; Abiathar was banished after siding with Adonijah (2:26–27). Zadok, Abiathar, and Benaiah go back to the time of David (2 Sam. 20:23, 25).[6] The influence of Zadok the priest and Nathan the prophet is evident in their sons continuing to hold high office.

The District Governors (4:7–20)

THE DISTRICTS OF Solomon's administration are defined according to tribal territory and groups of cities. This is the only administrative document pertaining to the official organization of the kingdom. Certain other lists exist within the biblical narrative as boundary descriptions and rosters of towns. There is much disagreement about the degree of authenticity to be found in such documents. Since the time of Alt this list in Kings has been regarded as an official administrative document of ancient Israel,[7] but it has recently been challenged by Ash as "the product of an oral/scribal transmission which selected, abbreviated, and garbled its source(s)."[8]

There are other comparable documents from this time that can serve as a basis for comparison with this list of Solomon's reign.[9] Some of these have a similar structure with a list of personal names of a governor, each followed by one or more place names.[10] Others begin each line with a number, sometimes referring to persons, houses, grain, horses, sheep, donkeys, or quantities of silver. Several features of these lists parallel the list of Solomon's governors. An introduction defines the contents of the list and designates the individuals listed; it is followed by a series of entries with a personal name and a place name, and finally there is a concluding entry distinctive from all its predecessors.

There are also other administrative lists that form part of a larger document. Solomon's list is typical of other archival sources. It is distinctive in

---

6. Zadok and Abiathar (v. 4b) appear in the same order in lists from the time of David (2 Sam. 8:18; 20:24).

7. A. Alt, in an article entitled "Israels Gaue unter Salamo" (1913), reprinted in *Kleine Schriften zur Geschichte das Volkes Israel* (Munich: Beck'sche Verlagsbuchhandlung, 1953), 2:76–89, defended this list as an official administrative document useful for understanding the geography and administration of the kingdom of Israel.

8. P. S. Ash, "Solomon's? District? List," *JSOT* 67 (1995): 84.

9. Tablets containing administrative lists of governors are known from the ancient cities of Ugarit and Alalakh (both on the northwestern border of Syria). These tablets date to the second millennium, several hundred years before Solomon.

10. Richard S. Hess has provided a comparative study: "The Solomonic District List," in *Crossing Boundaries and Linking Horizons*, ed. Gordon D. Young, Mark W. Chavalas, and Richard E. Averbeck (Bethesda, Md.: CDL, 1997), 279–92.

including notes about spouses and descriptions of additional territories. The administrative list in Kings has been incorporated into the narrative to show how the practical prudence of Solomon brings satisfaction to his citizens (4:20).

Five of the twelve names given in Solomon's list have the simple form "son of" ("Ben"), six others have a name followed by "son of" with a further identification. Only Ahimaaz (4:15) lacks any complementary element. These name forms are typical of those in other West Semitic name lists.[11] The element following "son of" may be a nickname, a tribal or national identity, or a place of origin. The form of these names does not provide any information about the social status of the individual.

Twelve individuals are named as governors over districts in northern Israel, but the text is uncertain. Judah is named as having a governor in the Greek text (4:19b),[12] which seems to be the intended meaning of the Hebrew text (RSV). Alternately, Judah is left out of the list altogether, and the concluding phrase of verse 19 is applied to Geber as the "only governor" of Gilead (NIV).[13] It is possible that Judah was regarded as a district using the expression "in the land" to describe the home territory.[14] It is more likely that the name Judah has been accidentally omitted (haplography), since the next verse begins with Judah. Judah is required as a twelfth district to provide for each of the months of the year (v. 7). The governor of Judah is not named.

The division of Israel into districts for political purposes is according to geographical areas that traditionally formed agricultural, social, and ethnic units.[15] It is most probable that Solomon follows and reorganizes David's district system.

> District 1 (v. 8) is the mountainous region of Ephraim, just north of Bethel and east to the Jordan Valley between Jericho and Jokmeam.
> District 2 (v. 9) borders on the Mediterranean just north of Philistine territory and south of the Yarkon River (just north of Joppa); it was

---

11. See J. Naveh, "Nameless People," *IEJ* 40 (1990): 108–21.

12. The Greek has a different order at this point in that Jehoshaphat (v. 17) is placed at the end of the list.

13. Verse 19 is often regarded as a repetition of the territory described in verse 13 (note "Geber," "Gilead," and "Bashan"). Further, the description of District 7 (v. 14) is limited to naming the district center. Montgomery (*The Books of Kings*, 122) is followed by Cogan (*I Kings*, 211) in making Judah a twelfth district.

14. Josephus took the phrase "one governor in the land" to refer to one person responsible for all the governors (*Ant.* 8.37–38), a role like that of Azariah (v. 5).

15. A detailed study identifying the districts and cities, with correspondence to modern-day place names, is provided by Yohanan Aharoni in *The Land of the Bible*, rev. and enlarged ed. (Philadelphia: Westminster, 1979), 309–17.

---

populated by Philistine and Canaanite clans who had no real connection to the mountain peoples.

District 3 (v. 10) is the coastal area north of the Yarkon, the Sharon plain. Only Socoh in the center of Sharon can be certainly identified. In ancient times this area was heavily forested with swamps on the coast and was not densely populated.

District 4 (v. 11) is the coastal area south of Carmel; the city of Dor was one of Solomon's few ports on the Mediterranean.

The boundaries of District 5 (v. 12) cannot be precisely determined. It included Megiddo on the west side and the Jordan Valley to the south of Beth Shean. It consisted of lowlands and valleys that formed a geographical and economic unit.

District 6 (v. 13) is in Transjordan in the area of Gilead and north into Bashan; this territory extended to the areas under the control of Damascus.

District 7 (v. 14) is in the Transjordan south of the Jabbok River down to the area north of the Heshbon Plateau. Mahanaim was on the border between Manasseh and Gad (Josh. 13:30), indicating that this district included the middle and southern settlements.

District 8 (v. 15) is the northern tribal territory of Naphtali, extending to the sources of the Jordan. It included the famous fortress of Hazor.

District 9 is western Galilee, the territory of Asher (v. 16). It originally included Acco in the southern plain, the territory Solomon later gave to Hiram of Tyre as payment.

District 10 (v. 17) is the territory of Issachar, including the central and eastern part of the Jezreel Valley, the southeastern hills of Galilee, and probably the northern part of the Jordan Valley.

District 11 (v. 18) is the district of Benjamin in the south, a pre-Israelite political unity that by the time of Saul included the Gibeonite cities. Verse 19 describes the Transjordan territory of the old Amorite kingdoms of Sihon and Og, the territory already named in District 6.[16] This district organization is distinct from the tribal system, which may have been the result of the geographical organization of various clan groups.

The district governors are to levy taxes and make provision for king and court (4:7). One of their duties is to provide the royal court with food and the draft animals with fodder (4:27–28). They also assist the official responsible for the forced labor (v. 6), required for the king's projects. Each governor is assigned one month in the year so that no period of time is missed. It is often

---

16. Aharoni finds a twelfth district to the south of district 7; he assumes the list originally contained a mention of Heshbon, the northern border of the Moabite tableland called the Mishor (*The Land of the Bible*, 314).

assumed that the officers worked on a twelve month calendar, each taking a month in turn, but this is not explicit. Each of the districts varies considerably in their potential to provide tribute, so it is unlikely that they provide equal services and goods. The divisions reflect social and political realities of tribes and territories that provided a reasonable division for administration and obligation, resulting in satisfaction for everyone (v. 20). Details of obligations are not given, so it is impossible to know how the various territories are taxed.

Provisions for the Kingdom (4:21–28)

THE EXTENT OF Solomon's kingdom and the prosperity of the people are fulfillments of the covenant with Abraham (Gen. 15:18). Solomon reigns from the Euphrates River to the border of Egypt (1 Kings 4:21). "The river of Egypt" (Gen. 15:18) is equivalent to the commonly known "Wadi of Egypt" (1 Kings 8:65), the usual Assyrian designation for the border of Egypt.[17] The territory from Tiphsah on the southern bend of the Euphrates, to Gaza on the southeastern Mediterranean coast (v. 24), encompass all of Syria and Palestine; it may include territory east of the Jordan as well.[18] The subservience of all these kings bringing tribute to Solomon is the farthest extent of the kingdom of Israel. It comprises a territory more vast than the land God had promised Abraham. This is a territory equal to that of David's conquests (2 Sam. 8:12–13). Both Judah and Israel enjoy security and prosperity under the reign of Solomon.

The list of provisions for a single day (v. 22) are for the entire palatial establishment, including servants and guests (v. 27).[19] A "cor" (a Mesopotamian measure) was equal to a "homer" (a West Semitic measure), equal to about 100 liters (just under three bushels) in preexilic times.[20] The foods are limited to

---

17. M. Görg, on the basis of Assyrian topographical names, identifies this area with Nahal Bezor and the town later known as Orda, just south of Gaza, somewhat to the north of Wadi el-Arish, which is commonly taken as the border; see his "Egypt, Brook of," *ABD*, 2:321.

18. "All the kingdoms west of the River" (v. 24) is an Assyrian administrative term, referring to the territory west of the Euphrates.

19. According to the Babylonian Talmud, about sixty thousand persons receive support from the royal coffers, not all of them necessarily residents at the capital (*b. B. Meṣiᶜa* 86b); other estimates also range in the tens of thousands (Cogan, *1 Kings*, 212).

20. The word "homer" is related to donkey, the approximate quantity of grain carried by one animal. An imperial bushel is 36.4 liters, the U.S. bushel is 35.24 liters. For these measures see Russell Fuller, "אֵיפָה," *NIDOTTE*, 1:384–85. In the postexilic period measures were realigned to Babylonian standards; Fuller estimates the postexilic cor to be about 180 liters. Estimating modern equivalents is problematic; others calculate cor to be approximately 220 liters (see Cogan, *1 Kings*, 212; cf. NIV footnotes).

grains that can be stored and animals that are kept in pens and fattened or are shot out on the open range.

The texts are not consistent on the number of stalls for horses (4:26). The Masoretic (Hebrew) text of Kings says Solomon had 40,000 stalls for his horses, but the parallel reference (2 Chron. 9:25) says he had 4,000 stalls, the number adopted by some modern translations for Kings (e.g., NIV). The LXX has 4,000 stalls for chariot horses in 1 Kings 10:26, where the Hebrew text has 1,400 chariots. The 4,000 stalls of the LXX is textually related to 2 Chronicles 9:25 rather than to its parallel reference in Kings; 1 Kings 10:26 in the LXX therefore is not a witness to 4,000 for the Hebrew text of 4:26.[21] The diversity but interrelatedness of the variants betray a text corrupted in transmission in such a way that it is impossible to speak with confidence about the original.[22] The number 4,000 of 4:26 compares favorably with other texts, but 40,000 has an independent textual tradition that cannot simply be dismissed (cf. NIV footnote).

A further question is whether the 12,000 pārāšîm (4:26) refers to horses or horsemen. If the reference is to 12,000 horses in 4,000 stalls, the text is saying that the horses were stabled together in groups of three to a pen. Three horses were reckoned as a chariot team in ancient Canaan, two harnessed and one in reserve. By this count Solomon had 4,000 chariots, comparable to the 3,000 chariots and 6,000 horses (or horsemen) the Philistines mustered in their battle against Saul (1 Sam. 13:5).[23] King Ahab deployed 2,000 chariots in the Aramean coalition against the Assyrians at Qarqar about one hundred years later.

The chariot steeds or teams are distinguished from the other horses in the mention of their fodder provisions (4:28). Solomon may have had stud horses or swift cavalry in addition to the well-trained chariot teams. A comparison of the texts for Solomon's stalls suggests that 4,000 is the original number.[24] The records indicated that Solomon has 12,000 horses in 4,000 stalls and probably about 3,000 chariots, a formidable force comparable to others of the time.

---

21. Barthélemy, *Critique textuelle de l'ancien testament*, 339.

22. Raymond B. Dillard, *2 Chronicles* (WBC 15; Waco, Tex.: Word, 1987), 74.

23. The Hebrew text of this verse says 30,000 chariots, a discrepancy like that of Kings.

24. Gooding, *Relics of Ancient Exegesis*, 46–47. The Greek has a different arrangement of these verses here. The present state of the textual witnesses seems to be the result of an attempt to correct 40,000 to the appropriate 4,000, but the wrong number was transmitted in some texts. The difference of a multiple of ten is found in other instances, such as 700 chariots in 2 Sam. 10:18, but 7,000 chariots in 1 Chron. 19:18. Such errors may have arisen from the use of ciphers.

The Wisdom of Solomon (4:29–34)

IN ADDITION TO the wisdom required for the governance of a vast kingdom, Solomon has a breadth of knowledge (4:29) that rivals that of all ancient time. Mesopotamia and Egypt were famous for wisdom, some aspects of which are preserved to the present time. The Wisdom of Amenemope (ca. 1000 B.C) has a notable similarity to Proverbs 22:17–24:22, both in content and style. Ethan and Heman are noted in their contribution to the Psalter (Ps. 88–89); they were choristers along with Calcol and Darda. "Sons of Mahol" (NIV) does not refer to physical ancestry but to their skill as musicians or dancers.[25] Wisdom, poetry, and music are closely connected. "Ezrahite" means native and may indicate that this knowledge of musical instruments and poetry goes back to the pre-Israelite occupants of Canaan. Wisdom is expressed with skill and impact by means of poetry and song.

Solomon is not only known for his songs (4:32), but also for his proverbs. "Proverb" has a considerable breadth of form. Most proverbs are poetic, a part of the skill exercised by the "men of song" mentioned earlier (v. 31). Proverbs often use analogy or comparison as a means of imparting wisdom. "Is Saul among the prophets?" comes to be a proverbial saying (1 Sam. 19:24), which invites comparison to the behavior of Saul; though his visible actions may sometimes be comparable to that of the prophets, he is not of them. Sometimes the comparison of a proverb is obscure, thus becoming a riddle.

Many proverbs are forceful memorable sayings. When confronted with the evil of Saul, David uses the proverb "from the wicked goes forth wickedness" (1 Sam. 24:13–14). David cannot exercise revenge, for then he will be wicked like Saul. There are collections of Solomon's proverbs, as indicated by the divisions in Proverbs. The "proverbs of Solomon" (Prov. 10:1–22:16) contain 475 proverbs, the numerical value of the name Solomon. The proverbs of Solomon inspire other collections of proverbs (e.g., 25:1) long after Solomon's death.

Ancient wisdom encompassed not only music and poetry, along with proverbial sayings for prudent conduct, but also much of what is now called science. The reference to Solomon's wisdom concerning nature (4:33) is not just that nature served as a basis for proverbial sayings. Some proverbial sayings are based on analogies to animals (e.g. Prov. 30:18–20, 24–31). The book of Job shows a considerable interest in the world of nature and knowledge of it, especially in the reference to meteorology and zoology in the speeches of God (Job 38:22–39:30; 40:15–41:34). Such knowledge is not

---

25. *māḥôl* means dance (Ps. 30:12; 149:3; 150:4); "sons of *māḥôl*" probably refers to membership in a guild of musicians.

only useful for analogies for conduct, but it also provides a perspective for understanding life in this world. Lists of natural phenomena are known from Egypt and Mesopotamia. Solomon's classification of creatures into beasts, birds, reptiles, and fish may have been another aspect of his comprehensive knowledge.

THE VULNERABILITY OF **success.** The purpose of including all these details about Solomon's wisdom, largesse, polity, and administration is not transparent.[26] There is no clear development between the sections dealing with Solomon's administration (4:7–19), empire (4:21–25), governors (4:27–28), wisdom (4:29–31), and science (4:32–34). Perhaps the author is simply following his sources, but this does not explain his own attitude toward these achievements.

Perhaps the author is emphasizing the wisdom of Solomon, an innovative sage of nature, who has advanced beyond Egyptian and Babylonian "enumerative science" by composing whole series of proverbs and songs.[27] But the whole section is more than wisdom. The Deuteronomist presents a king and its nation flourishing together. There is no explanation for how Solomon comes to have dominion over such a vast realm. Since it corresponds to the areas taken over by David (cf. 2 Sam. 1–14) and Solomon himself never wages war, he must have received this as an inheritance from David. The conscious connection between the reigns of David and Solomon indicates that their reigns complement each other. What David only hopes for, Solomon achieves.

Solomon succeeds his father as the designated heir and achieves the peace and security promised to David in Nathan's oracle (2 Sam. 7:10–12). Israel will live in security and no longer be troubled by its enemies; David is promised rest from all his enemies and a dynasty. As Solomon takes the next step in contacting Hiram to build the temple, explicit notice is made of the promise to David (1 Kings 5:3–4): Solomon has no adversaries or trouble. David was caught up in warfare and thwarted in his chief ambitions, battling foreign and familial foes. Solomon has a stable kingdom with officials in royal office, governors in all the districts, and a sound fiscal administration. He has security from foreign invasion, and all his citizens live with their own property (4:24–25).

---

26. Knoppers, *The Reign of Solomon and the Rise of Jeroboam*, 77–80.

27. Albrecht Alt, "Solomonic Wisdom," in *Studies in Ancient Wisdom*, ed. James L. Crenshaw (New York: KTAV, 1976), 102–12.

Consistent with Near Eastern royal ideology, Solomon's intelligent rule contributes to the wealth and stability of his realm. He not only benefits from the tribute of his own kingdom, but from the wealth of an empire stretching from the Euphrates River to the Philistines (4:21). Judah and Israel are "as numerous as the sand on the seashore" (v. 20), but Solomon's wisdom is equal to the task, "as measureless as the sand on the seashore" (vv. 29–30). His wisdom exceeds that of the nations to the east and south. Solomon's vast knowledge and wisdom is not an end in itself; for the Deuteronomist this perspicacity provides for unprecedented unity and repose.

The reigns of David and Solomon as the unprecedented era of economic, political, and religious success are developed extensively in Chronicles. The succession of Moses and Joshua becomes a paradigm for that of David and Solomon.[28] Both Moses and David are disqualified from achieving their chief goals. Both designate and announce their successors (Deut. 31:2–3; 1 Chron. 22:6; 28:6–8). Both Joshua and Solomon enjoy the wholehearted support of the people (Josh. 1:16–20; 1 Chron. 29:23–24) and lead the people into rest (Josh. 21:44; 1 Chron. 22:8–9).[29] This highly developed unity of the two kings as the ideal period in the history of Israel is not without basis in Kings. The Conquest was not Israel's finest hour, and certainly not the period of the judges. The inauguration of Solomon's reign is Israel's cultural zenith. This view of the first part of Solomon's reign as unmitigated blessing not only demonstrates the ideal of the monarchy, but the fulfillment of the divine promise to David.

This ideal of kingship depends on strict adherence to the requirements of the covenant. The problem for the Deuteronomist is that the success of the kingdom is the very thing that makes it vulnerable to demise. The king must not depend on military power or alliances, have many wives, or depend on wealth (Deut. 17:15–17). Wisdom brings Solomon wealth and power beyond that of any other king (1 Kings 10:23). While this is not stated in negative terms, this description of Solomon becomes the converse of what the covenant required (see 4:26–29). Solomon accumulates horses and chariots and makes silver in Jerusalem to be so plentiful it is like a common stone. Solomon goes to Egypt for his supply of horses, and he has many foreign wives (11:1–3). These statements reflect on the covenant requirement to trust God. While the statements about wealth and power may demonstrate the success of Solomon, they are also the point of his vulnerability.

The grace of God working through flawed people. In the context of the whole story of Solomon and the history of the nation, this period of

---

28. H. G. M. Williamson, "The Accession of Solomon in the Books of Chronicles," *VT* 26 (1976): 351–61.

29. Dillard, *2 Chronicles,* 4.

Solomon's glory is ambiguous. It is often assumed that when the Solomon story was incorporated into the final edition of the books of Kings, his reign was given a new assessment. There is no reason to think that it would take until the Exile before the reign of Solomon was evaluated critically in relation to the covenant.

Others find the elements of favor and failure in the structure of the story. Parker thinks that the negative assessment of 1 Kings 1–2 and 11:14–43 frame the story, and that within it chapters 3–8 are parallel to 9:1–11:13.[30] The first unit approves Solomon, but the second is hostile. Brettler proposes a different division;[31] the first section is Solomon's accession (chs. 1–2), the second his faithfulness and blessing (3:3–9:23), and the final one his punishment for the violation of the code of the king (9:26–11:43). These literary divisions have merit, but one must ask whether the authors actually intend two different portrayals of Solomon. Numerous other versions of irony and ambiguity have been observed in the Solomon narrative.[32] It is characteristic of the Deuteronomistic History to present the stark realities of failure of all the characters that in other respects are heroes.

Hays takes a different approach to the Solomon story. He thinks that what appears to be praise is in reality irony: "There are numerous clues that suggest to us that perhaps the narrator is playing literary games with his readers. He may be openly and overtly praising Solomon on the surface, but he does not tell the story with a straight face, and if we look closely, we see him winking at us."[33] The spectacular reign of Solomon has a subtheme that quietly points out the serious inconsistencies and serious problems that are not a part of the surface story. To use another metaphor, readers are given a tour of a spectacular and opulent mansion. However, without changing the inflection of his voice, the tour guide points out places where the façade has cracked. The guide uses nuances that tell us his glowing praise is not his honest opinion, and in the end tells us that the building is a fraud, covered with a thin veneer of glitz and hoopla.[34]

There certainly is plenty in the story from the start that is not complimentary to Solomon by the standards of Deuteronomy. The worship at the high places is not ideal, nor his marriage to Pharaoh's daughter. The organization of Solomon's empire, in being all an empire should be, has the very

---

30. Kim Ian Parker, "Repetition as a Structuring Device in 1 Kings 1–11," *JSOT* 42 (1988): 19–27.

31. Marc Brettler, "The Structure of 1 Kings 1–11," *JSOT* 49 (1991): 87–97.

32. A recent survey is provided by J. Daniel Hays, "Has the Narrator Come to Praise Solomon or to Bury Him? Narrative Subtlety in 1 Kings 1–11," *JSOT* 28 (2003): 164–67.

33. Ibid., 168.

34. Ibid., 169.

elements that Samuel warned about when Israel asked for a king. The king would take their sons and daughters, fields, vineyards, and flocks; the people would become slaves. When they would then cry out in distress because of their king, Yahweh would not hear (1 Sam. 8:16–18). Solomon's governors are assigned to collect taxes (1 Kings 4:7, 27), and one of his officials is in charge of conscripted labor (v. 6). It is consistent with an important motif within the Deuteronomistic History to regard kingship as oppressive and contrary to God's purpose.

If it was the sole purpose of the narrative to "bury" Solomon, then the Chronicler has developed a theology of the united kingdom that is completely contrary to that set out in Kings. If the glory of Solomon is a fraud, then the promise to David is never manifested within the history of the kingdom. The promise to David does survive in spite of Solomon, as it does during the reigns of other Judean kings, most notably Manasseh. Yet it is the viewpoint of the historian that God is actively at work directing the fulfillment of that promise. Solomon is a divine choice, just as the heroes of the past. In the days of the judges, the grace of God repeatedly ended in disaster, but that does not deny the reality of that grace at work through those who brought a temporary deliverance. The grace of God in Gideon ended with Abimelech, and the power of God in Samson ended with his death in the Philistine temple, but both were towering examples of missed opportunity.

All of the divinely chosen characters in the Deuteronomistic History, including David and Solomon, are flawed, but this is not to discount the grace of God at work through them. Whatever the failures of Solomon, his reign is a manifestation of God's power for Israel. His kingdom is not his own achievement; it is the grace of God because of the covenant and the promise. Solomon fails, but he is not a failure any more than all the others who in one way or another betray the grace of God. The Chronicler chooses to emphasize the possibility of receiving God's grace and properly finds in Solomon the most distinguished example.

The light and dark side of wisdom. The encomium to Solomon's wisdom is a typical tribute of court circles to their monarch (4:29–34).[35] At the time of Hezekiah, the fame of Solomon continues in collections of proverbs made and preserved in his name (Prov. 25:1). The whole story of Solomon can be read in terms of "Lady Wisdom" and the "foreign

---

35. The first cylinder commemorating the temple building of Gudea of Lagash (the third dynasty of Ur, ca. 2112–2004 B.C.) says, "The ruler (Gudea), being a man of wide wisdom, had been paying close attention, lauding (Ningirsu) with all great things," Richard E. Averbeck, "The Cylinders of Gudea," *The Context of Scripture*, ed. William W. Hallo, K. Lawson Younger (Leiden: Brill, 2003), 2.155 A i.12–13.

woman."[36] Wisdom and foreign women are significant and interrelated themes in the Solomon story, with ambiguous suggestive allusions. An irony of wisdom is that success in one realm endangers its application and function in another.

The wisdom of the Israelites is the teaching they receive through the covenant (Deut. 1–10). All nations marvel at the knowledge of life possessed by the Israelites (vv. 6–8); it enables them to be a great nation. The danger is that they will forget the source of their knowledge and blessings (vv. 9–10) and will subvert the very blessing that they have received.

The very passage that extols Solomon in the success of a vast empire (4:24–25) is implicitly a warning against the failure of wisdom. Administration, taxation, and military expertise require wisdom and are a necessary provision for an empire, but the success of these items brings reliance on them. The mention of the vast number of Solomon's horses is both a statement of his success as a wise man and his failure as a foolish man. Life in this world is never safe. Wisdom may bring the success of wealth and security, but wealth and security induce a reliance on material well-being that is a failure of wisdom. Though it is possible to have the wisdom that leads to success and the wisdom that is faithful to a trust in God, it is not easy to maintain both. Wisdom may be a victim of its own success.

There is a dark side to wisdom in the Old Testament. Wisdom can be used to achieve dubious ends. The serpent, wiser than any of the other creatures, led Adam and Eve to rebel against God and claim knowledge to govern their own lives and make their own decisions. Jonadab was a clever man (2 Sam. 13:3), able to devise a means for his friend Amnon to obtain forced sexual relations with his half-sister Tamar. The deceptive powers of the success of wisdom are just a step away from wisdom itself being used toward deceptive ends.

Though Solomon is portrayed as exceedingly wise, little is said about his mastery of the kind of wisdom that understands the fear of Yahweh—that instinctive and intuitive recognition of the total claim of God that is felt in religious and moral issues. The disjunction between the wisdom of Solomon in Kings and that of wisdom literature has led to the conclusion that Solomon's reputation as a wise man is simply legendary. It is asserts that the proverbs he composed are more like the lists of nature items found in Egypt and Mesopotamia (*onomastica*).[37] A poetic ditty describes this aspect of Solomon's wisdom:

---

36. Claudia V. Camp, *Wise, Strange and Holy: The Strange Woman and the Making of the Bible* (JSOTSup 320; Sheffield: Sheffield Academic Press, 2000).

37. James L. Crenshaw, *Old Testament Wisdom*, rev. ed. (Louisville: Westminster John Knox, 1998), 40–41. Such lists are now recognized as a didactic undertaking, not a scientific enterprise; M. J. Fox, "Egyptian Onomastica and Biblical Wisdom," *VT* 36 (1986): 302–10.

He spoke about the trees,
From the cedar in Lebanon
To the hyssop that grows from the wall;
He spoke about the animals,
The birds, the reptiles, and the fish. (1 Kings 4:33)

It is possible these collections of nature have been transformed into poetic compositions for moral instruction. Though this may have happened in particular instances, the collections of proverbs have no similarity to such collections.

The Hebrew word for wisdom (*ḥokmâ*) has a wide and unrelated range of meanings.[38] The wisdom of Solomon in Kings is regarded as superhuman, wisdom like that of God (3:28). Solomon asked for a "mind to listen" (3:9); knowing how to listen is an important component of proverbial wisdom (e.g. Prov. 12:15). Though the first datable identification of Solomon with proverbial wisdom is the collections of the men of Hezekiah (25:1), it is unusual for the court circles not to ascribe wisdom to their own king. The ruler of a vast empire and the builder of the nation's temple is regarded as having the discerning mind of the wise and a special dispensation of vast knowledge and insight that is possessed by no other. When asked for a sign, Jesus gives his inquisitors the sign of Solomon (Matt. 12:38—42); the Queen of the South will stand in judgment over them, for she came to seek out the wisdom of Solomon, and now a greater than Solomon is in their midst. Solomon himself becomes a proverb, exemplifying what it is to possess wisdom.

The kingdom of Solomon began as a paragon of wise governance, making the demise of that kingdom so much more tragic. The authors of Kings regard the kingdom of Solomon as more than the achievement of good government. God has granted Solomon wisdom that gives him fame among all nations, including the renowned wise men of the east (4:29—31). His achievements are possible only through such divine provision. Mastery of the skills of governance lead to a reliance on that knowledge and a failure to depend on God. Wisdom of the fear of Yahweh is displaced with carnal pursuits. The lofty achievements of Solomon are subverted by his failure to live by the fundamental requirement that wisdom demands.

The wealth of Solomon and the splendor of his building projects are to be regarded as a virtue. These are the accomplishments of a wise king, and they are the gift of God. This is not the "prosperity gospel" in the sense that God blesses individuals because they trust him for the things they want. The

---

38. Within the Hebrew Bible, Müller distinguishes aphorisms, mantic wisdom, magical wisdom, and artisans, apart from other more general meanings; "חכם," *TDOT*, 4:373—79. The onomastic lists are not included in his discussion.

kingdom of Solomon is an example of communal prosperity, which benefits a community and a nation when they are able to live together according to the virtues of wisdom and the fear of the Lord.

The wisdom of Solomon in the administration of his empire brings prosperity to the people. Wisdom as a "tree of life" brings long life in her right hand and wealth and honor in her left (Prov. 3:16–18). It is to understand the order of this world so that mortals (ʾādām) are able to live in harmony with the ground (ʾādāmâ) from which they have been taken. The function of such wisdom demands community. It is not good that man should be alone; as male and female they are to become a people who will appropriately exercise dominion and live for the benefit of each other. This is the knowledge that comes from God, the fruit of wisdom that brings favor and prosperity.

TAXES AND FAIRNESS. "Religions should 'rejoice' at the chance to pay taxes," writes John Longhurst in reference to the launch of "Taxation for the Common Good," a forty-page document by the Roman Catholoic Church designed to spark discussion about taxation and public services in the United Kingdom.[39] Bishop Howard Tripp says, "Taxes are very much based on the principles of solidarity, which is based on the commandment to love your neighbour." Christians should rejoice in the chance to contribute toward the sort of society that they want. "This document is suggesting taxes are a way to play our part and it is something we should be pleased to do," according to Tripp. "It is all a part of our duty to our neighbour." The Most Reverend Peter Smith, the Archbishop of Cardiff who headed the committee that created the report, said, "Taxation is a sign of social health, a moral good. Our willingness to pay it is a sign of our solidarity with one another, and of our humanity."

The glories of the reign of Solomon are based on the solidarity of taxation for the common good. These are the means to the people of Judah and Israel being "as numerous as the sand on the seashore; they ate, they drank and they were happy" (4:20). It is possible for a contemporary society to reach the ideals expressed of Solomon's reign: "During Solomon's lifetime, Judah and Israel, from Dan to Beersheba, lived in safety, each man under his own vine and fig tree" (v. 25). The power of government must include the responsibility of taxation in order to achieve a society with equity and prosperity. As some wag has expressed it, "The government needs to be glad we've got what it takes." Those who have the ability to pay

---

39. John Longhurst, "Faith," *Winnipeg Free Press* (March 6, 2004), E9.

taxes should be grateful for that capability and be willing to exercise it responsibly.

Longhurst reports on Alabama Governor Bob Riley, who attempted to implement the principle of taxation as a debt owed to fellow citizens.

> Riley, an evangelical Christian and Republican, stunned many of his conservative supporters ... when he advocated a tax reform plan that would have shifted a significant amount of the state's tax burden from the poor to wealthy individuals and corporations.... Riley argued that it was a matter of Christian duty to reform a tax system in which a family of four making as little as $4,600 a year paid more in taxes, percentage-wise, than the richest of the state's residents.

Riley made his case on the basis of the Bible. "I have spent a lot of time reading the New Testament, and it has three philosophies: love God, love each other, and take care of the least among you. It is immoral to charge somebody making $5,000 a year an income tax." Critics called Riley's proposal, "How Would Jesus Tax Us?" In his plan, just the top third of income earners, plus corporations and large farm and timber operations, would pay more taxes, while anyone earning less than $20,000 a year would pay no taxes at all.

The principles that Riley made on the basis of the New Testament for Christians in contemporary society are a prominent feature of the community ideal (Deut. 6:1–3; 14:28–29; 15:7–11). The tithe and the release of debts against property were part of the covenant of brothers and were not a matter of individual decisions of charity. Justice and economic equity were the responsibility of the king; their virtues were briefly achieved in the establishment of a united monarchy that brought all the regions together in one administrative system.

These values of collective responsibility to all society need to be fully appreciated by Christians in current times. Christians in Alabama were deeply divided over Governor Riley's plan. John Giles, president of the Christian Coalition of Alabama, opposed it saying, "Never in scripture does it say 'Render unto Caesar so he can take care of the poor.' It's the church's responsibility." Riley's tax reform plan was defeated by Alabama voters in September, 2003, but one observer, reflecting on the opposition of some churches, observed that for all the moral high ground those Christians claimed, their opposition showed that "they hate taxes more than they love Jesus."

There can be no simple comparison between a nation bonded by a covenant and the responsibility of the church. The church has a particular obligation to those who teach them the gospel and to those "of the household of faith" (Gal. 6:6, 10). The church cannot be responsible for all the poor of society, as was required in the old covenant. Neither can church members live in isolation from society, providing only for the poor in their own group. Christians are not only responsible for the benefits they derive from government. They are responsible to love their neighbors, in whom they encounter Christ, whoever they are and wherever they live. There is a moral foundation to taxation, to create a society that serves all, with a special concern for the most needy. There is no moral obligation to be happy when calculating tax, but it may help not to think of it as a burden, but as a way to serve God and neighbor.

In Judaism payment of taxes is a way to benefit all. Governments have a right to tax citizens, and anyone who doesn't pay "has violated the Torah prohibition against theft."[40] Such a provision is certainly in keeping with the principles of Old Testament covenant requirement and was so understood in the reign of Solomon. Government in turn must tax people fairly, or it is stealing from the taxpayer; government must be responsible for the money it collects because it belongs to the taxpayers collectively.

One of the lessons of the rule of Solomon is that government would seem to be incapable of holding itself accountable. At the death of Solomon, answerability is so little understood that his son Rehoboam rashly follows the counsel of youthful advisors to heavily increase taxation. They sarcastically suggest that the little finger of Rehoboam will be thicker than the waist of his father (12:10). When Rehoboam sends Adoniram, the officer in charge of conscripted labor (4:6), to recruit the required labor from the northern tribes, they stone him (12:18). Rehoboam flees for his life and the kingdom is permanently divided (v. 19). The glory of the kingdom of Solomon is achieved at an unsustainable price.

In stating the glories of that kingdom so boldly, the narrative accentuates the dangers of political success. That danger may be summed up in the famous saying of English historian Lord John Acton (1834–1902): "Power tends to corrupt, and absolute power corrupts absolutely."[41] The subversive corruption of power is often so subtle that it is unrecognized even by those with the best of intentions. The glory of the kingdom is equaled only in the tragedy of its demise, a factor that is of central concern to the Deuteronomistic Historian. The power of government control must be for the benefit of all those governed and not be controlled by the interests of those who govern.

Globalization and trade. Globalization, the phenomena of international trade agreements between virtually all industries, has created wealth that is

---

40. Longhurst refers to the website *torah.org* for this information.

41. This quote and information on the Acton Institute is provided by Stephen Henderson in "Talking Freely about Free Enterprise," *Milestones* (May 2004), a publication of the John Templeton Foundation.

unprecedented in human history. It also brings with it grave dangers that could end in a collapse no less spectacular than that of Solomon's empire. It affects justice and prosperity for virtually every worker in every country. Kris Mauren, cofounder and executive director of the Acton Institute for the Study of Religion and Liberty in Grand Rapids, Michigan, says that religious leaders in different parts of the world often misunderstand fundamental principles of free enterprise.

> The United States government likes to talk about free trade with other nations, yet it basically prevents third world countries from trading their agricultural products. So, although you have American religious leaders promoting humanitarian aid to places like Kenya, what Kenyans really want is the opportunity to engage the world market.[42]

The Acton Institute challenges the status quo of all political parties, especially the abuses that go on in the name of free enterprise.

In the context of globalization, the challenge of economic justice extends beyond the authority of one government. Taxation and trade tariffs affect the exchange of all commodities for both producers and consumers of distant countries. Exchange of food was fundamental in Solomon's administration, both for the supplies of his own palace (4:22–23)[43] and for obtaining goods and services for his building projects (5:11). Initially at least, this was beneficial for all concerned. With globalization, food has come to be one of the most debated and disputed areas of justice. The issues range from fair trade of coffee beans to the exchange of ruminant animals affected by what is popularly called "mad cow disease," a form of spongiform encephalopathy, which damages the central nervous system and brain tissue.

These issues are as disparate as they are complex. Trade regulations trap the producers of these products so their market value is less than what it costs to produce them. For example, trade barriers suddenly imposed on beef products, ostensibly because of health concerns, saddles farmers with the burden of having to feed animals that should be sold, and then selling them at a huge loss. Their fortunes are controlled by political factors completely out of their control. The issue is not health but the politics of food in the name of controlling disease. A part of the problem is that so little is known of the spread and danger of such diseases that it is difficult to set up reasonable regulations.

---

42. Ibid.

43. Solomon's requirements were modest when compared to those from Egyptian and Mesopotamian centers; A. R. Millard, "Story, History, and Theology," in *Faith, Tradition, and History: Old Testament Historiography in its Near Eastern Context*, ed. A. R. Millard, J. K. Hoffmeier, and D. W. Baker (Winona Lake, Ind.: Eisenbrauns, 1994), 47.

Fair trade is an ideal that good governments relentlessly pursue, with recognition of the limits to which it can be achieved. When a sector of industry suffers because of unanticipated and uncontrollable change, responsible governments come to the aid of the individuals affected as best they can. There is always a tendency for governments to seek retention of power as their first interest. When pursuit of power becomes a priority over pursuit of justice, the distress of those victimized by economic changes goes unaddressed. The beginning of the kingdom of Solomon is an example of wise and supportive administration for the citizens of the nation. But as so often happens with governments, the high ideals with which they begin is lost; the kingdom of Solomon exemplifies this hazard.

Wisdom is knowledge of how to live with other people and how to live in harmony with the world of nature. These two kinds of knowledge are the basis of getting on well in this world. Living in harmony with the world of nature is a continuing challenge. The "green revolution" has enabled the production of food many times beyond what previous generations could have imagined. It has also endangered plant species and polluted or dried up water supplies. The development of energy has been a vast resource, but there is the constant threat that demand will outstrip supply or that the consumption of energy will alter the earth so it becomes a much less hospitable place for human existence.

Wisdom of how to live with people is an even greater challenge. Conflict and violence are part of social relations from the smallest units of society to the largest: homes, communities, nations, and between nations. The ideals of Solomon's wisdom and administration are rightly remembered as the goal to which every society must strive.

1 Kings 5:1–7:51a

WHEN HIRAM KING of Tyre heard that Solomon had been anointed king to succeed his father David, he sent his envoys to Solomon, because he had always been on friendly terms with David. ²Solomon sent back this message to Hiram:

³"You know that because of the wars waged against my father David from all sides, he could not build a temple for the Name of the LORD his God until the LORD put his enemies under his feet. ⁴But now the LORD my God has given me rest on every side, and there is no adversary or disaster. ⁵I intend, therefore, to build a temple for the Name of the LORD my God, as the LORD told my father David, when he said, 'Your son whom I will put on the throne in your place will build the temple for my Name.'

⁶"So give orders that cedars of Lebanon be cut for me. My men will work with yours, and I will pay you for your men whatever wages you set. You know that we have no one so skilled in felling timber as the Sidonians."

⁷When Hiram heard Solomon's message, he was greatly pleased and said, "Praise be to the LORD today, for he has given David a wise son to rule over this great nation."

⁸So Hiram sent word to Solomon:

"I have received the message you sent me and will do all you want in providing the cedar and pine logs. ⁹My men will haul them down from Lebanon to the sea, and I will float them in rafts by sea to the place you specify. There I will separate them and you can take them away. And you are to grant my wish by providing food for my royal household."

¹⁰In this way Hiram kept Solomon supplied with all the cedar and pine logs he wanted, ¹¹and Solomon gave Hiram twenty thousand cors of wheat as food for his household, in addition to twenty thousand baths of pressed olive oil. Solomon continued to do this for Hiram year after year.

¹²The LORD gave Solomon wisdom, just as he had promised him. There were peaceful relations between Hiram and Solomon, and the two of them made a treaty.

¹³King Solomon conscripted laborers from all Israel—thirty thousand men. ¹⁴He sent them off to Lebanon in shifts of ten thousand a month, so that they spent one month in Lebanon and two months at home. Adoniram was in charge of the forced labor. ¹⁵Solomon had seventy thousand carriers and eighty thousand stonecutters in the hills, ¹⁶as well as thirty-three hundred foremen who supervised the project and directed the workmen. ¹⁷At the king's command they removed from the quarry large blocks of quality stone to provide a foundation of dressed stone for the temple. ¹⁸The craftsmen of Solomon and Hiram and the men of Gebal cut and prepared the timber and stone for the building of the temple.

⁶:¹In the four hundred and eightieth year after the Israelites had come out of Egypt, in the fourth year of Solomon's reign over Israel, in the month of Ziv, the second month, he began to build the temple of the LORD.

²The temple that King Solomon built for the LORD was sixty cubits long, twenty wide and thirty high. ³The portico at the front of the main hall of the temple extended the width of the temple, that is twenty cubits, and projected ten cubits from the front of the temple. ⁴He made narrow clerestory windows in the temple. ⁵Against the walls of the main hall and inner sanctuary he built a structure around the building, in which there were side rooms. ⁶The lowest floor was five cubits wide, the middle floor six cubits and the third floor seven. He made offset ledges around the outside of the temple so that nothing would be inserted into the temple walls.

⁷In building the temple, only blocks dressed at the quarry were used, and no hammer, chisel or any other iron tool was heard at the temple site while it was being built.

⁸The entrance to the lowest floor was on the south side of the temple; a stairway led up to the middle level and from there to the third. ⁹So he built the temple and completed it, roofing it with beams and cedar planks. ¹⁰And he built the side rooms all along the temple. The height of each was five cubits, and they were attached to the temple by beams of cedar.

¹¹The word of the LORD came to Solomon: ¹²"As for this temple you are building, if you follow my decrees, carry out

my regulations and keep all my commands and obey them, I will fulfill through you the promise I gave to David your father. ¹³And I will live among the Israelites and will not abandon my people Israel."

¹⁴So Solomon built the temple and completed it. ¹⁵He lined its interior walls with cedar boards, paneling them from the floor of the temple to the ceiling, and covered the floor of the temple with planks of pine. ¹⁶He partitioned off twenty cubits at the rear of the temple with cedar boards from floor to ceiling to form within the temple an inner sanctuary, the Most Holy Place. ¹⁷The main hall in front of this room was forty cubits long. ¹⁸The inside of the temple was cedar, carved with gourds and open flowers. Everything was cedar; no stone was to be seen.

¹⁹He prepared the inner sanctuary within the temple to set the ark of the covenant of the LORD there. ²⁰The inner sanctuary was twenty cubits long, twenty wide and twenty high. He overlaid the inside with pure gold, and he also overlaid the altar of cedar. ²¹Solomon covered the inside of the temple with pure gold, and he extended gold chains across the front of the inner sanctuary, which was overlaid with gold. ²²So he overlaid the whole interior with gold. He also overlaid with gold the altar that belonged to the inner sanctuary.

²³In the inner sanctuary he made a pair of cherubim of olive wood, each ten cubits high. ²⁴One wing of the first cherub was five cubits long, and the other wing five cubits—ten cubits from wing tip to wing tip. ²⁵The second cherub also measured ten cubits, for the two cherubim were identical in size and shape. ²⁶The height of each cherub was ten cubits. ²⁷He placed the cherubim inside the innermost room of the temple, with their wings spread out. The wing of one cherub touched one wall, while the wing of the other touched the other wall, and their wings touched each other in the middle of the room. ²⁸He overlaid the cherubim with gold.

²⁹On the walls all around the temple, in both the inner and outer rooms, he carved cherubim, palm trees and open flowers. ³⁰He also covered the floors of both the inner and outer rooms of the temple with gold.

³¹For the entrance of the inner sanctuary he made doors of olive wood with five-sided jambs. ³²And on the two olive wood doors he carved cherubim, palm trees and open flowers, and overlaid the cherubim and palm trees with beaten gold.

³³In the same way he made four-sided jambs of olive wood for the entrance to the main hall. ³⁴He also made two pine doors, each having two leaves that turned in sockets. ³⁵He carved cherubim, palm trees and open flowers on them and overlaid them with gold hammered evenly over the carvings.

³⁶And he built the inner courtyard of three courses of dressed stone and one course of trimmed cedar beams.

³⁷The foundation of the temple of the LORD was laid in the fourth year, in the month of Ziv. ³⁸In the eleventh year in the month of Bul, the eighth month, the temple was finished in all its details according to its specifications. He had spent seven years building it.

⁷:¹It took Solomon thirteen years, however, to complete the construction of his palace. ²He built the Palace of the Forest of Lebanon a hundred cubits long, fifty wide and thirty high, with four rows of cedar columns supporting trimmed cedar beams. ³It was roofed with cedar above the beams that rested on the columns—forty-five beams, fifteen to a row. ⁴Its windows were placed high in sets of three, facing each other. ⁵All the doorways had rectangular frames; they were in the front part in sets of three, facing each other.

⁶He made a colonnade fifty cubits long and thirty wide. In front of it was a portico, and in front of that were pillars and an overhanging roof.

⁷He built the throne hall, the Hall of Justice, where he was to judge, and he covered it with cedar from floor to ceiling. ⁸And the palace in which he was to live, set farther back, was similar in design. Solomon also made a palace like this hall for Pharaoh's daughter, whom he had married.

⁹All these structures, from the outside to the great courtyard and from foundation to eaves, were made of blocks of high-grade stone cut to size and trimmed with a saw on their inner and outer faces. ¹⁰The foundations were laid with large stones of good quality, some measuring ten cubits and some eight. ¹¹Above were high-grade stones, cut to size, and cedar beams. ¹²The great courtyard was surrounded by a wall of three courses of dressed stone and one course of trimmed cedar beams, as was the inner courtyard of the temple of the LORD with its portico.

¹³King Solomon sent to Tyre and brought Huram, ¹⁴whose mother was a widow from the tribe of Naphtali and whose

father was a man of Tyre and a craftsman in bronze. Huram was highly skilled and experienced in all kinds of bronze work. He came to King Solomon and did all the work assigned to him.

¹⁵He cast two bronze pillars, each eighteen cubits high and twelve cubits around, by line. ¹⁶He also made two capitals of cast bronze to set on the tops of the pillars; each capital was five cubits high. ¹⁷A network of interwoven chains festooned the capitals on top of the pillars, seven for each capital. ¹⁸He made pomegranates in two rows encircling each network to decorate the capitals on top of the pillars. He did the same for each capital. ¹⁹The capitals on top of the pillars in the portico were in the shape of lilies, four cubits high. ²⁰On the capitals of both pillars, above the bowl-shaped part next to the network, were the two hundred pomegranates in rows all around. ²¹He erected the pillars at the portico of the temple. The pillar to the south he named Jakin and the one to the north Boaz. ²²The capitals on top were in the shape of lilies. And so the work on the pillars was completed.

²³He made the Sea of cast metal, circular in shape, measuring ten cubits from rim to rim and five cubits high. It took a line of thirty cubits to measure around it. ²⁴Below the rim, gourds encircled it—ten to a cubit. The gourds were cast in two rows in one piece with the Sea.

²⁵The Sea stood on twelve bulls, three facing north, three facing west, three facing south and three facing east. The Sea rested on top of them, and their hindquarters were toward the center. ²⁶It was a handbreadth in thickness, and its rim was like the rim of a cup, like a lily blossom. It held two thousand baths.

²⁷He also made ten movable stands of bronze; each was four cubits long, four wide and three high. ²⁸This is how the stands were made: They had side panels attached to uprights. ²⁹On the panels between the uprights were lions, bulls and cherubim—and on the uprights as well. Above and below the lions and bulls were wreaths of hammered work. ³⁰Each stand had four bronze wheels with bronze axles, and each had a basin resting on four supports, cast with wreaths on each side. ³¹On the inside of the stand there was an opening that had a circular frame one cubit deep. This opening was round, and with its basework it measured a cubit and a half. Around its

opening there was engraving. The panels of the stands were square, not round. ³²The four wheels were under the panels, and the axles of the wheels were attached to the stand. The diameter of each wheel was a cubit and a half. ³³The wheels were made like chariot wheels; the axles, rims, spokes and hubs were all of cast metal.

³⁴Each stand had four handles, one on each corner, projecting from the stand. ³⁵At the top of the stand there was a circular band half a cubit deep. The supports and panels were attached to the top of the stand. ³⁶He engraved cherubim, lions and palm trees on the surfaces of the supports and on the panels, in every available space, with wreaths all around. ³⁷This is the way he made the ten stands. They were all cast in the same molds and were identical in size and shape.

³⁸He then made ten bronze basins, each holding forty baths and measuring four cubits across, one basin to go on each of the ten stands. ³⁹He placed five of the stands on the south side of the temple and five on the north. He placed the Sea on the south side, at the southeast corner of the temple. ⁴⁰He also made the basins and shovels and sprinkling bowls.

So Huram finished all the work he had undertaken for King Solomon in the temple of the LORD:

⁴¹ the two pillars;
the two bowl-shaped capitals on top of the pillars;
the two sets of network decorating the two bowl-shaped capitals on top of the pillars;
⁴² the four hundred pomegranates for the two sets of network (two rows of pomegranates for each network, decorating the bowl-shaped capitals on top of the pillars);
⁴³ the ten stands with their ten basins;
⁴⁴ the Sea and the twelve bulls under it;
⁴⁵ the pots, shovels and sprinkling bowls.

All these objects that Huram made for King Solomon for the temple of the LORD were of burnished bronze. ⁴⁶The king had them cast in clay molds in the plain of the Jordan between Succoth and Zarethan. ⁴⁷Solomon left all these things unweighed, because there were so many; the weight of the bronze was not determined.

⁴⁸Solomon also made all the furnishings that were in the LORD's temple:

the golden altar;

the golden table on which was the bread of the Presence;

[49] the lampstands of pure gold (five on the right and five on the
left, in front of the inner sanctuary);

the gold floral work and lamps and tongs;

[50] the pure gold basins, wick trimmers, sprinkling bowls, dishes
and censers;

and the gold sockets for the doors of the innermost room, the
Most Holy Place, and also for the doors of the main hall of
the temple.

[51a]When all the work King Solomon had done for the temple of the LORD was finished. . . .

THE ADMINISTRATION OF Solomon's kingdom
requires a large complex of buildings. The palace
serves as a residence and administrative center
for the king. It is larger in size than the temple
and takes thirteen years to build (7:1). No remains have been linked to the
palace of Solomon at Jerusalem. Remains of palaces are evident in their size,
layout, elaborate decorations, and contents, such as expensive furniture and
state archives. The ground plans of buildings at Megiddo from Solomon's time
are similar to the palaces at Zinjirli (the ancient Aramean city of Sam'al), suggesting that this may have been the plan of the Jerusalem palace.[1] Walls and
towers surround the three palaces and storehouses; to enter the complex it
was necessary to pass through two gates. Solomon develops a similar complex at Jerusalem, where the citadel encloses a number of buildings.

The typical ancient palace had a pillared porch that led into smaller halls,
a throne room, and open inner courts surrounded by smaller rooms, which
were living quarters for the royal household. The temple was closely associated with the palace.[2] The reign of the human king depended on the presence and power of the divine ruler on his throne. With the advent of dynastic
kingship in Israel, it is important to have a national temple to give legitimacy

---

1. D. Ussishkin, "King Solomon's Palace and Building 1723 in Megiddo," *IEJ* 16 (1966):
174–86.

2. Ussishkin proposes that adjacent temple and palace remains at Hamath and Tayanat
in Syria are comparable to those of Solomon; "Building IV in Hamath and the Temples of
Solomon and Tell Tayanat," *IEJ* 16 (1966): 104–10. See also Amihai Mazar, *Archaeology of
the Land of the Bible 10,000–586 B.C.E.* (ABRL; Doubleday, 1990), 377. Megiddo, Zinjirli, and
Alalakh have similar temples with adjacent palaces dating to the first millennium.

to the dynasty and signify the unity of the nation. The rule of Solomon has been legitimated by the God of Israel, but Solomon is subservient to the supreme King through the covenant. The citadel naturally stands predominantly over the city in the highest area on the eastern side. Its ideal location and the grandeur of its fortifications are celebrated in song as the envy of kings who visit there to bring their tribute (Ps. 48:1—14).

The palace complex of Solomon includes a great assembly hall, whose rows of pillars give it the appearance of a forest (7:2), a throne (judgment) hall (7:7), which may have been within the hall of pillars (7:6), the palace proper, and the residence of Pharaoh's daughter (7:8). Nothing is said about Solomon's house or that of the Egyptian queen, other than that they are built with a similar pattern in construction. The arrangement of these buildings on the temple mount is not given—a point of interest to the historian but not to the prophetic writer. In his exhaustive study of the Jerusalem temple, Busink makes the generally accepted proposal that the royal edifices were to the south of the temple.[3]

Solomon's own palace must have been the largest of the buildings to accommodate his large harem and all his retainers. It probably had an entrance to the inner court of the temple and another entrance into the larger outer court (7:8). The palace of Pharaoh's daughter would have been adjoined to that of Solomon. The great assembly hall and the hall of pillars would have been to the east of the two palaces, south of the temple court. The taxes collected by the governors went to these great building projects, a testimony to the greatness of the kingdom that God had given to Solomon in addition to his wisdom.

Preparations for Building the Temple (5:1–18)

THE ACCOUNT OF Solomon's building projects begins with the abrupt introduction of Hiram, king of Tyre. Hiram sends messengers to affirm Solomon's rule (5:1) because of his prior agreements with David. Hiram is a shortened form of Ahiram, a name that joins a divine epithet ("exalted") with "my brother." By the time of David, Tyre had become a maritime power, gaining preeminence over the rival cities of Sidon and Byblos. Tyrian expansion began in the time of Hiram; near the beginning of his reign he was involved in suppressing a rebellion on the island of Cyprus.[4] This was the beginning

---

3. T. A. Busink, *Der Tempel Salomos* (vol. 1 in *Der Tempel von Jerusalem von Salomo bis Herodes;* Studia Francisci Scholten memoriae dicata 3; Leiden: Brill, 1970), 128–61.

4. H. J. Katzenstein, *The History of Tyre* (Jerusalem: Schocken, 1973), 84–86. Josephus is a most important source for knowledge of Tyrian history; he has preserved several passages from Dius and Menander of Ephesus, two Hellenistic historians who used a translation of the annals of Tyre.

of colonization that came to extend as far as Carthage during the days of Israel. Ancient Tyre was an island fortress (Ezek. 27:32), about a half-mile from the shore. It was joined to the mainland by a dike at the conquest of Alexander the Great, and alluvial deposits over the centuries have turned it into a peninsula.

Hiram was involved in David's building projects, supplying wood, carpenters, and stone masons (2 Sam. 5:11). The attitude of the kings of Tyre toward Israel appears to have changed after David's victories over the Philistines. The Tyrians suffered from the power of the Philistines to rule over both land and sea. Perhaps the Phoenicians were allies with Israel against the Philistines; Israel attacked them on land and the Phoenicians at sea. Abibaal, the father of Hiram I and a contemporary of David, may have founded a new dynasty in Tyre and inaugurated a change in Tyrian foreign policy.[5] Hiram came to reign near the end of David's reign and was probably the head of the delegation sent to David by his father.[6] Hiram continued this loyal relationship with David and was fully prepared to continue that agreement with Solomon.

The political loyalty between Hiram and Solomon was probably based on a mutual need. Israel lacked technical skills for advancing its material culture, and Phoenicia lacked adequate agricultural production. Hiram took the initiative in affirming Solomon's accession to the throne. Palestine became Phoenicia's granary, supplying agricultural products for the king's household and workers. In return Solomon received skilled labor and materials for his massive building projects.

Tyre was famous for its skilled labor and building techniques (5:6). An example is the breakwater construction south of the city,[7] which were constructed from stones brought out from the mainland. The cornerstones were about ten feet by ten feet by two feet, and the stones in the wall about ten feet by three feet by two feet. Tyrian divers laid these massive stones in remarkable order that is still evident today.

Solomon's preparations for building are described in two sections. The first section (vv. 1–12) explains the alliance between Hiram and Solomon through which Solomon acquires the necessary materials and craftsmen. The second section (vv. 13–18) describes the workforce that Solomon marshals to accomplish his building projects. Though the two sections are complementary to each other, they are different in character. In the first section the prophetic authors recount the diplomatic exchange between Solomon and Hiram in

---

5. Ibid., 74.
6. Ibid., 96.
7. Ibid., 12–13.

terms that specifically recall the Davidic promise. Solomon's resolve to build
the temple (v. 5) repeats the very words of the promise to David concerning his son (2 Sam. 7:13). The second section has the character of administrative records, detailing the number of conscripted workers, the procedures
of rotation, the supervisors, and those responsible for the various aspects of
skilled work.

Alliance between Hiram and Solomon (5:1–12). The alliance of Hiram
with David and Solomon serves as the grounds for Solomon to make his
appeal, either through letter or as an oral communication (vv. 1–2). The actual
request is made at the conclusion of the appeal (v. 6). The delay in building
the temple must first be explained (vv. 3–5); David has been involved in warfare to gain control over his empire. No mention of this is made of the promise
to David given in Samuel (2 Sam. 7:12–13); the request of Solomon to Hiram
makes the declaration that Yahweh gave David rest from his enemies, the initial point made in Samuel (1 Kings 5:4; cf. 2 Sam. 7:1). The rest given to
David was a divine gift, a realization of the divine rest given to Joshua (cf. Josh.
21:43–45); Solomon experiences that rest with no adversaries.[8]

It was David's desire to provide a place of rest for God in the building of
the temple (2 Sam.7:1–2; cf. Ps. 132:7–8). Chronicles develops theologically
the reason why David could not build the temple; it was because of his shedding blood in warfare (1 Chron. 22:7–8; 28:2–3). The promise in Samuel
gives no reason why David could not build the temple; it merely emphasizes
what is more important: God will build a house for David. Solomon gives a
historical reason: David was too occupied by warfare. Chronicles gives the
theological reason: The peace of God's kingdom is incongruous with a person constantly involved in warfare. It is a man of peace (1 Chron. 22:9–10)
who is designated to build the temple.

Religion and politics were never separated in ancient times. Hiram's
response is to praise Solomon's God for the succession of a wise king like
Solomon (v. 7). Hiram is noted for his own temple buildings to the god
Melqart (Heracles),[9] but it is appropriate for him to give praise to Solomon's
God in observing the success of Solomon. Hiram's reply is constructed around
his obligation ("I . . . will do all you want") and Solomon's obligation ("you are
to grant my wish"); Hiram will give Solomon trees, and Solomon will give
Hiram food (vv. 8–9).

Lebanon is the territory north of Tyre; it refers to the double range of
mountains parallel to the Mediterranean coast, extending north on each side

8. The Hebrew word *śāṭān* ("adversary") later comes to be the name of the devil (cf.
Rev. 12:9); in earlier occurrences it simply means human adversaries.
9. Katzenstein, *The History of Tyre*, 86–94.

of the Litanni River to the el-Kabir River.[10] Solomon provides Hiram annually with over fifty thousand bushels of grain[11] and over one hundred thousand gallons of purified olive oil.[12] The treaty (v. 12) is a mutual benefit, since the cliffs of Tyre are not conducive to producing food and Solomon requires the skills and materials of the Phoenicians.

The cedar tree (vv. 8, 10) is identified as *Cedrus libani*, a tree renowned for its beauty and impressive height, reaching as high as thirty meters. The kings of Egypt, Mesopotamia, Phoenicia, Assyria, Babylon, Persia, and Greece all used cedar timber for building temples and palaces. Cedar wood was also desired for its fragrance.[13] The pine tree (often translated juniper or cypress) may be a collective name for several species of fir.[14] The trees are bound together in rafts (*dôberôt*) so they could be driven (*dbr*) by water as far as Jaffo (Joppa), where they can be disassembled and taken overland to Jerusalem (2 Chron. 2:15). Solomon in turn gives to Hiram food supplies that include the finest oil (v. 11), made by crushing olives into a mash, which was boiled until the oil floated to the top. The cooled oil was of exceptional quality for the lamps in the tabernacle (Ex. 27:20) and the preparation of flour offerings (29:40).

Administration of building projects (5:13–18). The second section of building preparations (vv. 13–18) gives some detail of the work of Adoniram (cf. 4:6), the chief officer in charge of the conscripted labor force. Thirty thousand workers serve for three-month periods, making an annual total of one hundred twenty thousand men. The rotation consists of one month of work in Lebanon and two months of work on the temple in Jerusalem. Hiram has determined that his workers will bring the wood down from Lebanon (v. 9), but according to this description they are assisted by Solomon's work force as well.

In addition to the wood workers there are seventy thousand workers transporting materials and eighty thousand quarrying rock in the hills of Palestine. Three thousand three hundred supervising officials provide a ratio

---

10. See Beitzel, *The Moody Atlas of Bible Lands*, #2, for the territory of Lebanon in the Promised Land.

11. A cor was equal to about one hundred liters or just under three bushels.

12. Following the numbers of LXX, which has 20,000 baths for the liquid quantity (cf. 2 Chron. 2:9). Twenty cors of oil (Hebrew text) seems too little, unless it is meant exclusively for Hiram's household. A "bath" is about 22 liters (5.8 U.S. gallons; 4.84 imperial gallons).

13. The legendary cedar forests of Lebanon go back as far as the beginnings of written script. By the mid-nineteenth century this rich resource was depleted; many efforts have been made to protect and restore these forests. In recent years the Lebanese government has made it a high priority to protect these trees from a wood wasp (*Cephalcia tannourinensis*); A. Daoud, "Tree Formations around Places of Worship in the Near East," *Unasylva* 213, 54 (2003): 49–51.

14. M. Zohary, *Plants of the Bible* (Cambridge: Cambridge Univ. Press, 1982), 106–7.

of one officer for every thirty-five workers. The amount of labor required to quarry and shape the stones to lay the foundation of the temple makes them costly (v. 17). The concluding verse explains that Solomon's workers are assisted by the men of Gebal to finish the stone and wood in preparation for the temple construction.

The city of Gebal (a mountain) was the northern boundary of the Promised Land (cf. Josh. 13:5). The Greeks called it Byblos, possibly because that was a port where they obtained material for making books. The craftsmen of Gebal were members of the commercial empire of Tyre (Ezek. 27:9).

The Construction of the Temple (6:1–7:1)

THE BUILDING OF the temple begins and ends with a chronological notice (6:1, 37–38). The foundation of the temple is laid in the fourth year of Solomon's reign, "in the month of Ziv" (*ziv* means "flowers"). It is completed in all its details and specifications in the eleventh year of Solomon's reign "in the month of Bul" (*bul* means "moisture").[15] The introduction sets the month in which the foundation is laid in reference to the Exodus. This is significant for two reasons. (1) The temple represents the worldview of the Israelites that Yahweh rules in all the earth (e.g., Ps. 24:1), so they calculate their chronology from the founding of the temple. (2) The Exodus is the redemptive event through which the Israelites experience the rule of God in the world (Ex. 15:13, 18; Ps. 24:6–10). The details of the temple are chronologically linked to the salvation event, which the temple represents.

The description of the temple is remarkable in that it contains detailed specifications of measurements, materials, and particular architectural features, but nothing about the preparation of the foundations or the orientation of the temple in relation to the other buildings. This has led to various conjectures about the sources of temple information, including suggestions that the data have come from craftsmen responsible for the building of the temple, an archival record of architectural specifications, or a priest who has studied in detail the temple and its furnishings. However, the peculiarities of the temple description elude explanation. The description of the building itself lacks details, except for a brief notice concerning the windows (6:4), but there is a detailed description of the doors to the inner sanctuary (vv. 31–32). The intention is to report selected details and ornamentations to illustrate the intricate designs and splendor of the temple as the edifice that represents the divine presence in Israel. The detailed engineering and layout of the building projects is not important to the prophetic objective.

---

15. The names of the months are old Canaanite, two of four mentioned in the preexilic period (see also Abib, Ex. 13:4 and Ethanim, 1 Kings 8:2).

The account of the temple construction consists of three sections. The first describes the exterior of the temple (vv. 2–14), the second its interior (vv. 15–28), and the third particular features of the furnishings of the temple and court (vv. 29–36).[16] The account contains a specialized use of many terms that have been understood in different ways. The meaning of such terms is surmised from analogies to other ancient temples or conjectured from a known common meaning of the word. The result is a description that is at times minutely detailed and difficult.

(1) **The exterior of the temple.** The description of the exterior concludes with a statement that the building has been completed (v. 9a); this is followed by a parenthetical note on the construction of the roof, the room extensions around the sides of the building, and the exterior paneling (vv. 9b–10). This section ends with an exhortation to obey the covenant (vv. 11–13); the covenant, not the temple, is the means to divine presence. The building account resumes with a repetition of the statement that Solomon built and completed the temple (v. 14; cf. v. 9); this repetition marks the transition to the second section.

The temple is a small structure adjacent to the much larger palace in the royal compound. The dimensions (v. 2) indicate the interior size of the building, not taking into account the thickness of the exterior walls or those that separated the three rooms. The length of sixty cubits includes the main hall and shrine; the porch is measured separately (v. 3). The temple is a long, narrow hall, twenty cubits wide, sixty cubits long, and thirty cubits high. The cubit varied in length in different periods (cf. 2 Chron. 3:3), but reasonable estimates can be established for modern equivalents. The temple of Solomon is about 27 meters long (87.5 feet), 9 meters wide (29 feet), and 13.5 meters high (44.8 feet).[17] The length and breadth of the temple are double the dimensions of the tabernacle constructed at Mount Sinai.

The porch runs the full width of the building and extends ten cubits in the front of the long room (v. 3). Windows are recessed in the walls (v. 4). The porch and windows may be better understood by those of a comparable temple at ʿAin Dara.[18] The entrance porch of the ʿAin Dara temple is

---

16. For the outline, see Burke Long, *I Kings with an Introduction to Historical Literature* (FOTL 9; Grand Rapids: Eerdmans, 1984), 85–86. Not all the features discussed in the third section are outside the inner shrine as indicated in his outline; the carvings and gold (vv. 29–30) include the Most Holy Place.

17. These dimensions assume a medium size cubit of 44.5 centimeters (17.52 inches); Fuller, "אַמָּה," *NIDOTTE*, 1:422–23.

18. John M. Monson, "The Temple of Solomon: Heart of Jerusalem," in *Zion, City of Our God*, ed. Richard Hess and Gordon Wenham (Grand Rapids: Eerdmans, 1999), 16–22; idem, "The New ʿAin Dara Temple: Closest Solomonic Parallel," *BAR* 26/3 (2000): 20–35. This temple is the closest to Solomon in size, date, and design.

integrated with an open courtyard and seems to have served as a type of transitional passageway linking the court and the temple. No doors lead to the porch of Solomon, nor is it stated that it has sidewalls, so that it may not have had a roof. The portico of the ʿAin Dara temple was open on one side, but the walls of the temple extended to form two walls, and two massive pillars (like Boaz and Jakin) supported a roof. This appears to be the model of the portico on Solomon's temple.

The windows in the walls are apparently ornamental; the wall panels in the first room of the ʿAin Dara temple included at least two window frames carefully cut into the stone. Each had a recessed indented frame all around the window, slightly arched at the top. The stone windows had reliefs featuring figure eight-shaped ribbons in the upper half.[19] The walls of Solomon's temple actually have similar decorative stone reliefs. Light and ventilation is apparently provided through openings on the upper part of the building.

A platform, built of large blocks, extends along the wall all around the building (v. 5) and serves as a foundation for three-storied auxiliary wings. These stones are placed as lifted from the quarry, without the use of iron tools in construction (v. 7). The outside walls of the temple are recessed at the level of each story so the adjoining wings are not bound into the temple walls (v. 6).[20] Each successive story is, therefore, one cubit wider. The architecture of the side chambers of Solomon's temple may be a feature like that of the multistoried hallways that flanked the ʿAin Dara temple.[21] These chambers had paved floors and beautiful wall reliefs. They were entered through doors on the main (south) side of the façade of the temple. Flights of stairs have been reconstructed based on wall sockets and debris found inside the wall joining the antechamber.

In Solomon's temple a door on the south side at the front of the temple serves as an entrance to the lower story (v. 8).[22] The second and third stories are reached by means of stairs, probably winding or reversing. The roof (v. 9) is constructed with rows of reticular beams (forming squares) and recessed panels (cofferwork). Each level of the side rooms has a ceiling (called a platform) adjoined to the

---

19. Based on the archaeological comparison, the Hebrew word *ʾaṭumîm* ("shut up, closed") is a description of the decorative stone window. The word *š*ᶜ*qupîm* ("lintel") refers to the framing around the windows. Rather than "narrow celestory windows" (NIV), the Hebrew describes windows "framed and blocked."

20. The Hebrew incorrectly refers to the foundation platform (*yṣ*ᶜ) rather than the level or story (ṣ*l*ᶜ), which is introduced in verse 5.

21. Monson, "The Temple of Solomon," 19–20. These are the first identifiable remains of this feature outside of third millennium Egypt.

22. The Hebrew text reads "middle" story, a textual error for the lower story, which is obviously meant; this is the reading of the LXX.

temple walls by cedar beams (v. 10).[23] The temple building is relatively simple and modest in size, especially in comparison to the assembly hall.

The use of undressed stones taken directly from the quarry conforms to the requirement that no iron tools were to be used on stones for altars used in worship (Ex. 20:25; Deut. 27:5–6), though dressed stones are used for the courts and the palace (cf. 1 Kings 5:32; 1 Chron. 22:2). The prohibition of dressed stones is another way of distinguishing an Israelite place of worship from the Canaanite shrines, which were often adorned with sculpted images of the gods. Israelite altars are to be unadorned, made of earth or unhewn stones and without steps (Ex. 20:24–26). The temple symbolizes the divine rule but in no sense the actual image of a king, not even in the construction of the building itself.

(2) **The interior of the temple.** The temple's interior is finished with costly materials: cedar for the wall panels and juniper for the floor panels (vv. 15–16).[24] The interior walls of the temple have carvings of gourds and open flowers, cherubs and palmettes (vv. 18, 29).[25] At the extreme interior of the hall a special area is constructed as the Most Holy Place (v. 16b). It is not evident whether it forms a separate room or area; it may have been constructed as a sacred throne space within the long hall, or it may have been a secondary room within the main hall.[26] It is constructed equal in all directions, extending twenty cubits into the hall and twenty cubits toward the ceiling (cf. 2 Chron. 3:8).

The building is thirty cubits high; thus, there may have been a space between the room and the roof, and it may have rested on an elevated platform like the shrine of other temples. The Most Holy Place is prepared as a repository for the ark, which contains the terms of the covenant. The interior of the Most Holy Place is covered with pure gold (v. 20), which may mean that it is gilded with liquid gold rather than covered with gold plating.[27]

---

23. The Hebrew of v. 10 is obscure, leading some commentators to regard this verse as a displacement from v. 5 (e.g., Gray, *I & II Kings*, 167; Montgomery, *The Books of Kings*, 147). However, the verse means that each platform (story) is five cubits in height (NIV), so the wings are half the height of the temple walls; cf. D. W. Gooding, "Temple Specifications: A Dispute in Logical Arrangement between the MT and LXX," *VT* 17 (1967): 158.

24. The Hebrew text should say the cedar paneling is from the "floor to the beams (*qôrôt*) of the roof" rather than to the "walls (*qîrôt*) of the roof" (*HALAT*, 1:1028). The Greek has a double reading, beams and walls; Hebrew *y* and *w* are frequently interchanged.

25. These may be compared to the stylized floral designs, lily patterns, palmettes, winged creatures, and lions of the main hall in the temple at ʿAin Dara.

26. The inner shrine of temple at Tell Taynat was separated from the hall by a substantial stone wall.

27. For the various meanings of cover (*ṣph*) see A. H. Konkel, "צפה," *NIDOTTE*, 3:832–33. In Prov. 26:23 the lips of an evil heart are compared to silver glazed on a clay pot; cf. Burney, *Notes on the Hebrew Text of the Books of Kings*, 73–74.

Nothing is said about the veil in front of the Most Holy Place (cf. 2 Chron. 3:14), but reference is made to gold chains pulled across its front (1 Kings 6:21). Perhaps the curtain is pulled with these chains.[28]

An altar built of cedar (v. 20) stands in front of the Most Holy Place. The LXX of verses 20–22 is simpler and superior, omitting most of verse 21 and the first half of verse 22; it describes the gold plating of the altar in front of the Most Holy Place, a point not actually stated in the Hebrew text. Though not stated, the altar inside the temple is for the offering of incense, as in the tabernacle (Ex. 30:1–10; 1 Chron. 28:18).

Cherubs were a distinguishing feature of thrones in ancient Mesopotamia, Syria, and Canaan. Keel provides numerous examples of cherub thrones comparable to those of Solomon's temple.[29] They were composite creatures (a bull, a lion, an eagle, and a human head), signifying union of the highest powers of strength, speed, and sagacity. Reproductions of ancient Egyptian temples found in Phoenicia show the throne of the deity supported by two animals.[30] The sides of ancient Canaanite thrones were commonly shaped as a cherub. The cherubs of Solomon's temple (vv. 23–28) are distinct because they are not designed to serve as a human throne. They are attached to the ark, which serves as a footstool to the throne (cf. 1 Chron. 28:2), with the wings touching in the middle and extending to the walls of the throne room. There is no actual seat to the throne, since none is necessary. They are made of costly wild olive wood and are covered with gold.

(3) **Particular features of temple furnishings.** The third section of the temple description (vv. 29–36) notes particular features about the larger temple complex. Cherubs, palm trees, and open flowers are engraved on all the walls, inside and outside. Special attention is given to the wood doors leading to the Most Holy Place.[31] The doorposts to the inmost shrine have five sides (v. 31), and those to the entrance of the main hall have four (v. 33). This may indicate that the posts and lintels to the door attachments are beveled.

The text describing the entrance to the main hall has been emended to

---

28. Cogan, *1 Kings*, 243–44. A curtain of this type is found in the desert tabernacle (Ex. 26:31–33), and it seems a wood partition of some type separated the inner shrine in the temple at ʿAin Dara (Monson, "The Temple of Solomon," 18).

29. Othmar Keel, *Symbolism of the Biblical World: Ancient Near Eastern Iconography and the Book of Psalms* (Winona Lake, Ind.: Eisenbrauns, 1997), 167–71 (figs. 231–36).

30. Ibid., 162 (figures 221, 222).

31. The identification of the wood of the cherubs (v. 23) and the doors (v. 31) is disputed. The olive tree (NIV) is otherwise specified as *zayit* (Neh. 8:15) in distinction from the "oil tree" (*ʿēṣ šemen*) named here. Cogan translates this as pinewood, with reference to the Aleppo pine (*pinus halepensis*), from which a rich resinous pitch and oil can be extracted (*1 Kings*, 244).

describe the doors as forming a square corridor.[32] The design of the doors is unclear, rendering emendations all the more tenuous.[33] Monson thinks that the expressions do not refer to the number of surfaces or structure of the entrance but to the number of recesses in the doorframe.[34] Doors in luxurious structures all over the ancient Near Eastern world had such recesses.[35] The two doors of juniper wood providing entrance into the main hall each have two panels (v. 34); the hinges may have been swivel pins for the doors (NIV) or a joint between the panels making them folding doors (RSV). For the first time it is explained that the gold is inlaid over the engraved figures (v. 35). A wall consisting of three layers of shaped stones with an ornate cedar beam on the top encloses the temple in an inner court (v. 36). The temple is a separate section within the great court, which includes the temple and the entire palace compound (v. 36; cf. 7:9, 12).

The concluding chronological reference to the seven years of temple building (vv. 37–38) includes notice of the thirteen years it took to build the palace (7:1). The royal residence receives mention as one of the structures in the description of all the buildings related to the whole palace complex (v. 8). Nothing more is said than that it follows the same pattern as the other buildings. The whole palace compound is a single building project; a brief account of the other buildings is included before returning to the various temple artifacts.

The Construction of the Palace Complex (7:2–12)

THE FIRST BUILDING described (vv. 2–5) is the great assembly hall, which also serves as an armory (1 Kings 10:17; Isa. 22:8). It is much larger than the temple, measuring 100 cubits by 50 cubits, but the same height of 30 cubits. Based on the medium size cubit, the structure is 44.5 meters (146 feet) long, 22.25 meters (73 feet) wide, and 13.35 meters (43.8 feet) high. The structure is supported by four rows of cedar pillars (v. 2) and cedar cross beams above them. It is known as the "Palace of the Forest of Lebanon" because its many pillars give it the appearance of a great forest. The structure of the building, however, is not clear; salient features are given to indicate its grandeur.

The description of the assembly hall is particularly ambiguous in 7:3, as a comparison of translations makes evident. The cedar roof is built over three "ribs" (ṣēlāᶜ), which are above the pillars. In the temple description "rib"

---

32. The Hebrew text has suffered in transmission; DeVries (*1 Kings*, 88) suggests a plausible emendation to "square corridor" (cf. Ezek. 42:5).

33. See A. Millard, "The Doorways of Solomon's Temple," *ErIsr* 20 (1989): 135–39.

34. Monson, "The New ᶜAin Dara Temple," 35.

35. This is known as rabbeting; several receding doorframes are fitted together.

describes stories of storage rooms (6:5, 8), rows of cedar boards (v. 15), and panels of a door (v. 34). The referent of the term in 7:3 may be either beams or storage rooms. It may mean that the roof rests on forty-five beams in three rows (NIV), though it is unclear how this would relate to the four rows of pillars. It may mean the roof is built over rooms that are constructed above the forty-five pillars arranged in rows of fifteen (RSV); this follows the LXX of verse 2, which says there are three rows of pillars. Alternately, the number forty-five may refer to three levels of fifteen rooms built along each side, a structure similar to the temple.[36] It is likely that the hall has storage rooms since it also serves as an armory.

Analogies to similar structures suggest that four rows of pillars form three long open naves, allowing a large assembly hall on the ground floor.[37] Three stories of rooms, fifteen at each level, are constructed on top each of the two outside naves. The middle nave may have been left open, allowing an open view to the roof over thirteen meters (forty-five feet) up. Each of the three stories has rows of windows at the ends of the great halls, each corresponding to or opposite the other at the three levels (v. 4).

The rooms likely do not extend to the end walls, so the windows furnish light and ventilation for the buildings. Such a structure would need to have included stairways to provide access to the various levels of rooms. The three sets of doorways serve as entrances to the great halls and are perhaps placed at the ends, opposite each other (v. 5).[38] The doorways and doorposts are square; the vocabulary of verse 5 is obscure but may describe the door openings and exits.[39] Whatever the arrangement of the rooms, doors, and windows, the "Forest of Lebanon" is a hall fit for a great assembly with plenty of rooms for an armory.

The hall of pillars (v. 6) does not seem to be an independent building but a colonnade that serves as an entrance to the great assembly hall. The length of 50 cubits (44.5 meters; 146 feet) is equal to the width of the assembly hall. It is unclear as to what structure is described in front of the colonnade. The obscure term translated as "overhanging roof" (ʿāb) occurs elsewhere only in Ezekiel 41:25—26, where it is taken to be a type of roof structure as a canopy. The Targums translate ʿāb as "threshold" and the Greek as "cross beam"; it more likely refers to a balustrade.[40] A hall along the front of the porch has a

36. Gray, *I & II Kings*, 177–78.

37. Cf. Montgomery, *The Books of Kings*, 163–64; G. H. Jones, *1 and 2 Kings* (2 vols.; NCBC; Grand Rapids: Eerdmans, 1984), 1:175–76.

38. Cogan says this is "unfathomable," suggesting the text may be a dittography (accidental repetition) from the previous verse (*1 Kings*, 255). The text of the chapter is problematic, but the architectural conceptions are also obscure.

39. DeVries, *1 Kings*, 101.

40. Ibid.

protective barrier guarding entrance into the building. It is likely that this porch is built to serve as the judgment hall (v. 7) where the king presides in court.[41] No separate measurements are given for the judgment hall, suggesting it is within the colonnade in front of the assembly hall. The judgment hall is paneled with cedar from the floor to the rafters.

The palace of Solomon (v. 8) and the quarters for all his servants are set in another court back (west) of the hall (cf. RSV). The public buildings are situated in a separate court; the palace is not accessible to the public but has an entrance to the public court as well as the inner court of the temple. The palace of Solomon and that of Pharaoh's daughter are similar in construction to the other buildings, since all of them are royal edifices.

Special notice is made of the costly stonework (vv. 9–12) that is part of the buildings and the courts. It is costly because the stones are all hewn to measure inside and outside.[42] Dressed stone is used from the foundation to the framework—or to the roof overhang,[43] if stonework is mixed with the woodwork, as is often done. This seems to have been the case in the royal buildings, as the stonework and woodwork are made to measure on the upper levels (v. 11). The stonework extends as far as the large public court. The foundation stones are large (3.5 to 4.5 meters; 11.5 to 14.6 feet), but not excessive by building standards. The larger outer court is built with three levels of stone and a row of cedar timbers (v. 12), like the inner temple court (cf. 6:36).

Artifacts for the Temple (7:13–51a)

THE ACCOUNT OF the artifacts for the temple describes first the bronze work (vv. 13–47) and then the gold work (vv. 48–50); the writer then has a concluding notice of the completion of the work (v. 51). The bronze work is done with the assistance of a skilled craftsman from Tyre who has the same name as the Tyrian king. Besides his skill in craftsmanship, he has Israelite connections to Naphtali. This is not surprising, as the Israelites have mixed with the Phoenicians from the days of the judges.[44] The tribe of Asher fails to drive out the inhabitants of various cities on the Phoenician coast (Judg. 1:31–32), such as Akko and Sidon. The Phoenicians were skilled in metal work, as they were in stone and woodwork. The gold work is credited to Solomon himself, though he certainly did not do it personally. The implication seems to be

---

41. Busink, *Der Temple Salomos*, 1:141.

42. The "saw" (NIV) was a smoothing tool dragged or pulled across the face of the stone to give it a smooth, polished look (based on the verb *grr*, "drag, pull"; Cogan, *1 Kings*, 256).

43. The Hebrew word *ṭapḥâ* is otherwise unknown as an architectural term; its usual meaning is "handbreadth."

44. Katzenstein, *The History of Tyre*, 65–68.

that the most precious objects are made by an Israelite rather than a hired foreign craftsman.

The first of the artifacts described are the two pillars set in the porch of the temple (vv. 15–22). They are made of bronze and are 8 meters (27 feet) in height. Their circumference was over 5 meters (17.5 feet), making them almost 2 meters (6 feet) in diameter. The LXX says the pillars are hollow with a thickness of four fingers (cf. Jer. 52:21).[45]

The height of each pillar is extended by a capital at the top formed of bronze, just over 2 meters (over 7 feet) in height (v. 16). These are ornately decorated with seven sets of tightly woven chain work in a net pattern and two rows of pomegranates around the network (vv. 17–18).[46] The two capitals have the shape of a lily, common for capitals; there is a bulge in the capital just below the lily, where two hundred pomegranates hang in rows (vv. 19–20).[47] The bulge may have been a collar to fasten the capital to the pillar. The pillar to the south is named Jakin and the pillar to the north Boaz (v. 20). The significance of the names can only be guessed; Jakin ("it is firm") may refer to the promise of the kingdom, and Boaz ("in strength") may have been a prayer for the king.[48] The pillars perhaps have a structural as well as symbolic function.

The second item described is a giant water container (vv. 23–26), over 4 meters (15 feet) in diameter and over 2 meters (7½ feet) in height, cast with two rows of gourds beneath its rim, which have the shape of a lily. Twelve bulls face outward beneath it, three in each direction. It holds about 11,000 gallons of water.[49] Its significance is to be found in the name "Sea." Another nonliteral use of the term is to designate chaos before creation (e.g., Ps. 74:12–14). In describing creation, "sea" is the equivalent of Leviathan and sea monster. In the Baal Epic "sea" is the adversary that must be destroyed before Baal can bring an orderly rule to creation.

Sea is a well-known motif in the ancient Near East. The famous picture of the sack of the temple of Muzazir in Urartu (northwest of Assur) depicts

---

45. The masoretic text apparently suffers from haplography (accidental omission of a phrase). Making the pillars hollow would significantly reduce their weight.

46. Instead of seven (*šib'a*) for each capital the Septuagint has a lattice (*śᵉbakâ*) for each capital (NEB); this conforms to the description in verse 42. The Hebrew of verse 18 also has pillars where it should read pomegranates (see NIV notes).

47. The text of vv. 19–20 is exceptionally difficult; v. 20 is described as "unintelligible" (Gray, *I & II Kings*, 183) or "incomprehensible" (Cogan, *1 Kings*, 263). The height of the capital (4 cubits) contradicts that given earlier (5 cubits). The textual history cannot be reconstructed.

48. See the discussion of R. B. Y. Scott, "The Pillars Jachin and Boaz," *JBL* 58 (1939): 143–49.

49. Excavations at Lachish have uncovered a broken jar, dated to about the eighth century B.C., inscribed as a "royal bath" (*bt lmlk*). Its volume is 5.8 gallons (22 liters).

two huge water basins set on bulls' feet. Bulls have been found on a large cult basin from Cyprus.[50] Water has a practical use in ritual cleansings in Solomon's temple (2 Chron. 4:6), but the size of the great water basin is not practical for that purpose. Its primary purpose in the temple court is to represent the rule of God over the cosmos.

In addition to the great Sea, the temple has ten water tanks in the shape of a bowl to distribute water for cleansing purposes (vv. 27–39). Each of these tanks was six feet in diameter and holds about 220 gallons of water (v. 38). It is estimated that the weight of each stand with its water reservoir full would be three and a half tons.[51] They are equipped with wheels, but they are not readily mobile. Artifacts like this are known. Perhaps most instructive are two found in Cyprus in the nineteenth century; one is from Larnaka, about twenty inches high, twelve inches wide, with wheels about six inches in diameter; the second is from Enkomi, nine inches in height and seven inches in width (the wheels are lost).[52] They illustrate well the supporting structures for the laver and the cherub figures engraved on the panels.

The bases of the lavers are six feet square and three feet high, made of bronze, with frames and supports (vv. 27–28). These are elaborately decorated with cherub figures and borders, above and below, with delicately worked spiral designs (v. 29). Each base is equipped with wheels, legs, and supports beneath the laver (v. 30), each of the supports adjacent to the spiral designs. The opening of the box-shaped frame has within it a circular rim to support the laver (v. 31), with engravings on the square frame that hold the laver support. The wheels are over two feet in diameter (v. 32), much as a chariot wheel with rims, spokes, and a hub cast together (v. 33) and attached to the legs with axles in sockets. The circular rim of the laver protrudes at the top of the base frame,[53] which have handles and supports (v. 35), possibly to assist in moving the laver. All the space on the panels, frames, and handles is appropriately filled with cherub figures and palm trees (v. 36). All ten lavers are identical (v. 37), disposed in two groups at the south and north corners at the temple (v. 39), with the great sea being further to the east on the south side.

Hiram is responsible for a variety of artifacts used for the altars (v. 40), including ash containers and shovels, and containers for sprinkling (cf. Exod. 27:3). The bowl shape of the capitals has not been mentioned previously

---

50. Keel, *Symbolism of the Biblical World*, 136 (figs. 139, 183).

51. Busink, *Der Temple Salomos*, 1:349.

52. Burney (*Notes on the Hebrew Text of the Books of Kings*, 91) provides publication data and figures; see also Keel, *Symbolism of the Biblical World*, fig. 188.

53. The dimensions of the laver (vv. 31, 35) are not clear or consistent; Gray thinks that numbers have been lost in both verses (*I & II Kings*, 192).

(v. 41); it is not certain if this is the same aspect as the "bulge" mentioned earlier (v. 20). The items are made with polished bronze (v. 45), smelted in earthen moulds in the Jordan Valley north of Jerusalem (v. 46), just north of the Jabbok River east of the Jordan. The clay in this area was particularly suitable for moulds. The amount of bronze is so extensive that the items are put in place without their weight being calculated.

The gold items are located inside the building next to the specially constructed throne room at the back (vv. 48–50). The incense altar (cf. 6:20, 22), the table with bread, and the ten lampstands (each with seven arms) are elements in the temple to represent access to the presence of the divine. Other floral decorations are part of the lampstands and lamps to provide decoration and light. The highest quality of metal distinguishes the sacredness of the area. All the equipment to service the lamps and the incense altar is gold as well: tongs, pans for hot coals, snuffers, sprinkling bowls, incense dishes, and pans for hot ashes. Gold sockets or hinges for the doors to the sacred throne room and the temple entrance are impractical (v. 50); the item may have been some sort of latching device as part of an entrance ritual.[54]

The incense altar provides for the transition from the common to the most holy.[55] As part of symbolizing the rule of God within creation, the lights of the lampstand likely represent the shining of the stars in the temple.[56] Solomon uses structures and artifacts familiar from the surrounding culture to represent the original state of the world under the rule of God.

Bridging Contexts

IT WAS DAVID'S intent to build a temple when God fulfilled the promise of granting him rest from his enemies (2 Sam. 7:1–3). Nathan the prophet affirmed this goal, but in a dream God revealed to him another priority. From the time of the Exodus through the years of the judges God had not required a house for the ark (7:11), and he did not require that provision from David. God did not ask David to build a house to represent the divine throne; instead, the divine King would build David the house of a continuing dynasty (7:12–17). The confirmation of Solomon's rule is the evidence that God has established the house of David. It is now

54. Ibid., 270.

55. Carol Meyers, "Realms of Sanctity: the Case of the 'Misplaced' Incense Altar in the Tabernacle Texts of Exodus," in *Texts, Temples, and Traditions*, ed. Michael V. Fox et al. (Winona Lake, Ind.: Eisenbrauns, 1996), 43–46.

56. Elizabeth Bloch-Smith, "Solomon's Temple: The Politics of Ritual Space," in *Sacred Time, Sacred Place: Archaeology and the Religion of Israel*, ed. Barry M. Gittlen (Winona Lake, Ind.: Eisenbrauns, 2002), 88–89.

time to build the house that will testify to the presence of God in his eternal kingdom (1 Chron. 28:2–7). The kingdom of Solomon is a gift of God; it is the continuation of the rest that God has given David in fulfillment of the covenant promise.

Covenant and temple. Two closely related themes are at the center of the Hebrew confession of faith: covenant and temple. The kingdom of Israel is not like the other kingdoms of the world. Other kings were mediators of the divine will, the means by which their gods exercised dominion in this world. In the theology of the Deuteronomistic prophets, the king could never be the mediator of divine grace. Rather, he is subordinate to the covenant, just like the people; he is one of the people as a brother. The king must have a copy of this covenant at all times (Deut. 17:18–19) so that he may live and govern according to God's will made known in the covenant.

The temple gives testimony to the role of the covenant in the kingdom. The ark contains the terms of the covenant with God as king. It serves as the footstool of the King who has made this covenant with his people (Ps. 132:6–8). The temple is the palace of the great King; symbolically his feet rest on the footstool that contains the declaration of his will. The temple is a symbol of Solomon's loyalty to God as his own King, and his commitment is to fulfill the will of God in his rule of the nation. All the other buildings of the royal complex stand in the shadow of the palace of the King of kings.

God's sovereignty. The Hebrew worldview has as its starting point the confession made repeatedly in their hymnbook: "The earth is the LORD's, and everything in it, the world, and all who live in it" (Ps. 24:1). This confession is complemented by a view distinct to the Hebrew faith: Their God is utterly transcendent, not to be identified with anything in this world:

> You saw no form of any kind the day the LORD spoke to you at Horeb out of the fire. Therefore watch yourselves very carefully, so that you do not become corrupt and make for yourselves an idol, an image of any shape, whether formed like a man or a woman, or like any animal on earth or any bird that flies in the air, or like any creature that moves along the ground or any fish in the waters below. (Deut. 4:15–18)

The temple represents this concept of God; it portrays him as the transcendent sovereign of this world, not to be identified with anything in the world. The throne room is devoid of any form of the sovereign God there, and it is inaccessible to all human sight. The cherubs mark the throne, and the words of the covenant in the footstool declare that the King of all kings is a God to them and they are his people (Ex. 19:5–6).

One of the indications of God's sovereignty over all peoples is the freedom Solomon has to ally with Hiram of Tyre in order to acquire materials and craftsmanship for his great building projects. Alliances with other nations were strictly prohibited when they were a matter of dependence for military purposes (Deut. 17:16–17) and a failure to trust in God. However, wholesome commitments with those of another religion were perfectly acceptable when they showed that all peoples are under the dominion of the sovereign Creator who rules on high (cf. Ps. 47). The treaty with Hiram triumphantly concludes by saying there was complete accord (*šālôm*) between Solomon and Hiram (5:12), a fine illustration of the primary meaning of the Hebrew word.

Beginning with the account of Omri, the book of Kings describes the devastating impact that alliances with the Phoenicians had on Israel, leading to the near extinction of the Davidic kingship. That was a totally different kind of alliance, not one that could be described as peace. It was a compromise of faith, because it involved military dependence and intermarriage with foreigners. The treaty with Solomon begins entirely differently; it is the means God uses to make possible the building projects that showed the wisdom of Solomon divinely received and the glory of God humanly portrayed.

The Exodus and the building of the temple. The prophetic authors of Kings begin with the founding of the temple 480 years from the time of the Exodus (6:1). This number appears to be schematic.[57] Matthew calculates the genealogies to the birth of Christ in much the same way: The time from the Exile to the birth of Christ was fourteen generations (1:17), which corresponds to fourteen generations from Abraham to David, and from David to the Exile. A generation was considered to be forty years (e.g., the time of the wilderness wanderings), so that Matthew's calculations are approximately correct. The birth of Christ was about 560 years after the Exile.

The time from the Exodus to the founding of the temple was twelve generations. The number twelve may have been derived from genealogical knowledge, but it also puts the founding of the temple at the midpoint of the history from the Exodus to the end of the Exile, the time period that is the concern of the Deuteronomistic History. The total number of years from Solomon to Zedekiah was four hundred thirty years, to which should be added fifty years from the destruction of the temple to the return from Babylon in the days of Cyrus. Noth has further developed the literary unity of the history by showing that the chronological data from Deuteronomy to the

---

57. For discussion, see K. A. Kitchen, "Exodus, The," *ABD*, 2:702–3. A total of over 553 years is given for this period in biblical chronologies. Biblical and Egyptian references place the Exodus in the thirteenth century.

building of the temple adds up to four hundred and eighty years.[58] A good deal of this data is also in the scheme of forty years being a generation. These numbers, as in the genealogy in Matthew, are not a precise chronology but a schematic way of showing the plan of God in the history of his people.

The cosmos, the mountain of God, and the temple. The reference to the Exodus in the introduction to the temple is important because the temple testifies to the continuing presence of God in the covenant, as he was encountered at Mount Sinai. The community entered into a covenant "before the LORD" (*lipnê yhwh*). This expression stems from the basic conception of the temple as a divine dwelling place and belongs to the temple's technical terminology.[59] It was not necessary to be within an actual building in order to be in a temple setting in the ancient Near East.[60] An encounter might take place between the deity and the person not in a temple building, but in a situation that has all the characteristics of a temple presence.

For the Israelites Mount Horeb was the great day when they stood before Yahweh and heard his words that they might fear him as long as they lived in the land (Deut. 4:10–13). The fire of the divine presence had blazed into the heart of the thick black cloud that covered the mountain. There was no form; only words could represent the Most Holy. Moses was to teach them the covenant, which was made with his people written on two tablets of stone and provided the regulations for living in the land. Once in the land there was the one place that Yahweh would choose for the presence of his Name, where the Israelites would rejoice *lipnê yhwh* (Deut. 12:12–14, 17–18). That place, chosen from one of the tribes (v. 14), could be none other than the temple Solomon built and dedicated.

A common theme to temples in the ancient Near East is that they were the architectural embodiment of the cosmic mountain. The Hymn to the Ekur (mountain house), the renowned temple of Enlil in Nippur, had as its refrain, "It is a mountain great," following lines that describe its darkness, its lofty gates, and its courts in much obscure terminology.[61] The conceptions of Mount Zion as a holy mountain are found in the prophets (Isa. 2:2) and in

58. Noth, *Überlieferungsgeschichtliche Studien*, 18–27.

59. Menahem Haran, *Temples and Temple-Service in Ancient Israel: An Inquiry into Biblical Cult Phenomena and the Historical Setting of the Priestly School* (Winona Lake, Ind.: Eisenbrauns, 1985), 26.

60. John M. Lundquist, "What Is a Temple? A Preliminary Typology," in *The Quest for the Kingdom of God: Studies in Honor of George E. Mendenhall*, ed. H. B. Huffmon, F. A. Spina, and A. R. W. Green (Winona Lake, Ind.: Eisenbrauns, 1983), 207.

61. For translation see James B. Pritchard, *Ancient Near Eastern Texts Relating to the Old Testament*, 3rd ed. with supplement (Princeton, N.J.: Princeton Univ. Press, 1969), 582. This hymn may have been composed as early as 2000 B.C.

the Psalms (Ps. 48:2).[62] The holy mountain of the Israelites was Mount Sinai. The temple of Solomon seems ultimately to be little more than the architectural realization and ritual enlargement of the Sinai experience.[63] The presence of Moses and the elders "before the LORD" is temple terminology; Mount Sinai itself is regarded as a temple.

The Sinai theophany may be compared with the enthronement of Enmeduranki of Nippur in the temple of Ebarra. Moses ascended to God and received the tablets from God; the encounter concluded with a sacred meal eaten in the presence of God (Ex. 24:11).[64] The meal and the sealing of the covenant with blood are the equivalent of royal enthronements in a temple. Sacral communal meals were frequently carried out in connection with temple ritual, during or at the conclusion of a covenant ceremony. The dedication of Solomon's temple is concluded with a great feast (1 Kings 8:62–66). Zion as a holy mountain goes back to the holy cosmic mountain of Israelite experience, Mount Sinai.

The doxology of Habakkuk expresses the homologous relationship that exists between the temple and the cosmos: "The LORD is in his holy temple; let all the earth be silent before him" (Hab. 2:20). The temple is depicted in cosmic terms that recall the language of creation. In the litany of God's actions for Israel, it is said, "He built his sanctuary like the heights, like the earth that he established forever" (Ps. 78:69).[65] The mention of the sanctuary immediately after the election of Judah and Mount Zion in verse 68 leaves no doubt that the temple in Jerusalem is in question. Usually Solomon is said to be the builder of the great Jerusalem temple; making God the builder of the temple accentuates the association with Genesis.

The description in Psalm 78:69 of the temple as the heavens and the earth may be hyperbole, like the claim that the low hill called Zion is actu-

---

62. The comparison of Mount Zion to the "utmost heights of Zaphon" (NIV) is a polemic against the Baal religion. *Sapanu* was the name of the mountain of *Ba'lu*, Mount Kasios/Casius of Hellenistic times, the present day Jebel Akra (1759 meters), about 40 kilometers north of Ugarit (the home of a great Baal temple). All Canaanites oriented themselves toward this holy mountain so that its name became synonymous with the word "north"; see de Moor, *An Anthology of Religious Texts from Ugarit,* 1.

63. Lundquist, "What Is a Temple," 207.

64. Geo Widengren, *The Ascension of the Apostle and the Heavenly Book* (King and Saviour III; Uppsala: Lundequist, 1950), 24.

65. Translation by Jon D. Levenson, *Creation and the Persistence of Evil: The Jewish Drama of Divine Omnipotence* (San Francisco: Harper & Row, 1988), 87. The heights (*rāmîm*) should be interpreted as a reference to the heavens rather than the mountains (NIV). The expression *šmm rmm* ("high heavens") in Ugaritic and Phoenician suggests that the terminology is close to Genesis 1:1: heavens (*šāmayim*) and earth; Mitchell Dahood, *Psalms II* (AB 17; Garden City, N.Y.: Doubleday, 1968), 247.

ally the great joy of all the earth (48:2). The comparison with the earth that is established forever "argues that the psalmist wishes to evoke the aura of cosmogony by associating the Temple with the belief that God 'founded [$y^e s\bar{a}d\hat{a}$] the earth upon the ocean/set it on the nether streams.'"[66] The temple is as unshakable as the earth itself because the same agent established them through parallel actions.

The temple may be described as the earth, but conversely the earth may be described as a temple:

> Heaven is my throne,
>   and the earth is my footstool.
> Where is the house you will build for me?
>   Where will my resting place be?
> Has not my hand made all these things,
>   and so they came into being?" (Isa. 66:1–2a)

Creation serves as the palace of the divine King; those who would build a temple in the world bring him no glory if they neglect the ethical implications of his cosmic rule (v. 2b).

The last of the Ascent Psalms suggests that the creation of heaven and earth is represented in the temple in Zion. Those going on or off night watch are invited to bless the God of the temple:

> Lift up your hands in the sanctuary,
>   and praise the LORD.
> May the LORD, the Maker of heaven and earth,
>   bless you from Zion. (Ps. 134:2–3)

"Zion" is the parallel term for "sanctuary" in the poem; in the closing two lines, "Yahweh" is parallel with the "Maker" and "Zion" with "heavens and earth." The poetic association is all the more reasonable if the temple in Zion represents the cosmos, the true, holy temple created as the residence of the great king.

The symbolism in the temple of Yahweh. Ancient sanctuaries claimed to house within their courts the primeval hill, which first emerged from the floods of chaos.[67] The great wall that surrounded the temple enclosure at Karnak was laid out in an undulating design to represent the primeval waters, which formerly lapped around the temple hill. The ordered world had its origin from this hill. The dead were portrayed on the primeval hill that they might be regenerated by its powers.[68]

---

66. Levenson, *Creation and the Persistence of Evil*, 87; the quotation is Ps. 24:2.
67. Keel, *Symbolism of the Biblical World*, 113 (cf. fig. 147).
68. Ibid., fig. 148. The pyramids were huge primeval hills, though that is not their only significance.

In Mesopotamia as well every temple had its "pure hill." In *Enuma Elish*, the Babylonian creation epic, the principal temple of Babylon, the Esagila, is described when Marduk, the principal deity of Babylon, had vanquished the powers of chaos.[69] The Esagila was the counterpart to Apsu, the primeval waters of the netherworld. The step-temple of Babylon is "house of the foundation of heaven and earth,"[70] the center and mainstay of creation. The step-temples form the bond between heaven and earth (cf. Gen. 11:4). In the Canaanite sphere, after Baal gains victory over the sea god Yam, he receives a temple on Zaphon.[71]

The style of the biblical temple and its artifacts are analogous to other temples of the period; the structure and symbols are designed in accordance with their cultural ethos. The temple at the southern fortress of Arad, which was founded in Solomon's time as a place of worship, was of the broad room type with entrance on the long side of the hall and the shrine on the opposite long side. The temple at Jerusalem was of the type common in Syria during the time of the Exodus, which in turn was similar to the Mycenaean long room type of building known in Anatolia and the Aegean.[72] The temple at Tell Tainat in the Amuq Valley at the northern Orontes had a portico, a long hall, and a raised platform for a shrine.[73] Archaeological parallels for the courtyard objects and the engravings of the temple help to explain their significance and the distinctives of Solomon's temple.

The enormous size of the courtyard items indicates their divine and cosmic significance. The two pillars flanking the porch entrance to the porch are generally agreed to attest to the presence and power of Yahweh.[74] The gilded reliefs of cherubs, palms, and calyxes, which adorn the doors of the temple and its walls, suggest the pillars have a relationship to the tree of life. The palm between two cherubs is a variation of the tree of life set between

---

69. For a translation see Benjamin R. Foster, "Epic of Creation," in *The Context of Scripture*, ed. William W. Hallo and K. Lawson Younger Jr. (Leiden: Brill, 2003), 1.111 vi 60–65.

70. See Keel, *Symbolism of the Biblical World*, fig. 150, for a reconstruction of the temple tower.

71. The defeat of Yam is found in Baal III (*KTU* 1.2 iv) and the building of the temple in Baal IV (*KTU* 1.4 vi); de Moor, *An Anthology of Religious Texts from Ugarit*, 40–42, 58–59.

72. See Volkmar Fritz, *An Introduction to Biblical Archaeology* (JSOTSup 172; Sheffield: Sheffield Academic Press, 1994), 153–55. These were temples with a long central hall.

73. See Fritz, Plate 9A. For a comparison of this and other temples with Solomon's temple, see Fritz, "Temple Architecture: What Can Archaeology Tell Us about Solomon's Temple," *BAR* 13/4 (1987): 38–49.

74. They have alternately been regarded as phalloi, stylish ornaments, fire altars, imitation Egyptian obelisks, and symbols for Yahweh; See Elizabeth Bloch-Smith, "'Who Is the King of Glory?' Solomon's Temple and Its Symbolism," in *Scripture and Other Artifacts: Essays in Honor of Philip J. King*, ed. Michael D. Coogan, J. Cheryl Exum, and Lawrence E. Stager (Louisville: Westminster John Knox, 1994), 19.

two animals, human beings, or divine beings, a motif originating in Mesopotamia that became widespread in Palestine.[75] The cherubs heighten the impression that the wondrous tree mediates mysterious powers.[76]

A wall painting from Mari during the time of Hammurabi (1728–1686 B.C.) depicts a huge date palm in the courtyard of a temple. Two trees, four cherubs, and two bulls flank a scene in which a goddess gives gifts to a king. One foot of each bull is planted on a mountain, and two fountain deities correspond to the two mountains.[77] The scene has all the motifs of creation, the place from which all life issues. Bloch-Smith thinks that temple pillars or posts, which resemble flowering trees or branches, symbolize the divine attributes of longevity and fruitfulness, or virility and fertility.[78] The floral appearance of the ornate capitals of the pillars of the Jerusalem temple then symbolize the life-giving power of God.

The cherub is the prominent motif of the temple interior. Its bodily parts signify strength and ferocity, the regalness of a lion with the flying capability of a bird and the reasoning of a human. In Ezekiel's temple the wall reliefs are carved palm trees with a cherub facing it on each side, one with the face of a human and one with the face of a lion (Ezek. 41:17–20). Cherubs guarded the tree of life in the original garden (Gen. 3:24), and cherubs served as chariots to depict the movement of God (Ps. 18:10 = 2 Sam. 22:11).[79]

The association of the cherub with the date palm (*tāmār*) evoke the tree of life from the garden and the tree that sustained the Israelites in the wilderness wanderings (Ex. 15:27; Num. 33:9). The closely related term of Kings (*timôrâ*) describes some ornament or carved representation of the palm tree (1 Kings 6:29, 32).[80] The lush appearance of the palm with its green leaves provides rich images of prosperity and becomes a symbol for the righteous followers of the covenant who remain vital and virile even into old age.

---

75. Keel, *Symbolism of the Biblical World*, 141–42. An ivory from Nimrud (9th–8th centuries B.C. depicts the tree of life in two scenes flanked by goats and by cherubs (fig. 189).

76. A gold lamella with its tree of life guarded by two cherubs was stitched to the breast of a deceased person, perhaps to mediate the powers of the tree of life (ibid., fig. 190).

77. Ibid., 142–44; fig. 191. For a color photo of the wall painting, see Lawrence E. Stager, "Jerusalem as Eden," *BAR* 26/3 (May/June 2000): 36–37. The painting is from the time of Hammurabi (1728–1686 B.C.).

78. Bloch-Smith, "Solomon's Temple and Its Symbolism," 23. Date palms flank the entrance to the Sin Temple at Khorsabad; similar depictions are found on cylinder seals from Tell Billa and Tell Agrab.

79. The Egyptian sphinx and the Mesopotamian cherub could be winged or non-winged, male or female; they are difficult to distinguish in Syrian art (Bloch-Smith, "Solomon's Temple: The Politics of Ritual Space," 85). The biblical cherub was always winged but unspecified in gender.

80. Larry L. Walker, "תִּמֹרָ," *NIDOTTE*, 4:308–9.

The righteous will flourish like a palm tree,
   they will grow like a cedar of Lebanon;
planted in the house of the LORD,
   they will flourish in the courts of our God.
They will still bear fruit in old age,
   they will stay fresh and green,
proclaiming, "The LORD is upright;
   he is my Rock, and there is no wickedness in him." (Ps. 92:12–15)

The association of the cherub with the palm is a powerful symbol of the source of vitality for creation. The cherubs guarding the tree of life in the Garden of Eden make the cherubs facing the tree a poignant motif in the temple of Solomon.

The immense cherubs in the Most Holy Place testify to the cosmic character of the King who rules there; the Israelite God is omnipotent and omnipresent and reigns for eternity (6:23–28).[81] The massive "Sea of cast metal" that rests on the backs of the twelve cast bronze oxen can serve no practical purpose (7:23–26). The great tank represents either the cosmic waters or the "waters of life" that emanated from the Garden of Eden. Divine forces subdue the waters of chaos ("sea") so that they provide life-giving nourishment for plant, animal, and human life. The temple is a depiction of Eden as the garden of God (Isa. 51:3; Ezek. 28:13).[82]

The cosmic mountain links heaven and earth (as *axis mundi*); from here order was established at creation, and through rituals and ceremonies it is continuously renewed.[83] In the temple depiction in the wall painting at Mari, two mountains probably indicate that the center of the court is located on a mountain; two fountain deities correspond to the two mountains. A stream with four branches (cf. Gen. 2:10) rises from the vessels held by the deities. A plant grows out of the stream. This is the place from which all life issues. In the garden of Eden, the presence of God was the source of all life-giving waters. The temple in turn is regarded as the source of life-giving waters (Ps. 46:4; Joel 3:18; Zech. 14:8). The garden that is the home of humankind leads to the garden of God, just as the portico of the temple leads to the Holy Place.

---

81. This may be compared to the giant footprints (three feet; one meter) in the portico and threshold of the temple at ʿAin Dara, representing the superhuman nature of the god (Ishtar) who lived there; John Monson, "The New ʿAin Dara Temple," 26–27. The step from the left foot to the right extends from the portico across the antechamber to the threshold leading to the main hall.

82. For a discussion of Eden as the garden of God in the Genesis context, see John H. Walton, *Genesis* (NIVAC; Grand Rapids: Zondervan, 2001), 168–69, 181–83.

83. Stager, "Jerusalem as Eden," 37.

The virtual garden of Eden is further manifested in the interior that includes the lamps (7:49). The lampstands stand five to either side of the entrance to the Most Holy Place. The seven lights of each lamp may have represented Pleiades, a cluster of stars mentioned several times in connection with God as the ruler of the universe (Job 9:9; 38:31; Amos 5:8).[84] The symbol of seven dots is known as early as the old Babylonian period and referred to as *sibittu*.[85] The biblical lamps are lit only at night; like the stars of the heavenly host, they shine from dusk to dawn.

The building of the temple conveys divine endorsement of Solomon's kingship. On Mount Zion, the mountain of God, Yahweh grants his decrees to the human community and its king. God is regarded as the father who speaks to the king as his son:

"I have installed my King
    on Zion, my holy hill."
I will proclaim the decree of the LORD:
He said to me, "You are my Son;
    today I have become your Father.
Ask of me,
    and I will make the nations your inheritance,
    the ends of the earth your possession." (Ps. 2:6–8)

The temple with its giant pillars is regarded as the fountain of life for its people:

They feast on the abundance of your house;
    you give them drink from your river of delights.
For with you is the fountain of life;
    in your light we see light. (Ps. 36:8–9)

The rich resources of the creative order resulting from the conquest of chaos are transferred to the king and his people. The names on the pillars (Jakin and Boaz) are best understood as prayers for endurance of the kingdom and strength for the king. In various Mesopotamian inscriptions, doors or gates of cities and palaces were given festive names that were blessings or wishes for the king.[86] An administrative text from Assur describes in detail

---

84. The word *kîmâ* ("to heap up") refers to the seven visible stars of "Pleiades" (*HALAT*, 2:450). Pleiades is a galactic cluster of over 400 stars.

85. Bloch-Smith, "Solomon's Temple: The Politics of Ritual Space," 89.

86. Victor Hurowitz, *I Have Built You an Exalted House: Temple Building in the Bible in the Light of Mesopotamian and Northwest Semitic Writings* (JSOTSup 115; Sheffield: Sheffield Academic Press, 1992), 257, n. 2. Sennacherib gave names to all fifteen gates of Nineveh, one of them being "Enlil (is the) establisher of my reign."

columns and their capitals transferred on order of the king.[87] A second section describes the inscription on the pillars of royal dedications made when the columns were set up during ritual offerings by the king. In a similar manner Kings records the details of the construction and furnishings of the temple at the time they are installed in the temple. The presence of the rule of God in the temple assures the endurance and security of Solomon's kingdom.

The structure and dimensions of the temple are modeled on those of the tabernacle. Solomon's temple was built to the scale of the tabernacle. The tabernacle was one third as high (10 cubits; 14.6 feet), half as wide (10 cubits), and half as long (30 cubits; 44 feet), set in a court that was one hundred cubits long (146 feet) and fifty cubits wide (73 feet). The temple can be alluded to by reference to its dimensions; the flying scroll of Zechariah (Zech. 5:2) was the size of the porch of the temple or the Holy Place of the tabernacle (20 cubits long and 10 cubits wide). A curse against a thief is written on one side, and a curse against a covenant violator on the other. Judgment is to begin at the house of God against all the impure in the land. The presence of the newly built temple and the purging of the transgressors signifies that God once again rules in the land. The presence of the temple is always a vital symbol of the rule of God in the land.

The orientation of the building in relation to the court is not given in Kings, but the tabernacle description tells us how it is conceived. The courtyard of the tabernacle is rectangular, with the east end of the building at the centerline. The back portion of the courtyard is fifty cubits, the building itself thirty cubits, so the center point of the Most Holy Place, ten cubits by ten cubits, is located in the very center of the back portion of the court.[88]

The gold of the temple is not simply a display of wealth and craftsmanship. The whole is conceived in a symmetrical pattern in which the gold of the Most Holy Place (the throne room) is at the very center, with materials of decreasing value found around it.[89] This is further indicated in the temple by all the gold furnishings in direct association with the Most Holy Place, in the description of the cherubs (1 Kings 6:28) and the temple artifacts (7:48–50). All bronze work of Hiram of Tyre (7:15–47) pertains to the courtyard and the porch at the entrance to the temple.

The furnishings of the temple. The furnishings of the temple include ten lampstands and apparently ten tables (1 Kings 7:48–49; 1 Chron. 28:15–16; 2 Chron. 4:19–20). The singular (table) in Kings must be understood col-

---

87. Ibid., 257.
88. Haran, *Temples and Temple-Service in Ancient Israel*, 150–53.
89. Ibid., 158–65.

lectively in a way known to biblical Hebrew.[90] The bread on the table is not only before God but belongs to God. This "bread of the Presence" is eaten by the priests (Lev. 24:5–9), a suggestion that they are eating from God's table. It symbolizes God's provision for his people, but is also a type of offering to God. The bread is left before the Lord, frankincense is sprinkled on it, and it becomes part of the offerings to the Lord (made) by fire. The bread is a type of sacrifice and signifies the participation of the transcendent God in the sharing of the bread. The consumption of the bread and burning it by fire represent a covenant meal between the two parties. The lamps are serviced daily (Ex. 27:20–21) to portray the light of creation as a continuous provision of God for his people.

The altar covered with gold within the temple that is named with the other gold items of the Most Holy Place must be the altar of incense described in the tabernacle (6:20, 22; 7:48; cf. Ex. 30:1–10). This altar is probably similar to those found in the temple at Arad.[91] The incense altar is part of the regular daily ritual of the sacred temple space, but it also has a central role in maintaining the sacred purity of the entire temple precincts. Inscriptions on incense altars from Lachish and Arad indicate that the wrath of Yahweh is appeased by soothing his nose with incense.[92] The same use of incense is found when Aaron is to make atonement to stop the plague (Num. 17:11).

The cloud also serves as a shield to protect the high priest as he enters the Most Holy Place on the Day of Atonement (Lev. 16:2, 13). Milgrom shows that it is not the incense itself that produces the cloud, but a smoke-raising substance ignited before entering the Most Holy Place. The incense is lit only after the high priest enters the Most Holy Place to placate God for the presumption of entering his presence.[93] After the high priest offers incense, he returns to get the blood of the purification offerings to sprinkle it on the gold cover of the ark (16:14).

The golden incense altar has a distinct function at the entrance to the Most Holy Place in line with the large bronze altar at the entrance to the temple.[94]

---

90. Ibid., 189, n. 1. This is the only mention of the bread of the presence in Kings. Chronicles also has the singular in two references (2 Chron. 13:11; 29:18), where the function of the temple is described in terms of the tabernacle.

91. Keel, *Symbolism of the Biblical World*, 149; fig. 248. If this is the altar of 1 Kings 6:20, it was made of cedar. According to Ex. 25:23–30 it was about 90 x 45 centimeters (36 x 18 inches) and about 65 centimeters high (26 inches).

92. Ibid., 147; fig. 197.

93. Jacob Milgrom, *Leviticus 1–16: A New Translation with Introduction and Commentary* (AB 3; Doubleday, 1991), 1028–31.

94. Meyers, "Realms of Sanctity: The Case of the 'Misplaced' Incense Altar in the Tabernacle Texts of Exodus," 38–46.

Both altars are at access points that allow movement to the innermost realm of holiness. They allow essential passage but risk the admission of anything that is not sanctified. As a golden object, the incense altar is set apart from the bronze altar of the courtyard, but it is homologous with respect to its shape and function. The basins used to carry the blood from the bronze altar into the sanctuary and the Most Holy Place on Atonement Day presumably are the bronze ones associated with that altar.

The incense altar participates in both the outer realm of the courtyard and the inner realm of the Most Holy Place. It is part of the ritual that prevents the pollution caused by transgressions from contaminating sacred space and from interfering with God's access to the community. It provides smoke that penetrates into the Most Holy Place; Hebrews actually places it inside the veil (Heb. 9:4). It functions as part of the regular daily ritual in the temple sanctuary, and on the Day of Atonement it receives blood from the outer altar. The connection of the golden altar with the three realms of sanctity make it distinct from the other items of gold in the temple sanctuary.

The temple, the people, and Jesus. Psalm 48 extols the city of Jerusalem as the place where the nations assemble and are astonished, even fearful, at the mighty fortress of God. The temple of Yahweh was mistakenly regarded as so significant and sacred that it could never be destroyed and would always provide deliverance (Jer. 7:1–11). That temple was destroyed by the Babylonians, as Jeremiah declared. After the Exile a second temple was built with the help of the Persians. In the time of Jesus, Herod had made the temple a magnificent complex, ornately embellished with many lavish offerings. As the disciples admired its splendid structures, Jesus informed them it too would be destroyed (Mark 13:1). That second destruction took place at the hands of the Roman general Titus as he was in command of subduing another rebellion in Palestine (Mark 13:14–19). The fortified city would be the most dangerous place to be. At two different times a glorious structure that represented God's presence in the world and his rule over the nations was destroyed by those nations as if it were of no significance to God.

The temple can only represent the glory of God within the context of a people of faith. This point interrupts the very account of the building of the temple structure (6:11–13), so that the statement of the completion of the structure must be repeated (6:9, 14). Israel reinvents her God in her own image, twisting the terms of his covenant to suit themselves and bringing the curses of covenant violation on themselves. These curses ultimately lead them into Exile, in order that the land might receive the Sabbaths of which it has been deprived (Lev. 26:27–35). The Sabbath is the primary sign of the covenant (Ex. 31:12–17), showing that these are the people that know their

Creator and accept his rule as the means of bringing peace to creation as it is meant to be (Gen. 2:1–3).

The temple functions according to the days of creation; the Sabbath observance is the equivalence of the seventh day. The seven days of creation are to be understood literally, though it is not clear if these incorporate a ceremonial setting, a declarative sequence, or something else.[95] In the Sumerian account of the construction of a temple for Ningirsu several items may be noted: The temple is a resting place for the gods; the ceremonies last seven days; the dedication ceremonies include a proclamation of the functions of the temple.

In the same way, the Genesis account sets up the functions and the functionaries for the cosmic temple.[96] Denial of the covenant was immediately evident in disregard of the Sabbath, and allegiance to the covenant was confessed in keeping the Sabbath (Isa. 56:4–6). The economic implications of the Sabbath extended to the years of release and Jubilee; failure to observe the Sabbath and all its cycles was a denial of the temple and the rule of God in the land. The destruction of the temple by the Babylonians was evidence that the temple had ceased to serve its purpose as representing the rule of God.

Jesus had respect for the temple of his day but declared that its purposes had again been violated, so that it had become a place of merchandise instead of a place of prayer (John 2:13–17). He drove out those conducting their business in the temple. When asked about what right he had to do this, he replied that if they were to destroy this temple, he would raise it up again in three days (2:18–19). This caused astonishment to those who heard it. Only later did the disciples come to realize that Jesus himself had replaced the function of the temple (2:20–22). He was in bodily form the very presence of God in their midst; he was everything that the temple had represented and more. The new covenant developed this in detail, particularly in Hebrews. It twice refers to the "new covenant" (Heb. 8:8–13; 10:16–18) in explaining that Jesus fulfilled every aspect of the temple symbolism. His body is now the means that leads believers through the veil into the very presence of God (10:19–20). Once the incarnation had taken place, there could be no more use for a physical temple.

---

95. Walton, *Genesis*, 156. Walton correctly shows that the primary purpose of the narrative in Gen. 1 is to describe the function of creation rather than the process by which the structure of the cosmos came into being.

96. Ibid., 151. The fourth day of creation is particularly significant in the narrative; it does not describe sun or moon, but "lights," the word used for the lamps of the sanctuary. The lights serve as signs for the festive seasons (liturgical celebrations) and natural seasons (days and years); see Walter Vogels, "The Cultic and Civil Calendars of the Fourth Day of Creation (Gen 1,14b)," *Scandinavian Journal of the Old Testament* 11.2 (1997): 167–75.

TRIVIALIZING GOD. What can ancient temples and their artifacts contribute to an understanding of life or theology? In ancient Israel the temple established the legitimacy of Solomon's reign, so its inclusion in the account of the kingdom of Israel was essential. The temple was important to the rule of Solomon because it expressed the sovereign and personal relationship between God, his world, and his people. It taught the Israelites about the exclusive dominion of God and the story of their experience with him. It served to declare the immanent presence of their transcendent and holy God.

The revelatory words of the temple are essential to understanding the God of the covenant. At times contemporary Christianity anthropomorphizes God so he is something of an extension of human power to manipulate the world. Such a God is scarcely worthy of worship. The Healer and Redeemer of mortals in this transient world is mysteriously and sovereignly present within it, not subject to it through human coercion of the divine will. The tendency to reduce God the Creator to a friend next door is an impediment to knowing him. It betrays conformity to a culture in which the majestic and marvelous are trivialized by analogy to that which is familiar.

When the robot Sojourner began roving the surface of Mars, the mysteries of the red planet were described as a version of a Disneyworld movie. Barbara Ehrenreich expressed it well:

> Isn't this just the cutest little universe you've ever seen? After centuries of technological striving, we finally got to Earth's strange sibling Mars—and found rocks named Yogi, Scooby Doo and Barnacle Bill. Someone high up in NASA must have issued a firm directive: "Keep it cuddly, guys. We don't want Mars to seem like, you know, outer space." So when Sojourner bumped into one of the rocks, we were told Yogi gave her a "boo-boo," and when she (yes, the robot is a girl) made a close approach to another one, we were informed that "Sojourner and Barnacle Bill are holding hands." Kind of made you look at the vast red deserts of the two-mooned planet and want to go "Coochy-coochy-coo!"[97]

The tendency to humanize the mysteries of the universe is an inhibition to understanding them. As Ehrenreich goes on to say, "When we turn the Martian terrain into a comic strip . . . we are making things seem tame and familiar before we even know what they are." Mars truly belongs to a realm

---

97. Barbara Ehrenreich, "What a Cute Universe You Have!" *Time* (Aug. 25, 1997), 82.

outside of human experience, but it is still in substance part of the universe in which we live. The God of the Scriptures does not belong to the realm of creation. The purpose of the temple was to show that the Creator could give life and meaning to the world because the Holy One of Israel is in no sense a part of it or dependent on it. Only by beginning with the mystery of God is it possible to begin to know him truly.

The reduction of the mysterious and incomprehensible to the banal happens readily in popular expressions of faith. The God of the prosperity gospel is scarcely the God of the temple Solomon built:

> Watch one of our shlockier televangelists, and you'll be introduced to an affable deity eager to be enlisted as your personal genie. Yes, the Great Spinner of Galaxies, Digger of Black Holes is available, for a suitable "love offering," to relieve the itch of hemorrhoids and help you prevail in office intrigues![98]

The temple was destroyed, but it is preserved in the scriptural record. The Scriptures warn against the atheism of serving a God who can be manipulated by our personal desires, who is less than the transcendent Creator. He is the giver of life only when he is in no sense dependent on the functions of the created order or manipulated by them.

For the prophets of the Deuteronomistic History, Israel's great failure is their inability to comprehend and worship the God of the temple (cf. 1 Kings 6:11–13). Solomon himself compromises this absolute exclusivity of God; he follows Ashtoreth, the goddess of the Sidonians, and Milcom, the abomination of the Ammonites (11:5). In Judah, in the days of Uzziah and Jothom, Isaiah sees Yahweh high and lifted up in the midst of the seraphs (Isa. 6:1–3), the One he will from that time on refer to as "the Holy One of Israel."

For the leaders of Judah, the temple was reduced to a place of ritual; their sacrifices, festivals, and even their prayers in the temple were an abomination to God (Isa. 1:11–15). Though they had fervent dedication to the temple, their city and land were equivalent to Sodom and Gomorrah (1:10). The grandeur of the temple was not sufficient to assure that God would be God in the land of Israel. God called them his enemies (v. 24); their utter failure to know God would bring them in subjugation to the gods of the Babylonians (39:6–8), the very concern of the authors of the books of Kings (2 Kings 20:17–18).

One of the most decisive influences in the lives of the faithful is their understanding of God. A subtle deception for Christians is the assumption that belief in the Bible will lead to a true understanding of the God of the

---

98. Ibid.

Bible. Though mortals can never understand God fully, it is possible and necessary to understand God truly. It is also possible to come to a seriously distorted understanding of God through improper, though sincere, reading of the Scriptures. Misunderstanding God may be no less disastrous for a church than it was for those who celebrated the construction of Solomon's temple.

In *Disappointment with God*, Philip Yancey writes about a congregation in rural Indiana who adopted a view of God that would accommodate their beliefs about faith in God. Yancey visited the church after reading about it in a *Chicago Tribune* series, which told of parents who had looked on helplessly as their children fought losing battles with medically treatable diseases. This church believed that to seek medical help was a failure of faith when God had promised to heal all those who asked. A *Tribune* artist had marked a map with fifty-two tiny tombstone symbols indicating the deaths of individuals refusing medical help. Yancey concluded with his assessment of their concept of faith:

> I went away from that Sunday service with a profound conviction that what we think about God matters—*really* matters—as much as anything in life matters. Those people were not ogres or child-murderers, and yet several dozen of their children had died because of an error (I believe) in theology. (Actually, the teaching of the Indiana church is not so different from what I hear in many evangelical churches and on religious television and radio; they simply apply the extravagant promises of faith more consistently).[99]

The significance of temple imagery. Understanding God is the task of biblical theology. Biblical theology seeks to take into account all of revelation in formulating a theology of the Bible itself. The details of the temple are a part of revelation, not only to teach us about Solomon and his glory, but also to teach us about the God of Israel and his relationship to his creation. The conception of the temple is a statement about the God of the universe and the history of Israel in particular. The lessons of Kings require the reader to understand the significance of the temple.

It is a complex task to construct a biblical theology in which an understanding of God, as communicated in the building of the temple, is incorporated into the lessons of God's work in the world. In his discussion of method in doing biblical theology, Rolf Knierim writes of the danger of going directly from texts, such as the building programs of Solomon, to application:

---

99. Philip Yancey, *Disappointment with God* (Grand Rapids: Zondervan, 1988), 26.

The problem of the theological validity of an individual text arises not only from its distance from our time; it arises, first of all, from the unresolved relationship between its own claim to truth and the multiple truth claims of all these texts with which it coexists.[100]

Texts do contradict each other if proper criteria are not established for how texts are to be related to each other. Knierim emphasizes that the central affirmation of the oneness of Yahweh and the oneness of his world provides a substantial theological reason for reconstructing the theology of the Old and New Testaments in their diversity.

Furthermore, Yahweh is not the God of creation because he is the God of the humans or of human history. He is the God of the humans and of human history because he is the God of creation. For the Old Testament, just as for the New Testament, the most universal aspect of Yahweh's dominion is not human history. It is the creation and sustenance of the world. This aspect is at the same time the most fundamental, because the creation does not depend on history or existence, but history and existence depend on and are measured against creation.[101]

The writings describing the temple and the role of the temple itself in ancient Israel testify to the God of creation, which subordinate all of human history to him. It is the doctrine that makes exclusive the obligations of the covenant.

The temple of Solomon was not the equivalent of other temples in its time. True, as a structure it resembled other temples. The symbolism and imagery of its features drew their meaning from the culture of the time, just as word symbols in language derive their significance from the culture in which they are used. But these similarities do not make the God it represented of the same order.[102] Israel lost the distinctives of the Solomonic temple to the tragedy of the empire of Solomon, and ultimately they lost the continuity of the nation. Their God became like the gods of the other nations, in spite of the distinct function of the adytum (the Most Holy Place), with its huge cherubs but no image. The God of Israel was not like that of the other nations; he was a holy and jealous God, unable to endure the worship of other gods (Josh. 24:19–20).

---

100. Rolf Knierim, *The Task of Old Testament Theology: Method and Cases* (Grand Rapids: Eerdmans, 1995), 68.

101. Ibid., 13.

102. A recent conversation with a couple that had viewed the ruins of ancient temples sharpened this point for me. They were impressed with how similar these temples were to the biblical model; their tendency was to assume that biblical meaning could be determined from observing archaeological remains. This is not necessarily the case; the similarities are essential to establishing communication, the differences are vital to the concept intended.

Israel could serve gods like those of the other nations, but the absolute demands of their God would prove impossible to keep.

The term *God* is frequently used with little reflection on the conception conveyed. A most important function of the structure of the temple was to express the incomparability of Israel's God, a function it continued to have literally when incorporated into this prophetic history of Israel. The temple, though comparatively small among Solomon's building projects, towered in significance. The other buildings, necessary to the function of the royal household and the kingdom, are subordinated to the magnitude of the temple. The God of Israel was ever present in the story of Israel; his identity and distinction were prominent in every aspect of that story. As in the present, the danger was that their God would be like those of the other nations.

When Stephen Hawking came out to Sudbury, Ontario, at the opening of the world's deepest laboratory investigating neutrinos, the smallest particles physically observed, a Canadian Broadcasting Corporation reporter asked him whether he believed in God. Hawking's reply was that he never answered that question, because he could not know that what the inquirer meant by God corresponded to his own understanding.[103] Chaim Potok in *The Book of Lights* tells of an American rabbi, an army chaplain during the Korean War, on leave in Japan. He and his Catholic friend passed a Japanese man praying devoutly at a shrine. He asks:

"Do you think our God is listening to him, John?"
"I don't know, chappy. I never thought of it."
"Neither did I until now. If He's not listening, why not? If He's listening, then—well, what are *we* all about, John? That's my thought for tomorrow. I think we ought to go back to the hotel."[104]

At some point an understanding of God, even when based on a reading of Scripture, comes to refer to a very different person. Not all monotheists worship the same God; though they may refer to the same individual, they can only worship according to what they know and believe about him.

The temple conveyed to the Israelites the concept of the world as a sacred space that belonged to its Creator. The word that most comprehensively describes the God of the temple is "holy." Holiness is the converse of the common; common is all that which belongs to the sphere of the world (universe) in which we live. Holiness in reference to God has nothing to do with morality; it connotes the essential nature that belongs to the sphere of God's being

---

103. For information on research at the Sudbury Neutrino Observatory Institute see http://www.sno.phy.queensu.ca/. Stephen Hawking was at the observatory April 29, 1998.
104. Chaim Potok, *The Book of Lights* (New York: Random House, 1981), 248.

or activity that is distinct from the created order.[105] The holy name can be the equivalent of the divine name: "The fear of the LORD is the beginning of wisdom, knowledge of the Holy One [*qᵉdōšîm*] is understanding" (Prov. 9:10). The holy name contrasts with everything creaturely; holiness is synonymous with the honor, reputation, and glory of God. The temple represented creation; it was a declaration that the earth and it fullness are Yahweh's (Ps. 24:1). The earth was created as the place where the majesty of the holy would be made known and where the presence of the holy might dwell.

Cosmic significance. The cosmic significance of the temple testifies to the reality that God's presence is to be extended throughout the whole earth. Eschatologically it reaches its fulfillment in the new heavens and new earth of Revelation (Rev. 21:1). The vision of John is best understood as picturing the final temple that will fill the entire cosmos.[106] The conception of Israel's temple is essential to understanding the relationship between the new creation and the city-temple that is the culmination of John's vision (21:1–22:5). The correspondence between pagan temples and Israel's temple provides a cultural context for revelation, but Beale thinks that conversely, pagan temples refracted a marred understanding of the true conception of the temple that was present from the very beginning of human history.[107] In the Bible, Eden is regarded as the first archetypal temple, upon which all Israel's temples are based. The restoration of Zion and its temple is described as making its "deserts like Eden, her wastelands like the garden of the LORD" (Isa. 51:3). The temple adumbrates the new creation.

The fulfillment of the temple promise is the restoration of the kingdom of God. In the Deuteronomistic History, the building of the temple signifies the divine approval of Solomon as the successor to the Davidic promise; the destruction of that same temple signifies judgment on the kingdom. Though prophets such as Jeremiah witness the destruction of the temple, they do not view it as ending the promise. God will establish a new covenant for his people (Jer. 31:31–34). The writer to the Hebrews understands Christ to be the fulfillment of the new covenant promise and, as the new high priest, is seated at the right hand of God's heavenly throne. This heavenly place of rule is not merely a king's palace; it is a sanctuary, the true tabernacle, the original Most Holy Place (Heb. 8:1–2). The rule of Christ in the heavenly temple

---

105. Jackie A. Naudé, "קדש," *NIDOTTE*, 3:879. Holiness in reference to humanity usually has a moral connotation (often referred to as sanctification), since it speaks of the character and conduct of those separated to God as creatures in the world and in social relations with each other (ibid., 882–83).

106. Gregory K. Beale, *The Temple and the Church's Mission: A Biblical Theology of the Dwelling Place of God* (NSBT 17; Downers Grove, Ill.: InterVarsity Press, 2004), 25.

107. Ibid., 29–30.

is the fulfillment of the intended design of the Old Testament temple. In Hebrews, the temple of Solomon is the shadow that represents the real temple where Christ rules at God's right hand.

Christ refers to himself in the Gospels as the "cornerstone" of the temple (Matt. 21:42; Mark 12:10; Luke 20:17). The fullness of the divine presence represented in the temple is found in the declaration that the glory of the only Son of the Father dwelt among us (John 1:14). The Word became flesh and "tabernacled among us."[108] He was in the world, and the world came to be through him, but the world did not know him (v. 10). The presence of the temple declared that the world belonged to God. Jesus was not a verisimilitude of the divine presence, but God incarnate in human form.

The Word was God (v. 1); he could claim the very name of God (8:24, 28, 58; cf. Isa. 43:10, 13). The unbelieving crowds could not understand the signs Jesus had done (John 12:37); they saw miracles, but for many in Israel they did not reveal the light of the world and the bread of life. As Isaiah had said, their minds were hardened so they could not believe (v. 40). Isaiah said these things when he had seen his glory (cf. Isa. 6:1–3) and, John says, "spoke concerning him" (John 12:41). As he had throughout his gospel, John equates the glory of Yahweh in the temple and in the vision of Isaiah with the Word that lived among us.

The physical presence of God in this world in the bodily presence of Jesus was taken away with his ascension. This did not mean that God's presence could no longer be perceived in the world. Peter declares that those who have come to Christ are living stones brought to Jesus, the chief cornerstone, and are a spiritual house in which are offered the sacrifices of praise (1 Peter 2:4–6). They are the people of the covenant, as was declared at Mount Sinai (2:9); they function as the temple in representing the rule of God in this world. Paul describes the church as the body of Christ making manifest the presence of God (Eph. 1:19–23). The church as the body of Christ is far above any other ruler or power, authority, or name that can be named. The church performs the will of God in his world, that his rule may be exercised on earth.

Sacred space, the people of God, and suffering. Christians have focused on the question of status with God rather than the question of sacred space in relation to God. The temple is a reminder that creation is God's sacred space; he is Lord over every dominion. The sacrificial system had to do with preserving sacred space. The objects of the Hebrew verb "atone" (*kāpar*) are typically those of the sanctuary; sacred space, not the person, is the focus of

---

108. These concepts are developed by Gregory K. Beale in "Eden, the Temple, and the Church's Mission in the New Creation," *JETS* 48 (2005): 20–21.

the ritual.[109] Individuals are beneficiaries of the ritual in that their status is restored because cleansing has taken place on their behalf. The sacrificial system of the temple was never intended to be a means of taking away sins from individuals (Heb. 10:1–4). The sacrifices were a means to purify a sanctuary (sacred space) tarnished by individual and corporate sin. Without a sanctuary, the sacrificial system becomes superfluous. The church, individually and corporately, is construed as the sanctuary in which Christ dwells and so becomes the object of the atoning sacrifice. The question of status is inseparable from the matter of the divine presence.

One generation before the Romans destroyed the temple, a most remarkable event took place: The veil in the temple was torn asunder (Matt. 27:51; Mark 15:38; Luke 23:45). The importance of this is so little understood because there is so little recognition of sacred space.[110] Christ's flesh is the veil that grants access to God (Heb. 10:20); his death is the end of restricted access to God. Paul uses the concept of sacred space to explain the ramifications of the cross for the Gentiles (Eph. 2:11–22). The Gentiles were formerly excluded from God's presence (outside the camp), but have now been brought near by the blood of Christ (v. 13). Peace is possible because the barrier that separated Gentiles from God has been broken down (v. 14). Jews and Gentiles both have access to the Father (v. 18); they are fellow citizens (v. 19); they rise together to become one holy temple (vv. 21–22).

The temple as a place of sacred space continues as a symbol of morality for the Christian and the congregation. Just as the temple had to be pure to be the place where God dwelt, so the Christian must be pure. This is Paul's argument in comparing the development of Christian character and the church to building on the foundation of the gospel of Christ (1 Cor. 3:10–17); the indwelling Spirit of God has made believers a temple that must be kept holy. The same argument is made in relation to sexual promiscuity (6:15–20); this sin involves the body itself with impurity, violating that sacred space that was purified with the most costly sacrifice.

As a representation of sacred space, the temple is a symbol of hope, calling the Christian to bear suffering with patience. According to Paul, the suffering of Christ restored the place of God in the world, bringing restoration and victory over suffering:

The creation waits in eager expectation for the sons of God to be revealed. For the creation was subjected to frustration, not by its own

---

109. John Walton, "Equilibrium and the Sacred Compass: The Structure of Leviticus," *BBR* 11 (2001): 298.
110. Ibid., 297.

choice, but by the will of the one who subjected it, in hope that the creation itself will be liberated from its bondage to decay and brought into the glorious freedom of the children of God. (Rom. 8:19–21)

This victory includes knowing how to suffer for the cause of Christ: "I want to know Christ and the power of his resurrection and the fellowship of sharing in his sufferings, becoming like him in his death, and so, somehow, to attain to the resurrection from the dead" (Phil. 3:10–11). The suffering of Christ was an atonement to purify the place of God's residence that life might be restored. Being one with Christ in his death is to share in the victory of his resurrection. The focus of the glorification of Christ (his crucifixion, resurrection, and ascension) is not his suffering but on his atoning sacrifice, which conquers the power of death and restores life.

Paul looks to the suffering of Christ as the explanation of his own sufferings for the gospel in the fulfillment of God's purpose for creation:

Now I rejoice in what was suffered for you, and I fill up in my flesh what is still lacking in regard to Christ's afflictions, for the sake of his body, which is the church. I have become its servant by the commission God gave me to present to you the word of God in its fullness— the mystery that has been kept hidden for ages and generations, but is now disclosed to the saints. To them God has chosen to make known among the Gentiles the glorious riches of this mystery, which is Christ in you, the hope of glory. (Col. 1:24–27)

The thought of the apostle must be followed with care.[111] What is the sense in which the sufferings of Christ are still lacking (v. 24)? The "still" is not in the Greek text and can be misleading. When Paul talks about his suffering, he does not relate it to some divinely set quota of afflictions. Suffering comes with living as a Christian; believers are always being given over to death for Jesus' sake, so that his life may be revealed in our mortal body (2 Cor. 4:11).

The struggle of the apostle to make the Word of God known brings suffering with it, a suffering that belongs to Christ. It is not the suffering of Christ at the cross that is incomplete, but the suffering of Christ in the apostle Paul. Paul rejoices because his own debt of suffering is being completed on behalf of the church, the body of Christ. If Christians are one with Christ in his burial and resurrection, they are one with him in his suffering. Christ continues to suffer in his church (Acts 9:4–5). What is still lacking is the bod-

---

111. See David E. Garland, *Colossians and Philemon* (NIVAC; Grand Rapids: Zondervan, 1998), 118–23.

ily presence of Christ.[112] Paul suffers as the representative of Christ, who is absent in the body but present in spirit. Paul presents himself as an example of the indwelling mystery of the work of the cross taking place in his life. Paul is suffering as Christ would suffer if he were bodily present. God's people have already begun to be his temple, where his presence is manifested to the world. Their task is to extend the boundaries of the temple until Christ returns.

Mel Gibson's movie *The Passion* has attracted a great many Christians but aroused the ire of many who disdain the implications of one human suffering for others and at the hands of others. I have been impressed with the many individuals—Christian, nominally Christian, and others—who have expressed the profound impact that viewing a crucifixion made on them and the impact it had for appropriating the grace of God on their behalf. I certainly feel there is great merit to such an experience. I have not viewed the film, in part because I do not enjoy watching movies, but in part because it seems to me to be distortive of the glorification of Christ in the Gospels. Christ identified in his suffering with the greatest of human suffering. His citation of the first line of one of the most intense lament psalms made such an impression that the Gospel writers recorded a Greek transliteration of the original Aramaic or Hebrew (Ps. 22:1; cf. Matt. 27:46; Mark 15:34). The choice of Christ to enter into our suffering is a profound demonstration of the love God has for us. Yet the gospel message does not emphasize a punishment borne on behalf of the world; the message is that this is a victory that transforms the world. God has reclaimed the world as his own.

Christ continues to suffer because he is present in the Christian and in his church, which is his temple. Salvation for the Christian must not be given a narcissistic twist, in which gratitude for what God has done makes believers think that faith is about themselves.[113] If the sanctity of God's presence is to be maintained and if people are to have access to it, they must be kept pure. The purpose of God is to be present in his temple. The evangelical emphasis on what Christ has done "for me" completely fails to understand the suffering and sacrifice of Christ. Walton appropriately quotes David Wells in the distortion of God's purpose for purity:

> The biblical interest in righteousness is replaced by a search for happiness, holiness by wholeness, truth by feeling, ethics by feeling good about one's self. The world shrinks to the range of personal circumstances; the community of faith shrinks to a circle of personal

---

112. The sense of lack may be understood from Phil. 2:30; the presence of Epaphroditus as the representative of the Philippians made up for their lack (ibid., 122).
113. Walton, "Equilibrium and the Sacred Compass," 298–99.

friends. The past recedes. The Church recedes. The world recedes. All that remains is the self.[114]

It is true that God loves me and that Jesus saves me, but this is not the sum total of Christian faith. Christianity is all about God and the sacred space of his temple.

Paul speaks of his life of suffering as being led in triumph so that through him the fragrance of knowing God is spread everywhere (2 Cor. 2:14–16). Paul here refers to two cultures: the Roman and the Hebrew. The triumphal procession in a Roman context was to lead prisoners of war to their death in giving thanks to the Roman gods.[115] The sentence of death is a metonymy for his suffering; Paul could say he "dies every day" (1 Cor. 15:31).[116] God used this suffering to make himself known; using the analogy of sacrifice in the Old Testament, Paul describes the dispersion of the knowledge of God as an aroma. "Fragrance" and "aroma" are used as synecdoche for a sacrifice pleasing to God.[117] Paul's suffering is the "fragrance" of Christ himself that rises up to God from Paul's life. Christ is the sacrifice, and Paul is the odor that rises from it. To the believer, Paul's suffering is an expression of glory, but to the unbeliever it is foolishness.

Words, actions, and places are interrelated in the expression of temple theology. It is this system of temple theology that carries the original Christian message.[118] The great seven-branched lamp is the tree of life; it is also God's presence with his people. The divine presence is described as the seven eyes or seven spirits (Zech. 4:10; Rev.4:5). The temple is rich with symbols that are daily reminders of the presence of a holy God. The rituals of sacrifice and cleanliness that are part of observing the temple function involve a daily consciousness of the presence of the King of kings.

Holiness and cleanness. The concepts of clean and unclean are not identical to modern ideas of sanitary and unsanitary. Uncleanness is opposed to holiness; the unclean is associated with death, while holiness is associated with life. The function of the temple in indicating this relationship between life and death has been illustrated well by Davies:[119]

---

114. Ibid., 298; quoted from *No Place for Truth* (Grand Rapids: Eerdmans, 1993), 183.

115. This should not be translated as "thanks be to God who causes us to triumph." Calvin gave the verb a causative sense that cannot be sustained; see Scott J. Hafemann, *2 Corinthians* (NIVAC; Grand Rapids: Zondervan, 2000), 108.

116. "Death" is used for suffering just as the word "crown" is used to refer to royalty or governance, as in the expression "crown land."

117. Synecdoche is a figure of speech where part of an object is used for the whole, as "fifty sails" to refer to a fleet of fifty ships.

118. Margaret Barker, *On Earth as It Is in Heaven: Temple Symbolism in the New Testament* (Edinburgh: T. & T. Clark, 1995), 10–12.

119. Douglas Davies, "An Interpretation of Sacrifice in Leviticus," *ZAW* 89 (1977): 394.

SACRED			PROFANE
God	Priesthood	People	Gentiles
Temple	Camp		Wilderness
Life			Death
Being	Transient Existence		Nothingness
ORDER	RITUAL		CHAOS

Care for the unclean included normal functions such as bodily discharges, particularly from sexual organs (Lev. 15:1–33). Vaginal blood and semen symbolized life, and their loss seemed to represent death. Childbirth too was dangerous; bodily fluids were lost, and the boundary between life and death was breached. Contact with animal and especially human corpses brought uncleanness (Num. 19:11–22). Purity regulated all areas of life where boundaries could become blurred. Mixtures, whether of cloth, agricultural practices, or animal breeding, were forbidden (Lev. 19:19; Deut. 22:9–11). Uncleanness had to be removed by rituals. Simple acts of bathing, washing one's clothes, and waiting until evening were normally required. Menstrual blood or contact with a corpse required seven days of waiting and even sprinkling with special water.

Food could also be clean or unclean. Since blood was associated with life and holiness, all food had to be kept pure from it (Lev. 17:10–14). Certain animals were also forbidden; animals that crossed distinct boundaries or did not clearly belong to certain categories were usually classified as unclean (e.g., Lev. 11:3–12, 29–31). Consciousness of clean and unclean was part of virtually every activity.

Since uncleanness was related to holiness, it had a vague connection with sin and guilt. The distinction of clean and unclean was a reminder of Israel's call to holiness. Holiness implied separation from the common or the profane. Restrictions on diet and requirements of order defined a self-identity in separation to God. The holy and the unclean were incompatible, so it was necessary for the sacred to be protected. This involved temple ritual and regular purification of the sanctuary. Once the symbolism of the temple was removed, none of the regulations concerning purity could be relevant or have significance. They all required the context of the temple, teaching the holiness of God as the Giver of life.

The church does not have a similar complement of rituals and activities to teach about life and the holiness of God. The presence (temple) of God in this world is made through baptism and the observance of communion. These symbols should never be minimized. They are no less significant than the proper observance of all the temple ritual. A deliberate conscious denial of these symbols is a denial of belonging to the temple of living stones—the body of Christ.

The rituals themselves are not efficacious, any more than the temple rituals, apart from accompanying faith. Faithless ritual led to the destruction of the physical temple, and faithless ritual will lead to the extinction of the temple fulfilled. Just as faith compelled the observance of covenant ritual in the physical temple, so faith is manifested in the rituals Jesus left for his followers. The followers of Jesus offer the sacrifice of praise in assembling together (Heb. 10:23–24), encouraging each other until the time of the fullness of the kingdom. Though the temple of living stones may not have the wealth of accompanying grandeur and ritual, it has a presence no less powerful in its confession.

Symbolism in the particulars. One of the most remarkable aspects of the construction of the temple is the detailed attention given to particular features. These were obviously of enormous interest, not only to craftsmen, but to all those who were familiar with them. Creativity and craftsmanship are part of the way we express the beauty of creation and the presence of God within it. Even utilitarian items like the ten water lavers in the temple court were ornately crafted that they might contribute to the effect of the whole. The gold and the carvings on the walls had a distinct function in manifesting the presence of the King, but art and beauty extended to the whole. Such items as church buildings need to be functional and utilitarian, but it is not a waste of resources to show their lofty purposes through the art of glass windows, bells, steeples, and other appropriate architectural features. They too represent the promise of the temple fulfilled in the church and awaiting its consummation in the temple of the new heavens and earth.

A few years ago I visited a friend in Enfield, on the north side of London. From the high vantage point of his veranda one could look out across the countryside for a number of miles. I knew from visiting the villages around Cambridge that a distinguishing feature of every village was a church with a steeple on the highest hill of the central street. I was struck by the scene as I looked out from that veranda across the miles of English countryside. The landscape was dotted with steeples—a testimony to the Christian heritage of the country at a time when the confession of a church building was regarded as a most important economic investment. Though these churches are enormously expensive to maintain and, in most cases, are no longer the center of village life, they are preserved as a heritage of the country and give constant testimony to the presence of God in the temple of his church.

Iconography is one of the most significant developments in the early history of the church. During the first centuries of Christianity, Christian symbols and artwork of the gospel message were the most important means by which the masses of the people learned gospel. Most were not literate, and few knew Latin, the language of the Bible at that time. The icons were very sophisticated; angles of the head, particular features in the faces, and other features were used to portray characters and their disposition. Old and New Testament were linked together in icons, so a biblical theology could be depicted.[120]

The sophisticated teaching method of icons has analogies to the temple and its artifacts. In modern societies, communication is largely done through written word, without question a desirable ideal. In the ancient world of Israel, the written word would have been limited for vast numbers of people, as it was in the early history of the church. Other visual symbols, which did not require the time and education required to acquire literacy or the tools necessary for it, became an important and efficient means of instruction. Even for the literate, symbols and pictures conveyed lasting impressions that could never be achieved the same way with words.

But one of the problems of iconography is that they can become venerated objects, as did the temple and its artifacts in ancient times. A second problem is that ritual tends to become thoughtless routine. Sacrifice without the more important aspects of justice is offensive to God (Mic. 6:6–8). All Christians must be reflective, for every person of faith has a tendency to skew the significance of objects or actions. Discipline to attend church or to pray regularly is necessary, but there is minimal value when motives are mostly obligatory. People of faith need to be vigilant about the routine things that they do, but they must not avoid routines. Visible symbols in a church make important contributions to worship; communion tables, crosses, glass windows, pictures, and so on have a vital role in creating a sense of God's presence.

One of the strengths of icons, as the temple rituals, is their potential for a consciousness of divine presence in every aspect of life. There are many ways of achieving this awareness of divine presence that must be cultivated. A relative of mine, an avid hunter and nature lover who does not attend church regularly, said to me, "The world is God's cathedral." This, of course, is true, as the imagery of the temple conveys. What does not follow is that seeing the world actually makes one aware of it as a God's cathedral. A friend of mine used to say, "It is better to be on the golf course thinking about God, than in church thinking about golf." That may be true; I would tell him that I was not convinced anyone on the golf course was thinking about God, not even when his name was used. The cathedral of God is his people joined together in worship and in extending the boundaries of God's temple in the world.

---

120. This is illustrated by Vivian K. Olender, "Iconography: Theology and Faith in Colour and Symbol," *Currents in Biblical and Theological Dialogue Proceedings* 2 (2003): 37–55.

The ongoing task of Christians is to serve God in his temple, in which they dwell and of which they are a part. They offer the sacrifice of their bodies, which is their service of worship (Rom. 12:1). In so doing they follow the Savior's example, who "gave himself up for us as a fragrant offering and sacrifice to God" (Eph. 5:2). The church's support of others to spread the gospel is also considered a sacrifice. Paul considered the financial support of the Philippians to be an acceptable sacrifice, well pleasing to God (Phil. 4:15–18).[121] The mark of the church is an expanding witness of the presence of God, first to our families, then to our communities and country, and ultimately to the whole earth.

"The Church is to be God's temple, so filled with his glorious presence that we expand and fill the earth with that presence until God finally accomplishes the goal completely at the end of time."[122] It is said that a small shark kept captive will stay a size proportionate to the aquarium in which it is confined. A shark turned loose in the ocean will reach a size of over twenty feet. The church must not be kept captive in a fishbowl or aquarium. Rather, the church must manifest the presence of Christ and his temple so the glory of God is manifest in the entire earth (Ps. 8:1, 9). The earth must be "full of the knowledge of the LORD as the waters cover the sea (Isa. 11:9; cf. Hab. 2:14). Only then can they fulfill the promise of the temple for the new heavens and new earth, in which everyone worships before God (Isa. 66:22–23).

121. Beale, *The Temple and the Church's Mission*, 398–400.
122. Ibid., 402.

SOLOMON] BROUGHT IN the things his father David had dedicated—the silver and gold and the furnishings—and he placed them in the treasuries of the LORD's temple.

8:1Then King Solomon summoned into his presence at Jerusalem the elders of Israel, all the heads of the tribes and the chiefs of the Israelite families, to bring up the ark of the LORD's covenant from Zion, the City of David. 2All the men of Israel came together to King Solomon at the time of the festival in the month of Ethanim, the seventh month.

3When all the elders of Israel had arrived, the priests took up the ark, 4and they brought up the ark of the LORD and the Tent of Meeting and all the sacred furnishings in it. The priests and Levites carried them up, 5and King Solomon and the entire assembly of Israel that had gathered about him were before the ark, sacrificing so many sheep and cattle that they could not be recorded or counted.

6The priests then brought the ark of the LORD's covenant to its place in the inner sanctuary of the temple, the Most Holy Place, and put it beneath the wings of the cherubim. 7The cherubim spread their wings over the place of the ark and overshadowed the ark and its carrying poles. 8These poles were so long that their ends could be seen from the Holy Place in front of the inner sanctuary, but not from outside the Holy Place; and they are still there today. 9There was nothing in the ark except the two stone tablets that Moses had placed in it at Horeb, where the LORD made a covenant with the Israelites after they came out of Egypt.

10When the priests withdrew from the Holy Place, the cloud filled the temple of the LORD. 11And the priests could not perform their service because of the cloud, for the glory of the LORD filled his temple.

12Then Solomon said, "The LORD has said that he would dwell in a dark cloud; 13I have indeed built a magnificent temple for you, a place for you to dwell forever."

14While the whole assembly of Israel was standing there, the king turned around and blessed them. 15Then he said:

"Praise be to the LORD, the God of Israel, who with his own hand has fulfilled what he promised with his own mouth to my father David. For he said, ¹⁶'Since the day I brought my people Israel out of Egypt, I have not chosen a city in any tribe of Israel to have a temple built for my Name to be there, but I have chosen David to rule my people Israel.'

¹⁷"My father David had it in his heart to build a temple for the Name of the LORD, the God of Israel. ¹⁸But the LORD said to my father David, 'Because it was in your heart to build a temple for my Name, you did well to have this in your heart. ¹⁹Nevertheless, you are not the one to build the temple, but your son, who is your own flesh and blood—he is the one who will build the temple for my Name.'

²⁰"The LORD has kept the promise he made: I have succeeded David my father and now I sit on the throne of Israel, just as the LORD promised, and I have built the temple for the Name of the LORD, the God of Israel. ²¹I have provided a place there for the ark, in which is the covenant of the LORD that he made with our fathers when he brought them out of Egypt."

²²Then Solomon stood before the altar of the LORD in front of the whole assembly of Israel, spread out his hands toward heaven ²³and said:

"O LORD, God of Israel, there is no God like you in heaven above or on earth below—you who keep your covenant of love with your servants who continue wholeheartedly in your way. ²⁴You have kept your promise to your servant David my father; with your mouth you have promised and with your hand you have fulfilled it—as it is today.

²⁵"Now LORD, God of Israel, keep for your servant David my father the promises you made to him when you said, 'You shall never fail to have a man to sit before me on the throne of Israel, if only your sons are careful in all they do to walk before me as you have done.' ²⁶And now, O God of Israel, let your word that you promised your servant David my father come true.

²⁷"But will God really dwell on earth? The heavens, even the highest heaven, cannot contain you. How

much less this temple I have built! ²⁸Yet give attention to your servant's prayer and his plea for mercy, O LORD my God. Hear the cry and the prayer that your servant is praying in your presence this day. ²⁹May your eyes be open toward this temple night and day, this place of which you said, 'My Name shall be there,' so that you will hear the prayer your servant prays toward this place. ³⁰Hear the supplication of your servant and of your people Israel when they pray toward this place. Hear from heaven, your dwelling place, and when you hear, forgive.

³¹"When a man wrongs his neighbor and is required to take an oath and he comes and swears the oath before your altar in this temple, ³²then hear from heaven and act. Judge between your servants, condemning the guilty and bringing down on his own head what he has done. Declare the innocent not guilty, and so establish his innocence.

³³"When your people Israel have been defeated by an enemy because they have sinned against you, and when they turn back to you and confess your name, praying and making supplication to you in this temple, ³⁴then hear from heaven and forgive the sin of your people Israel and bring them back to the land you gave to their fathers.

³⁵"When the heavens are shut up and there is no rain because your people have sinned against you, and when they pray toward this place and confess your name and turn from their sin because you have afflicted them, ³⁶then hear from heaven and forgive the sin of your servants, your people Israel. Teach them the right way to live, and send rain on the land you gave your people for an inheritance.

³⁷"When famine or plague comes to the land, or blight or mildew, locusts or grasshoppers, or when an enemy besieges them in any of their cities, whatever disaster or disease may come, ³⁸and when a prayer or plea is made by any of your people Israel—each one aware of the afflictions of his own heart, and spreading out his hands toward this temple—³⁹then hear from heaven, your dwelling place. Forgive and act; deal with each

man according to all he does, since you know his heart (for you alone know the hearts of all men), ⁴⁰so that they will fear you all the time they live in the land you gave our fathers.

⁴¹"As for the foreigner who does not belong to your people Israel but has come from a distant land because of your name—⁴²for men will hear of your great name and your mighty hand and your outstretched arm—when he comes and prays toward this temple, ⁴³then hear from heaven, your dwelling place, and do whatever the foreigner asks of you, so that all the peoples of the earth may know your name and fear you, as do your own people Israel, and may know that this house I have built bears your Name.

⁴⁴"When your people go to war against their enemies, wherever you send them, and when they pray to the LORD toward the city you have chosen and the temple I have built for your Name, ⁴⁵then hear from heaven their prayer and their plea, and uphold their cause.

⁴⁶"When they sin against you—for there is no one who does not sin—and you become angry with them and give them over to the enemy, who takes them captive to his own land, far away or near; ⁴⁷and if they have a change of heart in the land where they are held captive, and repent and plead with you in the land of their conquerors and say, 'We have sinned, we have done wrong, we have acted wickedly'; ⁴⁸and if they turn back to you with all their heart and soul in the land of their enemies who took them captive, and pray to you toward the land you gave their fathers, toward the city you have chosen and the temple I have built for your Name; ⁴⁹then from heaven, your dwelling place, hear their prayer and their plea, and uphold their cause. ⁵⁰And forgive your people, who have sinned against you; forgive all the offenses they have committed against you, and cause their conquerors to show them mercy; ⁵¹for they are your people and your inheritance, whom you brought out of Egypt, out of that iron-smelting furnace.

⁵²"May your eyes be open to your servant's plea and to the plea of your people Israel, and may you listen to them whenever they cry out to you. ⁵³For you singled

them out from all the nations of the world to be your own inheritance, just as you declared through your servant Moses when you, O Sovereign LORD, brought our fathers out of Egypt."

⁵⁴When Solomon had finished all these prayers and supplications to the LORD, he rose from before the altar of the LORD, where he had been kneeling with his hands spread out toward heaven. ⁵⁵He stood and blessed the whole assembly of Israel in a loud voice, saying:

⁵⁶"Praise be to the LORD, who has given rest to his people Israel just as he promised. Not one word has failed of all the good promises he gave through his servant Moses. ⁵⁷May the LORD our God be with us as he was with our fathers; may he never leave us nor forsake us. ⁵⁸May he turn our hearts to him, to walk in all his ways and to keep the commands, decrees and regulations he gave our fathers. ⁵⁹And may these words of mine, which I have prayed before the LORD, be near to the LORD our God day and night, that he may uphold the cause of his servant and the cause of his people Israel according to each day's need, ⁶⁰so that all the peoples of the earth may know that the LORD is God and that there is no other. ⁶¹But your hearts must be fully committed to the LORD our God, to live by his decrees and obey his commands, as at this time."

⁶²Then the king and all Israel with him offered sacrifices before the LORD. ⁶³Solomon offered a sacrifice of fellowship offerings to the LORD: twenty-two thousand cattle and a hundred and twenty thousand sheep and goats. So the king and all the Israelites dedicated the temple of the LORD.

⁶⁴On that same day the king consecrated the middle part of the courtyard in front of the temple of the LORD, and there he offered burnt offerings, grain offerings and the fat of the fellowship offerings, because the bronze altar before the LORD was too small to hold the burnt offerings, the grain offerings and the fat of the fellowship offerings.

⁶⁵So Solomon observed the festival at that time, and all Israel with him—a vast assembly, people from Lebo Hamath to the Wadi of Egypt. They celebrated it before the LORD our God for seven days and seven days more, fourteen days in all.

⁶⁶On the following day he sent the people away. They blessed the king and then went home, joyful and glad in heart for all the good things the LORD had done for his servant David and his people Israel.

⁹:¹When Solomon had finished building the temple of the LORD and the royal palace, and had achieved all he had desired to do, ²the LORD appeared to him a second time, as he had appeared to him at Gibeon. ³The LORD said to him:

"I have heard the prayer and plea you have made before me; I have consecrated this temple, which you have built, by putting my Name there forever. My eyes and my heart will always be there.

⁴"As for you, if you walk before me in integrity of heart and uprightness, as David your father did, and do all I command and observe my decrees and laws, ⁵I will establish your royal throne over Israel forever, as I promised David your father when I said, 'You shall never fail to have a man on the throne of Israel.'

⁶"But if you or your sons turn away from me and do not observe the commands and decrees I have given you and go off to serve other gods and worship them, ⁷then I will cut off Israel from the land I have given them and will reject this temple I have consecrated for my Name. Israel will then become a byword and an object of ridicule among all peoples. ⁸And though this temple is now imposing, all who pass by will be appalled and will scoff and say, 'Why has the LORD done such a thing to this land and to this temple?' ⁹People will answer, 'Because they have forsaken the LORD their God, who brought their fathers out of Egypt, and have embraced other gods, worshiping and serving them—that is why the LORD brought all this disaster on them.'"

A LONG SECTION on the dedication of the temple has its focus on the theology of the Deuteronomistic History. The central theological point is that the building of the temple and its dedication continue the promise made to David. Though the temple is an innovation in place of worship, it does not change the fact or manner of the relationship between God and his people. The installation of the ark, the various addresses of Solomon, and a vision provide assurance of divine guidance and approval of Solomon's work.

The temple dedication is effected with the installation of the ark (7:51b–8:10). Continuity with David is established immediately after the concluding summary of Solomon's completion of all the work of the house of Yahweh (7:51a). Solomon brings to the temple treasury the devoted articles of David (v. 51b), the ark, and the tent that housed it with its sacred vessels (8:4). With the ark in place, the glory of Yahweh settles on the temple (8:10–11), just as it had at the completion of the tabernacle (cf. Ex. 40:34–35).

Solomon's oration may be divided into four distinct speeches.[1] The first is an ancient poem, which can be regarded as an invitation to Yahweh to take up residence in his new temple (8:12–13).[2] Solomon opens by recalling the divine patronage of David and announces the fulfillment of the promise of 2 Samuel 7 (1 Kings 8:14–21). The prayer of dedication considers seven circumstances in which the God of the covenant is obligated to his people (vv. 22–53).[3] An exhortation reviews God's acts of faithfulness to Israel in granting them rest (cf. 2 Sam. 7:1) and exhorts Israel to keep the commandments (1 Kings 8:56–61).

The temple dedication is completed with offerings (8:62–66); the peace offerings bring the community together in a common meal (v. 63). A second appearance of Yahweh in a dream appears as a reply to the inaugural prayer (9:1–9); the promise of the kingdom and continuance of the temple are conditioned by absolute allegiance to God. Compromise will bring exile; the temple ruins will be a shock and horror, a testimony to the consequences of violating the covenant oath.

Installation of the Ark (7:51b–8:13)

AFTER THE BUILDING'S completion, its function as a temple must be established. The articles dedicated to God by a vow are brought to its treasuries (7:51b), and the ark is placed in the Most Holy Place. David devoted to sacred use gifts he had received and the spoils of war (2 Sam. 8:10–11). He

---

1. Following the model of Jon Levenson, "From Temple to Synagogue: 1 Kings 8," in *Traditions in Transformation*, ed. B. Halpern and J. Levenson (Winona Lake, Ind.: Eisenbrauns, 1981), 143–66.

2. See Weinfeld, *Deuteronomy and the Deuteronomic School*, 35, who suggests this poem might be parallel to Gudea's invitation to Ningirsu and Bau to come and reside in the rebuilt temple of Eninnu. Hurowitz thinks it possible that the lines are the incipit of a royal inscription in the temple courtyard (*I Have Built You an Exalted House*, 295, n. 1).

3. The stipulations are stated in a series of conditional clauses answered by the consequent independent clause; see Bruce Waltke and M. O'Connor, *An Introduction to Biblical Hebrew Syntax* (Winona Lake, Ind.: Eisenbrauns, 1990), 38.2 (pp. 636–38).

also brought to Jerusalem the sacred chest called the "ark of the covenant of the LORD Almighty, who is enthroned between the cherubim" (1 Sam. 4:4; 2 Sam. 6:2; 1 Chron. 13:6). The "song of the ark" in the days of the wilderness gave testimony to its function (Num. 10:35–36). When the ark set out, Moses would say, "Rise up, O LORD! May your enemies be scattered," and when it halted he would say, "Return O LORD, to the countless thousands of Israel." When the priests bring the ark into Solomon's sanctuary, the glory of the divine presence takes possession of it (1 Kings 8:11), just as the glory accompanied it in the desert.

Ceremony is the means by which ordinary objects receive sacred significance. The prophets regularly ridiculed the worship of idols made by human hands (Isa. 40:19–20; Hab. 2:18–19), because the gods supposedly present in the idol either had no real existence or were insignificant before Yahweh in his holy temple (Hab. 2:20).

In ancient Near Eastern ideology, the idol did not represent the presence of the god until the appropriate ceremony had taken place. This was accomplished through an "opening (or washing) of the mouth" ceremony, which may have been a cultic reenactment of the birth of the deity in heaven.[4] It was not sufficient merely to fashion an image; while in the sculptor's workshop (the "gold house"), the work of human hands was thought to come alive making the organs serviceable.[5] The dark niche in the temple, accessible only to the priest, was the home of the image and the residence of the god. At festivals, such as the coronation of the monarch, the deity would "appear"; that is, its image would leave the sanctuary and be carried by priests in a shrine on a barque.[6] In Coptic the word "festival" was actually derived from the word "to appear." The appearance of the deity was the central element of the festival.

Solomon assembles the elders of Israel, the heads of the tribes, the ancestral chieftains to bring the ark up to the temple (8:1). Several groups of people are distinguished: the ordinary people are brought together with their leaders, while the priests actually carry the ark (8:2–3).

The ark processional takes place in the seventh month. Since the temple was completed in the eighth month (6:38), the inauguration of the temple seems to be almost a year later. Perhaps the feast began in the seventh month, but temple building and ceremonies actually conclude in the eighth month,

---

4. Edward M. Curtis, "Idol, Idolatry," *ABD*, 3:377.

5. A similar ritual was apparently also performed on mummies; Siegfried Morenz, *Egyptian Religion* (London: Methuen, 1973), 155. Rituals performed on statues are known through pyramid texts and annals.

6. Ibid., 89.

since the festival is extended an extra seven days, with dismissal on the eighth day (cf. vv. 65–66). It is also possible that there are calendar changes, or even different calendars, as was certainly true at later times. The name of the month (Ethanim, meaning "constant flow," referring to the fall rains) is an old Canaanite name (the seventh month is usually called by its Babylonian name, Tishri); the ancient name probably belongs to the historical record.

The ark and the "Tent of Meeting" are brought up to the temple—the former to be put in the sacred throne room, the latter to be stored with the other sacred items. "Tent of Meeting" is the name used in Exodus to indicate the function of the building (e.g., Ex. 27:21), which was otherwise simply referred to as the dwelling indicating the divine Presence (e.g., 26:1).[7] When the Israelites entered the land, the tabernacle was set up at Shiloh (Josh. 18:1), and it was apparently also at Gibeon (2 Chron. 1:3–4). When David conquered Jerusalem and made it the capital, he made this location the place of worship (2 Sam. 6:17). With the building of the temple that tabernacle has no further function but is kept as a sacred treasure.

When the ark is placed beneath the cherubs, the poles are still visible (1 Kings 8:8). The details are insufficient to understand what is meant; if the ark is positioned with the long side across the front of the throne as a footstool, the poles would be at right angles to the length of the building. In this case, the visibility of the poles must be an allusion to a veil, which stands in front of the throne itself to shield the presence of the holy King from the priest as he enters. Such a veil was a part of the Most Holy Place (Ex. 26:31–34). If this is what is described, the poles are visible at the edges of the curtain as the priest comes through the doors into the Most Holy Place.[8] Gray thinks the verse is saying that the poles can be seen as the priest enters, but the ends of the poles cannot be seen because of the narrowness of the door.[9] Cogan thinks the ark is placed in an east–west orientation so the poles are visible.[10] The significant point is that the poles, as a permanent fixture, indicate the presence of the ark (Ex. 25:15). The ark contains only the tablets of the covenant (cf. Ex. 25:21; Deut. 10:5). The pot of manna (Ex. 16:33) and the branch of Aaron that budded (Num. 17:10) are also sacred objects associated with the temple or Holy Place, but are never said to be actually inside the ark in the Old Testament.

---

7. The tent mentioned earlier in 1:39; 2:28 was specifically prepared by David to receive the ark (2 Sam. 6:17). It should not be identified with the Tent of Meeting in Exodus (cf. Cogan, *I Kings*, 162).

8. Montgomery, *The Books of Kings*, 188–89.

9. Gray, *I & II Kings*, 210.

10. Cogan, *I Kings*, 280.

The ark is set in the Most Holy Place in thick darkness. A poem recited by Solomon celebrates the significance of this "magnificent temple" (vv. 12–13). God's temple is the heavens (8:39, 43, 49), but the Most Holy Place with the ark and the cherubs now represent his heavenly temple. In ancient temples the cella of the shrine where the statue resided was referred to as the dwelling place of the god.

Patronage of David (8:14–21)

THE BLESSING OF the assembly begins with a declaration of the blessedness of God (vv. 14–15). Blessedness is an epithet of God, an acknowledgment that he is the source and dispenser of blessing. The praise addressed to God is actually an exhortation to the assembly. It makes explicit reference to the prophetic word to David concerning the divine priorities of kingdom and temple (vv. 16–19). The delay of temple building was not only a matter of making the transition to one central place of worship; another factor was that David had been continuously embroiled in war (1 Kings 5:17). The rest David achieved was not the time for an undertaking like that of Solomon. The blessedness of God is his fulfillment of the promise that the son of David was destined to build a temple as a focus for Israel's prayers and worship.

Solomon's words express the importance of the temple in the history of the nation and the role it will have in future relationships between God and his people. The presence of the temple assures the people that God has secured a royal dynasty for his people (cf. 2 Sam. 7:12–17). The temple is the place where the ark of God's covenant finds its rest (1 Kings 8:21). The ark represents the special legal bond uniting God and Israel.[11] The presence of the ark of the covenant makes the temple the focal point for prayer, no matter where the prayer is uttered. God's eyes will constantly be directed toward the temple; prayers directed there will be received by God in heaven. The temple is central from this time forward; it represents the covenant bond and the establishment of the promised kingdom.

Dedication Prayer (8:22–53)

SOLOMON TAKES A position at the altar in front of all the people and begins his prayer of dedication. Standing with one's hands spread toward heaven is a customary posture of prayer (v. 22), though Solomon is later said to have been kneeling (v. 54). The Chronicler reconciles the discrepancy by having Solomon stand and kneel, explaining that a special dais was created for the occasion (2 Chron. 6:12–13).

---

11. Hurowitz, *I Have Built You an Exalted House*, 290.

Kneeling and standing are both depicted as postures in prayer, often with palms opened.[12] Standing before a seated deity signifies an attitude of readiness for service; kneeling or sitting depicts humility in the presence of the deity. Kneeling worshipers can be said to stand up in reference to divine service.[13] Terms for posture in prayer signify disposition, not only the external position of the body. The open palm expresses petition (cf. Ex. 9:29).

Solomon prays before the assembled crowd in the presence of the altar (vv. 22, 54). Presumably this is the bronze altar in the court (v. 64), though it has not been previously mentioned in the furnishings of the temple made by Hiram. Japhet thinks that the prayer "before the altar of the LORD" means the altar in the inner court.[14] Her argument is that the Chronicler changes the phrase to "before the court [ᶜazārâ]," inferring that the prayer takes place in the enclosure around the outer altar, because it is inconceivable to a later generation that the crowds could have been inside the temple. It is possible that Kings referred to the outer court.

The prayer emphasizes the loyal faithfulness of God in his covenant with those who are faithful (v. 23). "Covenant of love" is a paraphrase for loyalty; the Hebrew word *ḥesed* is used primarily to describe loyalty to a commitment made by oath. Complete faithfulness is one expression of love, one that is most critical in all relationships. Divine loyalty is evident in the promise to David already fulfilled (v. 24); Solomon's prayer is that the divine promise might now be fulfilled in the continuity of David's descendants on the throne (vv. 25–26). The covenant blessing is conditional on the faithfulness of the covenant partners; that is Solomon's particular concern in this prayer, for there is no person who does not sin and incur divine wrath (v. 46). Solomon pleads for the temple to receive the divine mercy when the people pray.

The presence of God is not to be conceived as limited to the temple, since even the heavens cannot contain the Creator (v. 27); this is the place God has chosen for his "Name" (v. 29). A place for "the Name" is one of the distinguishing features of Deuteronomistic theology. Worship at other shrines continued as long as there was no one place for God to dwell (3:2); Solomon's purpose is to build a central temple for "the Name" of God (8:17, 19). The Name is present as a guarantor of God's intent to save; it is a declaration of his election of Jerusalem.[15] Solomon prays that "the eyes of the LORD" will

---

12. Keel, *Symbolism of the Biblical World*, 314–18 (figs. 421, 422, 426).

13. D. R. Ap-Thomas, "Notes on Some Terms Relating to Prayer," *VT* 6 (1956): 225–28.

14. Sara Japhet, *I & II Chronicles: A Commentary* (OTL; Louisville: Westminster John Knox, 1993), 590.

15. For a discussion of name theology as hypostasis ("the Name" as the mode of divine presence), see Ernst Würthwein, *Die Bücher der Könige: 1. Könige 1–16* (ATD 11.1; Göttingen: Vandenhoeck & Ruprecht, 1977), 102–3.

always be open to the place where petitions are made (vv. 29, 52). The temple gives testimony to the divine election of Jerusalem and the dynasty of David; it is the assurance that God is the guarantor of the covenant.

The sins Solomon mentions are all in relation to the curses that come with covenant violation. Yahweh had set before his people a blessing and a curse, life or death (Deut. 27:11–28:69; 30:15–18). Sin was defined fundamentally as a violation of the relationship established between two individuals. The covenant contained terms of a relationship with God and with fellow humans (5:1–22); its conditions were written on the tablets contained in the ark. Rupture of the terms of the relationship brought with it consequences of betrayed commitment.

In the prayer, seven petitions are intended to be representative of any future situation that the people of the covenant might encounter. These include a plea for justice (vv. 31–32), being struck by enemies (vv. 33–34), drought (vv. 35–36), famine and plague (vv. 37–40), mercy for the foreigner (vv. 41–43), war (vv. 44–45), and exile (vv. 46–53).

The first circumstance describes a dispute that cannot be resolved, leading the parties to give testimony by oath to determine guilt and innocence (vv. 31–32). A case of this type is theft, an example used in the giving of the covenant at Mount Sinai (Exod. 22:7–9). Someone might give a neighbor items for safekeeping (money or other valuables), which disappear. Justice is nothing less than full restoration. If the thief were caught, he would repay double; if no thief is found, guilt and innocence cannot be easily determined. In such cases oaths are taken before God and the person determined to be guilty pays double. Solomon's first request is that justice might function as it should in the determination of guilt and innocence.

The petitions of Solomon make specific reference to the curses of Deuteronomy. One of the curses of covenant disobedience is that Israel will be struck by her enemies (v. 33; cf. Deut. 28:7, 25). This happened at numerous times, one of the most notable being the siege of Sennacherib, in which he left Hezekiah like a bird in a cage and deported thousands of captives (2 Kings 18:13–16). In that instance the king, with the encouragement of the prophet Isaiah, took the threatening letters of the Rabshakeh, went to the temple, and prayed to the God who sits between the cherubs (19:14–15). Immediately the prophet delivered an oracle assuring Hezekiah that the Assyrians would be defeated (19:21–28).

There may also come a time when no rain falls, when the sky turns to bronze and the earth to iron (1 Kings 8:35–36; cf. Deut. 28:23–24). Elijah the prophet places this curse on Ahab in the contest against Baal, the rider of the clouds, showing that Yahweh is in charge of the rain (1 Kings 17:1; 18:41–46). Famine, plague, hot dry winds, blight, and swarming grasshoppers are typical accompaniments of drought (8:37; cf. Deut. 28:21–22). Enemies will attack their fortified cities (1 Kings 8:37; cf. Deut. 28:52). War and illness are both matters of individual as well as national concern (1 Kings 8:38). God is the One who knows the inner attitude (8:39), the one who can forgive the truly penitent.

Knowledge of the covenant is the wisdom of Israel in the presence of all the nations (Deut. 4:6–8). There will be those from other nations who voluntarily join the society of the covenant. They no less than any others are the object of Solomon's concern; his prayer is that they, in the same way as other Israelites, might find mercy before God (1 Kings 8:41–43). The nations may hold Yahweh in derision (Ps. 2:1–3), but this should not be taken as an absolute statement, only a general description of their rejection of God. Jonah's great fear was that the Ninevites might respond in repentance, a fear that in fact became real (Jonah 4:2). It is fine for God to be merciful and compassionate, as the story of the golden calf made clear, but for this to extend even to Nineveh was too much for the reluctant prophet, who would rather die.

Solomon's petition returns to the themes of war (8:44–45) and exile (8:46–53). In war the people experience God's judgment (v. 45). Solomon prays that God may "uphold their cause." This is an appropriate rendering of God's acting on their case to give them justice. God made a commitment to his people at the time of the Exodus (cf. v. 53), so it is only appropriate to pray that God will act as their advocate in war. However, it may be impossible for God to defend his people in war because of their covenant violation.

Exile is the consequence of a ruptured relationship with God. The passage plays on the words "take captive" (*šbh*) and "turn" (*šwb*). These two words become virtual homonyms in their various forms. Captors may take them captive (*šabûm šōbêhem*) into an enemy land (8:46); if in the land where they were taken captive (*nišbû*) they turn in their minds (*hēšîbû*), turn (*šābû*), and make confession to God (vv. 47–48), if they turn (*šabû*) wholeheartedly to the city God has chosen, God may hear and forgive (vv. 49–50). Defeat by enemies is an evidence of sin and failure (v. 46); the only recourse in captivity is to turn back to God in repentance, remembering his covenant and his promise. God redeemed his people and made them his special possession at Mount Sinai (v. 53; cf. Ex. 19:5–6). Solomon's prayer is that God's work may be completed.

The prophetic concerns of a total exile are evident in the final two petitions of this prayer. Though it is not evident in translation, these petitions are distinguished by distinct formulas introducing a temporal circumstance (vv. 44, 46) and the consequent petition for mercy (vv. 45, 49).[16] The situation

---

16. The circumstances are introduced by the particle *kî*; cf. Gesenius, *Hebrew Grammar*, par. 164*d*. The apodosis uses the simple consecutive perfect (ibid., par. 112*oo*) rather than the pronoun with the imperfect.

of defeat in war has already been contemplated (vv. 33–34); it is now repeated (v. 44), with allusion to the curse of Deuteronomy (Deut. 28:36–37) that God may send them and their king into foreign territory. A petition for time of exile (1 Kings 8:46–53) follows that of being sent away in war (vv. 44–45). The curse of exile is described at length in the covenant (Deut. 28:64–68).

There were many exiles in the history of Israel, but complete destruction of Jerusalem and its temple will be the greatest challenge to faith. Solomon's petitions look to the temple as a resource for faith; in a foreign land the people might remember the chosen place and pray (8:44, 48). The mention of land, city, and temple suggests a total destruction, not a partial exile (v. 48). The promise of the Exodus (v. 53) has to be reaffirmed. The petitions (vv. 45, 50) and the covenant promise (vv. 51–53) are particularly important in a time when the temple might no longer be present. Even then, prayer could be directed to God in heaven, who would hear and forgive.

Dedication Exhortation (8:54–61)

FOLLOWING THE LONG dedicatory prayer Solomon stands to bless the people by giving praise to God for fulfilling his Word (8:56–58). God has given rest to his people; "rest" expresses the fulfillment of the promise that Israel would possess the land and live securely (Deut. 12:9–10). Once the Israelites entered that rest, they were to worship at the place God would choose to place his Name (Deut. 12:11). The place of worship is not necessarily limited to one location; the primary concern of the covenant stipulations is that the people not worship at the Canaanite high places. At the same time the covenant requirement for worship clearly anticipates the ideal of one single location for worship. With the dedication of the temple that ideal has been achieved.

The prayer switches to the first person with two concluding petitions (8:59–61). Solomon asks for justice as each day requires, so that all nations may know the truth declared at Mount Sinai: There is but one Lord (v. 60; cf. Deut. 4:35, 39). Solomon in turn petitions for undivided loyalty from the people (v. 61).[17] Ironically, this prayer fails to be realized in Solomon's lifetime (11:4).

Dedication Sacrifices (8:62–66)

THE CLOSING SUMMARY of the temple dedication at the Festival of Booths brings the account back to the events of the introduction (cf. vv. 1–2).[18] Further details are added; representatives have gathered from north to south,

17. "But your hearts must be fully committed to the LORD" (NIV) obscures the jussive construction (cf. Gesenius, *Hebrew Grammar*, par. 112aa). "Let your hearts therefore be wholly true" (RSV) preserves the parallel with the previous petition (v. 59).

18. Long, *1 Kings*, 106.

from Hamath to the Egyptian boundary.[19] Hamath on the Orontes is the most northern boundary of Israel at its maximum extent (Josh. 13:5; 2 Kings 14:25), probably the limit of David's conquests in his wars with the Arameans (2 Sam. 8:3–10).[20] The celebrations for the dedication of the temple last seven days, with an additional seven days of celebration of the feast (cf. 2 Chron. 7:9–10). Sacrifices were offered during the time of the installation of the ark (1 Kings 8:5), and they are offered continuously throughout the celebrations of dedication and the time of the festival.

The sacrifices previously described as being without number (v. 5) are here enumerated in terms of oxen and sheep (v. 63). Communal peace offerings introduce the sacrifices and appear to be the central aspect of the dedication. The main function of these offerings is to provide food for the table; these sacrifices are for joyous occasions of celebration.[21] Worshipers and priests share the peace offerings, providing a bonding of the community and a celebration of the covenant (Lev. 7:11–15, 30–36). The blood, fat, and entrails of the peace offering are devoted to God (3:3–5). The quantity of these offerings, plus the burnt offerings and grain offerings given to God, is so great that the great bronze altar does not have sufficient capacity (1 Kings 8:64). The entire court was consecrated for the occasion.

Sacrifices were an essential part of the ritual in ancient temple dedications. The central event was the divine possession of the temple (cf. vv. 11–12), which was necessarily accompanied with great celebration and sacrifices for the occasion. The significance of the temple dedication is expressed in the language of its own culture. Hurowitz is able to cite numerous parallel examples from Mesopotamian literature.[22] Esarhaddon dedicated the Assur temple by placing the god in his eternal dais and offered countless sacrifices. His dignitaries and the people celebrated for three days in the temple courtyard.

Covenant Confirmation (9:1–9)

THE LONG DEDICATION prayer and time of celebration require some type of divine response. This response is given in a vision like the one Solomon previously received at Gibeon. In the vision Solomon receives assurance that God has heard his prayer; this is the place to which the prayers of the people may be directed.

---

19. See comments on 4:21 for a discussion of the Egyptian border.
20. The "entrance to Hamath," is the general area to the south of Hamath providing access to the Euphrates; *lᵉbô ḥᵃmāt* may be the modern Lebweh south of Hamath near the source of the Orontes.
21. Milgrom, *Leviticus 1–16*, 220–21.
22. Hurowitz, *I Have Built You an Exalted House*, 273–77.

It is somewhat surprising that the vision is less an affirmation of the initiatives of Solomon in temple building than a warning of the dangers of covenant failure. The alliance with Egypt and the marriage to Pharaoh's daughter potentially constitute a foreign dependence rather than trust in God (Deut. 17:16–17), but this point has not been explicit.[23] The warning may qualify the high praise given to Solomon, but it does not repudiate the highly complimentary perspective that has been given.[24]

This vision powerfully expresses the prophetic theology of covenant present throughout Kings. God has been faithful in fulfilling the promise that he has given (9:5). The promise of an eternal house of David is always contingent on absolute faithfulness of the Davidic kings (9:6–7). This is not to dismiss the possibility of grace and forgiveness, which are a prominent part of Solomon's prayer. The problem is to expect grace while persisting in compromise of the covenant. This is the warning of the vision, with specific attention to the fact that no splendor of building[25] or eloquence of prayer can serve as a substitute for obedience (v. 8).

The vision is also an exhortation, which becomes personal in its use of the second person plural (9:6–9). The demand for obedience not only pertains to the king, it pertains to the entire people. The king has particular responsibility as the leader of the people, the constant viewpoint of the books of Kings. The vision is addressed to him, but in its literary form it is addressed to every reader. The astonishment and scorn of the nations at the destruction of the temple serve a solemn warning to all.

THE TIME OF DEDICATION. Houses in ancient Israel were dedicated by taking up residence in them, probably amid festivities, rituals, and prayers. If someone had built a house but had not dedicated it (*ḥᵃnākô*), he was not to go to war but to go back to his house, lest he die in battle and another dedicate it (*yaḥnᵉkennû;* i.e., go to live in it; Deut. 20:5).[26] A curse contained the converse of this dedication: One would build a house

---

23. Provan may be overstating the case when he finds an implicit condemnation in Solomon's giving priority to the palace of Pharoah's daughter (*1 & 2 Kings*, 44–45).

24. Knoppers, *The Reign of Solomon and the Rise of Jeroboam*, 111.

25. "This temple is now imposing" (NIV) is the reading of the Masoretic text "most high" (*ᶜelyôn);* other versions read "this house will become a heap of ruins" (RSV), following the Old Latin, Syriac, and Targums, which read the Hebrew word "ruin"(*ᶜiyyîn*).

26. The feast of *Hanukkah,* the celebration of the dedication of the temple under the Maccabees, is a transliteration of the Hebrew word for "dedicate." For discussion, see Hurowitz, *I Have Built You an Exalted House,* 266–69.

but not live in it (28:30). In similar fashion the temple is dedicated (*wayyaḥnᵉkû ʾet bêt yhwh*) with the visible signs of glory indicating that God has taken up residence within it, accompanied by prayers, sacrifices, and celebrations (1 Kings 8:63). The placement of the ark in the Most Holy Place as the divine footstool is the most significant symbol of the divine Presence.

The dedication of the temple takes place during the major fall festival of Sukkoth (Booths or Tabernacles), a seven-day festival that required a pilgrimage to the central place of worship (Deut. 16:13–15). The seventh month marks the completion of the Israelite harvest, when landowners (heads of houses) could leave for a week without concern for fields or crops. It is probable, however, that there is a theological significance to celebration in the seventh month (possibly almost a year after the completion of the temple in the eighth month; cf. 1 Kings 6:38). Seven-day celebrations, either in the spring or in the fall, were associated with creation and temple building.[27]

Gudea, king of the Sumerian city of Lagash (twenty-second century B.C.) held a seven-day festival of dedication for the building of Eninnu, the temple of Ningirsu.[28] Closer to Solomon, the building of the palace for the rule of Baal was a process of seven days.[29] The tabernacle was set up at the time of the spring equinox (Ex. 40:2, 17); Jeroboam dedicated his temples during Tabernacles (1 Kings 12:32–33), and after the Exile the altar was reconstructed at the time of Tabernacles (Ezra 3:1–6). Though the Bible does not explicitly relate the festivals with creation, the associations are present and become the occasion for temple dedication.

The seven-day festivals in the spring and fall were in part a celebration of the new year, similar to other practices in the ancient Near East. In Bablyon the *akītu* Festival of the New Year took place in the first eleven days of the vernal (spring) month of Nisan. On the fourth day the creation epic of Babylon, the *Enuma Elish*, was read—perhaps in order to reactualize the primordial events of the poem. The New Year's festival was not just a calendrical milestone, but an actual renewal of the created world. Social, political, and natural chaos were closely associated and were never far away; the efficacious recitation of creation events brought hope for the coming New Year. The New Year's celebrations in Israel were also associated with harvest and renewal and implicitly with creation itself. Levenson cites a debate between Rabbi

---

27. Levenson, *Creation and the Persistence of Evil*, 78–80.

28. Gudea Cylinder B, col. xviii 19, and Statue B, col. vii 30. For a full discussion of Gudea's temple building and dedication, see Hurowitz, *I Have Built You an Exalted House*, 33–57. Cylinder B deals entirely with the dedication of the new temple.

29. An instructive and readable translation of the Baal epic of Ugarit is provided by Michael Coogan, ed., *Stories from Ancient Canaan* (Philadelphia: Westminster, 1978); for the temple building episode, see 103–4.

Eliezer and Rabbi Joshua (both did their most important teaching about A.D. 80–120) concerning whether creation occurred during the fall festival (Tishri) or spring (Nisan).[30]

> Rabbi Eliezer says, From what text do we know that it was in Tishri that the world was created? Because the Bible says, "And God said, 'Let the earth sprout vegetation: seed-bearing plants, fruit trees. . . .'" In what month does the earth put forth vegetation and the trees are full of fruit? You have to say that this is Tishri, and that period was the rainy season, so that the rains fell and caused vegetation to sprout, as the Bible says, "a flow would well up from the ground."
>
> Rabbi Joshua says, From what text do we know that it was in Nisan that the world was created? Because the Bible says, "The earth brought forth vegetation: seed-bearing plants . . . and trees of every kind." In what month is the earth full of vegetation and trees are bringing out fruit? You have to say that this is Nisan, and that period was the season when cattle and game and birds mate, as the Bible says, "The meadows are clothed with flocks, [the valleys mantled with grain]."

Name theology. The blessings and prayer spoken by Solomon express the theological significance that the temple is to have in the life of the nation. There are fourteen references to the name of God in Solomon's prayer. In Deuteronomistic theology, God chose the temple as the place where his Name was to dwell. This theology of "the Name" is often regarded as a "demythologization" of the divine Presence. Whereas the divine glory filling the temple is thought to show that God himself dwelt there (8:1–14), the corrective taught that only the divine Name dwelt in the temple. The prayer locates God in heaven, which is interpreted to make him transcendent, invulnerable to any catastrophe that might affect his temple. The Name was regarded as a hypostasis of God, the very essence of him being present.

The ark of the covenant rested there, not as the footstool of God present on his throne but as a representation of the special legal bonding uniting God and Israel.[31] The temple became the focal point for prayers; prayers uttered in the city, in the land of Israel, or outside the land were to be directed toward the temple. God's eyes would be directed to the place where his Name dwelt. Under this interpretation the Name theology served to teach

---

30. Levenson, *Creation and the Persistence of Evil,* 72–73.

31. Marc Z. Brettler, "Interpretation and Prayer: Notes on the Composition of 1 Kings 8:15–53," in *Minḥah le-Naḥum: Biblical and other Studies Presented to Nahum M. Sarna in Honour of his 70th Birthday,* ed. M. Brettler and M. Fishbane (JSOTSupp 154; Sheffield: Sheffield Academic Press, 1993), 18; Hurowitz, *I Have Built You an Exalted House,* 290.

---

the transcendence of God and the centralization of worship. Farmers or soldiers did not need to resort to a local high place, since they could direct their prayers in the direction of the temple where God would hear.

The significance of a place for God's Name to dwell must be examined more carefully. Idioms have to be understood within their own language context. In the English language the word "hand" connotes different things in various expressions. We may give someone a hand (for a job well done), give a hand to someone (for help needed), give a handout (to someone in need), or give a hand up (to help someone become self sufficient). Nothing in the expression itself can determine the significance of "hand," nor can the meaning of hand in one of these idioms be used to determine its meaning in another. The distinct meaning in each expression is not shared with the others; the idioms are in no sense synonymous.

The significance of biblical Name theology must be related to similar expressions in other documents. The expression "to place the name" in the Amarna Letters, as has long been noted in Hebrew lexicons, signifies possession; it is an idiom for ownership.[32] Just as the pharaoh owned Jerusalem by placing his name there (EA 287, 288), so Yahweh owned the temple. In a study of comparative linguistics and various biblical name idioms, R. de Vaux was able to show that the Name theology of Deuteronomy did not represent any transformation of the Israelite perception of the mode of divine Presence. He showed that there were four name idioms that were linked to the election formula of the biblical text: the place that Yahweh has chosen in order to establish his Name; the place where Yahweh has chosen to place his Name; the place over which the Name of Yahweh has been pronounced; the place where Yahweh has named his Name.[33] De Vaux thought other expressions, such as "a place for the Name to be" and "to build a house for the Name," did address the issue of God's presence in the sanctuary.

Six of the references to "Name" in 1 Kings 8 come from the formula "to build a temple for the Name of the LORD" (vv. 17, 18, 19, 20, 44, 48). These are transparently quotations of the promise to Solomon, in which David is assured that his son will build a house and establish the kingdom (2 Sam. 7:13). Solomon is that son, so it is not surprising that this passage should be

---

32. The Amarna Letters constitute part of the diplomatic correspondence of the Egyptian Pharaohs Amenhotep III (1398–1361) and Amenhotep IV (1369–1353). Over forty of the letters are correspondence with Assyria, Babylonia, Hatti, and Mitanni. About three hundred letters were written by Canaanite scribes who had learned cuneiform second or third hand and lived in Palestine, Phoenicia, and southern Syria.

33. R. de Vaux, "Le lieu que Yahwé a choisi pour y établir son nom," in *Das ferne und nahe Wort: Festschrift L. Rost zur Vollendung seines 70 Lebensjahres*, ed. F. Mass (Berlin: Alfred Töpelmann, 1967), 224.

quoted frequently. The use of "the Name" in this promise is to establish a memorial in order to perpetuate a reputation.[34]

The Hebrew expression "to make a name" (*ʿāśâ šēm*) has much the same significance as in English (cf. Gen. 11:4). In the context of the promise, David will not build a house for Yahweh; rather, Yahweh will build a house for David; God will establish his dynasty and establish his name like that of the great ones who are in the earth (2 Sam. 7:9). As a result, the heir of David's house (Solomon) is appointed to build a house (temple) for the Name (reputation) of Yahweh. The result, David acknowledges, is that God will make his own Name great forever (1 Kings 8:26–27). Normally a king established the legitimacy of his rule by building or refurbishing a temple to the god that had granted his power to rule. The presence of the temple will ensure the continuity of the divine Presence and the security of the throne.

David was denied this symbolic assurance, but in its place God granted a promise by oath as an assurance that his kingdom was secure forever. Building a house for the Name of God in the promise to David signified reputation, not divine Presence. The house built for David (the royal dynasty) and the house built for God (the temple) will perpetuate the renown of both.

The fame or reputation of Yahweh for those from outside of the land is also expressed three times in Solomon's prayer (1 Kings 8:41–43). Others outside of Israel will have heard of God's great works, his outstretched arm, and will pray toward the temple. Solomon also considers the times when the people will suffer the curse because of their sin and will make confession (acknowledgment) of the Name (vv. 33, 35). In these instances the Name is simply a euphemism for God himself.

In one occurrence in the prayer the Name idiom is used to express purpose involving the case of the foreigner (8:43): that all may know "that this house I have built bears your Name." This expression is well known as signifying ownership by means of transference of property (e.g., 2 Sam. 12:28). In Deuteronomy this idiom communicates the elect nature of the people of Israel, whose redeemed state stands as a testimony to the nations of Yahweh's power to save.[35] In Solomon's prayer it stands as a testimony to Yahweh's power to save even those foreigners who come to the temple because of God's reputation for saving acts.

The prayer of Solomon utilizes these Name idioms to make the temple the ultimate symbol of the essentials of the Israelite faith. Two times in the prayer Solomon says that the temple will be a house where God's Name will

---

34. Sandra Richter, *The Deuteronomistic History and the Name Theology: lᵉšakēn šᵉmô šām in the Bible and the Ancient Near East* (Berlin: de Gruyter, 2002), 69–75.

35. Ibid., 84–85.

be present (vv. 16, 29); this formula makes the temple the place that fulfills the Deuteronomic promise. The temple is the house that fulfills the Davidic promise; it is the elect place over which God's Name is called; it is the place of covenant preservation, where God's Name is acknowledged in confession and praise. The temple is the embodiment of the land promised to Israel and marked by God's Name. The temple is the ultimate symbol of God's relationship with Israel; it served to memorialize and perpetuate God's great deeds of redemption amidst Israel and the nations. It is testimony to the reputation of Yahweh. The association between the election of Jerusalem and the election of David is made explicit in God's choosing the temple as the place for Yahweh's Name.

Theology of rest. In a concluding blessing Solomon declares that God has given rest to his people and that not a word of all the good things promised through Moses his servant has failed (8:56). This important confession is articulated in Joshua; rest was the consequence of Israel's inheriting the land, the uncompromised fulfillment of all God promised (Josh. 21:43–45; 23:1, 14). The temple is declared to be God's resting place; following David's relentless effort to restore the ark to its proper place, God is called to rise at his resting place (Ps. 132:8). God in turn avers to David that Zion, the temple mount and the seat of the divine throne, will be his resting place for all time (132:13–14). Not only the temple, but the whole land can be declared to be the place of God's rest (95:11). The concept of the land being God's resting place prompts David to seek to build a temple for God (2 Sam. 7:1). The mercies shown to him are the foundation of the hope of the nation (Ps. 89:1–4).

Divine rest is interpreted in two ways: Sabbath is to be observed in order to remember that Israel was delivered from the house of bondage in Egypt (Deut. 5:15) and to declare that Yahweh made the heavens and earth in six days (Ex. 20:11). Divine rest at creation was a declaration that the forces of chaos had been conquered. This victory served to ensure that the sure mercies promised to David would endure forever:

> You crushed Rahab like one of the slain;
>   with your strong arm you scattered your enemies.
> The heavens are yours, and yours also the earth;
>   you founded the world and all that is in it.
> You created the north and the south;
>   Tabor and Hermon sing for joy at your name.
> Your arm is endued with power;
>   your hand is strong, your right hand exalted.
> Righteousness and justice are the foundation of your throne;
>   love and faithfulness go before you. (Ps. 89:10–15)

The two interpretations of the Sabbath are in reality the same. Divine rest at creation not only signified the conquest of disorder, but also the establishment of justice and righteousness, the love and loyalty that were part of the covenant mercies to David. Sabbath was the central focus of the creation story (Gen. 2:1–3). The rest of God demonstrated that creative activity was complete and that the work of the Creator was perfect; further, "the explicit portrayal of the creator sleeping functioned as a statement of the deity's status as the supreme ruler of heaven and earth. The ability to sleep undisturbed was the symbol of the deity's absolute dominion over the heavens and the earth and the underworld."[36] In ancient Near Eastern creation stories this dominion included the provision of freedom: the emancipation of slaves, the repatriation of captives, restoration of land to the original owners, and provision of land for the poor. In the same way the Psalms declare that justice and right belong to the peace of creation:

> For the word of the LORD is right and true;
>   he is faithful in all he does.
> The LORD loves righteousness and justice;
>   the earth is full of his unfailing love.
> By the word of the LORD were the heavens made,
>   their starry host by the breath of his mouth.
> He gathers the waters of the sea into jars;
>   he puts the deep into storehouses. (Ps. 33:4–7)

Israel is not only the benefactor of the divine rest of creation, but is also expected to be a participant in it. The Sabbath, the sabbatical year, and the Sabbath of sabbatical years, the Jubilee, recall the primordial rest in a form in which humans can share. The collective existence of Israel is to participate in the divine rest that consummates creation. The prophets make acts of benevolence a part of right and justice that God seeks. Jeremiah provides an itemized list of such deeds: "Do what is just and right. Rescue from the hand of his oppressor the one who has been robbed. Do no wrong or violence to the alien, the fatherless or the widow, and do not shed innocent blood in this place" (Jer. 22:3). Justice and compassion are not distinguished in the call for righteousness: "Administer true justice; show mercy and compassion to one another. Do not oppress the widow or the fatherless, the alien or the poor. In your hearts do not think evil of each other" (Zech. 7:9–10).

The divine response to Solomon's prayer in the vision affirms both the election of the royal house and Jerusalem, and the necessity of maintaining

---

36. Bernard F. Batto, "The Sleeping God: An Ancient Near Eastern Motif of Divine Sovereignty," *Bib* 68 (1987): 156, 164.

the divine rest. God has placed his Name on Jerusalem forever (1 Kings 9:3); this idiom is used exclusively of the chosen place of worship and audience.[37] Blessing and cursing elements present in ancient Near Eastern inscriptions were intended to preserve the building against the ravages of time and future neglect and to preserve the memory of the king. These elements are given a distinct function in Solomon's vision.[38] This vision does not concern itself with a future king who might find the building in ruins; the future of the temple and the dynasty depend on allegiance to God and his commandments.

The prophetic concept of God is unlike that of any other religion in ancient time. God is incomparable and incomprehensible, an unrivaled God that all nations are to know (8:60–61). This God demands absolute faithfulness, loyalty, and justice (Deut. 10:14–18). External symbols and rituals can never in themselves secure a relationship with such a God. Circumcision means nothing if there was not a "circumcision of the mind" (10:16), that loyal faithfulness to the covenant that shows complete trust and reverence of God. The external symbols are all designed to show that the God of the covenant cannot be comprehended. The little poem of Solomon (1 Kings 8:12–13) is a reminder of this fact; God dwells where none can see him, for a visible throne room distorts a comprehension of the King of kings.

The prophets believe they know God truly, since he has entered into covenant with them. But they never believe it is possible to know God fully. Finite humans can know their majestic God by analogy, such as the comparison to a king as one of his functions. Israel succumbed to the seduction of idolatry because they failed to understand the absolute nature of God.

The majestic and imposing structure of the temple with all its associated ritual can never be far from the minds of the covenant people. In addition to the regular daily ritual of the priests, in which burnt offering is made to God, lights are maintained, and incense is poured on the hot coals, there are the daily requirements for individual Israelites to observe the regulations of diet, cleanliness, and sacrifice for sins. There is always the danger that rituals become routine, performed without thought for their significance. The dedication of the temple is a reminder of this danger. Building the temple does not fulfill the requirements of the covenant, nor does the meticulous observance of all its associated ritual. All these are a means of confessing the holy and majestic God of the covenant and his involvement in every aspect of daily life.

---

37. For a summary of this idiom and its variants in Kings and Chronicles, see Richter, *The Deuteronomistic History and the Name Theology*, fig. 4 (pp. 50–52).

38. Hurowitz, *I Have Built You an Exalted House*, 304.

TEMPLE THEOLOGY FOR the church. Paul describes Christians as those who have access into the presence of God the Father through Christ; peace has been proclaimed to those far and near from God (Eph. 2:16–18). God has brought all peoples together as fellow citizens. The church is described as a temple built on the foundation of the apostles and prophets. Christ is the cornerstone; he gives shape to this new edifice that rises as a holy sanctuary (vv. 19–22). In Christ Christians are built together as the new dwelling of God in the Spirit.

The Christian calling has a fundamental continuity with the function of the temple as expressed in Solomon's dedication prayer. The temple was a manifestation of God's elective choice of David and Jerusalem (1 Kings 8:16, 29; 9:3). God chose Zion to be his possession, and David was chosen to be ruler over God's people Israel. The dedication prayer taught the ultimate sovereignty of God over both land and people. The temple was a focal point to which prayers could be made; God, whose temple was the heavens, would attend to his earthly temple night and day (vv. 28–29) and respond in mercy to the prayers of his people.

Solomon's mission in building the temple was to memorialize and perpetuate the great works of Yahweh, the kingdom anticipated in the promise to David (2 Sam. 7; 1 Kings 8:60). The calling of the Christian church is to show the purpose of God for creation as it is accomplished in his world. In the letter to the Ephesians, Paul begins with God's desires before the cosmos came into being. God planned a family through adoption in Jesus Christ according to the good pleasure of his will, to the praise of his glory (Eph. 1:3–6a). God in time worked out this mystery, to bring all things together in Christ, earthly and heavenly (1:9–10). Those called to Christ are destined according to the purpose of the one who does all things according to the intent of his will, to be to the praise of his glory (1:11–12).

The fear of the apostle Paul is that Christians might not understand the significance of their calling in the world. In Ephesians, therefore, Paul prays that those in Christ might understand the hope of the Christian:

> I pray also that the eyes of your heart may be enlightened in order that you may know the hope to which he has called you, the riches of his glorious inheritance in the saints, and his incomparably great power for us who believe. That power is like the working of his mighty strength, which he exerted in Christ when he raised him from the dead and seated him at his right hand in the heavenly realms, far above all rule and authority, power and dominion, and every title that can be given, not only in the present age but also in the one to come. And

God placed all things under his feet and appointed him to be head over everything for the church, which is his body, the fullness of him who fills everything in every way. (Eph. 1:18–23)

Paul's whole life was driven by the power of this divine purpose; this great calling belongs to all Christians just as much as it did to the apostle. Paul, the least of all saints by his own estimation, felt compelled to go to the ends of the earth in order to proclaim this great mystery that had been hidden in previous times (Eph. 3:8–9). For the apostle, God's purpose in his choice of David and Jerusalem was but a partial revelation of the greater goal for creation. The proclamation of Solomon was a deeply veiled mystery of what God was doing in the world. Only the death and resurrection of Christ demonstrate how God is drawing all humankind to himself; the purpose of God is to be found in the church, whose reach is universal.

God's plan for the church must be made known to the greatest of the powers and authorities, particularly those in opposition to God, including those that exercise authority beyond this earth. Again Paul prays fervently that believers might understand this great work within creation, which they represent:

> For this reason I kneel before the Father, from whom his whole family in heaven and on earth derives its name. I pray that out of his glorious riches he may strengthen you with power through his Spirit in your inner being, so that Christ may dwell in your hearts through faith. And I pray that you, being rooted and established in love, may have power, together with all the saints, to grasp how wide and long and high and may be filled to the measure of all the fullness of God.[39] (Eph. 3:14–19)

Belonging to the church demands that Christians learn to live in accordance with that calling, learning harmony and unity with each other (Eph. 4:1–3). Fundamentally, living as a Christian requires a new way of thinking (4:17–24). Outside of Christ human values are governed by self-interest, the deceit of greed; the apostle calls believers back to the renewal of the original image, righteousness and holiness as they have learned it in Christ (4:22–24). All divisions of humanity are bridged in Christ; all races and classes are brought into harmony, as they are transformed in knowledge according to God's image (Col. 3:10–11).

Solomon called on God to show mercy to all who call on him, including those who did not belong to the nation (1 Kings 8:41–43). Israel must

---

39. The Greek does not say that Paul's prayer is to understand the love of Christ (vv. 18–19); it appears to be more comprehensive, of all that God has done in the fulfilling his purpose in Christ. All this may be described as love revealed in Christ.

represent God's kingdom in this world. Paul sees this kingdom as present across all national, ethnic, and cultural boundaries, through the transformation of mind. The peace of Christ is to rule in the lives of all those called to be one with him. The presence of the church is profoundly significant of that which the temple of Solomon is but a shadow. The temple declared God's ownership of land and his covenant with Israel; the church rises as God's holy temple in bringing all peoples in harmony as one household.

Discord within the church is a travesty. There is but one Spirit, one hope of the Christian calling, one God and Father of all, over all, through all, in all (Eph. 4:5–6). Failure to demonstrate this unity within the Christian community is a denial of the essence of the church; church leadership is to equip church members so they achieve the fullness of Christ in maturity (4:11–13). The temple declared the universality of God's grace and love. One who was wronged could find justice (1 Kings 8:31–32); those from a faraway land who had heard of the fame of Yahweh could seek mercy (vv. 41–43); Israel exiled in a distant land could pray and God would hear (vv. 48–50).

The church is to manifest the peace of Christ everywhere that it has a presence. Dissension within the church betrays its calling. Solomon acknowledged that failure would happen to all and they would suffer the consequences (1 Kings 8:46); he prayed that God's purpose for his inheritance might be preserved (vv. 51–53). The church, as the representation of God's mercy and love, must learn to forgive and show mercy just as they have received it (Eph. 4:32; 5:1–2).

Creation theology. With the dedication of the temple God had granted rest according to all that he had promised (1 Kings 8:56). The rest of the people of Israel testified to God's sovereign control of creation and fulfillment of redemption in the lives of the people of Israel. The celebration of the temple dedication on the festival of the New Year testified to the order and beauty of creation, as well as the progress of redemption. Christians need to celebrate both; Christians celebrate redemption on Sunday services and on special events such as Easter, but they often lack a corresponding confession to the beauty of creation. The restoration of creation is an important theme in relation to redemption. The apostle consciously links creation coming to its rest with the redemption of God's people:

> For the creation was subjected to frustration, not by its own choice, but by the will of the one who subjected it, in hope that the creation itself will be liberated from its bondage to decay and brought into the glorious freedom of the children of God. (Rom. 8:20–21)

The exhortation to live in the hope of a future redemption in which creation itself will be liberated from its present bondage is also a call to celebrate the beauty of creation in praise of the Creator. Christians of all people must be concerned about appropriately exercising dominion in the environment in which they live. Their responsibility, as those renewed in mind in the image of the Creator, is to live in his creation in a way that will respect the beauty of creation to the glory of the Creator.

Joseph Sittler declared the theological responsibility to ecological consciousness long before the first Earth Day celebration. He urged that environmental ethics should take its cue from the first question of the Westminster Catechism in the Calvinist tradition. "What is the chief end of man [and woman]? To glorify God and to enjoy him forever." The motivation for attention to environmental concerns is the delight of all the manifestations of God's glory in the natural world around us. Christian concern for the environment should not begin with the paralyzing fear of environmental catastrophe (as eminent as it might be), nor with crippling guilt over the human abuse of creation (as dreadful as it might be), but with the joy of living in God's world. Drawing on Augustine's distinction between what humans can "use" and what they can "enjoy," Sittler argues that in matters of ecological responsibility delight is the basis of right use.

The call to celebrate the beauty of creation was a central theme in the theology of Jonathan Edwards. It was his conviction that the natural world is a communication of God's glory that should fill us all with desire. Edward Parley goes so far as to say that in the work of Jonathan Edwards, "beauty is more central and more pervasive than in any other text in the history of Christian theology."[40] Humans have a particular capacity for joy at the marvel of creation and have a supreme role in the task of giving God glory along with the rest of the natural world (Ps. 8). Edwards understood the Christian to have a renewed capacity to sense the marvel of creation as one of the graces of receiving salvation.

Lane believes that in the thought of Edwards, divine grace included a renewed spiritual capacity to understand the magnificence of the natural world and a more integrated ability to perceive reality through the ordinary channels of sense experience.

> For Jonathan Edwards, creation functions as a school of desire, training regenerate human beings in the intimate sensory apprehension of God's glory mirrored in the beauty of the world. Humans are to respond, in turn, by articulating that glory, bringing it to full consciousness, and by replicating God's own disposition to communicate

---

40. Edward Parley, *Faith and Beauty: A Theological Aesthetic* (Burlington, Vt.: Ashgate, 2001), 43.

beauty as they extend the act of beautifying to the world around them. In other words, the natural world enlarges the human capacity to sense the fullness of God's beauty and the appreciation of that beauty subsequently leads to ethical action. Nature teaches us God's beauty which in turn drives us to its continual replication in time and space.[41]

The annual observance of Earth Day may be an occasion to remind Christians that their faith calls them to make confession of their Creator, as Israel did in the great fall festival of the seventh month, and of the rest that they have come to enjoy in Christ. Janet Schaeffler suggests that it might be good for us to become backyard biologists.[42] In your own backyard, mark off an area six feet square, preferably including a bush, a tree, or flowers, along with grass or bare soil. Make use of a magnifying glass, notebooks, and pencils to record the wonder of nature in this small area of God's creation. Be as thorough as you can. What plants do you find? What kinds of animals? What evidence do you find of creatures that may have passed through this area?

Another suggestion Schaeffler makes is to greet the rising sun. Find a place where you can see the sunrise clearly (this does require getting up before the sun). Each time you see a new color in the sky, thank God for something beautiful. Continue with new and different ideas until the sun is shining brightly, and then head to breakfast with a smile of thanksgiving on your face. (Because looking directly at the sun can damage vision, be sure to look at the sky around the sun or use approved sun blockers.) Or gather the family together to catch the setting sun, the sun's "closing act." Talk about how the power of the sun reflects the greatness of God.

Marvel too at the wonders of the night; go on a stargazing trip with your family, it can be in your own backyard.[43] Family celebrations should also include ceremony; this might include reading aloud the story of creation (Gen. 1:1–2:4) or a poem from Scripture that thanks God for the beauty of the earth (Ps. 8; 100; 150) or for the marvels of creation (Job 38:1–21; 22–38) and its creatures (38:39–39:30). Song, dance, poetry, or some other form of art can be used to express praise, or compose a prayer that expresses gratitude for the wonders of creation.

Justice and social order. For Israel, order within creation included justice; proper social order was an essential aspect of dominion over creation

---

41. Lane, "Jonathan Edwards on Beauty, Desire, and the Sensory World," 46.

42. Janet Schaeffler, "Summer Family Faith Suggestions to Celebrate Creation," *Catechist*, 37/7 (April/May 2004): 46.

43. The Star Gazer site at www.jackstargazer.com, a companion to the PBS program of the same name, offers tips on what to look for at various times of the year. The magazine *Sky and Telescope* (www.skyandtelescope.com) has a useful site with a weekly listing of sky highlights and a sky chart that you can customize to your viewing location.

as the representatives of God. The essence of the covenant oath was to act with justice. Repeatedly Solomon in his prayer asks that God remember his oath with Israel and act with justice (1 Kings 8:49, 59). Solomon does not ask that God "maintain their cause" (KJV, NRSV), which suggests partiality to Israel and misrepresents God; Yahweh was known for justice (Deut. 32:4; Isa. 61:8).

Covenant justice required just actions within society and between nations (Deut. 10:17–21). Justice began with fairness to individual people; the temple was the place of justice in the settlement of disputes between individuals (1 Kings 8:31–32). The rest of Israel was a sign of justice and peace; in the doxology of his prayer Solomon made God's faithfulness the basis of covenant fidelity (8:56–58). Sabbath observance was the essential sign of creation rest, observance of justice, and conformity to the covenant. Isaiah made it the central observance of all who would be joined to God and his people (Isa. 56:4–8). As Isaiah declared, the temple was a house of prayer for all people who loved the name of the Lord.

Sabbath observance moved from Saturday to Sunday for good early Christian reasons, but modern Christians must not neglect Sabbath. Martin Marty makes reference to Jewish interpretation in his exhortation to Christians to keep the Sabbath as a call to justice.[44] In Israel the climax of Sabbath rest was reached in the Jubilee year (š'nat bayyôbēl), times for enacting social justice and freeing the earth from human exploitation. The Sabbaths are to be times of release from attachments and habits, addictions and idolatries. Marty quotes Rabbi Abraham Joshua Heschel (who later marched alongside Martin Luther King Jr. against racism and the Vietnam War), who wrote following the Holocaust and Hiroshima, both grotesque mockeries of creation:

> To set apart one day a week for freedom, a day on which we would not use the instruments which have been so easily turned into weapons of destruction, a day for being with ourselves, a day of detachment from the vulgar, of independence of external obligations, a day on which we use no money ... on which [humanity] avows [its] independence of that which is the world's chief idol ... a day of armistice in the economic struggle with our fellow [humans] and the forces of nature—is there any institution that holds out a greater hope for humanity's progress than the Sabbath?[45]

---

44. Martin E. Marty, "Keep Holy the Sabbath," *Context* 36/3 (March 2004): 6–7. He quotes Rabbi Arthur Waskow, in *Take Back Your Time*, ed. J. DeGraff (San Francisco: Barrett-Koehler, 2003).

45. This is a quotation from Heschel's *The Sabbath* (New York: Noonday, 1951), 28.

Image of God and idolatry. For modern Christians, just as for Old Testament saints, constant vigilance is required to fulfill the purpose of mortals in showing the glory of God within creation, his true temple. The predisposition of Israel was to reduce God to the level of the gods of other religions (1 Kings 9:6–9); the exalted temple, representing the God of all nations, would then become the ridicule of the nations. Justice for Israel was to command the reverence of all nations in giving honor to Yahweh alone (8:43, 60). Abandoning God happened as soon as he was equated with gods of human conception (9:9). The same kind of reduction happens in contemporary thought. The term *God* is often used to refer to the impersonal (God does not communicate) or deistic (God has no involvement with earthly events). Any concept of God that is impersonal or deistic is not a biblical concept of God and is nothing more than human philosophizing.

The Creator of the universe made his representative image (humans) personal just as he is a person. A personal relationship assumes an awareness of self, an ability to expect respect and commitment from other individuals, and a willingness to show respect by keeping commitments. It is these two qualities that are emphasized about God. God has chosen to mediate his rule of the world through people. David and his people had a special function in this rule, because they were to make the name of God great (8:16, 25, 43, 60; 9:4–5). The church is the successor to the purpose of God in choosing David and Jerusalem; the calling of the church is to make the name of Christ known among all nations so that every knee may bow before him (Phil. 2:11). That honor is not given when God is made something less than a person in his sovereignty over creation, or when Christ is made less than God in choosing to live as a human.

Idolatry as expressed in the vision to Solomon has its origin in the mind. It is not so much a denial of God as a distortion, fashioning God in the ways of other religions or philosophies. Such idolatries may lead to worship of creation rather than the Creator, or they may lead to greed and the destruction of creation. Unhappily, such idolatries have been all too common among confessing Christians, just as they were in Israel. Solomon's prayers for forgiveness for such failures are most pertinent.

The renewal of the mind created after the image of God is not complete when a decision is made to believe in Christ. Putting off the old and putting on the new is a continual process (Eph. 4:17–24). Learning to know God must begin with his revelation of himself, uncompromised by other philosophies. Theology is of critical importance, as human thought is applied to understanding God in contemporary context. As in Israel, the danger is that those who would follow God may be self-deceived, so they do not even realize when they have become idolatrous.

The seduction of idolatry is evident in values destructive of creation or community. The symptoms of an inadequate concept of God are seen in the behavior of believers. Honor is given to God by delighting in his creation; wonder at the beauty of the earth is the basis for the right use of its resources. Exploitation of the earth for any reason is failure to know God, a sign of idolatry. Order in creation includes respect and honor to other individuals, the exercise of justice in all relationships. Equity must be a priority if respect is to be given to the Creator whose purpose is to bring rest to creation.

Indifference to justice is idolatry, a misrepresentation of who God is as a person. Idolatry is quite readily identified in serving mammon, but it is no less real in disrespect of any of God's creation or wrong done to other people. The evident examples of idolatry must not obscure the more subtle ways in which it is manifested. Christians must live with a renewed mind, clearly distinguished from the values of the "other nations" who do not know God.

1 Kings 9:10–10:29

A T THE END of twenty years, during which Solomon built these two buildings—the temple of the LORD and the royal palace—[11]King Solomon gave twenty towns in Galilee to Hiram king of Tyre, because Hiram had supplied him with all the cedar and pine and gold he wanted. [12]But when Hiram went from Tyre to see the towns that Solomon had given him, he was not pleased with them. [13]"What kind of towns are these you have given me, my brother?" he asked. And he called them the Land of Cabul, a name they have to this day. [14]Now Hiram had sent to the king 120 talents of gold.

[15]Here is the account of the forced labor King Solomon conscripted to build the LORD's temple, his own palace, the supporting terraces, the wall of Jerusalem, and Hazor, Megiddo and Gezer. [16](Pharaoh king of Egypt had attacked and captured Gezer. He had set it on fire. He killed its Canaanite inhabitants and then gave it as a wedding gift to his daughter, Solomon's wife. [17]And Solomon rebuilt Gezer.) He built up Lower Beth Horon, [18]Baalath, and Tadmor in the desert, within his land, [19]as well as all his store cities and the towns for his chariots and for his horses—whatever he desired to build in Jerusalem, in Lebanon and throughout all the territory he ruled.

[20]All the people left from the Amorites, Hittites, Perizzites, Hivites and Jebusites (these peoples were not Israelites), [21]that is, their descendants remaining in the land, whom the Israelites could not exterminate—these Solomon conscripted for his slave labor force, as it is to this day. [22]But Solomon did not make slaves of any of the Israelites; they were his fighting men, his government officials, his officers, his captains, and the commanders of his chariots and charioteers. [23]They were also the chief officials in charge of Solomon's projects—550 officials supervising the men who did the work.

[24]After Pharaoh's daughter had come up from the City of David to the palace Solomon had built for her, he constructed the supporting terraces.

[25]Three times a year Solomon sacrificed burnt offerings and fellowship offerings on the altar he had built for the LORD,

burning incense before the LORD along with them, and so fulfilled the temple obligations.

²⁶King Solomon also built ships at Ezion Geber, which is
near Elath in Edom, on the shore of the Red Sea. ²⁷And Hiram
sent his men—sailors who knew the sea—to serve in the fleet
with Solomon's men. ²⁸They sailed to Ophir and brought back
420 talents of gold, which they delivered to King Solomon.

¹⁰:¹When the queen of Sheba heard about the fame of
Solomon and his relation to the name of the LORD, she came
to test him with hard questions. ²Arriving at Jerusalem with a
very great caravan—with camels carrying spices, large quantities of gold, and precious stones—she came to Solomon and
talked with him about all that she had on her mind. ³Solomon
answered all her questions; nothing was too hard for the king
to explain to her. ⁴When the queen of Sheba saw all the wisdom of Solomon and the palace he had built, ⁵the food on his
table, the seating of his officials, the attending servants in
their robes, his cupbearers, and the burnt offerings he made at
the temple of the LORD, she was overwhelmed.

⁶She said to the king, "The report I heard in my own country about your achievements and your wisdom is true. ⁷But I
did not believe these things until I came and saw with my own
eyes. Indeed, not even half was told me; in wisdom and wealth
you have far exceeded the report I heard. ⁸How happy your
men must be! How happy your officials, who continually stand
before you and hear your wisdom! ⁹Praise be to the LORD
your God, who has delighted in you and placed you on the
throne of Israel. Because of the LORD's eternal love for Israel,
he has made you king, to maintain justice and righteousness."

¹⁰And she gave the king 120 talents of gold, large quantities of spices, and precious stones. Never again were so many
spices brought in as those the queen of Sheba gave to King
Solomon.

¹¹(Hiram's ships brought gold from Ophir; and from there
they brought great cargoes of almugwood and precious
stones. ¹²The king used the almugwood to make supports for
the temple of the LORD and for the royal palace, and to make
harps and lyres for the musicians. So much almugwood has
never been imported or seen since that day.)

¹³King Solomon gave the queen of Sheba all she desired
and asked for, besides what he had given her out of his royal

bounty. Then she left and returned with her retinue to her own country.

[14]The weight of the gold that Solomon received yearly was 666 talents, [15]not including the revenues from merchants and traders and from all the Arabian kings and the governors of the land.

[16]King Solomon made two hundred large shields of hammered gold; six hundred bekas of gold went into each shield. [17]He also made three hundred small shields of hammered gold, with three minas of gold in each shield. The king put them in the Palace of the Forest of Lebanon.

[18]Then the king made a great throne inlaid with ivory and overlaid with fine gold. [19]The throne had six steps, and its back had a rounded top. On both sides of the seat were armrests, with a lion standing beside each of them. [20]Twelve lions stood on the six steps, one at either end of each step. Nothing like it had ever been made for any other kingdom. [21]All King Solomon's goblets were gold, and all the household articles in the Palace of the Forest of Lebanon were pure gold. Nothing was made of silver, because silver was considered of little value in Solomon's days. [22]The king had a fleet of trading ships at sea along with the ships of Hiram. Once every three years it returned, carrying gold, silver and ivory, and apes and baboons.

[23]King Solomon was greater in riches and wisdom than all the other kings of the earth. [24]The whole world sought audience with Solomon to hear the wisdom God had put in his heart. [25]Year after year, everyone who came brought a gift—articles of silver and gold, robes, weapons and spices, and horses and mules.

[26]Solomon accumulated chariots and horses; he had fourteen hundred chariots and twelve thousand horses, which he kept in the chariot cities and also with him in Jerusalem. [27]The king made silver as common in Jerusalem as stones, and cedar as plentiful as sycamore-fig trees in the foothills. [28]Solomon's horses were imported from Egypt and from Kue—the royal merchants purchased them from Kue. [29]They imported a chariot from Egypt for six hundred shekels of silver, and a horse for a hundred and fifty. They also exported them to all the kings of the Hittites and of the Arameans.

Original Meaning

THE TEMPLE IS the focus of the grandeur of Solomon's kingdom. The account of that kingdom began with a description of its administration (4:1–34), listing the officials and governors, the provisions of the kingdom, and details on Solomon's wisdom. The concluding sections on the kingdom describe Solomon's vast trading relations and international influence (9:26–10:25); they end with summary statements of his military power, prosperity, and extensive trade relations (10:26–29).

The theme of the temple is continued in chapter 9, as is evident by a second notation that Solomon completed all the work of the house (9:25b). Though the content of 9:10–25 may seem to be disparate, it is all related to building projects with the temple as its focal point.[1] The displeasure of Hiram in his contract with Solomon (vv. 10–14) is related to the provision of materials for the royal buildings. A second section (vv. 15–23) reports on the labor provisions; it lists the various locations of building projects in Jerusalem and elsewhere (vv. 15–19), the divisions of labor (vv. 20–22), and finally the supervisors of the labor force (v. 23). This section concludes with a summary notation on the function of palace and temple (vv. 24–25).

The unit on Solomon's trade relations and international influence begins and ends with a report on his mercantile arrangements with Hiram (9:26–28; 10:22–25). The various references to Hiram have different points of interest; the first has to do with trade for gold (9:26–28), the second is part of the queen of Sheba story (10:11–12), and the third refers to a partnership in a trading empire to the west (10:22). The whole section on Solomon's grandeur has a focus on gold (9:28; 10:14–21; 22), which is complemented by his fame for wisdom in the queen of Sheba account. A concluding summary emphasizes Solomon's incomparable wealth and wisdom (10:23–25), tying together the threads that are interwoven throughout. The final summary reports (10:26–29) make Solomon's empire so grand that precious metals and articles are regarded as common household items.

Labor Provisions for Building Projects (9:10–25)

HIRAM WAS AN active partner in the building of the temple. Solomon's payment of cities to Hiram (9:10–14) is complementary to the report on labor provisions for temple building (cf. 9:15). At first there was harmony between Hiram and Solomon (5:7, 12), but as often happens in commercial relations, dissatisfaction develops. The building of the temple and Solomon's palaces takes a total of twenty years (6:38; 7:1). As part of the settlement at the end

---

1. Long, *1 Kings*, 111–17.

of that time Solomon allots to Hiram twenty settlements in Galilee. Hiram is displeased with them, so he named them Cabul. The digression provides an etymology for the name of a well-known territory, but the meaning of the name is not known.

It is not clear why Solomon gives territory to Hiram. Most translations make the cities a payment for timber and gold (e.g., NIV, RSV), but this creates two problems. Payment for building materials and wages of the workers was made in annual contributions of grain and oil (5:11); there is no indication Solomon has defaulted on his contract. Further, why does Hiram give Solomon gold if he felt cheated in a payment made by allotment of property (9:14)?

Solomon's payment of twenty settlements is not expressed as a sequel to the material contributions of Hiram (9:11). The temporal adverb introducing his compensation of cities in Galilee (ʾāz) expresses no chronological sequence with the preceding.[2] The main clause explains Hiram's displeasure when the transactions are completed at the end of twenty years (v. 12). This dissatisfaction is not a comment on the desirability of the property, which was fertile agricultural land readily annexed to Tyre. Hiram apparently thinks twenty settlements in northern Galilee are a miserly remuneration for the amount of gold given. The weight of a talent varied in different systems and times, but at minimum Hiram has given Solomon several tons of gold.

The city of Cabul is named in the boundary description of Asher (Josh. 19:27). An Arabic village called Kabul is located in lower Galilee, about eight miles south east of Akko. An historical, geographical, and chronological survey of the area of southern Galilee by Zvi Gal located a series of sites that correspond to the biblical description of the boundary between Asher and Zebulun.[3] The biblical Cabul may be identified with an Iron Age site called "the ruin of the head of the olive" (*Hurvat Rosh Zayit*), located on a narrow ridge less than a mile from the Arabic village. The site is an impressive fort, apparently built by Hiram to serve as an administrative center for the region.[4] Storage rooms contained hundreds of storage jars; carbonized remains show some were used to distribute grain; other jars were probably used to distribute olive oil and wine.

The account of conscripted labor (vv. 15–23) has a long introduction (vv. 15–19), which enumerates the various projects that form a part of

---

2. Verse 11 is asyndetic (usual conjunctions with the preceding verse are not present), making it parenthetical to the main thought.

3. Zvi Gal, "Khirbet Ros Zayit—Biblical Cabul: A Historical-Geographical Case," *BA* 53 (1990): 88–97.

4. Zvi Gal, "Cabul: A Royal Gift Found," *BAR* 19/2 (1993): 39–42.

Solomon's building activities. These include the fortifications of Jerusalem and strategic points in the provinces. Fortifications in Jerusalem include "supporting terraces" (v. 15, NIV), likely meaning embankments filled in to support retaining walls and buttresses for the buildings on the steep slopes of the southeast hill (the city of David).

Six cities are named as part of the fortifications: Hazor, Meggido, Gezer, Lower Beth Horon, Baalath, and Tamar. These form a line of defense from north to south. Hazor was a major northern fortification conquered by Joshua (Josh. 11:1), southwest of Lake Huleh. Megiddo was a fortress guarding one of the passes to the valley of Jezreel. Gezer was in the Judean foothills and served as protection against the Philistines to the south and west. Lower Beth Horon, to the northwest of Jerusalem, protected the road from the coast to the mountains west of Jordan. "Tadmor in the desert, within his land" (NIV) paraphrases a faulty text. Tadmor is found in the versions and in Chronicles (cf. 2 Chron. 8:4), but the Masoretic text reads Tamar, a city in Judah, located in the desert south of the Dead Sea on the border with Edom. This must be the location of the city intended in a north to south listing of fortifications.[5] Baalath might be Bealoth (cf. Josh. 15:24), but its identity remains uncertain.

The mention of Gezer includes a note about Solomon's relationship with the Egyptians (v. 16). Gezer is one of the cities named in the Merneptah Stele, a commemoration of Egyptian victories in Canaan that includes the earliest reference to Israel outside the Bible. It was in the interest of the Egyptians to control the Philistines, just as it was to Solomon. It would make perfectly good sense for the Egyptians to put Gezer under control of a loyal ally in Canaan. The list concludes with an inclusive reference to all centers developed for administrative and defensive purposes (v. 19). Excavations at cities like Lachish have revealed large buildings with long, narrow rooms that served for storage.

Conscripted labor that Solomon uses to maintain his building projects consists of native Canaanite peoples who lived as subordinates after the Conquest (vv. 20–21). These are to be distinguished from the temporary conscriptions that Solomon laid on the Israelites to construct the buildings (5:13). The Israelites were never subject to continuous servitude. They serve as military officers in charge of soldiers and chariotry.

A concluding summary on the temple (vv. 23–25) notes three disparate items: the number of the chief supervisors, the move of Pharaoh's daughter, and the three annual festivals (cf. Ex. 23:14–17). The offerings Solomon

---

5. Tadmor is the later Palmyra, an oasis city in Syria along the desert trade routes with Mesopotamia.

makes are not to suggest he is acting as a priest, but rather to show he makes provision for daily and yearly rituals of the temple. The translation "fulfilled the temple obligations" (v. 25b) interprets the Hebrew *šlm* in the context of temple maintenance; normally the verb conveys nothing more than the idea of completion (cf. 7:51).[6] "So he finished the house" (RSV) is the logical conclusion to the topic of temple building.

International Fame and Fortune (9:26–10:25)

IN ADDITION TO internal administration of his kingdom, Solomon has extensive involvement in foreign affairs. These include trade with distant lands, which he carries out in cooperation with Hiram (9:26–28; 10:22). Solomon's seaport is located at Ezion Geber on the Gulf of Aqaba (9:26); the length of time the ships travel is an indication of both the distance they go and they difficulties of the journey (10:22). The Phoenicians were experienced mariners, whose vocation was to ply the seas. They had ships and expertise, so it is natural for Solomon to rely on his alliance with Hiram to obtain imports. Gold, fine wood, and ivory are named as some of the chief imported items that were necessary for the artifacts of the temple and palace complex.

Ophir (9:28) is traditionally thought to be southwest Arabia. It is associated with the Queen of Sheba (10:11–12) and is located there in the Table of Nations (Gen. 10:28–29). Mention of ivory and exotic animals (10:22) has led to a search for Ophir in India or east Africa; Josephus locates Ophir in India. Tarshish[7] has been located on the coast of the Red Sea in Africa, an area rich with precious stones of the same name (e.g., Ex. 28:20; 39:13; Ezek. 28:13). Tarshish is also the name of a port on the Mediterranean known from Assyrian inscriptions and other biblical references (Gen. 10:4–5; Jonah 1:3); it is probably to be identified with Tharsis in southwestern Spain. It was colonized by the Phoenicians and was well known for its metals and precious stones.

"Ships of Tarshish" designates the cargo these ships carry rather than the destiny of their travels.[8] The expression extends to indicate the kind of ship used to transport the cargo. This type of ship was distinguished by its strength, large size, and peculiar shape, which allowed them to sail long distances in the open sea (cf. Ps. 48:7; Isa. 2:16; Ezek. 27:25). The shipbuilders of Tyre had access to many types of wood and imported materials for sails

6. Würthwein, *1. Könige 1–16*, 114.

7. Note that "fleet of trading ships" in 10:22 is literally "ships of Tarshish" (cf. NIV note).

8. Isaac Kalimi, "Tarshish," in *The Eerdmans Dictionary of the Bible*, ed. D. N. Freedman (Grand Rapids: Eerdmans, 2000), 1276.

and ornamentation.[9] Solomon used magnificent "ships of Tarshish" for voyages to fetch the treasures of Ophir.

The identity of the imports is uncertain (10:22). "Ivory" (NIV) translates a rare term (*šenhabbîm*), which is associated with a Sanskrit word meaning "elephant." This identification is suspicious in a language that regularly uses the common word *šēn* for ivory (v. 18). The reference may be to ebony (*hobnîm*; cf. Ezek. 27:15), a black wood highly valued for carving from trees in southern India and Sri Lanka. "Apes" (NIV) translates the Hebrew *qōpîm*, which appears in late Akkadian but may ultimately be derived from Egypt. The final item (*tûkkiyyîm*) may be a loanword of Indian origin meaning "peacocks" (RSV). "Baboons" (NIV) is based on an Egyptian etymology.

The account of the queen of Sheba further illustrates the fame, wisdom, and wealth of Solomon (10:1–13). A distinguished monarch as far away as southern Arabia is impressed by reports of his accomplishments. Southwestern Arabia was an important territory, controlling trade routes between India, east Africa, and the Mediterranean. The queen of Sheba controlled an enormous amount of wealth, as indicated in the size of the caravan that attended her (v. 2). She comes to test the wisdom of Solomon with riddles (v. 1), obscure metaphorical references like the kind Samson used to test the Philistines (cf. Judg. 14:14). His answers and accomplishments are enough to take away her breath (1 Kings 10:5).

Solomon's wealth is indicated by the enormous gifts the queen needs to give in order to be significant (v. 10); the gold alone is equivalent to what Solomon has received from Hiram (cf. 9:14). The ships of Hiram also bring almugwood (10:11), used to make supports for the temple (possibly pillars or balustrades) and musical instruments. Almug is well known in ancient writings (Ugaritic and Akkadian); its exact identity is uncertain, but it was a hard reddish brown wood. With the mention of Hiram, wealth is stressed as much as wisdom in the visit of the queen of Sheba.

The gold Solomon receives in one year may have been the income in one particular year rather than an annual income (10:14). Solomon also collects taxes from foreign traders and local merchants (v. 15). "Arabian kings" are probably merchant princes who use the routes from Edom to Damascus, and "governors of the land" are district officials.

Solomon makes two hundred large shields covered with gold and three hundred small shields (10:16–17).[10] Large shields were body length, possibly

---

9. Katzenstein, *The History of Tyre*, 112–13, 161.

10. Ornamental and ceremonial shields are well attested in Syria and Assyria; for discussion and illustrations see Alan Millard, "King Solomon's Shields," in *Scripture and Other Artifacts: Essays on the Bible and Archaeology in Honor of Philip J. King*, ed. Michael Coogan et al. (Louisville: Westminster John Knox, 1994), 286–95.

three sided; small shields were a light protection worn on the arm. The weight of gold in each small shield is three "minas," equal to about 150 "shekels" (just over three and a half pounds, just under two kilos). The weight measure of the large shields is not given, but shekel is likely to be inferred, a weight four times that of the small shields. The "bekah" (NIV, 10:16) is only half the weight of the shekel, which would have been double the small shield. Guards display the shields as the king goes up to the temple (cf. 14:27–28), a sight that appropriately impresses even the queen of Sheba.

The throne of Solomon is a work of grandeur. The six steps may indicate that the throne is situated on a platform, which constitutes the seventh step (10:19). Babylonian temple towers were built in seven stages to represent the entire cosmos; perhaps the ascent to the throne provided assurance that order in the world will prevail. Lion figures stand at the sides of each step and beside each armrest (vv. 19–20). The throne has ivory inlays and is covered with gold.

Prosperity and Security in Jerusalem (10:26–29)

THE WEALTH OF Solomon provides for a strong military, security, and spectacular luxury in the capital city. The enumeration of horses, chariots, and military cities summarizes information given earlier (4:26; 9:19). Solomon obtains his horses from Kue, located on the Cappadocian seacoast in Asia Minor near the Taurus Mountains (10:28). The Masoretic text says that Solomon also imports horses from Egypt, but the text is doubtful. The area of *muṣri* in Anatolia just north of the Taurus has likely been confused with the term for Egypt (*miṣrāyîm*) in the Hebrew text (cf. NIV). This area was rich in wood for chariots and was known as the home of horse breeders. Egypt was not a land for timber and was not known for the export of horses.

Solomon's merchants buy horses and chariots and trade them along the way with the Hittite and Aramean kings (10:29). Egypt may have been a recipient in the trade of horses and chariots. Jones suggests that Solomon may have controlled trade between Egypt and Syria.[11] As in the previous verse, the text may only be referring to the area of Cappadocia known as *muṣri*.

Bridging Contexts

THE GLORIFICATION OF GOD. An important phrase is included in the introduction of the visit of the queen of Sheba: She has heard of the fame of Solomon "for the sake of the name of the

---

11. Jones, *1 & 2 Kings*, 1:231. Making Egypt the recipient of military exports would require a change in preposition in the Masoretic text. Biblical references to reliance on Egypt for horses and chariots are all considerably later than Solomon (e.g., Isa. 31:1–3), and the numbers are much smaller than the thousands of animals recorded in Assyrian texts.

LORD" (lit. trans., 10:1). Though the phrase is often regarded as secondary, it expresses well the sentiments of the author.[12] The queen is compelled to acknowledge the fulfillment of God's promise to Solomon (cf. 3:12–13); his wisdom and great fortune are without parallel. The Gibeonites express a similar disposition in coming to Joshua (Josh. 9:9); Jeremiah says that the revival of Jerusalem will bring all the nations to acknowledge the fame of Yahweh (Jer. 3:17).

The kingdom of Solomon gives testimony to God's choice of David and Jerusalem; that kingdom becomes the occasion for the whole world to seek Solomon and bring him tribute (10:24–25). Their homage gives honor to God; the success of Solomon is entirely God's work. The concluding summary of Solomon's wealth and wisdom reinforces the accolades of the queen of Sheba, drawing to a conclusion the theme that has characterized his rule (10:23–25; cf. 10:6–7 and 4:29, 34). The world comes to seek Solomon, but the kingdom of Solomon makes the name of God known to the world.

The tribute brought to Solomon is often compared to the pompous lists of booty in Assyrian inscriptions.[13] Those lists boast of the achievements of the monarch in the rapacious pillaging undertaken in expansion of Assyrian control. But the greatness of Solomon's kingdom is not a tribute to Solomon and his military exploits. Unlike Assyrian annals, the memory of Solomon is not to immortalize a great king. The narrative will go on to make Solomon responsible for the failure of his kingdom. The greatness of Solomon is integrated with his building of the temple, particularly by the repeated reference to Hiram. Hiram was involved in providing materials, a skilled labor force, and a trade alliance that gives the empire international status. The temple is confirmation that God has fulfilled his promise to David in establishing his throne. The objective of the account is to show the kingdom established by God is not inferior to the greatest empires of its time.

Gold and other opulence. Royal status and divine favor are demonstrated by wealth and international influence. Gold is a constant topic of discussion; it serves to introduce the involvement of Hiram (9:14; 10:11, 22) and

---

12. See *BHS*. The phrase is not found in the corresponding passage in Chronicles (2 Chron. 9:1). It is syntactically somewhat harsh, but is certainly comprehensible. "His relation to the name of the LORD" (NIV) does not fully express the intent of the phrase; the kingdom of Solomon gave fame to God as the source of Solomon's wisdom and fortune.

13. An example is the list of booty taken from Jehu in the famous Black Obelisk: silver, gold, a golden bowl, a golden goblet, golden cups, golden buckets, tin, a staff of the king's hand, and javelins (Younger, *The Context of Scripture*, 2.113F). This is juxtaposed to a register from Gilzānu, a territory near Lake Urmia, paying similar tribute. By means of merism, the obelisk portrays booty from a vast territory from the north of Nineveh to the southern points of Judah.

links together a series of short notes on Solomon's wealth. Solomon receives annual revenues of gold (10:14–15); gold shields hang in the great meeting hall (vv. 16–17); gold covers the ivory throne (vv. 18–20). Gold is so plentiful that silver is considered inferior in the days of Solomon (v. 21). The amount of gold received in one year is approximately equal to the total of the payment of Hiram, gold brought by the ships of Hiram, and the enormous gift of the queen of Sheba (cf. 9:14, 28; 10:10).

The amounts of gold attributed to Solomon are fantastic, but there is evidence of enormous amounts of gold in ancient empires.[14] The claim that all Solomon's drinking vessels are gold (10:21) is unexceptional by ancient standards. Kings of the cultured Mesopotamian city of Ur, more than fifteen hundred years before Solomon (ca. 2600 B.C.), had palaces adorned with golden cups and dishes. Elegant specimens were discovered by Sir Leonard Wooley in excavations of the Royal Cemetery in 1927–31. The Cairo Museum boasts gold-plated furniture of ancient Egyptian kingdoms. Gold-plated furniture was buried with Queen Hetepheres, mother of Cheops, builder of the great pyramid (ca. 2600 B.C.).

The tomb of King Tutankhamun, who was buried about 1331 B.C., contained a carved wooden chair covered almost completely with gold. It still retains inlays of glass and colored stones. Gold was beaten into animal heads on the front of the armrests and claw feet on the chair legs. It gleams today much like the great throne of Solomon once did. Ivory was also common in the ancient world and was often covered with gold in an ostentatious display of wealth. In a tomb at Salamis, on the southern coast of Cyprus, a throne and a bed covered with ivory veneers were found smashed in a tomb. Thousands of ivory fragments found in the Assyrian palaces at Nimrud (ancient Kalah) are still being catalogued, drawn, and illustrated. Gold overlay on ivory surfaces has been preserved.

Gold was not limited to items of tableware and furniture. Pharaohs of the new kingdom period of Egypt (ca. 1550–1150 B.C.) were particularly lavish. Amenophis III (ca. 1386–1349) honored the great god Amun with a temple at Thebes that was "plated with gold throughout, its floor adorned with silver, (and) all its portals with electrum."[15]

Actual examples of large buildings covered with gold to substantiate the boasts of kings do not exist, but the evidence for them does. Pierre Lacau, a French scholar, examined exhaustively the pillars set up by Tuthmosis III (ca.

---

14. Examples with photographs are provided by Alan Millard, "Does the Bible Exaggerate King Solomon's Golden Wealth," *BAR* 15/3 (1989): 20–29, 30, 34.

15. James H. Breasted, *Ancient Records of Egypt* II (Chicago: Univ. of Chicago Press, 1907), par. 883.

1479–1425 B.C.) in front of the Temple of the Sacred Boat at Karnak (Thebes).[16] Each pillar is carved to resemble bundles of papyrus reed set on a flat round base. There are twelve pillars, each over eleven feet high, but textual descriptions indicate that an additional fourteen pillars, each about fifty-three feet from base to capital, were present in another hall. Narrow horizontal slits on the base and vertical slits around each column appear to have been designed to anchor sheets of gold that once covered these pillars. Elsewhere in the temple the stones of doorways, shrines, and obelisks all have slits or nail holes used to secure gold sheeting.

It is presumptuous to assume that biblical descriptions have no basis in reality. The biblical writers provide descriptions of gold items and weights of gold that are in accord with other records of those times. King Osorkon I of Egypt (921 B.C.) records a gift to the gods of 383 tons of gold and silver. Fragments on pillars in a temple at Bubastis (in the eastern Nile delta) show itemized lists of gifts to each god and goddess of Egypt and tally the vast gold treasure.[17] Such records are astounding and can no longer be verified, but care was taken to trace even small amounts of gold coming into official royal depots or storehouses.

The taxes Solomon receives are not regarded as negligible in comparison to the twenty-five tons of gold received in one year (10:14–15). Various grades of gold are often mentioned, and weights of gold given may have included the entire object. Though the amounts of gold attributed to Solomon cannot be determined with factual objectivity, the descriptions fit that of great kings of his time.

The enormous wealth of Solomon is sometimes regarded as exaggeration made to serve the purpose of the narrative; Solomon's "accruing of bullion, vessels, and other valuable artifacts in Jerusalem is not intended to be credible, but incredible."[18] The fashioning of shields and the king's stepped throne are examples of extravagant display of excessive wealth. Solomon, it is alleged, grew to be a figure larger than life as the ideal of his kingdom was perpetuated through the centuries.

DeVries provides a detailed analysis of the record of temple building (6:2–7:51) in which he distinguishes earlier records of measurements and removes all material he considers to be narrative embellishment. He asserts that once the original records are recovered, "it will be seen that 'Jerusalem the Golden' is a figment of someone's imagination."[19] Such literary conclusions

---

16. These pillars are illustrated by Millard, "King Solomon's Golden Wealth," 27–28.

17. These are illustrated by Kenneth A. Kitchen, "Where Did Solomon's Gold Go?" *BAR* 15/3 (1989): 30.

18. Knoppers, *The Reign of Solomon and the Rise of Jeroboam*, 130–31.

19. DeVries, *1 Kings*, 96.

are based on historical assessments. Davies helps clarify this issue: "The question of *historicity*—namely, how much use the text is to a modern historian operating with a rationalistic view of things as having either happened or not (or with quantifiable degrees of probability)—is a matter not for literary criticism but for historical criticism."[20]

The problem here is that historical criticism does not have the option of objectivity; data and methods open to the historian are subjective, even to the point that it is considered impossible to make any statements about the past that may be labeled true or false.[21] Such extreme skepticism is a discredit to the work of ancient historians. Information regarding Solomon's kingdom has been drawn from official records (11:41). These records had to be sufficiently precise to allow a vast empire to function. Early historians did distinguish between events, myths, legends, and deliberate invention in writing history. If the wealth of Solomon had no basis in reality, it could not have served to establish the claim of divine fulfillment, as it was obviously intended to do.

Solomon and Hiram. Historical records do leave diverse information for the historian; the texts describing Solomon's kingdom have some striking differences. A difficult example is the relationship that Solomon has with Hiram. The Hebrew text makes Solomon an independent king who establishes concord with Hiram because of a previous alliance with David. The LXX of 1 Kings 5:1 has quite a different statement: "And Hiram king of Tyre sent his servants to anoint Solomon in place of David his father, for Hiram always loved David." This account seems to make Solomon a subordinate to Hiram, not the architect of an alliance that became a vast empire. The historian seeking to judiciously assimilate all information in reconstructing the past cannot simply dismiss such a statement. At times the textual critic may despair in trying to explain the origin of differing texts.[22] But it is probable that the Greek is a corruption of the Hebrew, since later versions support the accepted Hebrew text.[23]

However preservation of such information must be accounted for; it is possible this version independently preserves another perspective on the relationship. The LXX reading of Solomon being subordinate to Hiram can be supported textually as a true reading.[24] Evaluation of this Greek version

---

20. Philip Davies, "Method and Madness: Some Remarks on Doing History with the Bible," *JBL* 114 (1995): 701.

21. Ibid., 703.

22. Katzenstein says, "We are unable to offer an explanation of this version" (*The History of Tyre*, 97).

23. Burney, *Notes on the Hebrew Text of the Books of Kings*, 53.

24. Jeffrey K. Kaun, "Third Kingdoms 5.1 and Israelite-Tyrian Relations during the Reign of Solomon," *JSOT* 46 (1990): 32–35.

---

requires a reexamination of other statements about the relationship between Hiram and Solomon.

The agreement between Hiram and Solomon results in substantial yearly obligations for Solomon. Hiram does determine certain conditions of the agreement (5:9–11), and the agreement is to be financially beneficial for Hiram because he is a superior in his dealing with Solomon.[25] The obligations of Solomon to Hiram may have included taxation, unmentioned by the accounts. Hiram probably controls the shipping operations as part of his commercial operations, with benefit to Solomon as a subordinate partner. None of this reduces the status of the empire of Solomon. The biblical description is not given as a full account of Solomon's international relations. The preservation of the Greek reading is an example of how the ancients retained data they had at their disposal, even when it was apparently contradictory.

The ideal king. A prophetic work such as Kings does not pretend to be modern history in its goals and purposes, nor is it inaccurate in its presentation. A comparison of Solomon in the account in Kings with that in Chronicles shows how much the objective of the writer determines the profile of his work.[26] The purpose of Kings is not to glorify Solomon; it is to show how the intention of God is at work in the rise and demise of the nation. The summary statement of Solomon's greatness is followed by a second conclusion (10:26–29). Reading this report together with the condemnation of Solomon in chapter 11 suggests that it is a negative evaluation of Solomon's reign against the ideal of the covenant king (cf. Deut. 17:16–17).[27] Peace in Jerusalem is not achieved by military might alone, nor can all the horses of Cappadocia preserve it. Silver as readily available as common stones and majestic cedars as plentiful as the ordinary sycamore of the Shephelah will not in themselves bring prosperity and justice to the people.

The prophet Zechariah has quite a different description of the great king who will come to Jerusalem to bring the peace security they so deeply desire:

> Rejoice greatly, O Daughter of Zion!
> Shout, Daughter of Jerusalem!
> See, your king comes to you,
> righteous and having salvation,
> gentle and riding on a donkey,
> on a colt, the foal of a donkey.

---

25. Ibid., 36–40.

26. See Raymond B. Dillard, "The Chronicler's Solomon," *WTJ* 43 (1981): 289–300.

27. Cogan points out that R. Isaac already made this connection in *b. Sanh.* 21b (*1 Kings*, 323).

I will take away the chariots from Ephraim
    and the war-horses from Jerusalem,
    and the battle bow will be broken.
He will proclaim peace to the nations.
    His rule will extend from sea to sea
    and from the River to the ends of the earth. (Zech. 9:9–10)

The humble king of Jerusalem does not arrive on a war steed or with military power. The connection of this king with Solomon is not to be lost. His rule will extend from sea to sea and from the river to the ends of the earth, just like the rule of the ideal king in the psalm attributed to Solomon (cf. Ps. 72:8). Solomon represents the kingdom of God as the greatest of all kingdoms. More than ostentation of gold, the ruler over God's people is to manifest justice and equity:

Endow the king with your justice, O God,
    the royal son with your righteousness.
He will judge your people in righteousness,
    your afflicted ones with justice.
The mountains will bring prosperity to the people,
    the hills the fruit of righteousness. (Ps. 72:1–3)

Presumably a king with the wealth and international reputation attributed to Solomon would be in the most advantageous position to bring prosperity and justice to the people. Ironically, in some ways the opposite is the case. The glory of Solomon places a heavy burden on his people, and his primary concerns are not those of justice. Initially Solomon has the wisdom that generates wealth and fame, but he does not retain the wisdom that is characterized by covenant loyalty, the wisdom of learning the fear of Yahweh. The ideal of King Solomon (Ps. 72) is only a memory to what his reign should have been.

WEALTH, ITS SIGNIFICANCE, **and its use.** Wealth is never an individual matter; no one can achieve wealth in isolation from a community or a broad work environment; people with wealth should always honor God as the Giver. We must live our Christian lives with these principles in mind. The use of money is fundamental to living out Christian values. The story of Solomon has important lessons on God's view of wealth, its significance, and its use.

Solomon's wealth was not his personally, nor were the riches he accumulated in Jerusalem an example of God's desire for individual wealth. In Kings the most significant theological statements are often found in speeches. The famed wisdom and wealth of Solomon that draw the attention of the distant queen of Sheba are not for the personal benefit or reputation of Solomon, but for the reputation of his God, as expressed by the queen herself: "Praise be to the LORD your God, who has delighted in you and placed you on the throne of Israel. Because of the LORD's eternal love for Israel, he has made you king, to maintain justice and righteousness" (10:9). God's reputation depends on Solomon's serving the entire nation with his wealth. To his credit, this is said to have been accomplished: "During Solomon's lifetime Judah and Israel, from Dan to Beersheba, lived in safety, each man under his own vine and fig tree" (4:25).

What control should individuals exercise over wealth? To what extent is wealth a personal achievement, and to what extent is it the product of the structure of a whole society? Should Bill Gates, the developer of the world's dominant computer operating system, be personally entitled to his forty billion dollars? Should corporate executives earn multimillions if their leadership earns shareholders billions in profits? The covenant of Deuteronomy contains warnings to the Israelites, not just to the Israelite king, about the accumulation of wealth in their new land:

> Be careful that you do not forget the LORD your God.... Otherwise, when you eat and are satisfied, when you build fine houses and settle down, and when your herds and flocks grow large and your silver and gold increase ... then your heart will become proud and you will forget the LORD your God.... You may say to yourself, "My power and the strength of my hands have produced this wealth for me." But remember the LORD your God, for he it is who gives you the ability to produce wealth, and so confirms the covenant, which he swore to your forefathers, as it is today. (Deut. 8:11–18)

The wealth of Israel was not the personal possession of individual Israelites, as though they earned it themselves, nor was it the possession of the king who made their national economy possible. According to Shmuel of Sokhokhow, a Hasidic rabbi of the early twentieth century, Israel endured slavery in Egypt in order to learn that wealth came from God, not from the Nile River.[28] God granted wealth in Israel the same way as he provided manna in the desert. The Israelites were to remember that they were unable to become independently wealthy. The very expression is an oxymoron. Theologically, resources are a gift from God; sociologically, they are received as a community and are a product of the collective work of individuals.

---

28. Cited by Lawrence Bush and Jeffry Dekro, "Who Owns Wealth?" *Tikkun* 14/2 (March/April 1999): 31.

Bush and Dekro refer to Albert Einstein in establishing the *"torah* of money" principle imbedded in the theology that the earth belongs to the Lord.[29] The paradigmatic "genius" of the twentieth century was firm in his insistence that "in science ... the work of the individual is so bound up with that of his scientific predecessors and contemporaries that it appears almost as an impersonal product of his generation."[30] The invention of a bright young computer scientist is not really his own; it is impossible without previous centuries of knowledge, skills, and resources. The scientist harvests the fruit of the labors of many before him.

The story of Solomon shows that wealth is a blessing from God. This does not validate what has come to be called the "prosperity gospel." The promise of this type of theology is that God desires wealth for each individual that can be generated by acts of faith and piety. It is often featured in the opulence of television personalities. Humorist Ray Stevens asks, "Would Jesus wear a Rolex on his television show?" The preacher had so inspired him he had already begun to write the check when the question came to his mind. Luxury can be successful in making financial appeals; evidence of material success inspires a desire to become a part of it. Viewers want to believe they can be as wealthy as the preacher; they need the preacher to be wealthy, and they respond by giving to be sure he remains wealthy.

Theologically the question of Stevens addresses a vital issue. A wealthy ruler came to Jesus with the question of what he needed to do to inherit eternal life (Mark 10:17–25). In answer to the question Jesus cites six social and ethical responsibilities. When the young man declares that he has observed these from the time he was young, Jesus shows special love for him and responds by telling him to sell what he has and give it to the poor. His wealth is a barrier to the good he desires; it has become his god.

The story continues with a lesson to the disciples. Peter observes that they have done exactly what Jesus urged the wealthy man to do. Jesus responds by assuring them that they have not given up anything that will not be restored to them one hundred times in this life, and in the world to come they will have eternal life. The blessing of wealth cannot be the end for which service is rendered to God. Service is rendered to the glory of God alone; God provides abundance to those who seek to magnify his name.

The story of the rich young ruler is usually interpreted as addressing the question of faith. Cranfield attempts to resolve the conflict between selling

---

29. A *torah* is an interpretation of scripture applied to a particular situation (e.g., Haggai 2:11).

30. Bush and Dekro, "Who Owns Wealth?" 31 (in reference to an article by Ronald W. Clark entitled "Einstein, Life and Times").

one's goods and salvation by faith alone. Selling one's goods and giving the proceeds to the poor is a meritorious act that will earn treasure in heaven (Mark 10:21); the reward is God's undeserved gift to those who are willing to receive it. But trust, willingness to accept God's gift as a gift, cannot help but show itself by outward tokens. Jesus, by commanding the man to show the tokens that are the outward expression of faith, is really appealing to him to have faith.[31] Faith always involves questions of use of wealth. Trust is difficult for the wealthy—more difficult than for a camel to go through the eye of a needle. The response of the disciples indicates that the words of Jesus have application beyond the particular case of the rich young ruler. Jesus is saying something about the use of possessions for all those who trust him.

The response of Jesus to the disciples after the encounter with the rich ruler indicates that all believers must make a decision regarding community loyalty. Those who follow Jesus become part of a new kinship group that represents the kingdom of God (Mark 10:29–30). Jesus assures Peter that both his relational and material needs will be satisfied in the context of the family of which he is a part. As argued by Hellerman:

> The promise to Peter assumes as its background a constellation of family values which characterized the patrilineal kinship groups of Mediterranean antiquity. Among these values were some tenaciously held convictions about the place of material goods in the family setting. Specifically, the sharing of material resources constituted a characteristic practice of Mediterranean family systems.[32]

The requirement that the young ruler give his goods to the poor is given in the context of the followers of Jesus; the obligation is not to disperse wealth indiscriminately to all who are poor but to invest it in those who are the followers of Jesus who have devoted their lives to his kingdom. The rich ruler has his place in a highly stratified class structure that isolates the wealthy elite from the agrarian peasants and the urban poor. Roman society was replicated in villages, cities, and provinces, in which class stratification was supported by an inequitable distribution of landed wealth. The difficulty for the rich ruler is to abandon the privileged place he has in larger society to join the community of the kingdom where such privilege does not exist. It is this choice of faith that leaves him grieved and troubled; it is a choice that must be made by all believers in all circumstances. The choice of joining

31. C. E. B. Cranfield, *The Gospel According to Saint Mark* (CGTC; Cambridge: Cambridge Univ. Press, 1959), 330.

32. Joseph H. Hellerman, "Wealth and Sacrifice in Early Christianity: Revisiting Mark's Presentation of Jesus' Encounter with the Rich Young Ruler," *TrinJ* 21 NS (2000): 160.

the alternate community established by Jesus makes it easier for a camel to go through the eye of a needle than for the rich to enter the kingdom.

Traditional ancient wisdom held that wealth invariably represented the blessing of God and that loss of wealth was evidence of a moral failure. Eliphaz and his accomplices defended this doctrine as they sought to correct Job. Eliphaz begins by commending Job, suggesting that his confidence should be found in knowing the just rules of retribution:

> Should not your piety be your confidence
>   and your blameless ways your hope?
> Consider now: Who, being innocent, has ever perished?
>   Where were the upright ever destroyed?
> As I have observed, those who plow evil
>   And those who sow trouble reap it. (Job 4:6–8)

In his second speech Eliphaz describes the terror of the wicked; they know their wealth cannot endure, that their vast possessions will be lost (Job 15:29). The rich ruler may well have held to the sentiments of the wisdom of Job's friends. If his wealth is a mark of divine favor, what more does he need to be part of the kingdom of God? His faith and his fear of God are evident in his life, because he has all the signs of being blessed by God. The book of Job does not deny this truth of traditional wisdom, but the story of Job is meant to show limits to the analogy of sowing and reaping.

Job is intransigent in resisting the arguments of his friends while he sits on the ash heap, because he is fully conscious of his integrity with God. His inner strength keeps him from yielding to the enormous pressure of traditional arguments, while he endures the harsh lessons of learning to trust God in his new circumstances. According to the subversive wisdom of Jesus, the rich are not necessarily within the kingdom of God and quite probably are outside of it.

Christians need to think carefully about their view of the world in relation to wealth. Industrialized societies tend to view the world as a resource of unlimited good. If this is so, wealth can be generated by hard work; hard work done honorably brings about God's blessing, and the wealth earned is the sole responsibility of the individual. Science and technology have taught well the lesson that the resources of this world are much more than is known. If current use of resources is not sustainable, new ways can be found to provide the same benefits. Christians need to remember that resources are limited for particular people in particular places. Not everyone is able to generate a living through relentless hard work, let alone wealth. Those in the kingdom of God must look beyond their own interests both in how they acquire wealth and how they share it with those who do not have the same opportunities.

In the kingdom of Solomon is a distinct recognition of limited resources, even though his trading ships do go to the farthest reaches of the world in search of treasures. When God established his people in the Promised Land, land was the most important limited resource, and it was to be carefully allotted so every family had a share (Num. 26:52–56). The year of release of debts for those whose land had been mortgaged, and the restoration of land to the original family in the Jubilee year, served as a protection against those who would join house to house and field to field until there was no place left for anyone else in the land (Isa. 5:8).

Priests and Levites received no share of land to prevent them from using their privileged status to control use of land in relation to temple service.[33] The blessing of God for Solomon was not to accumulate wealth in Jerusalem but to do what was just and right, as the Queen of Sheba said (1 Kings10:9). Justice would bring honor to God, even for a pagan queen, not the continuous acquisition of wealth.

In the days of Jesus it was particularly the religious leaders who were guilty of robbing the vulnerable. Jesus warned against those who liked to walk about in flowing garments, to have first place in the synagogue or at meals, but who devoured widow's houses and whose long prayers were nothing more than display of piety (Mark 12:38–39). A closely related evil was defrauding workers of their proper pay. Jesus warns against this in his response to the rich ruler; he follows the words of the covenant in saying do not kill, do not commit adultery, do not steal, and do not bear false witness, but he breaks the pattern by saying, "Do not defraud" (10:19). James refers to this same evil when he warns the rich that the wages they have failed to pay those who mow their fields are crying out (James 5:4). The Lord Almighty will hear the cries of the harvesters; the rich have reason to fear.

Sharing resources. The early Christians took seriously the challenge of forming a new community in which resources would be shared. The first believers shared everything in a single community, literally doing what Jesus had told the rich young ruler; they sold all their goods and distributed it to the needy. At first they were able to do this with complete harmony, and their numbers grew rapidly (Acts 2:44–47; 4:32–37). The specific example of Barnabas selling his property shows that the dispersal of landed wealth was not to give it up in monastic fashion, but was specifically given to assist the needy of the group that formed following the ascension.

This understanding of the Christian community is found in the first centuries of Christianity. Clement of Alexandria, who died early in the third

---

33. Heinrich Graetz was among the first to make this observation, contrasting Israelite practice with that of Egypt; *History of the Jews* (Philadelphia: Jewish Publication Society of America, 1891), 1:40.

century, wrote to people of some means a treatise entitled "Who Is the Rich Man Who Is Saved?"[34] He was attempting to interpret the words of Jesus to the rich man for wealthy believers. He did not take the command of Jesus to sell everything in a literal fashion; if all were in need of food and shelter, there would be no ability to meet the needs of the poor. Instead, he took the position that the church is a family; wealth and poverty were to be shared within this kinship group bound by faith, just as it might be in an ordinary family inheritance. Not every believer was expected to give up properties; resources were shared within the group without centralized ownership and control. The kingdom of God was to stand in opposition to the institutionalized greed of the world in which they lived.

Marx has called money our "jealous god" who can tolerate no other deity.[35] Marx found his own way to serve this same god; his solution was substitution of servitude. The failure of economic and political systems to provide justice is a lesson on the high calling given to Christians. Christians serve God rather than mammon; they work hard in order to be able to give to the one who has need (Eph. 4:28). Individuals are to have control over wealth they are able to earn; provision must be made so all can contribute to the common good.

The great challenge of living for the kingdom of God is that all Christians participate simultaneously in two worlds. Economically all members of a society participate in a system that serves the "jealous god." Political systems measure standard of living in material abundance; it seems to be the one common value held by all. Christians participate in a second kinship group, the family of God; they are responsible to do good for all, as they are able, especially to those of the household of faith (Gal. 6:9–10). They must not grow weary in doing well, because their work will not perish as the material gains provided by the "jealous god."

Wealth is an evidence of the blessing of God, but not all wealth is the result of God's blessing. The possession of wealth is not necessarily a blessing; wealth is probably responsible for as much unhappiness in this world as poverty. Those who have wealth must recognize the vulnerable spiritual circumstance that comes with prosperity. Those who do not have riches should not fear that opportunity for goodness in life has passed them by. The King of kings who fulfilled the promise to David after Solomon did not have a place to lay his head.

Solomon is an important example to all Christians who have considerable material well-being in comparison to other people of the world. God must

---

34. See Walter H. Wagner, *After the Apostles: Christianity in the Second Century* (Minneapolis: Fortress, 1994), 173.

35. Cited by John Kavanaugh, "Perils of Wealth," *America* 171/7 (Sept. 17, 1994): 31.

be honored through the riches he has given us through the collective support of a whole economic system. We are privileged to have the blessing; we need not apologize for it. Our challenge is to use this blessing to bring about peace and good, the kind of kingdom envisaged for Solomon (Ps. 72). We as Christians follow the king described by Zechariah, whose rule came through humility and sacrifice. The dominion of that kingdom will be "from sea to sea, and from the River to the ends of the earth" (72:8).

1 Kings 11:1–43

KING SOLOMON, HOWEVER, loved many foreign women besides Pharaoh's daughter—Moabites, Ammonites, Edomites, Sidonians and Hittites. ²They were from nations about which the LORD had told the Israelites, "You must not intermarry with them, because they will surely turn your hearts after their gods." Nevertheless, Solomon held fast to them in love. ³He had seven hundred wives of royal birth and three hundred concubines, and his wives led him astray. ⁴As Solomon grew old, his wives turned his heart after other gods, and his heart was not fully devoted to the LORD his God, as the heart of David his father had been. ⁵He followed Ashtoreth the goddess of the Sidonians, and Molech the detestable god of the Ammonites. ⁶So Solomon did evil in the eyes of the LORD; he did not follow the LORD completely, as David his father had done.

⁷On a hill east of Jerusalem, Solomon built a high place for Chemosh the detestable god of Moab, and for Molech the detestable god of the Ammonites. ⁸He did the same for all his foreign wives, who burned incense and offered sacrifices to their gods.

⁹The LORD became angry with Solomon because his heart had turned away from the LORD, the God of Israel, who had appeared to him twice. ¹⁰Although he had forbidden Solomon to follow other gods, Solomon did not keep the LORD's command. ¹¹So the LORD said to Solomon, "Since this is your attitude and you have not kept my covenant and my decrees, which I commanded you, I will most certainly tear the kingdom away from you and give it to one of your subordinates. ¹²Nevertheless, for the sake of David your father, I will not do it during your lifetime. I will tear it out of the hand of your son. ¹³Yet I will not tear the whole kingdom from him, but will give him one tribe for the sake of David my servant and for the sake of Jerusalem, which I have chosen."

¹⁴Then the LORD raised up against Solomon an adversary, Hadad the Edomite, from the royal line of Edom. ¹⁵Earlier when David was fighting with Edom, Joab the commander of the army, who had gone up to bury the dead, had struck down

all the men in Edom. ¹⁶Joab and all the Israelites stayed there for six months, until they had destroyed all the men in Edom. ¹⁷But Hadad, still only a boy, fled to Egypt with some Edomite officials who had served his father. ¹⁸They set out from Midian and went to Paran. Then taking men from Paran with them, they went to Egypt, to Pharaoh king of Egypt, who gave Hadad a house and land and provided him with food.

¹⁹Pharaoh was so pleased with Hadad that he gave him a sister of his own wife, Queen Tahpenes, in marriage. ²⁰The sister of Tahpenes bore him a son named Genubath, whom Tahpenes brought up in the royal palace. There Genubath lived with Pharaoh's own children.

²¹While he was in Egypt, Hadad heard that David rested with his fathers and that Joab the commander of the army was also dead. Then Hadad said to Pharaoh, "Let me go, that I may return to my own country."

²²"What have you lacked here that you want to go back to your own country?" Pharaoh asked.

"Nothing," Hadad replied, "but do let me go!"

²³And God raised up against Solomon another adversary, Rezon son of Eliada, who had fled from his master, Hadadezer king of Zobah. ²⁴He gathered men around him and became the leader of a band of rebels when David destroyed the forces of Zobah; the rebels went to Damascus, where they settled and took control. ²⁵Rezon was Israel's adversary as long as Solomon lived, adding to the trouble caused by Hadad. So Rezon ruled in Aram and was hostile toward Israel.

²⁶Also, Jeroboam son of Nebat rebelled against the king. He was one of Solomon's officials, an Ephraimite from Zeredah, and his mother was a widow named Zeruah.

²⁷Here is the account of how he rebelled against the king: Solomon had built the supporting terraces and had filled in the gap in the wall of the city of David his father. ²⁸Now Jeroboam was a man of standing, and when Solomon saw how well the young man did his work, he put him in charge of the whole labor force of the house of Joseph.

²⁹About that time Jeroboam was going out of Jerusalem, and Ahijah the prophet of Shiloh met him on the way, wearing a new cloak. The two of them were alone out in the country, ³⁰and Ahijah took hold of the new cloak he was wearing and tore it into twelve pieces. ³¹Then he said to Jeroboam, "Take

ten pieces for yourself, for this is what the LORD, the God of Israel, says: 'See, I am going to tear the kingdom out of Solomon's hand and give you ten tribes. ³²But for the sake of my servant David and the city of Jerusalem, which I have chosen out of all the tribes of Israel, he will have one tribe. ³³I will do this because they have forsaken me and worshiped Ashtoreth the goddess of the Sidonians, Chemosh the god of the Moabites, and Molech the god of the Ammonites, and have not walked in my ways, nor done what is right in my eyes, nor kept my statutes and laws as David, Solomon's father, did.

³⁴"'But I will not take the whole kingdom out of Solomon's hand; I have made him ruler all the days of his life for the sake of David my servant, whom I chose and who observed my commands and statutes. ³⁵I will take the kingdom from his son's hands and give you ten tribes. ³⁶I will give one tribe to his son so that David my servant may always have a lamp before me in Jerusalem, the city where I chose to put my Name. ³⁷However, as for you, I will take you, and you will rule over all that your heart desires; you will be king over Israel. ³⁸If you do whatever I command you and walk in my ways and do what is right in my eyes by keeping my statutes and commands, as David my servant did, I will be with you. I will build you a dynasty as enduring as the one I built for David and will give Israel to you. ³⁹I will humble David's descendants because of this, but not forever.'"

⁴⁰Solomon tried to kill Jeroboam, but Jeroboam fled to Egypt, to Shishak the king, and stayed there until Solomon's death.

⁴¹As for the other events of Solomon's reign—all he did and the wisdom he displayed—are they not written in the book of the annals of Solomon? ⁴²Solomon reigned in Jerusalem over all Israel forty years. ⁴³Then he rested with his fathers and was buried in the city of David his father. And Rehoboam his son succeeded him as king.

Original Meaning

SOLOMON DOES NOT KEEP the covenant. His violation is stated in a word from Yahweh (11:11–13), repeated in the message of the prophet Ahijah to Jeroboam (11:29–39). Solomon has three troublesome adversaries, sent by God to punish him; the most dangerous of these comes from within his own ranks. These threats to the kingdom of

Israel are not new: Edomites (vv. 14–22) and Arameans (vv. 23–25) have always been resistant to Israelite dominion. The enmity of Hadad goes back to the time of David, and Rezin is an adversary during all of Solomon's reign (v. 25). Few hints are given on the extent of Jeroboam's plot; the matter of his revolt is introduced, but the expected details do not follow (v. 27). Instead, the role he has in Solomon's labor force is given as an introduction to his encounter with the prophet. His flight to Shishak to escape Solomon suggests his mutiny has the support of the veteran leadership of the Ephraimite tribes.

The reign of Solomon concludes with the regularly styled notice that signals the transition to the next king (11:41–43). The length of reign is usually given in the introduction of a king, but the start of Solomon's reign began with a lengthy account of the establishment of the dynasty. His reign is forty years, like that of David (2:11), the length of one generation. These years are not integrated into the synchronized system of chronology in Kings. Precise length of reign is given for Rehoboam (14:21), and his successor is synchronized with the reign of Jeroboam (15:1).[1] When the biblical data are correlated with fixed Assyrian dates, the division of the kingdom can be dated at about 931 B.C.

Prophetic Judgment of Solomon (11:1–13)

THIS SECTION HAS been characterized as a theological review.[2] It contains offenses and judgment statements that evaluate the king according to prophetic orthodoxy. The prophetic indictment is given as a word from Yahweh without any specification as to the occasion or manner in which that word is delivered (vv. 11–13). The indictment is part of the narrative; the condemnation may have come through the written words of the covenant. Such reviews evaluate a reign (e.g., 2 Kings 10:28–31) or explain misfortune such as the northern exile (17:7–18). In this case the review does both, passing judgment on the reign of Solomon and explaining the reason for the division of the kingdom. Judgment against Solomon is mitigated by the promise to David (1 Kings 11:12–13). It does not take place during the time of Solomon, and the city of Jerusalem survives as part of the tribe of Judah.

Solomon attaches himself to foreign women (v. 2), accommodating their practices. He builds altars for them in the presence of the temple (vv. 7–8), though it is not said that he actually worships with them. The covenant

---

1. See appendix B for the chronology of Jeroboam and the end of the reign of Solomon. The factors involved with synchronisms and the establishment of an absolute chronology are complex and necessarily tentative.
2. Long, *1 Kings*, 123–34.

contained specific warnings about intermarriage with the nations (Deut. 7:1–5). This review of Solomon's reign has a particular focus on that failure.

Solomon builds altars instead of tearing them down in order to appease the women who are part of his harem. The size of his harem is given in schematic numbers, multiples of seven and three. The numbers of wives and concubines with their children are deemed beyond enumeration. The wives are princesses, women of high political rank (v. 3). The Moabites and Ammonites are subject nations under Solomon's domain; the Phoenicians and Egyptians are allies. Though these relationships may have begun as a matter of political expediency, the end result is the catastrophe Deuteronomy warned would happen.

"Ashtoreth" is a form of the name of the Canaanite goddess Ashtart (v. 5). The pronunciation is sometimes deemed to be a deliberate parody, changing the normal vowels to those of the word for shame (*bōšet*). She was the Canaanite counterpart to the Akkadian Ishtar and Sumerian Inanna, a goddess of war and sexuality. In Phoenician sources Ashtart is the patron goddess of both Tyre and Sidon, closely associated with Baal (perhaps as a consort).[3] Exported by the Phoenicians, worship of Ashtart thrived throughout the Mediterranean; her name is found in inscriptions in Carthage and Spain.

Milcom is the national god of the Ammonites (v. 5), also pronounced Molek (v. 7), a name that meant kingship. This god is associated with child sacrifice (2 Kings 23:10; Jer. 32:35). Chemosh, the national god of the Moabites, is also worshiped in Syria. A Moabite king offered his son in sacrifice to his god in desperation in his war with the Israelites (2 Kings 3:27).

Enemies of Solomon (11:14–25)

THE ADVERSARIES OF Solomon are human political opponents designated by God to punish Solomon (vv. 14, 23, 25). In later Hebrew this word for "adversary" meant "prosecutor" (*śāṭān*), in some instances a member of God's court (Job 1:9; 2:2; Zech. 3:1–2); eventually the term became a name for the devil.[4]

Hadad (meaning "thunder") is a common name for the fertility god known

---

3. The great Baal cycle is one of several literary works found among the tablets of various languages and scripts excavated at Tell Ras Shamra, north of modern Ladiqiye on the northeast shore of the Mediterranean. The city was destroyed ca. 1200. Mount Zaphon on the northern horizon (modern Jebel el-Aqraʿ) was the dwelling place of the storm god Baal.

4. Though *śāṭān* is often taken as "Satan" in 1 Chron. 21:1 (cf. NIV), this is unlikely the correct translation linguistically. Nothing in Chronicles indicates such a reconstructed development in the concept of evil (cf. Japhet, *I & II Chronicles*, 374–75). This figure is fully anchored in the human sphere, the antithesis of Joab, who tried to dissuade David from his foolish plan.

in the Bible as Baal ("master"). Two kings named Hadad are known from the genealogies of Edom (Gen. 36:31–39). David conquered Edom as one of the expansions of his empire (2 Sam. 8:13–14), an exploit remembered in the superscription to Psalm 60. There may have been more than one war in the effort to exterminate the Edomites. First Kings 11:15 is sometimes emended to say David carried out the massacre of the Edomites (RSV) rather than Joab (v. 16), but there is no need to postulate two different traditions in the brief account of the conquest of Edom (vv. 15–16).[5]

Nothing is said of the fate of Hadad,[6] but his servants take the young prince to Midian, east of the Gulf of Aqaba, then to Paran in the western Sinai. There they solicit the help of guides familiar with the territory and finally find refuge in Egypt. The reigning pharaoh not only gives the young prince a home, provisions, and land; he makes him a member of the royal family. Tahpenes is apparently a Hebrew transliteration of an Egyptian word meaning "wife of the king."[7] Like Moses, her son Genubath is raised in the Egyptian court. David and Joab are his dreaded enemies (v. 21); when they die, Hadad renounces the security and luxury of Egypt and enters into some type of guerilla warfare against Solomon (v. 25). The reintroduction of Hadad in connection with Rezon is abrupt, but it hints of a detail not noted earlier.

David's defeat of Hadadezer king of Zobah is described in some detail (2 Sam. 8:3–8). Aram Zobah was an Aramean kingdom located along the upper Orontes River in the Beqaᶜ Valley of Lebanon. Hadadezer (unknown outside of the Bible) ruled over a vast territory, allying with the Ammonites in the wars against David (10:6). David set up a garrison in Damascus with a governor to maintain control over the territory and enforce taxation. Rezon, a rebel against Hadadezer, organized a guerilla movement and eventually gained control of Damascus (1 Kings 11:23–24). Rezon founded a dynasty that became the kingdom of Aram-Damascus, the most powerful Syrian state in the days following Solomon.[8] As an independent power he resisted Solomon during the whole time of his rule.

---

5. Cogan, *I Kings*, 331. The emendation follows the LXX (cf. 2 Sam. 8:13), which has David fighting in Edom (*bhkwt*) rather than just being there (*bhywt*). The superscription to Psalm 60 suggests Joab was the perpetrator of the slaughter in Edom, while David was occupied with wars in Aram.

6. For a detailed study of this passage and the history of Hadad in Edom see J. R. Bartlett, "An Adversary against Solomon, Hadad the Edomite," *ZAW* 88 (1976): 205–26.

7. See K. A. Kitchen, *The Third Intermediate Period in Egypt (1100–650 B.C.)* (Warminster: Aris & Phillips, 1973), 273–75, n. 183.

8. For a brief Aramean history, see A. Malamat, "The Arameans," in *Peoples of the Old Testament Times*, ed. D. J. Wiseman (Oxford: Oxford Univ. Press, 1973), 134–55.

Revolt of Jeroboam (11:26—43)

JEROBOAM IS THE servant of Solomon who becomes his successor (vv. 11, 27—28). The name Jeroboam, "may the people be great," expresses opposition to his rival Rehoboam, "may your people be widespread." The name of Jeroboam's father (Nebat) is not found elsewhere as a personal name in the Bible. Zeruah apparently means a woman afflicted with a skin disease; such a name need not be regarded as a perversion intended to vilify Israel. "Son of a widow" is apparently an Akkadian expression to describe an unfit usurper seizing the throne; if this is such an idiom, the statement about Jeroboam's mother says nothing about his lineage.[9]

Solomon recognizes the capability of Jeroboam and makes him supervisor over the compulsory state service required from the house of Joseph, a likely reference to the district of Ephraim (cf. 4:8). The location of the two construction sites mentioned is not specified. Solomon may have needed to expand his fortifications to the south and east, which require building up the wall bases and closing the breaches.

"About that time" does not indicate chronological sequence (v. 29) but indicates a general temporal relationship with previous events. The prophetic endorsement comes sometime during Solomon's reign, because Jeroboam flees to Egypt and seeks refuge there until Solomon dies (v. 40). The prophet Ahijah has his home in Shiloh (cf. 14:2), the site that had been the home of the ark (1 Sam. 1—3) and the Tent of Meeting (Josh. 18:1). Where the prophet meets Jeroboam is not specified, but it is not a coincidental encounter. The prophet has a message for the young leader, which he communicates in dramatic fashion.

Prophets often communicate in dramatic fashion. Isaiah, for example, went about naked for three years to show that the Assyrians were going to conquer Egypt and take captive all who depended on them (Isa. 20:1—6). The action of Ahijah is particularly dramatic as he tears up the new garment of Jeroboam. The seizing of the garment indicates it belongs to Jeroboam (1 Kings 11:30), because such an action would not be pertinent to his own coat. The newness of the garment is stressed twice (vv. 29—30), making it a fit item for the prophetic sign.

Prophetic communications of this type have been variously interpreted.[10] Such actions have been thought to be inherently efficacious, setting in motion unavoidable events. Alternately, they may be expressions of reality, an act of power between prophet and audience, a persuasive use of street theater.

---

9. Cogan, *1 Kings*, 337—38.

10. For an analysis of prophetic sign messages see Kelvin Friebel, "A Hermeneutical Paradigm for Interpreting Prophetic Sign-Actions," *Didaskalia* 12/2 (2001): 25—45.

Friebel interprets them as rhetorical nonverbal communication, persuasive in nature and intent. They are communicative and interactive, a message with a persuasive dimension. The action of Ahijah persuades Jeroboam to initiate an insurrection against Solomon's autocracy, but it gains him nothing more than exile in Egypt (11:40). God will grant Jeroboam his desire to rule (v. 37), but it will not happen because of his own initiative. It is the work of a prophet to stir people to action in order that God's purposes may be accomplished through them in his time.

The words of Ahijah amplify the judgment given earlier in the narrative. Judgment is the result of Solomon's promoting worship of foreign gods (v. 33; cf. vv. 7–8); judgment is mitigated because of God's promise to David (vv. 34–36; cf. vv. 12–13). The leadership of David is described as a lamp at the time he was rescued from mortal danger by his soldiers (2 Sam. 21:17). A son of Solomon will continue to rule one tribe to preserve this light (1 Kings 11:36), a motif that is repeated (15:4; 2 Kings 8:19). Only one tribe is given to the descendants of Solomon (1 Kings 11:13, 36), an acknowledgment of the political reality that territorially the tribes of Benjamin and Simeon are absorbed, and Judah exists as a single territory.

Ahijah declares Jeroboam to be a true successor of David (v. 38); the promise of dynasty applies to Jeroboam as it had to David. The phraseology of Nathan's prophecy to David is strikingly adapted to Jeroboam, legitimizing the northern kingdom (2 Sam. 7:9a, 16a). But unlike David, where the kingdom is promised in perpetuity, the house of Jeroboam is made contingent on his uncompromised obedience. The house of David will be humbled, but a ruler will remain in Jerusalem for the sake of David (1 Kings 11:34).

Solomon becomes aware of Jeroboam's plot, which apparently is not limited to Jeroboam himself (cf. v. 26b). Jeroboam finds refuge in the court of Shishak, the first king of the Twenty-Second Dynasty in Egypt (ca. 945–924 B.C.). His treatment of Jeroboam is an indication of a change in Egyptian policy to Solomon. The length of his stay is not specified; Kitchen thinks the flight is soon after Shishak forms the new dynasty.[11] He reckons that the "government in exile" has to wait fifteen years before its next move.

Bridging Contexts

BLESSINGS AND CURSES. Blessings and curses are fundamental to the theology of Kings; these are the alternatives of the covenant relationship with God. The theology in Kings is not immediate retribution; grace is extended, particularly to the dynasty of David, but the

---

11. Kitchen, *The Third Intermediate Period in Egypt*, 294.

conditions of the covenant cannot be violated indefinitely. Of all the kings in the history of Israel, the review of Solomon is most mixed in terms of blessing and curse.

The divide between blessing and curse is said to be youth and old age (11:4), but the narrative itself indicates the process begins much earlier. Like any great monarch of ancient time, Solomon has many wives and concubines (v. 3), who retain their cultural and religious affiliations (vv. 7–8). Solomon builds shrines in their place of residence, an abominable compromise to the temple with its exclusive claims of kingship for Solomon's God. This can only be described as an offense; the final prophetic judgment of Solomon is the first of a refrain that applies to all kings that compromise the covenant (v. 6). The prophetic indictment of Solomon indicates that the punishment will be delayed until his death (vv. 11–12), but the adversaries begin their work during his lifetime (vv. 21–22, 25). The insurrection of Jeroboam begins sometime during the reign of Solomon and is serious enough that Solomon takes measures to dispatch him (v. 40).

Dissention within the kingdom in the latter part of Solomon's reign appears to be the result of seeds of rebellion planted early on, which only blossom when Solomon becomes old.[12] Note, for example, how Solomon tells Hiram his kingdom is at peace, there is no adversary (śāṭān), there is no trouble (rāʿ, 5:4). This terminology is retained to say that Yahweh raises up adversaries (śāṭān) against Solomon who cause trouble (rāʿâ) the entire time that Solomon is on the throne (11:25). Further, there is good reason to present the reign of Solomon as a failure, because the division of the kingdom takes place at his succession. The climactic judgment on the dynasty of David does not begin with the destruction of Jerusalem under the Babylonians.

Blessing and the curse are both integral within the reign of Solomon in Deuteronomistic theology. The blessing is present in that not one word of what God promised Moses fails (8:56); God has granted rest to his people. In Solomon the promise to David is fully realized (8:20–21); the choice of David and Zion is established with the construction of the temple (9:3). This fulfillment is nothing less than uncompromised glory that characterizes the kingdom of Solomon (10:9). God fulfills his promise with multiple tons of gold (v. 14), land for every citizen within a vast empire that stretches to the Euphrates, and security from any invader (4:24–25).

Though God has repeatedly fulfilled the promise of blessing, Israel has always been disobedient and suffers the curse. The division of the kingdom is a punishment, not a failure. The failure happens during the reign of

---

12. For a defense of this chronological harmonization, see D. A. Glatt, *Chronological Displacement in Biblical and Related Literature* (SBLDS 139; Atlanta: Scholars Press, 1993), 162–67.

Solomon just as much as the blessing. This pattern is consistent with Deuteronomistic understanding of the covenant with Moses. The evidence of blessing is present during the reign of Solomon; the signs of the curse become evident when the disintegration of the kingdom rapidly advances in Solomon's old age.

Marvin Sweeney has proposed that the narrative presents Solomon as an unfaithful king to serve as a foil to Josiah, the model of a faithful king.[13] The theme of apostasy permeates the narrative (chs. 3–11). Solomon compromises the covenant in his marriage to Pharaoh's daughter, apparently as a means to secure his kingdom, but in the end Jeroboam finds refuge in Egypt, and Pharaoh becomes a means through which the revolt is facilitated and the kingdom divided. It is also notable that the administrative taxation system (4:7–19) appears to have an imbalance that discriminates against the northern tribes, violating the principles of just rule. The summary of Solomon's rule is that he does what is wrong (11:4) while the summary of the rule of Josiah is that he does what is right without exception (2 Kings 22:2), just as David his father.

While it is true that the mixed presentation of Solomon is integrated into the account of Solomon's reign, it is unlikely that the prophetic authors intend to present Solomon as the opposite of Josiah.[14] The only explicit link between the narratives is in Josiah dismantling the cultic high places Solomon built (2 Kings 23:13; cf. 1 Kings 11:7). None of the other failures of Solomon, such as the amassing of wealth, horses, and foreign women, are specifically rectified in the reforms of Josiah. Scattered references to Pharaoh's daughter or allusions to the mistreatment of northern tribes allow for certain kinds of historical deductions, but cannot be said to conscientiously advance a literary intent to present a contrast of the two kings.

Amos Frisch finds nine units in the narrative of Solomon, which he defines as 1 Kings 1:1–12:24.[15] These are arranged in a concentric structure with the building and dedication of the temple at the center, but with implicit criticism of Solomon. The parallels give weight to the concept of reward and punishment, showing that blessing and curse are directly related to obedience and disobedience. Though the fulfillment of the prophetic word of Ahijah (12:1–24) might be considered to belong with the prophecy as part of the

---

13. Marvin A. Sweeney, "A Critique of Solomon in the Josianic Edition of the Deuteronomistic History," *JBL* 114 (1995): 607–22.

14. For a critique of Sweeney's methods see David A. Glatt-Gilad, "The Deuteronomostic Critique of Solomon: A Response to Marvin A. Sweeney," *JBL* 116 (1997): 700–703.

15. Amos Frisch, "Structure and Significance: The Narrative of Solomon's Reign (1 Kings 1–12:24)," *JSOT* 51 (1991): 3–14.

punishment (11:26–39), it is not made a part of the narrative of Solomon's reign. The closing formula to Solomon's reign indicates closure to his story (11:41–43). The focus then shifts to the reign of Jeroboam, who is the recipient of the prophetic word. The punishment of Solomon is explicitly said to occur after his reign (11:12, 35); though the fulfillment of the prophecy is about Solomon, it is not included as part of the narrative that deals with his reign.

Visions. The one unequivocal association that occurs in the narrative of Solomon's reign is that of the visions. Yahweh appears to Solomon a second time as he did at Gibeon (9:2). This point is taken up again in the prophetic judgment against Solomon; Solomon has turned away from his devotion to Yahweh in spite of the fact that God appeared to him twice (11:9). These deliberate literary repetitions are an important guide to narrative structure and the message of the story. The second vision, with its stern warnings, in contrast to the first vision of wisdom and wealth, shifts the evaluation of Solomon to reveal important lessons of the narrative.[16] Though the temple is prominent in the narrative, the counterpart is Solomon's high places built for his foreign wives (11:7–8). The contrast between worship at the temple and worship at the high places is an issue throughout the books of Kings.

The burden of the prophetic history in Kings is the problem of disobedience. The narrative of Solomon participates fully in that burden. Everything else about Solomon serves to accentuate the enormity of that tragedy. The greater his wealth and wisdom, the greater the tragedy of his fall. The visions have a central role in providing that orientation to the story. God has not failed Solomon in any way; from the start he is fully equipped to be the ideal king of the nation. The second vision provides the warning: Status and achievement have increased potential for vulnerability. Wisdom brings success; reliance on wisdom brings total disaster (9:6–9).

This lesson must be conveyed to everyone who hears about Solomon. The nations, who have no experience with God, will see the ruin of his exalted house and whistle in amazement, fully understanding that the problem is abandonment of the oath with God. All other sins or failures are a manifestation of this one sin (11:9). It reverses every other virtue and achievement.

Wisdom. The beginning of wisdom is to know and follow God's teaching, to know the fear of Yahweh. The great rewards of all other wisdom are lost unless they continuously find their starting point with the fear of Yah-

---

16. See Kim Parker, "The Limits of Solomon's Reign: A Response to Amos Frisch," *JSOT* 51 (1991): 19–20.

weh (Job 28:28). The gold of Solomon is many times what the sophisticated mining operation described in Job might yield (28:1–11). As the bitter experience of Job reveals, such wealth does not convey wisdom needed for living.

For entirely different reasons than Solomon, Job also loses his vast resources. It drives him to ask the question repeatedly: "From where does wisdom come?" (28:12, 20). No amount of the finest gold or any other treasure can begin to compare with the worth of such wisdom (28:15–19). In his hymn to wisdom, Job is fully conscious of the reality that the wisdom mortals need is completely outside their grasp (28:12–14, 20–22). Only God knows the way to such wisdom (28:23–27); God has revealed the one thing that all mortals must know; to turn from wrong is understanding (28:28).

Rather than turn from wrong (*rāʿ*), Solomon turns to wrong (1 Kings 11:6); that is not wisdom, no matter what other wisdom skills enable the greatest of power and fortune. This point of wisdom the Deuteronomistic Historians understand fully, and they portray its bitter reality with great skill in the life of Solomon. Tensions are allowed free reign: the grandeur of Solomon is real; the blessing of God is genuine in every respect. All this is in perfect conformity with covenant truth. The epitome of blessing and curse can be present in one individual virtually simultaneously. Blessing and curse do not operate in such mechanical fashion.

The further question of Job was not germane to the Deuteronomists: Can one who fears God still suffer the curse? This is the occasion for the profound eulogy to wisdom in Job. This question has profound implications for understanding God. This question is not pertinent to Solomon or to any part of Israel's past in the historiography of the Deuteronomists. The punishment is fully justified in every case, especially so when the blessing is palpable as in the case of Solomon. Such grandeur is not earned; the divine gift is not gained through merit, but is always lost through demerit.

Covenant. The prophets are responsible to maintain accountability to the covenant. It is the reason they have such a prominent role in the story of the nation. Transitions of kingship, for woe or weal, usually involve a prophet. In the case of Jeroboam it is some of both; hope for what is lost in the promise to David is present in him (11:35–38). Influence and power of prophets in political affairs are necessary and possible because of the covenant. The king is subordinated to the rule of God the same as every other Israelite. In this respect all are brothers. Kings who violate the brotherhood forfeit their right to rule (11:11). In Israel kingship is determined by covenant loyalty, not by dynastic succession. Dynastic succession continues in Judah, to maintain a lamp for David, but this will not be the case in Israel.

THE VALUE OF true wisdom. There is a story about a president who had a dream. God visited him in a vision; in the vision he was given a choice. He could have the wealth of Solomon, the fame of Solomon, or the wisdom of Solomon, but only one of the three. Being a pietistic individual, he naturally chose the wisdom of Solomon. Word soon spread about that the president had received the wisdom of Solomon. His cabinet quickly convened to hear what this wisest of all men would have to say. They waited breathlessly as he began to speak: "I should," he said, "have taken the money."

To most people most of the time the real deficiency seems to be money. It is always possible to think of what good things could be done if only there were more money. Wisdom is simple enough when there is money; those who have money also have wisdom. Advice is sought from those who are successful; success is measured in the wealth it brings. Though intellect may inform otherwise, the passions that govern life generally overrule rational thought.

The distinction between wisdom and folly is not as obvious as it would seem. Those with great wisdom may live as fools. John Ortberg says that one of the marks of the human condition is not to say it is depraved or lost but that it is ridiculous. Foolishness is not a series of bad choices; it is a choice to live as though God can be ignored.

> Foolishness, in this way of thinking, is not so much a disease of the intellect as of the will. The fool says in her heart that there is no God; or that she will live as god, which is perhaps the same thing. The fool thinks he needs bigger barns for the riches that he in his cleverness has accumulated, and forgets that the night when his construction project is finished is the night he has scheduled a massive coronary. You can be a fool and still find good work in Cambridge, Massachusetts, or on Madison Avenue. Sometimes it helps.[17]

For the prophetic writers of Kings, the dichotomy of Solomon is the problem, Ortberg observes. Solomon had wisdom in terms of intellect, but he came to live as a fool. Their description of this foolishness is monotonously simple: He followed other gods and built other high places. The very man who led in that marvelous prayer at the dedication of the temple did not abide by his own confession. His prayer was that the people of God's inheritance might follow in his directives, his decisions, his ways (8:58). Perhaps he

---

17. John Ortberg, "Living by the Word," *The Christian Century* 120/16 (Aug, 9, 2003): 16.

believed that he followed the desire of his prayer. The decisions of foolishness seem rational, or at least they are easily rationalized. Solomon denied God only by compromise; the prophets understood that this was nothing less than outright abandonment. For this he paid the price of the division of the kingdom.

Ortberg points out that Christians are no less foolish than Solomon. Christians fail in worship no less than Solomon in his building other high places:

> Paul says that as we relate to each other we are to sing psalms and hymns and spiritual songs, making melody to the Lord in our hearts and giving thanks to God at all times. But even in the church we end up spending more time fighting about the kind of melodies we should sing, and whether the Lord God prefers organ or guitar. People split churches over how loudly the songs should be amplified. We are ridiculous.[18]

It is tragic when intelligent people are ridiculous, especially when they can be wise in so many ways. It is a matter of perspective; it is a failure to focus on the one single value from which all other choices derive their relative importance.

It is easy to believe that glorifying God is the one thing that matters in this world. It is even easier to follow the sensualism of Ashtoreth of the Sidonians or the abominations of the Ammonites (11:5). Sidonians were allies of Israel; Ammonites contributed to Israel's wealth. If Solomon were to go back to the covenant and the warning about allying with other nations, he would have found that these were not in the list (cf. Deut. 7:1–7). Moabites, Edomites, Sidonians, and Hittites were not among the autochthonous nations of Canaan that Israel was to destroy.[19] Solomon could reason that this was another time, that clinging to these nations and their princesses did not come under the covenant restriction. This was not self-evidently contradictory to glorifying God in the temple. Whether or not Solomon thought along these lines, the prophets who wrote Kings knew better. All his wisdom is subverted in a foolish choice.

Solomon has been immortalized as the ideal king. In teaching his followers not to worry about clothes Jesus pointed to the beauty of the flowers

---

18. Ibid.

19. *Autochthonos* is the term used for the indigenous inhabitants of Canaan before the time of Israel. These are the Amorites who were to be destroyed because of their iniquity when the time came for Abraham's descendants to enter the land (Gen. 15:16, 18–21). Hittites in Kings is used in the later general sense of the peoples of Syria rather than the particular peoples that were part of the original Hittite empire.

of the field and reminded his hearers that not even Solomon in all his glory could compare. Jesus could use Solomon as an antitype of himself. The queen of the south would stand in judgment against religious leaders demanding a sign, because she came from distant regions to hear the wisdom of Solomon, and a greater than Solomon was present with them (Matt. 12:42).[20]

The glory of a king blessed by wisdom is a critical aspect of the story of Solomon, but the lessons of Solomon taught in the narrative of Kings are much more sobering. A great and wise king may at the same time be a foolish and weak king. This is the irony of Solomon's life; wisdom has the power to produce wealth, but the seductive power of wealth can erode the wisdom of following God. The narrative of Kings calls everyone to be a person greater than Solomon. None might compare to Solomon in the glory of his reign or the wisdom discovered by the queen of Sheba, but all need the wisdom of faithfulness to God.

Loyalty and faithfulness. Spirituality may be measured in different ways, but the critical standard is given in the story of Solomon. Spirituality is never anything less than uncompromised loyalty to God. If there ever was an individual with the opportunity to serve God with such loyalty it was Solomon. The Lord appeared to him twice. In the first instance God assured him of incomparable blessing because of the priority he had chosen. The fulfillment of this incomparable blessing should have been motivation to absolute devotion to God. The second vision comes as a warning—a reminder that such blessing is not an assurance of continued blessing. Neither the gift nor the warning is sufficient for Solomon. His heart is seduced, his kingdom divided; his life is a failure.

Jesus taught us to pray, "Lead us not into temptation," which needs to be interpreted as, "Cause us not to be led into temptation." It is not external enemies like Hadad and Rezon who are a threat to Solomon and his kingdom, though they trouble him the entire time of his rule. The revolt of Jeroboam is not the problem, and exiling Jeroboam to Egypt does not solve anything for Solomon. The problem for Solomon is the power of influences in his daily life, the people who are part of his household. This is the reason why the covenant gives such firm warnings against intermarriage and alliances with peoples of a foreign faith. Such intimacy is a source of constant conflict or fateful compromise. Certain distances must be maintained or they will cause

---

20. In later Jewish tradition, the wisdom of Solomon included knowledge of the structure of the universe and the operation of its elements as well as the power to cast out demons. The saying in Matthew is in the context of Jesus' casting out demons, which may be one of the ways his hearers understood his claim to be greater than Solomon. See Larry Perkins, "Greater Than Solomon (Matt 12:42)," *TrinJ* 19 (1998): 207–18.

us to be delivered to harm. The beginning of not being led into temptation, of being rescued from evil, is to avoid compromising situations.

There is no assurance for faithfulness. Solomon incurs the wrath and judgment of Yahweh, who appeared to him *twice* (11:9); the point is emphatic. Solomon did not come to know the God of the temple; his involvement with other gods led him into temptation. Faithfulness is not maintained by the greatest of past experiences. Faithfulness is to seek God daily; that is a wisdom for which there is no substitute. That wisdom is sufficient for every challenge life may have.

The persistent lesson of Solomon for those who live under a new covenant is the importance of faithfulness. Success at any one point in the life of an individual—spiritually, materially, or both—is no assurance of continued loyalty to God. This message is skillfully articulated in the prophetic portrayal of Solomon's reign.

Faithfulness requires an integration of various activities and relationship in life. Katharin Henderson asks whether God and mammon can be held together; can mammon be a means of service to God? Her answer comes in the testimony of Laura Jervis, who coined for her the term *seamlessness*. Laura has spent the past twenty years developing thousands of units of housing for the poor elderly on the west side of Manhattan. When asked if she considered this work a job, a profession, or ministry, she said that the personal, professional, and religious dimensions of her life all fit together as a whole. In her words,

> My life on the West Side is really life in community, and there is a sense of seamlessness to my life ... which I sometimes resent a little because it can feel like there's no escape.... That's hard. But most of the time I think it's the right way to live. But it is a kind of public life ... it's the community board, it's the churches and several synagogues, it's the community of my organization ... and it's all really one. There's a sense of symmetry and wholeness about it, which, if I were asked to, I don't think I could sacrifice.[21]

Few Christians can manage the kind of seamlessness described by Laura Jervis; life is segmented into obligations of employment, community, church, marriage, and family. Often these seem to have little to do with each other. But we must remember that our lives are judged as a whole. Christians live in realms of secular and sacred; each individual shares in several roles, and not all of those roles are performed with equal skill. Faithfulness cannot be

---

21. Katharin Rhodes Henderson, "Alchemists at Work: God, Money, and the Common Good," *Cross Currents* 53/2 (Summer 2003): 255–56.

limited to some of these responsibilities; in one life, each role relates to another. Faithfulness is learning to integrate rather than segregate. Life lived as a dichotomy is a life of harsh experience. Success and happiness in one role cannot compensate for faithlessness in another. Sorrows generated in one area of life will erode the joy of another.

Not long ago I received a rather curt and chastising response to an article I had written on work. It was my intent to show that God made the world as the crown of his work and that all human work is to be a part of God's work in the world. This is how I understand the sentiments of Psalm 104. The response came from the foreman of a crew doing roadwork, in which he asked how this was going to encourage the people he worked with in harsh weather conditions each day. My answer to that question is that meaningful work must have a greater purpose than earning a living; but further to the point, for the Christian all work is more than earning a living. Work regarded as nothing more than earning a living is a segmentation that dishonors God.

The work of Moses for most of his life consisted of desert wanderings, either herding sheep or, even worse, trying to lead people. The one psalm read as a prayer of Moses (Ps. 90) is a prayer that God will take human work and make it a part of his work. God will honor that prayer, even as he did in the life of Moses. This is the faithfulness that God requires. The mighty work of Solomon was not so honored; faithlessness in his divided life ended in the division of the kingdom and was the beginning of that great disaster that was to overtake the chosen city.

1 Kings 12:1–14:31

❦

REHOBOAM WENT TO Shechem, for all the Israelites had gone there to make him king. ²When Jeroboam son of Nebat heard this (he was still in Egypt, where he had fled from King Solomon), he returned from Egypt. ³So they sent for Jeroboam, and he and the whole assembly of Israel went to Rehoboam and said to him: ⁴"Your father put a heavy yoke on us, but now lighten the harsh labor and the heavy yoke he put on us, and we will serve you."

⁵Rehoboam answered, "Go away for three days and then come back to me." So the people went away.

⁶Then King Rehoboam consulted the elders who had served his father Solomon during his lifetime. "How would you advise me to answer these people?" he asked.

⁷They replied, "If today you will be a servant to these people and serve them and give them a favorable answer, they will always be your servants."

⁸But Rehoboam rejected the advice the elders gave him and consulted the young men who had grown up with him and were serving him. ⁹He asked them, "What is your advice? How should we answer these people who say to me, 'Lighten the yoke your father put on us'?"

¹⁰The young men who had grown up with him replied, "Tell these people who have said to you, 'Your father put a heavy yoke on us, but make our yoke lighter'—tell them, 'My little finger is thicker than my father's waist. ¹¹My father laid on you a heavy yoke; I will make it even heavier. My father scourged you with whips; I will scourge you with scorpions.'"

¹²Three days later Jeroboam and all the people returned to Rehoboam, as the king had said, "Come back to me in three days." ¹³The king answered the people harshly. Rejecting the advice given him by the elders, ¹⁴he followed the advice of the young men and said, "My father made your yoke heavy; I will make it even heavier. My father scourged you with whips; I will scourge you with scorpions." ¹⁵So the king did not listen to the people, for this turn of events was from the LORD, to fulfill the word the LORD had spoken to Jeroboam son of Nebat through Ahijah the Shilonite.

¹⁶When all Israel saw that the king refused to listen to them, they answered the king:

> "What share do we have in David,
>   what part in Jesse's son?
> To your tents, O Israel!
>   Look after your own house, O David!"

So the Israelites went home. ¹⁷But as for the Israelites who were living in the towns of Judah, Rehoboam still ruled over them.

¹⁸King Rehoboam sent out Adoniram, who was in charge of forced labor, but all Israel stoned him to death. King Rehoboam, however, managed to get into his chariot and escape to Jerusalem. ¹⁹So Israel has been in rebellion against the house of David to this day.

²⁰When all the Israelites heard that Jeroboam had returned, they sent and called him to the assembly and made him king over all Israel. Only the tribe of Judah remained loyal to the house of David.

²¹When Rehoboam arrived in Jerusalem, he mustered the whole house of Judah and the tribe of Benjamin—a hundred and eighty thousand fighting men—to make war against the house of Israel and to regain the kingdom for Rehoboam son of Solomon.

²²But this word of God came to Shemaiah the man of God: ²³"Say to Rehoboam son of Solomon king of Judah, to the whole house of Judah and Benjamin, and to the rest of the people, ²⁴'This is what the LORD says: Do not go up to fight against your brothers, the Israelites. Go home, every one of you, for this is my doing.'" So they obeyed the word of the LORD and went home again, as the LORD had ordered.

²⁵Then Jeroboam fortified Shechem in the hill country of Ephraim and lived there. From there he went out and built up Peniel.

²⁶Jeroboam thought to himself, "The kingdom will now likely revert to the house of David. ²⁷If these people go up to offer sacrifices at the temple of the LORD in Jerusalem, they will again give their allegiance to their lord, Rehoboam king of Judah. They will kill me and return to King Rehoboam."

²⁸After seeking advice, the king made two golden calves. He said to the people, "It is too much for you to go up to

Jerusalem. Here are your gods, O Israel, who brought you up out of Egypt." ²⁹One he set up in Bethel, and the other in Dan. ³⁰And this thing became a sin; the people went even as far as Dan to worship the one there.

³¹Jeroboam built shrines on high places and appointed priests from all sorts of people, even though they were not Levites. ³²He instituted a festival on the fifteenth day of the eighth month, like the festival held in Judah, and offered sacrifices on the altar. This he did in Bethel, sacrificing to the calves he had made. And at Bethel he also installed priests at the high places he had made. ³³On the fifteenth day of the eighth month, a month of his own choosing, he offered sacrifices on the altar he had built at Bethel. So he instituted the festival for the Israelites and went up to the altar to make offerings.

¹³:¹By the word of the LORD a man of God came from Judah to Bethel, as Jeroboam was standing by the altar to make an offering. ²He cried out against the altar by the word of the LORD: "O altar, altar! This is what the LORD says: 'A son named Josiah will be born to the house of David. On you he will sacrifice the priests of the high places who now make offerings here, and human bones will be burned on you.'" ³That same day the man of God gave a sign: "This is the sign the LORD has declared: The altar will be split apart and the ashes on it will be poured out."

⁴When King Jeroboam heard what the man of God cried out against the altar at Bethel, he stretched out his hand from the altar and said, "Seize him!" But the hand he stretched out toward the man shriveled up, so that he could not pull it back. ⁵Also, the altar was split apart and its ashes poured out according to the sign given by the man of God by the word of the LORD.

⁶Then the king said to the man of God, "Intercede with the LORD your God and pray for me that my hand may be restored." So the man of God interceded with the LORD, and the king's hand was restored and became as it was before.

⁷The king said to the man of God, "Come home with me and have something to eat, and I will give you a gift."

⁸But the man of God answered the king, "Even if you were to give me half your possessions, I would not go with you, nor would I eat bread or drink water here. ⁹For I was commanded

by the word of the LORD: 'You must not eat bread or drink water or return by the way you came.'" ¹⁰So he took another road and did not return by the way he had come to Bethel.

¹¹Now there was a certain old prophet living in Bethel, whose sons came and told him all that the man of God had done there that day. They also told their father what he had said to the king. ¹²Their father asked them, "Which way did he go?" And his sons showed him which road the man of God from Judah had taken. ¹³So he said to his sons, "Saddle the donkey for me." And when they had saddled the donkey for him, he mounted it ¹⁴and rode after the man of God. He found him sitting under an oak tree and asked, "Are you the man of God who came from Judah?"

"I am," he replied.

¹⁵So the prophet said to him, "Come home with me and eat."

¹⁶The man of God said, "I cannot turn back and go with you, nor can I eat bread or drink water with you in this place. ¹⁷I have been told by the word of the LORD: 'You must not eat bread or drink water there or return by the way you came.'"

¹⁸The old prophet answered, "I too am a prophet, as you are. And an angel said to me by the word of the LORD: 'Bring him back with you to your house so that he may eat bread and drink water.'" (But he was lying to him.) ¹⁹So the man of God returned with him and ate and drank in his house.

²⁰While they were sitting at the table, the word of the LORD came to the old prophet who had brought him back. ²¹He cried out to the man of God who had come from Judah, "This is what the LORD says: 'You have defied the word of the LORD and have not kept the command the LORD your God gave you. ²²You came back and ate bread and drank water in the place where he told you not to eat or drink. Therefore your body will not be buried in the tomb of your fathers.'"

²³When the man of God had finished eating and drinking, the prophet who had brought him back saddled his donkey for him. ²⁴As he went on his way, a lion met him on the road and killed him, and his body was thrown down on the road, with both the donkey and the lion standing beside it. ²⁵Some people who passed by saw the body thrown down there, with the lion standing beside the body, and they went and reported it in the city where the old prophet lived.

²⁶When the prophet who had brought him back from his journey heard of it, he said, "It is the man of God who defied the word of the LORD. The LORD has given him over to the lion, which has mauled him and killed him, as the word of the LORD had warned him."

²⁷The prophet said to his sons, "Saddle the donkey for me," and they did so. ²⁸Then he went out and found the body thrown down on the road, with the donkey and the lion standing beside it. The lion had neither eaten the body nor mauled the donkey. ²⁹So the prophet picked up the body of the man of God, laid it on the donkey, and brought it back to his own city to mourn for him and bury him. ³⁰Then he laid the body in his own tomb, and they mourned over him and said, "Oh, my brother!"

³¹After burying him, he said to his sons, "When I die, bury me in the grave where the man of God is buried; lay my bones beside his bones. ³²For the message he declared by the word of the LORD against the altar in Bethel and against all the shrines on the high places in the towns of Samaria will certainly come true."

³³Even after this, Jeroboam did not change his evil ways, but once more appointed priests for the high places from all sorts of people. Anyone who wanted to become a priest he consecrated for the high places. ³⁴This was the sin of the house of Jeroboam that led to its downfall and to its destruction from the face of the earth.

¹⁴:¹At that time Abijah son of Jeroboam became ill, ²and Jeroboam said to his wife, "Go, disguise yourself, so you won't be recognized as the wife of Jeroboam. Then go to Shiloh. Ahijah the prophet is there—the one who told me I would be king over this people. ³Take ten loaves of bread with you, some cakes and a jar of honey, and go to him. He will tell you what will happen to the boy." ⁴So Jeroboam's wife did what he said and went to Ahijah's house in Shiloh.

Now Ahijah could not see; his sight was gone because of his age. ⁵But the LORD had told Ahijah, "Jeroboam's wife is coming to ask you about her son, for he is ill, and you are to give her such and such an answer. When she arrives, she will pretend to be someone else."

⁶So when Ahijah heard the sound of her footsteps at the door, he said, "Come in, wife of Jeroboam. Why this pretense?

I have been sent to you with bad news. ⁷Go, tell Jeroboam that this is what the LORD, the God of Israel, says: 'I raised you up from among the people and made you a leader over my people Israel. ⁸I tore the kingdom away from the house of David and gave it to you, but you have not been like my servant David, who kept my commands and followed me with all his heart, doing only what was right in my eyes. ⁹You have done more evil than all who lived before you. You have made for yourself other gods, idols made of metal; you have provoked me to anger and thrust me behind your back.

¹⁰"Because of this, I am going to bring disaster on the house of Jeroboam. I will cut off from Jeroboam every last male in Israel—slave or free. I will burn up the house of Jeroboam as one burns dung, until it is all gone. ¹¹Dogs will eat those belonging to Jeroboam who die in the city, and the birds of the air will feed on those who die in the country. The LORD has spoken!'

¹²"As for you, go back home. When you set foot in your city, the boy will die. ¹³All Israel will mourn for him and bury him. He is the only one belonging to Jeroboam who will be buried, because he is the only one in the house of Jeroboam in whom the LORD, the God of Israel, has found anything good.

¹⁴"The LORD will raise up for himself a king over Israel who will cut off the family of Jeroboam. This is the day! What? Yes, even now. ¹⁵And the LORD will strike Israel, so that it will be like a reed swaying in the water. He will uproot Israel from this good land that he gave to their forefathers and scatter them beyond the River, because they provoked the LORD to anger by making Asherah poles. ¹⁶And he will give Israel up because of the sins Jeroboam has committed and has caused Israel to commit."

¹⁷Then Jeroboam's wife got up and left and went to Tirzah. As soon as she stepped over the threshold of the house, the boy died. ¹⁸They buried him, and all Israel mourned for him, as the LORD had said through his servant the prophet Ahijah.

¹⁹The other events of Jeroboam's reign, his wars and how he ruled, are written in the book of the annals of the kings of Israel. ²⁰He reigned for twenty-two years and then rested with his fathers. And Nadab his son succeeded him as king.

²¹Rehoboam son of Solomon was king in Judah. He was forty-one years old when he became king, and he reigned

seventeen years in Jerusalem, the city the LORD had chosen out of all the tribes of Israel in which to put his Name. His mother's name was Naamah; she was an Ammonite.

²²Judah did evil in the eyes of the LORD. By the sins they committed they stirred up his jealous anger more than their fathers had done. ²³They also set up for themselves high places, sacred stones and Asherah poles on every high hill and under every spreading tree. ²⁴There were even male shrine prostitutes in the land; the people engaged in all the detestable practices of the nations the LORD had driven out before the Israelites.

²⁵In the fifth year of King Rehoboam, Shishak king of Egypt attacked Jerusalem. ²⁶He carried off the treasures of the temple of the LORD and the treasures of the royal palace. He took everything, including all the gold shields Solomon had made. ²⁷So King Rehoboam made bronze shields to replace them and assigned these to the commanders of the guard on duty at the entrance to the royal palace. ²⁸Whenever the king went to the LORD's temple, the guards bore the shields, and afterward they returned them to the guardroom.

²⁹As for the other events of Rehoboam's reign, and all he did, are they not written in the book of the annals of the kings of Judah? ³⁰There was continual warfare between Rehoboam and Jeroboam. ³¹And Rehoboam rested with his fathers and was buried with them in the City of David. His mother's name was Naamah; she was an Ammonite. And Abijah his son succeeded him as king.

Original Meaning

THE STATE OF Israel begun by David in creating a national unity out of twelve quarreling tribes ends after the succession of the first king. The period of the united monarchy is more like a historical parenthesis.[1] David managed to forge a unity between north and south after a long struggle (2 Sam. 2:8–5:3). His first action as the leader of united Israel and Judah was to establish a capital city. He did this by conquering the Jebusite city of Jerusalem and establishing its fortress as the exclusive possession of his dynasty under the name "city of David" (5:6–9). The capital city was thus neutral in relation to the tribes since it was his by right of conquest.

---

1. Ahlström, *The History of Ancient Palestine*, 543.

Yet a strong central capital was insufficient to retain the unity of the nation. The main demand of the northern tribes was a relaxation of conscripted labor. Given their geographic and demographic superiority over Judah, the northern tribes seem to have felt they were shouldering a disproportionate share in supporting the central government, while at the same time receiving fewer benefits. Rehoboam is unable to reverse the tide of rebellion; he is depicted as callous and indifferent to the burdens of the people.

International relations deteriorate quickly. Egypt had been an ally in the days of Solomon, with the daughter of Pharaoh living in her own premises as queen. Only five years after Rehoboam begins to reign, Shishak king of Egypt plunders the gold that Solomon gathered. The kingdom of David disintegrates under Solomon, divides under Rehoboam, and soon comes into open civil war between north and south.

Jeroboam Made King over Israel (12:1–24)

DYNASTIC SUCCESSION DID not have an established procedure in the early days of the kingdom. Solomon had to overcome the forces of Adonijah in succeeding David to the throne. In the same way Rehoboam, son of Solomon, has to travel to Shechem to develop a consensus on his claim to the throne. Shechem was the original center of tribal commitment to the rule of Yahweh, their covenant god. Deuteronomy was structured around the requirement of a tribal commitment at Mounts Ebal and Gerizim, where Shechem was located (Deut. 11:29–32; 27:1–14). The fulfillment of this requirement was made a central point in the arrangement of the book of Joshua. Immediately after entering the land the assembly at Shechem fulfills the requirement of Deuteronomy (Josh. 8:30–35). Joshua concludes with a lengthy description of this assembly (24:1–27); an enduring monument was placed there as a memorial to the covenant that not only maintained the unity of the tribes but their faithfulness to serving Yahweh. If Rehoboam is to secure the loyalty of the northern tribes, he must do so at Shechem.

When Rehoboam arrives in Shechem, the representatives of the northern tribes, referred to as "the whole assembly of Israel," begin negotiations to gain concessions from the heavy load of taxation and conscripted service. The king is not at liberty to make an independent decision on this vital matter. He sets a time of three days to take counsel with the "elders" and the "young men," two groups who have a critical role in the political process.

Elders traditionally exercised considerable influence in royal decisions. When Ben Hadad, king of Aram of Damascus, attacked Samaria, the elders were decisive in rejecting his harsh terms of surrender (1 Kings 20:7–9). When Absalom revolted against David, the elders of Israel were an influential force in critical decisions (2 Sam. 17:4, 15; 19:11). These elders were distinguished from officials, nobles, and guardians (Judg. 8:14; 1 Kings 21:8; 2 Kings 10:5) who had official roles in governance.

The "young men" are described as those who have grown up with Rehoboam (12:8). This designation has a parallel to an Egyptian term referring to the children of officials and palace personnel. Evidence of Israelite court officials indicates that such "young men" are descendants of officials and courtiers of both royal and nonroyal descent who serve in various capacities.[2] Since Rehoboam is forty-one years old when he becomes king (14:21), they are not particularly youth. They belong to another generation and have different values from the more experienced elders. The elders held some type of official standing during the days of Solomon (12:6), and it is likely that the "young men" also had a high standing in the court. It is not apparent that these two groups are official bodies that convene to render decisions on vital matters,[3] but the king needs the support of one of these groups before he can proceed with a decision.

As might be expected, the opinions of the two groups of advisors are diametrically opposed. The elders, well tempered by years of political experience, urge moderation; they remind the king that he is the servant of the people (12:7), and only by acting in that capacity can he expect the people to be willing to serve him. The younger princes, having enjoyed a sense of power and status all of their lives, urge the new king to proceed in an autocratic manner, using political force to increase control over the populace. Their rhetoric is designed to inspire fear: "My little finger is thicker than my father's waist" (v. 10); "my father chastised you with whips, I will use scorpions" (v. 11). The sting of the "scorpion" is apparently a weighted or spiked lash that can be wielded by a taskmaster. The younger counselors see no need for conciliation. They cannot conceive of a leader as a servant to the people.

Rehoboam chooses not to follow the counsel of the elders. Though this is a foolish political choice, it is not just politics that influences his choice. The values of the covenant and the role of the king as a brother have already been lost by Solomon. The judgment of the prophets has already been declared; this turn of events is from Yahweh's fulfilling the declarations of the prophet Ahijah (v. 15). Yet it is wrong to interpret this statement as divine control over Rehoboam's mind. Rehoboam has no inner desire to follow Yahweh or the way of the covenant. He makes choices in accordance with his own values, which he has learned through his father.

---

2. Nili Fox, "Royal Officials and Court Families: A New Look at *yldym* (*yᵉlādîm*) in 1 Kings 12," *BA* 59 (1996): 225–32.

3. A case for such official status is made by A. Malamat, "Kingship and Council in Israel and Sumer: A Parallel," *JNES* 22 (1965): 248–51.

Rehoboam proceeds to follow the path of political coercion and sends Adoram, the commissioner over those conscripted into royal service, to deal with the unrest. Adoram may be an abbreviation of Adoniram, the commissioner who regulated the conscripted workers during the time of Solomon (4:6). Whether or not he is known from an earlier regime, the people are in no mood to listen to new policies for regular terms of state service. They kill him, and Rehoboam flees to Jerusalem.

Rehoboam has not lost all capacity to respect the prophetic word. In accordance with the advice of the "young men," Rehoboam prepares a considerable army to enforce his will over the rebellious tribes (12:21). A godly man named Shemaiah reminds him that though these tribes have rejected his rule, they are still brothers of the covenant. Their rejection of his rule is not a judgment against them, but the evidence of a divine judgment against Rehoboam himself. Rehoboam respects this judgment sufficiently to refrain from further political conflict and self-destruction.

The death of Solomon and the revolt of the northern tribes provides the occasion for Jeroboam to return from his exile in Egypt and assume leadership over the new political entity of Israel (12:20). His role in the revolt has been a matter of considerable discussion. It seems that Jeroboam is not summoned to the assembly until after the murder of Adoram, when it becomes known he has returned from Egypt (v. 20). Earlier references to Jeroboam indicate he is present during the negotiations at Shechem (vv. 2–3, 12). Presumably, Jeroboam has had a role in inspiring the verdict that Israel has no inheritance in the dynasty of David (12:16).

Innovations in the Northern Kingdom (12:25–32)

JEROBOAM CREATES A distinct kingdom in the north through various changes. He fortifies Shechem to make it a royal residence, then Penuel across the Jordan (12:25), and finally Tirzah (cf. 14:17). He establishes places of worship in Bethel and Dan so the people will not go to Jerusalem for the pilgrimage festivals; he makes the Canaanite bull the symbol of divine presence and providence (12:27–31). Archaeological evidence indicates that in the days of Jeroboam the sanctuary at Dan extended over a relatively large area (approximately 150 feet or 45 meters by 200 feet or 60 meters). This area, with its various structures, storerooms, and open spaces paved with stone, may be the various "houses on the high places" (v. 31).[4]

Jeroboam alters the priesthood, ordaining those not from the tribe of Levi; he establishes the eighth month as the time of the great fall pilgrimage

---

4. Biran Avraham, "Tel Dan: Biblical Texts and Archaeological Data," in *Scripture and Other Artifacts: Essays in Honor of Philip J. King*, ed. Michael D. Coogan, J. Cheryl Exum, and Lawrence E. Stager (Louisville: Westminster John Knox, 1994), 7.

(12:32). These changes establish him as a legitimate king and serve to isolate those who are inclined to loyalty toward Jerusalem.

The name Shechem ("shoulder") is probably derived from the location of the city on the slopes of Mount Ebal to the north or Gerizim to the south. This strategic valley of fertile soil provides access to the central hill country from the Jordan. The ascent follows the deeply faulted Wadi Faria from the river fords at Adam to Tirzah, and from there to Shechem. Shechem replaces Shiloh (to the south) as a religious and political center. From there inner montane roads lead to the west through the valley and to points north through the Dothan Valley and Jezreel.

Tirzah ("beauty") is about seven miles (eleven kilometers) northeast of Shechem. It is destroyed shortly after Jeroboam, possibly during the siege of Omri when Zimri burns down his own palace (16:17—18). Penuel is east of the Jordan at a crossing of the Jabbok Valley. It was a sacred site as the place where Jacob wrestled with the angel (Gen. 32:22—32). Jeroboam's fortification assists in the control of Gilead, an area that remained loyal to David in the revolt of Absalom.

The ordination of nonlevitical priests may have been part of the policy to forge a separation between the kingdoms of David and Jeroboam. The Levitical settlements were agents of David and Solomon in preserving Israelite faith and culture as Canaanite territories were added to the kingdom (1 Chron. 26:29—32).[5] The settlements in southern Benjamin may have been designed to resist the influence of the family of Saul. Levitical priests would naturally have had a loyalty to the temple as well as David, and most may have been unwilling to serve at a separate shrine.

An annual pilgrimage festival was common in the religions of Syria and Mesopotamia. Rehoboam would have used the occasion of the fall festival to seek the confirmation of his rule in Shechem. If that were the case, it would have been necessary for Jeroboam to counter that festival in the next month to establish his own independent dominion. The fall Festival of Booths was connected to the completion of harvest; it was the Feast of Ingathering (Ex. 23:16). Harvest is dependent on weather; in Palestine the more tropical south generally has an earlier harvest than the more moderate north. The Gezer Calendar, from about the time of Jeroboam, was based on agricultural cycles and appears to have had flexibility for the time of the fruit harvest festival.[6] David set up Jerusalem as a new capital between Shechem and Hebron; Solomon centralized worship and established an exclusive priesthood.

---

5. Gray, *I & II Kings*, 296. This thesis was developed by B. Mazar in "The Cities of the Priests and Levites," *Congress Volume* (VTSup 7; Leiden: Brill, 1960), 193–205.

6. S. Talmon, "Divergencies in Calendar-Reckoning in Ephraim and Judah," *VT* 8 (1958): 55–56.

Prophetic Condemnation of Jeroboam (12:33−13:34)

JEROBOAM'S ASCENT TO the altar on the first day of the festival is the initiation of the high place he has built.[7] A man of God from Judah calls Jeroboam to account for his worship at Bethel (13:1−10).[8] There is an old prophet from Bethel who tests this word from Yahweh (vv. 11−32). Literary analysts often treat this narrative as two different stories, each with its own distinct though related focus.[9] They see the first as a polemic against the cultic establishment of Jeroboam, the second as a narrative about importance of obedience to the divine word. There is, however, a literary unity to this chapter that has its focus on the religious reforms of Jeroboam.[10]

The disobedience of Jeroboam to the word of Yahweh leads him to the same fate as the disobedience of the man of God who came from Judah. The faithful man of God becomes unfaithful, just as Jeroboam, the anointed king of Israel, goes his own way and becomes the object of the word of judgment. The man of God from Judah proclaims God's word in declaring the folly of Jeroboam, but then chooses the way of folly himself in disobeying what he knows to be God's word given to him.

A second revelation given to the man of God from Judah is pivotal in understanding the message of this story about two prophets. Three times we are told the man of God from Judah is not to eat bread, drink water, or return by the way he came. The first occurs in his encounter with Jeroboam. The king suffers paralysis of his arm in demanding that the prophet be seized (13:4). The prophet prays for the king and his arm is restored (v. 6), and the king in turn offers the man of God hospitality (v. 7), possibly as a sign of solidarity and affirmation of his new position. The prophet refuses, citing the prohibition of Yahweh given to him (vv. 8−10).[11]

---

7. The virtual repetition of the previous verse introduces the condemnation of the altar; mention of the altar is sufficient to bring the entire place of worship under judgment.

8. "Man of God" is a term synonymous with prophet (cf. 13:1, 18).

9. See, e.g., Werner E. Lemke, "The Way of Obedience: 1 Kings 13 and the Structure of the Deuteronomisitc History," in *Magnalia Dei: The Mighty Acts of God: Essays on the Bible and Archaeology in Memory of G.Ernest Writght*, ed. F. M. Cross, W. E. Lemke, and P. D. Miller (Garden City, N.Y.: Doubleday, 1976), 305−6; D. W. van Winkle, "1 Kings XIII: True and False Prophecy," *VT* 39 (1989): 35−36.

10. In a later study van Winkle proposes that 1 Kings 12:25−13:34 forms a literary unit, with the result that the condemnation of the altar at Bethel and the disobedience of the prophet are meant to point to Jeroboam's disobedience; see "1 Kings XII 25-XIII 34: Jeroboam's Cultic Innovations and the Man of God from Judah," *VT* 46 (1996): 102−9.

11. D. J. Wiseman, in *1 & 2 Kings: An Introduction and Commentary* (TOTC; Downers Grove, Ill.: InterVarsity Press, 1993), 146−47, observes that fellowship would be tantamount to a withdrawal of judgment, and returning the same way would mean contact with a cursed people.

When the old prophet from Bethel invites the man from Judah to return for food and drink, the latter repeats the prohibition, which he knows to be Yahweh's word (vv. 16–17). The prophet from Bethel lies (v. 18), averring that a messenger from Yahweh has told him the man from Judah should return and eat bread with him. Following the lie does not excuse the man from Judah, who has demonstrated with a sign that he knows the word of Yahweh (v. 5). When the word of judgment comes to the prophet from Bethel the prohibition of eating and drinking is repeated (v. 22). The disobedience of the prophet from Judah with its attendant judgment becomes a demonstration of the judgment that rests on the house of Jeroboam.

The context and sequences of the story depict the judgment that awaits Israel.[12] Jeroboam has built altars, which become a sin for the people (12:25–33). The obedient man of God proclaims judgment against the altar at Bethel as Jeroboam stands by (13:1–10). But the prophet himself compromises his mission returning to eat and drink, contrary to God's word (vv. 11–19). The prophet of Judah is condemned by a word of Yahweh given by the prophet from Bethel and falls prey to a lion (vv. 20–25a). The donkey stands helplessly beside his body, just as Jeroboam stood beside the shattered altar. In subtle terms this scene shows Jeroboam to be an dumb animal.[13]

In the final scene the prophet from Bethel retrieves the body from the presence of the lion, which has not molested the body or mauled the donkey (vv. 25b–32). The lion's abstention from eating serves to emphasize retrospectively the transgression of the man of God in eating prohibited food.[14] The warning at the altar does nothing to change the ways of Jeroboam (vv. 33–34). He proceeds to ordain priests to serve at the high places. This is the sin of Jeroboam that leads to the dissolution of the nation and its ultimate destruction.

Prophetic Judgment against Jeroboam (14:1–20)

JUDGMENT AGAINST THE house of Jeroboam begins with the illness and death of his son Abijah. The name of his son meant "my father is Yah(weh)," suggesting a pretentious claim on the part of the king. The illness of the son is so severe the king seeks the help of the prophet Ahijah, who brought him the original oracle of his appointment as king. He sends his wife from his residence in Tirzah (v. 17) to Shiloh in Ephraim, where the prophet resides. She is to be disguised so Ahijah will not know who is coming with the request, possibly because Jeroboam hopes to receive a more favorable

---

12. James K. Mead, "Kings and Prophets, Donkeys and Lions: Dramatic Shape and Deuteronomistic Rhetoric in 1 Kings XIII," *VT* 49 (1999): 194–97.

13. Ibid., 202.

14. Ibid., 204.

response. She carries a modest gift (cf. 2 Kings 5:22–23) as a tribute to the prophet. The physical sight of Ahijah has failed, but he has inspired vision, which not only enables him to identify his visitor but declare the harsh message he has for her.

The condemnation of Jeroboam is in terms of his call (14:7–11; cf. 11:33–35). Jeroboam has received the kingdom at the expense of the Davidic dynasty because Solomon failed to be loyal to God. That Jeroboam is "more evil than all who lived before [him]" (v. 9) is stereotyped language found repeatedly in Kings; David was not evil as Jeroboam, but Jeroboam has committed the same sins as Solomon and leaders before David. The judgment that came on Solomon will also come on Jeroboam. His whole royal house will die without receiving a proper burial (vv. 10–11). The idiom "him that pisseth against the wall, and him who is shut up and left in Israel" (v. 10, KJV) refers to royal descendants. The expression refers to males who are privileged to relieve themselves in royal quarters, those who are to be a ruler and deliverer.[15] A comparison of related verses (16:11; 2 Kings 14:26) indicates a reference to leaders as helpers or deliverers, and the contexts are always in reference to the royal family.

The judgment against Jeroboam begins the moment his wife enters the city (vv. 12–13). His son will die and will be mourned by all Israel. Only this child of the house of Jeroboam will be buried with dignity. Yahweh will raise up another king in place of the descendants of Jeroboam (v. 14), but ultimately the whole nation will go into exile beyond the Euphrates because of his sins (vv. 15–16). The metaphor of a reed shaken in the water may refer to the many dynastic changes that will shortly take place or to the uncertainty that comes with the instability of leadership. The Asherah poles, which are so offensive to Yahweh (v. 15; cf. Judg. 6:25, 28), are associated with the worship of Baal, representing the goddess of fertility. Jeroboam has introduced the key elements of Canaanite worship that will be a continual sin in Israel, known thereafter as "the sins of Jeroboam son of Nebat."

The concluding notice of the reign of Jeroboam makes special note of his great feats in warfare and rule (14:19–20). His twenty-two years are 930–908 B.C. Information from the royal annals of the kings, referred to as "the book of the annals of the kings of Israel," must have been incorporated into the sources the prophetic authors used to compile their history.[16] Reference to

---

15. Shemaryahu Talmon and Weston W. Fields, "The Collocation *mštyn bqyr ʿṣwr wʿzwb* and its Meaning," *ZAW* 101 (1989), 85–109. Rather than "slave or free" (NIV), the expression is a hendiadys meaning "ruler-deliverer." This assumes a second root for ʿzb meaning "arrange, order" rather than "abandon," a word also attested in Ugaritic.

16. Menahem Haran, "The Books of the Chronicles 'of the Kings of Judah' and 'of the Kings of Israel': What Sort of Books Were They?" *VT* 49 (1999): 156–62.

these records becomes a fixed and formalized framework for the reign of each king. The authors adapt information from their sources to serve their purposes and are responsible for giving the regnal résumé its standard form. The flow of thought around common themes is developed from the story of each king, and the sequence is indicated by standard summaries of each reign.

The Reign of Rehoboam (14:21−31)

THE INTRODUCTORY REGNAL résumé introduces Rehoboam at the death of Solomon (vv. 21−24; cf. 11:43); he reigns from 930−913 B.C. Rehoboam reigns in Judah, the name for the southern kingdom in the books of Kings, with the term Israel restricted to the northern kingdom. It is noted that Rehoboam is the son of an Ammonite woman, one of the many foreign wives who were a part of Solomon's court.

Most notable about Rehoboam is the way he leads Judah in the sins of Canaanite worship, no less than what Jeroboam does in the north. This includes the erection of sacred stones along with the sacred poles representing Asherah, the goddess of fertility. It was legitimate to set up stones as a memorial (Gen. 28:18; 35:14), or as a witness (31:45), but it was not permissible to follow the practice of the Canaanites to use such stones for worship (Ex. 23:24). Worship "on every high hill and under every spreading tree" may be a way of referring to the domain of the deity and the associated fertility. Worst of all are the "shrine prostitutes," a collective term that perhaps refers to both males and females. Sexual relations were part of sacrificial rites as a means of achieving fertility and prosperity (Hos. 4:14). Cult practices and prostitution were explicitly forbidden by the covenant (Deut. 23:18).

One of the main events of the reign of Rehoboam is the invasion of Shoshenq I of Egypt, known to the Hebrews as Shishak (14:25−28). The division of Israel, along with internal union and peace in Egypt, provide opportunity for political and commercial exploitation. A fragmentary victory stela from Thebes (Karnak) provides a description of a border skirmish that may have been the immediate occasion for the invasion.[17]

The general course of Shishak's campaign can be inferred from a topical list inscribed on the pylon of a temple in Karnak.[18] Shoshenq with the main army goes up a well-traveled route by Ajalon and Gibeon to secure the submission and tribute of Rehoboam in Jerusalem. From there he travels north to Megiddo, possibly through Tirzah, the capital of Jeroboam. Of greatest

---

17. Kitchen, *The Third Intermediate Period in Egypt*, 292−94.
18. For interpretations of this list see the excursus in ibid., 442−47.

significance is the cost of the campaign to the wealth and splendor that Solomon accumulated. The temple and palace are stripped; mere bronze shields replace the gold ones Solomon made. The ceremonial marches to the temple lose much of their former splendor.

LONG-STANDING DIVISIONS. David's kingdom suffered from internal conflict even while it was emerging as a powerful empire in Palestine. Absalom shook the foundations of the kingdom in gaining the sympathy of the most influential people by taking advantage of the tribal institutions of eldership that David had transcended in a unified state (2 Sam. 15:13). David was forced to take refuge in Mahanaim in Transjordan, which was generally interested in a strong central monarchy. However, the deep division between Israel and Judah surfaced on his return, with David reliant mainly on his kinsmen in Judah and unable to internally unite them in one monarchical administration (19:15, 40−44). The action resulted in the revolt of Sheba the son of Bichri (20:1−2). Joab was able to stamp out the revolt without destroying any Israelite cities, but the internal division between Israel and Judah remained.

The words of Sheba in his rejection of David (2 Sam. 20:1) came to be used against Rehoboam after the death of Solomon (1 Kings 12:16):

> What share do we have in David,
> what part in Jesse's son?
> To your tents, O Israel!
> Look after your own house, O David!

Poetic sayings like this circulated widely in oral form and were long remembered because they expressed deeply held feelings during the time of the united monarchy. This saying appears to be the converse of an earlier saying used to rally support for David. The Chronicler provides such a saying at the center of a chapter designed to show growing support for David (1 Chron. 12:18):

> We are yours, O David!
> We are with you, O son of Jesse!
> Success, success to you,
> and peace to those who help you, for your God will help you.

These words expressed support for David from a group that came from Benjamin and Judah (1 Chron. 12:17). It seems reasonable to suggest that such a saying arose early in David's rise as a slogan of support.[19] Later antag-onism to David on the throne led to such a saying being developed beyond a personal level in the classic formulation of Sheba in his attack on David. When it surfaces again at the division of the kingdom, it takes on dynastic dimensions with the addition of the line, "Look after your own house, O David!"

The death of Solomon shows again how divided Israel remained during the time of Solomon's reign. Matters seriously deteriorated toward the end of Solomon's reign, as one of his highest officials over the house of Joseph (1 Kings 11:28) was exiled to Egypt (v. 40). It is not clear that Jeroboam's "mutiny" is a revolt by the north against Solomon, but it enhances his can-didacy for the throne of Israel.

What is significant in this account of highly complex political turmoil is the role of the prophets. It was a "man of God" named Shemaiah who averts a civil war by persuading the contestants to behave in accordance with Yah-weh's word (12:21–24). Rehoboam has 120,000 elite troops ready to whip the northern tribes back into submission, but he does not use them. Even as the words of the prophet Ahijah are being fulfilled in giving ten parts of the kingdom to Jeroboam (v. 15; cf. 11:31), the words of Shemaiah have the effect of averting a disastrous war.

Tactics of Jeroboam. Jeroboam does not prove more faithful than Solomon in following the demands of the covenant. Political motivations lead him to establish cult centers in the north (12:26–29) and a different time of the Passover (vv. 32–33). Not only does Jeroboam compromise the unity of worship with his innovations, he introduces syncretistic elements. The bull was the common symbol for the Canaanite fertility cult in the worship of Baal. The whole message of the temple was that the Creator could not be repre-sented by any form, since he could not be limited to any element of creation. The counsel given to Jeroboam is no doubt shrewd in its accommodation of popular culture (12:28), but it is destructive of the exclusive worship of Yah-weh; worship at Dan and Bethel become the sin that characterizes the north-ern kingdom.

The two cult shrines are particularly offensive. The offense is not just that it is contrary to worshiping at the one place (Deut. 12:4–7), since Shiloh and Gibeon were legitimate places of worship. The problem is syncretism with Canaanite religion; they are like the high places of the nations, which the Israelites were to destroy (12:2–3). The figure of the bull serves as a

19. H. G. M. Williamson, "'We Are Yours, O David': The Setting and Purpose of 1 Chronicles xii 1–23," in *Remembering All the Way*, ed. B. Albrektson (*OtSt* 21; Leiden: Brill, 1981), 174–75.

footstool for the king, much as the ark did in the temple. Canaanite iconography depicts Baal as standing on the back of a bull with the lightning rod and the thunder club in his hands.

The use of such a symbol has a certain logic. Jeroboam cannot imitate the temple in Jerusalem; if the symbols are not those of the covenant, they must have some other connection to the world of the people. The calf is readily understood as a representation of fertility and prosperity, aspects of Yahweh that the people desire to affirm. They also readily understand the calf as a symbol of an invisible god, as the Canaanites do. Though Jeroboam intends the calves to be a symbol of Yahweh who brought them up from Egypt (v. 28; cf. Ex. 32:1, 4), they can never be dissociated from the Phoenician god Hadad. They further limit the representation of Yahweh to specific elements of creation and providence and as such are a complete distortion of the Lord of the covenant. The shrines are a continual offense and lead to Phoenician practices so that in the days of Elijah there is virtually no one who has not bowed the knee to Baal.

Solomon fully established centralization of worship with the building of the temple; the pilgrimage festivals then had to be observed at the same time. In breaking with this innovation Jeroboam is able to establish himself as maintaining the traditions of God, who brought them up from Egypt (12:28).[20] Not only does Jeroboam counter the claim of Rehoboam at Shechem, he counters the innovation of a centralized festival during the seventh month, before the harvest in the north is complete.

The calendar was a complex and often contentious issue in Israel. It was complex because it had to be based on annual solar cycles relating to harvest, but the year was based on lunar cycles, which do not coincide with the solar cycle. It was necessary to add a month approximately every three years in lunar calendar reckoning.[21] It is possible that Jeroboam adds a month in a year when Judah does not, a convenient means of discouraging citizens of Israel to make the pilgrimage to Jerusalem.[22] The decision to observe the feast in a different month would not be a radical change.

Though God has called Jeroboam to be king over ten tribes of Israel (11:31, 35), the success of his reign depends on obedience (vv. 37—38), the same conditions that pertained for David. Jeroboam's reforms are well designed to establish an independent kingdom, but they do not foster wor-

---

20. Talmon, "Divergencies in Calendar-Reckoning in Ephraim and Judah," 50.

21. J. B. Segal provides tables showing how the calculations may have been derived using heliacal risings and settings in conjunction with the moon; see "Intercalation and the Hebrew Calendar," *VT* 7 (1957): 271—72.

22. Ibid., 257—59, 275.

ship of Yahweh. Prophetic judgment against Jeroboam comes at the great festival as the king ascends the altar at Bethel to make his dedication offering (12:33). Bethel had long been a sacred place of worship. Jacob built an altar there (Gen. 35:1, 6–7), Deborah presided near Bethel (Judg. 4:5), and the ark of the covenant was brought there (Judg. 20:27). Jeroboam follows sacred tradition in building an altar there, but his worship is not acceptable.

Jeroboam does not understand the lordship of Yahweh, which cannot be compromised by foreign symbols. The situation is exactly as Joshua said it would be when the covenant was first made at Shechem (Josh. 24:19–22). Though the people vowed to serve Yahweh, they did not understand the nature of such a commitment. Yahweh was not like other gods; he did not share his dominion.

The two prophets. A man of God from Judah brings the word of Yahweh in condemning Jeroboam's place of worship. The mission of this prophet demonstrates both the inspiration of his message and the importance of unconditional obedience. The mission of this prophet is to deliver his message and return to Judah without accepting any hospitality (13:8–9). An old prophet from Bethel tests the man of God on this point, urging him to return and accept his offer of hospitality. Judgment comes on the prophet; a lion kills him, and in very unlion-like fashion stands guard over his body with the donkey standing by. The death of the man from Judah for his disobedience is proof for the prophet at Bethel that the man from Judah has indeed proclaimed the word of Yahweh. If the man of God had arrived safely home, it would have proved he did not truly bear a word from God.

The story about the two prophets illustrates the problem of false prophecy in Israel. Even during the last days of Judah, a prophet named Hananiah took a stand against Jeremiah, promising that the yoke of Babylon would be broken and the valuables plundered from the temple would be restored (Jer. 28:1–4). Death was his fate for false prophecy (v. 17). The prophetic warning against Jeroboam has an ironic twist. In the words of Crenshaw, "Here one sees the true prophet become false to his commission, and the 'false prophet' takes up the genuine word of God and lets it fall with shattering force upon the erring man of God."23

In the present case, the problem of a lying prophet serves the interests of prophecy itself. The word of the prophet from Judah is truly a word from Yahweh (13:32). The narrative shows that Jeroboam had ample warning from a genuine man of God, thus magnifying his guilt.24 The prophet from Judah

---

23. James L. Crenshaw, *Prophetic Conflict: Its Effect upon Israelite Religion* (BZAW 124; Berlin: de Gruyter, 1971), 48.
24. Ibid., 43.

demonstrates unwittingly the critical requirement of obedience. A man of God, prophet or king, must be so committed to transcendent truth that his entire life is controlled by it. The old prophet from Bethel shows him tremendous respect. The prophet fetches the body, buries it in his own tomb, laments over him as a brother, and requests that his own body be placed alongside that of the venerable prophet (vv. 27–31). The unmolested body is a sign that the word of judgment against the man of God from Judah is authentic. Disobedience to the divine word is a fearful matter. The prophet from Judah was false to himself and paid the ultimate price.

In every age there are those who claim to speak for God. These chapters provide the clearest test for recognizing words from God: obedience by the prophet. A prophetic message apart from obedience cannot be assured as coming from God. In this regard the man from Judah fails, but in so doing proves that he was a true prophet. The judgment of death applied to both prophet and king. Ahijah the prophet, the man who promised Jeroboam ten parts of the kingdom, delivers the message that his dynasty will come to an abrupt end because of his disobedience (14:7–11). His son Nadab is murdered in a conspiracy after a two-year reign. The only member of Jeroboam's family to have a honorable burial was a young, innocent child who dies of illness.

The sin of Jeroboam ultimately leads to the death of the nation because he leads them in the way of disobedience. The situation in the southern kingdom is not much different. A dynasty of kings is preserved as a light for David in Jerusalem, as Ahijah has said (11:36). The temple holds hope of true worship of Yahweh in Jerusalem, but it does not assure that worship. Rehoboam leads the nation in a way that provokes the anger of Yahweh as none before him (14:22), a foreboding omen for the future of that nation as well.

The way of the Canaanites. The Former Prophets of the Hebrew Bible (Joshua–Kings) show a pattern of apostasy from the covenant. The book of Joshua is a compilation of materials that show how God fulfilled his promise of giving Israel the land of Canaan as an inheritance. Judges shows how the Israelites themselves became indistinguishable from the Canaanites. Joshua shows how Canaan became Israelite, and Judges how Israel became Canaanite.

The complete apostasy of Israel is illustrated in Judges 19. A Levite on his return home refuses to lodge in the foreign city of Jebus (pre-Davidic Jerusalem), but goes on to the Benjamite city of Gibeah (Judg. 19:11–14). The Levite and his company are ignored until finally an old man returning from work provides hospitality (vv. 15–21). That night the Benjamites demanded sexual relations with the Levite. When this is refused, they abuse the concubine of the Levite until she dies (vv. 22–28). These verses have precise verbal parallel to the account of Lot receiving the two messengers in Sodom (Gen. 19:4–11). This technique is called echo narrative; it is a means of using a previous account to interpret a new event.[25] Sodom is the quintessence of Canaanitism in the Scriptures (e.g., Isa. 1:7–10). The end of the story of Judges shows that apostasy has made the Israelites indistinguishable from the Canaanites.

The apostasy of Jeroboam in Kings shows that Israel and Judah once again as indistinguishable from Canaanites. The Davidic promise in 1–2 Samuel explains how after the period of the Judges God has again provided rest for the Israelites in their land (2 Sam. 7:1; cf. Josh. 21:43–45). In spite of all the struggles in David's house, God has provided for his chosen son to receive the throne. But at the end of his reign the nation divides and is in constant internal conflict. Though the majestic temple gives testimony to the incomparable God of the covenant, both Israel and Judah adopt the ways of the Canaanites.

Prophetic worldview. The history of Kings makes the sins of Jeroboam son of Nebat the influence that sets the pattern for all the kings that follow after him and sets the kingdom on a fateful course of annihilation. This persistent reminder is given in the negative evaluation of virtually every Israelite king. The fall of Israel is summarized in the following words:

> When he tore Israel away from the house of David, they made Jeroboam son of Nebat their king. Jeroboam enticed Israel away from following the LORD and caused them to commit a great sin. The Israelites persisted in all the sins of Jeroboam and did not turn away from them until the LORD removed them from his presence, as he had warned through all his servants the prophets. So the people of Israel were taken from their homeland into exile in Assyria, and they are still there. (2 Kings 17:21–23)

Jeroboam has been described as an *Unheilsherrscher*.[26] The closest English equivalents are "calamitous ruler" or "ill-fated ruler," but the German term connotes the elements of the king's own instrumentality in bringing about misfortune through real or alleged misdeeds. This portrayal of Jeroboam as being responsible for the fall of Israel is peculiar to the history of Kings. The

---

25. For an analysis of this technique, with specific application to this story, see Daniel Block, "Echo Narrative Technique in Hebrew Literature: A Study in Judges 9," *WTJ* 52 (1990): 325–31.

26. Carl D. Evans, "Naram-Sin and Jeroboam: The Archetypal *Unheilsherrscher* in Mesopotamian and Biblical Historiography," in *Scripture in Context II: More Essays on the Comparative Method*, ed. William W. Hallo, James C. Moyer, and Leo G. Perdue (Winona Lake, Ind.: Eisenbrauns, 1983), 99.

Chronicler does not take account of the fall of Israel, since his focus is on the history of Judah, but he does offer a lengthy censure of Jeroboam (2 Chron. 13:4–12). Though Jeroboam is soundly condemned for his idolatry, there is no suggestion that he is responsible for the ultimate disappearance of Israel. Isaiah gives a vivid description of the moral decay that led to the ruin of the northern kingdom, but he does not make Jeroboam the primary culprit in the matter (Isa. 9:7–21). Kings alone assigns blame and culpability for the fall of Israel to Jeroboam.

This kind of historical perspective is known in other history writing of the ancient Near East. Perhaps the closest parallel is a ruler named Naram-Sin of the third millennium (ca. 2230–2100 B.C.). Naram-Sin followed Sargon I as ruler of the empire of Akkad. His rule has been described as "the most brilliant period that the Sargonic empire—and perhaps any Mesopotamian empire—was to know."[27] In a poetic writing called the Curse of Agade, Naram-Sin is said to have incurred the curse of the gods by sacrilege. The Gutians from the distant mountains invaded the land like a swarm of grasshoppers. The gods pronounced a lengthy curse against Akkad, dooming it to utter destruction. Naram-Sin, in spite of all his political achievements, became the paradigm of an *Unheilsherrscher* as an example to other dynasties.

In spite of his divine calling and privileged position as a successor to Solomon, Jeroboam is remembered as the king who brought destruction to himself and to his land. Though Israel has a long history with many wicked kings, the prophetic historians view the fall of Israel as the responsibility of Jeroboam. This king violated three fundamental theological propositions of the kingdom of God: The promise of God belonged to the Davidic dynasty (cf. 12:26–27); only the temple could represent the divine presence (12:28–29); the worship of God was to take place in Jerusalem (12:30–33). Ahijah condemns Jeroboam on each of these three counts.[28] Jeroboam's dynasty ends because he established other symbols of worship so the people would not go to Jerusalem (14:9–11). The prophetic interpretation of Israel's history is that Jeroboam has fundamentally undermined loyalty to God and is thus responsible for the nation's destruction.

It is often said that those who do not learn from history are bound to repeat it. The problem is that the lessons of history are not so transparent. History is a complexity of factors; many different causes are involved in the events that transpire. The lessons of historians are themselves shaped by the

---

27. W. W. Hallo and William K. Simpson, *The Ancient Near East: A History* (New York: Harcourt Brace Jovanovich, 1971), 60.

28. John Holder, "The Presuppositions, Accusations, and Threats of 1 Kings 14:1–18," *JBL* 107 (1988): 27–38.

worldview of the history writer. According to the Mesopotamian legends, Naram-Sin caused the fall and destruction of Akkad. In their worldview the gods were responsible for the prosperity of their cities, so the fall of a city was logically explained by sacrilege against the gods. In this respect the prophets of Israel follow the same method; they believe that Yahweh has given the land to Israel; he is offended and brings judgment on the land.

Modern historians are different in their worldview; they interpret historical events according to their own economic, social, or anthropological theories, often without making their controlling assumptions explicit. Insofar as worldview is an expression of faith, modern histories are nevertheless controlled by religion, just as were those of the ancients.

 DO NOT BE CONFORMED **to this world.** The division of the kingdom is a sobering reminder of the danger of conforming to surrounding culture, all the while believing that confessions of faith are being followed and supported. The condemnations from Ahijah and the prophet of Judah make the sin of Israel seem self-evident. The story of the prophet from Bethel who lies in contradiction to the prophet from Judah is a reminder that Jeroboam had his supporting cast of prophets and priests who regarded their version of worship to be an acceptable expression of their faith in God.

Jeroboam goes back to earlier traditions in some of his innovations: a northern capital, northern sites of worship, and a northern time of the fall festival. In spite of the sign of a broken altar and a withered arm, Jeroboam refuses to change his ways. The nation of Israel follows him, even though they see the cost of disobedience in the death of the prophet from Judah. The conflict Judah has with the north is not because of idolatry, for Rehoboam leads Judah down the same path of syncretism. Political agendas and cultural pressures have an enormous power to distort adherence to faith in God and obedience to a divinely ordered way of life.

Jesus, in his high priestly prayer for his disciples, did not ask that God take them out of the world, but that God would keep them from the evil one; they were not of this world, just as Jesus himself was not of this world (John 17:15–16). Christians have struggled with this concept and debated it in many ways. Christians understand that they live by the values and conduct of the kingdom of God, but it is not easy to know how these are to be exercised in particular circumstances. To some extent believers must conform to the culture around them as part of the world they live in, but in certain ways their lives need to manifest a different value system.

It is easy for Christians to become consumed with the pursuit of wealth and a better standard of living. Such a standard is a good goal, but not if it becomes the purpose for work and use of one's time. Christians understand that good relationships within family and community must be a high priority, but it is difficult to maintain good relations in the stress of daily life and encounters with difficult individuals. Some would even say "Christian businessman" is an oxymoron, since the interaction of business often requires dealings that are contrary to values of the Christian community. It is easiest to maintain a form of faith by certain practices like prayer and worship, even though much else of importance has been critically compromised.

Even maintaining an expression of Christian faith has become a challenge. Many churhces are facing an acute shortage of pastors. One denomination reports that it will need one hundred new pastors each year for the next ten years to replace those who are now between fifty-five and sixty-five years old. At the same time their seminary has half as many students as it did twenty years ago. The growth in pastoral needs is an indication that the influence of the church and the work of pastoral teaching are implicitly held to be of inferior value.

There are various reasons for pastoral work not being a career of choice for gifted young Christians. A modern society occupied with individual rights and activist concerns for political agendas has increasingly marginalized the church. There was a time when the opinion of a minister was respected in ethical discussion, but more often now values based on faith are regarded as illegitimate in public life. There is a type of state religion established by government and courts on moral and ethical issues. Instead of recognizing this as a counter religious force, some Christians seem to be prepared to conform to these cultural norms. There is little encouragement for gifted young people to take up the challenge of thoughtfully articulating their faith in a society of a contrary religion. Christian leaders are pursuing careers where their opinion can be respected. This is important, but if it happens at the expense of thoughtful leadership in Christian congregations, there will be an increasing conformity to the culture and standards of a self-centered, self-absorbed, secular society.

The existentialism of the mid-twentieth century led to a postmodern culture with its own view of life and the world. Truth has become an individual matter, and spirituality is related to one's emotional health. Evidence is growing that this culture has begun to compromise Christian faith, much as the calves and calendar of Jeroboam and the sacred stones and Asherah poles of Rehoboam led to the dissolution of faith in Israel and Judah. Many are aware of this compromise of faith, but too many deny it. Without thoughtful and informed leadership, the church is in danger of becoming more religiously obscurantist and irrelevant.

As in the days of Jeroboam and Rehoboam, there is an expression of faith that has compromised biblical life and values so it is indistinguishable from the surrounding culture. Jesus did not ask that his followers be taken from the world, but that they would be sanctified in the truth of God's Word and sent into the world (John 17:17–18). Purity from this world must begin with clear Christian thinking. Failure to clearly distinguish Christian faith from postmodern relativism will lead Christians to conform to the ways of the world.

Interpreting the signs. The story of the division of the kingdom should cause Christians to give careful thought to present history and life in this world. Believers are often prepared to explain the unfolding of political events in terms of divine judgment. It was the prerogative of inspired prophets to offer such analysis, especially when passing judgment on false worship as flagrant as that of Jeroboam. Jeroboam knew well the power of Ahijah to pass judgment on his reign, since his coming to power had been through Ahijah's word from the beginning.

Jesus discouraged his disciples from looking for signs of final judgment in the events of their times. He said they would hear of wars and insurrections, but they were not to fear; this was a sign that the end was *not yet* (Luke 21:9). All these things are part of the times of this age, but those who belong to the kingdom of God need not fear. The falling of kingdoms is not in itself an indication that the end is immanent. The story of Jeroboam and Rehoboam beckons Christians to be vigilant about doing God's will on earth as it is in heaven so that they will be distinguished from the ways of the world, but they should not be occupied with explaining how God is working in the events of the present time that his kingdom may come.

The prophets of Israel were able to proclaim boldly the work of God in their own history, declaring that the fall of the kingdom was the immediate result of disobedience. Prophetic activity was not without conflict in its own context, and it was possible for a true prophet to be deceived and to fail. It is necessary to have an understanding of the work of God in history, but it is not self-evident how God is at work in political events. Web sites such as *raptureready.com* track events that are a sign of the end: earthquakes, floods, plagues, crime, false prophets, and economic measurements like unemployment that add to instability and civil unrest. These are taken as signs of the arrival of Antichrist or the judgment that will bring the end of the world.

There is a danger in looking for the end of the world by an average of end-time activity. The warning of the apostle Paul to the Thessalonians was that the end would come when they were thinking everything was safe (1 Thess.

5:1–3). Though warfare, earthquakes, famine, pestilences, and fearful events will precede the time of the end, Jesus warns that the end will come when his followers are not ready (Luke 21:34–36). They will be weighed down with the pleasures and anxieties of life, and the final day will arrive as a trap. Efforts to read prophecy in terms of calamitous events may actually be a distraction from the critical issues of being ready for the kingdom. It is important to watch the signs of the times, but these in themselves can never tell us precisely what God is doing in his great work of bringing his kingdom to this world.

Catastrophic events have always led to a rising interest in the end of the world. When Rome was sacked in A.D. 410 masses of people were convinced the end was near; similar thoughts surfaced when the Black Death wiped out one-third of the population of fourteenth-century Europe or when the Lisbon earthquake in 1755 created shudders all across Europe. As reported by Nancy Gibbs, events of the twentieth century have led believers to fit more recent events like the attacks on the World Trade Center into a scriptural grid of end-time events.

> The rise of Hitler, a wicked man who wanted to murder the Jews, read like a Bible story; his utter destruction, and the subsequent return of the Jews to Israel after 2,000 years and the capture of Jerusalem's Old City by the Israelis in 1967, were taken by devout Christians and Jews alike as evidence of God's handiwork.[29]

The Old Testament prophets consistently confessed that God was at work in the political events of this world. Isaiah declared that Assyria was the rod of God's anger against Israel (Isa. 10:5), but Assyria would itself be destroyed under God's judgment. The axe should not pride itself over the one who swings it, nor should the staff try to lift the one that is not wood (10:15). Believers may be confident that God is at work in present events to bring about the consummation of redemption and the judgment of the Babylon of the last days (Rev. 18:2). But this does not grant a license to explain present catastrophes as judgments of God against particular nations in a scheme of how the world must end, nor can anyone know how soon the final judgment will come. The New Testament warns believers against attempts to judge the events of their times, since God has chosen not to reveal the times and the seasons that he has put under his own authority (Acts 1:7). Instead, they are called upon to be witnesses to the kingdom of God to the ends of the earth.

Just as there is danger in trying to interpret present events for the future, there is also danger in laying blame for the events of the past. When Abijah

---

29. Nancy Gibbs, "Apocalypse Now," *Time* (Canadian Edition) (July 1, 2002), 36.

the son of Jeroboam became ill, the king sent a disguised messenger to the prophet who had commissioned him. The death of the child was not merely a judgment against Jeroboam but against his whole dynasty (14:10–11). This judgment was a judgment against the entire nation, which would go into exile (vv. 15–16). It was never the role of Jesus' followers to ordain kings into power or to proclaim judgment against particular rulers. The gospel of the kingdom operates on a different order, where the last will be first and the great ones will be servants (Luke 22:24–30). The kingdom of Jesus transcended all earthly kingdoms.

Trivializing sacred symbols. A significant challenge for Christians, living in a hostile society, is the adoption of sacred symbols and times for purposes that make them trivial. A cartoon of a businessman bunny being crucified on a tax form in the *New Yorker* roused the passions of Wendy Zoba:

> Every year during the holiest week on the Christian calendar, believers' remembrances of the passion and resurrection of Christ must compete with egg-dropping expeditions of ubiquitous bunnies. But, as in the case of the fat guy in the red suit, we put up with a degree of secular mythology. It goes with our society's pluralistic territory.
>
> So maybe Christians should not be surprised when secular images are melded with the sacred and plastered on the cover of a respected magazine. Who can know what muse moved Art Spiegelman to sketch "Theology of the Tax Cut," a businessman-bunny crucified on a tax form? Or what the editors of the *New Yorker* had in mind when they ran it on their cover during Holy Week?
>
> But it is one more affirmation that the impact of the cross has lost its meaning for many in our society. Madonna's frivolous use of the cross to define her quasi-religious persona has spurred its marketability within mainstream culture. But its significance has also been lost more generally, as evidenced by the jewelry store clerk who asked a customer if she wanted the plain cross necklace or the one with the "little man" on it.
>
> Spiegelman's work has sarcastically exploited the image in an attempt to engage in a political discussion (tax reform) that has little to do with the essence of the crucifixion.[30]

Zoba's concerns have their analogy with the golden calves of Jeroboam. The calf cannot be an ark, just as the Passion story is not about taxation. The adoption and adaptation of sacred symbols invariably brings a mixed or

---

30. Wendy Murray Zoba, "Trivializing the Cross," *Christianity Today* 39/7 (June 19, 1995): 17.

compromised message. The cross is the most sacred symbol for the Christian, representing the *incomparable* act of God in reconciling humankind to himself. Zoba is not asking society to adopt Christian doctrine but to respect their expression of it, just as people do with other culturally significant symbols. She cannot imagine Spiegelman depicting Santa Claus expiring in a gas chamber during Yom Kippur; such an offense is unthinkable, as it should be.

As is the case with Jeroboam and Rehoboam, social and political forces often control the use of symbols with a force that cannot be challenged. It becomes all the more imperative for believers to keep clear for themselves the sacred distinctions represented in their symbols and to use them appropriately as expressions of faith.

Christianity has a history of giving spiritual significance to pagan festivals and emblems. The time of the Christmas celebration, just after solstice, green trees, Yule logs, and lights are all accretions around the birth of Christ adopted from pagan festivities; the church has used them successfully in making its own confessions. In modern times the reverse is taking place. In the name of tolerance and freedom, a crèche may not be displayed in a public place, and there has even been talk that the term *Christmas* itself is offensive to other religions and should not be used in signs and advertising. Christmas has been extensively taken over for commercial purposes, so Christians must self-consciously retain the sacred significance the day has for them. Times and symbols of Christian confession are as challenging as when Jeroboam set up his calves and Rehoboam his sacred stones and Asherah poles.

Dividing over religious calendars. One final important lesson from the reforms of Jeroboam is the power for division around the dates of festal celebrations. Some of the greatest controversies in the Christian church have been over the celebration of Easter. From the earliest times there has been division. It is clear from the Gospels that the death of Jesus was associated with Passover, but the time is not clear. According to the Synoptics, the Last Supper was a Passover meal, with the death of Jesus the next day, but according to John the death of Jesus occurred at the time of the Passover. By the second century some churches celebrated Easter at the time of the Passover, whatever day of the week it occurred, and some celebrated it on Sunday. With four different methods used to calculate the date of Easter by the beginning of the fourth century, the Council of Nicea (325) decided Easter should be celebrated on the first Sunday after the full moon following the spring equinox.

In modern times division over the celebration of Easter occurs because of the use of Gregorian and Julian calendars. The Gregorian calendar shortened the length of a calendar year to bring it more into conformity with the actual solar year. The date was then adjusted to bring the calendar months closer to the seasons, so that currently thirteen days separates the two calendars.

The division of calendar is most painful in regions where Christians of Eastern and Western churches live in close proximity. Various attempts have been made to bring Christians into harmony on the celebration of Easter.[31] Three solutions are possible to harmonize celebration of Easter: a fixed date like Christmas; a common mobile date related to the spring equinox; a fixed Sunday with a mobility of about seven days. The questions are difficult; should Easter be related to the season of spring (which does not pertain in the southern hemisphere), or to the date of the Jewish Passover? The one goal that should not be lost is giving a unified and common witness to the resurrection of Jesus Christ in the celebration of Easter. Calendar is powerful in dividing communities; it has an equal power to unite faith confessions, if a way can be found to provide harmonization.

---

31. For a review of various ecclesiastical and legislative initiatives in the twentieth century, see Dagmar Heller, "The Date of Easter?" *Ecumenical Review* 48/3 (July 1996): 392–401.

1 Kings 15:1–16:34

𝒱

IN THE EIGHTEENTH YEAR of the reign of Jeroboam son of Nebat, Abijah became king of Judah, ²and he reigned in Jerusalem three years. His mother's name was Maacah daughter of Abishalom.

³He committed all the sins his father had done before him; his heart was not fully devoted to the LORD his God, as the heart of David his forefather had been. ⁴Nevertheless, for David's sake the LORD his God gave him a lamp in Jerusalem by raising up a son to succeed him and by making Jerusalem strong. ⁵For David had done what was right in the eyes of the LORD and had not failed to keep any of the LORD's commands all the days of his life—except in the case of Uriah the Hittite.

⁶There was war between Rehoboam and Jeroboam throughout Abijah's lifetime. ⁷As for the other events of Abijah's reign, and all he did, are they not written in the book of the annals of the kings of Judah? There was war between Abijah and Jeroboam. ⁸And Abijah rested with his fathers and was buried in the City of David. And Asa his son succeeded him as king.

⁹In the twentieth year of Jeroboam king of Israel, Asa became king of Judah, ¹⁰and he reigned in Jerusalem forty-one years. His grandmother's name was Maacah daughter of Abishalom.

¹¹Asa did what was right in the eyes of the LORD, as his father David had done. ¹²He expelled the male shrine prostitutes from the land and got rid of all the idols his fathers had made. ¹³He even deposed his grandmother Maacah from her position as queen mother, because she had made a repulsive Asherah pole. Asa cut the pole down and burned it in the Kidron Valley. ¹⁴Although he did not remove the high places, Asa's heart was fully committed to the LORD all his life. ¹⁵He brought into the temple of the LORD the silver and gold and the articles that he and his father had dedicated.

¹⁶There was war between Asa and Baasha king of Israel throughout their reigns. ¹⁷Baasha king of Israel went up against Judah and fortified Ramah to prevent anyone from leaving or entering the territory of Asa king of Judah.

¹⁸Asa then took all the silver and gold that was left in the treasuries of the LORD's temple and of his own palace. He entrusted it to his officials and sent them to Ben-Hadad son of Tabrimmon, the son of Hezion, the king of Aram, who was ruling in Damascus. ¹⁹"Let there be a treaty between me and you," he said, "as there was between my father and your father. See, I am sending you a gift of silver and gold. Now break your treaty with Baasha king of Israel so he will withdraw from me."

²⁰Ben-Hadad agreed with King Asa and sent the commanders of his forces against the towns of Israel. He conquered Ijon, Dan, Abel Beth Maacah and all Kinnereth in addition to Naphtali. ²¹When Baasha heard this, he stopped building Ramah and withdrew to Tirzah. ²²Then King Asa issued an order to all Judah—no one was exempt—and they carried away from Ramah the stones and timber Baasha had been using there. With them King Asa built up Geba in Benjamin, and also Mizpah.

²³As for all the other events of Asa's reign, all his achievements, all he did and the cities he built, are they not written in the book of the annals of the kings of Judah? In his old age, however, his feet became diseased. ²⁴Then Asa rested with his fathers and was buried with them in the city of his father David. And Jehoshaphat his son succeeded him as king.

²⁵Nadab son of Jeroboam became king of Israel in the second year of Asa king of Judah, and he reigned over Israel two years. ²⁶He did evil in the eyes of the LORD, walking in the ways of his father and in his sin, which he had caused Israel to commit.

²⁷Baasha son of Ahijah of the house of Issachar plotted against him, and he struck him down at Gibbethon, a Philistine town, while Nadab and all Israel were besieging it. ²⁸Baasha killed Nadab in the third year of Asa king of Judah and succeeded him as king.

²⁹As soon as he began to reign, he killed Jeroboam's whole family. He did not leave Jeroboam anyone that breathed, but destroyed them all, according to the word of the LORD given through his servant Ahijah the Shilonite—³⁰because of the sins Jeroboam had committed and had caused Israel to commit, and because he provoked the LORD, the God of Israel, to anger.

³¹As for the other events of Nadab's reign, and all he did, are they not written in the book of the annals of the kings of Israel? ³²There was war between Asa and Baasha king of Israel throughout their reigns.

³³In the third year of Asa king of Judah, Baasha son of Ahijah became king of all Israel in Tirzah, and he reigned twenty-four years. ³⁴He did evil in the eyes of the LORD, walking in the ways of Jeroboam and in his sin, which he had caused Israel to commit.

¹⁶:¹Then the word of the LORD came to Jehu son of Hanani against Baasha: ²"I lifted you up from the dust and made you leader of my people Israel, but you walked in the ways of Jeroboam and caused my people Israel to sin and to provoke me to anger by their sins. ³So I am about to consume Baasha and his house, and I will make your house like that of Jeroboam son of Nebat. ⁴Dogs will eat those belonging to Baasha who die in the city, and the birds of the air will feed on those who die in the country."

⁵As for the other events of Baasha's reign, what he did and his achievements, are they not written in the book of the annals of the kings of Israel? ⁶Baasha rested with his fathers and was buried in Tirzah. And Elah his son succeeded him as king.

⁷Moreover, the word of the LORD came through the prophet Jehu son of Hanani to Baasha and his house, because of all the evil he had done in the eyes of the LORD, provoking him to anger by the things he did, and becoming like the house of Jeroboam—and also because he destroyed it.

⁸In the twenty-sixth year of Asa king of Judah, Elah son of Baasha became king of Israel, and he reigned in Tirzah two years.

⁹Zimri, one of his officials, who had command of half his chariots, plotted against him. Elah was in Tirzah at the time, getting drunk in the home of Arza, the man in charge of the palace at Tirzah. ¹⁰Zimri came in, struck him down and killed him in the twenty-seventh year of Asa king of Judah. Then he succeeded him as king.

¹¹As soon as he began to reign and was seated on the throne, he killed off Baasha's whole family. He did not spare a single male, whether relative or friend. ¹²So Zimri destroyed the whole family of Baasha, in accordance with the word of the LORD spoken against Baasha through the prophet Jehu—

¹³because of all the sins Baasha and his son Elah had committed and had caused Israel to commit, so that they provoked the LORD, the God of Israel, to anger by their worthless idols.

¹⁴As for the other events of Elah's reign, and all he did, are they not written in the book of the annals of the kings of Israel?

¹⁵In the twenty-seventh year of Asa king of Judah, Zimri reigned in Tirzah seven days. The army was encamped near Gibbethon, a Philistine town. ¹⁶When the Israelites in the camp heard that Zimri had plotted against the king and murdered him, they proclaimed Omri, the commander of the army, king over Israel that very day there in the camp. ¹⁷Then Omri and all the Israelites with him withdrew from Gibbethon and laid siege to Tirzah. ¹⁸When Zimri saw that the city was taken, he went into the citadel of the royal palace and set the palace on fire around him. So he died, ¹⁹because of the sins he had committed, doing evil in the eyes of the LORD and walking in the ways of Jeroboam and in the sin he had committed and had caused Israel to commit.

²⁰As for the other events of Zimri's reign, and the rebellion he carried out, are they not written in the book of the annals of the kings of Israel?

²¹Then the people of Israel were split into two factions; half supported Tibni son of Ginath for king, and the other half supported Omri. ²²But Omri's followers proved stronger than those of Tibni son of Ginath. So Tibni died and Omri became king.

²³In the thirty-first year of Asa king of Judah, Omri became king of Israel, and he reigned twelve years, six of them in Tirzah. ²⁴He bought the hill of Samaria from Shemer for two talents of silver and built a city on the hill, calling it Samaria, after Shemer, the name of the former owner of the hill.

²⁵But Omri did evil in the eyes of the LORD and sinned more than all those before him. ²⁶He walked in all the ways of Jeroboam son of Nebat and in his sin, which he had caused Israel to commit, so that they provoked the LORD, the God of Israel, to anger by their worthless idols.

²⁷As for the other events of Omri's reign, what he did and the things he achieved, are they not written in the book of the annals of the kings of Israel? ²⁸Omri rested with his fathers and was buried in Samaria. And Ahab his son succeeded him as king.

²⁹In the thirty-eighth year of Asa king of Judah, Ahab son of Omri became king of Israel, and he reigned in Samaria over Israel twenty-two years. ³⁰Ahab son of Omri did more evil in the eyes of the LORD than any of those before him. ³¹He not only considered it trivial to commit the sins of Jeroboam son of Nebat, but he also married Jezebel daughter of Ethbaal king of the Sidonians, and began to serve Baal and worship him. ³²He set up an altar for Baal in the temple of Baal that he built in Samaria. ³³Ahab also made an Asherah pole and did more to provoke the LORD, the God of Israel, to anger than did all the kings of Israel before him.

³⁴In Ahab's time, Hiel of Bethel rebuilt Jericho. He laid its foundations at the cost of his firstborn son Abiram, and he set up its gates at the cost of his youngest son Segub, in accordance with the word of the LORD spoken by Joshua son of Nun.

THE END OF the house of Jeroboam, as announced by the prophet Ahijah (14:10–12), comes with the conspiracy of Baasha (15:27–28). The failure of dynastic succession in the northern kingdom results in a series of conspiracies and civil war. The boundary between Israel and Judah is a contentious issue that results in continuous warfare (15:6–7, 16, 32). This pattern continues until the establishment of the dynasty of Omri. Omri brings stability to Israel and establishes an alliance with Judah, the smaller, more dependent state.

Politically Omri is a highly successful king. A daughter of Ahab, son of Omri, is married to the Judean king Jehoram, son of Jehoshaphat (2 Kings 8:16–18), who is the successor to Asa. Omri restores an active alliance with Tyre, reinforced by the marriage of his son Ahab to Jezebel, daughter of Ethbaal, king of the Sidonians (1 Kings 16:31). The wealth and influence of Tyre are significant; its colonies spread out as far as Spain and Africa. This results in great political strength, but it is spiritually disastrous, almost resulting in the extermination of the house of David in Judah (2 Kings 11:1–3). The spiritual conflict results in the struggles of Elijah and Elisha against the Baal fertility cult. These prophetic stories constitute a major section in Kings (1 Kings 17–2 Kings 8). The political achievements of Omri result in the Assyrians referring to Israel as "the land of Omri" for centuries, but knowledge of the God of Israel is almost lost.

The principal foreign power during this period is the Arameans. Rezon founded Aram-Damascus in the latter days of Solomon, making Damascus his capital (11:23–25). Rezon carries the meaning "high official" and may be the royal title of Hezion, father of Ben-Hadad, or these may be phonetic variants of the same name (15:18).[1] Aram-Damascus benefit from the division of Israel (15:18–19). Asa appeals to Ben-Hadad, king of Aram-Damascus, for assistance in his war against Baasha. Ben-Hadad willingly obliges by invading Israel, so Asa is able to rebuild Ramah (about five miles north of Jerusalem) as a border fortress. The boundary is stabilized until the fall of Israel.

Conflict between Judah and Israel (15:1–24)

ABIJAM (HEBREW), MORE usually known as Abijah (some Hebrew manuscripts, the versions, and Chronicles), succeeds Rehoboam. Abijah is the more orthodox form of the name, which means "My father is Yahweh."[2] The eighteenth year of Jeroboam is given in Israelite nonaccession year reckoning (v. 1); in accession year reckoning of Judah, Rehoboam is said to have reigned only seventeen years (14:21). This is one of the many apparent contradictions of the synchronisms in Kings, indicating the authors retain the data as found in royal records. Ahijah has a short reign, from 913–910 B.C. (following the chronology outlined in Appendix B).

Abijah's mother is Maacah daughter of Abishalom, understood to be a variation of Absalom (cf. 2 Chron. 11:20–23). Maacah may have been a foreigner (cf. 1 Kings 2:39), possibly of Aramean descent (Gen. 22:24), which may account for her idolatry (1 Kings 15:13).[3] The Chronicler says the mother of Abijah is Micaiah (a scribal variant of the same name), daughter of Uriel (2 Chron. 13:2). Tamar is the only known daughter of Absalom (2 Sam. 14:27). If Uriel married Tamar, then Maacah would have been granddaughter of Absalom (NEB).[4] The mother of Absalom is named Maacah (2 Sam. 3:3), as well as the mother of Asa (1 Kings 15:10), though Asa is son of Abijah, not a brother (v. 8). It is not possible to identify the mother of Abijah as

---

1. The meaning of Rezon is established in a bilingual Phoenician inscription from Karatepe (*KAI* 26 A iii 12). B. Mazar has proposed that Rezon is a royal title and that the personal name of the king was Hezion; see *The Early Biblical Period: Historical Essays* (Jerusalem: Israel Exploration Journal, 1986), 157. For a scholarly discussion, see W. T. Pitard, *Ancient Damascus: A Historical Study of the Syrian City-State from Earliest Times until its Fall to the Assyrians in 732 B.C.E.* (Winona Lake, Ind.: Eisenbrauns, 1987), 138–44. The name Hezion of a later king of Damascus is found in an Akkadian inscription on the Pazarcik Stela; see A. K. Grayson, *Assyrian Rulers of the Early First Millennium B.C. II (858–745 B.C.)* (RIMA 3; Toronto: Univ. of Toronto Press, 1996), 239–40.

2. Abijam has a Canaanite name meaning, "My father is Yam" (Yam is the Canaanite god of the sea).

3. Ahlström, *The History of Ancient Palestine*, 361, 567.

4. So indicates the genealogy of Josephus, *Ant.* 8.249.

---

daughter to Absalom the son of David. It is best to accept the information given, rather than to harmonize or assume contradictions. It is unlikely that Rehoboam would have married a daughter of Absalom, a cousin through his father's older brother.

Kings condemns Abijah; he follows in the idolatry of Rehoboam. His territory is preserved only because Yahweh desires to keep the lamp of David preserved in Jerusalem (15:3–5; cf. 11:36; 2 Sam. 21:17). Abijah continues his father's policy of war with Israel (1 Kings 15:6–7; cf. 14:30),[5] but there is no acknowledgment of divine blessing on his reign. The Chronicler presents him in a more favorable manner (2 Chron. 13:1–20). His account of the war with Jeroboam is probably based on other sources independently preserved; it provides him with the information concerning Abijah's decisive victory over Jeroboam.

The forty-one years of Asa are from 910–869 B.C. (15:9–10). He takes initiative against the male and female cult prostitutes serving at the country shrines and removes Maacah as the leading lady (vv. 12–13). Maacah holds the office of "queen mother" (v. 13), a position she continues to hold after the short reign of Abijah; more precisely, she is grandmother to Asa. The queen mother is the first lady of the realm, taking precedence over all the women of the harem (cf. 2:19; 11:19; 2 Kings 10:13). Normally she holds the office as long as she lives, and on her decease the title passes on to the mother of the heir apparent.

Official functions of the office of queen mother in Israelite monarchy are nowhere more specific than in 15:13. In Hittite practice the queen mother had both state and cultic functions and sometimes continued to exercise influence after the death of her husband.[6] The patronage of Maacah to the Asherah cult may have been one aspect of fulfilling her court responsibilities to legitimizing the rule of the king, but this is speculative.[7] Maacah may have been a woman with particular personality force and influence.

Asherah in the Bible is usually a pole, possibly a phallic symbol (cf. 2 Kings 23:4). She is well known from the Canaanite Ugaritic literature, where she is the wife of the supreme god El and the mother of seventy children, includ-

---

5. A few Hebrew manuscripts read Abijam instead of Rehoboam in 15:6; this verse is a duplicate of 14:30, possibly a textual dittography.

6. R. De Vaux, *Social Institutions* (New York: McGraw-Hill, 1961), 117–19.

7. S. Ackerman, "The Queen Mother and the Cult in Ancient Israel," *JBL* 112 (1993): 385–401. Based on the inscription from Kuntillet ʿAjrûd, which identifes Asherah with Yahweh, Ackerman presents Jezebel and Athaliah as official representatives of Asherah in the monarchy. Zafrira Ben-Barak shows that none of the examples of *g*ʿ*bîrâ* ("queen mother") in Kings mean anything more than mother or wife of the reigning sovereign; "The Status and Right of the *g*ʿ*bîrâ*," *JBL* 110 (1991): 23–34.

ing Baal.[8] At Ugarit her title is "the lady who treads the sea," probably a coastal version of her Akkadian title "the lady of the steppe (plains)." In Canaanite mythology she is not to be confused with Ashtoreth (11:5), the goddess of war and sexuality. The queen mother has a shrine dedicated to this goddess, possibly located on the hill to the east of Jerusalem where Solomon located other foreign shrines (11:7). Asa has the object cut down and burned in a dumping ground in the Kidron Valley (cf. 2 Kings 23:6, 12). Though Asa is unable to remove the shrines, he is committed to the restoration of the temple treasuries (1 Kings 15:14–15). He was able to restore some of the artifacts of the temple through booty, which he and his father dedicate for temple use.

The war with Baasha brings the Arameans into conflict with Israel (15:16). Baasha apparently attempts to prevent Israelites from having contact with Asa by fortifying Ramah (v. 17). Ramah is located on the high road on the border of Ephraim, about five miles north of Jerusalem. This was probably the home of Samuel (1 Sam. 7:17). Asa takes whatever treasures Shishak has left and whatever he has managed to restore and sends them as a bribe to the Aramean king Ben-Hadad to attack Baasha. The mention of Asa's father may indicate that Abijah has already made an agreement with Ben-Hadad (1 Kings 15:19).

Ben-Hadad (son of Hadad, the equivalent of the storm god Baal in Canaan)[9] was a common name for Aramean kings. A ninth-century Aramean inscription to the god Melqart (the chief god of Tyre) names Barhadad (the Aramean equivalent of Ben-Hadad) as a king of Aram. The reading of the second line is uncertain, but it has been thought to refer to Tabrimmon, son of Hezion, who leads the Aramean armies against Israel.[10] The Arameans are bitter enemies of Israel until the Assyrians destroy both in the last half of the eighth century.

---

8. Judith M. Hadley in *The Cult of Asherah in Ancient Israel and Judah: Evidence for a Hebrew Goddess* (Cambridge: Cambridge Univ. Press, 2000) lists over six hundred bibliographic items in her critical review of all inscriptions and cult objects related to Asherah. There are several indications that Asherah is of eastern, probably Amorite origin. Hadley thinks that in Israel Asherah gradually lost her identity as a fertility goddess.

9. Hadad means "the Thunderer," the equivalent of *Rammanu* in Assyria. The Hebrews parodied the latter as Rimmon (pomegranate), as seen in the name Hadad-Rimmon (Zech. 12:11). Tabrimmon (1 Kings 15:18) may mean "Rammon is bountiful" or "Rammon is willing."

10. John C. L. Gibson, *Aramaic Inscriptions* (vol. 2 of *Textbook of Syrian Semitic Inscriptions*; Oxford: Clarendon, 1975), 1. This identification is disputed, as the inscription has been severely damaged. See also Wayne T. Pitard, "The Identity of the Bir Hadad of the Melqart Stela," *BASOR* 272 (1988): 3–21; he defends the reading br'trhmk (son of 'Attarhamek). This king is not the same as any of those known in Damascus.

Ben-Hadad is more than willing to accept money from both Baasha and Asa in their war against each other (15:19–20). The Aramean breaks his treaty and attacks northern Israel, capturing all the land of Naphtali. That means all Galilee is taken, almost all the country north of the Jezreel Valley and east of Lake Kinnereth.[11] Ijon is a large village in the southern Beqaᶜ Valley, on the southern border of modern Lebanon. It is usually listed together with Abel Beth Maacah, Dan (Laish), and Hazor in northern Israel. Abel Beth Maacah is located near a major waterfall of the Jordan tributaries, at the juncture of the Huleh Valley and the Beqaᶜ Valley in Lebanon. ᶜEn Gev on the eastern side of the lake is likely taken by the Arameans as well.[12]

The absence of Hazor from the list of cities taken by Ben-Hadad is remarkable, since it was the major fortified city of the area. Baasha may have been able to resist the Aramean army and retain the territory around Hazor. Ben-Hadad gains control over the corn land of the Hauran and the trade routes, which run to Tyre and Sidon and south to the plain of Jezreel. The northern attack forces Baasha to abandon his southern fortification.

After the withdrawal of Baasha, Asa conscripts workers to use the materials at Ramah to rebuild Geba and Mizpah. Mizpah is usually identified with Tell en-Nasbe, which is about four miles north of Ramah and about two miles from Bethel. Gebaᶜ is likely located three miles beyond the watershed east of Gibeah, protecting a wadi[13] leading down to Jericho and the sanctuary at Gilgal. According to the concluding formula, Asa fortifies other cities in Judah as well (15:23–24). His death from disease was regarded as an evidence of divine disfavor, a point developed at some length by the Chronicler (2 Chron. 16:7–12).

Civil War and Idolatry in Israel (15:25–16:34)

THE ONLY SON of Jeroboam to succeed him is Nadab, whose two-year reign according to nonaccession year reckoning of Israel is chronologically somewhat more than a year (909–908 B.C.). Baasha assassinates him while he is occupied with a siege at Gibbethon (15:25–31), a Levitical city belonging to the tribe of Dan (Josh. 19:44; 21:23). It appears in a list of cities conquered by Thutmose III (1468 B.C.) and again in a campaign of Sargon II against the

---

11. Kinnereth appears in the New Testament as Genesareth, the name apparently derived from harp-shaped bays around the lakeshore. The name also appears as a city of Galilee.

12. Ahlström, *The History of Ancient Palestine*, 565.

13. A wadi is a depression, which carries off the winter rains but is mostly dry in the summer. It is neither a river nor a valley. If the water runs year round, the term "river" is further qualified as continuous (ʾêtan).

kings of Ashdod (712–713). It was located in Philistine territory about three miles west of Gezer and probably served as a military post guarding the Israelite-Philistine frontier. It was under the control of the Philistines (16:15).

Baasha not only assassinates Nadab but also carries out a blood purge against the entire royal lineage of Jeroboam, fulfilling the judgment that Ahijah the prophet proclaimed against him. None of Jeroboam's house receives an honorable burial, except for the sick child who died. The regnal summary of Nadab does not include burial in the royal cemetery.

The war between Baasha and Asa is discussed as part of the reign of Asa (15:17–21), so Baasha's reign can be summarized with the synchronism and length of his reign (15:32–33) and a theological assessment (v. 34). His guilt lies in following the sins of Jeroboam; Jehu son of Hanani delivers the sentence. The Chronicler mentions Jehu the prophet in judgment against Jehoshaphat king of Judah about thirty-five years later (2 Chron. 19:2; 20:34), but nothing more is said about him.

The speech against Baasha (16:1–4) is given in the rhetoric found in the judgment against Jeroboam. Baasha is appointed as a leader over Israel (16:2; cf. 14:7), but causes Israel to sin and offends Yahweh (16:2; cf. 14:9). The threat to "consume Baasha" is an abbreviation of the threat to "burn up the house of Jeroboam as one burns dung" (16:3; cf. 14:10). Exposure of the corpses is described in the same manner (16:4; cf. 14:11). Content of the prophetic speeches provides a conscious continuity between the house of Jeroboam and the house of Baasha. The regnal summary provided for the reign of Baasha includes the activity of Jehu the prophet (16:5–7), which makes explicit the parallel to Jeroboam.

The house of Baasha ends with the type of violence Baasha inflicted on the house of Jeroboam (16:8–14). Elah reigns for two years, like Nadab son of Jeroboam (886–885 B.C.). Zimri, an army commander responsible for half of the chariot force, murders Elah in a conspiracy. The conspiracy is facilitated by the drunkenness of Elah in the house of the administrator of the palace property. While half the army is occupied with the war in Gibbethon (16:15), Elah is dissipated in the capital at Tirzah. Arza is either complicit in the conspiracy or actively a part of it (16:9). All the potential heirs to the throne are killed (16:11; cf. 14:10). The judgment announced by the prophet Jehu is fulfilled, just as that announced by Abijah against Jeroboam (16:12–13; cf. 15:29–30). Elah dies because of false worship of "worthless idols," meaning gods of no real existence (16:13).

Zimri is reckoned as one of the kings of Israel even though his reign only lasts seven days (v. 15). When Omri, the field commander in Gibbethon, hears the king has been killed, he has himself proclaimed king by the army. He marches to Tirzah and lays siege to the capital. When Zimri sees his cause is lost, he chooses death in the flames of the palace rather than execution by Omri. Foundations of unfinished structures have been found over the burned debris at the site (Tell el-Farʿah), possible evidence of the abandonment of Tirzah as the capital in Israel.[14]

Omri is unable to claim the kingship of Israel with the death of Zimri. Apparently some influential individuals of the royal court and the army there resist him. Tibni the son of Ginath makes a bid for the throne (16:21), so the country is divided for a period of about four years (cf. vv. 21–22). At the death of Tibni, Omri becomes the undisputed king. The death notice of Tibni is short; the LXX says that Joram his brother dies with him, suggesting Tibni comes to a violent end as well. Zimri is given the usual theological assessment for the Israelite kings (16:19) and concluding note about the records of his reign (v. 20).

The cause of the civil war is not given. Rival factions of the army may have been jostling for control in a volatile situation. Omri is not a common Israelite name, but it certainly is West Semitic (from the root ʿmr, "to reap" or "live long, develop"). It is possible Omri is an aggressive young general whom Tibni and his party attempt to prevent from taking over the throne. They fail, and with Omri a whole new era begins for Israel. The decimation that the Arameans have exacted in the attacks of Ben-Hadad (15:18–20), with the loss of trade routes through the Transjordan, will be reversed through the alliances forged by Omri. The civil war is over, and a lengthy new dynasty begins.

The twelve-year reign of Omri is shared with Tibni for the first five years (885–874 B.C.). Omri receives the briefest attention; his great deeds are mentioned in a general summarizing fashion (16:27), but that brief evaluation does not compare with the prominence attributed to him in other historical sources. The one achievement mentioned is the establishment of a new state capital, neutral to the warring factions within Israel (16:24). This is a strategic move, exchanging the eastward low hilltop of Tirzah for the westward high isolated hill of the tribe or community of Shemer (modern *Sebastiyeh*).

The biblical names for the site, *Shamir* (Judg. 10:1–2) or *Shomeron* (1 Kings 16:24), mean "watch" or "watchman." "Samaria" is the Greek version for the name of the hill. Its summit reaches over 1,400 feet overlooking the main coastal road connecting Egypt and Judah with the Jezreel Valley[15] and north-

---

14. Tirzah has been used as an example of widespread Hebrew appropriation of pagan Canaanite shrines. Careful scrutiny of archaeological evidence at Tirzah does not support this conclusion; see Mervyn D. Fowler, "Cultic Continuity at *Tirzah*: A Re-examination of the Archaeological Evidence," *PEQ* 113 (1981): 27–31.

15. Latin versions rendered this *Via Maris* ("way of the sea," Isa. 9:1); during the Middle Ages the route to Damascus was known by this name, but it is not known as such in any ancient Roman source.

ern routes to Phoenicia and Damascus. Excavations on the western half of the summit have revealed much of the royal palace and a storeroom complex.[16] Dozens of shipping documents record the transfer of commodities from the outlying villages to the capital during the later periods of the Israelite monarchy. Though the hill was occupied before Omri, the earlier buildings indicate the presence of a family estate producing oil and wine.

The twenty-two-year reign of Ahab ends with the battle at Qarqar (874–853 B.C.). His regnal summary occurs several chapters later (22:39–40), since the account of his reign is intertwined with the Elijah stories. Ahab extends the idolatry of Israel, making worship for the Baal cult exclusive. He builds a temple for Baal in Samaria and promotes the cult of Asherah (16:32–33). Alliance with the Phoenicians, with the marriage of Ahab to Jezebel, daughter of the Sidonian king (v. 31),[17] facilitates the state promotion of the Baal cult.

Rebuilding Jericho, one of many cities Ahab restores, brings about the curse of Joshua (16:34; cf. 22:39; Josh. 6:26). It results in the death of the sons of Hiel of Bethel (otherwise unknown).[18] Some argue here for a ritual of foundation sacrifices, in which infants were placed in jars and inserted into the masonry to propitiate the gods and ward off evil.[19] More likely, however, the text means that during the building of Jericho his entire family dies because of the curse of Joshua. Specification of the eldest and youngest sons is a merism ("from oldest to youngest"), indicating the death of all the children of Ahiel. Laying the foundations is the first stage of building, and hanging the doors its completion.

Bridging Contexts

KINGS AND CHRONICLES. The historiographic intent of the Deuteronomistic authors is perspicacious in this section on internecine warfare. Idolatry is the curse that resulted in the exile of the nation. As good historians, they must be true to their sources as they find them in the archives of the kings. The complementary account in Chronicles

---

16. For the archaeology of Samaria, see Larry Stager, "Shemer's Estate," *BASOR* 277/278 (1990): 93–107.

17. The name Jezebel is also a parody on a Canaanite name. The original probably was ⁱzebul, meaning "where is the prince?" (cf. C. H. Gordon, *Ugaritic Textbook* [Rome: Pontificium Institutum Biblicum, 1965], 393). The title *zebul*, used for Baal, has been perverted to *zebel*, "dung" (foliage piled up to make manure).

18. Hiel is an abbreviation of Ahiel, as it is found in the Greek; the first part of the name means "my brother."

19. Gray, *I & II Kings*, 370–71, discusses examples of foundation burials and possible implications for this notice in Kings.

provides quite a different perspective on the first rulers of Judah (2 Chron. 10–16). The account of Abijah leaves the impression that Rehoboam is an unsuccessful digression as a successor to Solomon. Rehoboam is humbled by Shishak (2 Chron. 12:7), but Abijah becomes the true descendant of Solomon. His speech to Jeroboam establishes two points: the legitimacy of the Davidic dynasty and the purity of worship at Jerusalem (13:4–12). With the succession of a true Davidide, normalcy is restored. In Chronicles, Jerusalem and its kings continuously represent all Israel.

The first point is important in Kings, but the evidence for it after Solomon is found only in the survival of the dynasty as a divine concession to preserve a light for David (15:4). Worship at Jerusalem is somewhat corrected by good kings such as Asa, but specific mention is made of continuing worship at the high places (v. 14), as in the days of Solomon (3:2). Ahab's constructing a temple for Baal in Samaria is not regarded as substantially different than Solomon's erecting various shrines for worship to accommodate his foreign wives in Jerusalem. In Kings, substantial change in Judah does not come into effect until the purification of Josiah, and that is immediately ended by Manasseh, the worst of all the idolaters.

The positive picture of Abijah in Chronicles cannot be explained as a development from the account in Kings (2 Chron. 13:1–20). Chronicles tells of war with Jeroboam, in which the army of Judah is outflanked by the Israelites. Abijah addresses the people with a speech highly charged with devout faith. He appeals to Jeroboam not to fight against the true Davidide kings in Jerusalem; he further claims divine support because true worship of God is taking place at the temple in Jerusalem. His appeal is rejected, but Yahweh grants Judah miraculous victory. Abijah is able to take the territories surrounding Ephron, Bethel, and Jeshanah from Israel (13:19). These, together with Mount Zemaraim (13:4), form a coherent and logical geographical unit (cf. Josh. 18:22–23). All these are in the hill country on the northern border of Judah. The subsequent history of this territorial gain is not known; by the time of Amos (ca. 760 B.C.) Bethel is a major cult shrine in Israel.

The portrait of Abijah as a righteous king who fights and wins Yahweh's battles and follows the covenant requirements to the letter must have been derived from an authentic source. Such a depiction posed certain tensions for the Chronicler's own view of divine providence in dealing with kings. Righteousness is rewarded with success, which normally means a long rule. The long rule of a wicked king like Manasseh or the death of a just monarch like Josiah are both circumstances that required theological justification. The short rule of Abijah should have inclined the Chronicler to view Abijah with the judgment found in Kings; instead, he finds a king blessed by God with an impressive military victory over the forces of a superior army.

Japhet finds the Chronicler's report of the results of the war tendentious. At the end of the war the Israelites are subdued, and Yahweh smites Jeroboam so he dies (15:18–20). The inference that Jeroboam dies before Abijah and other comparisons to Kings "remind us that the Chronicler's literary procedure may entail—even in these extreme cases—not an entirely fictitious composition, but the reversal of a given source."[20] The Chronicler himself recognizes that the war with Jeroboam is not a subjugation of Israel, as he immediately reports the war between Asa and Baasha (16:1). The war does not bring Israel back under Davidic rule, but it does yield limited occupation of Benjamite territory on the border of Ephraim.

Jeroboam indeed outlives Abijah, but battle reports often include an account of the death of the defeated leader, so it seems appropriate to the Chronicler to mention Jeroboam's death.[21] Japhet acknowledges that the implications may be viewed from alternate perspectives; one may see limited results of what is intended as a major campaign against the northern kingdom and link this outcome with the untimely death of Abijah, or regard the limited military action as the historical event that is developed into a comprehensive confrontation between south and north.

In the Chronicles account, the achievements of Abijah have continuing influence for the reign of his son Asa: the land has peace ten years (2 Chron. 13:23). This statement provides a direct transition to Asa, so the usual introductory formula is omitted. This time of peace provides Asa with opportunity to refortify his cities (14:5–6); twice the Chronicler calls this divine rest—the term used in Kings for a redemptive state (cf. 1 Kings 5:18). The Chronicler further reports a rebuff of Zerah the Ethiopian on the southern border of Judah, in which Yahweh grants Asa a great victory and booty for Jerusalem (2 Chron. 14:9–15). The purification from idolatry is developed at considerable length under the inspiration of Azariah the son of Oded (15:1–19).

Chronicles returns to the Kings account to report the war with Baasha (2 Chron. 16:16), the only major event reported for Asa in Kings (1 Kings 15:17–22). Asa is censured for his reliance on the Arameans, through the prophetic word of Hanani; for his troubles, Asa throws Hanani into stocks (2 Chron. 16:7–10). Condemnation of Asa comes with the twice-repeated motif that the imprisonment is solely because of the king's anger, not for any transgression of the prophet. Asa is judged with a disease in his feet, for which he fails to seek the Lord; as a result he dies from his illness (16:12–13). For all the achievements of Asa, he dies under divine discipline. For the Chronicler, Asa is a less exemplary king than Abijah.

---

20. Japhet, *I & II Chronicles*, 698–99.
21. Williamson, *1 & 2 Chronicles*, 255.

The Chronicler has structured his account to show reward for faithfulness and judgment for rebellion. In Kings, the division of the kingdom and the ensuing warfare between the two nations is predominant, explained by idolatrous pursuits of subsequent kings. In Chronicles, the speech of Abijah introduces the implications of the division for the Davidic dynasty and the purity of worship at Jerusalem (2 Chron. 13:4–12). The Chronicler regards each generation as being responsible to God for its actions, without reference back to previous circumstances. The weakness of Rehoboam provides explanation for the division (13:7), allowing that this was an irregular circumstance. With the accession of Abijah, a true Davidide, normalcy is restored. The rule of Rehoboam over the city God has chosen is treated as a past event (12:13–14).

The northern kingdom is never given separate consideration in Chronicles. The Israelites live in the cities of Judah, with Rehoboam ruling over them (2 Chron. 10:16-17). "All Israel" in this context includes the north (cf. 10:1, 3, 18). In this way the Chronicler reconciles the tension of the division of the kingdom and the continued state of rebellion by the northerners.

This brief comparison of two accounts of the first kings of Judah shows both the importance of historiographic intent and the means used to achieve it. Both of these are essential to understanding the narrative and its lessons. Chronicles includes significantly more material on Abijah and Asa, perhaps not known to the Deuteronomistic writers. His use of terminology, the ordering of his material, and his evaluative judgments all serve to show that the legitimate rule of God and worship of God continue at Jerusalem and at no other place. This is accomplished in part by his use of the term *Israel*, which is inclusive of all the people of both kingdoms who are under the rule of the Davidide king and of all who find their true worship at Jerusalem. It is further accomplished by only recognizing the kings at Jerusalem as legitimate. The northern kingdom does not have its own independent story of how God deals with them.

The purposes of historiography are governed by circumstance. Chronicles was written in the last days of the Persian Empire, as is evident in the genealogy of Jehoiakim, which extends several generations beyond Zerubbabel (1 Chron. 3:17–24). The tiny province of Judah had little political influence within the vast reaches of the empire. The mighty Persian horses charged about, maintaining order for a government in distant Susa. It took a special vision to have any sense of the divine presence at work in the world (Zech. 1:7–17). The Chronicler has to establish that the promise of David was represented in the small struggling community of Judah. He does this by showing that the promise is never lost; all Israel is present when the kingdom divided, all Israel is present when the exiles regroup in Jerusalem (1 Chron. 9:3), and a son of David continues to serve as leader of the people. The quarrels of the divided kingdom are distant events that no longer have relevance. The nation long ago paid the ultimate price for its disobedience.

The Chronicler must provide hope for a people who have no political future, a hope that was originally given in terms of an eternal kingdom. That hope can only be established by a review of the past. For the Chronicler, that past is largely available in the book of Kings, but not only there. An account written to explain the destruction of Assyrians and Babylonians cannot provide hope for a sometimes-disillusioned people. The integrity of the original promise must be established. For the Chronicler, the glory of Solomon is possible if the formula of Solomon given in his prayer dedicating the temple is followed: Be humble, pray, seek God's face, turn from your wicked ways, so God can heal (2 Chron. 7:14). The goal of the Chronicler in the story of each of the kings of Jerusalem is to show the efficacy of this principle.

Prophecy, fulfillment, and judgment. In the accounts of Kings and Chronicles, there is the consistent perspective that God is about the business of bringing his purposes to fruition. The book of Kings struggles with the division of the nation and the internal conflicts that represent God's kingdom. God is seen to be actively at work in each of the capitals, in discipline and judgment, but with continued frustration of the covenant relationship.

Jehu son of Hanani rebukes Baasha for causing the people to sin, pointing out that God has raised him up from the dust (1 Kings 16:2). Like Jeroboam his predecessor, Baasha has no royal connections and is not entitled to the throne of Israel. He is the instrument of divine punishment against the house of Jeroboam, exterminating his dynasty as Ahijah has announced (15:27–30). As is so often the case in Israelite history, the aggressor, acting as a rod of judgment used by God, ends up being guilty of the same sins. Jehu pronounces against Baasha the same judgment he has executed against the house of Jeroboam (16:3–4; cf. 14:10–11). A concluding note on the message of Jehu the prophet censures Baasha for causing idolatry in Israel and exterminating the house of Jeroboam (16:7). The cycles of political vengeance are all part of divine judgment on rebellious and arrogant kings.

It seems contradictory to speak of Baasha as raised from the dust to carry out judgment, and then to rebuke him because he has carried out that judgment. Würthwein thinks that this is an instance of later reevaluation, as the actions of Jehu (2 Kings 10:7–11; cf. Hos. 1:4).[22] Another suggestion is that this statement against Baasha is concessive; in spite of the destruction of the house of Jeroboam, Baasha has acted meritoriously in fulfilling God's word through Ahijah.[23] It is necessary to let the prophetic tensions stand; when an aggressor carries out a judgment announced by the prophets, that aggressor is not absolved of any crimes committed. Baasha acts out of his own interests,

22. Würthwein, *Das Alte Testament Deutsch*, 195.
23. Gray, *I & II Kings*, 361.

seen in how he leads Israel to sin, and one of his sins is the elimination of the house of Jeroboam.

The prophets never find it contradictory to hold wicked individuals responsible for their actions, even when God accomplishes his purposes through them. Peter in addressing the men of Israel on the day of Pentecost speaks in exactly the same terms as the condemnation of Baasha in Kings. The leaders in Jerusalem through their own wicked deeds have carried out the purpose of God in killing Jesus of Nazareth, a man they knew to be of God through the great deeds he did in their midst (Acts 2:22–23). For this act they are guilty, even though through it God overcomes the power of death and fulfills the promise he made to David (vv. 24–31). Human deeds are never regarded as a divine coercion. Humans act freely of their own volition for good or ill. In the prophetic viewpoint, all are responsible for the choices they make. At the same time, God never fails to accomplish his purpose, whatever may have been the human volition and intent.

Events in Israel must also be understood as part of international events. During the reign of Omri, Assyria entered a period of westward expansion. Within a decade after his accession, Ashurnasirpal II (882 B.C.) reached the Phoenician coast. Though he took tribute from Tyre, Sidon, and Byblos, Israel is not mentioned as a subject state. Omri not only stabilized the entire country of Ephraim, he made extensive conquests in Transjordan. The Moabite Stone says Omri controlled the territory east of Jordan as far south as Medeba.[24] His conquests in Transjordan during the period of Assyrian westward expansion were a remarkable achievement.

Shalmaneser III (858–824 B.C.) overran the Aramean states between the Habur and Euphrates, including the well-known Bit-Adini, in the first years of his reign.[25] This defeat served as an intimidating example of Assyrian power even 150 years later (2 Kings 19:12). Assyrian expansion brought Israel into coalition with their old enemy the Arameans; Ahab was present in the famous battle of Qarqar on the Orontes River in 853 B.C.[26] Though Shalmaneser claimed an overwhelming victory, it is likely the confederates carried the day, as the same coalition appeared again in successive years. Israel and the Arameans repeatedly resume their old conflicts, with Ahab dying in his attempt to regain Ramoth Gilead (1 Kings 22). Ahab's son Ahaziah dies within a year and is succeeded by another son Joram, named after the son of Jehoshaphat in Judah. It is probably during his reign that Samaria is besieged

---

24. For the Moabite stone, see Pritchard, *An Anthology of Texts and Pictures*, 209–10; plate 74; T. C. Mitchell, *The Bible in the British Museum: Interpreting the Evidence* (London: British Museum, 1988), 51.

25. Hallo and Simpson, *The Ancient Near East*, 127.

26. James B. Pritchard, ed., *Ancient Near Eastern Texts Relating to the Old Testament*, 3rd ed. (Princeton: Princeton Univ. Press, 1969), 278–79.

by Ben-Hadad II of Aram, producing conditions of cannibalism in the city (2 Kings 6:24−7:20). Joram was the last king of the Omride dynasty.

Though the establishment of the capital of Israel at Samaria is never declared to be the divine will and is not accomplished by a king subservient to the covenant, Samaria becomes an icon of political success. With the strategic location of the capital and the alliances with neighboring countries, Israel became a nation of considerable political force. The splendor of Samaria can still be seen in the ruins uncovered by archaeologists:

> ... the buildings of Samaria are of monumental character. Ashlar masonry was lavishly used in the various structures, and in particular the construction of the casemate walls with ashlar stones should be noted. At least some entrances to the monumental buildings had been decorated with stone-carved Proto-Ionic capitals mounted on pillars or pilasters, and several such capitals were uncovered in the excavations.[27]

Samaria was a grand capital, described as a crown at the head of a rich valley. It was a capital of decadence destined for destruction. The prophet Isaiah uses the fading flowers in the garland of its drunkards as a suitable metaphor for the dissolution of the city.

> Woe to the proud crown of the drunkards of Ephraim,
> and to the fading flowers of his glorious beauty,
> set on the head of a fertile valley
> of those overcome by wine.
>
> See, the Lord has one at his bidding
> who is powerful and strong,
> like a hailstorm, a destructive tempest,
> like a storm of massive overflowing waters,
> he will hurl it forcefully to the ground.
>
> That crown, the pride of Ephraim's drunkards,
> will be trampled underfoot.
>
> And the fading flower of his glorious beauty,
> set on the head of the fertile valley,
> will be like an early fig before the summer harvest;
> whoever sees it devours it
> as soon as it is in his hand. (Isa. 28:1−4)[28]

---

27. David Ussishkin, "Jezreel, Samaria and Megiddo: Royal Centers of Omri and Ahab," in *Congress Volume: Cambridge 1995* (VTSup 46; Leiden: Brill, 1997), 358.

28. The translation is that of Brevard S. Childs, *Isaiah* (OTL; Louisville: Westminster John Knox, 2001), 201.

This prophetic tradition against Samaria is more than 150 years after Omri established it as the magnificent capital of a new kingdom. This invective likely had its origins in the decadent days of luxury and greed described by the prophet Amos. Its destruction came with the fierceness of a hailstorm; the city was swallowed the way an early fig would be swallowed by one passing by. The city of glorious beauty was trampled underfoot by invading armies. Those who lived in wealth, luxury, and dissipation in the grand capital could not have imagined such ignominy.

By the time Kings was composed, the glory of Israelite Samaria had long passed from living memory. Their only comment on the achievements of Omri was that "he did what was wrong, more than all those who had gone before him" (16:25–26). No more needed to be said about the proud achievements of Israel's greatest kings. Though the kingdom of Israel ends in oblivion, there is a remnant within the kingdom of Israel that is very much a part of the kingdom of God. The prophet Isaiah has a further word for Samaria:

In that day the LORD of hosts will become
a crown of glory,
and a diadem of beauty for the remnant of his people,
and a spirit of justice to him who sits in judgment,
and strength for those who turn back the battle at the gate.
    (Isa. 28:5–6)[29]

This word of promise, which seems to intrude on the word of warning directed against Samaria in this section of Isaiah (Isa. 28:1–13), has close connections to other passages of hope that speak about "that day" (e.g., 4:2–4). The Lord of hosts will be the crown of glory and diadem of beauty of the faithful remnant, not the capital city of a vain nation long forgotten. Yahweh will provide a spirit of justice (4:4; 28:6) that will characterize his holy mountain as a place of beauty and glory (4:2; 28:5). Though Jerusalem and Samaria will never share in a national glory like that of Solomon, the prophetic vision for the kingdom of God represented by his palace in Jerusalem remains undiminished.

The writers of Kings have to deal with exile. Their challenge is a crisis of faith that comes with loss of national identity. Their answer is in terms of the divine word: The circumstance of exile is not because God's word had failed, but because it has been fully established. The postexilic prophets have the same message:

"But did not my words and my decrees, which I commanded my servants the prophets, overtake your forefathers?

---

29. Ibid.

"Then they repented and said, 'The LORD Almighty has done to us what our ways and practices deserve, just as he determined to do.'" (Zech. 1:6–7)

Turmoil at the division of the kingdom continues to spiral toward complete dissolution of both nations. Politically the explanation is simple: Israel and Judah occupy the bridge between the mighty empires of Mesopotamia and Egypt. Their survival as independent entities is never viable. That is not the prophetic viewpoint. The history of Kings is written well; divine judgment and blessing operative in the kingdoms of Judah and Israel are no less significant for the present.

 MOST OF THE CHRISTIAN past involves conflict, like the history of Israel and Judah. This conflict goes back to the earliest times of the New Testament itself. The apostle Paul encounters intense conflict with the church at Corinth and avoids a further personal confrontation by writing a painful letter (2 Cor. 1:23–2:4). There are those who took satisfaction in the suffering and imprisonment of the apostle Paul and preached Christ with the goal of adding affliction to his imprisonment (Phil. 1:15–18).

As Christians look back on their past it is important to have clearly understood perspectives. Only then is it possible to understand the way in which the church struggles and fails in dealing with the forces of this age. It is then more possible to respect considerable divergences within the Christian faith. Above all, it is important to see how God continues to be at work accomplishing his purposes, sometimes through the deeds of wicked individuals who seek only to promote their own interests and sometimes through individuals willing to sacrifice their lives in doing the will of God on earth.

The church and political power. The absolute claims of the Christian faith must not lead to intolerance, but tolerance must not lead to compromise of the faith. This may be an impossible goal. Ernst Wilhelm Benz in *The New Encyclopaedia Britannica* describes Christianity as an intolerant religion, itself responsible for the conflict and persecution against it.

Christianity consistently practiced an intolerant attitude in its approach to Judaism and paganism as well as heresy in its own ranks. By practicing its intolerance vis-à-vis the Roman emperor cult, it thereby forced the Roman state, for its part, into intolerance.[30]

---

30. E. W. Benz, "Christianity," *Encyclopaedia Britannica*, 15th ed., 4:492.

According to Benz, the mighty force of the Roman empire could not be tolerant of Christians who refused to bow to the emperor cult. "Early Christianity aimed at the elimination of paganism—the destruction of institutions, temples, tradition, and the order of life based upon it. After Christianity's victory over Greco-Roman religions, it left only the ruins of paganism still remaining."[31] This view of the early Christian history is an admission that religions of human deification enforced by political power were no match for the simple power of the truth claims of the Christian gospel. The earliest Christian church had nothing more than the power of the Word to overcome the oppressive darkness of their world (John 1:1–5). The "forced" persecution of the Roman empire could not stop the light of the claims of Christ from being seen.

It is sadly true that Christianity became a religion of political power with vested interests in control. Exclusive claims for truth could not be separated from the power of the state. Benz again credits intolerance of religion as the cause of political wars within Christian countries.

> When the Reformation churches asserted the exclusive claim of possessing the Christian truth, they tried to carry it out with the help of the political and military power at their disposal. In the religious wars of the 16th and 17th centuries, Christian intolerance developed into an internal fratricidal struggle in which each side sought to annihilate the other party in the name of truth.[32]

In biblical terms, the church is not to be just another social-political force. It is to be the kingdom of God present amidst the kingdoms of humans. The power of the church over state in the Reformation period obscures this ideal. The religious wars of Europe are a dark period in the story of the kingdom of God.

Religious wars are a reminder that faith can never achieve its ends through political force. The problem is that political ambitions are not easily separated from religious issues, so political conflict over religion is the result. This was most evident in the intolerance of revolutionary groups of the Reformation period. The threats to the life of Martin Luther, the execution of radical Anabaptist reformers, the revolts led by the German radical reformer Thomas Müntzer, and the attempt of fanatical John of Leiden (Jan Beuckelson) to establish the New Jerusalem in the city of Münster are all examples of using political force to enforce truth claims on others.

This small sampling illustrates the tragic history of the Christian church in its failure to distinguish between the role of government to maintain peace

---

31. Ibid.
32. Ibid.

and order between divergent groups and the responsibility to peacefully represent Christian truth against hostile forces. Religious wars did not arise because of the absolute claims of Christian faith, as Benz asserts; rather, religion was made a political matter. The conflicts of the Reformation were as political as those of Israel and Judah. Conflict between Israel and Judah, as well as civil war within Israel, was not caused by the absolute claims of the covenant, since none of the political leaders maintained the covenant requirement of exclusive worship of God. All claims of covenant allegiance were quickly subordinated to other political ambitions.

There are continuing lessons here for the Christian church. Each Reformation Day (October 31) all Christians should recall Luther's intent in nailing his ninety-five theses to the Wittenburg church door on the eve of All Saints Day. He was responding to the sale of indulgences, the receipt of money for the forgiveness of sins. He was extending an invitation to debate a number of theological propositions. But debating these propositions had serious political implications. Indulgences served many useful purposes. Luther's university at Wittenberg, even his own salary, was partly funded from the offerings of the pious who flocked to pray before the famous relic collection of Elector Frederick the Wise, displayed periodically in the Castle Church at Wittenberg. Though Luther was inviting theological debate, he was inadvertently stirring up a hornets' nest of political interests.

It is the responsibility of churches to maintain the integrity of their own faith confessions. This is not intolerance, since those who do not share these confessions are not expected to have membership within the group. This is a separate question from tolerance in relation to a larger society. Christians should not expect the state to conform to their values and cannot expect that laws of state will always support their values.

A greater tension arises when the state proposes legislation that is explicitly contrary to Christian values or ethical convictions. If Christians are compelled by law to participate in an activity contrary to their convictions, like the Christians in the time of the Roman empire, they will have no choice but to obey God rather than government. To lay blame for such disobedience as Christian intolerance is itself a manifestation of intolerance of minorities that is inimical to democratic ideals. The viewpoint of Benz is completely undemocratic and intolerant.

Israel and Judah could not survive as political entities. They did survive as entities of faith, present in a small way in the days of Chronicles and still present when the mighty Roman empire enforced its own version of peace on the entire Western world. It emerged in the followers of the Way, who found the man Jesus to be the fulfillment of the promise to David. It became a force that eventually transformed a pagan Greco-Roman culture, as Benz describes it.

Conflict and war following the division of the Israelite kingdom show the difficulty of integrating faith and powers of state. Under the covenant, civil and religious authorities were to be separate; kings were not to function as temple officials, and prophets could challenge the conduct of kings. However, the Deuteronomistic Historians did not envision a pluralistic state tolerant of other faiths. The covenant specified that certain groups could not be part of the state, such as the indigenous nations of Canaan and individuals supporting their religious practices (Deut. 7:1–6; 18:9–13). The covenant commitment of Israel was not sufficient to bring about homogeneity of faith in God, much to the anguish of the historical writers. Quest for power invariably brought dissension and violence, undermining the ideal of a nation living in obedience to God.

The new covenant of the church was of a different order; in the vision of Jeremiah, its power would be in a transformation of mind, and for this reason would succeed where the old covenant failed (Jer. 31:33–34). The church was not to be a state power but an expression of faith within the pluralism of many faiths. People of faith may be profitably involved in political power, but in a pluralistic society the function of political control is to maintain order in the midst of a divergence of worldviews. The power of faith is its ability to change the lives of individuals; its goal is not to control them.

Chronicles is in this respect a most helpful complement to Kings in understanding the history of faith. While Kings focuses on the conflict and failure of the political, Chronicles focuses on the perspective of the divine kingdom. There is a continuity of faith in the people the Chronicler called "Israel" who survived the Exile and the end of the nation. Though politically powerless, they represent the hope of David, the possibility a theocratic kingdom. The church represents the continuity of doing God's will on earth as it is in heaven, in a sometimes-difficult dialectic with the political forces around it.

The church and conflict. The church will always need to deal with conflict in its institutional life. The great battles of the church for truth are sobering reminders of the inevitability of conflict. In writing to the churches of Asia the apostle John gave stern warnings to deal with those who threatened the church from within and an exhortation not to fear those without. Pergamum had to deal with the "throne of Satan," which involved the "teaching of Balaam" and the doctrines of the "Nicolaitans" (Rev. 2:13–15). They paid a high price; Antipas, the faithful witness (*martyr*) paid the ultimate price for being faithful to the truth.

Battles against Gnosticism in the second century, the establishment of orthodoxy about the incarnation Christ, and the ecclesiastical conflicts of the Reformation are all examples of the dangers of false religion. In the New

Testament, the response of the church is never to defend itself with the powers of state. Instead, it is the example that shows the limitations of state power. In his Revelation, John sees a great number from every tribe, tongue, and nation surrounding the throne of God, giving praise to his power forever (Rev. 7:9–12). Those suffering in great tribulation in the kingdoms of this world gain their victory as members of a kingdom that transcends earthly kingdoms.

A great tragedy in the story of the church is its attempt to be a political kingdom in this world. An even greater tragedy is the church's attacks against itself. Days like those of the Reformation period are unlikely to return; Christians have recognized that power of a faith group over state is a source of great trouble and conflict. But this has not removed the problem of open conflict within the church, most especially within particular congregations. It is most tragic when the disputes of believers are much more trivial than political power and have no concern with even minor points in church doctrine. Most church disputes are over personalities and church culture. Susan Lang uses the metaphor of a ship at sea to describe the voyage of a congregation:

> As the crew of the good ship Our Congregation plots the course of ministry together, they have high hopes for smooth sailing. The ship sails out of the docks and begins its journey of worshiping, witnessing and learning together. The seas are calm and spirits are high.
>
> Then someone suggests a small change. What about introducing a new worship book? Or, even more dramatic, a contemporary worship service to draw in a younger crowd? Suddenly the seas begin to churn. The boat starts to rock.
>
> Other ideas surface, such as major renovations to a sanctuary that has never been changed in its 150-year history. Someone else suggests moving the altar so the pastor can face the congregation while presiding over communion. The waves swell and begin to crash on the deck.
>
> Passionate disagreements about what should be done occur. Thick, dark clouds appear. Visibility decreases and it's impossible to see where the ship is headed. The leadership fears it is caught in a maelstrom of conflict and will sink. Perhaps all is lost.[33]

Michael Smith (a pseudonym) is a chaplain and history teacher at a private secondary school. Of the myriad of problems in the church receiving media attention, from membership losses to sexual abuse, a hidden crisis

---

33. Susan M. Lang, "Navigating the Seas of Congregational Life," *The Lutheran* 16/8 (August 2003): 36.

lurks in the proliferation of congregational conflicts. Local churches, denominational officials, and clergy perpetuate the problem by being loathe to acknowledge it. The former find ignoring it easier than dealing with it, the latter want to avoid professional stigma. The problem is congregational conflicts in which the pastor is the target.

Particularly in the so-called free churches, in which decisions to hire and fire clergy rest with the members and not with denominational officials, clergy are vulnerable to assault by small but committed factions of critics. I am referring not to situations in which a pastor's poor performance or scandalous behavior has ignited a controversy, but to conflicts that arise from unhealthy congregational dynamics, and that target pastors who are innocent of malfeasance and are usually caught unawares.

It is impossible to say how common this kind of conflict is, or how many clergy have become casualties. One denomination that offers some statistics, the Southern Baptist Convention, reported that during an 18-month period ending in 1989, some 2,100 pastors were fired—a 31 percent increase since 1984. Other denominations are less forthright, but my own experience of a bitter church fight and its surprising aftermath suggests that the SBC's figures are a good indication of what is happening in many denominations.[34]

"Smith" suggests that one of the reasons for such conflict lies within the nature of the congregations; they have become clubs, sociological fellowships rather than theological communities. A club is closed, exclusive, and inward looking; it can be the friendliest of places and put on the best potluck dinners, but the congregation-as-club is essentially concerned with past and present friendship circles.

Richard Kaufman recognizes that the church is often embattled and dysfunctional, but it is still where God chooses to meet us:

Sometimes you have to suffer as much from the church as you do for it, said Flannery O'Connor. Some of my friends share her sentiment. Caught in the crossfire of church conflict, they considered giving up on the church entirely. Bruised and abused, they wondered, is it worth all the hassle? And they asked me, "Church, who needs it?"

"I gave up my faith in the church a long time ago, even though I still believe in it." I told them that my faith isn't ultimately in the church. "That is misplaced faith, idolatry. My faith is in God. But I still

---

34. "Pastors Under Fire: A Personal Report," *The Christian Century* 111/6 (Feb. 23, 1994): 196.

believe in the church because it is central to what God is doing in the world—forming a reconciled and reconciling people who are a light to the nations."[35]

The people of faith have never had a Golden Era. The Old Testament is a continuous story of conflict and failure, not only between kings as heads of idolatrous states, but conflict between prophet and prophet. The New Testament would be a much smaller volume if all the passages dealing with church conflict were excised. Some of Paul's letters would virtually disappear. In terms of conflict, the New Testament church is remarkably modern. Kaufman provides a reminder of both the church's significance and function:

> The church is a common community with an uncommon cause. The foundation of our corporate life is what God has done for us in Jesus Christ. We have been brought into being by the utterly unique and gratuitous act of God's reconciling work in Jesus Christ. By this act, God has forgiven our sins and welcomed us into his family. And the very act that brought the church into being should be what characterizes the life of the church. Our life should be marked by forgiveness, reconciliation, and by welcoming people into God's family. Perhaps that is why we get so discouraged over conflict.[36]

Christian faith holds promise of reconciliation for some of the world's greatest conflicts. South Africa, Cambodia, and Rwanda are examples where this is happening. Justice is not possible in situations of terror and genocide. Justice is restoration of what has been lost; lives lost in the atrocities of terror and genocide cannot be restored. In such extreme cases, many of the individuals involved in such atrocities are not dangerous; they were caught up in circumstances much bigger than they could manage. The past cannot be undone; the present must be restored. Forgiveness and reconciliation are the only hope for such countries.

The church has had a most significant role in teaching forgiveness that can reconcile families torn asunder by violence. In the examples of South Africa, Cambodia, and Rwanda, virtually every family has members who were lost through terrorist violence and members who were a part of committing those terrorist acts. Forgiveness and reconciliation are the only possibility for the restoration of those communities. The Truth and Reconciliation hearings of Bishop Desmond Tutu are legendary. These are also part of the church's story.

---

35. Richard Kaufman, "Don't Give Up on the Church," *Christianity Today* 41/11 (Oct. 6, 1997): 18.
36. Ibid., 19.

There is a tendency among some to regard religion and racism as the cause of all conflict. Such a charge is an utter dearth of creativity. Religion is universal and inescapable; those who call themselves nonreligious are only oblivious to the religion they live and espouse or to the narrow definition they have given to religion. It is as inevitable as having race, language, and culture. Every conflict in some respect involves religion as a part of the circumstances. The universality of both conflict and religion does not establish a causal relationship between the two; both are inseparable aspects of the human condition.

In writing about human conflict of the past, it is important to have a clearly articulated historiography. This aspect of history writing is exemplary in both Kings and Chronicles. Their circumstances, presuppositions, and goals for writing are translucent. The reader is unable to know how historical material has been selected, but it is clear how it was used. Such method gives historical data a context from which it can be assessed and appropriate lessons learned. Christians must write their own story, with all its conflicts, with clarity of conviction and viewpoint. It may appear as one unmitigated tale of conflict, but it may also be the one story that holds out hope for resolution in a world continuously in conflict.

1 Kings 17:1–19:21

❧

NOW ELIJAH THE Tishbite, from Tishbe in Gilead, said to Ahab, "As the LORD, the God of Israel, lives, whom I serve, there will be neither dew nor rain in the next few years except at my word."

²Then the word of the LORD came to Elijah: ³"Leave here, turn eastward and hide in the Kerith Ravine, east of the Jordan. ⁴You will drink from the brook, and I have ordered the ravens to feed you there."

⁵So he did what the LORD had told him. He went to the Kerith Ravine, east of the Jordan, and stayed there. ⁶The ravens brought him bread and meat in the morning and bread and meat in the evening, and he drank from the brook.

⁷Some time later the brook dried up because there had been no rain in the land. ⁸Then the word of the LORD came to him: ⁹"Go at once to Zarephath of Sidon and stay there. I have commanded a widow in that place to supply you with food." ¹⁰So he went to Zarephath. When he came to the town gate, a widow was there gathering sticks. He called to her and asked, "Would you bring me a little water in a jar so I may have a drink?" ¹¹As she was going to get it, he called, "And bring me, please, a piece of bread."

¹²"As surely as the LORD your God lives," she replied, "I don't have any bread—only a handful of flour in a jar and a little oil in a jug. I am gathering a few sticks to take home and make a meal for myself and my son, that we may eat it—and die."

¹³Elijah said to her, "Don't be afraid. Go home and do as you have said. But first make a small cake of bread for me from what you have and bring it to me, and then make something for yourself and your son. ¹⁴For this is what the LORD, the God of Israel, says: 'The jar of flour will not be used up and the jug of oil will not run dry until the day the LORD gives rain on the land.'"

¹⁵She went away and did as Elijah had told her. So there was food every day for Elijah and for the woman and her family. ¹⁶For the jar of flour was not used up and the jug of oil did not run dry, in keeping with the word of the LORD spoken by Elijah.

¹⁷Some time later the son of the woman who owned the house became ill. He grew worse and worse, and finally stopped breathing. ¹⁸She said to Elijah, "What do you have against me, man of God? Did you come to remind me of my sin and kill my son?"

¹⁹"Give me your son," Elijah replied. He took him from her arms, carried him to the upper room where he was staying, and laid him on his bed. ²⁰Then he cried out to the LORD, "O LORD my God, have you brought tragedy also upon this widow I am staying with, by causing her son to die?" ²¹Then he stretched himself out on the boy three times and cried to the LORD, "O LORD my God, let this boy's life return to him!"

²²The LORD heard Elijah's cry, and the boy's life returned to him, and he lived. ²³Elijah picked up the child and carried him down from the room into the house. He gave him to his mother and said, "Look, your son is alive!"

²⁴Then the woman said to Elijah, "Now I know that you are a man of God and that the word of the LORD from your mouth is the truth."

¹⁸:¹After a long time, in the third year, the word of the LORD came to Elijah: "Go and present yourself to Ahab, and I will send rain on the land." ²So Elijah went to present himself to Ahab.

Now the famine was severe in Samaria, ³and Ahab had summoned Obadiah, who was in charge of his palace. (Obadiah was a devout believer in the LORD. ⁴While Jezebel was killing off the LORD's prophets, Obadiah had taken a hundred prophets and hidden them in two caves, fifty in each, and had supplied them with food and water.) ⁵Ahab had said to Obadiah, "Go through the land to all the springs and valleys. Maybe we can find some grass to keep the horses and mules alive so we will not have to kill any of our animals." ⁶So they divided the land they were to cover, Ahab going in one direction and Obadiah in another.

⁷As Obadiah was walking along, Elijah met him. Obadiah recognized him, bowed down to the ground, and said, "Is it really you, my lord Elijah?"

⁸"Yes," he replied. "Go tell your master, 'Elijah is here.'"

⁹"What have I done wrong," asked Obadiah, "that you are handing your servant over to Ahab to be put to death? ¹⁰As surely as the LORD your God lives, there is not a nation or

kingdom where my master has not sent someone to look for you. And whenever a nation or kingdom claimed you were not there, he made them swear they could not find you. [11]But now you tell me to go to my master and say, 'Elijah is here.' [12]I don't know where the Spirit of the LORD may carry you when I leave you. If I go and tell Ahab and he doesn't find you, he will kill me. Yet I your servant have worshiped the LORD since my youth. [13]Haven't you heard, my lord, what I did while Jezebel was killing the prophets of the LORD? I hid a hundred of the LORD's prophets in two caves, fifty in each, and supplied them with food and water. [14]And now you tell me to go to my master and say, 'Elijah is here.' He will kill me!"

[15]Elijah said, "As the LORD Almighty lives, whom I serve, I will surely present myself to Ahab today."

[16]So Obadiah went to meet Ahab and told him, and Ahab went to meet Elijah. [17]When he saw Elijah, he said to him, "Is that you, you troubler of Israel?"

[18]"I have not made trouble for Israel," Elijah replied. "But you and your father's family have. You have abandoned the LORD's commands and have followed the Baals. [19]Now summon the people from all over Israel to meet me on Mount Carmel. And bring the four hundred and fifty prophets of Baal and the four hundred prophets of Asherah, who eat at Jezebel's table."

[20]So Ahab sent word throughout all Israel and assembled the prophets on Mount Carmel. [21]Elijah went before the people and said, "How long will you waver between two opinions? If the LORD is God, follow him; but if Baal is God, follow him."

But the people said nothing.

[22]Then Elijah said to them, "I am the only one of the LORD's prophets left, but Baal has four hundred and fifty prophets. [23]Get two bulls for us. Let them choose one for themselves, and let them cut it into pieces and put it on the wood but not set fire to it. I will prepare the other bull and put it on the wood but not set fire to it. [24]Then you call on the name of your god, and I will call on the name of the LORD. The god who answers by fire—he is God."

Then all the people said, "What you say is good."

[25]Elijah said to the prophets of Baal, "Choose one of the bulls and prepare it first, since there are so many of you. Call

on the name of your god, but do not light the fire." ²⁶So they took the bull given them and prepared it.

Then they called on the name of Baal from morning till noon. "O Baal, answer us!" they shouted. But there was no response; no one answered. And they danced around the altar they had made.

²⁷At noon Elijah began to taunt them. "Shout louder!" he said. "Surely he is a god! Perhaps he is deep in thought, or busy, or traveling. Maybe he is sleeping and must be awakened." ²⁸So they shouted louder and slashed themselves with swords and spears, as was their custom, until their blood flowed. ²⁹Midday passed, and they continued their frantic prophesying until the time for the evening sacrifice. But there was no response, no one answered, no one paid attention.

³⁰Then Elijah said to all the people, "Come here to me." They came to him, and he repaired the altar of the LORD, which was in ruins. ³¹Elijah took twelve stones, one for each of the tribes descended from Jacob, to whom the word of the LORD had come, saying, "Your name shall be Israel." ³²With the stones he built an altar in the name of the LORD, and he dug a trench around it large enough to hold two seahs of seed. ³³He arranged the wood, cut the bull into pieces and laid it on the wood. Then he said to them, "Fill four large jars with water and pour it on the offering and on the wood."

³⁴"Do it again," he said, and they did it again.

"Do it a third time," he ordered, and they did it the third time. ³⁵The water ran down around the altar and even filled the trench.

³⁶At the time of sacrifice, the prophet Elijah stepped forward and prayed: "O LORD, God of Abraham, Isaac and Israel, let it be known today that you are God in Israel and that I am your servant and have done all these things at your command. ³⁷Answer me, O LORD, answer me, so these people will know that you, O LORD, are God, and that you are turning their hearts back again."

³⁸Then the fire of the LORD fell and burned up the sacrifice, the wood, the stones and the soil, and also licked up the water in the trench.

³⁹When all the people saw this, they fell prostrate and cried, "The LORD—he is God! The LORD—he is God!"

⁴⁰Then Elijah commanded them, "Seize the prophets of Baal. Don't let anyone get away!" They seized them, and Elijah had them brought down to the Kishon Valley and slaughtered there.

⁴¹And Elijah said to Ahab, "Go, eat and drink, for there is the sound of a heavy rain." ⁴²So Ahab went off to eat and drink, but Elijah climbed to the top of Carmel, bent down to the ground and put his face between his knees.

⁴³"Go and look toward the sea," he told his servant. And he went up and looked.

"There is nothing there," he said.

Seven times Elijah said, "Go back."

⁴⁴The seventh time the servant reported, "A cloud as small as a man's hand is rising from the sea."

So Elijah said, "Go and tell Ahab, 'Hitch up your chariot and go down before the rain stops you.'"

⁴⁵Meanwhile, the sky grew black with clouds, the wind rose, a heavy rain came on and Ahab rode off to Jezreel. ⁴⁶The power of the LORD came upon Elijah and, tucking his cloak into his belt, he ran ahead of Ahab all the way to Jezreel.

¹⁹:¹Now Ahab told Jezebel everything Elijah had done and how he had killed all the prophets with the sword. ²So Jezebel sent a messenger to Elijah to say, "May the gods deal with me, be it ever so severely, if by this time tomorrow I do not make your life like that of one of them."

³Elijah was afraid and ran for his life. When he came to Beersheba in Judah, he left his servant there, ⁴while he himself went a day's journey into the desert. He came to a broom tree, sat down under it and prayed that he might die. "I have had enough, LORD," he said. "Take my life; I am no better than my ancestors." ⁵Then he lay down under the tree and fell asleep.

All at once an angel touched him and said, "Get up and eat." ⁶He looked around, and there by his head was a cake of bread baked over hot coals, and a jar of water. He ate and drank and then lay down again.

⁷The angel of the LORD came back a second time and touched him and said, "Get up and eat, for the journey is too much for you." ⁸So he got up and ate and drank. Strengthened by that food, he traveled forty days and forty nights until he reached Horeb, the mountain of God. ⁹There he went into a cave and spent the night.

And the word of the LORD came to him: "What are you doing here, Elijah?"

¹⁰He replied, "I have been very zealous for the LORD God Almighty. The Israelites have rejected your covenant, broken down your altars, and put your prophets to death with the sword. I am the only one left, and now they are trying to kill me too."

¹¹The LORD said, "Go out and stand on the mountain in the presence of the LORD, for the LORD is about to pass by."

Then a great and powerful wind tore the mountains apart and shattered the rocks before the LORD, but the LORD was not in the wind. After the wind there was an earthquake, but the LORD was not in the earthquake. ¹²After the earthquake came a fire, but the LORD was not in the fire. And after the fire came a gentle whisper. ¹³When Elijah heard it, he pulled his cloak over his face and went out and stood at the mouth of the cave.

Then a voice said to him, "What are you doing here, Elijah?"

¹⁴He replied, "I have been very zealous for the LORD God Almighty. The Israelites have rejected your covenant, broken down your altars, and put your prophets to death with the sword. I am the only one left, and now they are trying to kill me too."

¹⁵The LORD said to him, "Go back the way you came, and go to the Desert of Damascus. When you get there, anoint Hazael king over Aram. ¹⁶Also, anoint Jehu son of Nimshi king over Israel, and anoint Elisha son of Shaphat from Abel Meholah to succeed you as prophet. ¹⁷Jehu will put to death any who escape the sword of Hazael, and Elisha will put to death any who escape the sword of Jehu. ¹⁸Yet I reserve seven thousand in Israel—all whose knees have not bowed down to Baal and all whose mouths have not kissed him."

¹⁹So Elijah went from there and found Elisha son of Shaphat. He was plowing with twelve yoke of oxen, and he himself was driving the twelfth pair. Elijah went up to him and threw his cloak around him. ²⁰Elisha then left his oxen and ran after Elijah. "Let me kiss my father and mother good-by," he said, "and then I will come with you."

"Go back," Elijah replied. "What have I done to you?"

²¹So Elisha left him and went back. He took his yoke of oxen and slaughtered them. He burned the plowing equipment to cook the meat and gave it to the people, and they ate. Then he set out to follow Elijah and became his attendant.

THE BATTLE WITH the Baal cult is a major constituent within the Deuteronomistic History. The confrontation of Elijah with the state-supported prophets of Baal at Mount Carmel is a significant component of their narration (cf. 18:19). This account is important on several counts. It authenticates worship of God as Creator of all against the perpetrators of a false religion; it proves the truth of the words of the prophets, who are opposed by the state to the point of death (18:4; 19:10). It shows how faithlessness to the covenant in pursuit of politically expedient ends lead Israel in a deceptive downward spiral to eventual extinction, and it shows how a small faithful remnant of prophets preserve a presence of true worship of God in Israel.

The story of Elijah at Mount Carmel is known from prophetic sources apart from the books of the annals of the kings of Judah and the kings of Israel. Nothing can be definitely known about the groups that preserved these stories or the process through which they have been incorporated into the Deuteronomistic History, though the subject has been much discussed. DeVries has proposed three distinct literary complexes: the Elijah cycle, the Elisha cycle, and the Omride-war cycle.[1] He believes that these cycles of prophetic tradition were later heavily edited by those sympathetic with the revolt of Jehu. By the time of Jehu, the anguish caused by the Arameans created excessive bitterness, and the Omride dynasty was given the blame for the humiliating subjugation Israel suffered.

At this distance, the nature of prophetic records and the process of their integration with royal archival information cannot be established. Literary assessment of the sources depends on the judgment of the literary critic.[2] Much depends on the reader's attitude to the supernatural. The details of place, persons, and events are sufficient to establish a firm historical basis for these stories, which cannot be said for the evidence ranged against the traditions.[3] Historicity does not mean that the stories are told in chronological order.[4] For example, Elijah's ascension is obviously after a letter sent to wicked Jehoram, the last king of the Omride dynasty (2 Chron. 21:12–15), though in Kings it is recounted immediately after the death of Ahaziah (2 Kings 2:1). The account of Elijah at Carmel is not given to advance the history of the kingdom of Ahab. It starts off a cycle of prophetic stories that show the character of that kingdom and the consequences of religious syncretism.

---

1. Simon J. DeVries, *Prophet against Prophet* (Grand Rapids: Eerdmans, 1978), 112–27.
2. DeVries catalogues eleven different subgenres of prophetic story (or legend) on the basis of their respective functions (ibid., 56–72).
3. Wiseman, *1 & 2 Kings*, 45.
4. See the introduction.

Drought in Israel (17:1–24)

ELIJAH IS INTRODUCED as a prophet from Gilead, though the precise place of his origin remains in doubt. He is introduced as a Tishbite (*hattišbî*) "of the settlers" (*tōšābê*) of Gilead (NASB; see NIV note).[5] The description of "settler" makes Elijah a non-Israelite, indicating he is an immigrant. The location of Tishbe in the Transjordan is not attested in ancient sources, though it has been identified with el-Istib eight miles (thirteen kilometers) north of the Jabbok in the proximity of a shrine for St. Elijah. Perhaps the text says nothing more than that Elijah is a settler in the wild, forested, and largely unsettled territory east of Jordan between the Yarmuk and Jabbok brooks in Gilead.

The message to King Ahab is given with divine sanction: lit., "by the life of Yahweh," which invokes an oath asserting the truth of the words spoken. If Yahweh withholds the rain, it will prove Baal to be powerless. Yahweh's will is represented through the word of prophet; the oath announces an irrevocable state of affairs that will weigh on the rule of Ahab.

The threat of drought by the oath of Yahweh is a direct challenge to the powers of Baal. Baal was the rider of the clouds, the god of rain and fertility, and therefore of riches. The image of Baal was a bull, which represented productivity and wealth that came through the god. He is depicted standing on a bull with the club of thunder in one hand and a sprig representing lightning in the other.[6] The psalmist's praise to Yahweh as the rider of the clouds is a direct challenge to the powers of Baal as the god of rain (Ps. 104:3–4). The protagonists in the present story are Yahweh and Baal, represented by Elijah and Ahab respectively.

Immediately after delivering the message, presumably in Samaria, Elijah is directed to go outside Ahab's territory. He hides by a little brook overlooking the Jordan called Kerith.[7] The need to make the journey to the river directly indicates that the drought will take immediate effect. Elijah needs sustenance and protection from Ahab. The divine provision for Elijah is similar to that of the Israelites in the desert after the crossing of the Red Sea (Ex. 16:8, 12). Provision for Elijah becomes even more dramatic after the brook dries up. Elijah is directed into the heart of Baal territory in Phoenicia, to a little town called Zarephath, about seven miles (thirteen kilometers) south of Sidon. Not only is Baal incapable of overcoming the drought, but the provision of Yahweh for the faithful prophet takes place right in the heart of Baal territory.

---

5. This is the pronunciation of the Hebrew; the Greek says he is from Tishbe (Thesbon) in Gilead (NIV).

6. Pritchard, *An Anthology of Texts and Pictures*, plates 136, 140.

7. Usually this is taken to mean east of the Jordan (e.g., 11:7, east of Jerusalem), but *ʿal pᵉnê* is often not specific (Gen. 18:16). Gileadite territory is home territory to Elijah.

A widow in this foreign territory provides for Elijah. Usually widows were the poorest of all the citizens, though the reference to her household may suggest she is a woman of some means (17:15, 17). She is herself preparing to die with her son because the drought has exhausted their entire food supply (v. 12). Her favorable response to the prophet's request for water prompts him to ask her for bread as well. The woman, though a Sidonian, answers in the name of the God of Elijah. Elijah tests her faith and self-renunciation by asking that she first provide a small loaf for him, then another for herself and her son. Yahweh will ensure that the flour in the jar and the oil in the jug will be sufficient until the rains again restore the fertility of the ground. The woman trusts the God of the prophet and does as he instructs. Her faith is rewarded, the prophetic word is confirmed, and the God of Israel is shown to be the giver of life.

The raising of the woman's son is usually considered to be supplementary, joined by the vague phrase "after these things" (17:17; "some time later," NIV). It is often thought to be derivative from the much more detailed story of the raising of the son of the Shunammite widow by Elisha (2 Kings 4:8– 37). Schmitt considers it to be a prophetic narrative that creates a parallel between Elijah and Moses.[8] In any case, the raising of the son is additional evidence that God alone has the power of life in addition to food. Parallels between Elijah and Moses, or Elijah and Elisha, are a deliberate aspect of the prophetic presentation, but they cannot in themselves serve as criteria for an artificial linking of extraneous stories.

The illness and death of the woman's son (17:18, 20, 21–22) is taken as evidence that Elijah is not a benevolent prophet to a foreign woman; instead, she is being punished for her sins. The woman addresses Elijah in great distress; the idiom (lit.) "what have I to do with you" (17:18) expresses the same harsh dissociation as that of Jesus when asked by his mother to provide wine at the wedding in Cana (John 2:1–4). The woman implies that Elijah has come to meddle in her affairs and is causing her grief.

Elijah takes the lad upstairs to his own private room, where he stretches himself over the lifeless body three times (17:21). Normally this would be a violation of the prohibition of touching a dead body (e.g., Num. 9:6–7). The action may be an acted-out prayer typical of the prophets, but it could be a self-sacrificial intercession in which he takes the role of the sacrificial victim, identifying himself with the ultimate uncleanness of death.[9] Moses identified fully with the plight of the people at the sin of the golden calf, praying that his name be stricken from the book of life if the people were not forgiven

---

8. Armin Schmitt, "Die Totenerweckung in 1 Kon. XVII 17–24," *VT* 27 (1977): 454–74.

9. Nobuyoshi Kiuchi, "Elijah's Self-Offering: 1 Kings 17:21," *Bib* 75 (1994): 74–79.

(Ex. 32:32). The action should not be regarded as contactual magic by analogy to similar Babylonian practices. This story is set in the context of a Hebrew worldview where magical practice is forbidden. It should not be thought that Elijah prays for the restoration of the "soul" of the child to the body (1 Kings 17:21, KJV), because the Hebrew word *nepeš* indicates breath or life such as animals possess as well (e.g., Gen. 1:20–21, 24). Life is restored to the child, demonstrating that God, not Baal, is the giver of life.

Confrontation on Mount Carmel (18:1–46)

THERE ARE THREE episodes in the account of the confrontation at Mount Carmel. Elijah meets Obadiah the prophet and asks him to inform Ahab he is present (18:1–15); Elijah confronts the prophets of Baal at Mount Carmel (18:16–40); and rain comes on the drought-stricken land (18:41–46).

Elijah and Obadiah (18:1–15). "The third year" indicates the extent of the drought according to the prophetic word (18:1). It does not mean three full years of drought, which would have been entirely destructive. It describes a severe drought that did not end the year after it began, but continues on into a third year.

Elijah arrives back in Israel when Ahab and Obadiah, his administrator of palace property (cf. 4:6), are scouting the land in the hope of finding sufficient provision so the animals will not need to be destroyed. Obadiah is a God-fearing man, who has risked his own life when he hid and fed a hundred prophets in caves to preserve them from the sentence of death by Jezebel (18:3–4). Ahab has completely misplaced priorities. He is busy trying to preserve the animals (v. 5), but apparently has no concern for the prophets whom Jezebel has cut off (v. 4). There are two droughts in the land; while hunger from drought is severe (v. 2), hunger for the prophets is caused by the wiles of a wicked woman. Ahab and Obadiah are not only going in different directions geographically in their search for water (v. 6), they are in pursuit of opposing values.

The encounter between Elijah and Obadiah (vv. 7–15) reveals how Elijah is in control of life in Samaria. Obadiah the prophet has the opposite response of the widow in Zarephath when Elijah asks him to report to Ahab (vv. 8–9). While the pagan widow immediately complied with a demanding request (17:13–15), the man who fears Yahweh responds with fear. As the widow makes Elijah responsible for the death of her son by bringing her sin to light (17:18), so Obadiah feels that Elijah will be the cause of his death if he should report to Ahab (18:9, 12, 14). The king has sought relentlessly to find Elijah, demanding on oath to be assured that no one is hiding him (v. 10). Elijah will likely prove as elusive to Obadiah as he does to Ahab, disappearing at the critical moment, so he will suffer the same fate as the prophets found by Jezebel (vv. 12–14).[10]

A further irony is that Ahab has utterly failed to find any trace of Elijah among the nations, but Elijah appears when he is busy seeking food for his animals. Both of the king's searches are pointless; Elijah appears as he wills, and he alone can make possible the life-saving provision of water.

Elijah and the prophets of Baal at Mount Carmel (18:16–40). The meeting between Elijah and Ahab contrasts his apostasy with the faithfulness of Obadiah (18:16–20). While the latter has respectfully greeted Elijah by falling to the ground (v. 7), Ahab accuses Elijah as being the one who had put a hex on Israel (v. 17). This accusation of Ahab is itself a contradiction. If Baal is truly god, Elijah could have no power over Israel at all. If Elijah does have power to bring drought, then Baal is not really god.

Ahab accepts the order to gather the prophets of Baal and Asherah to Mount Carmel (18:19–20). His acquiescence may have been because of his fear of Elijah, since Elijah does have control over the kingdom in spite of Jezebel's zeal. Ahab may have secretly realized that promotion of the Baal cult is disastrous. Though Elijah has appeared to announce the coming of rain, it is first necessary to demonstrate to all the people that the Baal cult is powerless.

The choice of Mount Carmel is significant as the center for the worship of a local deity that functioned as Canaanite Baal. Its proximity to the Phoenician border places the challenge to Jezebel right at her doorstep. The luxurious valley in the area of Carmel is a natural place for the worship of a fertility god (cf. Amos 1:2). The plain of Acco drains two rivers, the Naᶜaman and the Kishon, which supply the area with a heavy layer of rich topsoil from the erosion of the Galilean highlands, providing for plenteous agricultural productivity. The much narrower plain of Dor to the south is blanketed with a thicket-like forest.[11] Carmel is also the natural place to worship the storm god who can calm the winter gales and turn the storms into rain.

The contest at Mount Carmel shows that the Lord of Israel will tolerate no compromise; Elijah challenges the people to "stop hopping between two boughs."[12] The word for "bough" (*seᶜippîm*) is also used to refer to thoughts

---

10. There are a number of structural parallels between the scenes of Elijah and the widow and Elijah and Obadiah. In both cases Elijah overcomes human protest to fulfill the word of the Lord; see Robert L. Cohn, "The Literary Logic of 1 Kings 17–19," *JBL* 101 (1982): 339, n. 11.

11. Beitzel, *The Moody Atlas of Bible Lands*, 27, 30.

12. The meaning of the verb (*psḥ*) is uncertain. It describes the lameness of Mephibosheth because of a childhood accident (2 Sam. 9:13) and a condition that disqualifies one from holding the office of priest (Lev. 21:18). Milgrom proposes that *pesaḥ* (relating to the

---

(e.g., Job 4:13). Just as boughs branch off from trees, so thoughts and opinions can branch off in more than one direction. This wordplay describes the prevarication of the people in their professed worship; prayers and homage at the bull shrine can have nothing to do with Yahweh. The silence of the people is a concession to the truth of Elijah's words.

The contest Elijah proposes shows the folly of attempting to serve two masters (18:22–24). Lightning will signal the advance of rain; only if the prophets of Baal are able to produce a burnt offering can worship of Baal be justified. The prophets of Baal hop about, seeking a response from their god (v. 26); this ritual dance, which may have included music and song, is meant to attract the attention of Baal. Elijah may have alluded to this ritual in describing the people as hopping between two opinions.

Baal ritual seems to be alluded to in Elijah's taunting questions (v. 27).[13] The question about sleep probably refers to the death of Baal; sleep is often used as a metaphor for death (e.g., Job 3:13; Ps. 13:4). In the assumption that Baal rituals follow a seasonal pattern, the death of Baal in the ritual would signify the hot dry period of summer. The customary gashing with knives and blades may be part of a blood ritual seeking the first rainfall.[14] Blood letting was a rite of imitative magic to prompt a release of vital rain. Ecstatic prophesying may be a frenzied activity indistinguishable from mad behavior (cf. 1 Sam. 19:24). These rituals would take place at a fall festival for the Baal cult in anticipation of the early rains.

Once the time for the Baal offering has passed, Elijah makes preparations for the evening burnt offering (18:29). This takes place on an altar restored for the purpose (v. 30), indicating that the worship of God is not fully centralized with the building of the temple. Disrepair of the altar is presumably a result of the oppression Jezebel has inflicted on the prophets. The animal is prepared on the wood, and everything is soaked with water three times. Elijah then prays that the hearts of the people will be turned back to Yahweh (vv. 36–37), bringing fire to consume the offering.

The "fire from God" anticipates the advance of the rain. The fiery apparition indicates the divine presence (cf. Ex. 3:2; 19:18; 24:17). Fire also attests

---

Passover blood) means protection (Ex. 12:27; Isa. 31:5), citing other apotropaic rites; *Leviticus 1–16*, 1081. It may then have the sense of paralysis, but this hardly describes animals unfit for sacrifice (Mal. 1:8) or the ritual dance of the Baal prophets about the altar (1 Kings 18:26).

13. H. Jagersma, "YŠN in 1. Könige xviii 27," *VT* 25 (1975): 674–76.

14. *KTU* 1.3, 30–42; DeMoor, *An Anthology of Religious Texts from Ugarit*, 6–7. An Akkadian text at Ugarit attests to lacerations as part of ecstatic prophecy; see J. J. M. Roberts, "A New Parallel to 1 Kings 18:28–29," in *The Bible and the Ancient Near East* (Winona Lake, Ind.: Eisenbrauns, 2002), 102–3.

the divine acceptance and approval of the sacrifice (1 Chron. 21:26). Fire may indicate both approval of the sacrifice and the divine presence, as with Gideon (Judg. 6:20–22) and Moses (Lev. 9:22–24).

The actions of Elijah signal the restoration of Israel. An altar of twelve stones (v. 31) and twelve dousings with water (four jars emptied three times) both recall the twelve tribes and the crossing of the Jordan (Josh. 4:1–7, 19–24). Building an altar, forsaking false gods, and restoring the name Israel (1 Kings 18:30–31)[15] follow the pattern of Jacob when he built the altar at Bethel (Gen. 35:1–9). The Carmel event is no less significant than the Exodus; the renewal of Israel does not allow for the continuance of Baalism (1 Kings 18:40).

Elijah and the resumption of rain (18:41–46). With Israel reborn, Elijah turns his attention to Ahab. Ahab must prepare for a feast to celebrate the coming of rain. A sevenfold repetition indicates the fullness of prayer (vv. 43–44); each time the servant ascends one of the peaks of Carmel for the best view. At the first sign of a small cloud the company begins its descent from the mountain lest the rain bog them in the valley below. As Ahab rides furiously towards Jezreel, Elijah runs on ahead. Running before the king indicates service to that king,[16] now with the intent that the king will fulfill his proper mission in service to God.

Confirmation at Mount Horeb (19:1–21)

WITH THE SLAUGHTER of the prophets of Baal, Jezebel asserts her authority as the patron of the Baal cult (19:1–2). Her reputation is well established (16:31; 18:4, 13, 19); now she appears in person with an oath against the life of Elijah. The names of the protagonists reveal the combatants: Jezebel (meaning "Where is the prince [Baal]?") is pitted against Elijah (meaning "Yah[weh] is my God"). The warfare is initially psychological, as Jezebel sends her messenger with a verbal threat rather than her bailiffs to arrest him for the crime committed against her prophets. She prefers to avoid personal confrontation, perhaps because of the following Elijah has achieved at Carmel. If she can persuade Elijah to leave the country, she can pursue her ends without interference from the prophet and without exacerbating the situation by violent conflict.

The prophet Elijah appears to be a contradiction of himself in his fearful withdrawal from Jezebel (18:3–8) and his accusations against the faithlessness

---

15. A trench sufficient to contain two seahs of seed (about fifteen liters or four gallons) is a reasonable measure, commensurate to the water poured on the altar (vv. 32, 38).

16. The royal chariot was customarily escorted by a team of runners, who were part of the palace guard (1 Sam. 8:11; 21:8; 22:17); see P. K. McCarter, *1 Samuel* (AB 8; Garden City, N.Y.: Doubleday, 1980), 158, 364.

of the people (18:9–11). He seems to have felt confident in confronting Ahab, but he is not prepared to face the real proponent of the Baal cult, in spite of the dramatic victory that has just taken place on the mountain. He ignores the dramatic conversion of the people (18:39), forgets the courageous faithfulness of the prophet Obadiah (18:3–4), blames the people for the vengeful attack of Jezebel (19:10, 14), and regards himself as utterly isolated in his struggle against the Baal cult.

The despair of Elijah demonstrates the frailty of human strength and the power of God that is liberated within human weakness. Elijah is shown to be a true prophet in the tradition of Moses, and God is shown to be sovereign in the forces of nature, a monarch over the kings of this world and the Redeemer of his people.

Jezebel achieves her desired ends in her threats against Elijah. Elijah flees south out of Israel to Beersheba, the southern limit of Judah. There he dismisses his servant (19:3), signifying that he intends to leave the land of Israel's heritage altogether. After another day's journey south Elijah finds shelter under a broom tree (v. 4), a desert shrub that grows four to twelve feet high with straight long branches and small leaves. Shelter under a broom tree is the converse of each under their own vine and fig tree (4:25).

Alone in the desert, Elijah desires nothing other than death. "No better than my ancestors" (v. 4) may recall Moses, who asks for death when the people grumble about their conditions in the desert (Num. 11:15). As with Moses, Yahweh intervenes at the critical moment. The "angel of the LORD," the agent of divine presence, appears, as he did to Moses when he fled to Midian from the threats of Pharaoh in his journey toward Horeb (Ex. 3:2). Elijah is twice strengthened by divine provision of food and refreshed by sleep (1 Kings 19:5–7) before he continues his journey toward Horeb for forty days and forty nights (v. 8). Forty is a typical number for completion; Moses similarly spent forty days on the mountain at Horeb receiving the words of the covenant (Ex. 24:18; 34:28).

Driven by fear from the Promised Land, Elijah arrives at the mountain of God where he takes up residence in a cave (19:9a). God not only continues to be with his servant in flight, but also prepares him to receive the divine commission again.

At Mount Horeb, just as Moses before him, Elijah hears the word of Yahweh (19:9b), addressing him twice with the same question: "What are you doing here, Elijah?" (vv. 9c, 13c). Repetition is characteristic of the Elijah narrative. At times it serves to advance the narrative, as when Elijah goes before the people to challenge their duplicity (18:21) or when the people go before Elijah following the failure of the Baal prophets (18:30). In other instances it serves to emphasize a point, such as the faithfulness of Obadiah (18:4, 13) or the failure of Baal to respond to his prophets (18:26, 29).[17]

In this instance, the repetition puts into perspective the flight of Elijah to the mountain. The introduction depicts a prophet fleeing in fear at the threats of his opponent (19:2–3). The repetition of the question, introduced as "the word of the LORD" (v. 9b), brings the narrative back to the principal characteristic of the prophet as one who follows God's word.[18] Elijah's answer to the question shows that he is a prophet worthy of encountering Yahweh at his mountain (v. 11a); his function as a prophet is restored.

The narrative intentionally makes Elijah a prophet like Moses. Storm, earthquake, and fire recall the original appearance of God to the people at Mount Sinai (cf. Ex. 19:16; 20:18; Deut. 4:11, 24). Fire and storm were characteristic ways for God to manifest himself, as in the challenge to the prophets of Baal: Fire consumed the offering, fierce rain descended on the mountain. Jealous zeal for Yahweh is appropriate for a jealous God (1 Kings 19:10, 14; cf. Ex. 20:5; 34:14). Elijah wraps his face in his garment, the equivalent of Moses being protected by the rock as the glory of Yahweh passed by (1 Kings 19:13; cf. Ex. 33:21–22).

Elijah has restored the people to a relationship with God after failure. Like Moses, Elijah has brought God's word to the people (cf. Deut. 18:16–18); he occupies a position above that of the other prophets (Num. 12:6–8a).[19] Elijah experiences the divine Presence, though it is not possible for him to encounter directly the divine majesty. After the storm, earthquake, and fire, God speaks in the silence.[20] The divine word comes to Elijah renewing his commission to judge the compromise of the covenant and bring about a renewal.

The commission of Elijah is the pledge that conflict with Baal will end in victory over the house of Ahab (19:15–18). Anointing the kings of Aram and Israel is the harbinger of judgment on the nation for its political compromise and a purge of the Baal cult within Israel. The Arameans will eventually control all the territory on the east side of the Jordan, from the Arnon at the Dead Sea northward, all of Gilead and Bashan (2 Kings 10:32–33). Jehu, the successor to the Omride dynasty, carries out a total purge of the Baal cult and is rewarded with a dynasty of four generations, even though he does not

---

17. This technique in the Elijah narrative is demonstrated by R. A. Carlson, "Élie á l'Horeb," *VT* 19 (1969): 420–25, 432.

18. Ibid., 433.

19. Ibid., 437.

20. "A sound of sheer silence" (NRSV) captures the assonance of the text. In the apparition described by Eliphaz there is "silence" and a "sound" (Job 4:16). Walton suggests that the sound (*qôl*) was the echo after the storm, indicating that the destructive effects of the divine Presence has passed so the audience with God can take place; "Still," *ISBE*, 4:620.

institute pure Yahweh worship (10:30–31). The anointing of Elisha assures Elijah that the prophetic challenge will not end with him.

Elijah's place of sojourn after his renewal at Horeb is the Desert of Damascus (19:15), the edge of the desert just to the east of the Sea of Galilee. Somewhat like Galilee in the life of Jesus, it is the region of his activity from which his mission continues. Elisha, the successor in the mission, has his family property at Abel Meholah (19:16), just east of the Jordan in the direction of Jabesh Gilead.[21] The worship of Yahweh is preserved by seven thousand who have not bowed to Baal (the number of fullness multiplied by a thousand).

From Horeb Elijah proceeds to commission Elisha (19:19) as he makes the journey northward to Abel Meholah. Elisha (meaning "God is my salvation") is in charge of twelve pairs of oxen ploughing in succession, he being the twelfth. Elisha evidently comes from a relatively prosperous family. The hairy mantel that Elijah throws over Elisha is a garment distinctive to some type of prophet, especially significant to Elisha (cf. 2 Kings 2:8, 13–14) but known in other circles (cf. Zech. 13:4). Transfer of the garment signifies a transmission of the mission and the ability to accomplish it. The custom was also known in Mesopotamian circles; Gray provides examples from Assyrian rituals and Mari descriptions of prophets.[22]

Elisha recognizes God's call and prepares to separate from his family (19:20). Elijah grants permission with an enigmatic question: "What have I done to you?" There is no indication the question is a rebuke. It may indicate that the calling of Elisha does not need to sever natural family affection, but without clarification it leaves the future mission of Elisha a mystery.[23] Elisha's sacrifice is a thank offering for his call, in which neighbors are naturally invited to join. The burning of the yoke of the oxen signifies a complete break with the past. From that time on Elisha becomes the protégé of Elijah.

Bridging Contexts

ARRANGEMENT OF MATERIAL. The battle with the Baal cult is set in the context of a Phoenician manifestation of Canaanite fertility worship. The Baal epic preserved in the tablets of the ancient city of Ugarit on the northern Mediterranean coast is an example of this religion.

---

21. For the location see Aharoni, *The Land of the Bible*, 284 n. 222, 429. It was a ford of the Jordan possibly to be identified with modern Tel Abû Sûs. It was the eastern boundary of district five of Solomon's administration (1 Kings 4:12) and the scene of Gideon's victory over the Midianites (Judg. 7:22).

22. Gray, *I & II Kings*, 413. This ritual is not magic, as Gray suggests.

23. Elijah challenges Elisha by denying that there is any significance to his action or that he demands anything of him (Cogan, *1 Kings*, 455).

Originally the Baal myth at Ugarit was told in six large tablets and, according to one interpretation, described the mythological prototype of the normal agricultural and cultic year of the people of Ugarit.[24]

The narrative starts with a description of the supposed autumnal New Year festival when Baʿlu[25] celebrates his victory over Death and his return to his holy mountain. The epic tells of the struggle between Yammu, the sea god, and Baʿlu, the god responsible for rain, storms, and fertility, the mythological prototype of the short Syrian winter with its gales, rain, hail, and occasional high tides.[26] Tablet 4, column 5 tells of the building of a giant palace of silver and gold in seven days so that Baʿlu may rule again. The purpose of the palace is stated in lines 6–9 of the column:

> Also it is the prime time for his rains,
> Baʿlu should designate the time of the barque with snow,
> and of the giving forth of his voice in the clouds,
> of his letting loose the lightnings to the earth.[27]

The reference is to the so-called "latter rains" in the early spring (first half of March). The timing of these rains was of crucial importance to the standing crops. These rains came with thunderstorms, and occasionally took the form of snow and hail. The holy voice of Baʿlu was the thunder. A version of this cult was fostered by Jezebel and is the basis of the challenge given by Elijah (17:1). The question is whether Baal or the God of Elijah will determine the time of the rains. It is a test of the true prophet as well as the true God.

The confrontation with the Baal cult is told in a series of stories. Once the challenge to Baal has been laid down (17:1), the life of the prophet is in grave danger. God first grants provision for Elijah by a brook east of Jordan (vv. 2–7) and then by a widow in the foreign territory of Phoenicia (vv. 8–16). This provision is tested by the illness of the widow's son (vv. 17–24); the gift of life brings faith to a foreigner as the prophet is confirmed as a man of God (v. 24). The restoration of life stirs a greater awe than the gift to sustain life (v. 16).

The contest at Mount Carmel (18:1–46) settles the question of who controls the rain, but it does not settle the question of worship in Israel. Elijah fears for his life, and it is not until he has a confirmation on the order of the call of Moses at Mount Horeb that his prophetic ministry resumes (19:1–18).

---

24. J. C. de Moor, *The Seasonal Pattern in the Ugaritic Myth of Baʿlu* (AOAT 16; Neukirchen; Neukirchener Verlag, 1971).

25. Baʿlu is the Ugaritic word for the god Baal.

26. Ibid., 140–42.

27. J. C. de Moor, *An Anthology of Religious Texts from Ugarit* (Leiden: Brill, 1987), 54.

The continuity of this prophetic affirmation is assured with the passing of the mantel on to Elisha (vv. 19–21).

This sequence is the result of a conscious arrangement of material.[28] The contest at Mount Carmel (8:1–46) is at the center of the composition. The movement of the first section shows the fulfillment of the divine word, beginning with the prophetic announcement (17:1; 18:1) and ending in the fulfillment of pouring rain (18:41–46). The initial provision for the well-being of Elijah (17:2–24) is demonstrated mightily in his victory over the Baal prophets (18:20–40). The second section repeats the theme of challenge at the mountain. The first challenge at Mount Carmel is between Yahweh and Baal, and Ahab and Elijah. The second challenge at Mount Horeb is between the death threat of Jezebel and the death wish of Elijah (19:1–4), to the deliverance that Yahweh provides (vv. 11–18). The provision in the desert (vv. 5–8) and at Horeb (vv. 9–14) prepare the way for the pledge of ultimate victory (vv. 15–21). The fulfillment of the prophetic word and victory over the threat of death at Carmel and at Jezreel both focus attention on the confrontation with the Baal cult and the divine triumph over it.

Materialism. The Baal cult against which Elijah battles is in essence a religion of materialism. The detailed study of de Moor[29] can be regarded as substantially correct in finding a seasonal pattern in the Baal ritual at Ugarit. The rule of Baal and the timely appearance of the fall and winter rains were crucial to agricultural success and the economic success of Israel. The alliance of Ahab with Phoenicia, with his marriage to Jezebel, daughter of Ethbaal, king of Sidon (16:31), made both Israel and Phoenicia dependent on the powers of Baal.

The Phoenician worship of Melqart of Tyre was a variation on the more ancient cult known at Ugarit.[30] The name Melqart means "king of the city," either Tyre or the dwellings of the dead. This god is probably a deified king or hero who has evolved into a cosmic god of prosperity.[31] Ezekiel's oracle against the king of Tyre (Ezek. 28:1–19) may have been directed against Melqart. Jezebel feverishly advocates some version of the religions of Baal and Melqart in Israel. Opposition to Baal is regarded as the cause of the bitter famine that drives the population to the point of starvation (1 Kings 18:17). The basic meaning of "trouble" (ʿkr in 18:17) is to "stir up," used in Mish-

---

28. Long, *1 Kings*, 175–76.

29. de Moor, *The Seasonal Pattern in the Ugaritic Myth of Baʿlu*.

30. Gibson, *Textbook of Syrian Semitic Inscriptions*, 1.

31. Brent A. Strawn, "Melqart," *Eerdmans Dictionary of the Bible*, ed. D. N. Freedman (Grand Rapids: Eerdmans, 2000), 882. Philo of Byblos connects Melqart to Heracles (cf. Herodotus, *Hist.* 2.44; 2 Macc. 4:18–20).

naic Hebrew to describe turgid liquids and murky waters. Elijah is regarded as a traitor disturbing the tranquility and prosperity of Israel. Baal is worshiped for his powers of providing wealth, but during the time of Elijah that worship does not bring about the desired results. The conclusion might be that Baal is unhappy with Israel and has withdrawn his life-giving power, or that his power over the forces of nature is being thwarted.

Materialism has the power to bring about a strange kind of double-mindedness. Desire for wealth displaces allegiance to God, though loyalty to God is claimed just the same. Ahab blames Elijah for the drought that has overtaken his land, apparently oblivious to the implicit irrationalism of doing so. If Baal truly had the power to rule the rains and bring wealth, as was supposed, Ahab's zeal to the extent of killing the prophets of Yahweh should have brought prosperity, and Elijah should have been powerless to cause famine in the land (17:1). Recognition that Elijah's devotion to Yahweh has brought about famine is in itself a concession to the fact that Baal did not have control over the rains.

The failure of Baal does not change the policy of Ahab. He is determined to promote the Baal religion, apparently with the belief that this course of events will make Israel wealthy. The fact that Elijah can temporarily interfere in his course of action only stirs up resistance rather than a change of mind. Even the defeat of the Baal prophets and the downpour of the rain do nothing to incite Ahab to change his own course of action. Ahab does not support Elijah against the threats of Jezebel; perhaps he is powerless to do so. If Jezebel is the patron of the Baal cult (18:19), possibly through her Phoenician connections, Ahab may not have been able to intervene.

The introduction of the four hundred prophets of Asherah (18:19), with no further mention of them,[32] has sometimes been taken as evidence of Ahab's impotence before Jezebel.[33] In addition to the oath of Jezebel against Elijah (19:2), the Greek adds the phrase "as you are Elijah and I am Jezebel." The ominous sound of the words—"you may be Elijah, but I am Jezebel"— are completely in keeping with the dominating and self-confident depiction of Jezebel. Materialism also has the power to trap its adherents in a web of circumstance from which it is virtually impossible to extricate oneself. This may have been part of Ahab's dilemma, though nothing explicitly suggests his actions were anything but voluntary.

Israel does come to be wealthy in time. Several generations after Elijah, the prophet Amos denounces the wealth and luxury of Israel because it was

---

32. The Greek does mention them again in verse 22.
33. For references, see Cogan, *1 Kings*, 439. The medieval commentator Qimhi provides a fanciful explanation that the queen does not permit them to participate in the contest.

gained at the expense of the poor and through the corruption of unjust practices. In the midst of this wealth Amos speaks of a famine in the land—not a famine from drought but a famine of inability to hear God's word (Amos 8:11–14). These Israelites will wander the length of the land in a futile search for truth. They will take their oaths by Ashima (v. 14), a deity brought by Aramean settlers from Hamath to Samaria (2 Kings 17:30). They will swear by the god of Dan and Beersheba, the two cities that encompassed the entire land, but they will never rise again. Final judgment has come on Israel, and they will go into exile. During the days of Elijah there are two famines in the land. The famine of food is the result of a famine of the word of the covenant. The nation will survive the famine of food, but it cannot survive the famine of the divine word.

There is not a complete famine of the prophetic word during the days of Elijah. Though Elijah himself despairs in his zeal against Baal's prophets, God does not abandon him. Elijah flees south into the desert in order to escape Jezebel, but God leads him to discover again the power of his mission. God finds Elijah at Mount Horeb in order to commission him again; Elijah is that prophet who will continue the work of Moses. Elijah anoints Hazael the Aramean, Jehu the Israelite, and Elisha the prophet as instruments by which Baal will be purged from the land.

Though materialism akin to that of the Baal cult may pervade Western society, the voice of the church is a hope in the midst of the spiritual famine. Worship of the god Mammon will lead to destruction; greed is unaware of the drought of better values, a drought that will lead to the decimation of an entire society. Though Christians in the Western world may feel threatened and despised like Elijah, the Word of God is present and may be heard as that still small voice. We are commissioned to follow our vocation or calling (19:15);[34] our mission is to call a decadent society to the life of the kingdom of God. Though our society often gives lip service to the values of the kingdom, it is deceived in its attempt to serve two masters.

Significance of Elijah. In scriptural tradition Elijah has come to occupy a position as a successor to Moses in prophetic authority. The narrative of Elijah creates an association with Moses as a prophet with a distinguished mission in the life of Israel. Like Moses, Elijah is forced to flee at the wrath of a king (Ex. 2:15; 1 Kings 17:2–6). Like Moses in his challenge to Pharaoh, Elijah contests with Ahab and the prophets of Baal. Like Moses, Elijah spends forty days in the region of Mount Horeb in order to appear before God (1 Kings 19:8, 11). Like Moses, Elijah needs and receives assurance of the glory and the presence of God in order to fulfill his mission (Ex. 33:18–23;

---

34. For this translation see Carlson, "Élie á l'Horeb," 437.

1 Kings 19:13–17). Like Moses, Elijah feels the burden of the failure of the people to the point that he desires death (Num. 11:14–15; 1 Kings 19:3–4).[35]

Though Elijah is a successor to Moses in his zeal for Yahweh, he is not to be regarded as an equal to Moses.[36] Storm, fire, and earthquake are present at the mountain, though the voice of God is only heard in "the sound of sheer silence" (NRSV). While Moses was promised that worship at the mountain would be a sign that he was sent and commissioned by God (Ex. 3:11–12), God twice asks Elijah what he is doing at the mountain (1 Kings 19:9, 14). There can only be one Moses who gives the covenant and the way of life for God's people. There needs to be a prophet like Moses to preserve a remnant who will not bow the knee to Baal.

The role of Elijah in relation to Moses is found in the conclusion to Malachi ("my messenger"), the last of the prophetic writings.

> Remember the law of my servant Moses, the decrees and laws I gave him at Horeb for all Israel.
>
> See, I will send you the prophet Elijah before that great and dreadful day of the LORD comes. He will turn the hearts of the fathers to their children, and the hearts of the children to their fathers; or else I will come and strike the land with a curse. (Mal. 4:4–6)

These verses must not be regarded as a "legalistic corrective" stemming from some disgruntled priestly editor.[37] The reference to Moses is a reminder to the whole nation that it stands under the regulation of the covenant as given at Mount Horeb. The prophet's attacks on the nation's sins must not be misunderstood as an additional requirement for the faithful. The law and the prophets are not to be heard as rivals but as an essential unity within the divine purpose. Nor must the words of Malachi be used to add to the covenant and call into question the single voice of divine revelation.

At the same time the mention of Elijah is to point the direction to the future of the covenant. The messenger who will come to prepare the way of Yahweh will reconcile and unify the people just as Elijah did in the time of Ahab and Jezebel (Mal. 3:1). The future messenger will have the role of Elijah in making possible the renewal of a relationship with God.

Elijah becomes a popular figure in the emergence of Judaism. He is given a lengthy review in the Apocrypha (Sir. 48:1–11), concluding with the words

---

35. John Olley, "YHWH and his Zealous Prophet: The Presentation of Elijah in 1 and 2 Kings," *JSOT* 80 (1998): 38–39.

36. Brevard S. Childs, "On Reading the Elijah Narratives," *Int* 34 (1980): 135.

37. Brevard S. Childs, "The Canonical Shape of the Prophetic Literature," *Int* 32 (1978): 51–52.

of Malachi, saying that his mission will be the restoration of the tribes of Jacob. Mention is also made of him in the Ethiopic book of *Enoch* (*1 Enoch* 89:51–52). The book of *4 Ezra* (ca. A.D. 100) mentions Elijah's prayers for rain and the resuscitation of the child (*4 Ezra* 7:109). The same book has a prophecy that those who have been taken up and not tasted death from birth will appear before the Messiah (6:26).

Elijah plays a significant role in modern Judaism. He is mentioned when grace is said after meals: "May God in his mercy send us the prophet Elijah." At a circumcision the child is placed on a seat and the following words are said:

> This is the throne of Elijah; may he be remembered for good!
> For thy salvation I have waited, O Lord. I have hope, O Lord, for
> thy salvation; and have done thy commandments. Elijah, thou angel
> of the covenant, lo, thine is before thee. Do thou stand at my right and
> sustain me. I have hoped for thy salvation, O Lord.[38]

Elijah also plays a significant role in the Passover. After the drinking of the third cup of wine, a fourth cup of wine is poured and the door is opened for Elijah the prophet. Everyone rises, and the following prayer is said:

> Pour out Thy wrath upon the nations that know Thee not, and
> upon the kingdoms that call not upon Thy name; for they have con-
> sumed Jacob and laid waste his habitation. Pour out Thy rage upon
> them and let Thy fury overtake them. Pursue them in anger and
> destroy them from under the heavens of the Eternal.[39]

After the prayer the door is closed and all are seated. The book of Malachi ends with the promise that Elijah will bring reconciliation to the people and a warning that God may set a curse on the earth preparing it for destruction. The redemption celebrated in the Passover ceremony looks forward to the reconciliation of Israel and the destruction of all the ungodly.

Elijah also has a prominent role in Christian tradition. John the Baptist carries out the work of the messenger of Malachi (Mal. 3:1–3), coming as a refiner to prepare the people for the coming of Yahweh. John baptizes in the Jordan River as a sign of the purification of repentance (Matt. 3:4–12; Mark 1:4–8; Luke 3:7–14). He warns a generation of snakes that they need to change their ways. His generation needs to bear the fruit of their confession of sin or they will be cut down; the ax is already laid at the root of the tree.

The Baptist is identified as Elijah in the quotations of the angel to Zechariah (Luke 1:16–17) and the quotations of Zechariah concerning the

38. Hyman A. Segal, *Siddur Tifereth David* (New York: Hebrew Publishing, 1951), 122–23.
39. Nathan Goldberg, *Passover Haggadah* (New York: Ktav, 1966), 33.

child (1:76–77). Jesus himself affirms the identification of John the Baptist as the last prophet, the messenger Elijah who was to come (Matt. 11:7–15; Luke 7:24–28). The quotation from Malachi not only shows that John is the forerunner of the Messiah but presupposes that Jesus is conscious of the finality of his own mission to Israel.[40] It is only fitting that Moses and Elijah join Jesus on the mount of Transfiguration (Matt. 17:1–8; Mark 9:2–8; Luke 9:28–36). Moses was the initiator of the covenant with Israel, as Malachi had said, and Elijah was the messenger who would restore that covenant before the coming of the Lord.

Only Luke makes reference in the Transfiguration to the hour of fulfillment, saying that the conversation with Moses and Elijah was about the *exodos* ("departure") of Jesus (Luke 9:31). The reference to Jesus' death as an exodus is a deliberate allusion to the redemption that had begun under Moses. The messenger for whom Elijah has prepared the way is now here, and the time has now come for those events to be fulfilled in Jerusalem.

Though Elijah came in the person of John the Baptist and the Lord brought about redemption in his death and ascension, the church awaits the Second Coming when this redemption will be consummated. The apostle John in Revelation unveils those events for the Christians being martyred under the tyranny of the Roman empire. With the blast of the seventh trumpet we are told that "the kingdom of the world has become the kingdom of our Lord and of his Christ, and he will reign forever and ever" (Rev. 11:15). In preparation for this great event God sends the two witnesses who prophesy day and night during the days of great persecution (11:3).

A mixture of images is woven into the description of these two witnesses. The references to the witnesses calling down fire, shutting up the heavens so it cannot rain, and striking the earth with plagues (Rev. 11:5–6) recall the work of Moses and Elijah. It may be that John expects a glorified Moses and Elijah to return in person to prepare the way for redemption, as at the Mount of Transfiguration. However, the witnesses are identified with the two olive trees and the two lampstands (11:4), an interpretation of Zerubbabel and Joshua the high priest in Zechariah (cf. Zech. 4:2–3). Since John uses the lampstands to represent churches, it seems he wishes to indicate that the witnesses are the churches of Christ.[41]

As prophetic witnesses the churches fulfill the role of governors like Zerubbabel and priests like Joshua. Earlier John symbolized the whole church by seven lampstands (Rev. 1:20), but the two witnesses are depicted as lamps

---

40. Leon Morris, *The Gospel According to St. Luke: An Introduction and Commentary* (TNTC; Grand Rapids: Eerdmans, 1974), 143.

41. G. R. Beasley-Murray, *The Book of Revelation* (NCBC; Greenwood, S.C.: Attic, 1974), 183–84.

corresponding to the work of Moses and Elijah. The churches of Asia are given the function of Moses and Elijah to prepare the way for the coming of the Lord, when the kingdoms of this world become exclusively his own.

MATERIALISM. In ancient times, material well-being required that the gods be satisfied in order for them to bestow their bounty. In part religion served materialist desires; to a measure, materialism was the basis for religion. In modern times, materialism has itself become a religion.

Philosophical materialism is the theory that physical matter is the only reality and that everything, including thought, feeling, mind, and will, can be explained in terms of matter and physical phenomena. Ethically, materialism is the theory or attitude that physical well-being and worldly possessions constitute the greatest good and highest value in life. Socially and spiritually, materialism may be defined as a desire for wealth and material possessions with little interest in ethical or spiritual matters; it is the tendency to give undue importance to material interests, a devotion to the material nature and its wants. All of these definitions of materialism are related to each other, and all of them are an expression of religious values and viewpoints.

Modern society continues to operate largely on the materialistic premises of such thinkers as Charles Darwin, Karl Marx, and Sigmund Freud. Convinced that the only reality is material, true explanations become reductive. If you want to understand a flower, you explain its cell structure, not its beauty. If you want to explain humans, you do not look to their great achievements but to the raw materials that make them up. Thought is treated as the irrational product of environment or brain chemistry; reductionism permeates society from politics and social sciences to literature and the performing arts.

C. S. Lewis attacked such reductionism.[42] A section of *The Pilgrim's Regress* is entitled "Through Darkest *Zeitgeistheim*" (the darkest abode of the spirit of the age). A giant who represents materialistic reductionism apprehends Pilgrim. The eyes of the giant have the property of making whatever they look upon transparent. Pilgrim does not recognize a woman seated near him because what he sees is her skull, her brains, the passage of her nose, the larynx, the saliva in her glands, and the blood in her veins. Dropping his head,

---

42. For a discussion of the various aspects of materialism attacked in the writings of Lewis, see John G. West Jr., "C. S. Lewis and Materialism," *Religion and Liberty* 6/6 (November–December, 1996). This article can be found at http://www.acton.org/publicat/randl/article.php?id=211.

he sees only the inner workings of his own body. This, of course, is not what it means to be human; so dissected, a human does not become visible but dies. Lewis likens life to a drama; the reality of the drama is not the elements of the set but the production of the play. Materialists are caught in their own web of reasoning; if all thought is irrational, then so is the philosophy that propounds materialist ideas.

One of the legacies of materialism is coercive utopianism; this is the belief that the perfect society may be engineered through social science and planning. One version of this is the modern welfare state, in which government becomes ever more intrusive as planners ally themselves with the tools of materialist social science. In the name of social science and humanity, social scientists claim the right to remake society without having to obtain its consent. They believe in their own power to bring about complete material well-being and implicitly believe that this is the highest good, since it is the basis of fulfilling all other desires.

Such materialist objectives, even if achievable, cannot bring about the utopian promise. Materialist doctrines of moral relativism and denial of personal responsibility undermine the ideal society of materialist dreams. Materialist religion is as deceptive, destructive, and pervasive as Baalism in Ahab's Israel.

Harvey Cox tells of his initiation into what a friend of his called the "real world" of business. Having studied religion all his life, he took the advice with a fear of the unknown; his angst, he says, was unnecessary:

> Expecting a *terra incognita*, I found myself instead in the land of *déjà vu*. The lexicon of the *Wall Street Journal* and the business sections of *Time* and *Newsweek* turned out to bear a striking resemblance to Genesis, the Epistle to the Romans, and Saint Augustine's *City of God*. Behind descriptions of market reforms, monetary policy, and the convolutions of the Dow, I gradually made out the pieces of a grand narrative about the inner meaning of human history, why things had gone wrong, and how to put them right.[43]

At the apex of the system of "business theology" Cox found its god, which he capitalizes as the Market, to signify the mystery that enshrouds it and the reverence that it inspires in business folk. Since the earliest stages of human history there have been bazaars, rialtos, and trading posts, but the Market was never God, because there were other centers of value and meaning, other "gods." The Market operated within a plethora of other institutions that

---

43. Harvey Cox, "The Market Is My Shepherd, and I Shall Want and Want and Want ...," *U. S. Catholic*, 65/2 (February 2000): 38.

restrained it. Only in the past two centuries has the Market risen above these demigods and spirits to become today's First Cause.

Cox suggests that of all the religions of the world, however they may differ from one another, the Market is their most formidable rival, particularly because it is scarcely recognized as a religion. Christianity and Judaism believe that the earth is the Lord's and all that is in it. In the religion of the Market, humans own anything they buy, and within certain limits, can dispose of anything they choose. As the markets for material goods become increasingly glutted, such previously unmarketable states of grace as serenity and tranquility are now appearing in the catalogues. These can handily be bought, without an unrealistic demand on one's time, in a weekend workshop at a Caribbean resort, with a sensitive psychological consultant replacing the crotchety retreat master. It does not seem that traditional faith will rise to challenge this new religion; it seems more likely that it will be absorbed by it.

Since no religion, new or old, is subject to empirical proof, this version of materialism is a contest between faiths. In the words of Cox, "Much is at stake. The Market, for example, strongly prefers individualism and mobility. Since it needs to shift people to wherever production requires them, it becomes wrathful when people cling to local traditions."[44] Valuing family or community relationships, for example, belongs to the older dispensations, and like the high places of the Baals, should be plowed under. It is more likely, as in Ahab's Israel, new syncretisms will arise; new religions have ingenious ways of incorporating preexisting ones. There is one contradiction that cannot be accommodated in the religion of the Market; it is to know how much is enough. The first commandment of the Market is that there is never enough; the market that stops expanding dies.

Jesus gave a strong warning against the religion of the Market. It is not possible to make the pursuit of treasure on earth your life ambition and to serve God at the same time (Matt. 7:19–24). To do so is an attempt to serve two masters, God and Mammon. Mammon is known in both Aramaic and Greek languages as the name of a Syrian deity, the god of wealth or riches.[45] Mammon is nothing other than some form of continuation of ancient religions that goes back to the time of Elijah. God demands that wealth be used in the furtherance of his kingdom; to use wealth for any other reason, even in giving, is a contradiction to devotion to God (Matt. 6:2–4).

It may seem strange that even giving can be a way of serving Mammon, but sometimes that is the case. It happens when motives for giving are dom-

44. Ibid., 42–43.
45. See. e.g., H. G. Liddell and R. Scott, *Intermediate Greek-English Lexicon* (Oxford: Oxford Univ. Press, 1945), sub *mammonas*.

inated by something other than doing service for the kingdom of God. It may be for the sake of using money to obtain personal prestige. There is no indication Ahab has any intention of using his wealth for anything as noble as giving, but he presumes he can serve his Mammon and his God at the same time. The opposition of Elijah is a prominent example of the impossibility of serving two masters.

In an historical case study approach of American culture, Colleen McDannell examines the relationship of the sacred and the secular.[46] In six studies, she argues for the shared meanings people derive from their religious material culture.[47] "Christian commitments, musical taste, economic achievement, and domestic stability—none of these elements can be easily separated from the other." "The practice of Christianity brings together the disparate elements of life that possess meaning: everything from our sense of style and social status to our trust in God."[48]

The gap between official definition of religious significance and ordinary practice is intriguingly present in the use of Mormon "garments." By refusing to offer official definitions, the church's hierarchy assumes that God will reveal the true meaning to each wearer. As a result, members are left to conjure meaning on their own. McDannell discovered that physical discomfort and occasional personal embarrassment aside, garments reminded Mormons of their covenant with God and, especially for the religiously ambivalent, indicated communal loyalty. Her main point is that religion must be understood as part of the everyday lives of ordinary people who engage in the construction of meaning and surround themselves with the things that remind them of their connections to God.

Leigh Eric Schmidt offers another perspective on the relationship between consumerism and religion.[49] John Wanamaker, an active Presbyterian businessman, transformed the interior of his department store in Philadelphia into a religious spectacle for Christmas and Easter. It displayed candlesticks, statues, religious tapestries, and flags to create an awe-inspiring ambience.

---

46. Colleen McDannell, *Material Christianity: Religion and Popular Culture in America* (New Haven, Conn.: Yale Univ. Press, 1995). For reviews see Nancy T. Ammerman, *Sociology of Religion*, 58/3 (Fall 1997): 289–90; Michele Dillon, *Commonweal* 123/5 (March 8, 1996): 25–26.

47. Her six case studies review religious practices over the last 150 years: the Bible in Victorian homes, the creation of Philadelphia's Laurel Hill cemetery, the use of Lourdes water among American Catholics, the definitions and uses of *kitsch*, the experience of wearing Mormon garments (previously unmentionable outside Mormon circles), and the burgeoning Christian retail market.

48. Ibid., 16, 273.

49. Leigh Eric Schmidt, *Consumer Rites: The Buying and Selling of American Holidays* (Princeton N.J.: Princeton Univ. Press, 1995); this book is reviewed by Dillon, along with McDannell's *Material Christianity*.

This was aided by what was then the largest pipe organ in the world, with its own musical director and hymnals. Customers' letters thanked Wanamaker for honoring Jesus Christ and for inspiring a feeling of communal togetherness. The success of such intentional blending of religion and commerce shows how integrated sacred and secular are in popular culture.

The possibility of self-deception is a constant reminder that faith requires rigor in examining every deed. There are always many motives for why actions are taken. Too often Christians are ready to make rules to guard the actions of others without ever taking sufficient time to examine themselves. It is easy to be picking at a speck in someone else's eye while ignoring a beam in one's own eye (Matt. 7:1–5). This is especially true in relation to materialism.

A public gift to a worthy Christian project can be a testimony of devotion to doing the work of God on earth. Just as easily, it can be a way of using money to draw attention to personal achievement. One is quite noble, while the other is quite vain. The difference is the attitude of the giver and remains hidden in the motives of the giver. Passing judgment on someone who chooses to give a public testimony to values of another kingdom is hypocrisy unworthy of true faith. The motives of others are between them and God; no one can read the mind of another, and presuming to do so by judging a public gift may just be a sign of rendering a service to Mammon.

Faith and its motivations can all too easily degenerate into indefensible rationalization, not so different from the hypocrisy attacked by Elijah. Jesus had gone all about the regions of Galilee, cities such as Korazin and Bethsaida on the north side of the Sea of Galilee (Matt. 11:21), the very regions that had been Ahab's domain. There he performed many examples of healing and helping the people, so much so that it was evident the promise of Isaiah was fulfilled. This was the servant who would not quench the flickering wick or snap off the broken reed, but would bring justice and deliverance (Matt. 12:18–21; cf. Isa. 42:1–4).

Immediately after the quotation about the servant in Matthew, we are told about the healing of someone made blind and deaf by a demon (Matt. 12:22–23). Some immediately denied this possibility; they were willing to suggest instead that Jesus cast out demons by the prince of demons (v. 24). This was absurd on two grounds: first, a kingdom divided against itself cannot stand, and the kingdom of Satan was doing very well (vv. 25–26); second, the disciples of such Pharisees were also casting out demons, presumably by the same power (v. 27). The work of Jesus was nothing other than the coming of the kingdom of God (vv. 28–30).

Those who resort to such idiosyncrasies in defense of their own service of two masters have passed the point of no return. This is the kind of mental rejection of God, a blasphemy of his Spirit, that cannot be forgiven (Matt.

12:31—32). Ahab, in his rejection of Elijah, even after the defeat of the prophets of Baal, had crossed such a line. It was not possible for him to understand his fatal compromise with materialism.

Western religious hypocrisy. Jesus judged the hypocrisy of certain religious people with a direct reference to Elijah. According to Luke, Jesus customarily attended a synagogue in Nazareth, where he had grown up (Luke 4:16). On a given Sabbath he was given the opportunity to read from the Prophets. He chose words of Isaiah about bringing good news to the poor and the proclamation of the year of the Lord, a reference to the year of Jubilee and the redistribution of wealth (Isa. 61:1—2). Jesus declared his mission was to fulfill these words (Luke 4:16—21). Those who heard him were astonished at the knowledge and eloquence of someone from their own town (v. 22). They demanded the same demonstration of healing they had heard about from Capernaum. They were skeptics and did not believe such things happened in a distant locality.

Jesus reminded these townsfolk that their situation was no different than it had been in the days of Elijah. There were many poor widows during the drought of three and one-half years.[50] Elijah was not sent to anyone in the land of Ahab but to a widow in Phoenician territory, in the city of Zarephath. A foreign Phoenician woman was quite prepared to accept by faith the word of Elijah (1 Kings 17:11—16) and to trust the God of Elijah when her son was restored to life (v. 24). Ahab and his leaders refused to leave their devotion to Baal, even when it was evident that their course of action was not bringing the prosperity they sought. The discouragement of Elijah was an indication how dismal the situation had come to be (19:10). Similarly, Jesus saw no value in seeking to convince the people of Nazareth.

Recognizing that they were being compared to the apostates of the time of Ahab, the people of Nazareth tried to kill Jesus (Luke 4:28—29). Jesus passed through their midst (v. 30), and as far as is known never went back to Nazareth again. The rejection of God can be final.

As in the case of the widow at Zarephath, true faith in God may be found in unexpected places, and it may happen in unexpected ways. Lamin Sanneh is the D. Willis James Professor of Missions and World Christianity and professor of history at Yale Divinity School. Gambian born, Sanneh is a descendant from the *nyanchos*, an ancient African royal line. His earliest education was with the sons of fellow chiefs. Following graduation from the

---

50. The length of time was traditional, based on the reference to the third year in the Kings story (1 Kings 18:1). Three years meant the drought extended beyond a year at the beginning and end, though Josephus, on the evidence of Menander, refers to a drought of a year (*Ant.* 7.13.2). Three years may have included time spent with the widow at Zarephath.

University of London with a Ph.D. in Islamic history, he taught at the University of Ghana and in the University of Aberdeen (Scotland). He served for eight years as assistant and associate professor of the history of religion at Harvard University before moving to Yale University in 1989.[51] Most significant is his conversion to Christianity.

Lamin Sanneh was raised in an orthodox Muslim family. Emphasis was placed on the community, tradition, fidelity to past models, respect for parents and elders, rote memorization of knowledge, and scarce material resources offset by a wealth of social capital. He became interested in Christianity through reading about Jesus in the Qurʾan. He had no access to the Bible or to a church, so the Qurʾan was his only source for knowledge of Jesus. He kept his interest to himself, because his teachers would react unpredictably and his Muslim friends would be scandalized.

Once Sanneh's choice was made about the significance of Jesus in God's work of salvation, it was not difficult to make the decision to join the church. But getting accepted in a Protestant church was another matter because of their suspicion and skepticism. Unofficially the Methodist church he approached welcomed his decision to seek baptism, but officially they put off the decision. They asked that he go to the Catholic Church, which he did for a year, with the same result. It took over two years until he was finally baptized in the Methodist church, as a result of an ultimatum he gave them.

With interest undiminished, Sanneh made the request to be allowed to study theology. This permission was denied, with the indication that the decision was final, with no appeals to be made to mission headquarters in London. In his words, "It so happened that I was so profoundly affected by the message of Jesus, so inexplicably transformed at the roots of faith and trust, that I felt myself in the grips of an undeniable impetus to give myself to God, whatever my ultimate career path. I never had cause to fret about the work which God might call me; so steadfast are God's promises."

Sanneh never went to a mission school and knew no missionaries when he embarked on his inquiry. The Protestant church remained incredulous of him; the Catholic Church eventually relented "after years of ignoring and wishing me away." The reasons for this reluctance are unclear; it could be liberal distrust of religion, residual hostility toward converts as illegitimate fruits of mission, unfamiliarity with nonwhite people, presumptions about political motives, or some combination of the above.

Sanneh recalls a visit to Germany when he was on vacation from school

---

51. Lamin Sanneh was interviewed by Jonathan Bonk in "Defender of the Good News," *Christianity Today* 47/10 (October, 2003): 112−16. Jonathan Bonk is the executive director of the Overseas Ministries Studies Center.

in Africa. He saw a sign that said "The Episcopal Church Welcomes You," and duly going there on Sunday discovered he was most unwelcome. His secular white American friend felt vindicated for ceasing to be a practicing Christian; it was all one big cultural pretense. He caustically observed that there would have been no problems if the guest were a white person; his advice was to never get literal with Christian slogans. A cultural paradigm had usurped the place of God in this enlightened scheme of things. That was one reason why for so long the church tried to make a sincere black convert feel guilty and untrustworthy for claiming the Christian name. The religious orientation of Sanneh was such that he was unable to reconcile himself to that fundamental compromise with the world. For him, Jesus was for real in spite of the prevarications of the church.

The testimony of Sanneh helps to put the experience of the widow at Zarephath in the days of Elijah or the experience of Jesus in Nazareth into modern perspective.[52] The church is no less guilty of having faith so jaded by prejudice and surrounding culture that it is unable to recognize truth when confronted by it. Sanneh's assessment is that the cultural captivity of Christianity in the West is nearly complete, and it is open season on the West's Christian heritage. Without a moral center, the prospects of facing the ideological intolerance of a politically resurgent Islam are disturbing.

For Sanneh, the cultural captivity has not spared evangelicals. They tend to make religious militancy a partner with military might in a joint assault on the war on terror. There is the danger that the flag becomes a more prominent symbol than the cross. In the words of Sanneh, "With respect to cultural biases, we see the speck in the other person's eye, but are blind to the splinter in our own" (Matt. 7:3).

According to Sanneh, an extraordinary new world of Christianity is unfolding; it is unprecedented, more vibrant, more varied, more widespread. The church of the post-Christian West views this unprecedented church growth with suspicion. It represents an unwelcome resistance to the cultural change they believe is the church's mission. A post-Christian West sees religion as contagion and mobilizes behind a domesticated view of culture for safeguard. The West limits its role in this new, growing Christianity to taking precautions against too close an encounter with it. Religion is not about rejection of the old but about willingness to embrace the new. Sanneh believes that in the mystery of God, the energy of the revitalized global church will find its own channels for expression of biblical faith.

---

52. Lamin Sanneh's recent book, *Whose Religion Is Christianity:The Gospel beyond the West* (Grand Rapids: Eerdmans, 2003), addresses the difficult questions of Christian social impact in Africa (South Africa, Rwanda) in the Yale environment of an Ivy League long marked by subliminal agnosticism and deep suspicion of Christianity, especially evangelicalism.

1 Kings 20:1–43

❦

NOW BEN-HADAD king of Aram mustered his entire army. Accompanied by thirty-two kings with their horses and chariots, he went up and besieged Samaria and attacked it. ²He sent messengers into the city to Ahab king of Israel, saying, "This is what Ben-Hadad says: ³'Your silver and gold are mine, and the best of your wives and children are mine.'"

⁴The king of Israel answered, "Just as you say, my lord the king. I and all I have are yours."

⁵The messengers came again and said, "This is what Ben-Hadad says: 'I sent to demand your silver and gold, your wives and your children. ⁶But about this time tomorrow I am going to send my officials to search your palace and the houses of your officials. They will seize everything you value and carry it away.'"

⁷The king of Israel summoned all the elders of the land and said to them, "See how this man is looking for trouble! When he sent for my wives and my children, my silver and my gold, I did not refuse him."

⁸The elders and the people all answered, "Don't listen to him or agree to his demands."

⁹So he replied to Ben-Hadad's messengers, "Tell my lord the king, 'Your servant will do all you demanded the first time, but this demand I cannot meet.'" They left and took the answer back to Ben-Hadad.

¹⁰Then Ben-Hadad sent another message to Ahab: "May the gods deal with me, be it ever so severely, if enough dust remains in Samaria to give each of my men a handful."

¹¹The king of Israel answered, "Tell him: 'One who puts on his armor should not boast like one who takes it off.'"

¹²Ben-Hadad heard this message while he and the kings were drinking in their tents, and he ordered his men: "Prepare to attack." So they prepared to attack the city.

¹³Meanwhile a prophet came to Ahab king of Israel and announced, "This is what the LORD says: 'Do you see this vast army? I will give it into your hand today, and then you will know that I am the LORD.'"

¹⁴"But who will do this?" asked Ahab.

The prophet replied, "This is what the LORD says: 'The young officers of the provincial commanders will do it.'"

"And who will start the battle?" he asked.

The prophet answered, "You will."

¹⁵So Ahab summoned the young officers of the provincial commanders, 232 men. Then he assembled the rest of the Israelites, 7,000 in all. ¹⁶They set out at noon while Ben-Hadad and the 32 kings allied with him were in their tents getting drunk. ¹⁷The young officers of the provincial commanders went out first.

Now Ben-Hadad had dispatched scouts, who reported, "Men are advancing from Samaria."

¹⁸He said, "If they have come out for peace, take them alive; if they have come out for war, take them alive."

¹⁹The young officers of the provincial commanders marched out of the city with the army behind them ²⁰and each one struck down his opponent. At that, the Arameans fled, with the Israelites in pursuit. But Ben-Hadad king of Aram escaped on horseback with some of his horsemen. ²¹The king of Israel advanced and overpowered the horses and chariots and inflicted heavy losses on the Arameans.

²²Afterward, the prophet came to the king of Israel and said, "Strengthen your position and see what must be done, because next spring the king of Aram will attack you again."

²³Meanwhile, the officials of the king of Aram advised him, "Their gods are gods of the hills. That is why they were too strong for us. But if we fight them on the plains, surely we will be stronger than they. ²⁴Do this: Remove all the kings from their commands and replace them with other officers. ²⁵You must also raise an army like the one you lost—horse for horse and chariot for chariot—so we can fight Israel on the plains. Then surely we will be stronger than they." He agreed with them and acted accordingly.

²⁶The next spring Ben-Hadad mustered the Arameans and went up to Aphek to fight against Israel. ²⁷When the Israelites were also mustered and given provisions, they marched out to meet them. The Israelites camped opposite them like two small flocks of goats, while the Arameans covered the countryside.

²⁸The man of God came up and told the king of Israel, "This is what the LORD says: 'Because the Arameans think the

LORD is a god of the hills and not a god of the valleys, I will deliver this vast army into your hands, and you will know that I am the LORD.'"

²⁹For seven days they camped opposite each other, and on the seventh day the battle was joined. The Israelites inflicted a hundred thousand casualties on the Aramean foot soldiers in one day. ³⁰The rest of them escaped to the city of Aphek, where the wall collapsed on twenty-seven thousand of them. And Ben-Hadad fled to the city and hid in an inner room.

³¹His officials said to him, "Look, we have heard that the kings of the house of Israel are merciful. Let us go to the king of Israel with sackcloth around our waists and ropes around our heads. Perhaps he will spare your life."

³²Wearing sackcloth around their waists and ropes around their heads, they went to the king of Israel and said, "Your servant Ben-Hadad says: 'Please let me live.'"

The king answered, "Is he still alive? He is my brother."

³³The men took this as a good sign and were quick to pick up his word. "Yes, your brother Ben-Hadad!" they said.

"Go and get him," the king said. When Ben-Hadad came out, Ahab had him come up into his chariot.

³⁴"I will return the cities my father took from your father," Ben-Hadad offered. "You may set up your own market areas in Damascus, as my father did in Samaria."

Ahab said, "On the basis of a treaty I will set you free." So he made a treaty with him, and let him go.

³⁵By the word of the LORD one of the sons of the prophets said to his companion, "Strike me with your weapon," but the man refused.

³⁶So the prophet said, "Because you have not obeyed the LORD, as soon as you leave me a lion will kill you." And after the man went away, a lion found him and killed him.

³⁷The prophet found another man and said, "Strike me, please." So the man struck him and wounded him. ³⁸Then the prophet went and stood by the road waiting for the king. He disguised himself with his headband down over his eyes. ³⁹As the king passed by, the prophet called out to him, "Your servant went into the thick of the battle, and someone came to me with a captive and said, 'Guard this man. If he is missing, it will be your life for his life, or you must pay a talent of silver.' ⁴⁰While your servant was busy here and there, the man disappeared."

"That is your sentence," the king of Israel said. "You have pronounced it yourself."

⁴¹Then the prophet quickly removed the headband from his eyes, and the king of Israel recognized him as one of the prophets. ⁴²He said to the king, "This is what the LORD says: 'You have set free a man I had determined should die. Therefore it is your life for his life, your people for his people.'" ⁴³Sullen and angry, the king of Israel went to his palace in Samaria.

THIS CHAPTER IS very different in character from those describing the battles against the Baal cult. It deals with the wars against the Arameans and is identified as having come from a different cycle of source material dealing with the Omride wars.[1] Though prophets are key players in the war stories, Elijah does not appear. In the LXX this chapter is joined with the last chapter of 1 Kings, while the story of Naboth's vineyard follows the account of Elijah battling Ahab as leader of the Baal cult.[2] In that arrangement of Kings, the Elijah stories are grouped together, as well as those about the wars against the Arameans.

This chapter on the wars between Ahab and Ben-Hadad is prophetic in showing how Yahweh works through historical events in order to accomplish his purposes. Victory does not come through the might of Ahab's armies but through divine intervention; the prophet or man of God (20:13, 28) plays the decisive role in determining the outcome of events.

There are two wars against the Arameans here. The first is a siege against Samaria (20:1–21), the second a battle at Aphek, a town east of Lake Tiberias (vv. 22–34). Each battle has a similar structure: consultation and mustering of forces (vv. 12–15, 22–28), confrontation and battle (vv. 16–20, 29–30), and report of results (vv. 21, 31–34). In the second battle Ben-Hadad suffers a humiliating defeat (vv. 22–34). After his victory Ahab is confronted by a prophet in disguise and condemned for his dismissal of Ben-Hadad (vv. 35–43). Ahab does not realize he is pronouncing judgment on himself when he exacts judgment on a presumed negligent soldier.

The Battle for Samaria (20:1–21)

THE BATTLE FOR Samaria results when negotiations break down between the Aramean king and his Israelite vassal (20:1–11). The demands begin when the

---

1. DeVries, *1 Kings*, 208.

2. See the appendix for a brief discussion of the composition variations of Kings.

Aramean forces are able to break down Israelite control of its provinces and besiege Samaria (v. 1). The thirty-two kings may be compared with the ten states under the hegemony of Ben-Hadad son of Hazael in the Zakkur inscription.[3] These kings were not heads of state but tribal chieftains who roamed with semi-independence in the area of Damascus. Damascus was a great oasis southeast of the southern extremity of the Anti-Lebanon mountain range. Tribesman of the north Arabian steppe roamed and settled in the area of Damascus. The title "king of Aram" (v. 1) refers to the control Ben-Hadad has in mustering these chieftains against Ahab. Aram is an ethnic rather than a geographic term, and the "kings" are rulers of various tribes or confederacies.

The negotiations are arranged in three sets of dialogue between Ben-Hadad and Ahab: verses 2–4, 5–9, and 10–11. In the middle set Ben-Hadad addresses Ahab (vv. 5–6), Ahab has exchanges with his elders (vv. 7–8), and he finally responds to Ben-Hadad (v. 9). The whole is governed by the word "send" (*šlḥ*) as exchanges of messengers conduct the negotiations (vv. 2, 5, 6, 7, 9, 10). The subordinate situation of Ahab is indicated by his acceptance of the Aramean king as "my lord the king" (v. 4) and a willingness to be subservient to his demands of taxation.

Ben-Hadad demands that his officers conduct the taxation as they see fit, including possession of members of the royal family, leaving Ahab to rule as a vassal (vv. 5–6). Ahab follows the advice of his elders in resisting this demand. Ahab still defers to the Aramean king as his "lord" (v. 9) and concedes to his original demands, but Ahab will not be reduced to Aramean occupation of his territory. Ben-Hadad responds to this with an oath that he will turn Samaria into dust scooped up by his soldiers (v. 10), but Ahab replies with a proverb of his own (v. 11): Boasting only comes after the battle.

On hearing this response, Ben-Hadad orders his troops to attack Samaria (20:12). It is likely that his army is based in Succoth in the Jordan Valley at the mouth of the Jabbok.[4] The Hebrew *sukkôt* can refer to the city or to army encampments (cf. NIV footnote), but the use of *sukkôt* to mean field bivouacs (temporary encampments) is unusual.[5] By midday Ben-Hadad has become scandalously drunk. Ahab in turn is given assurance by an unnamed prophet

---

3. H. Donner and W. Röllig, *Kanaanäische und Aramäsche Inschriften* (Wiesbaden: Otto Harrassowitz, 1968), #202, A, 4–5.

4. This was the location of the wars of David against Ammon (2 Sam. 11:1), where *sukkôt* (v. 11) may be a place name rather than "tents" (NIV). The case for *sukkôt* as the location of the war has been made by Y. Yadin, "Some Aspects of the Strategy of Ahab and David," *Bib* 36 (1955): 332–51.

5. The Greek translator took *sukkôt* as a place name in the second occurrence (v. 16); 2 Sam. 11:11 is the only other location where *sukkôt* may be used instead of the more usual "tents" (*ʾōhālîm*). It is not certain that *sukkôt* was ever used to refer to army encampments.

that God will win the battle as in the time of the Exodus, so the Israelites may know the meaning of the name Yahweh (v. 13; cf. Ex. 7:5; 10:2; 15:3). The word of proof offered by the prophet (1 Kings 20:14–15) is that Ahab will appoint 232 elite troops engaged in the protection of the provinces, who will be joined by seven thousand of the regular troops marshaled for the occasion. As at Mount Sinai (cf. Ex. 3:12), the meaning of "Yahweh" ("Yah will be with you") will be seen in the defeat of his enemies.

The report goes out to Ben-Hadad that the troops have left the capital of Samaria. In his drunken and arrogant state, Ben-Hadad demands they be seized alive, whether their intentions are for peaceful negotiations or war. The Israelites meet the Aramean army man for man, pursue them, and inflict heavy casualties. Ben-Hadad manages to escape with his horsemen, but the Israelites decimate their cavalry as well (20:21).[6]

The Battle for Aphek (20:22–34)

THOUGH BEN-HADAD SHOULD have been forced into a conciliatory position, it is Ahab who continues to be reticent. Ahab is given a prophetic warning to strategize carefully, because the Arameans will be back at the "turn of the year" (20:22). Spring is a usual time for military expeditions; weather is more favorable, and crops are available for marching armies (e.g., 1 Sam. 23:1). Ben-Hadad revises his battle strategy to make better use of his superior cavalry, determining to engage the battle on level terrain rather than the mountains (vv. 23–25). The Aramean king is advised to abandon the ineffective alliances with area chieftains and bring his military forces directly under his control, with officials he appoints himself. He further needs to tally a force equal to the troops and cavalry that desert him.[7]

When the entire Israelite army is mustered, it has the appearance of two exposed flocks of goats (20:27).[8] The prophet responds with a message identical to the one given before the first battle (v. 28; cf. v.13), with the same assurance the God of the Exodus will be with them in defeat of his enemies.

The battle at Aphek is described briefly (20:29–30), depicting the victory in terms of holy war. The armies face each other seven days and the walls of Aphek fall. The parallels to Jericho must be tempered by the fact that no ceremony precedes the attack (cf. Josh. 6:12–21). The Israelites shatter the

---

6. Following the Greek, some translations say he seized the horses and chariots (e.g., RSV). The Greek is not a different text, but a translation error based on a wrong interpretation of "seize" in Josh. 15:16; Barthélemy, *Critique textuelle de l'ancien testament*, 373–74.

7. The sense of the verb *npl* is that they "desert," though most translations say "lost" (cf. NIV).

8. The Hebrew adjective is derived from *ḥśp* ("to strip, lay bare"). It governs the meaning of the noun in a genitival relationship.

Arameans; 100,000 are struck down in one day, and another 27,000 are crushed by the falling walls. Ben-Hadad himself manages to seek security within a secret room.

Ben-Hadad is left with no alternative but to appeal to treaty loyalty, which he expects from Ahab (20:31). "Merciful" (*ḥesed*) is a covenant term denoting loyalty to a relationship. Submission, made evident in their garments, is the basis of appeal to someone who can respect agreements. Course black cloth attached to the waist is a sign of penitence, a sign of suspension of normal activities to focus on critical relational matters. A rope on the head indicates servitude, either as a prisoner of war or as someone who has given up his rights to one who has the power of life and death.[9]

Ahab responds to this with a willingness to continue a treaty relationship: "He is my brother" (20:32). The envoys are looking for an omen, some sign that their mission will succeed; they test Ahab by suggesting a renewed loyalty (v. 33).[10] Ahab sends for Ben-Hadad and invites him into his chariot. Ben-Hadad agrees to restore territory he has taken and to set up preferential commercial relations in Damascus; in return Ahab agrees to release Ben-Hadad.

Prophetic Confrontation with the King of Israel (20:35—43)

A MESSAGE FOR Ahab comes from one of the "sons of the prophets," a group associated with Elisha, mentioned only here in connection with Elijah (v. 35).[11] The message of the prophet is delivered through an enacted parable. The prophet demands that someone from his company strike and injure him. The refusal of his request is a disobedience that results in death by a lion (v. 36), a fate consistent with that of the disobedient prophet from Judah (cf. 13:24). A second companion does strike and injure him, allowing him to disguise himself for the king.

When the king comes by, he sees a wounded soldier crying out for justice. The story of the prophet to the king assumes that a prisoner of war was the property of his captor and that his escape is a breach of pledge demanding restitution. A talent of silver is an exorbitant price for a poor man to pay, about a hundred times the price of a slave provided for in the covenant code (Ex. 21:32).[12]

---

9. Gray, *I & II Kings*, 429—30.

10. The verb *nḥš* is to practice divination or to learn through that method. One such means was to find omens through chance utterances considered endowed with meaning.

11. For the significance of the expression "sons of the prophets" see the story of the ascension of Elijah (2 Kings 2).

12. The talent was the largest unit of weight in the Near East. It consisted of sixty minas, the mina consisting of sixty shekels in the Babylonian system and fifty in the Canaanite system (cf. Ezek. 45:12). A talent would have been about 3,000 shekels.

The debt would have driven such a wounded soldier into slavery. The exorbitant price for the loss of a slave may have been a way of impressing the king with the severity of breaching the divine covenant and causing the death of the entire nation.[13] The king in rendering his judgment assumes he is indicting a wounded soldier with a punishment determined by the soldier himself. He does not realize that "your life for his life" (1 Kings 20:39) is a verdict he is bringing on himself and his people.

The king recognizes the prophet the instant he removes his disguise. The king may have known the man; there is no indication he has some distinguishing mark as is occasionally mentioned (cf. Isa. 44:5; Zech. 13:6). The doctrine of "holy war"—wars where God acts as the warrior in defeating the enemy—requires that the spoils belong entirely to God (as at Jericho, cf. Josh. 6:18). A prisoner in such a case cannot be treated as common property; anything so devoted cannot be sold or redeemed by substituting something else (cf. Lev. 27:28; Deut. 7:2; 20:16–17). According to prophetic theology, the Aramean king is under such a ban (*ḥerem*, 1 Kings 20:42), and it is not Ahab's prerogative to make a treaty with him. The king, learning of the judgment pronounced on him and his country, returns to his capital resentful and angry.

Bridging Contexts

ISSUES OF HISTORY. The accounts of the wars of Ahab against the Arameans (1 Kings 20, 22) have been integrated into the Elijah narratives to show the resistance of the king to following the word of the prophets. Historians have grave reservations in using these stories as historical sources for the time of the Omride dynasty.[14] These episodes occur near the end of Ahab's life, beginning about three years before his death at the hands of the Arameans (22:1–2, 37). This is near the time of the battle of Qarqar, when Ahab is allied with the Arameans against the Assyrians, making it untimely for them to be at war with each other. Further, Ahab is only able to muster seven thousand troops to resist Ben-Hadad (20:15), compared to the ten thousand troops said to be present just a couple of years later at the battle of Qarqar.[15]

---

13. Jones, *1 and 2 Kings*, 348–49.

14. Stefan Timm, *Die Dynastie Omri: Quellen und Untersuchungen zur Geschichte Israels im 9. Jahrhundert vor Christus* (Göttingen: Vandenhoeck & Ruprecht, 1982), 214.

15. A. Leo Oppenheim, "Shalmaneser III (858–824): The Fight against the Aramean Coalition," in *An Anthology of Texts and Pictures*, ed. J. Pritchard (Princeton, N.J.: Princeton Univ. Press, 1958), 190. The numbers in the Assyrian inscriptions are doubted by many historians; Cogan, *1 Kings*, 474, n. 5.

According to Assyrian inscriptions, the Aramean king at the battle of Qarqar is not Ben-Hadad but Hadadezer, who is not named as king until 845 B.C. Whitley thinks the submission of Israel to the Arameans must have been after the destruction that Hazael inflicted on Israel during the reign of Jehoahaz son of Jehu the usurper (2 Kings 13:1–9).[16] Further, the establishment of a treaty by which the Arameans return cities to Israel corresponds to the victories of Jehoash, son of Jehoahaz over Ben-Hadad the son of Hazael (1 Kings 20:34; cf. 2 Kings 13:25).

A further ambiguity is suggested because Ahab is named only four times (1 Kings 20:2, 13, 14; 22:20); the king of Israel is usually mentioned but not named (20:7, 11, 21, 22, 28, 31, 32), indicative of the name being secondary to the account. Whitely believes that the author of Kings has arranged and supplemented his sources to make the Aramean wars part of the Omride dynasty rather than that of Jehu.[17] The prophetic achievements of Elijah and Elisha are deliberately arranged to contrast with national calamities attributed to the reign of Ahab because of his profligate violation of Israelite religion.

It is the goal of the prophetic authors to provide a theological interpretation of events; as in any historiography, chronology serves ideological ends. But chronological strategy must retain historical integrity, or past events cannot substantiate the viewpoint presented. Revisionist histories can be nothing more than ideological propaganda. The transposition of events from one dynasty to another would fail to accomplish a historiographic purpose.

There are serious historical difficulties with such a transposition of events. If the battle against the Moabites took place during the reign of Jehoash (1 Kings 22), son of Jehoahaz, then the king of Judah present as his ally would have been Amaziah, the son of Joash (2 Kings 14:1–4). Given the inimical relations between Jehoash and Amaziah (vv. 8–14), this is an unlikely scenario; Jehoshaphat must have been the compliant Judean king supporting the king of Israel. While the Ben-Hadad in these Aramean wars with Ahab is not otherwise known, it is a common name for Aramean kings; it may have been a throne name rather than a personal name.

The Arameans were continually in hostilities with Israel and in part shared its territory. The upper Transjordan region to Ramoth Gilead in the south was a buffer zone with mixed Israelite-Aramean population (cf. 1 Chron. 2:23; 7:14), and it periodically changed hands. Assyrian pressure during the days of Ahab, as evident in the battle at Qarqar, need not have prevented an attack from Damascus. It could also explain why Ahab defeated Ben-Hadad,

16. C. F. Whitley, "The House of Omri," VT 2 (1952): 144.
17. Ibid., 147.

so the latter was compelled to return towns in the Transjordan conquered by the first Ben-Hadad.[18] Israelite merchants were granted preferential rights in Damascus (1 Kings 20:34), like those previously enjoyed by the Arameans at Samaria. Ben-Hadad II was also forced to reconstitute his vassal states to provinces in order to consolidate his empire (20:24–25).

Know that I am Yahweh. Twice the prophetic message to Ahab is that he will learn the significance of the name of God: "You will know that I am the LORD" (1 Kings 20:13, 28). This signifies victory after the manner of holy war, one in which God joins the army as a soldier. In the first instance God brings triumph through a small band led by untrained junior officers, normally assistants to the regional commanders (v. 14).[19] Ahab is to prepare for battle by mustering his troops; seven thousand is a small but complete force (v. 15). In the second instance the Aramean army is forced into retreat to Aphek, where the soldiers who manage to escape are crushed under the rubble of falling walls (v. 30). Ben-Hadad begins with demanding the surrender of Ahab, but ends with imposing on himself humiliating concessions in order to earn his own release. The prophetic word declares these wars to be of the same order as the great battles of the past in which the few triumph over the many under divine direction (e.g., Judg. 7:1–8). Victory comes through allegiance to the name of Yahweh.

Learning to know the name was at the heart of the Exodus story. God spoke to Moses saying, "I am the LORD" (Ex. 6:2). Before that time God had been known as the Almighty (šadday), but from that time on the Israelites understood the meaning and significance of the name Yahweh (6:3). The name was identified with the covenant promise that God would give the land of Canaan to his people (6: 4). The name was associated with redemption, bringing the oppressed people out of bondage into the land of their inheritance (6:5–6). God's word of the covenant was: "I will take you as my own people, and I will be your God" (6:7). "I am the LORD" not only makes confession of redemption; it signifies the oath of the promise (6:8).

The battle against Pharaoh will teach the meaning of the name as revealed to Israel. Pharaoh had a logical question for Moses from an Egyptian point of view: "Who is the LORD, that I should obey him?" (Ex. 5:2). Pharaoh had no reason to believe this God would be a threat to his own divine status. His

---

18. A. Malamat, "The Arameans," in *Peoples of Old Testament Times*, ed. D. J. Wiseman (Oxford: Clarendon, 1973), 144.

19. It is well established that the word for youth (naʿar) includes high-ranking military officers; Victor Hamilton, "נַעַר," *NIDOTTE*, 3:124. For its use in a Canaanite context, see B. Cutler and J. MacDonald, "Identification of the naʿar in the Ugaritic Texts," *UF* 8 (1976): 27–35. In this context of divine victory, the word must be given its more usual meaning where it stands in contrast to "elder" (zāqēn) as a merism.

---

question set the motif for the narrative to follow; the whole story of the plagues and the crossing of the Reed Sea was the answer to this question. Egyptians and Israelites learned the meaning of the name as judgment came against Egypt in the redemption of Israel (7:5, 17; 8:18; 10:2; 14:4, 18; 16:12).

At the Song of the Sea the Israelites triumphantly declared their victory in the name of Yahweh; he is the "man of war," he delivered them by casting the Egyptians into the sea (15:3–6). The sign of the Sabbath was a fundamental confession of the covenant, setting this people apart from all the others (31:13); the distinction of this sanctification was to know what it meant for God to say, "I am the LORD." The divine provision through forty years in the desert taught Israel the name, so they would be prepared to enter the land of promise (Deut. 29:5).

The power of God's name is as effective in bringing judgment against Israel as it is in victory. The call of Ezekiel fell during that brief period between the first exile of Nebuchadnezzar (598 B.C.) and the fall of the city of Jerusalem (586 B.C.). His task was to deal with the recalcitrant and corrupt leadership in Jerusalem, who treated the covenant promises as unconditional guarantees. Convinced that the city was theirs for exploitation, they used the temple as the place to plot their schemes (Ezek. 11:1–5). It fell to Ezekiel to bring the message of doom: Their corpses would fill the streets; God was wielding the swords that came in the hands of the Babylonians (11:6–8). The God of Ezekiel was the cosmic king whose chariot moved effortlessly and instantly to the farthest corners of the earth, but in the exercise of his authority over the nations, his focus was always on Israel.

From beginning to end, God is passionate about his relationship with his people and is willing to stake his reputation on their fate or fortune.[20] Ezekiel repeatedly uses the covenant formula: "I will be your God and you will be my people" (Ezek. 11:20; 14:11; 34:24, 30–31; 36:28; 37:23). His prophecy leaves the impression that when Yahweh acts in judgment against his people, it is not primarily to punish them but that they and the world may know him. Ezekiel uses the redemptive declaration from the Exodus story over seventy times: "You will know that I am the LORD." God's primary goal in bringing down foreign powers is not to destroy the enemies of Israel (such as Gog and his hordes), but to manifest his greatness, glory, and holiness.

Ezekiel makes the revelation of the name of God the time of his election of the nation. He paraphrases Exodus so the self-revelation of God becomes an oath, whose substance is redemption from Egypt and deliverance in the Promised Land.[21]

---

20. Dan Block, "Ezekiel: Theology of," *NIDOTTE*, 4:618.

21. M. Greenberg, *Understanding Exodus* (New York: Behrman House, 1969), 133–35.

On the day I chose Israel

> a and raised my hand to the seed of . . . Jacob
>   b and made myself known in the land of Egypt
> a′ when I raised my hand to them
>   b′ saying "I am YHWH your God"—

On that day I raised my hand to them to bring them out of the land of Egypt, to a land that I scouted for them (a land flowing with milk and honey). (Ezek. 20:5–6, pers. trans.)

The oath of God revealed in his name guarantees that judgment on the relentless idolatries of Israel is unavoidable:

> The end has come—the end, upon the four corners of the land.
> Now the end is upon you, I am sending my wrath against you.
> I will judge you according to your deeds; I will set your abominations on you.
> My eye will not pity you; I will not spare you.
> I will set your ways upon you, your abominations will be in your midst.
> You will know that I am Yahweh. (Ezek. 7:2b–4, pers. trans.)

These sentiments are not unique to Ezekiel, though no other prophet expresses them so consistently. The prophetic message against Ahab shares that same view. Mercy may be granted repeatedly, but violation of the oath necessitates judgment. Ahab has released the man whom God brought under the ban, the judgment of holy war (1 Kings 20:42). The judgment destined for the Aramean enemy will devolve on Ahab and bring an end to his dynasty. Ahab will come to know Yahweh, as the prophets have said, not in victory but in death. The accounts of the Aramean wars serve the purpose of the Deuteronomistic History well. That history demonstrates the repeated violation of the covenant and disregard for the repeated warnings of the prophets. Ahab is an example par excellence of how desecration of the name has inevitable consequence.

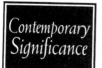

GOD, MERCY, AND JUDGMENT. The prophets writing the Deuteronomistic History had the task of explaining divine judgment. Judgment had come on Israel repeatedly throughout the history of the kingdom; in the end it removed the nation entirely. Their belief that God was committed to make them his people demanded that these catastrophes be explained in terms of divine judgment.

This judgment was necessarily understood in the context of divine love. The blazing mountain at Sinai was an everlasting testimony to God's freely loving his people and bringing them out of bondage with great power (Deut. 4:37); the Lord of the highest heavens and all peoples had chosen them, his love was revealed in them (10:15). The love of God was utterly unconditional; there was nothing Israel had done to earn the privilege of a relationship with God. Such faith and such a calling had to be reconciled with the circumstances of Israel in the midst of the nations. The Aramean wars with Ahab served the prophets well in teaching the truth about God, mercy, and judgment.

Judgment is conspicuously absent in contemporary concepts of God. Judging is a bad odor, always equivalent to judgmentalism. Knowing God in acts of divine judgment is regarded as primitive, even primordial in the development of moral understanding. Unconditional love is regarded as equivalent to unconditional forgiveness. The God of popular imagining is less father than uncle. Judgment, especially in relation to God, is regarded as arbitrary and capricious.

The church may shoulder its share of blame for this perception; divine punishment has often been attached to rules that have little to do with morality or requirements of faith that have little to do with biblical theology. It may also be the consequence of a permissive culture in pursuit of personal freedom without responsibility for the consequences of such choices. A therapeutic culture has replaced judgment with validation of feelings.

The scandal of divine judgment has its transfer to evaluation of human conduct. Those who found it offensive that a president in office would take advantage of a young intern with sexual dalliances were charged with being condemnatory. The only questions for such noble office should concern effective management of matters of state. A dichotomy is driven between character and concern for justice; concern about character means lack of concern about social-political issues, while concern for large scale issues of justice leaves questions of personal virtue as a minor, bourgeois matter. Jean Elshtain relates a debate in the Clinton affair with an ethics professor and pastor who argued that God loves sinners, and everyone needed to assist the president in his "quest for maturity" by not judging his behavior.[22] There is an assumption that any judgment leads to a punitive way of understanding life. This, of course, is itself a judgment and passes judgment on all those who are victims of power.

Thomas Jefferson trembled for the nation when he reflected that God was just. Abraham Lincoln saw the American Civil War as visited on his

---

22. Jean Bethke Elshtain, "Go Ahead, Use Good Judgment," *U. S. Catholic* 69/6 (June 2004): 27.

country by a just God's punishment for the sin of slavery. The God of the fathers and the God of Jesus the Christ was the judge of the nations, a God who paid attention to what was done and who had done it, and in time he would act as the judge of all. Charles Colson reminds Christians that they must ask the question of God's judgment in time of a terrorist attacks.[23] It must not be asked in terms of laying blame; like the prophets of old, it must be asked in terms of learning to know God and to know ourselves. It is a serious question. If terrorist attacks are a sign of divine judgment on a decadent and presumptuous society, then Marines, cruise missiles, satellites, and smart bombs will be powerless to save. The only thing that can save is a deep sense of repentance.

Mercy is implicit in the Ahab narrative. The attack of Ben-Hadad is nowhere said to be because of the sin of Ahab or the nation. At the same time, Ahab is consistently presented as culpable; even if the Aramean attack itself is not divine judgment, Ahab not only fails to seek divine guidance, he appears to resist it each time it is given. His failure to pass God's judgment on Ben-Hadad is fatal. He responds to the announcement of his own judgment with anger and resentment, to his own demise and that of his nation.

No doubt the attacks of the Arameans seem as unjustified to Ahab's wealthy and comfortable state as the highjacking of an airplane and turning it into a suicidal and homicidal bomb to bring down twin towers representing the fruits of industry and freedom. Both may be judged to be capricious evil attacks against the undeserving and unsuspecting. Both should be regarded as a time for self-evaluation and for discerning the requirements of judgment and justice.

Judgment always begins with God's own people. The first message of the church in turbulent political times must point to its own need for repentance. If Christians are honest, they have much for which to repent. Their values and use of resources do not suggest that their lives are committed to seeking first the kingdom of God. The idols of the church look little different from that of the surrounding culture. Colson reminds Christians of William Wilberforce, a member of parliament who fought to abolish slavery in the British empire. During a crucial moment in the campaign he said that his hope for Britain depended "not so much on her navies and armies, nor on the wisdom of her rulers, as on the persuasion that she still contains many who love and obey the Gospel of Christ, that their prayers may yet prevail." If Wilberforce is right, then the role of the church is of life-and-death importance.

Jesus was confronted with the question of why bad things happen to good people. Herod had killed some of the Galileans, making them a part

---

23. Charles Colson, "Wake-Up Call," *Christianity Today* 45/14 (November 2001): 112.

of their own sacrifices (Luke 13:1—5). Jesus added a situation of his own, one that did not involve direct human volition; a tower had fallen and killed eighteen people in Jerusalem. Jesus warned against passing judgment on such situations or against seeking to lay blame. The lesson was the same for every person: All will perish unless they repent.

A call to accountability. Disasters and troubles are always a reminder of the same lesson; it is not a question of self-justification or faultfinding. Repentance was always central to the life of Christ. God is not to be blamed for evil, whether it originates with political tyranny or natural disaster. God does not create evil but does use it to his purposes. Troublesome times are a time to cry out for God's mercy—personally, for the church, for the country. Peace and security prevail not so much because of diplomatic or military efforts but because God in his mercy forgives, heals, and restores.

John Garvey relates a conversation with a woman in his parish who had come from a Muslim background and had been baptized as an adult in her husband's Orthodox Christian faith. It was important for a couple to share religion, she said, but what really matters is belief in God. His fear was that she would follow that observation with the standard response: "We are all going the same way, but by different paths." Instead she said, "I think that I am able to trust a person more if he knows that someday he will be judged."[24] For her, belief in God was tied to a belief in judgment. A God of unconditional love and knowledge with the power to judge provides confidence in the midst of many travesties of personal experience. It is at the same time a sobering reminder of accountability not only for deeds actually done, but also for those intended.

The God of the Bible is not beyond good and evil. He has made us in his image to represent his will in this world, and in turn he demands accountability. This is not a matter of human choice; it is the human situation in this world. Judgment is demanded by the belief that God is revealed in those he has created. Knowledge of God is comprehended in compassion and in accountability for what has been given and done. It is not possible to enter into the joy of the Lord without judgment. God's judgment is not the external verdict of a magistrate passing judgment on someone he hardly knows. It is the judgment present in an intimate relationship with a personal God.

As with the prophet who confronts Ahab for his failure to execute judgment, there is a role for Christians to call for accountability. The warning Jesus gave against judgment is not a prohibition against all judgment; it is a reminder that judgment be given with the same measure it should be received

---

24. John Garvey, "Dies Irae," *Commonweal* 128/9 (May 2001): 9. (*Dies irae* is a medieval Latin hymn describing judgment day, used in some masses for the dead.)

(Matt. 7:1). It is a warning against vindictive judgment, but not against all judgment. The behavior of terrorists must not be excused; alleged efforts to find "root causes," attempting to correlate terrorism with poverty and despair, turns analysts into apologists. Instead of looking at extenuating circumstances, there is a tendency to recite exculpatory conditions.

This well-intentioned effort leads to cultural condescension. Terrorists are held to a different moral standard than is normally applied. In refusing to judge violence, justice is denied to the majority, who never engage in such destructive acts. Politics is an arena in which tough judgments must be rendered; irresolute leaders who refuse to judge are incapable of carrying out the responsibility of their own office.

Judgments of conduct are inseparable from the function of integrity in home, community, church, and social relationships. There are many things wrong with the "system," but the faults of the system do not absolve individuals of their own conduct within it.[25] The judgments of the prophets against the nation were not separable from the choices made by individuals. Systems do not work apart from the integrity of individuals involved. Failure to deal with plagiarism not only undermines the education of the student concerned but also the function of the entire class.

There needs to be judgment of work if learning is to take place. Responsible parenting requires a parent to assess a child's behavior at all points; judging behavior and attempting to understand it are not mutually exclusive. Choosing the route of irresponsibility ("Who am I to judge?") stems from moral weakness more than a sense of appropriate humility. Judging involves calling things by their right names. This includes the use of powerful words like evil and sinful. "An enormously enlarged empathy" does not suffice to sustain the critical capacity called judging.[26] The harder truths of life and politics must be confronted.

There is a tendency to see the God of the Old Testament as much harsher and judgmental than the Jesus of the New Testament. The stern judgments of God against the nations, including Israel, seem incompatible with him who insists that we love our enemies. N.T. Wright says the good news is that Western culture needs to come to terms with this sterile sort of antithesis. Theologians and church leaders are facing the challenge of articulating

---

25. An anonymous article entitled "Common Character" in *The Christian Century* laments the irresponsibility of individual officials in the Enron-Andersen debacle to responsibly follow the spirit of the law (119/5 [February–March, 2002]: 5). The result has been enormous hardship for thousands who have lost jobs, savings, and investments; key institutions have been undermined.

26. Elshtain, "Go Ahead, Use Good Judgment," 28.

a worldview in which individuals may find their way forward in their thinking, their communities, and their reading of texts.

> If any journalist had predicted, thirty-four years ago, that a black archbishop of Cape Town would preside over the Truth and Reconciliation Commission for the whole community, he or she would have been laughed off the airwaves as hopelessly optimistic. The image of white secret policemen and black terrorists together confessing their atrocities and seeking reconciliation with their victims ought to be recognized as one of the great moral landmarks of the late twentieth century.[27]

The commission faced attack from both sides: those who wanted vengeance rather than reconciliation, and those who wanted to let bygones be bygones, not to stir up the past. Both wanted to live with the antithesis of judgment and mercy, distorting both by keeping them separate. Like many Bible readers, they were unable or unwilling to face the possibility that in their highest form, judgment and mercy are inseparable.

---

27. N. T. Wright, "Judgment and Mercy," *Bible Review* 16/2 (April 2000): 10.

1 Kings 21:1–29

SOME TIME LATER there was an incident involving a vine-yard belonging to Naboth the Jezreelite. The vineyard was in Jezreel, close to the palace of Ahab king of Samaria. ²Ahab said to Naboth, "Let me have your vineyard to use for a vegetable garden, since it is close to my palace. In exchange I will give you a better vineyard or, if you prefer, I will pay you whatever it is worth."

³But Naboth replied, "The LORD forbid that I should give you the inheritance of my fathers."

⁴So Ahab went home, sullen and angry because Naboth the Jezreelite had said, "I will not give you the inheritance of my fathers." He lay on his bed sulking and refused to eat.

⁵His wife Jezebel came in and asked him, "Why are you so sullen? Why won't you eat?"

⁶He answered her, "Because I said to Naboth the Jezreelite, 'Sell me your vineyard; or if you prefer, I will give you another vineyard in its place.' But he said, 'I will not give you my vine-yard.'"

⁷Jezebel his wife said, "Is this how you act as king over Israel? Get up and eat! Cheer up. I'll get you the vineyard of Naboth the Jezreelite."

⁸So she wrote letters in Ahab's name, placed his seal on them, and sent them to the elders and nobles who lived in Naboth's city with him. ⁹In those letters she wrote:

"Proclaim a day of fasting and seat Naboth in a prominent place among the people. ¹⁰But seat two scoundrels opposite him and have them testify that he has cursed both God and the king. Then take him out and stone him to death."

¹¹So the elders and nobles who lived in Naboth's city did as Jezebel directed in the letters she had written to them. ¹²They proclaimed a fast and seated Naboth in a prominent place among the people. ¹³Then two scoundrels came and sat oppo-site him and brought charges against Naboth before the people, saying, "Naboth has cursed both God and the king." So they took him outside the city and stoned him to death.

¹⁴Then they sent word to Jezebel: "Naboth has been stoned and is dead."

¹⁵As soon as Jezebel heard that Naboth had been stoned to death, she said to Ahab, "Get up and take possession of the vineyard of Naboth the Jezreelite that he refused to sell you. He is no longer alive, but dead." ¹⁶When Ahab heard that Naboth was dead, he got up and went down to take possession of Naboth's vineyard.

¹⁷Then the word of the LORD came to Elijah the Tishbite: ¹⁸"Go down to meet Ahab king of Israel, who rules in Samaria. He is now in Naboth's vineyard, where he has gone to take possession of it. ¹⁹Say to him, 'This is what the LORD says: Have you not murdered a man and seized his property?' Then say to him, 'This is what the LORD says: In the place where dogs licked up Naboth's blood, dogs will lick up your blood—yes, yours!'"

²⁰Ahab said to Elijah, "So you have found me, my enemy!"

"I have found you," he answered, "because you have sold yourself to do evil in the eyes of the LORD. ²¹I am going to bring disaster on you. I will consume your descendants and cut off from Ahab every last male in Israel—slave or free. ²²I will make your house like that of Jeroboam son of Nebat and that of Baasha son of Ahijah, because you have provoked me to anger and have caused Israel to sin.'

²³"And also concerning Jezebel the LORD says: 'Dogs will devour Jezebel by the wall of Jezreel.'

²⁴"Dogs will eat those belonging to Ahab who die in the city, and the birds of the air will feed on those who die in the country."

²⁵(There was never a man like Ahab, who sold himself to do evil in the eyes of the LORD, urged on by Jezebel his wife. ²⁶He behaved in the vilest manner by going after idols, like the Amorites the LORD drove out before Israel.)

²⁷When Ahab heard these words, he tore his clothes, put on sackcloth and fasted. He lay in sackcloth and went around meekly.

²⁸Then the word of the LORD came to Elijah the Tishbite: ²⁹"Have you noticed how Ahab has humbled himself before me? Because he has humbled himself, I will not bring this disaster in his day, but I will bring it on his house in the days of his son."

Original Meaning

THE NARRATIVE OF Naboth's vineyard has a loose chronological affiliation with the events of the time of Ahab (21:1). The story also has variant positions in the canon; in the Greek versions it is connected with the Elijah stories (following ch. 19). It has an important role in the fulfillment of prophetic judgment; in the purge of Jehu, Joram the son of Ahab was cast into the vineyard to avenge the blood of Naboth (cf. 2 Kings 9:25–26).

In the development of the royal properties Ahab desires a field that will enhance his residence in Jezreel. Such appropriations of property were not uncommon; Samuel warned that this would happen if Israel were to choose a king like the other nations (1 Sam. 8:14). Naboth's refusal to give up his ancestral property is in the spirit of each family retaining its heritage in Israel (Num. 36:7–8), which is provided for in the regulations of the Jubilee year (cf. Lev. 25:13, 23). There is no indication Naboth would give up his rights as a citizen if he sold his property, but it could have prejudiced his status making his family a royal dependent.[1] For Naboth the heritage is worth more than any monetary compensation.

Judicial Murder of Naboth (21:1–16)

NABOTH, FROM JEZREEL, has property in Jezreel; the double mention of Jezreel in 21:1 is not superfluous, because a significant point in the story is that the property is located in his hometown. Jezreel is a royal center of the Omride dynasty, though Omri established a capital in Samaria (16:24). Jezreel is about ten miles (fifteen kilometers) east of Megiddo, on a ridge extending along the southern edge of the Valley of Jezreel.

On the basis of archaeological evidence in relation to Samaria, Ussishkin thinks that Jezreel was established as a fortified military center to serve as a strong central base for a large army, including substantial units of cavalry and chariotry.[2] It was built concurrently with Samaria; the planners and architects of both sites followed the same architectural layout. The various buildings included a central building that served as a royal residence. The Hebrew for palace (*hêkal*) is a Sumerian loanword (*ekallu*) that normally refers to a temple, but occasionally has a secular referent (cf. 2 Kings 20:18).

The size and imposing nature of the fortifications clearly serve the purposes of propaganda.[3] They express the need to show the strength and

---

1. Alexander Rofé, "The Vineyard of Naboth: The Origin and Message of the Story," *VT* 38 (1988): 90.

2. Ussishkin, "Jezreel, Samaria and Megiddo: Royal Centers of Omri and Ahab," 352–56, 361–63.

3. H. G. M. Williamson, "Jezreel in the Biblical Texts," *Tel Aviv* 18 (1991): 72–92.

---

position of the royal dynasty. These grandiose public works are a means of social control over the local population. This function of Jezreel in the royal possessions conforms well to the desire of Ahab to enhance his presence by taking possession of Naboth's vineyard.

The specification of Ahab as "king of Samaria" (21:1) is important to the story; the vineyard is in Jezreel, some distance from the capital. This explains the need for written correspondence from Samaria to Jezreel (21:8). Naboth refuses Ahab's offer of purchase from the viewpoint of ancestral inheritance: All the land belongs to God; the Israelites are sojourners. It is not their prerogative to sell land in perpetuity or to alienate it from the family.

Ahab responds in the manner of an exacerbated king, but apparently does not intend to overcome Naboth's opposition. Jezebel perceives Ahab's response as weakness. She intends to exercise royal authority in his name in order to obtain the property (v. 7). She writes letters and signs them in the name of the king. According to the covenant, the king was to protect the rights of the citizens as fellow brothers (Deut. 17:14–20), but in Israel the corruption of authority extended to supervising elders and freemen with the power to exercise judicial authority.

Naboth himself appears to have been the head of an influential local family, as he is given a place of honor at the sacred occasion (v. 9). However, his refusal to cooperate with the royal request makes him a rival to the supporters of the king. It is an offense to curse a ruler of the people (Ex. 22:28), so it is not difficult for unscrupulous witnesses to bring a sentence of death against Naboth. The ease with which such a plot is accomplished demonstrates the pervasive corruption of Ahab's reign. Once Jezebel receives word of the execution, she informs her husband that the vineyard is now his for the taking. This criminal act has been achieved with full judicial authority.

Judgment of Ahab (21:17–29)

JEZEBEL CAN ESCAPE legal consequences for murder and appropriation of property by acting through corrupt judges, but she cannot escape the judgment of the Owner who gave the land to Israel (cf. Lev. 25:23). Yahweh commissions Elijah to confront Ahab in Naboth's vineyard. Ahab has gone from Samaria to Jezreel to inspect his property (21:16, 18b); Ahab "who is in Samaria" (v. 18; KJV, RSV) is a reference to his normal habitat at his royal residence rather than his personal presence there (NIV). Elijah is to confront Ahab at the scene of the crime.

The judgment against Ahab is that the dogs will lick up his blood just as they did that of Naboth (21:19). The dogs do literally lick up the blood of

Ahab in Samaria when the chariot in which he dies is washed (22:38), but they also lick up his blood in the vineyard of Naboth when the body of his son Joram is thrown there (2 Kings 9:25–26). Human injustice is succeeded by divine judgment in a double sense; Ahab will die in battle, and his dynasty will end with the death of his son. The judgment against Ahab is not that every male will be cut off (1 Kings 21:21; cf. NIV), but that all the royal descendants will be exterminated.[4] His death, and that of Jezebel, are described in the terms of Jeroboam and Baasha (21:23–24; cf. 14:10–11; 16:4). The fire of divine judgment will pursue his sons (21:21) until the last of the royal descendants dies.

Ahab's response to Elijah betrays knowledge of his own guilt: "So you have found me, my enemy!" (21:20). Elijah is Ahab's enemy because the latter has violated his responsibility as a king under the covenant. Elijah describes Ahab's guilt for what it is: "You have sold yourself to do evil" (v. 20). Greed has led Ahab into the sin of murder and theft, so there is none who can be compared to him (v. 25). Though Jezebel is an accomplice in his crime, Ahab is still culpable as the instigator of her actions. Murder and theft are the results of desecrating the covenant (v. 26), a manifestation of his disrespect for God and the relationships that are divinely ordained.

The ending of the narrative offers a surprising turn on the character of Ahab (21:27–29). One would not expect a king described as more abominable in his deeds than the Amorites (vv. 25–26) to have a change of heart at the proclamation of judgment. Ahab shows his repentance by wearing sackcloth, fasting, sleeping in sackcloth, and conducting his affairs with gentleness. Though Elijah is not commissioned with any message for Ahab, God does inform the prophet that his punishment will be mitigated and will come to fruition in the days of his son. Though Ahab does die violently in battle, he is buried in the royal sepulcher (22:39–40), and his dynasty continues for another fourteen years under the rule of his sons.

INHERITANCE RIGHTS IN ISRAEL. The matter of Naboth's vineyard became a cause célèbre in Israel. The blood of Naboth was declared to be avenged at the death of Ahab (22:38) and further served to justify the revolt of Jehu in ending the Omride dynasty (2 Kings 9:24–26). This story is often regarded as secondary to Ahab, but we must accept the text as it has been received, with its testimony that Naboth was

---

4. "Slave or free" (NIV) is a hendiadys meaning "ruler-deliverer" (cf. 1 Kings 14:10); hence it is not every male, but every member of the royal family.

murdered in the reign of Ahab and that judgment for this act finally ends his dynasty with the death of Joram.

A further question is the location of the vineyard. Naboth is a Jezreelite; his ancestral land is in Jezreel (21:1, 3), the location Ahab established as a royal residence (cf. 18:45–46). The capital of Israel is Samaria (cf. 16:24), and the fulfillment of the prophecy of Elijah concerning the death of Ahab takes place in Samaria (22:37–38). These differences have been used to say the story has been adapted from elsewhere as a condemnation of Ahab. But the narrative is consistent; as recorded it assumes a distance between the palace in Samaria and the vineyard of Naboth, because Jezebel corresponds with the leaders of the city of Naboth through letters (21:8–9). In the narrative, the dogs licking up the blood of Ahab in Samaria is the equivalent of the dogs licking up the blood of Naboth outside the city of Jezreel. The vineyard is adjacent to the royal residence in Jezreel (21:1), but the burial of Ahab is in Samaria (22:37–38). The prophetic judgment declares only that the king will suffer the same ignominious death he inflicted on Naboth. The location of the actual event is not the point of the statement.

Kingship in Israel began with an account of how power was abused and the basic right of land violated. Saul was anointed as Israel's first king, but his violation of that trust led to his rejection and the anointing of David in his stead. Saul was afflicted with an evil temperament (1 Sam. 16:14), which tormented him and led him to violence. After David's victory over Goliath, Saul envied him and tried to kill him (18:9, 11). David was eventually forced to flee (19:10), driven from his home by the very person whose responsibility it was to protect it at all times.

It is possible that David's experience is expressed in a psalm ascribed to him. David expresses his hope in God as that which has superseded the loss of his inheritance:

LORD, you have assigned me my portion and my cup;
  you have made my lot secure.
The boundary lines have fallen for me in pleasant places;
  surely I have a delightful inheritance. (Ps. 16:5–6)

The terminology of this passage is derived from the division of the land to the tribes. The land was apportioned to each family as an inheritance as determined by the casting of a lot (Num. 26:52–56), which determined the divine choice for the allocation of land each tribe would receive. The fields (portions) were assigned on the size of each tribe according to the listed names.[5]

---

5. Jacob Milgrom, *Numbers* (JPS Torah Commentary: Philadelphia: Jewish Publication Society, 1990), 227, 480–81.

The Jubilee year was the means of ensuring that once in every generation the land would return to its original owners, so that each family would always be able to enjoy the divine provision.

Psalm 16 is a celebration of trust when all means of support are lost. Yahweh is the only portion left to the psalmist (16:5); he is the One who makes the boundaries of the situation pleasant. Once when Saul had driven David into the desert, David had opportunity to dispose of his enemy. David and his men had invaded the cave where Saul was sleeping and could have killed him (1 Sam. 26:6–8). David rejected this opportunity because he lived by another rule: "From evildoers come evil deeds" (24:14). If David were to be as vengeful as Saul, then he would be indistinguishable from Saul.

Instead David insisted that Saul's fate was in the hands of Yahweh, who had anointed him (26:9–11). David left with Saul's spear and water jug, then made appeal to his enemy. David said that if he had sinned so that the anointed king was compelled to pursue him, he would make an offering (26:19). However, if this pursuit was of human design, then those pursuing him were cursed. They had driven him away from securing his rightful inheritance, and in so doing had abandoned him to serve other gods.

This line of thought is consistent with the covenant; all who belong to the covenant have a share in the land that God has given. If they do not rightfully possess that land, they belong to the Canaanites. However, the psalmist left without land will not be separated from his God. Though enemies can drive him from his land, they cannot drive him from his God. In such circumstances God is his inheritance and his portion. Murderous individuals who drive people from their rightful inheritance are under a curse. This was demonstrated in the case of Saul, and the same principle pertains in the judgment against Ahab.

The injustices of Israel that eventually drive them into exile involve the violations of land rights. Isaiah, in the introduction of his prophecy, sets out an alternative for Jerusalem. They need to cease from their evil, learn to do good, seek justice, and assist the oppressed (Isa. 1:16b–17a). If they learn to do justice, they will eat from the prosperity of the land, but if they refuse and rebel, they will be consumed by the sword (1:19–20). The very first of the woe oracles against Jerusalem is because of the violence of land appropriation: "Woe to those who add house to house and join field to field, till no space is left and you live alone in the land" (5:8). Those who act in such greed will never get to live in their houses or enjoy the produce of the land because of Yahweh's judgment (5:9–10).

Land is among the most sacred of human rights in the biblical understanding of justice. Those whose rights to land are violated become the object of God's concern, the violators the objects of his judgment. Naboth's death will not go unnoticed; Ahab rightly fears the appearance of the prophet.

ECONOMIC OPPRESSION. Murder and the confiscation of land are perhaps the most common crimes of state against individual citizens. Virtually every country has within it a segment of citizens who believe they have experienced the tyranny of the state in their past. Some may be refugees from another country; others may feel they have been robbed within their own country.

The story of Naboth is a biblical paragon for such injustices, as it exemplifies how the powerful take advantage of the weak to add to their wealth. It has all the features that are typical of such instances. The actions are done "legally" because they are in the power of the state; they are justified by the people in power, so the victims may not even be able to make a case for their deprivation being unjust. Naboth is vilified as being an enemy of the state (21:13), which he is in that he has resisted the desires of the king. The leaders of the community can justify their actions as being loyal to their king (21:11), for they receive their instructions from the palace. The witnesses are described as "scoundrels" (NIV), sons of *beliyyaʿal* (21:10, 13), malicious individuals who "swallow up" others. As a society becomes corrupt because of oppressive leaders, there is increased opportunity for such individuals to ply their trade.

My mother was born in Novgorodskoye, a village in eastern Ukraine to the east of the city of Donetsk. In 1926, when she was three years old, her parents fled Ukraine as the terror of Stalinism became increasingly oppressive. I grew up hearing the stories of how my grandparents were dispossessed and gradually realizing how this had profoundly affected not only the life of my mother but the lives of her children as well. It was only later that I began to understand the horror of what happened in Ukraine under Stalinism and what I had been spared, even though my grandparents lost all their property.

Between 1929 and 1932 the Soviet Communist Party struck a double blow at the peasantry of the USSR; the elimination of *kulaks*[6] enabled the state to dispossess and deport millions of peasant families, and collectivization abolished all private ownership of land. This was followed in 1932–33 by a "terror-famine," which the state inflicted on the collectivized peasants of Ukraine. The state demanded impossibly high grain quotas, removed every other source of food, and prevented any outside help from reaching the starving millions. The state dispossession of property and food grown on collectivized farms led to the greatest genocide in human history. The story of Ukraine is Naboth's vineyard multiplied many millions of times.

---

6. *Kulaks* were landowners, sometimes able to hire labor and loan money.

This state confiscation of property is well documented by Robert Conquest, senior research fellow and scholar-curator of the East European Collection at the Hoover Institution, Stanford University.[7] At the end of the war the peasants owned or rented out four times the land held by other owners. The collapse of the old regime in March 1917 resulted in the peasantry forcibly taking over the large estates. The land decree of November 1917, immediately following the Bolshevik seizure of power, was a conscious maneuver to gain peasant support. All land, including state land, was to be given to the use of those who worked on it. Lenin explained: "We Bolsheviks were opposed to the law. . . . Yet we signed it, because we did not want to oppose the will of the majority of peasants."[8]

The next stage in collectivization was to ally the poor peasant against the *kulak*, those who presumably oppressed the peasant through loans and mortgages. The *kulak* in the sense of a rich man exploiting a peasant was in reality a mythical figure. The real struggle was not that of the poor against the rich, but the abolition of the peasant's right to sell his grain. A decree in May 1918 "on the monopoly of food" empowered the Commissariat of Food to extract from the peasants any grain held in excess of quotas set by the Commissariat, with the claim that "this grain is in the hands of *kulaks*."[9] Quotas were set impossibly high, and *kulaks* who failed to meet their quotas were expropriated and exiled.

Those who escaped these deportations thought no fate could be worse than that of the *kulaks*. They did not realize that confiscation of grain to meet procurement targets would result in the ultimate penalty of death. R. Conquest provides a conservative estimate of approximately seven million premature deaths due to famine from 1926–37, and four million deaths because of deportation and collectivization.[10] This was rationalized and defended on the basis of creating a just state of equality for workers.

Similar accounts of dispossession and death can be told for every continent in every era, and individual stories can be found in every community. Adjacent territories can be described in different ways, such as nations neighboring each other in an increasingly global economic system. Don Helder Camara, diminutive Brazilian archbishop, used the Naboth story as illustrative of political force where the greed of multinationals could export entire factories to paradises of investment where salaries are low and dispute impossible.[11]

7. R. Conquest, *The Harvest of Sorrow: Soviet Collectivization and the Terror-Famine* (Edmonton: Univ. of Alberta Press, 1986).
8. Ibid., 43–44.
9. Ibid., 46.
10. Ibid., 304–5.
11. Davie Napier, "The Inheritance and the Problem of Adjacency: An Essay on 1 Kings 21," *Int* 30 (1976): 4.

He said that the pessimist in him mocked his receipt of a degree in law when "Law is ever more a hollow word, resonant but empty, in a world increasingly dominated by force, by violence, by fraud—in a word, by egoism;" when civil law permits "the progressive and rapid increase of oppressed people who continue being swept toward ghettos, without work, without health, without instruction, without diversion and, not rarely, without God;" when under so-called international law "more than two-thirds of humanity (exist) in situations of misery, of hunger, of subhuman life;" and when agrarian law or special law permits "today's powerful landowners to continue to live at the cost of misery for unhappy pariahs" and whereby "modern technology achieves marvels from the earth with an ever-reduced number of rural workers (while) those not needed in the fields live sub lives in depressing slums on the outskirts of nearly all the large cities."[12]

Justice is not a simple matter. Most North American citizens are part of an economic system in which economic power involves exploitation of others. Camara almost suggests that all individuals in industrialized states are an Ahab. This is an unfair comparison. The problems of economic justice will not be solved by one individual, one government, or in one generation. These injustices ought not to be compared with the kind of state terror that took place in Ukraine, as sometimes seems to be implied. At the same time it must never be denied that there are injustices between industrialized states and others on a different economic system. Consumers are part of these systems just as much as the marketers, and it will take the cooperative and consistent effort of all to provide a proper inheritance for those economically oppressed. Individuals can have an influence for good and must consistently seek how they can make a difference in the lives of other individual people.

12. Ibid.

1 Kings 22:1-50

FOR THREE YEARS there was no war between Aram and Israel. ²But in the third year Jehoshaphat king of Judah went down to see the king of Israel. ³The king of Israel had said to his officials, "Don't you know that Ramoth Gilead belongs to us and yet we are doing nothing to retake it from the king of Aram?"

⁴So he asked Jehoshaphat, "Will you go with me to fight against Ramoth Gilead?"

Jehoshaphat replied to the king of Israel, "I am as you are, my people as your people, my horses as your horses." ⁵But Jehoshaphat also said to the king of Israel, "First seek the counsel of the LORD."

⁶So the king of Israel brought together the prophets—about four hundred men—and asked them, "Shall I go to war against Ramoth Gilead, or shall I refrain?"

"Go," they answered, "for the Lord will give it into the king's hand."

⁷But Jehoshaphat asked, "Is there not a prophet of the LORD here whom we can inquire of?"

⁸The king of Israel answered Jehoshaphat, "There is still one man through whom we can inquire of the LORD, but I hate him because he never prophesies anything good about me, but always bad. He is Micaiah son of Imlah."

"The king should not say that," Jehoshaphat replied.

⁹So the king of Israel called one of his officials and said, "Bring Micaiah son of Imlah at once."

¹⁰Dressed in their royal robes, the king of Israel and Jehoshaphat king of Judah were sitting on their thrones at the threshing floor by the entrance of the gate of Samaria, with all the prophets prophesying before them. ¹¹Now Zedekiah son of Kenaanah had made iron horns and he declared, "This is what the LORD says: 'With these you will gore the Arameans until they are destroyed.'"

¹²All the other prophets were prophesying the same thing. "Attack Ramoth Gilead and be victorious," they said, "for the LORD will give it into the king's hand."

¹³The messenger who had gone to summon Micaiah said to him, "Look, as one man the other prophets are predicting

success for the king. Let your word agree with theirs, and speak favorably."

14But Micaiah said, "As surely as the LORD lives, I can tell him only what the LORD tells me."

15When he arrived, the king asked him, "Micaiah, shall we go to war against Ramoth Gilead, or shall I refrain?"

"Attack and be victorious," he answered, "for the LORD will give it into the king's hand."

16The king said to him, "How many times must I make you swear to tell me nothing but the truth in the name of the LORD?"

17Then Micaiah answered, "I saw all Israel scattered on the hills like sheep without a shepherd, and the LORD said, 'These people have no master. Let each one go home in peace.'"

18The king of Israel said to Jehoshaphat, "Didn't I tell you that he never prophesies anything good about me, but only bad?"

19Micaiah continued, "Therefore hear the word of the LORD: I saw the LORD sitting on his throne with all the host of heaven standing around him on his right and on his left. 20And the LORD said, 'Who will entice Ahab into attacking Ramoth Gilead and going to his death there?'

"One suggested this, and another that. 21Finally, a spirit came forward, stood before the LORD and said, 'I will entice him.'

22"'By what means?' the LORD asked.

"'I will go out and be a lying spirit in the mouths of all his prophets,' he said.

"'You will succeed in enticing him,' said the LORD. 'Go and do it.'

23"So now the LORD has put a lying spirit in the mouths of all these prophets of yours. The LORD has decreed disaster for you."

24Then Zedekiah son of Kenaanah went up and slapped Micaiah in the face. "Which way did the spirit from the LORD go when he went from me to speak to you?" he asked.

25Micaiah replied, "You will find out on the day you go to hide in an inner room."

26The king of Israel then ordered, "Take Micaiah and send him back to Amon the ruler of the city and to Joash the king's son 27and say, 'This is what the king says: Put this fellow in prison and give him nothing but bread and water until I return safely.'"

²⁸Micaiah declared, "If you ever return safely, the LORD has not spoken through me." Then he added, "Mark my words, all you people!"

²⁹So the king of Israel and Jehoshaphat king of Judah went up to Ramoth Gilead. ³⁰The king of Israel said to Jehoshaphat, "I will enter the battle in disguise, but you wear your royal robes." So the king of Israel disguised himself and went into battle.

³¹Now the king of Aram had ordered his thirty-two chariot commanders, "Do not fight with anyone, small or great, except the king of Israel." ³²When the chariot commanders saw Jehoshaphat, they thought, "Surely this is the king of Israel." So they turned to attack him, but when Jehoshaphat cried out, ³³the chariot commanders saw that he was not the king of Israel and stopped pursuing him.

³⁴But someone drew his bow at random and hit the king of Israel between the sections of his armor. The king told his chariot driver, "Wheel around and get me out of the fighting. I've been wounded." ³⁵All day long the battle raged, and the king was propped up in his chariot facing the Arameans. The blood from his wound ran onto the floor of the chariot, and that evening he died. ³⁶As the sun was setting, a cry spread through the army: "Every man to his town; everyone to his land!"

³⁷So the king died and was brought to Samaria, and they buried him there. ³⁸They washed the chariot at a pool in Samaria (where the prostitutes bathed), and the dogs licked up his blood, as the word of the LORD had declared.

³⁹As for the other events of Ahab's reign, including all he did, the palace he built and inlaid with ivory, and the cities he fortified, are they not written in the book of the annals of the kings of Israel? ⁴⁰Ahab rested with his fathers. And Ahaziah his son succeeded him as king.

⁴¹Jehoshaphat son of Asa became king of Judah in the fourth year of Ahab king of Israel. ⁴²Jehoshaphat was thirty-five years old when he became king, and he reigned in Jerusalem twenty-five years. His mother's name was Azubah daughter of Shilhi. ⁴³In everything he walked in the ways of his father Asa and did not stray from them; he did what was right in the eyes of the LORD. The high places, however, were not removed, and the people continued to offer sacrifices and

burn incense there. ⁴⁴Jehoshaphat was also at peace with the king of Israel.

⁴⁵As for the other events of Jehoshaphat's reign, the things he achieved and his military exploits, are they not written in the book of the annals of the kings of Judah? ⁴⁶He rid the land of the rest of the male shrine prostitutes who remained there even after the reign of his father Asa. ⁴⁷There was then no king in Edom; a deputy ruled.

⁴⁸Now Jehoshaphat built a fleet of trading ships to go to Ophir for gold, but they never set sail—they were wrecked at Ezion Geber. ⁴⁹At that time Ahaziah son of Ahab said to Jehoshaphat, "Let my men sail with your men," but Jehoshaphat refused.

⁵⁰Then Jehoshaphat rested with his fathers and was buried with them in the city of David his father. And Jehoram his son succeeded him.

THE DEATH OF Ahab comes at the hands of the Arameans in his attempt to regain Ramoth Gilead, a city of refuge located in the eastern portion of the tribal territory of Gad (Deut. 4:43; Josh. 20:8; 21:38).[1] The battle takes place in alliance with Jehoshaphat king of Judah, the son of Asa, who became king over Judah in the fourth year of Ahab (1 Kings 22:41) and entered into a treaty with the prosperous Omrides.

Jehoshaphat may have entered into this alliance for potential benefits from Israel's position in the Transjordan; Judah retained control over Edom and the southern port at Ezion Geber (22:48). The alliance was sealed through the marriage of Ahab's daughter Athaliah to Judah's crown prince Jehoram (2 Kings 8:18). Judah may have been a vassal, or it was a treaty of equals.[2] Israel was the stronger of the two states, and until disaster hit both dynasties under Jehu, Judah participated in most of Israel's wars. Jehoshaphat is consistently depicted as seeking to be faithful to Yahweh and his prophets (1 Kings 22:43), and therefore in constant tension with his ally Ahab, who was devoted to the Phoenician religion.

---

1. It is likely to be identified with Tell Ramith, based on the etymological ties with Ramoth, namely, a strategic location as a "height"; Iron Age pottery at the site dates from the time of Solomon to the latter period of the kingdom of Israel. Gilead was added to the toponym to distinguish it from other towns with the same name.

2. Ahlström, *The History of Ancient Palestine*, 574.

The Battle for Ramoth Gilead (22:1–40)

AHAB'S PREVIOUS WAR with Aram concluded with a treaty (20:34), which brought peace for a short period of time. Three years is a typological number rather than an exact chronological statement. Plans for the attack are laid during a state visit by Jehoshaphat. Judah has no interest in the battleground between Israel and the Arameans at the northeastern frontier of the heavily forested Gilead. Ahab's question concerning Ramoth Gilead is intended to arouse shame and resentment (22:3), since the Arameans are violating the agreement made earlier at Aphek.

Ahab does not have sufficient resources to attack the Arameans on his own (22:4), so solicits help from his ally in enforcing the treaty. Jehoshaphat affirms his support with a traditional expression (cf. 2 Kings 3:7), but he refuses to proceed unless there is divine confirmation that the venture is within the divine will.

Consultations with the prophets interrupt the preparations for war (22:5–28). Such inquiries were a normal procedure (Num. 27:21; Judg.1:1; 20:27–28; 1 Sam. 23:2, 9–10; 30:7–8). Ahab apparently knows the Lord is not with him in this battle, as stated in his response to Micaiah son of Imlah (vv. 8, 15–16). But Ahab has determined his course of action irrespective of the outcome of the consultations. It seems the function of the royal prophets was to sanction the decisions of the king rather than provide actual guidance. The episode reveals the problem of false prophecy among the official prophets of the king and the dilemma of conflict with other prophets who did not conform.

The inquiry unfolds in two scenes. In the first, four hundred prophets of the king (cf. 1 Kings 18:19) affirm Ahab's intention to go to war (22:5–6). They carry on their ecstatic behavior before the two kings, who sit in their royal regalia in the open space at the entrance of the city gate.[3] The message of Ahab's prophets is affirmed and reiterated in a circumstantial amplification (22:10–12). Their leader Zedekiah makes himself iron horns to act out the message of how the Arameans will be utterly defeated.[4]

In the second Micaiah is first persuaded to verbally confirm the message of Ahab's prophets (vv. 7–23): Yahweh will give Ramoth Gilead over to the king's control (vv. 6b, 15b).[5] But the king knows Micaiah is only giving him

---

3. The designation "threshing-floor" preserves an item from ancient life. Space was a premium in ancient walled cities; the only open space for a public gathering was at the city gate. At Samaria this space was used for winnowing; since this was a seasonal activity, it provided a space for large assemblies at other times.

4. For an interpretation of these sign acts see comments on 11:29–30. These actions are rhetorical nonverbal communication, persuasive in nature and intent.

5. The answer of the four hundred prophets uses the honorific *ʾadonay* ("Lord") rather than the divine name *Yahweh* used by Micaiah. This difference may only be textual; the

the answer that will confirm the loyalty of his prophets rather than the divine word. At the request of Ahab, Micaiah elaborates that the armies of Israel will be scattered like sheep without a shepherd and will return home without leaders (22:17). In other words, Ahab will die. The contradiction with Micaiah's first response is clarified with a vision (vv. 19–23), which explains the behavior of Ahab's prophets and how it is possible for the initial words of Micaiah to conform to them.

The lengthy inquiry involving Micaiah is a verbal drama to establish prophetic legitimacy.[6] Prophetic enmity against Micaiah is longstanding; Ahab's messenger expects a discordant message, so he prevails on the prophet to conform to the word of the other prophets (22:13). Micaiah makes clear that he can do nothing other than speak the word of Yahweh; this he does, to the end that the deceit of the royal prophets of Ahab is fully disclosed. The vision serves to explain the willful self-deception of the false prophets and legitimates Micaiah's word.

Micaiah does not claim, as charged by Zedekiah (22:24), that the spirit of Yahweh has left Zedekiah and gone over to him. Micaiah can only speak the truth he has seen in the vision (v. 14).[7] The prophets, in their desire to affirm the intent of the king, have carried out God's will as decided in the heavenly court. The false prophets confirm the self-determined decision of the king, because divine judgment has already been decided against him (v. 20). Both the false prophets and the king are culpable in their resolve to carry out their own purposes, irrespective of God's guidance. This is not a situation of being unknowingly misled. Their deception lies in the belief they can deny the word of Yahweh and succeed.

In Micaiah's vision, the heavenly court is the counterpart of a royal council (cf. Job 1:6); the King is surrounded by his attendants, each assigned to fulfill specific roles (1 Kings 22:19). "Host of heaven" is the term for celestial bodies worshiped by foreign nations (Deut. 4:19; 2 Kings 17:16; 21:3). In that vision these are divine beings in service to God.[8] The question to the

---

Targums and most Hebrew manuscripts have Ahab's prophets say Yahweh (v. 6b). However, these may be harmonistic readings (cf. v. 12); on the basis of comparative texts, Daniel Block ("What Has Delphi to do with Samaria?") believes that the prophecy was deliberately ambiguous (forthcoming in *Writing and Ancient Near Eastern Society: Papers in Honour of Alan Millard*, ed. Piotr Bienkowski [British Academy Monographs in Archaeology; Oxford: Oxford Univ. Press], 185–212).

6. Long, *1 Kings*, 234–35.

7. Volkmar Hirth, "Der Geist in I Reg 22," *ZAW* 101 (1989): 114.

8. The divine attendant is referred to as a spirit (*rûaḥ*); in other instances the divine attendants are described as "sons of God" (Job 1:6) or "seraphim" (Isa. 6:2). A messenger (*malʾāk*) describes a heavenly intermediary who appears in bodily form (Judg. 6:11). In this case the divine messenger directly informs the minds of the earthly participants.

heavenly court is how to entice Ahab to go into battle at Ramoth Gilead. The persuasion of Ahab is to accomplish the invincible will of God.[9] This persuasion is to guarantee that Ahab will fall in battle; his judgment is decreed.

The effective accomplishment of the divine will can take place without the conscious participation of his prophets—either positively, as in the case of Jeremiah (Jer. 20: 7, 10), or negatively, as in the case of Ahab's prophets (1 Kings 22:21–22). Ezekiel understands God to be adding to the punishment of the prophets by misguiding them to evil acts (Ezek. 14:9–10). The punishment on Ahab and his prophets is determined by their own hardness of heart, just as Pharaoh hardened his heart and then came under divine judgment of an unchanging will that led to his destruction.

A crux in this passage is the intent of the enticement as a "lying spirit" (22:23). The LXX renders this as a "false spirit" (*pneuma pseudes*), taking the Hebrew *rûaḥ šeqer* as deception by the divine messenger. However the question as to how the spirit will try to persuade Ahab suggests that the *rûaḥ šeqer* is not a deception on the part of the messenger, but a description of the effect his message will have on the king.[10] Ahab is deluded; this delusion begins with his adoption of the message of his own prophets and his implicit recognition that Micaiah speaks the truth, contrary to Ahab's own prophets.

The confrontation with Micaiah reaches its climax in the assault of Zedekiah (22:24) and the confinement imposed by the king until the truth of his words can be verified (vv. 26–27). "Amon the ruler of the city" and "Joash the king's son" represent civil and regal authority. They are jointly responsible for sustaining Micaiah with sufficient physical provision until the king returns safely from battle. Restraint imposed on the prophet will prevent him from disseminating his pernicious views among the people. Micaiah for his part simply responds according to the prophetic test of truth as found in Deuteronomy 18: 21–22. If Zedekiah and Ahab are vindicated, death is his well-deserved fate.

Ahab's resolve to attack at Ramoth Gilead does not leave the question long in limbo. With the consultation at an impasse, the scene moves to the battlefront. His plan is to go into the battle disguised as a soldier, with Jehoshaphat filling the role of military leader. Ahab is the chief military leader, but disguises himself as an ordinary soldier because of the prophecy

---

9. M. Saebo, "פתה," *THAT*, 2:497.

10. Block, "What Has Delphi to do with Samaria?" This is not only an Old Testament phenomena; Paul declares that the activity of Satan with all his signs and wonders and wicked deception will cause people to reject the truth. For this reason God sends them a strong delusion (*planēs*) so they believe a lie (*pseudei*), in order that they may be condemned (2 Thess. 2:9–12).

that the army will return without its king (22:17).[11] Though he has chosen to disregard the oracle, he is not able to ignore it.

The strategy of the Aramean chariot commanders is to single out the king of Israel (22:31). Since Jehoshaphat alone is distinguished by the insignia of the military leader, the warriors focus their attention on him (v. 32). The outcry of Jehoshaphat informs them he is not the king of Israel, or it is a cry of alarm by which they recognize they have the wrong person. Ahab is hit by an inadvertent shot that pierces the scales of his armor at a vulnerable point. The shot is not an accident, however; it confirms the judgment that has been pronounced by Micaiah.

The wounded king demands to be taken from the troops; this is the first step in separating his fate from that of the army (22:34). The battle intensifies throughout the day, while the king faces the army propped up in his chariot. The end of the day seals the separate destinies of king and army. At evening the king dies (v. 35b), the blood from his mortal wound draining and collecting at the bottom of the chariot. At sunset, the army disperses; each of the soldiers returns to his own place of residence (v. 36). By the end of the day the king's effort to subvert the word of doom spoken against him fails (v. 35).[12] The central occurrence of the battle is the death of the king at Ramoth Gilead and the return of the armies in peace without their shepherd.

The death of the king is the first oracle to receive fulfillment on that fateful day. The body of the king is returned to Samaria, where the chariot is washed (22:37–38). Dogs lick up the blood of the slain king, fulfilling the judgment pronounced by Elijah for slaying Naboth (cf. 21:19).[13] In that day confrontation between king and prophet is resolved. The whole event is about the fate of Ahab. The Aramean commander has no obvious interest in victory over the Israelites. His charioteers were commanded to target the king of Israel (v. 31); they passed up an opportunity to capture his ally (vv. 32–33). The defiance of Ahab in his death stands as a stark contrast to his humility when Elijah denounced him for the murder of Naboth (21:27–29).

---

11. DeVries follows Malamat in translating *ḥpś* as "girding for combat" rather than disguise, the essential contrast that of Jehoshaphat wearing the royal insignia, while the king of Israel is armed as an ordinary soldier (*Prophet against Prophet*, 40, n. 10).

12. DeVries finds narrative and theological significance in the phrase "at evening." The phrase "in that day" telescopes an event and its consequences into one day. Evening designates its termination, bringing a denouement to the climactic events; Simon J. DeVries, *Yesterday, Today and Tomorrow* (Grand Rapids: Eerdmans, 1975), 112–13.

13. The reference to prostitutes bathing in water stained by the king's blood is not explained. The versions emend it to the washing of the king's armor (*zᵉyānôt*) rather than prostitutes (*zônôt*). Another possibility is to read pigs (*ḥazîrîm*) for prostitutes; dogs and swine were the scavengers of ancient cities.

The epilogue on Ahab's reign notes his significant achievements and his royal burial as a great king (22:39–40). The peaceful death of Ahab is recorded as a standard feature of the regnal framework.[14] The paneling and furniture of his palace were inlaid with ivory, a sign of affluence and commercial relationships in the Iron Age (cf. Amos 3:15).[15] He fortified and developed various cities, including Samaria the capital. The ninth-century period at Megiddo (Stratum VA-IVB) had several monumental palatial buildings built of ashlar masonry, some of which may have been Ahab's work. Ahaziah took refuge in Megiddo at the time of Jehu's revolt, indicating the administrative importance of the city until that time.[16] Jericho is mentioned as another city rebuilt by Ahab at a terrible cost (cf. 16:34). The reign of Ahab is among the most influential and, by temporal standards, an almost incomparable success.

The Reign of Jehoshaphat (22:41–50)

ACCORDING TO THE Hebrew text, Jehoshaphat begins his reign in the fourth year of Ahab (22:41), so that his twenty-five year reign extends into the fifth year of Joram son of Ahab (2 Kings 8:16).[17] This chronology accounts for Jehoshaphat's being present in the battle against Moab during the time of Joram (2 Kings 3:1–27). The synchronisms of the Old Greek text (Lucian) sets the reign of Jehoshaphat earlier, beginning in the eleventh year of Omri (Ahab's father), so that his death would have occurred during the brief reign of Ahaziah, just after the twenty-two year reign of Ahab (1 Kings 16:29).

However, the Hebrew text has two synchronisms for the beginning of the reign of Jehoram son of Jehoshaphat. Jehoram is already in the second year of his reign when Ahaziah son of Ahab dies (2 Kings 1:17); this accords with the Greek chronology. A second synchronism states that Jehoram begins to reign in the fifth year of Joram son of Ahab when Jehoshaphat is still king

---

14. The phrase is usually taken as positive proof that the account of his violent death has been secondarily applied to him. This tension is no greater than the statement that his punishment was postponed because of his humility (21:29). The phrase is usually lacking for kings taken over by a coup or dying in battle; Naʾaman thinks Ahab is an exception: "Prophetic Stories as Sources for the Histories of Jehoshaphat and the Omrides," *Bib* 78 (1997): 167.

15. For a survey of major known ivories and the techniques of the craft, see Hershel Shanks, "Ancient Ivory: The Story of Wealth, Decadence and Beauty," *BAR* 11/5 (1985): 40–53.

16. See Ussishkin, "Jezreel, Samaria and Megiddo," 358–61.

17. Ahab reigned twenty-two years (1 Kings 16:29) and his son Ahaziah just over one in nonaccession year reckoning (22:52); thus, the twenty-five year reign of Jehoshaphat extends to the fifth year of Ahab's son Joram.

(2 Kings 8:16). According to the Hebrew text, Jehoshaphat appoints his son Jehoram as coregent during the reign of Ahab and before the battle against Moab. The sole rule of Jehoram begins only in the fifth year of Joram son of Ahab. The reign of Jehoshaphat does extend into the reign of Joram son of Ahab, which explains his presence at the battle of Moab. Jehoshaphat thus begins his reign in the fourth year of Ahab, not during the time of Omri.

In Kings, events of the reign of Jehoshaphat are related in accounts of his wars with Israelite kings. His own reign is recounted in a regnal résumé. He is given credit for purging the "male shrine prostitutes." His resolution of hostilities with Israel includes the marriage of his son Jehoram to Athaliah, daughter of Ahab (2 Kings 8:18). Edom is still subject to Judah in the time of Jehoshaphat (v. 47); during the reign of Jehoram, Edom revolts and set up its own king in perpetuity (2 Kings 8:20–22; 2 Chron. 21:8–10). Like Solomon, Jehoshaphat controls the seaport at Ezion Geber on the Gulf of Aqaba (1 Kings 22:48; cf. 9:26), but his effort to launch a sailing fleet fails. Apparently he attempts to renovate the ships used by Solomon, but they prove to be unseaworthy and never leave port.[18] The Judean mariners are not prepared for such voyages, but Jehoshaphat refuses the assistance of Ahaziah, whose alliance with Phoenician expertise may have been of great assistance (22:49).

The two kingdoms ally themselves against the Arameans, but Jehoshaphat determines to maintain his economic and territorial independence. His control of Edom supports Israel because it cuts off Aramean access to the Red Sea. For this reason Israel, Judah, and Edom unite to resist Moabite aspirations for independence (2 Kings 3:4–27).

Bridging Contexts

ISRAEL AND ARAM. The biblical narrative asserts a treaty alliance between Ahab and the Arameans (1 Kings 20:34), though not always a peaceful one. The Kurkh Monolith inscription of Shalmaneser III, which describes the Aramean coalition at Qarqar, likewise shows that Ahab stood in a treaty relationship with the Aramean king.[19] But Israel was not a satellite state of Aram-Damascus; Ahab was able to retrieve territory that had been lost. The war with Ramoth Gilead was an attempt to enforce the terms imposed on Ben-Hadad at the treaty of Aphek. These events must have been shortly after the battle of Qarqar, since that coalition

---

18. The text is not clear (see *BHS*); a change in verse division would say "a deputy of King Jehoshaphat made Tarshish-style ships to journey to Ophir for gold" (22:48b–49). For this type of ship and the location of Ophir, see the discussion at 10:22.

19. K. Lawson Younger Jr., "Kurkh Monolith," in *Context of Scripture*, 2.113A, ii 86b–102.

took place in the last year of his reign.[20] Dispute over a treaty did not preclude a coalition against a common enemy.

The same western alliance seems to have remained intact confronting Shalmaneser again in 849, 848, and 845 B.C.[21] The change in Aramean dominance over Israel is most easily explained with the coup of Hazael and his wars with Joram at Ramoth Gilead (2 Kings 8:28–29). The disintegration of the coalition enabled the Assyrian victories beginning in 841 B.C.

Israelite kings and God's will. If the prophetic message recorded in Kings was to have validity, it had to be anchored in the official annals of the kings of Israel.[22] The truth about God and the people was established in accepted political events. Prophetic records complemented the archival annals. The visions of Micaiah son of Imlah were not retained in royal sources, which merely recorded that "Ahab slept with his fathers" (1 Kings 22:40). The Deuteronomistic prophets retained this appraisal, even though it was obviously contrary to the usual epitaph for an ignoble death. They found it sufficiently consistent to juxtapose this with the irrational behavior of a king who virtually brought his death on himself.

Fully realizing that Micaiah was being pressured into conformity by Ahab's own prophets, the king willfully challenges what he knows to be a word from Yahweh. A word of prophecy given by those who follow false worship has no more integrity than the life of such prophets. Micaiah confirms in a vision the culpability of following such prophecies. It is an evidence of divine judgment already determined against a recalcitrant king.

A distinction between the function of the government and the practice of faith is necessary, even under the ideal of a theocracy (the belief that God is the real ruler of the nation).[23] Nations around Israel practiced a kind of theocracy in which the king was anointed by his god so long as he ruled; his rules were the rules of the gods.[24] Citizens of the state could not question

---

20. Cf. Cogan, *1 Kings*, 498. See appendix B for the chronology of Ahab.

21. Malamat, "The Arameans," 144–45.

22. It is true that populist agitators such as Michael Moore create political propaganda in the guise of documentary. In an online publication "Slate," Christopher Hitchens described Michael Moore's movie *Fahrenheit 9/11* as "a sinister exercise in moral frivolity, crudely disguised as an exercise in seriousness" (reported by Richard Corliss, "The World According to Michael," *Time* 164 (July 12, 2004): 52. Ancient historians should not be compared to manipulation in modern media for election purposes. They saw themselves as prophets carrying out the solemn task of revealing the work of God in the history of the nation.

23. Gideon, for example, refused the offer of kingship with the declaration that only God could be the king over Israel (Judg. 8:22–23).

24. The contrast between the biblical view of kingship and law to that of the other nations is developed by Moshe Greenberg, "Some Postulates of Biblical Criminal Law," in *The Jewish Expression*, ed. Judah Goldin (New York: Bantam, 1970), 18–37.

---

his legitimacy. The king made the rules for citizens as if received from the gods. An offense against the rules of state was an offense against the king himself.

In the biblical world, the values of life are given by God, not by the king; offenses are against the victim and against God, not against king and state. The king did not establish the law, but under the covenant he was responsible to enforce the law as given. God declared the way of life that was right for his people; prophets and priests told the king whether he was fulfilling that role. God did not rule through the king alone; the function of the king was to obey the will of God, punish offenders, and provide for their victims. Prophet and priest provided guidance, accountability, and reconciliation; when they failed in their task, the will of God also failed.

The roles of king, priest, and prophet were clearly specified (Deut. 17:14–18:22). The responsibility of the king was to know the covenant, which was managed by the priests, and to fulfill its requirements (Deut. 17:18–20). The king had no privileged status in religious practice or knowledge of the divine will. He was dependent on other mediators to know God's will. Priests or Levites were normally consulted for divination under the covenant, usually through the use of the Urim and Thummim. When the priest wore his vest in the inner sanctuary, he not only represented the people to God but also inquired for divine judgment on their behalf. In the choice of Joshua as successor to Moses, Eleazar the priest consulted the Urim on his behalf before the entire assembly (Num. 27:12–23). This method was capable of giving more than a positive or negative reply (Judg. 1:1–2; 20:18; 1 Sam. 10:22; 2 Sam. 5:23–24).[25]

Consultation with prophets rather than with priests in preparation for battle was outside usual procedure. Instead of the venerable Urim and Thummin were ecstatics who brandished symbolic tools (1 Kings 22:11–12). Jehoshaphat's suspicion appears well founded. Nevertheless, prophecy was a legitimate means of discerning the divine will. God promised to raise up a prophet like Moses who would continue to fill the revelatory role, as opposed to other forms of divination that were the abomination of the nations (Deut. 18:9–22). The role of the prophets was serious; failure to deliver the divine word was at the cost of their own life.

---

25. The method of communication is not known. A possible solution is that Urim and Thummim encompassed the letters of the alphabet, the name designating the first (ʾ [*urim*]) and last (*t*[*ummim*]) letters (a merism, like A to Z). For discussion see Milgrom, *Numbers*, 484–86. In support of this is a word found in the Dead Sea Scrolls: ʾwrtwm (1QH 4:6, 23; 18:29). It is probably formed from the words light (ʾwr) and perfect (*twm*). This would also explain why *Urim* and *Thummim* were chosen to represent the alphabet; God first created light (ʾwr) and finally declared creation as completed (*tmm*).

In governance Israel distinguished between the sacred and the common, or what we might call the secular. Among the other nations the king mediated the laws of the gods, so religion and governance functioned as a seamless entity. The king regulated and enforced the religion of the people. In Israel kings could be called to account by priests and prophets.

The prophet Amos, for example, was a farmer from Tekoa in the hill country of Judah (Amos 1:1). God called him to leave his own country to confront the evils of Jeroboam II king of Israel. Amaziah was serving as the priest of Jeroboam at Bethel (7:10). The judgment pronounced by Amos was unacceptable to him, as it threatened king and country, so he demanded the prophet leave (7:12–13). Amos in turn declared his unqualified independence from the religion of the state. He was not a prophet, nor the son of a prophet; he was called by God from his vocation as a farmer to speak God's word against the house of Jeroboam and the state of Israel (7:14–15). This calling of Amos could not be altered by the protestations of a priest in the service of the king. Israel was destined for exile according to the truth of his word (7:16–17). Neither king nor priest had control over the message of the prophet.

The indictment of the prophets who wrote Kings is that the kings of Israel never followed the covenant. They attempted to create a state religion of their own making, like the other nations. Ahab had his prophets who made it their priority to say what the king wanted to hear (22:13). The king also maintained the cult centers where the people worshiped. Ahab was typical of the other kings with whom he made alliances. There was only one exception to the support of the prophets: Micaiah. In the end Micaiah had no influence over the four hundred prophets in the service of the king; he merely determined the fate of the king in his declaration of God's plan.

Jehoshaphat is presented as a vacillating king; he calls for additional prophetic consultation, yet he submits to Ahab in going to war and risking his life. His reign is briefly summarized in Kings, as compared with the detailed account of his reforms and conquests in Chronicles (2 Chron. 17:1–20:36). The Chronicler read Kings as expressing a negative view of Jehoshaphat and is unequivocal in retaining that viewpoint. Jehoshaphat does follow the policies of Asa his father, who removed cult prostitution and idolatry (2 Chron. 20:32). Like Asa, he fails to remove the country shrines, which compromise worship at one central sanctuary (v. 33).

Particularly reprehensible is the alliance Jehoshaphat has with the northern kingdom, the one sin for which he is severely castigated. After the battle at Ramoth Gilead, Jehu the son of Hanani confronts Jehoshaphat in the palace to reprimand him and declare that great wrath rests on him, though no consequence is noted (2 Chron. 19:1–3). Later, Eliezer son of Dodavahu declares that the achievements of Jehoshaphat will be destroyed (20:37); the loss of his trading fleet is because of his union with Ahaziah son of Ahab.

In Chronicles, one of the lessons to be learned from Jehoshaphat is that judgment can be mollified, if not averted, by timely action. The warning of Jehu is followed by the report of a major judicial reform (2 Chron. 19:4–11), as justice comes more centrally under the jurisdiction of the king in Jerusalem. More significantly, judicial reform is followed by an account of a major war against the hordes from Transjordan. Unlike the war against Moab reported in Kings, Jehoshaphat acts in complete dependence on God without any reliance on Israel or other allies (20:1–30). The result is an outstanding triumph for the Judean armies without any warfare on their part; their only action is the recovery of an enormous spoil.

The importance of humility, repentance, and complete reliance on God in the face of grave danger needs to be made repeatedly. For all this Jehoshaphat is not completely exonerated; approval for his reign remains qualified. Jehoshaphat does not achieve purity of worship. He continues to experience divine wrath to the extent that his efforts at economic success fail with the loss of his ships, but that judgment is certainly not what it might have been.

FREE HUMAN BEINGS and God's will. Life is dangerous. There is much outside of human control and much that cannot be known. At times decisions need to be made that involve danger. Without adequate knowledge or control in such circumstances, mortals are driven to seek power and knowledge outside their sphere. For Christians this is natural. Christians believe that God, the Creator, is in control of events and that he has a personal interest in those who trust him. The question for Christians, as it was for Ahab and Jehoshaphat, is how to access that power, how to obtain the knowledge that is necessary for particular decisions.

Magic and manipulation stand in contradiction to a Christian view of God. God is sovereign in every aspect of his providential care. The account of Ahab and Jehoshaphat in the war at Ramoth Gilead confirms this view of God. There was no question about the sovereignty of God; their intent was to learn the divine purpose to guide them in their course of action.

Situations like this are complicated by human volition. Ahab and Jehoshaphat both declared their desire to know the divine will, but neither of them seems to have been willing to follow through on the implications of that desire. Ahab chose to follow his own prophets, though he did not really believe they declared the will of Yahweh; Jehoshaphat thought it expedient to follow Ahab, though he specifically challenged Ahab's prophets and found them wanting. Perhaps they presumed on divine mercy or thought that their decision to proceed could influence the divine response. Their situation is not different from that of contemporary Christians. Often there seems to be ambiguity about God's will in particular situations; it is also difficult to distinguish between human volition and a genuine commitment to follow his will in all ways.

Another problem in discerning God's will for particular situations is the question of knowing how to ascertain it. Mysticism is practiced is various forms; one form is an encounter with God in which his word is immediately received for guidance in a particular situation. Sometimes such encounters are completely unsolicited and have made the recipients aware of information that is most pertinent to their situation. Most pastors have encountered such experiences, and in many instances they have been genuinely edifying. At the same time there is much that is declared to be God's will received in some form, sometimes even an interpretation of the Bible, which has no more to do with his will than the asseverations of Ahab's prophets.

Christians are agreed on the efficacy of prayer in discerning and doing God's will. This is not in contradiction to God's sovereignty over all things, nor is it a denial of humans to make their own decisions, for which they are fully responsible. Terrance Tiessen proposes a model of divine sovereignty that affirms meticulous providence and human freedom of a spontaneous or voluntary kind.[26] In a significant sense God fully determines human history and responds to his creatures within it. This responsiveness is facilitated by his possessing knowledge of how creatures will act in particular circumstances. This has been called God's "middle knowledge."

God's "natural knowledge" is those events that are determined by the past; God's "free knowledge" is the sum of all events that God knows because he has freely determined them; God's "middle knowledge" is that which God knows could happen if particular circumstances existed prior to and at the moment of the events in question. The "middle knowledge" model of providence proposes that God has determined the future on the basis of how people will freely respond to situations, including their response to his own persuasions or actions. Fully knowing how people will respond does not in any sense limit the freedom of that response; such knowledge is necessary if God is to carry out his sovereign purposes.

Libertarian freedom demands that it is impossible to have knowledge of how a free volitional being will necessarily respond given a certain set of circumstances. The actions of Ahab and Jehoshaphat are portrayed as being

---

26. For a summary of this view see Terrance Tiessen, *Providence and Prayer: How Does God Work in the World* (Downers Grove, Ill.: InterVarsity Press, 2000), 289–90.

their own pure volition, but fully within God's sovereign knowledge of their choices. God's will in this instance does not have to do with the outcome of the battle at Ramoth Gilead; it has to do with divine judgment of Ahab for choices that he has voluntarily made. Ahab knows this judgment through the prophet Micaiah well enough to fear it; he demands that only Jehoshaphat be identified as the military leader in battle.

This could do nothing to avert divine judgment. The Aramean soldiers were especially charged with targeting the king of Israel in battle; this was their own choice as a military strategy. When that attempt fails, they quite freely carry out God's judgment with the random shot of an arrow that pierces the king's armor. The divine will is carried out within the freely chosen actions of all the individuals involved. Ahab is not deceived; he fully knows that his prophets are lying and is told why they are lying. There is every reason for Ahab to have chosen differently, but he has passed the point of no return. He operates under delusion, a self-imposed blindness. The divine message plunges him headlong into judgment. This judgment does not violate Ahab's volition; it comes because of it.

Prayer is not only a means for discerning God's will; it is also a means for achieving it. Tiessen summarizes the importance of prayer in providence; in his eternal purpose God does not act alone.

> He has given his children the privilege of participation in his program for establishing his kingdom on earth. One of the most significant means of our involvement is through petitionary prayer, because it is here that we attempt to discern God's will in particular situations, we align our own desires with his, and then we ask God to do what we believe he wants to do. Although God could work without us, he delights to answer the prayers of his children, and to be glorified by their thanksgiving when he does so.... In prayer we do not seek to change God's mind. We seek to discern his will and to pray accordingly, believing that there are some things that God has determined to do in answer to prayer so that our prayers are a necessary—though not a sufficient—"cause" of the ultimate outcome.[27]

This is prayer as God intends it; it is not simply a desire to be prudent in a course of action. Even if we grant Ahab the most generous allowance in his desire to know God's will, it hardly appears that his desire is to align his desires with God's greater plan of providence. Prayer is not to manipulate God to achieve a particular personal desire, which seems more likely Ahab's motive in consulting with his prophets.

---

27. Ibid., 337.

Pressures on Christians to conform. A further issue for Christians is to live with integrity within a society that has a conflicting worldview. This was the problem for Jehoshaphat; while he desired to know God's will, he was unable to counter the worldview of the political forces arrayed against him. All advanced societies must come to terms with two fundamental issues.[28] One is the relation of the individual to society, the world of people. The second is the relation of the individual and society to the world of nature and to the universe itself. The first issue is addressed in law and government; the second issue finds expression in religion; in this respect every person in the world is religious.

The answers given to religion are largely determinative of the answers provided for law and government. In ancient cultures religion was a significant force on law and government. As part of its culture, the Bible is a work of history in which an understanding of political fortunes is determined by a particular view of the universe or the relationship of God with the peoples in his world. At the same time a defense of faith in the divine covenant could only be provided through an explanation of how God was at work in the history of his people. The Israelite answer to the question of the relation of society to the cosmos proceeded from the affirmation that a sole and omnipotent Lord is responsible for all creation. His ways are just and purposeful, and destiny is largely determined by a readiness to embrace and uphold his eternally valid covenant. Israel had a share in its destiny and was required to accept the challenge of this responsibility. Responsibility for their destiny granted them dignity and hope.

The issues of law and religion are interdependent, but they are seldom in true equilibrium. "It is this that makes for the immemorial rivalry between church and state."[29] It is evident that law and government in modern secular societies have been influenced by fundamental concepts of faith. American coins bear the phrase "In God We Trust." The name "The Dominion of Canada" was adopted from Psalm 72:8[30] through the influence of Sir Samuel Leonard Tilley, a Baptist from New Brunswick, representing confederation in 1864.

As law evolves in North America it reflects the changing influences of fundamental values. Advocacy for religious freedom has led to the restriction of

---

28. Speiser, "The Biblical Idea of History in its Common Near Eastern Setting," 2.
29. Ibid., 2.
30. Psalm 72 is a prayer for the king, with the request that his "dominion [will be] from sea to sea and from the river unto the ends of the earth" (72:8, KJV). This prayer concludes the declaration of the king coming to bring peace to the nations in Zech. 9:10. Jesus self-consciously undertook to enact this entry of the king into Jerusalem in his triumphal entry in the Gospels (Matt. 21:1−11; Mark 11:1−11; Luke 19:28−40; John 12:12−19).

religious freedom, such as the right to display a Christmas crèche in a public place or the right to have religious instruction in a public school. Advocacy of animal rights has brought restrictions to traditional livelihoods such as the fur industry and to the use of animals in scientific research. The metaphysical or religious views of those in control in a society determine the laws that govern individual rights and relationships of a society.

Conflict of belief is as intense in secular societies as it was in Israel. Faith in the God of history and order is confronted by a view of individual liberties and rights as a self-sustaining value that can be imposed by legal authority. Social values that began as liberalism have become a religion.[31] Liberalism arose as a solution to the destructive religious wars of Europe's past and succeeded because it allowed people of different perspectives to live together in the same society. Meaning in life was sought outside of politics itself. Contemporary social liberals have neither an ultimate purpose nor a pattern of virtue, so only the belief system itself can supply these essential elements of life.

Liberalism grants meaning to life by making its prescribed individual freedoms a moral necessity to be imposed on all, including those who do not hold to the same norms of human relationships. There is a continual expansion of concepts like racism and political correctness to create instances of "oppression." Racism once meant hatred of a person from another race, but it can now be freely applied to anyone who voices opposition to affirmative action, which is often racist and oppressive.

The feminism of Betty Friedan in *The Feminine Mystique* characterized the suburban home as a "comfortable concentration camp" for women. The use of Holocaust metaphors for a way of life she did not like was meant to endow the feminist crusade with an apocalyptic sense of urgency and significance. The right to kill the unborn, even when in the process of birth, is regarded as essential to freedom for women, and any alternative to abortion is regarded as oppressive of women.

As a religion, liberalism has become illiberal, incapable of even entering into reasonable debate over its own policies and values. Free speech and judicial restraint have been replaced by talk of oppression and rights as a way of reproducing good versus evil. Viewpoints based on faith or long-standing principle are demonized as a threat to social engineering according to individual choice as defined by liberal values.

Though the secular role of the state is necessary, it is absurd to think that faith is a purely private matter. If religion has no role in public society, then

---

31. Stanley Kurtz, "The Church of the Left: Finding Meaning in Liberalism," *The National Review Online* (May 31, 2001); see www.nationalreview.com/contributors/kurtz053101.shtml. Kurz is a fellow of the Hudson Institute.

secularism becomes a state religion of its own, imposing its own values on people of all faiths and religion.[32] This is really no different than Ahab choosing his own prophets who always say what he wants them to say. Values for ethics and law cannot be established apart from convictions that have a personal faith base, and in that sense are always religious. Freedom of religion in the secular state must not only allow for the public expression of various faiths, it must also allow for rational expression of faith convictions. To the extent that a state fails to do this, it will succumb to its own vices, just like Ahab and the state of Israel in listening only to their own prophets.

Christians, in this manifestation of a postmodern society, often find themselves in the unhappy lot of Jehoshaphat. Having a desire to seek an independent course of action, they are pressured in various ways to conform, even at risk to their own well-being. While they seek to do what is right, the high places remain and compromise the way of life they value most.

---

32. Professor David Novak illustrated this point in a lecture entitled "Can One Be Religious and Secular?" at Providence College, Otterburne MB, February 19, 2003.

1 Kings 22:51–2 Kings 1:18

❧

A HAZIAH SON OF Ahab became king of Israel in Samaria in the seventeenth year of Jehoshaphat king of Judah, and he reigned over Israel two years. ⁵²He did evil in the eyes of the LORD, because he walked in the ways of his father and mother and in the ways of Jeroboam son of Nebat, who caused Israel to sin. ⁵³He served and worshiped Baal and provoked the LORD, the God of Israel, to anger, just as his father had done.

¹:¹After Ahab's death, Moab rebelled against Israel. ²Now Ahaziah had fallen through the lattice of his upper room in Samaria and injured himself. So he sent messengers, saying to them, "Go and consult Baal-Zebub, the god of Ekron, to see if I will recover from this injury."

³But the angel of the LORD said to Elijah the Tishbite, "Go up and meet the messengers of the king of Samaria and ask them, 'Is it because there is no God in Israel that you are going off to consult Baal-Zebub, the god of Ekron?' ⁴Therefore this is what the LORD says: 'You will not leave the bed you are lying on. You will certainly die!'" So Elijah went.

⁵When the messengers returned to the king, he asked them, "Why have you come back?"

⁶"A man came to meet us," they replied. "And he said to us, 'Go back to the king who sent you and tell him, "This is what the LORD says: Is it because there is no God in Israel that you are sending men to consult Baal-Zebub, the god of Ekron? Therefore you will not leave the bed you are lying on. You will certainly die!"'"

⁷The king asked them, "What kind of man was it who came to meet you and told you this?"

⁸They replied, "He was a man with a garment of hair and with a leather belt around his waist."

The king said, "That was Elijah the Tishbite."

⁹Then he sent to Elijah a captain with his company of fifty men. The captain went up to Elijah, who was sitting on the top of a hill, and said to him, "Man of God, the king says, 'Come down!'"

¹⁰Elijah answered the captain, "If I am a man of God, may

fire come down from heaven and consume you and your fifty men!" Then fire fell from heaven and consumed the captain and his men.

¹¹At this the king sent to Elijah another captain with his fifty men. The captain said to him, "Man of God, this is what the king says, 'Come down at once!'"

¹²"If I am a man of God," Elijah replied, "may fire come down from heaven and consume you and your fifty men!" Then the fire of God fell from heaven and consumed him and his fifty men.

¹³So the king sent a third captain with his fifty men. This third captain went up and fell on his knees before Elijah. "Man of God," he begged, "please have respect for my life and the lives of these fifty men, your servants! ¹⁴See, fire has fallen from heaven and consumed the first two captains and all their men. But now have respect for my life!"

¹⁵The angel of the LORD said to Elijah, "Go down with him; do not be afraid of him." So Elijah got up and went down with him to the king.

¹⁶He told the king, "This is what the LORD says: Is it because there is no God in Israel for you to consult that you have sent messengers to consult Baal-Zebub, the god of Ekron? Because you have done this, you will never leave the bed you are lying on. You will certainly die!" ¹⁷So he died, according to the word of the LORD that Elijah had spoken.

Because Ahaziah had no son, Joram succeeded him as king in the second year of Jehoram son of Jehoshaphat king of Judah. ¹⁸As for all the other events of Ahaziah's reign, and what he did, are they not written in the book of the annals of the kings of Israel?

Original Meaning

THE REIGN OF Ahaziah was only somewhat more than a year (cf. 1 Kings 22:51; 2 Kings 3:1). The sins of his mother and father are both mentioned (1 Kings 22:53), since they are so instrumental in the ultimate demise of the kingdom of Israel. They actively pursued the Phoenician cult and resisted the true prophets of the covenant. Jeroboam son of Nebat presumed to worship Yahweh at the calf shrines rather than at the temple. Ahaziah offends Yahweh with his active pursuit of the Phoenician Baal cult, following the practice of his parents.

Reign of Ahaziah (1 Kings 22:51–2 Kings 1:1)

THE INTRODUCTORY SUMMARY of the reign of Ahaziah is regular in providing a synchronism with Jehoshaphat and giving the length of his reign.[1] The last year of the reign of Ahab was the battle of Qarqar in 853 B.C., a firm date in ancient Syrian chronology.[2] The reference to the rebellion of Moab complements the chronological data and the events of the reign of Ahaziah. A similar notation of the independence of Moab at the death of Ahab is found in the account of Joram allying with Jehoshaphat to restore Moabite subjection (2 Kings 3:5).

This is confirmed by the Mesha Inscription, in which the king of Moab refers to the occupation of Israel during the time of Omri and half that of his sons, a total of forty years.[3] Omri, Ahab, Ahaziah, and Joram rule a total of forty-eight years. The inscription affirms that the rebellion took place during the time of Omri's sons, approximately forty years from the time of Omri. The ambiguities of the inscription do not intend a precise calculation of time.[4] A closer correlation with the biblical chronology of the Omride dynasty is not possible.

The death of Ahab brings about a new era in the Omride dynasty. Moab rebels almost immediately, with both Edom and Libnah gaining independence during the reign of Joram (cf. 1 Kings 22:47; 2 Kings 8:20, 22). The days of the Israelite empire are over. The alliance of Ahab with the Arameans at the battle of Qarqar is the end of a period of international influence for Israel.

Confrontation with Elijah (1:2–18)

AHAZIAH IS AN apostate like his parents, but his particular sin is the act of seeking an oracle from Baal-Zebub, a god of the Philistines (2 Kings 2:2). He seeks a message for restored health after being injured in a fall from the upper level of his palace in Samaria. Baal-Zebub (lit., "lord of the flies") may have been a god to control disease, much as Zeus the healer was the "averter of

---

1. The Old Greek (Lucianic) text gives the synchronism as the twenty-fourth year of Jehoshaphat, to harmonize with the statement that Joram son of Ahab came to reign in the second year of Jehoram, son of Jehoshaphat (2 Kings 1:17). For the end of the twenty-five year reign of Jehoshaphat see comments on 1 Kings 22:41–42.

2. For the chronology see Appendix B.

3. K. D. Smelik, "The Inscription of King Mesha," in *Context of Scripture*, 2.23 line 8.

4. This is the conclusion of Donner and Röllig, *Kanaanäische und Aramäische Inschriften*, 2:174 (#181). They reject the proposal of Cross and Freedman that the Mesha Inscription refers to the midpoint of Joram's reign, which would be a total of 42 years (Omri 12 years, Ahab 22 years, Ahaziah 2 years, and Joram 6 years).

---

the flies."[5] However, Ahaziah is suffering from injury and not disease. It is likely that the name was originally Baal-Zebul ("lord of a lofty or exalted place"), an epithet used for Baal in Ugaritic literature.[6] This is the equivalent of the "lord of heaven" and would have been the name of the storm god Baal in Ekron.

The name Baal-Zebub is found repeatedly in the New Testament, with many manuscripts providing the alternate Baal-Zebul (cf. Matt. 10:25; 12:24; Mark 3:22). Baal-Zebub appears to have been a derogatory pun on the original name. Ekron is identified with Khirbat al-Muqanna, the northernmost of the five Philistine cities on the border of the territory settled by Israel (cf. Josh. 13:3). It is a prudent place for Ahaziah to stay when seeking an oracle from a Baal prophet.

The desire to receive an oracle from Baal-Zebub, as if there were no God in Israel (2 Kings 1:3), becomes the occasion for Elijah to confront once again the apostate house of Omri. The messenger of Yahweh commissions Elijah to intercept the messengers of the king with an oracle of doom, telling the king that he will not recover from his injuries (1:3–4). This incites a conflict between Elijah and the messengers of the king, which in reality is a conflict between Ahaziah and Yahweh.

The impact of the struggle in the narrative is achieved through the double meaning of the word "messenger" (malʾāk).[7] This Hebrew word refers to both the "angel [of the LORD]" and to the "messengers [of the king]" (v. 3). God exercises his authority through the first messenger, while King Ahaziah can do nothing more than extend his power through military messengers. The divine messenger counters the first messengers of the king, subverting their quest. The king's messengers in effect return with an oracle from Yahweh rather than Baal-Zebub (1:5–6).

The king recognizes Elijah by his description as a hairy man (1:8)[8] and takes up the challenge by immediately sending a military unit to arrest him (vv. 9–14). The military officers are no match for the power of Yahweh

---

5. Montgomery, *The Books of Kings*, 349.
6. The phrase *zbl bʿl ʾrṣ* ("prince lord of the earth") is found parallel with *aliyn bʿl* ("exalted lord") when Anat announces the death of Baal (*KTU* 1.6 i 41, 42), and repeatedly in the column seeking the fate of Baal (iii 1–2, 8–9, 20–21).
7. Burke O. Long, *2 Kings* (FOTL 10; Grand Rapids: Eerdmans, 1991), 12–13.
8. The description of Elijah as the "owner of hair" (*baʿal śēʿār*) refers to his appearance rather than to his wearing a "garment of hair" (NIV). Elijah did have a mantle (cf. 1 Kings 19:13, 19), and perhaps even a hairy one (cf. Zech. 13:4), but the tradition taken up by John the Baptist as part of his costume developed in later times (Matt. 3:4). If all the prophets had worn a hairy garment, the king could not have recognized immediately that his messengers had encountered Elijah.

through Elijah and are repeatedly consumed by fire. In the end the king's messengers finally get their way (vv. 15–16), but it has nothing to do with their power. The messenger (angel) of Yahweh comes to Elijah again, instructing him to go down to the king, so that Elijah may personally deliver the same oracle to the king.

Ahaziah is portrayed as someone relentlessly driven to his own destruction. The king intends to solicit the power of foreknowledge and healing from the god of Ekron, but when frustrated in his efforts by the messenger of Yahweh, he turns his focus on Elijah. In treating Elijah as his enemy he inadvertently keeps coming into direct conflict with Yahweh through his military messengers. Obsessively calling down Elijah the Tishbite is in reality to summon the Lord of Israel whom he is seeking to deny. Though the king refuses to acknowledge this reality, it is evident to the reader that he cannot escape the presence and judgment of Israel's God.

When the king gets his request to meet his nemesis Elijah face to face, the result is nothing more than a repetition of the inevitable oracle of doom. The repeated exchange of the messengers dramatizes the superior and dangerous power of God connected with the prophetic oracle. God emerges from his remote recess and takes control, first delivering his prophecy through the messengers of Ahaziah and then through Elijah. Each of Ahaziah's actions moves him inexorably toward the judgment reserved for him because of his rejection of the God of the covenant.

The account of Ahaziah does not tell about his life but about his death. With the appearance of Elijah before the king, Ahaziah's death according to the divine oracle is simply reported. The narrative concludes with the summary of his reign and the introduction of the next king. The usual formula appears somewhat disjointed in the Hebrew text. The accession of his successor is given before the typical concluding summary (1:17b–18); the synchronism to the second year of Jehoram is marked as separate in the Hebrew text by a long spacing.[9] The intrusive phrase is the only synchronism to introduce the reign of Joram brother of Ahaziah as the next king. Though the origin of this synchronism is in doubt, it is in harmony with the chronology of Joram son of Ahab. Jehoshaphat appoints Jehoram his son as king during the reign of Ahab, before he goes to war against Moab. The sole rule of Jehoram began in the fifth year of Joram son of Ahab (8:16), at the end of the twenty-five year reign of Jehoshaphat.

---

9. The Greek text does not include the synchronism to Jehoram but has here four extra verses, most of which are found in the introduction to Joram son of Ahab (2 Kings 3:1–3). These include a synchronism with the eighteenth year of Jehoshaphat.

Bridging Contexts

CHALLENGING GOD'S AUTHORITY. The account of Ahaziah provides no information about political developments; it reports his tragic personal history and his devotion to the religion of his parents. The narrative advances the succession of the Omride kings and demonstrates the incorrigibility of their religion.

The reign of Ahaziah is a time of transition between the prophet Elijah and the prophet Elisha. One of the last acts of Elijah is to declare the judgment of death on Ahaziah because he has denied God in seeking help from Baal-Zebub, god of the Philistines in Ekron. The king inadvertently comes into confrontation with the prophet when his royal messengers are intercepted as a result of divine intervention.

DeVries classifies the encounter of Ahaziah with Elijah as a "prophet-authorization narrative."[10] In these narratives the theme of conflict with institutional authority becomes a constant constitutive factor. The institutional authority under challenge is that of the king. In the Elijah-versus-Baal story, the direct conflict is with the rival cult sponsored by Ahab (1 Kings 18–19). In that story the royal threat comes through Jezebel, and the power of the prophet is reaffirmed at Horeb. In the confrontation with Ahaziah, a regal threat may be implied, but the king's only demand is that the prophet meet him at his palace. The conflict is with the king directly, but in his capacity as a sponsor of the Baal cult.

The king apparently avoids Elijah in an attempt to avert divine judgment. The prophet is commissioned to intervene, but his identity is not revealed to the king's messengers. They only know him as "a man" (v. 6); the king is able to identify the prophet through their description. He is determined to intimidate the prophet and thereby destroy the evil oracle spoken against him. But the overwhelming authority of the prophet is more than abundantly demonstrated; the military commander of the third contingent can only plead that his life and the lives of his soldiers be spared. Elijah consents to meet the king, not to be arrested or exiled but to confront him with a word that he can no longer resist. The fulfillment of that prophetic word is merely reported; all the details of the narrative focus on the person and authority of the prophet. Elijah is vindicated as decisively as at the contest at Mount Carmel.

Ahaziah's rejection of Yahweh in his time of deep distress results in an irrevocable judgment. His fate is stated unequivocally three times: "You will

---

10. DeVries, *Prophet against Prophet*, 58–59. He includes in this classification the account of the Bethel altar (1 Kings 12:1–32), the famine in the siege against Samaria (2 Kings 6:24–7:17), and the confrontation between Elijah and Baal (1 Kings 17–18).

not leave the bed you are lying on. You will certainly die" (2 Kings 1:4, 6, 16). Ahaziah knows well the experiences of his father with this prophet. He has chosen to continue the policies of his father, also under the pressure of his mother, who continues to take royal matters into her own hands as she did in the case of Naboth (cf. 1 Kings 22:53; 2 Kings 9:36–37). Seeking a prophet outside of Israel is necessitated by his allegiance to his mother and his unwillingness to abdicate her religion.

The prophetic authors have a well-focused objective in recording the demise of the Omride kings. Their goal is to teach the truth of the words of the covenant that serve as the charter for the nation:

> See, I set before you today life and prosperity, death and destruction. For I command you today to love the LORD our God, to walk in his ways, and to keep his commands, decrees and laws; then you will live and increase, and the LORD your God will bless you in the land you are crossing the Jordan to enter and possess. . . .
>
> This day I call heaven and earth as witnesses against you that I have set before you life and death, blessings and curses. Now choose life, so that you and your children may live. (Deut. 30:15–16, 19)

The life of Ahaziah calls on the Israelites to make a choice. They can be the people of God and have life, or they can follow the ways of the nations and have death. Will the Israelites choose life in hearing the words of the prophets, or will they be like Ahaziah and seek to escape the divine word of judgment? For the authors of Kings, this power struggle between king and prophet is not a question of political control. Rather, it is a question of the survival of the nation itself. The appeal of the third captain makes this choice clear (1:14); the king is powerless before the messenger of Yahweh. He can do nothing more to save the nation than to save himself.

Elijah's role is to intervene in the crisis facing the nation. The destruction of the elite soldiers of the king needs to be understood in this context. Elijah is remembered as the spokesperson for the guarantor of the covenant. As Ben Sirach says, "Never in his lifetime did he tremble before any ruler nor could anyone intimidate him at all" (Sir. 48:12, NRSV). Elijah is the means of hope and life: "Happy are those who saw you and were adorned with your love! For we also shall surely live" (v. 11). Elijah provides yet another opportunity for the nation to enjoy the blessing of life. Failure to follow the appeal of the prophet is to share in the fate of the king.

The questions of authority and life extend into the New Testament and the life of the church. The question of authority is the central issue leading up to the crucifixion. Like Ahaziah with Elijah, the authorities were unable to arrest Jesus except by his permission. When they did get their way in the crucifixion, they did not succeed in establishing their authority but brought judgment on themselves.

The triumphal entry of Jesus into Jerusalem was an explicit declaration of authority and power. Jesus deliberately mounted a donkey and rode into the city, declaring himself to be the king spoken about by Zechariah the prophet. Zechariah prophesied that the king of Zion would come riding on a donkey; without weapons of war he would bring peace to the nations and establish a universal dominion (Mark 11:1–11; cf. Zech. 9:9–10). Jesus proceeded into the temple and tossed out those exchanging money for sacrifices, declaring their business to be fraudulent. This so offended the temple officials that they were prepared to kill Jesus, but they were thwarted by his authority (Mark 11:15–18). His authority was the power of his teaching, which captivated the minds of the crowds (v. 18).

Later Jesus was confronted directly by the officials with the demand that he declare the source of his authority (Mark 11:27–33). Jesus diverted their attempt to trap him by asking whether the baptism of John was of God or human beings. Authority again rested in the opinion of the people; since the people held John to be a prophet, it was impossible to say it was not of God, even though the officials did not accept it as from God.

The parable of the vineyard (Mark 12:1–12) was a particular affront to the power of the officials. The comparison to the leaders of Jerusalem condemned by the prophet Isaiah was unmistakable. Isaiah had compared the leaders of the nation to a treacherous vineyard that yielded rotten fruit in spite of the best provisions for its yield (Isa. 5:1–7). Jesus adapted the parable to make it applicable to himself as the Son of God killed by the caretakers of the vineyard. This enraged the leaders so they sought to kill him immediately, but they feared the people (Mark 12:12).

A series of questions followed in which the authority of Jesus was challenged in the hopes of accusing him of false teaching. These included questions about the duty to pay taxes, always a hot topic (Mark 12:13–17), questions about resurrection (vv. 18–27), and a question about the most important commandment (vv. 28–34). Jesus then finally asked them a question about David's Son, quoting from Psalm 110 to show that the Son of David was to be greater in authority and position than David himself (vv. 35–37). This delighted the crowds but exasperated the leaders and officials since it vindicated the claims of Jesus against them. He concluded with a warning against authority found in official position, because it all too readily becomes a masquerade for greed and self-interest (vv. 38–40). Such authorities stand under a greater judgment.

IN THE CATACOMBS. The authority of Elijah was grounded in his uncompromising allegiance to God in the teaching of the covenant. The divine purpose was revealed through Elijah in his confrontations with King Ahaziah. The authority of Jesus was established with the people through his use of the Scriptures. Those who purported to represent the truth of the Scriptures backed by official authority were powerless when confronted by a teacher whose use of the Scripture convinced the crowds of his authenticity. Through the power of God his death was a victory. His parting words to his disciples were that "all power in heaven and on earth has been given to me" (Matt. 28:18). He promised that this power would be with his followers always, even to the end of the world.

This power continues to be the authority of the church. The church has often claimed and used temporal powers, but often not to the advancement of its mission in the world. The kingdom of God is not like those of this world. In the kingdom of God the last will be first and the first will be last (Matt. 20:16); those who wish to be great must be those who serve, just as Jesus did not come to be served but to serve (vv. 27–28). Temporal power does not assist the church in the accomplishment of its mission, but neither can temporal power prevent the growth of the church.

It is vital that church leaders always adhere to the genuine source of their authority, which is found in faithfulness to the revelation of God for his world. Their power lies in teaching this truth to the people. Government powers of this world cannot control this power. The Reformation stands as a testimony to this truth. Martin Luther, with the truth of Scripture, was able to confront the power entrenched in the church of his time with all its backing of government authority. In the five hundredth anniversary of the year of his birth, *National Geographic* featured a major article on Luther, including a reproduction of a painting that depicts the events and people at the Diet of Worms in April 1521.[11] At Worms Luther was asked two questions: Were these his books? And was he ready to revoke the heresies they contained? The second question required time to consider.

> At 6:00 p.m. the following day Luther was led into a larger, torchlit room packed to suffocation with the empire's notables. To disown some of his books would be to condemn simple Christian morality.... Dark eyes flashing, voice clear and strong, he ended with ringing defiance: "Unless proved wrong by Scripture and plain reason ... my conscience

---

11. Merle Severy, "The World of Luther," *National Geographic* 164/4 (October 1983): 418–63.

is captive to the Word of God. I cannot and will not recant.... God help me. Amen." Here he stood. Being Luther, he could do not other.[12]

The church today can do no other. The spirit of Elijah is no less necessary for the church today, than it was in the times when a king of Israel sought Baal-Zebub for an oracle.

The examples of Jesus and Martin Luther are only partially analogous to Elijah; neither brought fire down from heaven to consume their adversaries. The Gospels make clear that Jesus' life was not taken from him; he chose to give his life to his aggressors with the words, "Father, forgive them, for they know not what they are doing" (Luke 23:34). The triumph of his authority was in the resurrection rather than the death of those who came to arrest him.

Luther staked his authority on the Word of God and prayer, but his actual survival depended on the temporal powers of Frederick the Wise. Frederick obtained a promise from Emperor Charles V that Luther should not be condemned unheard and should appear before the Diet. Luther traveled to the imperial Diet at Worms under the safe custody of a heretic, though the cavalcade of German knights that attended him made it more like a triumphant procession. The Diet did pass an edict that declared Luther to be an outlaw whose writings were proscribed. In order to protect him on his return, high in the Thuringian Forest, Luther's wagon was set upon by horsemen. In a mock abduction, Luther was spirited off to Wartburg Castle. Disguised as a bearded squire—Junker Georg—Luther lived for ten months alone with God and the devil under the protective custody of Frederick. The edict shadowed Luther and fettered his movements all his days.

In a free and democratic society, temporal power of government ought not to be a threat to any law-abiding citizen. This does not mean absence of discrimination in favor of a separate set of values favored and promoted by the state. Thomas Berg offers the following analogy of the church in America.

This is not a good time for religious freedom in American law. More and more, U.S. courts are explicitly embracing arguments that religious freedom extends only to those religious practices that are confined and compartmentalized. Religious practices are explicitly receiving reduced protection if the practice pervades the believer's life rather than being limited to one facet, and if the believer applies his or her faith in the broader world rather than limiting it to the person's religious community. These trends can be captured in the proposition that today one can enjoy religious freedom only in the catacombs, as the first-century Christians did. They lived daily in the broader Roman

---

12. Ibid., 449.

society. But in the periodic times of persecution, they could not exercise the faith publicly. They could only worship and practice the faith at night and underground.[13]

Berg immediately makes clear that restricted freedoms simply because of faith must not be compared with the violent persecutions that drove early Christians underground. Nevertheless public policy has a religion of its own that is intolerant of other values. Berg's first example of restricted freedom is a decision in which the Supreme Court held that a student at an evangelical college could be denied a state scholarship for which he qualified in every stipulation of grades and financial need. The reason was that he chose to major in theology in preparation to be a pastor. The court held that the state was not obligated because it could treat clergy training as a "distinct category of instruction" from all other courses of study. It argued that the procurement of taxpayer's funds to support church leaders in the past was a source of popular unrest.

In another decision, the California Supreme Court ruled against a program of Catholic Charities seeking to provide prescription-drug insurance coverage for employees that did not include contraceptives. Private employers are not obligated to provide such insurance, but if they do so, they cannot stipulate limitations for such coverage. Catholic Charities believes that social justice and religious conscience requires it to provide such coverage, but their understanding of sexual acts prevents them from including contraceptives. The exemption of contraceptives would have been permissible if the purpose of the entity were the inculcation of religious values, but this did not pertain because the plan offered its service to the needy irrespective of religious values. The mindset is that any social service that reaches out to the community indiscriminately must also lose its religious identity. The church may maintain its values within its insular community—in the catacombs—but outside of that narrow limitation may not retain its own lines of conscience in social support.

The prophet Elijah did not envision a pluralistic society that would seek to equally accommodate all versions of faith and values. In his context it was intolerable that the king should actively adhere to the religious values of a surrounding culture. In this he fearlessly confronted the state authority. The modern ideals of pluralism are good and necessary; coercion in matters of faith is not God's way. However, justice in such a plurality is an exceedingly difficult matter, and the church increasingly will find the power of the state oppressive. This should not cause fear or despair; Christ will build his church, and government authority will not prevail against it.

---

13. Thomas C. Berg, "Religious Life in the Catacombs," *America* 190/19 (June 2004): 17–18.

2 Kings 2:1–25

WHEN THE Lord was about to take Elijah up to heaven in a whirlwind, Elijah and Elisha were on their way from Gilgal. ²Elijah said to Elisha, "Stay here; the LORD has sent me to Bethel."

But Elisha said, "As surely as the LORD lives and as you live, I will not leave you." So they went down to Bethel.

³The company of the prophets at Bethel came out to Elisha and asked, "Do you know that the LORD is going to take your master from you today?"

"Yes, I know," Elisha replied, "but do not speak of it."

⁴Then Elijah said to him, "Stay here, Elisha; the LORD has sent me to Jericho."

And he replied, "As surely as the LORD lives and as you live, I will not leave you." So they went to Jericho.

⁵The company of the prophets at Jericho went up to Elisha and asked him, "Do you know that the LORD is going to take your master from you today?"

"Yes, I know," he replied, "but do not speak of it."

⁶Then Elijah said to him, "Stay here; the LORD has sent me to the Jordan."

And he replied, "As surely as the LORD lives and as you live, I will not leave you." So the two of them walked on.

⁷Fifty men of the company of the prophets went and stood at a distance, facing the place where Elijah and Elisha had stopped at the Jordan. ⁸Elijah took his cloak, rolled it up and struck the water with it. The water divided to the right and to the left, and the two of them crossed over on dry ground.

⁹When they had crossed, Elijah said to Elisha, "Tell me, what can I do for you before I am taken from you?"

"Let me inherit a double portion of your spirit," Elisha replied.

¹⁰"You have asked a difficult thing," Elijah said, "yet if you see me when I am taken from you, it will be yours—otherwise not."

¹¹As they were walking along and talking together, suddenly a chariot of fire and horses of fire appeared and separated the two of them, and Elijah went up to heaven in a

whirlwind. ¹²Elisha saw this and cried out, "My father! My father! The chariots and horsemen of Israel!" And Elisha saw him no more. Then he took hold of his own clothes and tore them apart.

¹³He picked up the cloak that had fallen from Elijah and went back and stood on the bank of the Jordan. ¹⁴Then he took the cloak that had fallen from him and struck the water with it. "Where now is the LORD, the God of Elijah?" he asked. When he struck the water, it divided to the right and to the left, and he crossed over.

¹⁵The company of the prophets from Jericho, who were watching, said, "The spirit of Elijah is resting on Elisha." And they went to meet him and bowed to the ground before him. ¹⁶"Look," they said, "we your servants have fifty able men. Let them go and look for your master. Perhaps the Spirit of the LORD has picked him up and set him down on some mountain or in some valley."

"No," Elisha replied, "do not send them."

¹⁷But they persisted until he was too ashamed to refuse. So he said, "Send them." And they sent fifty men, who searched for three days but did not find him. ¹⁸When they returned to Elisha, who was staying in Jericho, he said to them, "Didn't I tell you not to go?"

¹⁹The men of the city said to Elisha, "Look, our lord, this town is well situated, as you can see, but the water is bad and the land is unproductive."

²⁰"Bring me a new bowl," he said, "and put salt in it." So they brought it to him.

²¹Then he went out to the spring and threw the salt into it, saying, "This is what the LORD says: 'I have healed this water. Never again will it cause death or make the land unproductive.'" ²²And the water has remained wholesome to this day, according to the word Elisha had spoken.

²³From there Elisha went up to Bethel. As he was walking along the road, some youths came out of the town and jeered at him. "Go on up, you baldhead!" they said. "Go on up, you baldhead!" ²⁴He turned around, looked at them and called down a curse on them in the name of the LORD. Then two bears came out of the woods and mauled forty-two of the youths. ²⁵And he went on to Mount Carmel and from there returned to Samaria.

THE CONFRONTATION OF the apostasy of Ahaziah is the last activity of Elijah reported in the book of Kings.[1] With Elijah's ascension to heaven, prophetic responsibility to hold Israel accountable for covenant fidelity is transferred to Elisha. This transition is the focal point of the final activities of Elijah, as he announces the death of Ahaziah and is then translated from the land by the heavenly cavalry.

Two contingents of prophets receive and relay the same message: Elijah is to be removed as the leader "today" (2:3, 5). The expression "today" calls attention to the central epitome of the narrative, in this case marking the transition to the next phase of prophetic activity.[2] Elisha's acknowledgment of these messages is indicative of their being preparatory to the climactic declaration of the story: "The spirit of Elijah is resting on Elisha" (2:15). This confirms what happens at the translation of Elijah (vv. 10–11). Elisha will become the rightful heir to the office of Elijah (i.e., the double portion of his spirit) on condition that he observes Elijah being taken from his presence. The removal of Elijah is further confirmed by the search of the band of fifty prophets who are unable to locate him (vv. 16–18). Elijah's succession is established by prophetic revelation and by prophetic witness to his disappearance.

Departure of Elijah (2:1–18)

THE TOPIC OF the chapter is introduced by saying that Elijah is taken up to heaven in a storm. The "whirlwind" ($s^{e\,c}\bar{a}r\hat{a}$) was the same phenomenon by which God made himself known to Job (Job 38:1; 40:6). The force and power of the wind are symbolic of the majestic and holy presence of the divine. The storm is the means by which the immanence of God can be perceived, somewhat like the storm on Mount Sinai (Ex. 20:18–19).

Gilgal is most often identified with the site of Israel's first encampment in the land. Just a few kilometers east of Jericho, the Israelites erected a memorial of twelve stones to commemorate their crossing of the Jordan. During the time of Samuel Gilgal became an important religious center and may have been the site of an ancient temple.[3] Gilgal also seems to have been a

---

1. Chronicles has a further confrontation with Jehoram son of Jehoshaphat, after the revolt of Edom, sent in the form of a letter (2 Chron. 21:1–15). For a discussion of the chronological arrangement of Kings, see the introduction.

2. Simon DeVries, *Yesterday, Today and Tomorrow*, 233–34, 275–76.

3. Zevit counts Gilgal as among a possible seventeen temples in Iron Age Israel, all characterized by a lack of uniformity (*The Religions of Ancient Israel*, 254–55). Literary allusion to a temple is indicated when a sacrifice is said to be done "before the LORD" (cf. 1 Sam. 11:15).

location in the southern hill country of Samaria near Bethel.[4] Elisha had been discipled by Elijah and anointed to be his successor (1 Kings 19:19−21) and became the leader of a prophetic guild. Elisha ("my God saves") was son of Shaphat, originally from Abel Meholah on the east side of Jordan toward Jabesh Gilead (19:16). The prophets of his band made a living through normal occupations, just as Elisha did until anointed as a disciple of Elijah.

The whole narrative is designed to build suspense. Elijah suddenly receives the revelation that he is to go as far as Bethel and urges Elisha to stay behind. When they arrive at Bethel, they are met with news of a prophetic revelation. Elijah then receives a message that he is to go to Jericho. A second band of prophets from Jericho comes with news of the same revelation. Mixed emotions of impatience, sorrow, and anger may be intended in the words (lit.), "I know. Be quiet!"[5] (2:3, 5). Yahweh then calls Elijah to the Jordan; Elisha is determined to follow his master, refusing to compromise his vow, though repeatedly challenged.

Elisha asks for a double portion of Elijah's spirit, an expression used elsewhere to refer to the right of inheritance of the firstborn as double that of the others (Deut. 21:17). Elisha is not requesting twice the prophetic spirit of Elijah, but rather the right to the office of Elijah, double the portion of other heirs of the prophetic office. "My father" is repeated (2 Kings 2:12), an expression of the honor attributed to the leader.[6] The terms "father" and "son" do not distinguish exact relationships, but are the representatives of the older and younger generation, making the term "father" suitable as an expression of honor. There is no evidence to designate this as a term for the leader of a prophetic group or an interpreter of prophetic utterances.

"The chariots and horseman of Israel" (2:12) must refer to the vision of Elijah departing into glory. The expression is associated with Elisha and is repeated by King Joash when Elisha is about to die (13:14). Elijah introduced the cloak as a symbol of succession (2:13) when he first anointed Elisha as his successor (1 Kings 19:19). In the return crossing of the Jordan Elisha calls for the same demonstration of divine provision as was given Elijah (2 Kings 2:14).[7] The same miraculous crossing assures Elisha that he is indeed the true successor to Elijah.

---

4. Mark F. Rooker, "Gilgal," *NIDOTTE*, 4:683−84. It may be the location of the present Jiljilia. The geographical movements, which apparently began at Mount Carmel (2 Kings 1:9; cf. 1 Kings 18:20), end at that same location (2 Kings 2:25), demonstrating the transference of prophetic authority from Elijah to Elisha.

5. The Hiphil perfect (*heḥᵉšû*) should be read an imperative (*HALAT*, 1:347).

6. H. Ringgren, "אָב," *TDOT*, 1:7−8.

7. The translation "Where now is the LORD" (NIV) follows the Greek translation in reading *ʾēpô*, rather than the awkward Masoretic text "even he" (*ʾap hûʾ*), which is connected to the following clause.

The prophetic band in Jericho confirms that Elisha will continue the work of Elijah (2:15–18). When they see Elisha coming from the direction of the river, they recognize he has received the spirit of Elijah and render him respect accordingly. Elisha resists their request to search for Elijah, but they need to confirm that Elijah has departed and not simply been moved by divine power into another location, as happened on other occasions (v. 16; cf. 1 Kings 18:12). The search confirms the prophetic message and the anointing of Elisha; it also assures them that the body of Elijah has not been left unburied in disgrace. The attitude of Elisha in saying they should not have gone on the search is ambiguous (2 Kings 2:18). It would seem that the prophets regard their failure to find the body of Elijah as a success. Their search is not to doubt the prophetic word but to confirm it beyond dispute.

Confirmation of Elisha (2:19–25)

THE FIRST EVENT to confirm that Elisha has succeeded Elijah as the prophet like Moses is the curing of the waters at Jericho. The context suggests that this was the city, and the story is still preserved in the tradition of the abundant spring called ᶜ*Ain as-Sultan* at the base of the mound of ancient Jericho.[8] The effect of the sterility caused by the water is not clear; it could be that it caused the land to be unproductive (NIV), or it caused the people to be childless. The latter is the interpretation of the old Greek translation (*ateknounta*).[9] Gray suggests that the waters at Jericho may have been affected by radioactivity, which can cause sterility.[10] The frequent earthquakes of the area may have caused the water to come in contact with radioactive geological strata. Theologically the problem might have been regarded as a result of the curse of Joshua (cf. Josh. 6:26).

Elisha asks for a "new bowl" (2 Kings 2:20); the jar is distinguished by being unused and by its distinct nature. The word for "bowl" (*ṣᵉlōḥît*) is found only here in the Old Testament; in later Hebrew it is used for a glossy type of bottle. There is no explanation for the use of salt in curing the water.[11] The

---

8. M. Cogan and H. Tadmor, *II Kings: A New Translation with Introduction and Commentary* (AB; Garden City, N.Y.: Doubleday, 1988), 36. Identification of the spring was made by Edward Robinson in 1838.

9. It is usually assumed that the Greek translates *mᵉšakkᵉlîm* rather than the Masoretic text *mᵉšakkālet* (the feminine modifies "land"). In both instances (vv. 19, 21) the use of the word is grammatically problematic.

10. Gray, *I & II Kings*, 477–78.

11. Jones (*1 & 2 Kings*, 2:388–89) compares this to sowing a city with salt as a ritual act of separation (cf. Judg. 9:45), in this case separating Jericho from the curse of Joshua. Hobbs (*2 Kings*, 23) suggests that Abimelech used salt to curse a city while Elisha used salt to restore it.

point of the salt in the new jar is to distinguish this prophetic action from all other common techniques that might be used in "healing" the water. The waters remain pure until the time the accounts of Elisha are recorded (2:22).[12] The power of Elisha is reminiscent of that of Moses in "healing" the waters at Marah (cf. Ex. 15:22–26).

The first event confirming the anointing of Elisha demonstrates the power of prophetic blessing to those who affirm the prophet. The second event demonstrates the power of a curse that rests on all who deny him. The taunting of the young men should not be viewed as immature juvenile activity (2:23). If a prophet were known because he was a hairy man (1:8), taunting Elisha as a bald man is to deny that he is a prophet, or at least to deny that he is a prophet like Elijah.[13] The mauling of the youthful mob is not vindictive anger on behalf of Elisha but divine judgment for culpable denial of the divine purpose. The bears are no less divinely appointed than the whale that swallowed Jonah. With the return to Mount Carmel Elisha completes the transition to being successor to Elijah (2:25).

Bridging Contexts

PROPHECY IN ANCIENT **Israel and prophetic succession.** The transition of prophetic authority from Elijah to Elisha is demonstrated through geographical movements. Ahaziah attempted to summon Elijah while he was residing on the mountain summit (2 Kings 1:9), evidently a reference to Carmel, where Elijah had confronted the prophets of Baal (1 Kings 18:20). Elisha joins Elijah as he journeys to Bethel and on to the Jordan. After crossing the Jordan, Elijah is taken from earthly duties in the same location as Moses before him. The commissioning of Elisha is demonstrated at Jericho in the removal of toxicity from a water source that made the prophetic location virtually uninhabitable. Judgment consumes those who ridicule the prophetic office as Elisha makes his way to Bethel. Elisha finally returns to Carmel to resume the prophetic activity that had been the responsibility of Elijah (2:25).

The stories that initiate the prophetic role of Elisha (2:19–25) have a parallel with the final challenge of Ahaziah against Elijah (1:9–14).[14] The status of the prophet is challenged in both episodes. Elijah is ordered to come down from Carmel to face Ahaziah (1:9) and Elisha is taunted by the disbe-

---

12. For a discussion of "until this day," see the introduction.

13. Leigh Eric Schmidt, "Elisha's Locks and the She-Bears," *Journal of Reform Judaism* 34 (1987): 25–26.

14. T. R. Hobbs, *2 Kings* (WBC 13; Waco, Tex.: Word, 1985), 18.

lieving juveniles to go up to Carmel (2:23). Elijah is described as "hairy" (1:8) while Elisha is ridiculed for being bald (2:23). The judgment in each case is described in parallel phrases. Fire came down from heaven and consumed the king's soldiers (1:10), while two female bears come out from the forest and maul the insolent taunters (2:24). Together, the two chapters constitute a succession of the prophetic office.

These events are intended to show that Elisha is the successor to Elijah just as Joshua was the successor to Moses. Elisha was previously anointed to succeed his master (1 Kings 19:19–21), just as Joshua had been divinely ordained through the office of the priest to succeed Moses (Num. 27:18–23). The miraculous crossing of the Jordan (2 Kings 2:8, 14; cf. Josh. 3:11–13); the presence at Gilgal (cf. 2 Kings 2:1; Josh. 4:19), Bethel (2 Kings 2:2, 23; cf. Josh. 7:2), and Jericho (2 Kings 2:4, 15; cf. Josh. 2:1); and the ascension of Elijah at the same location where Moses died (2 Kings 2:9; cf. Deut. 34:1) all show that Elijah and Elisha are the equivalent of Moses and Joshua in their own time. Josephus exploited this connection, linking the ignorance of the burial place of Moses (Deut. 34:6) with the mysterious end of Elijah (2 Kings 2:11).[15] The motif of Elijah as a second Moses found in his flight to Sinai (1 Kings 19:11–13) is further developed in his departure.

The anointing of a new leader was a means of demonstrating divinely appointed authority. However the anointing of Elisha as a successor to Elijah is unusual because prophecy was not an office of official leadership. Prophets often had a vital role to play in the transition of leadership, but they usually received their own authority independently by a direct divine call. Elijah and Elisha are each given a role in anointing Jehu as successor to the house of Omri (1 Kings 19:15–16; 2 Kings 9:1–3), in order to promote purity of worship by a change in political succession. Both Elijah and Elisha are also given a role in anointing Hazael as successor to Ben-Hadad in Syria (1 Kings 19:15; 2 Kings 8:7–15), as an act of judgment against the sons of Omri for their promotion of Baal cult worship. Elijah anointed Hazael, Jehu, and Elisha as a means of accomplishing his mission after his departure. Elijah's concern was not the succession of office. Elisha is commissioned to continue the unfinished task of Elijah with the same power and authority.

It is not unusual for prophets to be called from their normal vocation to confront apostasy. Amos was a herdsman from Tekoa (Amos 1:1) called to pronounce judgment against Jeroboam II and the worship at Bethel. His

---

15. Josephus echoes the Greek translation of the death of Moses, likening the unknown location of the burial place (*taphē*) of Moses with the end (*teleute*) of Elijah (*Ant.* 9.28). In that same paragraph he compares the departure of Elijah with that of Enoch and implicitly with that of Moses, saying that no one knows of his death.

warnings of the death of Israel (e.g., Amos 3:12) were met with hostility and a demand that he return home. The priest at Bethel requested an edict from the king to have him evicted (7:10–11). Amos was welcome to carry on his preaching activity in his own country (7:12–13), but there was no room for him in Israel. Amos responded by reminding Amaziah the priest that he was merely a herdsman, "neither a prophet nor a prophet's son" (7:14). His authority had nothing to do with an official anointing. He was not there by some special commission from the authorities in Jerusalem. Amaziah could use political power to remove him from Bethel, but he could do nothing to change the word of judgment that Amos had delivered (7:15–16). The lion had roared (3:8); Amos could do nothing other than prophesy (3:3–6). The profession of herdsman did not diminish his calling or authority as a prophet, nor did he need an official commission for it to be effective.

Unique to Elisha is his association with a group called "the company [lit., sons] of the prophets." They are first mentioned in the story of Naboth's vineyard when one of them confronts King Ahab (1 Kings 20:35). They are introduced as a well-known group without need of explanation. They are mentioned eleven times; all the other references occur in connection with the figure of Elisha (2 Kings 2:3, 5, 7, 15; 4:1, 38; 5:22; 6:1; 9:1).

There are other groupings of prophets. Saul encountered a "procession of prophets" coming down from the high place, presumably after worship (1 Sam. 10:5, 10). Their activity involved a number of musical instruments, and whenever a special divine power came on them, their actions manifested something distinctly identifiable as "prophesying." King Ahab retained his own prophets to guide his political decisions (1 Kings 22:6). These official prophets were reviled by other prophets as only giving words that would bring pay, even if they led the people into self-destruction (Mic. 3:5–8). References to groups of prophets has led to the assertion that in the early monarchic period there were professionally trained prophets organized into bands with a leader referred to as "father."[16] It was the responsibility of the leader to train the members of the band in their specific practice of prophetic activity and to instruct them in the true worship of Yahweh. The "sons of the prophets" are sometimes thought to be members of a guild of professionally trained prophets.

Linguistic and literary evidence is insufficient to support the concept of professionally trained prophets.[17] Josephus does refer to Elisha as the "disciple" (*mathētēs*) of Elijah (*Ant.* 9.28, 33), as well as the prophet sent to anoint Jehu (2 Kings 9:1; *Ant.* 9.106), but he does not use "disciple" as a technical

---

16. See J. Lindblom, *Prophecy in Ancient Israel* (Philadelphia: Muhlenberg, 1962), 69–71.
17. Hobbs, 2 *Kings*, 25–26.

term. He also uses the word disciple for the Hebrew term "elder" (*zqn*) when referring to Elisha at home with the leaders of Israel (2 Kings 6:32; *Ant.* 9.68). The limitation of the term "sons of the prophets" to the activity of Elijah (once) and Elisha indicates that this is a specific designation for followers of these prominent prophets. The mention of other bands of prophets in the early monarchic period shows that this phenomenon is not unique. There is nothing to indicate that Elisha was one of the "sons of the prophets" before his anointing or that the term "father" referred to someone who trained disciples in prophetic activity.

Elijah and Elisha had a particular calling and mission during a critical period of Israel's history, when power of the Baal cult was extended through the alliances of Israel and Judah and the intermarriage of the royal families. The supporters of these two prophets in their struggle against the Baal cult were designated as "sons of the prophets." Prophecy manifested itself in a variety of forms in ancient Israel; its function was always to call for faithfulness to the covenant. Inspired prophecy was the means God used to confront false teaching at the highest levels of power. Followers of Elijah who had not bowed before Baal were both recipients of a revelation that the mantel would be transferred to another prophet and witnesses to the anointing of Elisha as the prophet who would bring an end to the power of the house of Omri.

SUCCESSION OF THE **prophetic office.** The authority of the kingdom of God must always be kept separate from the power of the state and must not be dependent on dynastic succession of office. In the Elijah and Elisha stories, "royal power is repeatedly characterized as weak and ineffective, while the prophet can bring victory, healing, and even life."[18] God has always chosen and empowered his leaders for times of political threat against his people.

Jesus gave his followers the same assurance that the kingdom of God would prevail. At Caesarea Philippi Peter recognized Jesus as the Anointed One ("the Christ"), who fulfilled the promises of the prophets for the kingdom of God (Matt. 16:16). This confession was not by means of some special discernment but was itself a revelation granted by God (v. 17). As the one who had received this revelation Peter became that rock on which the church would be built (v. 18), with the assurance that "the gates of hell shall not prevail against it" (KJV). The "keys of the kingdom" were entrusted to Peter

---

18. Judith M. Hadley, "Elijah and Elisha," *NIDOTTE*, 4:572, citing Wesley J. Berger in *Elijah and Elisha in Socioliterary Perspective* (ed. R. B. Coote, 1992).

(v. 19), with the assurance that no earthly power would ever be able to stop the will of God on earth.

This famous rock saying does not support the doctrine of apostolic succession. That doctrine declares that Christ appointed the original apostles and entrusted to them his full spiritual authority; they then appointed overseers (bishops) for the churches founded by them and passed on to them, through the sacramental laying on of hands, their authority of office. These men transmitted the office of overseer to their successors also by the laying on of hands. In this manner, apostolic succession guaranteed the legitimacy of episcopal church government, episcopal doctrine, and the validity of the sacraments dispensed by the bishops.[19]

The claim of the Roman Catholic Church to be the one legitimate continuation of the community established by Jesus Christ is based on apostolic succession. This does not mean that there are apostles, nor does it mean that individual apostles transmitted some or all of their commission to others. The officers of the church, the bishops, are a college (organized group or body) that continues the college of the apostles, and the individual bishop is a successor of the apostles only through his membership in the college.

Roman Catholic, Eastern Orthodox, Old Catholic, Swedish Lutheran, and some other Christian churches accept the doctrine of apostolic succession and believe that the only valid ministry is based on bishops whose office has descended from the apostles. This does not mean, however, that each of these groups necessarily accepts the ministries of the other groups as valid. Roman Catholics generally regard the ministry of the Eastern Orthodox churches as valid but do not accept the Protestant ministry. Protestants consider episcopacy or leadership necessary to the "well-being" but not to the "being" of the church; therefore, they not only accept the ministries of the other Christian groups as valid, but they encourage associations with all Christian groups that do not accept apostolic succession.

The prophetic authority of the church is not different from that of Elijah and Elisha, which was sovereignly granted for the preservation of the faith when it was threatened by political and social forces. In his famous rock saying, Jesus was not bestowing the name Peter on the apostle as an indication of succession, but was interpreting it. The Greek word *petros* did not exist as a name in pre-Christian times. The word "stone" in Aramaic (*kepa'*) was known, probably originating as a surname (e.g., 1 Cor. 1:12). The term referred to a small round stone. Peter (*petros*) would have been a literal translation of the Aramaic name *kepa'*. Greek speakers would have understood

---

19. See the article on "Apostolic Succession" and the article on "Roman Catholicism" in *Enclopedia Britannica Online*.

the play on words in which the stone (*petros*) would become a rock (*petra*), which would serve as the foundation for the church.[20] Peter, "the stone," something like a gem, perhaps known for his hardness and decisiveness, would become a massive rock. The meaning of *petra* is best illustrated by the famous city of that name (Petra), located in southwest Jordan and built on a massive terrace. Such a rock would serve as the foundation of the church.

In the rock saying, the phrase "my church" designates a time when the Christian communities existed alongside the Jewish synagogues as a distinct collective assembly. This distinct assembly began as the small group of followers identified as a congregation of God and grew to become a separate community. Though Jesus directed the beatitude specifically at Peter (Matt. 16:17), it must be remembered that the blessing belonged to all the disciples (cf. 13:16–17; 18:18). The heavenly Father had revealed his Son to his disciples (11:25–30), to those who were not skilled in intricacies of the traditions that grew up as a protection of the covenant, but who had seen the values of the covenant lived and fulfilled in the life of Jesus. The church was built on the foundation of the apostles and prophets (Eph. 2:20) as a sacred temple to the Lord. Peter is singled out as a representative apostle, the first person to be called a disciple, the son of John called Cephas (John 1:42), who loved Jesus and was called to feed his sheep (21:15–17).

The authority of the church. The authority of Jesus was continued in the one church described as a building. Members of the community of Qumran often referred to themselves as a temple or "holy house,"[21] a metaphor that would have had a ready application in the earliest days of the church. "The gates of Hades" (Matt. 16:18) is a standard expression that means death or mortal danger. The powers of death are those forces that wish to bring an end to the church. Though these powers might manifest themselves in political movements, behind them are the forces of darkness that emerge from the abyss itself (Rev. 20:3, 7–10). Even these forces can never prevail against the church built on the rock.

Jesus' words are his assurance to the church even in such a time when apostasy might infest the church, just as Elijah is assured that God's power for his kingdom will prevail when he thought he alone remained faithful (1 Kings 19:15–21). Elijah will not only be succeeded by a prophet like himself, but will have a role in determining political leadership, both foreign and domestic. The church in the same way must not fear the oppression of political and religious leadership, but must recognize that faithfulness in times of threat

---

20. Ulrich Luz, *Matthew 8–20: A Commentary* (Minneapolis: Augsburg Fortress, 2001), 358–59.

21. See, e.g., *The Community Rule* 8.5–10, 9.6, 11.9; *The Damascus Document* 3.19.

is the assurance of their indestructible prophetic role. The church stands on the rock of the authority of Christ himself. Should the church come to be supported by political and social authority, she has reason to fear. Political authority serves the kingdom of humanity rather than the kingdom of God; political authority crumbles on foundations of sand.

As in the days of Elijah and Elisha, the church in the West is facing social pressures that might seem to threaten its prophetic voice, if not its very existence. Individual liberties and human rights have become the trump cards that supersede all other values. They serve as the basis for moral decisions, such as the right of life and death itself in questions of abortion and euthanasia. They are the argument for the redefinition of family, the very foundation of society itself. The momentum of social forces is to relegate the church to the periphery of social influence, as nothing more than one among many competing religious expressions that have no place in public life or in the academy.

The church must not be frightened by such threats; God has his succession of prophetic authority for the preservation of his kingdom, just as he did in the days of Elijah and Elisha. Rulers and skeptics who seek to challenge its role for human good will themselves prove to be weak and ineffective.

In the rock saying, the authority of the church is further developed in another image. Peter holds "the keys of the kingdom" (Matt. 16:19), the manager who has authority over all the buildings of the estate. The function of the keys is explained as a "binding and loosing." The primary meaning is that of forbidding and permitting in the interpretation of the law. Rabbinic conviction held that God or the heavenly court recognized the decisions made on earth in relation to the Scriptures. Jesus was speaking of the teaching of the Scriptures, which would serve to introduce people into the kingdom.

The interpretations of the teachers of the law and the Pharisees excluded people from the kingdom (Matt. 23:13), but the teaching of Jesus' followers would permit entrance into the kingdom. The "service of Peter" in the church is the "constant uncompromising advocacy of the teachings of Jesus."[22] Matthew concentrates this authority on Peter, but it is evident later in his Gospel that the same authority is given to every disciple and every community (18:18). Church discipline is one aspect of carrying out Jesus' teaching that provides entrance to the kingdom.

Elijah and Elisha established their prophetic authority by means of divine intervention. Fire consumed the soldiers who sought to apprehend Elijah; bears destroyed the mockers who disbelieved the prophetic authority of Elisha. The prophets could turn deadly water into a life-giving source and influence change in political powers. Though God may grant such powers

---

22. Luz, *Matthew 8–20*, 365.

to the church in particular circumstances, the designated authority of the church is the "binding and loosing" that is the power of the gospel message. The prophetic word is complete in Christ.

The church must ever be faithful to this authority of Christ, recognizing it as the rock on which it stands. In his darkest days of tribulation, Martin Luther wrote the hymn "Ein feste Burg," confessing that no temporal power can stop the work of the church. Luther recognized in the forces arrayed against him the work of the old serpent spoken of by the apostle John (Rev. 12:1–6). "For still our ancient foe, doth seek to work us woe, his craft and power are great, and armed with cruel hate, on earth is not his equal" (trans. by Frederick H. Hedge). Luther continues:

Did we in our own strength confide,
our striving would be losing;
were not the right man on our side,
the man of God's own choosing.
Dost ask who that may be?
Christ Jesus, it is He;
Lord Sabaoth His name,
from age to age the same,
and He must win the battle.

The attacks of temporal powers against God's people should cause no fear. They will not prevail against the church any more than the house of Omri could prevail against Elijah and Elisha. Attempting to establish a power of spiritual authority on the basis of temporal powers is always a compromise of the real power of God in this world. Just as God called his prophets to teach the true worship of the covenant, so today he calls his ministers to give testimony to the teaching of Jesus. The keys of the kingdom do not belong to an ordained office but to all who minister in the service of Peter in advocating the teachings of Jesus.

2 Kings 3:1–27

JORAM SON OF Ahab became king of Israel in Samaria in the eighteenth year of Jehoshaphat king of Judah, and he reigned twelve years. ²He did evil in the eyes of the LORD, but not as his father and mother had done. He got rid of the sacred stone of Baal that his father had made. ³Nevertheless he clung to the sins of Jeroboam son of Nebat, which he had caused Israel to commit; he did not turn away from them.

⁴Now Mesha king of Moab raised sheep, and he had to supply the king of Israel with a hundred thousand lambs and with the wool of a hundred thousand rams. ⁵But after Ahab died, the king of Moab rebelled against the king of Israel. ⁶So at that time King Joram set out from Samaria and mobilized all Israel. ⁷He also sent this message to Jehoshaphat king of Judah: "The king of Moab has rebelled against me. Will you go with me to fight against Moab?"

"I will go with you," he replied. "I am as you are, my people as your people, my horses as your horses."

⁸"By what route shall we attack?" he asked.

"Through the Desert of Edom," he answered.

⁹So the king of Israel set out with the king of Judah and the king of Edom. After a roundabout march of seven days, the army had no more water for themselves or for the animals with them.

¹⁰"What!" exclaimed the king of Israel. "Has the LORD called us three kings together only to hand us over to Moab?"

¹¹But Jehoshaphat asked, "Is there no prophet of the LORD here, that we may inquire of the LORD through him?"

An officer of the king of Israel answered, "Elisha son of Shaphat is here. He used to pour water on the hands of Elijah."

¹²Jehoshaphat said, "The word of the LORD is with him." So the king of Israel and Jehoshaphat and the king of Edom went down to him.

¹³Elisha said to the king of Israel, "What do we have to do with each other? Go to the prophets of your father and the prophets of your mother."

"No," the king of Israel answered, "because it was the LORD who called us three kings together to hand us over to Moab."

¹⁴Elisha said, "As surely as the LORD Almighty lives, whom I serve, if I did not have respect for the presence of Jehoshaphat king of Judah, I would not look at you or even notice you. ¹⁵But now bring me a harpist."

While the harpist was playing, the hand of the LORD came upon Elisha ¹⁶and he said, "This is what the LORD says: Make this valley full of ditches. ¹⁷For this is what the LORD says: You will see neither wind nor rain, yet this valley will be filled with water, and you, your cattle and your other animals will drink. ¹⁸This is an easy thing in the eyes of the LORD; he will also hand Moab over to you. ¹⁹You will overthrow every fortified city and every major town. You will cut down every good tree, stop up all the springs, and ruin every good field with stones."

²⁰The next morning, about the time for offering the sacrifice, there it was—water flowing from the direction of Edom! And the land was filled with water.

²¹Now all the Moabites had heard that the kings had come to fight against them; so every man, young and old, who could bear arms was called up and stationed on the border. ²²When they got up early in the morning, the sun was shining on the water. To the Moabites across the way, the water looked red—like blood. ²³"That's blood!" they said. "Those kings must have fought and slaughtered each other. Now to the plunder, Moab!"

²⁴But when the Moabites came to the camp of Israel, the Israelites rose up and fought them until they fled. And the Israelites invaded the land and slaughtered the Moabites. ²⁵They destroyed the towns, and each man threw a stone on every good field until it was covered. They stopped up all the springs and cut down every good tree. Only Kir Hareseth was left with its stones in place, but men armed with slings surrounded it and attacked it as well.

²⁶When the king of Moab saw that the battle had gone against him, he took with him seven hundred swordsmen to break through to the king of Edom, but they failed. ²⁷Then he took his firstborn son, who was to succeed him as king, and offered him as a sacrifice on the city wall. The fury against Israel was great; they withdrew and returned to their own land.

ELISHA'S CONTINUATION OF Elijah's work is illustrated in the battle against Moab. It bears obvious similarities to the coalition of Jehoshaphat with Ahab in the battle against Ramoth Gilead (1 Kings 22). In both events there is an alliance between Jehoshaphat, the God-fearing king of Judah, and the apostate northern king following in the ways of Jeroboam son of Nebat. Jehoshaphat asks for the assistance of a true prophet of God. The confirmation of the prophetic word and the power of the God of Israel in the covenant are seen in the outcome of the events.

The similarity extends to the phrases used in the solicitation of the alliance (1 Kings 22:4; 2 Kings 3:7) and of the prophet (1 Kings 22:7; 2 Kings 3:11). These stories were a part of prophetic tradition expressed in its own distinct vocabulary and literary style. The war against Moab in prophetic history shows how political events concerning Israelite and Judean relations with surrounding nations accomplishes the work of Yahweh through the word of his prophets.

A minimum of historical information about relations with Moab is provided in the Kings account because of the prophetic interests of the Deuteronomistic History. Not much more can be learned from the Moabite black basalt stone, which is a war report designed to enhance the Moabite king, the loyal servant of the national deity.[1] As a royal victory stele it records the heroic deeds of Mesha, king of Moab, through the sanctification of his god Chemosh. It reports a long period of oppression beginning with Omri, because of the wrath of Chemosh. Mesha records a long series of victories in the territory north of the Arnon (the land of Medeba) that had been controlled by the house of Omri for some forty years.[2] These extended as far as Nebo, where Mesha claims to have slaughtered seven thousand Israelite citizens in devotion to Chemosh and to have taken sacred vessels from there as booty.

The stele describes events of several decades, confined to victories over Israel. Mesha does not mention the attack of Joram and his allies, since such an event was contrary to his political and religious propaganda. Military victories of the type described in the stele would provide for a revolt for independence as described at the death of Ahab (cf. 2 Kings 3:5). They also explain

---

1. The stone, just over three feet high, was discovered by missionary Klein in 1868 in the vicinity of Dibon in the Transjordan. Translation and commentary is provided in *Kanaanäische und Aramäische Inschriften*, no. 181. A translation by W. F. Albright is provided in Pritchard, *An Anthology of Texts and Pictures*, 209–10; the stele is illustrated in plate 74.

2. For the geography of the various places named in the stele see Ahlström, *The History of Ancient Palestine*, 580–81, and map 18.

why the attack needed to come from Edom in the south (v. 8). By the time of Joram the territory north of the Arnon was totally under the control of Moab.

Political and Military Crisis (3:1–12)

THE REGNAL SUMMARY of Joram (3:1–3) is given with a synchronism to the eighteenth year of Jehoshaphat. A coregency of Jehoshaphat with his son Jehoram is assumed in the Masoretic text. The synchronism for Ahaziah states that Joram came to rule in the second year of Jehoram son of Jehoshaphat (1:17), and the synchronism for Jehoram is in the fifth year of Joram king of Israel (8:16). According to the chronology of the Masoretic text, both Jehoram and Jehoshaphat were kings in Judah at the time of the battle against Moab.

Joram is credited with removing the memorial pillar (*maṣṣēbâ*) that Ahab had set up in honor of Baal (3:2). Ahab built a Baal temple and altar in Samaria, along with a sacred pole (1 Kings 16:31–33); his monuments to Baal also included an upright memorial stone. From the Middle Bronze Age onward stones lacking pictures or inscriptions are grouped with one bearing a picture, with a statue, or with other stone memorials. Biblical texts report such standing stones at relatively few sites in Israel. The fundamental intention of such pillars may have been applicable in various dimensions, including the cultic and religious; to this extent the *maṣṣēbâ* could portray or represent the worshiper and not always (merely) the venerated deity.[3]

Standing stones were objects of veneration and worship, conventionalized aniconic representations of a deity. Such stones were not symbols of the transcendent being but evoked an actual presence.[4] The *maṣṣēbâ* in the Baal temple in Samaria may have presented the deity, as it was removed but not destroyed. Apparently it was sequestered somewhere in that temple; Jehu had it destroyed in his purge of the Baal cult (10:26–27).[5] Joram did not turn from devotion to Baal but may have removed memorials that were specifically erected as a memorial to his father.

Moab had been subservient to Israel from the time of David (2 Sam. 8:2). Solomon had allowed a place of worship for his Moabite wife in Jerusalem (1 Kings 11:7). Mesha ("savior"), from the area of Dibon, was a sheep herder. As a vassal of Israel he was required to pay a levy of one hundred thousand lambs and the wool of one hundred thousand rams (NIV), or possibly the wool only of the lambs and rams (NEB). The large numbers are comparable

---

3. J. Gamberoni, "מַצֵּבָה," *TDOT*, 8:485–86.

4. Zevit, *The Religions of Ancient Israel*, 256–59.

5. The text of these verses is problematic; for discussion see Cogan and Tadmor, *2 Kings*, 116.

with other reports of booty taken.[6] Mesha's refusal to bring tribute is the result of the weakening military control of Israel.

Joram attempts to regain dominance over Moab by mustering his forces and reinforcing them with assistance from Judah.[7] Edom is still subservient to Judah at this time, so Edom's army is part of the alliance. Edom does not have an independent king until the independent reign of Jehoram in Judah (2 Kings 8:20; cf. 1 Kings 22:48). The king of Edom in the story must refer to the viceroy or ruling representative of Edom.[8]

The route of attack takes the armies through Edom around the southern end of the Dead Sea. The southern territory of Moab, including the city of Horonaim, had been occupied by the "house of David." It may be that Horonaim is occupied by the forces of Judah as a logistic base in support of the campaign on the Moabite plateau above.[9] The journey around the Dead Sea would have taken considerable time. In typical prophetic style it is described as "a journey of seven days," the emphasis being on the time-consuming effort of a difficult journey rather than a precise calculation of time. It is an arduous military undertaking, with a large number of burden-bearing animals necessary to carry the supplies. The whole expedition is jeopardized by a lack of water as the armies march through desert land.

Joram realizes that the eminent failure of his armies is a sign of divine judgment on him (3:10). Jehoshaphat comes to the rescue in a nonmilitary fashion by proposing they seek direction from a true prophet (v. 11). Elisha is introduced abruptly through the information of a nameless third party. He is known through Elijah; "pouring water over the hands" was apparently a gesture of respect shown by a servant to his master or a host to his guest. Jehoshaphat recognizes Elisha as a true prophet who can bring them a word from Yahweh (v. 12). Joram has been alienated from Elisha (v. 13) and could not have sought his assistance without the mediation of Jehoshaphat.

---

6. The numbers are high and may have been intended to indicate total submission of Moab. Thutmose III lists a vast booty taken from the city of Megiddo; livestock includes 1,929 cows, 2,000 goats, and 20,500 sheep (*Context of Scripture*, 2.2A 96–102a).

7. The idiom "my people as your people, my horses as your horses" (cf. 1 Kings 22:4) emphasizes the unity of purpose in the alliance, not a "what is mine is yours" nuance (NEB).

8. It is not at all unusual for the same official to be referred to as a deputy in a chronistic source (as 1 Kings 22:48) and a king in a prophetic narrative (as 2 Kings 3:9). The meaning of terms is determined by the genre in which they are used. In the Tel Fekharye inscription the local ruler is referred to as "king of Gozan" in the Aramaic text, but "governor" in the Akkadian text (see Cogan and Tadmor, *II Kings*, 44–45).

9. For discussion see Anson F. Rainey et al., *The Sacred Bridge* (Jerusalem: Carta, 2006), 204–5. The Moabite stone boasts that Mesha conquered Hauronen, but the text is too broken to indicate more than that. Since its purpose was to glorify Mesha and his deity, it naturally makes no reference to the invasion by Israel and its allies.

The Prophetic Assurance (3:13–20)

WHEN THE KING of Israel appears before Elisha, the prophet confronts him in uncompromising and forceful terms. The king ought to be consistent with his own policy of following in the ways of Jeroboam the son of Nebat (v. 13). Though Joram follows the prophets of his parents in official policy, he also knows that his dire situation is a result of the judgment of the God of Elisha (cf. v. 14).

Joram is logical enough in the context of Canaanite religion. Opposing political and cultic groups each had their own gods, and the success of the group depended on the disposition of their god. As Mesha said in his inscription, "Omri, king of Israel, oppressed Moab many years, for Chemosh was angry with his land."[10] Joram knows that only the God of Elisha can be of assistance. Elisha grants Joram a concession (v. 14); though he regards Joram, the leader of the group, with disdain, Jehoshaphat is worthy of receiving a word from Yahweh.

The procedures for entering the mystic state of prophecy are veiled in tantalizing incidental comments. Elisha calls for music in order that he might experience the power of the Lord. When Saul was anointed king, he encountered a band of prophets at Gibeah, led by a band playing lyres, drums, flutes, and zithers as they prophesied (1 Sam. 10:5–6). When Saul met them, he was empowered by God and exercised the same mystic behavior. The "wind/spirit" (rûaḥ)[11] that came on Saul is not different from the "hand" that came on Elisha (2 Kings 3:15). Both are metaphors for describing an invisible force or power that inspires a changed behavior and enables the individual to come into direct communication with God. The use of music is only one means of entering the mystical experience.

The word of Yahweh through Elisha declares that every depression in the dry valley bed will become a receptacle for water. The prophet is not commanding them to make ditches (v. 16);[12] the valley itself will become pools. It is common for wadis to become streams after a cloud burst, leaving behind pools of water in the hollows of the valley rift. The storm may occur far enough away that no sound of wind or rain can be heard, but the water gathers and rushes down the valleys, often taking travelers by

---

10. Translation of Cogan and Tadmor, *II Kings*, 333 (Appendix I).

11. The tendency of translations to capitalize spirit as a translation of *ruach* (e.g. NIV) is a distortion of the Hebrew metaphor, which does nothing more than describe this power as an unseen force like wind.

12. The infinitive absolute (ʿāśōb) should not be translated as an imperative (NIV), because in this instance it does nothing more than indicate the immediacy of inspiration on the prophet (Burney, *The Books of Kings*, 269–70; GKC 113ff). No human intervention is necessary (v. 17), and the appearance of the water is not in artificially constructed trenches (vv. 22–23).

surprise.[13] Though such occurrences are not infrequent, there is nothing natural about the deliverance experienced by the three armies. The water comes according to the word of the prophet.

The mere deliverance of the armies perishing for lack of water would have been a partial victory. The prophetic word assures Joram and his allies that they will be successful in the battle against Moab (v. 19). The ruin described in the victory over Moab is a contradiction to the rules for war provided in the covenant (Deut. 20:19). The object of attack in warfare is enemy soldiers, not the resources of the land that are necessary for civil life. It is true that "war supersedes all wisdom as well as benevolence even in allegedly Christian nations,"[14] but the prophetic word is not an order in contradiction to the covenant. Elisha does not order the destruction of trees and arable land but describes the totality of the ruin that will come to Moab in the conflict.

The Military Outcome (3:21–27)

WHEN THE MOABITES realize the coalition is at their boundary, they muster what army they can to stop them at the border (3:21). The border of Moab in the south is probably Nahal Zered (cf. Deut. 2:13). As a newly independent regime the Moabites do not have a highly organized army. Their soldiers are described as "bearing arms," meaning lightly armed skirmishers or those carrying a sword. In the light of the early morning sun the water gathered in the hollows appears to the Moabites to be red like blood (v. 22). Though this may be regarded as a natural phenomenon caused by the rays of the rising sun reflecting in the waters,[15] the event itself is ordained as an act of God as promised by Elisha.

There is a notable wordplay here; while waiting in the red sandstone ground of Edom (ʾedôm), the Moabites mistake water that appears blood red (ʾᵃdummîm) for actual blood (v. 22). They come to the conclusion that the coalition has turned on itself and the spoil is theirs for the taking (23). This is a fatal error (v. 24); as the Moabite army moves into the Israelite camp, the Israelites continue on the attack against the Moabites. The resulting destruction is exactly as the prophet said (v. 25); the cities are overthrown, every field ruined with stones, the water sources filled, and the trees felled.

The Israelites advance as far as the city of Kir Haresheth. This is usually

---

13. These sudden rushes of water could be life threatening; Israel would have been swallowed up by its enemies like a traveler by a torrential flood if Yahweh had not delivered them (Ps. 124:3–5).

14. Montgomery, *The Books of Kings*, 361.

15. Hobbs (2 *Kings*, 37) thinks that the Moabites have lost the tactical advantage and are now facing east, as the coalition army has circumvented them and entered the land.

identified with a southern fortified city described by Isaiah as the "city of Moab" (Isa. 15:1), the modern Kerak. It was situated on a strategic plateau surrounded by steep valleys overlooking the wadi Kerak, which flows into the Dead Sea. The steep approaches to the city may have been a factor in Mesha's successful resistance to the Israelite attack. Warriors with slings lay siege to the fortification and attack it in an effort to capture the Moabite warriors.

The Moabites attempt to break out of the siege by breaking through the Edomite line, the weak link in the circle of forces that surround the city (v. 26).[16] When this fails, the king of Moab sacrifices a young man on the walls of the city in full view of the attacking armies (v. 27). The result is a "great fury" that causes a reversal of the campaign and a withdrawal of the coalition forces. The source of this fury is not explained; it may have been the anger of one of the armies or one of the deities. Rabbinic exegetes took it to be the anger of the king of Edom who turns against Joram and Jehoshaphat because of the sacrifice of his son who has been taken captive by the Moabites when they attempt to break through the Edomite ranks.[17] Josephus took it to be the anger and despair of the Moabites that so affects the invading armies they abandon their goals and return (*Ant.* 9.43).

The most natural reading of the pronouns in verse 26 is that the king of Moab sacrifices his own son under conditions of distress. The offering may have been in the fulfillment of a vow like Jephthah (Judg. 11:30–31) or an attempt to satisfy the anger of Chemosh (referred to in the Moabite Inscription). If the sacrifice is a propitiatory act offered to Chemosh, the nature of the "great fury" is still unexplained. It must be inferred that only the wrath of Yahweh, who grants deliverance, can cause army foes to retreat. In Deuteronomistic theology the cause must be a failure of Israelite faith. The prophetic source gives no indication how the army loses its nerve and retreats. The equivocal wrath is sufficient to explain the retreat and the failure of the campaign to regain control of the territory.

The final outcome of the campaign fails to regain control over the territory and restore the tribute of Moab. Neither the presence of Jehoshaphat nor the word of Elisha can turn the tide of judgment against Israel. In spite of the rout of the Moabites through divine intervention, Joram cannot achieve his goal to subjugate Mesha; rather, he is forced to retreat precipitately.

---

16. The use of the preposition usually meaning "to" (ʾel), and the unusual verb (bqʿ) usually meaning "divide, cut," has led to various speculations. Long proposes that the Edomites have deserted to Moab during the long campaign, and the two armies are attempting to ally ("2 Kings III and the Genres of Prophetic Narrative," *VT* 23 [1973]: 340–41). But the context indicates that the Moabites attempt to break through an army line to escape rather than to ally.

17. This explanation is followed by Y. Aharoni et al., *The Carta Bible Atlas*, 4th ed. (Jerusalem: Carta, 2002), 99; see also Rainey, *The Sacred Bridge*, 205.

GOD AS A WARRIOR. During the days of the judges Moab was dominant over Israel and demanded tribute (Judg. 3:12–30). Ehud was commissioned to bring tribute to Eglon at Jericho. The animosity of Israel for Moab can be felt in the telling of the story. The king of Moab was a very fat man, whose name in the story is related to the word "calf" (ʿegel). After delivery of the tax, Ehud returned with a secret "message from God" (v. 20), delivered in the form of the blow of a knife that buried itself completely into Eglon. Ehud managed to lock the corpse in a room that contained a latrine and exit so the bodyguards of Eglon did not suspect anything.

The smells made these guards think they knew what was going on behind the locked doors, so they waited and waited, not wanting to disturb the king. In the meantime Ehud had sufficient time to rally an army and capture the fleeing Moabite soldiers at the fords of the Jordan. This is the second instance in Judges where God was merciful to a recalcitrant Israel and granted them deliverance through special enablement. The story of Joram is along the same lines, except in this instance it is Moab that fails to pay tribute. The armies survive but do not achieve their desired ends. Moab continues to become an increasingly despised enemy.

The battle against Moab is an indictment against the house of Ahab and demonstrates the irreversible destiny of the nation of Israel. Joram is not like his father and mother, but the distinction carries no significance because he has compromised the covenant just like his predecessors (vv. 2–3).[18] The rebellion of the king of Moab is indicative of the political failure that is a result of Israel's failure to abide by the covenant, which set before them the alternatives of a long stay in the land or quickly perishing from it (Deut. 30:15–18).

The initial crisis is the revolt of Moab (2 Kings 3:4–5), but the attempt of the king of Israel to resolve the situation leads to a potentially much greater disaster (vv. 6–12). The allied armies are in danger of perishing for lack of water. Through the influence of Jehoshaphat Elisha is brought to the scene and gives a promising oracle, not only assuring them that the second crisis will be averted but that victory will be achieved (vv. 13–20). The word of the prophet is fulfilled in the course of battle, but in the end the victory is compromised by the failure of the Israelites (vv. 21–27). The cause of Israelite withdrawal is vague, but the judgment against Israel in its failure to regain control of the territory north of the Arnon is clear.

---

18. "Only [raq] not as his father and mother, but he removed [wayyāsar] the pillar of Baal . . ." (v. 2) has a precise parallel in "only [raq] he clung to the sin of Jeroboam, . . . he did not turn [sār] from it" (v. 3).

Remarkable in the story of the battle against Moab in Kings is the claim that Yahweh is the One who instigates the military action (3:10, 13). The initial decision to invade Moab is entirely that of the Israelite king, who musters his troops and seeks the alliance of Jehoshaphat to subdue Moab when they no longer produce tax revenues (vv. 5–8). Divine involvement through the prophet takes place after the kings have become hopelessly entangled in a losing cause. Failed military policy often seeks a scapegoat, and in this instance Joram has the audacity to claim the failure is a result of divine inaction. The king's capacity for duplicity is astonishing, but in the context of this story it serves to show God's mercy in spite of misguided actions.

Joram gives no indication of repentance or trust in spite of acknowledging his utter dependence on God. He appears to expect that God is obligated on his behalf. The consequences of his arrogance and presumptuousness are transparent at the end of the story. Joram does not receive deliverance but divine wrath and abject failure, in spite of the mighty action of God on his behalf. Mercy is shown in deference to Jehoshaphat, but the power of God does not reverse the consequences of the power of sin.

The battle against Moab demonstrates the Hebrew belief that Yahweh is a man of war for the deliverance of his people (Ex. 15:3; cf. Isa. 42:13).[19] The Exodus experience was a fundamental revelation of God's character. The revelation of the name Yahweh to Moses assured the Israelites of God's presence in the covenant at all times (Ex. 3:12–14). "To call God a Warrior is to use anthropomorphic language, the language of immanence."[20] The sign that God was with Moses was the giving of the covenant at Mount Sinai, where Moses had encountered the burning bush. The journey to Mount Sinai was by means of the defeat of the Egyptians. When confronted, Pharaoh challenged Moses and Aaron with a question: "Who is Yahweh that I should obey him?" (5:2). His stubbornness revealed the significance of the name Yahweh to both the Egyptians and the Israelites (e.g., 7:3–5; 10:1–2).

The battle was not between Pharaoh and Moses, but between Pharaoh and Yahweh (7:1). Pharaoh learned that the battle belonged to Yahweh in delivering his people (cf. 17:16). The final lesson to the Egyptians in learning the meaning of the name came when they attempted to capture the Israelites at the Reed Sea (14:4, 18). The only responsibility of the people was to be still and see the salvation of Yahweh (v. 13). The song of Moses and Israel celebrated the meaning of the name Yahweh (15:1–18). The eternal King (v. 18) was the Redeemer of Israel (v. 13) by being the man of war (v. 3) who tossed the chariots of Egypt into the sea.

---

19. See T. Longman, "לחם," *NIDOTTE*, 2:786.

20. Peter C. Craigie, *The Problem of War in the Old Testament* (Grand Rapids: Eerdmans), 39.

This significance of the name of Yahweh is celebrated triumphantly in Psalm 24. The gates of the temple are insufficient for the entrance of the King of glory (vv. 6–10). "Who is this King of glory? The LORD strong and mighty … mighty in battle" (v. 8)—terminology directly reminiscent of the Redeemer revealed in the Exodus from Egypt. This "King of glory" is "the LORD of hosts" (v. 10, NRSV), a title most often connected with the armies of Israel. The name Yahweh invoked in the worship of the temple signifies that the God of the covenant will fight on behalf of his people in order to redeem them.

The self-revelation of God in the Exodus was not typical of all his participation in Israelite history. If the Israelites were to stand still and see the salvation of Yahweh when the chariots of Pharaoh pursued them, the conquest of the Promised Land revealed a different aspect of God's actions on behalf of his people. During the Conquest real wars were fought against real enemies, but God granted victory through his participation with them in battle. God determined the outcome of events by acting as warrior through the fighting of his people.

That is why the kings of Israel were instructed not to trust in horses or to seek alliances with other nations; rather, their first priority was to know and keep the terms of the covenant so the kingdom would endure (Deut. 17:16–20). As expressed by the psalmist, "Some trust in chariots and some in horses, but we trust in the name of the LORD our God" (Ps. 20:7). Though Joram follows in the ways of Jeroboam son of Nebat, in time of distress he turns to Jehoshaphat and through him to the God of the covenant. Though rejected by the prophet, he claims that Yahweh has led these three kings into battle (2 Kings 3:10, 13) and that it is not Yahweh's purpose to enter a conflict and then give up his armies to defeat.

If Yahweh is to win the battle, it needs to be initiated by him. Israel is not the one to determine which battles Yahweh will enter on their behalf. It is always necessary to inquire whether a battle is according to the divine will prior to its start. Even faithless Ahab in his desire to restore Ramoth Gilead to Israel cooperated with Jehoshaphat to know the will of Yahweh so that he could be successful in battle (1 Kings 22:5–8). This quest led to the conflict between Micaiah and the prophets loyal to the king. Ahab determined to proceed against the divine will anyway and died in battle, as Micaiah had said (v. 17).

Inquiry before Yahweh is not mentioned in the case of Joram going to war against Moab, but when the armies come to grief in the journey through the barren hills, Yahweh does come to fight on their behalf through the word of the prophet. But the victory is compromised by a failure of trust explained as a "great fury" that comes on Israel (2 Kings 3:27). Such failure is consistent with the theology that victory is possible only through divine initiation of the battle.

The doctrine that God acts as a warrior to silence his enemies is consummated in bringing his kingdom to earth. The victory of the divine warrior is not limited to particular battles but is celebrated as the event by which salvation will come to the world. The "enthronement psalms," which celebrate Yahweh as King, are examples of God acting as warrior. Psalm 98 is a "new song" praising God for his salvation (vv. 1–3), declaring that "the LORD reigns" (vv. 4–6), and anticipating his future judgment of the earth (vv. 7–9).[21] The parallels to the song of Moses at the crossing of the sea (Ex. 15:1–18) are obvious. While Yahweh is extolled as a "man of war" in that particular event, Psalm 98 has no reference to an historical event but describes God as Savior, Ruler, and Judge.

God as a man of war also fought against Israel in bringing about his rule. The prophets recognized that the divine warrior was at work in Babylon's conquest of the nation of Judah. The prophet Habakkuk found it unfair, but there was no denying God's war against Israel.

O LORD, are you not from everlasting?
My God, my Holy One, we will not die.
O LORD, you have appointed them to execute judgment;
O Rock, you have ordained them to punish.
Your eyes are too pure to look on evil;
you cannot tolerate wrong.
Why then do you tolerate the treacherous?
Why are you silent while the wicked
swallow up those more righteous than themselves? (Hab. 1:12–13)

The theme of God as the divine warrior may be described as moving through five stages with some overlap.[22] In the first stage God fights for Israel; in the second he fights against Israel. The wars in the period of Elijah and Elisha have elements of both. The third stage looks forward to the advent of the divine warrior who will conquer all nations: "In that day the LORD will punish with his sword, his fierce, great and powerful sword, Leviathan the gliding serpent, Leviathan the coiling serpent; he will slay the monster of the sea" (Isa. 27:1). This third stage acknowledges an underlying motif, namely, that the real battle of the divine warrior is against cosmic forces that disrupt the created order. Fourth, the Gospels and New Testament letters portray Jesus as the conqueror of all the principalities and powers that are arrayed

---

21. See Tremper Longman III, "Psalm 98: A Divine Warrior Victory Song," *JETS* 27 (1984): 267–74.

22. Tremper Longman III and Daniel G. Reid, *God Is a Warrior* (Grand Rapids: Zondervan, 1995), 17.

against the kingdom of God (Eph. 1:19−21). Finally, Jesus will come as the divine conqueror over all temporal and spiritual forces: "I saw heaven standing open and there before me was a white horse, whose rider is called Faithful and True. With justice he judges and makes war" (Rev. 19:11). This is the New Testament version of the ultimate victory of God as King.

Moab was never a major military power, but it was a vexing neighbor of Israel and Judah and came to be representative of human resistance to God's purposes. Moab became a recurring subject in Israel's prophetic oracles against the nations, where Israel expected God's mighty judgment (Isa. 15−16; Jer. 48; Ezek. 25:8−11; Zeph. 2:8−9). One of the most notable oracles against Moab occurs in a section of Isaiah often referred to as the "Little Apocalypse" (Isa. 24−27). A remarkable characteristic of this passage is that cities and nations remain nameless; Moab is the only exception (25:10). The "city of ruin" (24:12) is mentioned several times but is never named. All suggestions to provide a historical setting for these events fail because of the ambiguities of time and place.

This passage of Isaiah has been considered *sui generis*, with little connection to the book as a whole. It is significant as a sequel to the judgments against the nations (Isa. 13−23), which deal with the purposes of God in exercising his sovereignty over the nations. The ruler of Babylon who presumed to ascend to the highest heaven found himself instead in the deepest pit (Isa. 14). In the sequel to the judgments against particular nations, the eschatological focus is raised to the ultimate purpose of God, portraying the cosmological judgment of the world and its final glorious restoration. The redemption of Israel is depicted as emerging from the ashes of the polluted and decaying world. Not just a remnant is redeemed, but all peoples share in the celebration of God's new order in which death is banished forever (25:8).

The announcement of the continuing punishment of Moab in a context of universal judgment and deliverance (Isa. 25:10−12) is frequently deemed highly inappropriate, an example of a late Jewish author's deep hatred of Moab. Often this short section is regarded as an appendix that could have had no part in the original.[23] It is evident that there was a longstanding animosity between Israel and Moab, but the mention of Moab is not singled out for personal spite. Moab becomes the symbol of arrogance and pride that rejects the inclusion of all nations under the rule of the Lord of hosts.[24]

The mystery of God's salvation of the world is such that the possibility of rejecting the divine mercy remains. Isaiah 24−27 anticipates the conclusion

---

23. Hans Wildberger, *Jesaja Kapitel 31−27*, 2nd ed. (BKAT 10/2; Neukirchen: Neukirchener Verlag, 1978), 900.

24. Childs, *Isaiah*, 185.

of Isaiah (Isa. 66:24). The universal restoration of creation does not remove all tension between good and evil. The same offense of the gospel is to be found in the culmination of the world in the New Testament (Rev. 20:14b–15; 21:27). The final conquest of the divine warrior (19:11–18) will not result in a universal inclusivity. In the eschatology of Isaiah, Moab represents those outside of divine salvation in the restoration of all things.

GOD AND CONTEMPORARY WAR. Christians must reconcile the doctrine of the divine warrior with the particular historical wars that are a part of the present order. Just as God was active in human affairs in times past, exercising his rule among human kingdoms and giving them to whomever he willed (Dan. 5:21), so God continues to be at work in human affairs.

When a war seems justified, it is natural for believers to assume that God is with them in battle. Before the Allied Forces landed in Normandy during the World War II, General (later Field Marshall) Montgomery encouraged his troops with a message that concluded with a prayer: "Let us pray that the Lord Mighty in Battle will go forth with our armies, and that his special providence will aid us in the struggle."[25] A second example is the "Soldier's Prayer" of General George S. Patton, recorded on January 1, 1944: "God of our fathers, who by land and sea has ever led us to victory, please continue your inspiring guidance in this the greatest of our conflicts. . . . Grant us the victory, Lord."[26] Both these men were Christians who believed that God would fight for them in battle.

Scriptures have a mixed view of the goodness of human government. It is to be respected as ordained by God for the control of evil (1 Peter 2:11–17), but often is a beast that tramples and devours the faithful (Dan. 7:7–8). Christians often must make discomforting compromises in their participation in government and society.

A particularly difficult question for the faithful is how to relate to the government in its legitimate role of the control of violence and the exercise of judgment. Though this is a God-ordained function, it is scarcely possible to point to a government at any time that consistently carried out this function as a legitimate representative of divine authority.[27]

---

25. As reported by Craigie, *The Problem of War in the Old Testament*, 33.
26. Ibid., 33–34.
27. August H. Konkel, "Christians in Conflict and at Peace," *The Messenger* 40/6 (March 27, 2002): 3.

War is always a matter of fallible human governments making judgments in matters of life and death. At their best they have their share of evil, and at their worst they are the greatest enemy to their own people.

The dilemma of the Christian has an analogy to the alliance of Jehoshaphat with Joram. Joram could claim for himself the right of regaining control over lost territory, though his issues were strictly political. Failures within his regime had resulted in a loss of power and the revolt of a subject territory. He needed the assistance of Jehoshaphat, because Mesha had apparently developed impenetrable fortifications north of the Arnon, or he feared reprisals from the Arameans or the Ammonites.[28] The relations between the two countries had become interdependent (3:7); the words of Jehoshaphat indicate they had been formalized in a treaty relationship. The alliance with Edom, a vassal of Judah, was also expedient and necessary from a military point of view.

Nothing in the proceedings bears any relationship to the usual criteria for God entering into war on behalf of his people. All of this was an undertaking motivated by a desire to control resources; the success of the venture depended on carefully calculated military power. The circumstances of the battle with Moab have many parallels with contemporary wars. The leading of the Lord and the furtherance of his kingdom were not an issue. Once engaged in battle, the intervention of the prophet was sought to avoid disaster. A general who believes in his cause can do nothing other than pray that God may honor his goals, as Joram and Jehoshaphat did through Elisha. There was no certain victory, like that of the Israelites in the crossing of the sea. The many factors of intended good and imbedded evil led to a "great fury" that subverted the outcome (2 Kings 3:27).

There is a danger of hypocrisy in seeking divine assistance for national causes. Insincerity in the case of Joram may be observed in the response of Elisha when the king sought his assistance: "Go to the prophets of your father and the prophets of your mother" (3:13). Only the presence of Jehoshaphat provided for any association to the God of Elisha. The self-deception of Joram is apparent in his following the idolatries of Baal condemned by the covenant (v. 3), even while believing that he was somehow following the leading of Yahweh (v. 10).

Jehoshaphat is the one who brings up the matter of actually seeking a prophet of Yahweh (v. 11). Elisha's first response is to castigate the king of Israel fearlessly and severely for even daring to ask for divine assistance. The king is culpably duplicitous in stating that Yahweh has led them into battle. The enigmatic requirement that music be provided may have had something

---

28. Rainey et al., *The Sacred Bridge*, 205.

to do with the circumstances of conflicting interests and compromise, perhaps as an accommodation to Joram. Elisha requires no such assistance in other circumstances.

Modern national causes are most often equally equivocal. Populations can scarcely be said to be in pursuit of Christian values but have no hesitation in turning to prayer for politically expedient purposes. Even Christians within a society may largely live for self-serving values, but assume, like Joram, that they are led of the Lord and that they should expect divine assistance in time of need. This is not to suggest divine assistance is never deserved or that failures of faith disqualify one from petitioning God. It is a reminder that failure to pursue the kingdom of God is not reversed in time of peril. Such peril is an opportunity to examine motives and actions. Joram failed to search his own mind (Ps. 139:23–24); he was spared disaster for his forces but incurred enormous loss for his country.

Truth is the first casualty in war, but perhaps the problem is as much self-deception as simple deception. No rationalization is more readily available than one required to justify national security. Clare Short, secretary of State for International Development under the British Labor government of Tony Blair, is known for her passionate, outspoken commitment to the poor and vulnerable.[29] She is a firm believer in just war: The cause must be just, any use of force must be proportionate, and it must be a last resort. She did not believe that Iraq could be ignored; it was right to contemplate the use of force to back up the authority of the United Nations.

Ms. Short resigned her post because she was convinced her prime minister ignored the commitments he had made to her. In her resignation letter to Prime Minister Tony Blair, she charged that the Security Council resolution negotiated between the Prime Minister and the foreign secretary contradicted the assurance she was given in the House of Commons and elsewhere about the legal authority of the occupying powers and the need for a United Nations-led process to establish a legitimate Iraqi government. This betrayal made her position impossible. She felt the American and British leaders were saying, "We might have exaggerated a bit, but we couldn't trust you to be brave enough to take this option, and Saddam Hussein was a bad man." Her own response was blunt: "If our governments are going to lie to us about matters of life and death, war and peace, then integrity is gone from public life." Short further indicated that for the first time in American history, most of the Christian churches were united in saying that the conditions for a just war were not fulfilled in this instance.

---

29. Short was interviewed by Jim Wallis in "Lies Leaders Tell," *Sojourners Magazine* 33 (January 2004): 20.

When a nation engages in conflict for the advancement of its own prosperity, the result is suffering for its people. While Joram considered his ambition justified, his intent being the restoration of wealth to Israel (cf. 2 Kings 3:4), the outcome of the war with Moab was judgment for Israel. The prophetic conclusion was that "the fury against Israel was great" (3:27); war had brought God's punishment of Israel.[30] The failure of the campaign is stated clearly: Kir Hareseth, a major fortification, probably located in southern Moab,[31] remained intact (v. 25).

The words of Elisha contain a certain ambiguity; the man of God could not promise success for Joram's ambition. Though the Israelites did plunder Moab in their attack and struck every city (cf. v. 19), there was one major city they did not overthrow.[32] Moab remained independent and was never reconquered by Israel. Joram, following in the sins of Jeroboam son of Nebat (v. 3), caused his army and his people to suffer. Good that may be intended is compromised when the people and their leader lack integrity; the consequences of such aggression result in an enduring pain.

World War II is an example of a long and agonizing legacy of "a great fury." One of the great challenges following the war was coming to terms with the Holocaust. More than a generation since that event, Germany has made a remarkable and outstanding effort to deal with the past horror in that country. Jalowiecki notes that efforts to reconciliation have included monetary payments to victims, memorials, and demonstrations of remorse.

> After the collapse of Communism and the country's reunification, Germany began to provide assistance to non-Jewish victims of Nazism in Central and Eastern Europe as well, in particular, hundreds of thousands of former forced laborers. All told, Germany's voluntary payments for past wrongs amount thus far to more than $55 billion over a period of almost six decades, and are unparalleled in history.

---

30. Wrath (*qeṣep*) describes punishment against wrongdoers. The wrath of God must be intented; to attribute the wrath to Chemosh, god of Moab, would grant a foreign deity equal status and suggest that the sacrifice of Mesha's son was in some sense efficacious. The wrath of the God of Israel was not because of the sacrifice, since it obviously was made to Chemosh.

31. The city has been identified with a strategic plateau above wadi Kerak, mentioned on the sixth century Madeba mosaic map, though actual archaeological confirmation is scarce.

32. Most translations do not distinguish a point that seems to be significant in Hebrew in v. 19; Elisha did not strictly declare that the cities of Moab would be "overthrown" (NIV). Elisha said the Israelites would strike every fortified city (*wᵉhikkîtem kol ʿîr mibṣār*), which need not mean "overthrow"; see Raymond Westbrook, "Elisha's True Prophecy in 2 Kings 3," *JBL* 124 (2005): 530−32. The report (v. 25) says the Israelites overthrew all the cities (*wᵉheʿārîm yahᵃrōsû*), with the exception of Kir Hareseth. They did strike it (*wayyakkûbā*) with the stones of the slingers, but this was rather harmless on a large fortified city.

Nor have the Germans limited their efforts to the monetary realm. In 1999, in an act of great symbolic significance, the German parliament voted to establish a "Memorial to the Murdered Jews of Europe." Designed by the American architect Peter Eisenman and consisting of 2,700 concrete steles arranged in a terror-inspiring maze, the monument will be situated adjacent to Berlin's Brandenburg Gate, that venerable icon of Prussian might, and within eyeshot of the Bundestag. To be completed this year [2004], it is aimed at forcing the memory of Germany's greatest crime upon all who visit the German capital.

Demonstrations of shame and remorse extend far beyond the political elite. When Germany's then-chancellor Willy Brandt traveled to Poland in 1970 and knelt before the memorial to the Jewish heroes of the Warsaw ghetto uprising, his gesture struck a chord among the German public at large. Innumerable documentary films recounting the barbarities of the past have been shown regularly on German television to vast audiences. The German language itself has registered the impact of this national impulse to self-recrimination and penitence. When I lived in Munich in the 1980's, many of my acquaintances regarded the very designation "German" as a reproach; words associated with the Nazi era, like "Sieg" (victory), had virtually disappeared from the spoken and written vocabulary of my German contemporaries.[33]

Germans themselves suffered enormously during the war and in the aftermath of the war. Yet Germans understandably are not content to be viewed as monsters unlike any other country in history. Historian Martin Broszat has argued that the twelve-year Nazi dictatorship in Germany should no longer be treated as a discrete and exceptional phenomenon, but rather be placed within a larger European context and examined like any other chapter of the Continental past.

Another historian, Ernst Nolte, has asserted that there was nothing exceptional about the Nazi Holocaust. The extermination camps, in Nolte's judgment, merely mirrored and copied atrocities previously committed on a mass scale by the Bolsheviks under Lenin and Stalin; the incessant harping on the peculiar enormity of Nazi crimes served an unhealthy political agenda, one that amounted to a deliberate attempt to keep Germany from assuming its rightful place among the nations of Europe and the world.

Norman Finkelstein has written *The Holocaust Industry* (1999), a book widely received in Germany. The book contends that Holocaust reparations were

---

33. Bartosz Jalowiecki, "Lies the Germans Tell Themselves," *Commentary* 117 (January 2004): 43.

a fraud perpetuated on German taxpayers by avaricious Jewish organizations, out to enrich their coffers and furnish aid to the state of Israel in its campaign to oppress Palestinian Arabs. Jalowiecki queries whether Germany has succeeded in coming to terms with its past in becoming a normal country.

The prophetic judgment at the end of the war against Moab was not malicious refusal to allow an Omride king undiluted victory.[34] Neither the actions of Joram nor the Nazis can be justified, nor is it helpful to excuse such conflict in comparison with others. The consequences of such conflict are a pain that endures over generations. Reparations are to be encouraged, insofar as possible, but they cannot be expected to resolve the burden.

---

34. D. N. Freedman regards the conclusion of the account as a comment indicting a hated Israelite dynasty: "In spite of the prophet and the decision of God against the Moabites, in the end, Jehoram was not allowed to enjoy the fruits of the victory, but had to retreat precipitately" (noted by Cogan and Tadmor, *II Kings*, 52).

2 Kings 4:1–44

T HE WIFE OF a man from the company of the prophets
cried out to Elisha, "Your servant my husband is dead,
and you know that he revered the LORD. But now his
creditor is coming to take my two boys as his slaves."

²Elisha replied to her, "How can I help you? Tell me, what
do you have in your house?"

"Your servant has nothing there at all," she said, "except a
little oil."

³Elisha said, "Go around and ask all your neighbors for
empty jars. Don't ask for just a few. ⁴Then go inside and shut
the door behind you and your sons. Pour oil into all the jars,
and as each is filled, put it to one side."

⁵She left him and afterward shut the door behind her and
her sons. They brought the jars to her and she kept pouring.
⁶When all the jars were full, she said to her son, "Bring me
another one."

But he replied, "There is not a jar left." Then the oil
stopped flowing.

⁷She went and told the man of God, and he said, "Go, sell
the oil and pay your debts. You and your sons can live on
what is left."

⁸One day Elisha went to Shunem. And a well-to-do woman
was there, who urged him to stay for a meal. So whenever he
came by, he stopped there to eat. ⁹She said to her husband, "I
know that this man who often comes our way is a holy man of
God. ¹⁰Let's make a small room on the roof and put in it a bed
and a table, a chair and a lamp for him. Then he can stay there
whenever he comes to us."

¹¹One day when Elisha came, he went up to his room and
lay down there. ¹²He said to his servant Gehazi, "Call the
Shunammite." So he called her, and she stood before him.
¹³Elisha said to him, "Tell her, 'You have gone to all this trouble for us. Now what can be done for you? Can we speak on
your behalf to the king or the commander of the army?'"

She replied, "I have a home among my own people."

¹⁴"What can be done for her?" Elisha asked.

Gehazi said, "Well, she has no son and her husband is old."

¹⁵Then Elisha said, "Call her." So he called her, and she stood in the doorway. ¹⁶"About this time next year," Elisha said, "you will hold a son in your arms."

"No, my lord," she objected. "Don't mislead your servant, O man of God!"

¹⁷But the woman became pregnant, and the next year about that same time she gave birth to a son, just as Elisha had told her.

¹⁸The child grew, and one day he went out to his father, who was with the reapers. ¹⁹"My head! My head!" he said to his father.

His father told a servant, "Carry him to his mother." ²⁰After the servant had lifted him up and carried him to his mother, the boy sat on her lap until noon, and then he died. ²¹She went up and laid him on the bed of the man of God, then shut the door and went out.

²²She called her husband and said, "Please send me one of the servants and a donkey so I can go to the man of God quickly and return."

²³"Why go to him today?" he asked. "It's not the New Moon or the Sabbath."

"It's all right," she said.

²⁴She saddled the donkey and said to her servant, "Lead on; don't slow down for me unless I tell you." ²⁵So she set out and came to the man of God at Mount Carmel.

When he saw her in the distance, the man of God said to his servant Gehazi, "Look! There's the Shunammite! ²⁶Run to meet her and ask her, 'Are you all right? Is your husband all right? Is your child all right?'"

"Everything is all right," she said.

²⁷When she reached the man of God at the mountain, she took hold of his feet. Gehazi came over to push her away, but the man of God said, "Leave her alone! She is in bitter distress, but the LORD has hidden it from me and has not told me why."

²⁸"Did I ask you for a son, my lord?" she said. "Didn't I tell you, 'Don't raise my hopes'?"

²⁹Elisha said to Gehazi, "Tuck your cloak into your belt, take my staff in your hand and run. If you meet anyone, do not greet him, and if anyone greets you, do not answer. Lay my staff on the boy's face."

³⁰But the child's mother said, "As surely as the LORD lives and as you live, I will not leave you." So he got up and followed her.

³¹Gehazi went on ahead and laid the staff on the boy's face, but there was no sound or response. So Gehazi went back to meet Elisha and told him, "The boy has not awakened."

³²When Elisha reached the house, there was the boy lying dead on his couch. ³³He went in, shut the door on the two of them and prayed to the LORD. ³⁴Then he got on the bed and lay upon the boy, mouth to mouth, eyes to eyes, hands to hands. As he stretched himself out upon him, the boy's body grew warm. ³⁵Elisha turned away and walked back and forth in the room and then got on the bed and stretched out upon him once more. The boy sneezed seven times and opened his eyes.

³⁶Elisha summoned Gehazi and said, "Call the Shunammite." And he did. When she came, he said, "Take your son." ³⁷She came in, fell at his feet and bowed to the ground. Then she took her son and went out.

³⁸Elisha returned to Gilgal and there was a famine in that region. While the company of the prophets was meeting with him, he said to his servant, "Put on the large pot and cook some stew for these men."

³⁹One of them went out into the fields to gather herbs and found a wild vine. He gathered some of its gourds and filled the fold of his cloak. When he returned, he cut them up into the pot of stew, though no one knew what they were. ⁴⁰The stew was poured out for the men, but as they began to eat it, they cried out, "O man of God, there is death in the pot!" And they could not eat it.

⁴¹Elisha said, "Get some flour." He put it into the pot and said, "Serve it to the people to eat." And there was nothing harmful in the pot.

⁴²A man came from Baal Shalishah, bringing the man of God twenty loaves of barley bread baked from the first ripe grain, along with some heads of new grain. "Give it to the people to eat," Elisha said.

⁴³"How can I set this before a hundred men?" his servant asked.

But Elisha answered, "Give it to the people to eat. For this is what the LORD says: 'They will eat and have some left over.'" ⁴⁴Then he set it before them, and they ate and had some left over, according to the word of the LORD.

THESE STORIES OF Elisha appear independent of chronological sequence or of political events. The events with the wealthy woman of Shunem are simply said to happen "one day" (4:8, 11, 18),[1] and there is no indication of the time of the famine (v. 38). There is no mention of the names of officials; the woman from Shunem has no connection to the king or his associates (v. 13). Even the power of the prophetic word is subordinated, being mentioned only in the final miracle (v. 43). These accounts do not further the history of Israel but serve to illustrate the power and authority of Elisha. Elisha does the work of God, the true King of Israel. The duty of the king was to provide for justice, protection, and the well-being of the people.[2] In the fading days of the Omride dynasty, the responsibilities of the king in Israel are fulfilled in particular times and places through the man of God.

Oil for a Widow (4:1–7)

THIS NAMELESS WIDOW of the prophets is rescued from anonymity early on in Jewish tradition.[3] Josephus makes her the wife of Obadiah, the servant of Ahab (1 Kings 18:3–4), who risked his life to save a hundred prophets otherwise to be slain by Jezebel (*Ant.* 9.47–48). The cause of the debt is that Obadiah borrowed money for the maintenance of the prophets while in hiding. After he died his widow and her children are in danger of being carried off into slavery. The widow's plea is that Elisha will have mercy on her because of the noble deed of her husband in preserving the prophets. The Targums also identify the widow as the wife of Obadiah.

The company of prophets who supported Elijah and Elisha maintained their own properties and families. Quite apart from the tradition that this woman is the widow of Obadiah, these followers of the covenant would have paid a high price for their commitment in the hostile environment of the official Baal cult. The time and sacrifice required to support this movement against the prevailing economic forces left little reserve when the family provider died. Even in normal times families could become so indebted that some members were given as servants to their creditors (cf. Ex. 21:1–11).

---

1. In contrast to other occurrences of this expression, here it is nothing more than a specific time identifier as the day of the event (DeVries, *Yesterday, Today and Tomorrow*, 235). It is used to facilitate transitions in the narrative.

2. "A prominent theme in the political legends is Elisha's ability to save the nation when the king has failed" (Marsha White, "Elisha," *Eerdmans Dictionary of the Bible*, 399).

3. See L. Ginzberg, *The Legends of the Jews* (Philadelphia: Jewish Publication Society, 1913), 4:240–42.

God in his law provided that this would be a temporary situation (six years at the most), or that the servants could voluntarily enter into a new family relationship (especially if marriage and children were involved). Servanthood would be a dismal end for a family that had already endured so much.

The story of God's provision is told without embellishment.[4] Elisha asks two questions about the widow's need and resources, to which she responds. He then tells her what to do, and she dutifully obeys. The provision of oil takes place behind closed doors, with only the woman and her sons present. The oil is a divine gift that is not dependent on the presence of the man of God and cannot be viewed as some kind of trick. The unusual form of the verb "pour" seems to indicate that the oil is made to pour continuously until all the jars are filled (v. 5).[5] No details are given following Elisha's final instruction (v. 7), but it may be assumed that the woman obeys without question. Her debts are paid, and her family remains together.

A Son for the Childless (4:8–37)

IN THE PREVIOUS STORY, a widow of one of the prophets supporting Elisha seeks out his assistance in her dire need. In this second story a woman of means urges the prophet to accept her hospitality whenever he passes by on his journeys through the Jezreel Valley (v. 8). Shunem, also the home of Abishag (1 Kings 1:3), was in Issachar (Josh. 19:18), near Gilboa; the valley between Shunem and Jezreel formed a pass to the Jordan.[6] The name may have been a description of the place where one of the prophetic groups met and received oracles from God.[7]

Elisha has occasion to pass the location regularly on his journeys from Carmel (4:9); like Samuel (1 Sam. 7:15–17), he probably follows a circuit in the administration of his duties. Elisha is regarded as a holy man, distinguished from the other prophets who continue to have regular vocations. This status may have been the reason for providing a separate room for him; separate quarters protect the family from having inappropriate intimacy with this man of God. The woman's reverence is also expressed in the vocabulary used to describe her hospitality (2 Kings 4:13); Elisha says she "trembled"

---

4. The unusual feminine endings and the rare word for a jar (ʾasûk) of oil (v. 2) may be relics of the dialect of northern Israel (Cogan and Tadmor, *II Kings*, 60).

5. The Piel form of the verb (myṣqt) is found only in this verse; the Masoretic vocalization (qere) is Hiphil.

6. It is on the slopes of the Hill of Moreh (Teacher's Hill), the area where the Midianites encamped before Gideon's attack. It is identified as the modern Sôlem; see Aharoni et al., *The Carta Bible Atlas*, #75.

7. Gray (*I & II Kings*, 494) notes that in Arabic times it was crowned with a saint's tomb, possibly indicating the ancient sanctity of the location.

(*ḥāradtᵉ*) with "fear" (*ḥᵃrādâ*) for him,[8] expressing the care she has taken not to infringe on his sanctity as a man of God. The room is furnished simply but adequately for a regular guest. This woman is not independently wealthy, but secures permission from her husband to build a special hospitality suite for this notable guest.

The second part of the story introduces Gehazi, the assistant to Elisha, as intermediary between Elisha and the woman (4:12–17). The scene depicts a deference and appropriate protocol between Elisha and his patron, who holds him to be a holy man of God. Through Gehazi, she first makes herself available to Elisha (v. 12), then she comes to be present in the doorway (v. 15); a similar procedure occurs at the end of the section, where the woman is first summoned (v. 36) and then enters the room (v. 37).[9]

Elisha poses the same question for his benefactor as he did for the widow who came to plead her case: "What can be done for you?" (v. 13; cf. v. 2). His suggestions of intervening with the king or military commander show that Elisha has come into a position of political influence, perhaps enhanced by his involvement in the Moabite campaign. As wealthy people, the woman and her husband carry a heavy liability for maintaining the state and its military. The woman declines political intervention, saying she is secure within her clan. Such independence is typical of communities that take responsibility for their neighbors seriously. She has no need of social and material assistance, unlike the first woman who is about to lose her sons.

Discussion with Gehazi reveals her real need: Unlike the widow, she cannot lose her children, because she has none. Elisha asks her to be present in person for his announcement that in a year she will embrace a son.[10] Like Sarah at the announcement of Isaac (Gen. 18:12), the woman finds the promise incredible (2 Kings 4:16); she does not dare to hope lest she be disappointed. In spite of her doubts, her desire for a child is fulfilled.

The narrative immediately advances to another day, some years later, when the child has grown (4:18). The third division of the story deals with the disappointment the woman fears (vv. 18–28); in spite of the miraculous birth, she does not now have a son. The woman is depicted as resolute in her plight. When the child dies in her arms, she immediately lays the body on the bed of the man of God and prepares to confront him. Her husband is pre-

---

8. See Genesis 27:33 for the same expression, as Isaac responds to Esau just after he has blessed Jacob. The context in Kings suggests concern, effort, and respect.

9. Montgomery (*The Books of Kings*, 368) observes the various nuances of the word come (*bôʾ*) used to depict the movements of the woman in relation to Elisha.

10. "At the time of reviving" (*kāᶜet ḥayyâ*) probably refers to spring (cf. Gen. 18:10, 14), distinguishing it from the explicit "same time next year" (Gen. 17:21). Alternately, the idiom may be equivalent to the Akkadian *ana balat*, "to life," meaning next year at the same time.

sented as uncompassionate and skeptical (vv. 22–23). Her request for release of a farm worker from harvest is met with the protest of inopportune time; Sabbath or feast days were the normal times to travel to Carmel, when work ceased and matters of faith were given priority. The woman silences her husband with a single word for well-being (*šālôm*); an amorphous term, it can be interpreted as a dismissal or a confidence.

The woman goes with all the speed she can manage (4:24), resolved to express her distress to the man of God himself. Elisha sees her coming and sends Gehazi to meet her (v. 26); she dismisses his inquiry with the same uncertain response she had for her husband (*šālôm*). Like the woman at Zarephath, who held Elijah responsible for the death of her son (1 Kings 17:18), the woman from Shunem feels that there is something sinister about this man of God; he has deceived her (2 Kings 4:28). From the start she has been loath to believe it was possible she should have a son. Surprisingly, Elisha confesses to being mystified by this turn of events (4:27). He admits to Gehazi that he has received no word from Yahweh on this matter.

The final division of the story shows that the woman has not lost her faith in God or his servant (4:29–37). She is hurt, confused, and anxious. Elisha treats the situation with urgency, sending Gehazi to the lad with instructions that he not be delayed by courtesies to those he might meet along the way (v. 29). The mission to place the staff of Elisha on the lad is an assurance that the prophet himself is on his way to Shunem. The woman refuses to go with Gehazi; her vow to stay with Elisha is identical to that of Elisha in his refusal to leave Elijah (v. 30; cf. 2:2, 4, 6).

When Elisha arrives he shuts the door so the miracle will be private (4:33), just like the multiplication of the oil (vv. 4–5). The actions of Elisha are similar to those of Elijah in reviving the child of the woman at Zarephath, but are described in significantly more detail (vv. 33–35; cf. 1 Kings 17:20–21). Elisha places his own living body over the boy in place of the staff;[11] his intensity is seen in pacing back and forth, waiting for signs of life. The first response of the child is a sneeze (NIV); it represents some physical or spiritual substance that leads to the cause of death being expelled.[12] Seven sneezes assure complete restoration. The actions of the woman are similar to her reporting the death of the child (v. 27); she falls prostrate at the feet of Elisha, this time in gratitude rather than grief.

---

11. The posture of Elisha on the bed is described as "crouching" (*ghr*), the same verb used to describe the posture of Elijah praying for rain with his head between his knees (1 Kings 18:42).

12. Mark Phelps, "זרר I," *NIDOTTE*, 1:1155. The root *zrr* appears to be closely related to *zwr*, used to describe the expulsion of pus (Isa. 1:6). The Aramaic used the same word in this verse as it did for the sneezes of Leviathan (Job 41:18); the Latin has "yawned," and the Greek omits the word.

Food in Time of Famine (4:38–44)

THE FINAL TWO STORIES deal with another fundamental need of life. Both stories involve the prophetic bands that support Elisha in his efforts to teach the ways of the covenant in a state devoted to the Baal cult. In the first story (4:38–41), a famine leaves the band short of food, with the necessity of foraging for what they can find. Ignorance results in a "death pot" that threatens the health of the men. Elisha responds immediately to the crisis with the authority that is his alone as the man of God; the food is made wholesome and the welfare of the band preserved.

In the second story a stranger offers food to the band, but it is insufficient for the entire group. Elisha twice gives exactly the same command: "Give it to the people to eat" (vv. 42, 43). The protest that it will be insufficient is met with a word from Yahweh indicating that it will be more than sufficient. This word is fulfilled (v. 44); Elisha provides for his prophets, just as he had for the widow. Each of these events establishes the authority of Elisha with the prophets as well as his ability to care for them.

These stories give a glimpse into the life of the prophetic bands and how God provides for them in times of need. Elisha is the leader of the band at Gilgal near Jericho (cf. 2:1), where they gather before him for instruction, encouragement, and direction.[13] "The famine" (4:38) probably refers to the seven-year famine described in a later encounter with the Shunammite woman (8:1–6). Elisha assumes responsibility for the preparation of the meal, asking that the large pot be set to boil with potage. In searching for edible food,[14] someone from the group finds a wild vine with gourds. These are probably to be identified with a small yellow melon popularly called the "Apple of Sodom." It is a strong purgative and known to be fatal.[15] The addition of flour to the potage absorbs the bitterness and makes it edible.

The land of Shalishah is found together with the lands of Shaalim and Zuph, all of them family districts of Benjamin in Mount Ephraim (1 Sam. 9:4–5). The city of Baal Shalishah cannot be identified with certainty, but the name may be preserved in the modern *Kefr Thilth* to the southwest of Shechem. "The first ripe grain" would be the time when the famine is most severe. This grain, usually barley, belongs to Yahweh (Lev. 23:20), and it may be that the gift is brought as part of the provision for a sacramental

---

13. Montgomery (*The Books of Kings*, 369) suggests that the noun *yᵉšibâ*, meaning session or academy, a technical term used to this day, may be related to the verb *yāšab*, which describes the sons of the prophets before Elisha.

14. The rare Hebrew word for "herb" (*ʾōrâ*) is probably related to the verb *ʾrh*, meaning pluck (Ps. 80:12; Song 5:1).

15. A member of the *citrullus colcynthus*; Cogan and Tadmor, *II Kings*, 58.

meal. "Some heads of new grain" (NIV) is often translated "fresh ears of grain in his sack" (RSV). The word translated "sack" (ṣqln) is otherwise unknown. The man brings fresh heads of grain (cf. Lev. 2:14) along with the twenty barley loaves made from the firstfruits. This amount of bread appears to be inadequate to the servant, but at the instruction of Elisha it feeds the hundred men with some left over.

GOD'S CARE FOR the individual. In this chapter Elisha shows that his name, "my God saves," is a truth to live by. In the first example (vv. 1–7), a destitute widow of one of the sons of the prophets appeals to Elisha. The creditors have come to take her two children as slaves. Elisha may have some obligation to provide for those who have joined his band of followers as a prophet, but the Hebrew covenant always places a special emphasis on God's concern for needs of widows and orphans (e.g., Deut. 10:18; 24:17–22; Isa. 1:17).

In the second example a nameless but wealthy woman from Shunem suffers from the poverty of childlessness, a pain no less than that of the poverty that causes loss of children. Her generosity in providing for the prophet is rewarded with the gift of life. The miracle child is reclaimed by Yahweh, but the faith of the woman prevails and her child is restored (vv. 8–37).

In the final two episodes Elisha provides food for the band of the prophets; in the first instance he makes it edible (vv. 38–41), in the second sufficient (vv. 42–44). In all of these instances God shows his care for his prophets and his provision for his people in a way that is beyond the power of human kings.

The miracles of these stories have counterparts in the activities of Elijah. The multiplication of oil (vv. 4–5) and of bread (vv. 43–44) and the revival of a widow's son (vv. 33–35) are similar to the provisions of Elijah for the widow of Zarephath (1 Kings 17:14–16, 20–22). Elisha is again shown to be the worthy successor of Elijah.

This chapter provides an insight into the function of prophets and the great variety of their individual vocations. Within the larger Deuteronomistic History the unique ministries of Elijah and Elisha call for loyalty to the covenant, with the power to confront and control political and military forces. The stories of this chapter, however, reveal another dimension of the prophetic task not directly related to the battle against the imperial cult. Caught up in the larger conflict are many victims with individual struggles; others live with personal sorrows not rectified by victories against political oppression. These stories show that God's compassion and care for individuals in their need is no less significant than his triumph over organized resistance to his dominion.

Elisha is the focus of these stories, to the exclusion of all other detail. None of the other characters or events is given so much as a name, let alone some context in other events of their life and times. Elisha is the ordained benefactor who brings mercy in times of need.

The strength of the Shunammite woman. There are other remarkable features to be observed not central to the story, and the modern reader may well note their considerable significance.[16] The story of the Shunammite woman assumes a subtle protocol for the status of the prophet, maintaining a respectful distance between Elisha and the woman. The woman strains against such formalities in the pursuit of her aims, first of all urging Elisha to accept her hospitality (v. 8), then prevailing on her husband to provide a permanent furnished room for the prophet as a regular guest (vv. 9–10).

When her child dies this woman takes matters into her own hands; she secures the assistance of one of the farm workers and a donkey to assist her in a hasty journey to the prophet, efficiently silencing the objections of her husband (vv. 22–23). Though Elisha sends Gehazi to meet her, she is undeterred by such proprieties and dismisses him just as she had her husband (v. 26). When she meets the man of God, in a manner scarcely appropriate for a married woman of some status, she seizes and clings to his feet. The impulse of Gehazi is to forcibly provide a respectable distance, but the woman has her way through the concession of Elisha (v. 27). When the life of the child is revived, she again expresses both reverence and intimacy in falling at the feet of the prophet (v. 37). This exchange between the woman and the prophet is just as irregular as the miracle itself, though it is incidental in the presentation of the story, scarcely observed by the reader taken up with the central focus on the prophet.

The story of the Shunammite and her son reveals the compassion and power of Elisha, but the impact is considerably enhanced by the strength of her character. The status of Elisha as a holy man is not reduced (v. 9), but he is also shown to be human, approachable, and vulnerable as are other humans. He accepted her hospitality as assistance to his travels, preferable to other choices. Shunem is only about fifteen miles from the traditional location of Elijah's sacrifice (*Deir al-Mahraq*), and the name of the hill at Shunem (Moreh) makes it likely there is a prophetic community located there where Elisha can

---

16. See Burke O. Long, "The Shunammite Woman: In the Shadow of the Prophet," *Bible Review* 7/1 (1991): 12–19, 42. Sometimes referred to as deconstruction, this type of reading focuses on interests of the reader; it observes aspects of the narrative that subtly determine the force of its central theme.

receive hospitality. Elisha determines to give to the woman in turn, even though she is reluctant to accept any assistance (vv. 13, 16).

The death of the child comes as a complete surprise to Elisha (v. 27), so the woman appropriately challenges the efficacy of the promise concerning the gift of the child (v. 28). She refuses to leave the prophet (v. 30), insisting that he personally be present at the side of the child (v. 32). Once at Shunem, the resuscitation is a process in which the woman participates; she waits outside the room as Elisha first prays for the child (v. 33), then warms the body of the child by stretching (*ghr*) his own body over it (v. 34),[17] and after pacing the house returns to repeat the motion until the child sneezes and opens his eyes (v. 35). The Shunammite is then invited into the room, where she receives the child alive into her arms and reverences the man of God for his care and provision in her time of grief.

The nature of miracles. The miraculous nature of the divine provision in each of these stories is not to be rationally explained.[18] By their very nature miracles transcend explanation and stand outside of historical investigation. Miracles are an act of grace that cannot be controlled or predicted, but are a provision of the sovereign God in time of need. It is not the mission of Elisha to demonstrate the power of God by performing miracles at his own will. The ability to perform miracles is not in and of itself a sign of God's power (cf. Ex. 7:8—13). The vocation of Elisha is to bring the message of God's faithfulness wherever he goes. In each instance the miraculous is God's gracious compassion to particular human need.

Not all prophets perform miracles, and not all situations of distress are resolved by miraculous intervention. The nature of the miraculous must remain in the mysteries of heaven. In these stories the miraculous comes to those powerless to address their own need, but are submissive to the divine will in looking to the man of God as their spiritual leader and provider in time of need. The prominence of Elisha in these stories emphasizes his vocation, not only to call for faithfulness to God but also to demonstrate God's faithfulness to those who trust him.

---

17. Montgomery notes the difficulty that the Greek translators had with this verb (*The Books of Kings*, 372); if the word shares an etymology with the Arabic root for "fight" (the noun *jihad* is used for holy war), it might indicate a vigorous motion, a nuance apparently known to the Greek translators (*diakamptô*).

18. The similarity of these stories to magic makers in other cultures has been noted, though to be sure, similarity of phenomena does not indicate similarity of cause. For comparisons with "shamanism," see T. W. Overholt, "Seeing Is Believing: The Social Setting of Prophetic Acts of Power," *JSOT* 23 (1982): 3—31. Overholt views these "acts of power" as legitimating the authority of the prophets concerned, as they received responses of affirmation from their supporters. African parallels have also been cited; see E. R. Wendland, "Elijah and Elisha: Sorcerers or Witch Doctors? Tonga Interpretation," *BT* 43 (1992): 213—23.

CONCERN FOR THE HELPLESS. Life in this world is characterized by need and struggle as typified in these stories about Elisha. The pain of various situations and individuals is not really comparable; who is to say that losing a child to a creditor is more painful than never to have had a child at all (vv. 1, 14), or that the pain of food deprivation is more injurious than the loss of children (vv. 38, 43)? Empathy is a somewhat risky business, since one can never know the feelings or pain of another. Perhaps this unknown is part of the divine mystery of grace. God sovereignly dispenses his mercy to particular situations in his care for all his children. Mercy by its very nature is not justice, so the children are not able to demand whatever they consider to be their right, nor can they expect that their experience with God will be like that of someone else.

Every age has a need for a mission like that of Elisha: to care for the needy, intervene for justice, and provide for the well-being of the marginalized. The needs of women, rich and poor, have been rightly emphasized in our time. There is less agreement on values to be pursued, concepts of how equality can be defined and how justice may be advanced. The role of faith groups has been challenged in various ways; generally, faith is marginalized to a personal pursuit of existential spirituality that is not allowed to have a role in public life. In its place is a set of state-controlled values that are not to be violated, the Baalism of our time. Those with a mission like that of Elisha must find a way to work within the system, much as Elisha in his own time.

A society preoccupied by rights and individual indulgence has established its own valuations of what is just, necessary, and possible. The justification of abortion on demand, in defense of the reproductive right of choice for women, assumes that this right must receive primacy over the rights of an unborn child, its father, her parents, and anyone related to her situation. Such values determine the way health care dollars are invested in state-provided medical care. Allocation of funds for abortion should equally require that childless couples receive assistance for conception. Childless couples unable to conceive are deprived of assistance, while those seeking to end the life of an unborn child are assisted without question. The care of Elisha for the childless woman of Shunem shows that the pain of barrenness is not to be subordinated to that of economic loss and hardship.

Even those committed to the right of abortion on demand concede the injustice of rights in the laws of abortion, not only against the unborn but also against the childless. Gordon Sinclair, a Winnipeg freelance writer, tells of an unusual request for an obituary that came his way. A couple was expecting twins after eleven years of trying to conceive, but they lost the children before they were born. The husband was writing to say that his wife needed something tangible to acknowledge the lives that had been lost; she wanted the names of their babies in an obituary notice so that knowledge of their existence might be preserved. Sinclair expresses the outrage that he feels about the situation of childless couples.

"Choice," for those couples, is getting in line at private infertility clinics and paying $8,000 per attempt.

The government will fund abortion without blinking.

But there is no health-care money for those whose "choice" is to try to have babies with the assistance of medical technology. There is no marching in the street for these women from either the pro-life or the pro-choice movements.

If I sound angry, it's because I am.[19]

Both technology and the systems of medical delivery are a painful injustice to such couples. They are in need of divine grace no less than the woman at Shunem. The least that can be done is to pray that they may have a sense of divine mercy and that God in his grace may also grant them the gift of life. Elisha as the man of God can assure the Shunammite of a son in a year's time, but even Elisha is unable to anticipate the child's death (4:27). Elisha also lives under submission to the divine will, waiting on Yahweh as he tries three times to bring life back to the lad. Medical services are a divine gift and need to be applied justly, but they can never be a replacement for prayer and trust in the Lifegiver.

How God provides. A society made wealthy by technological success, a result of the pursuit of understanding cause and effect, functions with a scientific explanation for events. Acceptance of miracles requires an act of faith in which the normal processes of empirical investigation are suspended. Adherence to the scientific method as the explanation for all phenomena regards such stories as the projection of faith in a desperate effort to address the problem of pain. The point of these stories, however, is just the reverse. Miracles are the result of faith, not the inspiration of faith.[20] Faith is a process of learning to trust God; these stories of Elisha are intended to teach the life of trust in God and to show the power of such a faith in dealing with pain. Such faith does provide oil to pay debts, revive the dead, and provide food for the hungry. Such faith also acknowledges that God provides through a

---

19. Gordon Sinclair Jr., "Some Dreams Will Never Be Forgotten; Infertile Couples Know Both Hope . . . and Sorrow," *Winnipeg Free Press* (June 28, 2003), C3.

20. Hobbs, *2 Kings*, 54.

better understanding of how to live in harmony with his earth, a knowledge gained through scientific research.

The miracles of Jesus follow the same pattern of care for the needy—the act of faith, however fledgling, being a prerequisite to the experience of divine grace. The Gospel of Mark illustrates this truth in two touching stories. Jairus, the ruler of the synagogue, was persuaded that Jesus could save his daughter from imminent death (Mark 5:22−23). As Jesus went with him, a woman with a chronic hemorrhage joined the crowd. She believed that if she could but touch the garment of Jesus, she would be delivered (vv. 25−28). Though her faith bordered on magic, it was honored by Jesus, and she was healed. Jesus was not content to allow her faith to be unacknowledged, so he led her to make confession and exhorted her to continue in a life of trust (vv. 30−34).

In the meantime the daughter of Jairus died, and the crowd exhorted him not to trouble Jesus any further. Jesus encouraged Jairus not to waver in his trust (Mark 5:36). Jesus dismissed the mourners who scorned his exhortation and entered the girl's chamber with the parents alone. The impact of his words were remembered and repeated in Aramaic, just as they were heard: *talitha koum* (v. 41), simply translated as "maiden, arise." Jesus then exhorted them not to make this known, for the skepticism of the unbelieving could never be objective with such an event. Their denial and rationalizations would compromise the experience of grace received. Trusting people must be careful not to cast their pearls before swine.

The experiences of the widow of the prophet and the woman of Shunem are both very private affairs, concealed from the skeptical world of Baal around them, preserved as a miracle of grace for the need of the occasion. This is often the way it should be. As a pastor, there have been a select number of sacred occasions when I have observed such a miracle. One of the cases was a diagnosis of meningitis in an adolescent girl. Her mother called me while I was out of town to request prayer for surgery that was to take place immediately, because the physicians had determined the case to be critical. Many joined in prayer.

I returned the next day to pay a visit in the hospital and learn how serious the situation was, wondering if this young woman would be able to function normally again. I called her parents and found that she was at home and well. When the actual time for surgery arrived, I was informed, no trace of the dreadful disease could be found. Her family asked about the diagnosis; they were informed that meningitis had been observed as clearly as a cow on their front lawn. Together with the family, those informed were most grateful for the grace received, in whatever form it had come. Such matters of course were not confidential; the family received calls from various well-meaning individuals wanting the story to be shared. All were wisely declined. God's miracles of grace for his people are not to be paraded about as if this could prove the power of God to the skeptics. As with these miracles of Elisha, the grace of God is for his trusting people in time of need, however tentative they may feel their faith to be.

A society indulged by wealth struggles to solve its problems of pain and injustice. It tends to regard affirmation of the miraculous as the inspiration of faith; the miraculous is not compatible with methods they pursue in dealing with pain. The faithful must recognize that material and technological achievements are a gift of God and a further reason to trust God in faith. Victims of poverty, hunger, and unjust loss of life will not be delivered by more promises of the just society. Such victims need God's grace no less than the victims of Joram's kingdom. The contemporary world must have its servants of God, those anointed like Elisha, who can challenge arrogance and self-sufficiency but extend divine grace to the needy and trusting.

While technology and wealth can never be a replacement for trust in God, they have been used by God to provide for widows and children. AIDS and civil war have become twin scourges for women and children in Africa; they are left homeless and without food as providers in the family die. In Uganda alone, two million children have been orphaned by these calamities. Kampala Pentecostal Church in Uganda (a 12,000 member cell-based community church) has established Watoto Child Care Ministries (*wahtoto* means "children" in Swahili).[21] To date over one hundred homes have been built, forming three Watoto villages, and a fourth village is now under way. Presently over eight hundred orphans and eighty widows are being cared for through this program. Each village has a school and clinic.

Echo Farm is an organization in Fort Myers, Florida, involved in the research and production of crops and livestock that will survive and flourish under the various conditions of Third World countries.[22] Missionaries both full time and short term can come to intern and learn how to take this knowledge to other areas of the world. Recently, Watoto hired a director of agriculture to help their villages become self-sufficient; this created a great need for the director to learn more about agricultural research. An entrepreneur aware of both organizations brought the two groups together and introduced them in Fort Myers.[23] Two individuals from the Watoto head office in Tampa came down to Fort Myers, and they met and toured Echo Farm. Both

21. See www.watoto.com.

22. See www.echonet.org.

23. Warren and Bonnie Toles, a Canadian business couple residing half time in Florida, have facilitated the link between the two organizations. This took place in October, 2004.

technology and financial support are helping the widows and orphans of Uganda, in the same way that the endless supply of oil provided for the widow of one of the prophetic bands. One is not more the provision of God than the other. In a great diversity of ways God provides for his children. The name "my God saves" is as pertinent today as in the time of Elisha.

2 Kings 5:1–27

NOW NAAMAN WAS commander of the army of the king of Aram. He was a great man in the sight of his master and highly regarded, because through him the LORD had given victory to Aram. He was a valiant soldier, but he had leprosy.

²Now bands from Aram had gone out and had taken captive a young girl from Israel, and she served Naaman's wife. ³She said to her mistress, "If only my master would see the prophet who is in Samaria! He would cure him of his leprosy."

⁴Naaman went to his master and told him what the girl from Israel had said. ⁵"By all means, go," the king of Aram replied. "I will send a letter to the king of Israel." So Naaman left, taking with him ten talents of silver, six thousand shekels of gold and ten sets of clothing. ⁶The letter that he took to the king of Israel read: "With this letter I am sending my servant Naaman to you so that you may cure him of his leprosy."

⁷As soon as the king of Israel read the letter, he tore his robes and said, "Am I God? Can I kill and bring back to life? Why does this fellow send someone to me to be cured of his leprosy? See how he is trying to pick a quarrel with me!"

⁸When Elisha the man of God heard that the king of Israel had torn his robes, he sent him this message: "Why have you torn your robes? Have the man come to me and he will know that there is a prophet in Israel." ⁹So Naaman went with his horses and chariots and stopped at the door of Elisha's house. ¹⁰Elisha sent a messenger to say to him, "Go, wash yourself seven times in the Jordan, and your flesh will be restored and you will be cleansed."

¹¹But Naaman went away angry and said, "I thought that he would surely come out to me and stand and call on the name of the LORD his God, wave his hand over the spot and cure me of my leprosy. ¹²Are not Abana and Pharpar, the rivers of Damascus, better than any of the waters of Israel? Couldn't I wash in them and be cleansed?" So he turned and went off in a rage.

¹³Naaman's servants went to him and said, "My father, if the prophet had told you to do some great thing, would you not have done it? How much more, then, when he tells you, 'Wash

and be cleansed'!" ¹⁴So he went down and dipped himself in the Jordan seven times, as the man of God had told him, and his flesh was restored and became clean like that of a young boy.

¹⁵Then Naaman and all his attendants went back to the man of God. He stood before him and said, "Now I know that there is no God in all the world except in Israel. Please accept now a gift from your servant."

¹⁶The prophet answered, "As surely as the LORD lives, whom I serve, I will not accept a thing." And even though Naaman urged him, he refused.

¹⁷"If you will not," said Naaman, "please let me, your servant, be given as much earth as a pair of mules can carry, for your servant will never again make burnt offerings and sacrifices to any other god but the LORD. ¹⁸But may the LORD forgive your servant for this one thing: When my master enters the temple of Rimmon to bow down and he is leaning on my arm and I bow there also—when I bow down in the temple of Rimmon, may the LORD forgive your servant for this."

¹⁹"Go in peace," Elisha said.

After Naaman had traveled some distance, ²⁰Gehazi, the servant of Elisha the man of God, said to himself, "My master was too easy on Naaman, this Aramean, by not accepting from him what he brought. As surely as the LORD lives, I will run after him and get something from him."

²¹So Gehazi hurried after Naaman. When Naaman saw him running toward him, he got down from the chariot to meet him. "Is everything all right?" he asked.

²²"Everything is all right," Gehazi answered. "My master sent me to say, 'Two young men from the company of the prophets have just come to me from the hill country of Ephraim. Please give them a talent of silver and two sets of clothing.'"

²³"By all means, take two talents," said Naaman. He urged Gehazi to accept them, and then tied up the two talents of silver in two bags, with two sets of clothing. He gave them to two of his servants, and they carried them ahead of Gehazi. ²⁴When Gehazi came to the hill, he took the things from the servants and put them away in the house. He sent the men away and they left. ²⁵Then he went in and stood before his master Elisha.

"Where have you been, Gehazi?" Elisha asked.

"Your servant didn't go anywhere," Gehazi answered.

²⁶But Elisha said to him, "Was not my spirit with you when the man got down from his chariot to meet you? Is this the

time to take money, or to accept clothes, olive groves, vineyards, flocks, herds, or menservants or maidservants? [27]Naaman's leprosy will cling to you and to your descendants forever." Then Gehazi went from Elisha's presence and he was leprous, as white as snow.

Original Meaning

THE HEALING OF Naaman is a story of need met by God through the agency of the prophet, but the provision itself is subordinate to other moral and theological issues. Historically the story is related to the wars with the Arameans, though neither the Aramean king nor the Israelite king is named. The role of Elisha is complemented by that of a captive Israelite maiden, and the fate of Naaman is contrasted with that of Gehazi. The story shows the powerlessness of the king and the power of the prophet, the reign and grace of God extending outside Israel, the commendation of a foreign military chief, and the condemnation of a deceitful assistant to the prophet. Naaman's healing points toward a changed relationship between Israel and Syria as the worship of God extends beyond the borders of Israel by a general who has been raiding the land of Israel.

The Cure of a Mighty Leper (5:1–14)

NAAMAN IS THE field marshal of the king of Aram, the commander of all the army units of fifty, hundred, or thousand, each of which is led by its own officer. The fame and valor of Naaman is expanded three times to emphasize his distinction: He is a great man before his lord; he is of high renown because of the victories he has won; he is a hero of valor (v. 1). He also has one other distinction; he is a leper. This one single word at the end of a string of accolades compromises all the others.

The term *leper* is usually avoided in modern medical usage. The Greek translates the Hebrew term *ṣāraʿat* consistently as *lepra*. In Hellenistic times both the Hebrew and Greek terms referred to a wide variety of cutaneous (skin) diseases, most of them benign.[1] The term also refers to molds and fungi on clothes and buildings. In the law its distinctive signs include

---

1. The Hebrew word group *ṣrʿ* forms a generic term for a variety of cutaneous diseases, most of which were benign (R. K. Harrison, "צרע," *NIDOTTE*, 3:846–47). The signs and symptoms of leprosy in Leviticus are generally considered to preclude Hansen's disease (*Elephantiasis Graecorum*), with its symptomatic swellings, facial distortions, and mutilations; see further Gordon G. Wenham, *The Book of Leviticus* (NICOT; Grand Rapids: Eerdmans 1979), 189–214; Milgrom, "Scale Disease," *Leviticus 1–16*, 816–26.

scales and blotches (Lev. 13). Naaman's disease has caused whiteness
(v. 27), something like vitiligo in which pigment is lost from areas of the
skin. Naaman continued to have access to the court of the king of Aram
in Damascus (v. 4), an indication that his distress is more aesthetic than
contagion.

Naaman has been conducting raids in the territory of Israel, and in the
course of war has taken citizens captive, including a young girl who serves
in his household. The "little maiden" now rescues the "great man"; the captive saves the commander. She suggests to her mistress that if her master
were to go to the prophet in Samaria he might be cured.[2] Her remark begins
a series of transmissions that travel like lightning.

No mention is made of the report to Naaman; he abruptly reports this
information to the Aramean king, who in turn promptly prepares a letter for
the Israelite king.[3] Naaman prepares a large gift to establish diplomatic relations with the king of Israel (v. 5). He takes five times the amount of silver
required to purchase the hill of Samaria (cf. 1 Kings 16:24), plus six thousand
shekels of gold and ten changes of garments.[4] Naaman then sets out for Israel
with the letter and with the enormous royal gift.

The content of the letter is not disclosed until Naaman has actually
delivered it. This shifts the focus to the dramatic response of the king, who
takes the letter as an incitation to war. Requests from Damascus to Samaria
require official diplomatic exchange, with the natural assumption on the
part of the Arameans that prophets function under royal auspices.[5] The king
of Israel, knowing his precarious situation with the Aramean armies and the

---

2. The verb "gather" (ʾsp) is used for readmission into the community (cf. Num. 12:14–
15) and can also mean "heal"; Milgrom, Numbers, 99. Gray (I & II Kings, 505, following Montgomery) is in error in linking ʾsp to the Akkadian noun āšiptu(m), meaning exorcist. The noun
is found in the list of conjurers in the court of Nebuchadnezzar (Dan. 1:20; 2:2), but there
is no verb form; see Wolfram von Soden, Akkadisches Handwörterbuch (Lieferung 16, Wiesbaden: Harrassowitz; 1981), 1485–86; CAD A 2.431–35.

3. The form of ancient Hebrew and Aramaic letters has been studied extensively from
extant samples. This example is limited to mention of the letter (sēper), the sending of the
letter (šālaḥ), and a brief summary of its contents (vv. 5–6). The transition from the greet-
ing to the contents follows the standard formal transition in the phrase "and now" (wᵉʿattâ),
paraphrased as "with this letter" (NIV). For a brief analysis see Hobbs, 2 Kings, 62.

4. The shekel was a standard weight for measure; the name is a cognate of the verb for
weigh (šql). The talent was sixty minas, and the mina fifty shekels in the Palestinian system.
A shekel weighs about 4/10 oz. (10–13 grams). The sets of clothing (NIV) are rolls of cloth
used as payment rather than garments ready to wear.

5. The four hundred prophets of Ahab agreed unanimously that he should go to make
war against Ramoth Gilead (1 Kings 22:6). If it had not been for the presence of Jehoshaphat,
who represented another country, the national prophets would have been unanimous in their
support of the king.

prophets of Elisha, reads the letter as a demand that he demonstrate his authority over matters of life and death (5:7). Though a follower of Baal, he apparently knows that such powers belong to God alone (cf. Deut. 32:39). The king of Aram can hardly be expected to know that the king of Israel actively opposes the worship of the God of the prophets in the camp of Elisha, at times even seeking to kill them. The story mocks the impotence of kings and royal protocol, especially when the God of the covenant is being actively rejected.

The account now brings Elisha directly onto the scene as the main character of the first division (5:8). The narrative sequence may suggest that Elisha is still at Gilgal, where he fed the prophets, when he hears about the letter (cf. 4:38), in which case it makes sense for him to ask Naaman to dip in the Jordan. Elisha interrupts the royal exchange, telling the unbelieving king of Israel that an Aramean general will come to know the power of a true prophet.

Naaman proves to have a pride of his own (5:9–12). He interprets the prophet's indifference to royal protocol as an affront to his own status as someone esteemed by the mighty king of Aram. The prophet refuses to grant even a personal audience and does not come out to pray and offer a gesture of healing. Instead, he suggests the cure can be found in waters vastly inferior to those of his own country. The Abana and Pharpar were two rivers of the Anti-Lebanon Range, the first descending from Mount Amanah[6] into plain of Damascus, the second descending eastward from the heights of Hermon. As a great man he expects some "great thing." His own servants intervene with their own logic on the simplicity of faith; if Naaman were willing to do some great thing, why should he object to the simple instruction of the prophet?

The Conversion of a Conqueror (5:15–19)

THOUGH NAAMAN CONSENTS to abiding by the words of the prophet, his attitude remains a mystery. His return to the prophet settles the question of his disposition. His arrogance has become humility, and he now qualifies for his wish to have a direct audience with the prophet. He makes his confession to the God of Israel (5:15), proving the earlier words of Elisha to be true (v. 8). His confession also confirms the introductory verse: His victories are a provision of the God of Israel. The master of the servant girl now becomes the servant of the Israelite prophet.

Elisha refuses his proffered reward with a vow (5:16); Elisha can accept no responsibility for the mercy received. Grace granted by God cannot be rewarded with material benefits. As a confirmation of his confession, Naaman

---

6. The river takes its name from the mountain, known as Amanah in the only other biblical reference (Song 4:8) and in all extrabiblical references.

then makes two further requests of his own. He has changed his attitude toward the land of Israel; earlier he disparaged the river of Israel, but now wants two mule loads of earth to take back to the land of Aram.[7] The earth is to build an altar to worship in Aram, because he acknowledges no God in all the earth except the God of Israel. The second request is related to the first. As a servant of his lord he will be required to worship the God of thunder.[8] His seeming rambling request for forgiveness is actually a perfectly symmetric chiasm with the problem at the center.[9]

> For this thing
>> may the LORD pardon your servant
>>> when my lord comes to the house of Rimmon to worship there
>>>> and he leans on my hand
>>> and I worship in the house of Rimmon (when I worship in
>>>> the house of Rimmon)
>> may the LORD pardon your servant
> for this thing.

As the esteemed soldier, Naaman will be required to participate with the king as his right hand man. Elisha dismisses him with a simple blessing: "Go in peace." Elisha does not question Naaman's loyalty. His humble petition serves as its own affirmation of his genuine faith.

The Curse of Envy (5:20–27)

THOUGH NAAMAN DEPARTS (5:19), the story is not over, for he does not get very far. The entrance of Gehazi puts the transformation of Naaman and the power of Elisha into a fuller perspective. Naaman is shown to be truly generous, and Elisha is shown to be uncompromising in his integrity. Naaman shows the true character of faith while Gehazi, the servant of the prophet, betrays his master and his trust in God. Gehazi vows in the name of God to obtain at least a portion of the gift (v. 20), though his master has vowed that he cannot accept material gifts for a gift of grace (v. 16).

Gehazi sets off in hot pursuit to rectify what he thinks to be an injustice, but Naaman expresses concern only for the well-being of the prophet (v. 21).

---

7. The Hebrew term *ṣemed* refers to a team of animals, yoked together for work such as plowing a field (cf. 1 Kings 19:19). The mule (*pered*) was a hybrid offspring of the stallion and female donkey, the Akkadian *perdum* (Michael S. Moore and Michael L. Brown, "פֶּרֶד," *NIDOTTE*, 3:675–76). The mule is a royal animal (cf. 1 Kings 1:33, 38, 44); their presence with Naaman is an indication of their strength and common use as beasts of burden.

8. For the name Rimmon as thunder, see comment on 1 Kings 15:18.

9. Robert Cohn, "Form and Perspective in 2 Kings V," *VT* 33 (1983): 179.

Though Gehazi professes that all is at "peace" (v. 22), he is in the very process of violating that peace. He not only prepares to lie, but puts the lie in the mouth of his master. Naaman has been sent to Elisha by his master (v. 6), but Gehazi acts on his own with treachery to satisfy his own greed. Somehow Gehazi knew about the size of gift that Naaman planned (v. 5) and contrives his request accordingly (v. 22).

When Naaman urges him to take more, he packs the loot and readily accepts the help of two servants to take it back (v. 23).[10] While Naaman's reputation precedes him (v. 1), the servants precede Gehazi with the booty of his treachery (v. 24). As soon as they are back at the safety of the acropolis in Samaria,[11] Gehazi deposits the goods in the house and dispatches the servants (v. 25). Naaman is again on his way, and Gehazi resumes his position in the presence of his master as though nothing has happened.

The closing episode shows Elisha to be a true prophet who is fully aware of the implications of what has transpired. The duplicitous response of Gehazi to the question of where he has been does not deceive Elisha (5:25–26a).[12] The sharp rebuke of Elisha comes in the form of an enigmatic question (v. 26b). The self-evident answer to the rhetorical question is that this is not the time to be receiving money, clothes, and lands. Yet the form of the question leaves open the possibility that there may be a time to receive such gifts (cf. Hag. 1:4).

Strangely, Elisha goes on to name items Gehazi has not actually taken: fields of olives and vineyards, sheep, cattle, and servants. At most it may be thought that Gehazi intends to purchase these with the money he has acquired. The sin of Gehazi is deception, unbelief, and the disparagement of "this Aramean" (5:20). The question indicates that the sin of Gehazi is not merely greed and theft. The envy of Gehazi is immoral, as is his indifference to the profound conversion of Naaman to trust in the God of Israel. Gehazi cannot even consider how his envy of the goods of Naaman the Aramean is a subversion of God's grace. No doubt he intends the money and goods to provide a more comfortable life for the sons of the prophets, but Elisha understands that this is not the way of contentment with God's provision.

---

10. The two "bags" in which the silver is packed are large pieces of cloth, otherwise listed among women's apparel (Isa. 3:22). Gevirtz ("ḥereṭ in the Manufacture of the Golden Calf," *Bib* 65 [1984]: 377–81) thinks that this same word is found in Ex. 32:4 for a cloth Aaron used to gather up the gold for the calf, much like the procedure of Gideon (cf. Judg. 8:25).

11. The city is not named, but the citadel (ʿōpel) would be part of the capital; Gehazi, like his master, must have had a residence within the fortifications of the royal residence.

12. The idiom ʾānâ wāʾānâ (lit., "here and there") is deliberately ambiguous. In the prohibition against Shimei (1 Kings 2:36, 42), it meant nowhere outside of Jerusalem. The answer of Gehazi suggests he had not gone anywhere in particular ("out and about").

THE IRONY OF GRACE. This story of Naaman has three distinct divisions. Each division introduces another main character, so the miraculous healing is superseded by the lessons of subsequent events.[13] The first division deals with the healing of Naaman (vv. 1–14); it describes how the words of a young maiden (v. 2) come to restore the skin of the leprous general to be like that of a young lad (v. 14).

The second division (vv. 15–19) shows how someone whose skin has returned to that of a youth then returns to face his healer (v. 15), so that he is both physically and spiritually transformed.

In the final section (vv. 20–27), the humility and generosity of Naaman, disparagingly referred to as "this Aramean" (v. 20), is starkly contrasted with the presumptuousness and greed of Gehazi. While the foreigner submits to the prophet, Gehazi the servant of the prophet takes matters into his own hands in doing what seems right to him. The miracle of the healing initially brings about the greater miracle of the conversion of a foreign general. Events then evolve so the prophet's servant is afflicted with the disease the general originally suffered. The divisions that follow the initial healing transform the lesson on the miraculous to a lesson on faith and grace.

In the larger historical context, Gehazi shows himself to be like the rest of Israel, in violation of covenant trust.[14] Naaman the foreigner and invader has voluntarily come to seek God and has turned to him. Israel steadfastly refuses covenant fidelity and trust in God. The Arameans have been God's appointed agent for bringing judgment against Israel. This is not the time for Gehazi and the people of Israel to seek peace and security from the land of Naaman, with the hope of living securely on their own farms. Naaman judges the land of Israel by his acceptance of their God as the one and only (v. 15b); Gehazi betrays trust in God by attempting to derive peace and security through Naaman. The return of Naaman in peace and health is part of the prophetic indictment against Israel. Elisha knows this to be a time of judgment; the opportunism of Gehazi is completely misplaced.

The actions of Gehazi bring a whole new dimension to understanding divine grace. The grace of God begins with a series of miracles. A servant in a foreign household testifies to her own faith; her lord takes it seriously enough to undertake a diplomatic exchange, with the thought that help may

---

13. Robert Cohn shows how art and theology are "symbiotically related" in this story ("Form and Perspective in 2 Kings V," 171–84).

14. D. P. O'Brien, "'Is This the Time to Accept . . . ?' (2 Kings V 26b): Simply Moralizing (LXX) of an Ominous Foreboding of Yahweh's Rejection of Israel (MT)?" VT 46 (1996): 448–57.

be found in the royal courts of an adversary. The distress of the king of Israel gains the attention of the prophet, but the distance of the prophet only brings anger to the great foreign general. The servants of the mighty warrior bring him to a state of humility that fits him to be a recipient of divine healing. This leads to the real miracle; a foreign general, whose mission is to attack Israel, turns to trust their God as the only Lord of all the earth.

The irony of Naaman and Gehazi. To make his point Naaman requests some earth to take back to his own land (5:17), presumably so he can make an altar according to the requirements of his newly found faith (Ex. 20:23–25). The profundity of that miracle is brought into perspective by Gehazi. The miracle of conversion is lost on the servant of the prophet; he cannot rejoice with an enemy who has become a friend of God. Gehazi does not even seem to realize he has succumbed to the same kind of self-serving religion as the Baal worshipers of Joram.

The situation for Naaman is difficult. The king of Aram, in a polytheistic culture, would not object to Naaman worshiping another god from Israel; the problem would come in worshiping God alone, which seems to have been his intent. In his own land he will be required to show political loyalty, which means worshiping the national god of Aram; failure to do so will be regarded as treason. There can be no sympathy for a political leader denying the god of his own land for exclusive adherence to the God of Israel.

In another country a half a millennium earlier an Egyptian Pharaoh attempted to establish a type of exclusive supremacy of a native god. Pharaoh Akhenaten (ca. 1350–1334 B.C.) came to the throne as Amenophis IV; he changed his name to Akhenaten to show his strict devotion to one aspect of the sun god (Re), the Aten, specifically "the disk of the sun." In conjunction with his new devotion he built a new capital in Middle Egypt at what is now called el-Amarna. All other priesthoods and localized religious practice were condemned. The names of traditional gods were removed from monuments to blot out all memory of their presence.

The Hymn to Aten[15] is a well-known literary expression of his monotheistic belief. Similarities to Psalm 104 indicate that this poem was known in Israel (parallels are found esp. in 104:11–14, 20–27).[16] This effort at creating a monotheistic religion with a native god was not well received; after Akhenaten's death there was a rapid return to traditional polytheism. What was scarcely possible for a pharaoh regarded as divine was certainly not

---

15. Pritchard, *An Anthology of Texts and Pictures*, 226–31; figs. 108, 110.

16. For a study of the relationship between the Hymn to Aten and Psalm 104 see P. Dion, "YHWH as Storm-god and Sun-god: The Double Legacy of Egypt and Canaan as Reflected in Psalm 104," *ZAW* 103/1 (1991): 43–71.

possible for a subordinate Aramean general who wants to acknowledge exclusively, as God of all the earth, the deity of an enemy land. At the same time he cannot acknowledge the God who has given him healing without confessing the exclusive claims of his universal sovereignty as Creator.

Naaman asks for pardon in advance for showing loyalty to his lord; it is his only choice if he is to survive. To do otherwise in his own land will make him a traitor and a deserter to his own army, crimes punished by death. Gehazi, on the other hand, criticizes his lord for sparing Naaman a cost for his newly found faith and excuses himself in advance for his treachery. In so doing he places material concerns above his devotion to God. The followers of Elisha are expected to give up their lives under charges of treason if they are not delivered by some other means (cf. 1 Kings 18:40). They are prepared for death as a necessary testimony to their commitment to the God of all the earth, who has granted the gift of their land. No doubt Gehazi, in his own ideals, is prepared for death, and for this reason chose to be a follower of Elisha. The treason of the house of Omri against God will not be successful in coercing the submission of the loyal followers of the covenant.

Though Gehazi understands this, he does not understand the material implications of his confession. The gift of divine grace is not to be reimbursed with gifts of money and clothes. His God is the Lord of the whole earth, who desires to give grace to all. This includes the land of the Arameans and the general he despises. Gehazi gives testimony to a God limited to the interests of his own nationality, a belief that they alone deserve his grace.

The prophet Isaiah, speaking of the time of the Exile, not only appeals to his people to wait for God's deliverance, but reminds them that their salvation is intended for the world:

> Listen to me, my people;
>   hear me, my nation:
> The law will go out from me;
>   my justice will become a light for the nations.
> My righteousness draws near speedily,
>   my salvation is on the way,
>   and my arm will bring justice to the nations.
> The islands will look to me,
>   and wait in hope for my arm. (Isa. 51:4—5)

Gehazi does not think of the land of the Arameans as those who might be viewed as waiting for God to bring his salvation to the whole earth. He cannot even think of one converted Aramean as an example of God reaching out to his world. Instead, he becomes a representative of his own apostate society, even while he thinks the contrary. His preoccupation with the struggles and needs of his group seduce him.

God and the nations. It was never easy for the Israelites, who experienced such relentless judgment at the hands of the nations, to think of them as the recipients of divine mercy. The book of Jonah was written for Israelites who had difficulty in thinking of the nations as objects of God's mercy. It focuses on what is evil. The expansion of the Assyrian empire, deporting peoples and demanding tribute, is not unique or more evil than the conduct of other nations, including Israel, but it is evil (Jonah 1:2). Under the preaching of Jonah, the Ninevites come to realize the evil of their ways (ironically, Jonah lived during a time when Israel did not); they repent, even to the extent of making their cows wear sackcloth and fast (3:7–8).

God sees that they have turned from their evil ways and in turn relents from the evil of judgment he intended for them (Jonah 3:10). In plain words, for God to destroy the Ninevites is not justice but punishment and harm. The response of Jonah comes in 4:1; in the Hebrew there is a double emphasis on the word "evil": "It was evil for Jonah, a very great evil, and he was angry." Jonah then explains: "Was this not exactly what I thought while in my own land, the reason why I fled to Tarshish?" (4:2).

At that point, Jonah quotes the statement about God in the Exodus story of the golden calf: "I knew that you are a gracious and compassionate God, slow to anger and abounding in love, a God who relents from sending calamity" (Jonah 4:2). In the Exodus story, mercy is the very essence of the name of God (cf. Ex. 33:19; 34:6). In Exodus such mercy pertained to Israel; in Jonah it pertained to Nineveh. Jonah has no problem with the mercy of God in relation to Israel, but he has great difficulty with the mercy of God to those agents who victimize Israel, preferring death to having to preach such mercy.

Gehazi may be viewed as manifesting the attitude addressed in Jonah. He has no sense of the mercy shown to Naaman; he is completely self-absorbed, thinking only about the way that the mercy of God can be shown to him. Rather than rejoicing in mercy, he is scheming in selfish concerns. The needs of the schools of the prophets are no excuse; Elisha has provided for their needs repeatedly (e.g., 2 Kings 4:38–44). The problem is his self-interest in how justice should operate. Like Jonah, he presumes that mercy pertains to him and his group in a way it does not apply to those wicked Arameans.

The conversion of Naaman the Aramean is one of the examples Jesus uses to show what faith must mean for the Christian and their understanding of the Bible. His rebuke of the religious leaders of his day shows their propensity towards cultural blindness; they fail to recognize their own faithlessness and condemn whatever does not conform to their own interpretations. Luke introduces the sermon at Nazareth, where Jesus grew up, with words from the prophet Isaiah about the anointed servant (Luke 4:18–19; cf. Isa. 61:1–2a). The servant in Isaiah is anointed to bring good news to the poor, liberty to the captives, sight to the blind, and freedom to the broken, and to preach the year of Jubilee. This servant identifies with the eschatological Son of David (Isa. 11:1–4) and the Suffering Servant (42:1–5).[17]

When Jesus identifies himself as this servant, those who know him simply ask, "Is this not the son of Joseph?" (Luke 4:22). Jesus meets their unbelief by pointing out that Elijah in his time was sent to the Sidonian woman of Zarephath (v. 26), and Elisha was sent to the Aramean general Naaman (v. 27). Both prophets found faith outside of Israel, to the judgment of those without faith within Israel, who thought they were following God. The crowd at Nazareth has a faith much like that of Gehazi. Though they think themselves to be the true followers of the Scriptures, they are not prepared to hear the Scriptures. They can no more accept Jesus as the servant of Isaiah than Gehazi can accept Naaman the Aramean as one who belongs with the sons of the prophets as he himself does.

THE INFLUENCE OF **the vulnerable.** This is not another story about the miracles of a prophet; the presence of the man of God is minimized in the conversion of Naaman. The point of the story is set out in the introduction: Naaman, whose high position in the Aramean court has been achieved at the expense of Israel, does not realize that his good fortune is the work of the God of Israel. A servant girl in his service, a victim of his exploits, is the means of introducing him to his benefactor and eventually to the exclusive worship of the God of Israel.

In this remarkable account, God is at work to demonstrate that the world is his and that all those who live in it belong to him (Ps. 24:1). Naaman the Aramean is of concern to God, not because he suffers from a rather harmless form of vitiligo but because God cares about the worship of Arameans as well. God chooses the small things of this world to confound the wise, the weak to confound the mighty (1 Cor. 1:27). Naaman, the potent Aramean, is reached through a captive of one of his mighty campaigns. All the forces of intimidation are present for the young Israelite maiden. She has no support group of her own; she is in a household expected to be contemptuous of her faith; she is in the lowest possible social status; she has no right to express any of her own opinions and might expect serious consequences for

---

17. Childs, *Isaiah*, 505.

so doing. However she cannot be silent; in voicing her faith, she puts in motion of a chain of events that brings about an entire change of life.

God continues to bring about the work of his kingdom through the influence of the vulnerable. Mary Getui, senior lecturer of the department of religious studies at Kenyatta University, Nairobi, uses this servant girl as an example of what is needed in her continent today.[18] She notes that African governments suppress or even eliminate intellectuals and others who try to speak out about the true situation of their people. Appalling conditions prevail. Like Naaman, solutions are often anticipated from the grand and spectacular. The great economic and political forces of the world have been frustrated by the turbulence of Africa. Christians of Africa practicing their faith and values may be the ones who can begin to turn the tide of relentless disease and violence that is destroying a continent. Christian morals can be a means to bring about the conversion of a people no less dramatic than the genuine worship of God coming to Syria in the person of Naaman.

The University of Winnipeg was recently graced with the presence of Archbishop of Matabeleland in Zimbabwe.[19] Pius Ncube advocated abstinence and monogamous relationships as the necessary counter to the AIDS epidemic of Africa. University students recognized these practices as distinctly Christian; for them the proposition of the archbishop was unacceptable as the promotion of one religion and culture. He was specifically challenged by activist students on his position; for them sex education was the exclusive solution to AIDS. The archbishop replied that condoms were available everywhere as well as knowledge of what they were about. Many people simply live in denial of their effectiveness, which in truth is limited. Christian conviction has influence, not only in stemming the advance of AIDS, but also in establishing functional family units in which children receive care.

This was the viewpoint of the archbishop; Christianity potentially has more power for the problem of AIDS in Africa than all the money of the United Nations (which will never be enough, according to special envoy Stephen Lewis) and all of its influence (which is often ineffective). In the story of Namaan, the words of a young girl proved to be more powerful than the might of a soldier, the faithfulness of Elisha more influential than diplomacy with a king. Though faith may be expressed in ever so simple a fashion, it has the power to move mountains.

The struggles of newfound faith. There are always dangers and risks. The work of faith often falters, but faithfulness is the means God uses to accomplish

---

18. "Wash and Be Clean," *Ecumenical Review* 49/4 (1997): 467.
19. The archbishop visited Winnipeg in October, 2004; he addressed a student assembly at the university.

his purpose. That purpose is nothing less than worship appropriate to the one who alone is Lord of the whole earth, as Naaman comes to understand (5:15). The kingdom of God depends on cross-cultural diffusion, but conversion across cultures is a complex process.

Andrew Walls points out that conversion involves more than a cognitive shift from incorrect to correct theological propositions.[20] A transformation process aiming to redirect a culture toward Christ requires a "deep translation" that penetrates to "the very DNA of that culture." Such a process takes multiple generations to accomplish. Walls believes that if such qualitative conversion occurs in African societies, there may come to be mature, discriminating standards of Christian living. If such a transformation does not occur, African Christianity will be reduced to a hollow echo of European Christian forms, with distortion, confusion, uncertainty, and almost certain hypocrisy on a large scale.

Naaman needs a concession regarding the practice of his newfound faith upon return to his land (5:18). Elisha dismisses him with a simple beatification; he does not further direct the genuine faith of the new convert. An article produced by the Overseas Ministries Study Center reminds us:

> To be spoken for implies a degree of powerlessness on the part of those who are represented by the voice of another. This incapacity may issue from intrinsic reasons having to do with one's degree of maturity, mental development, or medical condition; or it may be the result of extrinsic conditions that foster and perpetuate marginalization, rendering certain individuals and groups voiceless.[21]

Elisha the man of God affirms the new convert in the articulation of his newfound faith.

Conversion within another culture is a complex process. Whether the conversion of Naaman may have influenced the court of the Aramean king or those under his influence is not part of the story. The story of Naaman demonstrates God's purpose that "all the families of the earth may receive his blessing" (Gen. 12:3). This purpose lies at the basis of Christian mission; however, the transformations necessary for the practice of faith are complex.

An article by Anatoliy Ablazhei, chiefly addressed to scholars in Russia, illustrates how an indigenous people in Siberia were not transformed by the lordship of Christ, but how Christianity was itself subverted without

---

20. Andrew Walls, "Christian Scholarship in Africa in the Twenty-first Century," *Journal of African Christian Thought* (December 2001): 46.

21. *International Bulletin of Missionary Research* 29 (2005): 113.

appropriate cultural transformation.[22] The missionaries traveled through the localities where the baptized population had lived from time immemorial, relating to them within the confines of their customary dwellings and establishing close contact with representatives of traditional society. The culture of the aboriginals was shaped by the practice of "shamanism," an irrational belief in the power of traditional ceremonies that forced natives to live and struggle with visible and invisible enemies under the most severe and burdensome conditions.

The shaman was a challenge to the missionaries; he entered into communication with invisible spirits in a trance to learn their demands. The shaman performed the task of protector and guarantor of traditional beliefs. The missionaries did perceive correctly several constituent parts of the aboriginal religious consciousness. The adoption of Christianity took the form of incorporating individual Christian elements as additions to the existing structures, rethinking and interpreting them as appropriate.

The ideological transformation of the traditional aboriginal belief centered on the figure of St. Nicholas the Miracle Worker. He was the most popular Christian saint between both the Russian and aboriginal populations of the area. A church building of St. Nicholas was established in almost every newly founded Russian settlement. Accounts from different periods show the evolution of religious stereotypes and the gradual adaption of figures of the Christian pantheon by traditional religion. The idol (the family spirit protector) came to be called the brother of St. Nicholas the Miracle Worker. As the authority of the saint rose, the aboriginals came to consider him a Russian god stronger than the pagan ones. The Khanty Mikola came to be a substantially new deity subsuming within itself traits of various religious traditions. Ostiak religion came to contain elements of a whole range of beliefs, identifying Christian saints with Ostiak deities or heroes of the national epic.

As a result of Christianization, a new cult rooted in traditional observances developed; "vows" were made to Mikola to ward off danger or misfortune. Baptism, important to the church, had little significance for the newly baptized person. It was a perfunctory superficial formality; certain Christian propositions and formalities were adopted into the structure of the traditional worldview. Only in the few places where the Ostiaks were significantly influenced by the culture of the Russian population was there a modification of the general Ostiak worldview.

---

22. Anatoliy M. Ablazhei, "The Religious Worldview of the Indigenous Population of the Northern Ob' as Understood by Christian Missionaries," *International Bulletin of Missionary Research* 29 (2005): 134–39.

Conversion can lead to the appropriate transformation of an entire culture. The promise to Abraham, adumbrated in the conversion of Naaman, is not an impossible ideal. Jennifer Trafton in an article on Samuel Fairbank shows how the gospel was good news to the people of Wadale, India, in the mid-nineteenth century.[23] The *kirtan*, an indigenous style of teaching and singing, was adapted to Christian purposes to communicate the gospel. Socially, those subsisting as landless laborers, sharecroppers, or beggars, whose woes were compounded by droughts, blights, and famines, were given assistance through the development of industrial schools, agricultural work, and English classes. The caste of Untouchables was given the capacity to truly live the Christian faith. Conversion should be good news.

The practice of faith must be thoughtfully pursued even in the context of a worldview of the kingdom of God. Gehazi is an example of a failure to be consistent with the sovereignty of God in Israel and the school of the prophets. His own sense of justice led him to appropriate that which was not his and to depreciate what had happened to the "foreigner."

As a pastor I have too often observed those who would reprimand others for failure of faith, with little understanding of their own compromises in their accusations. Not long ago I was ordering a meal on Sunday in a town well known for its abundance of churches. When the pleasant and cheerful table waiter came to take the order, I thanked her for such delightful attention to her customers, even when she had to work on a Sunday. She responded by saying my appreciation was a rather different attitude than the one she had just received. A couple had ordered their meal and discovered that the person serving them was a church member. They gave her a long lecture on the sin of working on Sunday, seemingly quite oblivious to the fact that if they thought such work on Sunday was a sin, they would do well to do their eating where someone else did not need to work for them.

Jesus often replicated the prophets. He both healed lepers and illustrated faith through them. On one occasion Jesus healed ten lepers (Luke 17:11–19). His instructions followed conventional requirements; the lepers were to show themselves to the priests to authenticate their healing. Only one of the lepers returned to show the gratitude of faith as a genuine trust in the gift of God. The one who returned was not among those of traditional faith, but was a Samaritan. Though the narrative makes no explicit reference to Namaan the Syrian, the parallel is obvious. Thanksgiving is the proper evidence of faith, for faith is to know and trust God's grace. This one leper had what the others, who simply followed the rules, were lacking. Like Namaan, he may

---

23. Jennifer M. Trafton, "The Legacy of Samuel Bacon Fairbank," *International Bulletin of Missionary Research* 29 (2005): 144–49.

have faced his own threats in declaring the wonder of healing in his home country.

Elisha's assurance of peace to Naaman when he should go to the house of Rimmon in the service of his master is a reminder that believers must be given freedom to choose how they can best give witness to their faith. The question is not whether believers should be faithful, but how they most effectively give testimony to their faith. Believers in hostile circumstances must make decisions about what constitutes a situation where they must be faithful to death. Though Naaman would likely have been banished rather than martyred for his refusal to go to the Rimmon temple, Ngan asks the question for those who might face death for confession of faith:

> If, like Naaman, a new convert must return to a hostile environment, should martyrdom be demanded of such person? It may be an honor to be a faithful witness unto death, but should this not be a decision each person makes before God? Naaman knows the realities of life when he returns. His newfound faith will bring conflict to his life in Syria. He does not justify what he must do but recognizes the contradictions that he cannot avoid and asks for forgiveness.[24]

Von Rad correctly observes that Elisha leaves Naaman "completely to his new faith, or better, to God's hand which has sought and found him."[25] Naaman submits to the mercy of God in the line of duty, in order that testimony to the divine mercy may continue to be confessed.

---

24. Lai Ling Elizabeth Ngan, "2 Kings 5," *RevEx* 94 (1997): 593.
25. Gerhard von Rad, "Naaman: A Critical Reading," in *God at Work in Israel*, trans. John H. Marks (Nashville: Abingdon, 1980), 54.

2 Kings 6:1–8:15

THE COMPANY OF the prophets said to Elisha, "Look, the place where we meet with you is too small for us. ²Let us go to the Jordan, where each of us can get a pole; and let us build a place there for us to live."

And he said, "Go."

³Then one of them said, "Won't you please come with your servants?"

"I will," Elisha replied. ⁴And he went with them.

They went to the Jordan and began to cut down trees. ⁵As one of them was cutting down a tree, the iron axhead fell into the water. "Oh, my lord," he cried out, "it was borrowed!"

⁶The man of God asked, "Where did it fall?" When he showed him the place, Elisha cut a stick and threw it there, and made the iron float. ⁷"Lift it out," he said. Then the man reached out his hand and took it.

⁸Now the king of Aram was at war with Israel. After conferring with his officers, he said, "I will set up my camp in such and such a place."

⁹The man of God sent word to the king of Israel: "Beware of passing that place, because the Arameans are going down there." ¹⁰So the king of Israel checked on the place indicated by the man of God. Time and again Elisha warned the king, so that he was on his guard in such places.

¹¹This enraged the king of Aram. He summoned his officers and demanded of them, "Will you not tell me which of us is on the side of the king of Israel?"

¹²"None of us, my lord the king," said one of his officers, "but Elisha, the prophet who is in Israel, tells the king of Israel the very words you speak in your bedroom."

¹³"Go, find out where he is," the king ordered, "so I can send men and capture him." The report came back: "He is in Dothan." ¹⁴Then he sent horses and chariots and a strong force there. They went by night and surrounded the city.

¹⁵When the servant of the man of God got up and went out early the next morning, an army with horses and chariots had surrounded the city. "Oh, my lord, what shall we do?" the servant asked.

¹⁶"Don't be afraid," the prophet answered. "Those who are with us are more than those who are with them."

¹⁷And Elisha prayed, "O LORD, open his eyes so he may see." Then the LORD opened the servant's eyes, and he looked and saw the hills full of horses and chariots of fire all around Elisha.

¹⁸As the enemy came down toward him, Elisha prayed to the LORD, "Strike these people with blindness." So he struck them with blindness, as Elisha had asked.

¹⁹Elisha told them, "This is not the road and this is not the city. Follow me, and I will lead you to the man you are looking for." And he led them to Samaria.

²⁰After they entered the city, Elisha said, "LORD, open the eyes of these men so they can see." Then the LORD opened their eyes and they looked, and there they were, inside Samaria.

²¹When the king of Israel saw them, he asked Elisha, "Shall I kill them, my father? Shall I kill them?"

²²"Do not kill them," he answered. "Would you kill men you have captured with your own sword or bow? Set food and water before them so that they may eat and drink and then go back to their master." ²³So he prepared a great feast for them, and after they had finished eating and drinking, he sent them away, and they returned to their master. So the bands from Aram stopped raiding Israel's territory.

²⁴Some time later, Ben-Hadad king of Aram mobilized his entire army and marched up and laid siege to Samaria. ²⁵There was a great famine in the city; the siege lasted so long that a donkey's head sold for eighty shekels of silver, and a quarter of a cab of seed pods for five shekels.

²⁶As the king of Israel was passing by on the wall, a woman cried to him, "Help me, my lord the king!"

²⁷The king replied, "If the LORD does not help you, where can I get help for you? From the threshing floor? From the winepress?" ²⁸Then he asked her, "What's the matter?"

She answered, "This woman said to me, 'Give up your son so we may eat him today, and tomorrow we'll eat my son.' ²⁹So we cooked my son and ate him. The next day I said to her, 'Give up your son so we may eat him,' but she had hidden him."

³⁰When the king heard the woman's words, he tore his robes. As he went along the wall, the people looked, and

there, underneath, he had sackcloth on his body. [31]He said, "May God deal with me, be it ever so severely, if the head of Elisha son of Shaphat remains on his shoulders today!"

[32]Now Elisha was sitting in his house, and the elders were sitting with him. The king sent a messenger ahead, but before he arrived, Elisha said to the elders, "Don't you see how this murderer is sending someone to cut off my head? Look, when the messenger comes, shut the door and hold it shut against him. Is not the sound of his master's footsteps behind him?"

[33]While he was still talking to them, the messenger came down to him. And the king said, "This disaster is from the LORD. Why should I wait for the LORD any longer?"

[7:1]Elisha said, "Hear the word of the LORD. This is what the LORD says: About this time tomorrow, a seah of flour will sell for a shekel and two seahs of barley for a shekel at the gate of Samaria."

[2]The officer on whose arm the king was leaning said to the man of God, "Look, even if the LORD should open the floodgates of the heavens, could this happen?"

"You will see it with your own eyes," answered Elisha, "but you will not eat any of it!"

[3]Now there were four men with leprosy at the entrance of the city gate. They said to each other, "Why stay here until we die? [4]If we say, 'We'll go into the city'—the famine is there, and we will die. And if we stay here, we will die. So let's go over to the camp of the Arameans and surrender. If they spare us, we live; if they kill us, then we die."

[5]At dusk they got up and went to the camp of the Arameans. When they reached the edge of the camp, not a man was there, [6]for the Lord had caused the Arameans to hear the sound of chariots and horses and a great army, so that they said to one another, "Look, the king of Israel has hired the Hittite and Egyptian kings to attack us!" [7]So they got up and fled in the dusk and abandoned their tents and their horses and donkeys. They left the camp as it was and ran for their lives.

[8]The men who had leprosy reached the edge of the camp and entered one of the tents. They ate and drank, and carried away silver, gold and clothes, and went off and hid them. They returned and entered another tent and took some things from it and hid them also.

[9]Then they said to each other, "We're not doing right. This

is a day of good news and we are keeping it to ourselves. If we wait until daylight, punishment will overtake us. Let's go at once and report this to the royal palace."

¹⁰So they went and called out to the city gatekeepers and told them, "We went into the Aramean camp and not a man was there—not a sound of anyone—only tethered horses and donkeys, and the tents left just as they were." ¹¹The gatekeepers shouted the news, and it was reported within the palace.

¹²The king got up in the night and said to his officers, "I will tell you what the Arameans have done to us. They know we are starving; so they have left the camp to hide in the countryside, thinking, 'They will surely come out, and then we will take them alive and get into the city.'"

¹³One of his officers answered, "Have some men take five of the horses that are left in the city. Their plight will be like that of all the Israelites left here—yes, they will only be like all these Israelites who are doomed. So let us send them to find out what happened."

¹⁴So they selected two chariots with their horses, and the king sent them after the Aramean army. He commanded the drivers, "Go and find out what has happened." ¹⁵They followed them as far as the Jordan, and they found the whole road strewn with the clothing and equipment the Arameans had thrown away in their headlong flight. So the messengers returned and reported to the king. ¹⁶Then the people went out and plundered the camp of the Arameans. So a seah of flour sold for a shekel, and two seahs of barley sold for a shekel, as the LORD had said.

¹⁷Now the king had put the officer on whose arm he leaned in charge of the gate, and the people trampled him in the gateway, and he died, just as the man of God had foretold when the king came down to his house. ¹⁸It happened as the man of God had said to the king: "About this time tomorrow, a seah of flour will sell for a shekel and two seahs of barley for a shekel at the gate of Samaria."

¹⁹The officer had said to the man of God, "Look, even if the LORD should open the floodgates of the heavens, could this happen?" The man of God had replied, "You will see it with your own eyes, but you will not eat any of it!" ²⁰And that is exactly what happened to him, for the people trampled him in the gateway, and he died.

^{8:1}Now Elisha had said to the woman whose son he had restored to life, "Go away with your family and stay for a while wherever you can, because the LORD has decreed a famine in the land that will last seven years." ²The woman proceeded to do as the man of God said. She and her family went away and stayed in the land of the Philistines seven years.

³At the end of the seven years she came back from the land of the Philistines and went to the king to beg for her house and land. ⁴The king was talking to Gehazi, the servant of the man of God, and had said, "Tell me about all the great things Elisha has done." ⁵Just as Gehazi was telling the king how Elisha had restored the dead to life, the woman whose son Elisha had brought back to life came to beg the king for her house and land.

Gehazi said, "This is the woman, my lord the king, and this is her son whom Elisha restored to life." ⁶The king asked the woman about it, and she told him.

Then he assigned an official to her case and said to him, "Give back everything that belonged to her, including all the income from her land from the day she left the country until now."

⁷Elisha went to Damascus, and Ben-Hadad king of Aram was ill. When the king was told, "The man of God has come all the way up here," ⁸he said to Hazael, "Take a gift with you and go to meet the man of God. Consult the LORD through him; ask him, 'Will I recover from this illness?'"

⁹Hazael went to meet Elisha, taking with him as a gift forty camel-loads of all the finest wares of Damascus. He went in and stood before him, and said, "Your son Ben-Hadad king of Aram has sent me to ask, 'Will I recover from this illness?'"

¹⁰Elisha answered, "Go and say to him, 'You will certainly recover'; but the LORD has revealed to me that he will in fact die." ¹¹He stared at him with a fixed gaze until Hazael felt ashamed. Then the man of God began to weep.

¹²"Why is my lord weeping?" asked Hazael.

"Because I know the harm you will do to the Israelites," he answered. "You will set fire to their fortified places, kill their young men with the sword, dash their little children to the ground, and rip open their pregnant women."

¹³Hazael said, "How could your servant, a mere dog, accomplish such a feat?"

"The LORD has shown me that you will become king of Aram," answered Elisha.

¹⁴Then Hazael left Elisha and returned to his master. When Ben-Hadad asked, "What did Elisha say to you?" Hazael replied, "He told me that you would certainly recover." ¹⁵But the next day he took a thick cloth, soaked it in water and spread it over the king's face, so that he died. Then Hazael succeeded him as king.

ELISHA THE MAN of God continues his mission of confronting the religion of Baal, but in a less direct manner than Elijah. Elisha makes it his work to support the sons of the prophets, to meet needs as he encounters them, and to assist the king of Israel (usually unnamed) in the hostilities that confront him. The story of Naaman is followed by a series of encounters at a variety of geographical locations that take place during the time of Aramean incursions.

These stories do not follow any chronology of events; the account of Elisha delivering Israel from the Aramean raids (6:8–23) is followed immediately by a story of Samaria under a severe siege (6:24–7:20). These accounts are joined by a literary phrase linking independent narratives (6:24).[1] They do not provide a political history but are examples of the sovereign work of God through his prophet during times of apostasy and conflict.

Mercy at the Jordan (6:1–7)

THE ACCOUNT OF the building project for the sons of the prophets at the Jordan is given in sketchy details. Nothing is said about the time of the project, the circumstances that create the need, or the reason for moving to the Jordan. The story is abruptly introduced with the notice that the meeting place is too cramped.[2] It may have been inadequate from the beginning, the prophetic group may have grown, or the time may have come to build an improved building.

There must have been some advantage in moving to the Jordan, since that is not an ideal location for finding timbers. Elisha as the leader of the group

---

1. The Hebrew phrase *wayᵉhî 'aḥᵃrê kēn*, translated "some time later" (NIV), has no chronological significance; it is a narrative technique to transition to a sequel, a story from another place and time. In 2 Samuel, where events are arranged around topics, it is correctly translated "in the course of time" (NIV; cf. 2 Sam. 8:1; 10:1; 13:1; 15:1; 21:18).

2. For a discussion of the expression "sitting before him" (v. 1), see comments on 4:38.

is asked to join in the project and is thus present when the axhead was lost. This iron instrument no doubt was a valuable instrument and was "borrowed" (v. 5; lit., it was "begged or prayed for"), making the loss so much more distressing. The story's focus is entirely on the miracle of recovering the axhead from the Jordan; the only connection for its being placed here in the Elisha collection of stories is that it relates another miracle of Elisha at the Jordan (cf. the Naaman story).

Military Secrets at Dothan (6:8–23)

THE FIRST EPISODE of this story presents Elisha as a spy in the Aramean camp, warning the Israelites where the enemy is planning to attack (6:8–10). The episode is artistically arranged to link the actions of the Aramean king, the man of God, and the king of Israel.[3] The Aramean king plans an attack against Israel (cf. NEB),[4] but Elisha sends a warning to the king of Israel about the place of attack (v. 9).[5] The king then sends a warning to his commander (v. 10), so the Arameans are stymied repeatedly, and no attack actually takes place.

In the second episode (6:11–14), a frustrated Aramean king rages against his own advisors, accusing one of them of being a spy for Israel. It is not clear whether he really believes his ranks have been infiltrated or is venting his frustration in seeking someone to blame. Apparently the king has his own spies in the Israelite camp, because one of his assistants is able to inform him that the prophet Elisha can hear what is said in the walls of his bedroom. The king further learns that the prophet is residing at Dothan, a city north of Samaria on the road leading into the Jezreel Valley.[6] The king is determined to capture Elisha, either to avenge the sabotage of his army or to enlist him as an intelligence informant in his own forces. In order to ensure the success of his efforts, he dispatches a heavy force deep into the Israelite territory. The force enters under the cover of darkness and surrounds the city.

The third episode contrasts the army of the Arameans with the army of

---

3. For the artistic elements of the narrative see Robert LaBarbera, "The Man of War and the Man of God: Social Satire in 2 Kings 6:8–7:20," *CBQ* 46 (1984): 639–45.

4. The anomalous *taḥᵃnōtî* of the Masoretic text, paraphrased as "I will set up my camp" (NIV), is an error for the verb attack (*nḥt*), repeated in the warning of Elisha (v. 9), about where the Arameans are "going down" (NIV). The verb is also found as a military term for attack in the prophets (cf. Jer. 21:13; Joel 3:11). The text should say *tinḥᵃtû*.

5. The Masoretic adjective "descending" (*nᵉḥittîm*) should be vocalized as a participle of the verb (*nōḥᵃtîm*).

6. Joseph was sold by his brothers to the Ishmaelite/Midianite caravan in the pasture-land of Dothan (Gen. 37:13–25). The Iron Age II remains at Dothan are the most significant, including several domestic and public buildings. A major ninth-century destruction may be associated with the Arameans.

God (6:15–17). The Arameans have surrounded the city with horses and chariots, but to the vision of the trusting eye, the hill on which the city stands is filled with horses and chariots of fire. The sense requires that the divine contingent is serving as a protective cordon around the city of Dothan.[7] The mighty army of the Arameans surrounding the city (v. 15) is no match for one man of God surrounded by the chariots of Yahweh's army (v. 17).

The Aramean army is not struck down by the swords of soldiers but by a blinding light (*sanwērîm*). This is not ordinary blindness (*ʿiwwārôn*), but a bright light that causes a temporary distortion of vision.[8] In this fourth episode the Aramean army is taken captive by Elisha and led to the capital (6:18–20). The original command of the Aramean king is to go and find Elisha (v. 13); once they get to the city they are unable to find him, but instead are led to the city where they will find him. Elisha then prays a prayer virtually identical to the one that enabled his servant to see the heavenly armies (v. 20; cf. v. 17). The eyes of the soldiers are opened and they see their man, but they also see that they are now surrounded by the enemy army.

In the final episode the king of Israel believes he has an opportunity to inflict a debilitating defeat on the Aramean army (6:21–23). Matters, however, are not in his control; he has not been responsible for taking the soldiers captive and requires permission from the prophet, respectfully and unusually addressed as "father" (v. 21). The prophet instead follows the wisdom of a proverb: "If your enemy hungers, give him food to eat; if he is thirsty, give him water to drink. In doing this, you will heap burning coals on his head, and the LORD will reward you" (Prov. 25:21–22). These soldiers are not to be slain or taken captive as the spoils of war and made slaves; instead, they are treated lavishly with food and drink and sent on their way. The result is a halt of the border wars.

Famine in Samaria (6:24–7:20)

THIS STORY BEGINS with a siege by Ben-Hadad against the city of Samaria. The mention of Ben-Hadad does not assist in locating this story historically. Ahab fought against Ben-Hadad (cf. 1 Kings 20; 22), an Aramean king otherwise historically unknown by that name. Ben-Hadad was probably a dynastic name for Aramean kings.

The usual assumption of historians is that the Ben-Hadad in this Elisha story is Ben-Hadad son of Hazael (cf. 13:3). This is consistent with the assumptions

---

7. Cogan and Tadmor, *II Kings*, 74.

8. The same affliction struck the predators at Lot's door (Gen. 19:11). The sense is known from the Akkadian (*šunwārum*), "to make the eye (vision) sharp" (*CAD* N 1.218), a derivative of *nāmaru* (cf. the Hebrew root *mwr*), used of gleaming metal (e.g., a mirror).

of historians that Aramean conquests such as this siege of Samaria take place during the Jehu dynasty when Israel is weak.[9] Since the Israelite king is not named, the siege is not remembered for its political significance.

One of the tactics of siege warfare was to create famine so the citizens within a fortified city would be forced to surrender. Montgomery refers to Plutarch (*Artaxerxes* 24.3), who says that the Kadisians divided up the draft animals so that a donkey's head was worth almost sixty drachmas, and to Pliny the Elder (*Historia naturalis* 8.82), who says that during a siege by Hannibal a mouse rose in the market to 200 denarii.[10] A "cab" (6:25) was a dry measure equal to one sixth of a seah (7:1); thirty seahs made an omer, equal to about 100 liters. A seah was just over three liters, and a cab about half a liter.[11] Linguistic comparisons show that the Masoretic text's "dove's dung" (*ḥir'yyônîm*) was slang for an edible "seed pod" as a carob.[12] It is possible that "donkey's head" is a similar type of idiom. Siege warfare reduces populations to extremes, which can include cannibalism.

The pathos of the story surfaces in the appeal of the woman who cries out to the king for help (6:26–31). Her complaint is not that she had been reduced to eating the corpse of her own child for food, but the injustice she feels when her neighbor refuses to honor the agreement they have to equally share their grisly fare. Her complaint to the king is legal; it is an appeal for justice in the deception of her neighbor. The revulsion of the story is her apparent lack of feeling for the death of her own child and that of her neighbor; the normal compassion of motherhood is subordinated to the desperation to survive.

The king betrays his own feelings of futility when the woman appeals for help. He initially assumes she is asking for food, and his helplessness is seen in the retort that only God can provide help in such circumstances (6:27), for the royal storehouses have been exhausted. When he learns of the real concern of the woman, he can only tear his clothes in grief. The rip reveals his own despair, as it exposes the coarse cloth of lament he is wearing underneath his regular tunic.

Contrary to the previous story, where Elisha is in total control, the prophet is now threatened with death by his own king. Just as Elijah was held responsible for causing the drought in the days of Ahab (1 Kings 18:17), so Elisha

9. See Jones, *1 & 2 Kings*, 2:430–31.

10. Montgomery, *The Books of Kings*, 384.

11. Fuller, "אֵיפָה," *NIDOTTE*, 1:384–85. Israel derived its measures of capacity from Egyptian, Mesopotamian, and West Semitic sources. Ratios between capacities are found in biblical and postbiblical sources. Amounts can only be approximately calculated and they varied between regions and over time (like the American and Canadian gallon).

12. See Gray, *I & II Kings*, 518; Cogan and Tadmor, *II Kings*, 79.

is held responsible for the siege that has caused such famine. After all, Elisha preached divine judgment against the descendants of Ahab (e.g., 2 Kings 3:13), and the encounter with Naaman and his treatment of the Aramean army in Samaria demonstrate his good standing with the Arameans. Elisha is a logical target for the frustrations of an impotent king.

The threat the king makes against Elisha is irrational, but it is not idle. He dispatches a messenger to ambush the prophet while he is conferring with the leaders of the city (6:32–33); it is not only the members of the prophetic band who listen to Elisha. Elisha is fully aware of the king's intentions and instructs the elders to block the door and hold the executioner until the king arrives. He knows the king is right behind and that he has relented from his rash order.

The apocopated style of the Hebrew narrative makes it seem as if the king arrives ahead of the executioner, because he arrives while Elisha is still issuing instructions to the elders (RSV; cf. NLT).[13] This may be paraphrased by saying the messenger arrives; then the king as the subject for the speech is supplied (NIV). Josephus provides a similar reconstruction, saying that the king hastened after the messenger to prevent the killing (*Ant.* 9.69–70). The narrative moves quickly, showing the control of the prophet and the despair of the king. This disaster is part of God's sovereign purpose; the king can do nothing, not even pray.

Elisha responds to the king with a word from Yahweh pertaining to the next day; it sounds like the cry of a vendor in the marketplace of Samaria (7:1). The open plaza at the city gate serves as a main marketplace. The prices announced indicate a break in the famine, and though they may still be many times the normal prices, it will be taken as a great blessing to the starving residents of Samaria.[14] The officer who is the immediate assistant to the king finds this announcement unbelievable (7:2). The prophet assures the officer that he will see this reversal of fortune but not enjoy the benefits. The warning is not given in the usual formula of a judgment oracle. It serves to reinforce the truth of the change of circumstances as well as the helplessness and skepticism of the political leaders responsible for the well-being of the citizens of Samaria.

---

13. The Masoretic text says the messenger (*malʾāk*) arrived (v. 33), but this is a textual error for the king (*melek*); this is evident in the sequel, which repeats the words of Elisha's pronouncement to the king (7:17–18).

14. For documentation on normal costs of food see Jonas C. Greenfeld, "Dove's Dung and the Price of Food: The Topoi of II Kings 6:24–7:2," in *Storia e tradizioni di Israele: scritti in onore di J. Alberto Soggin*, ed. Daniele Garrone (Brescia: Paideia Editrice, 1991), 123–25. Ashurbanipal boasts that ten homers of barley could be bought for a shekel; if the shekel had the same value in Israel, the relief announced by Elisha was not great.

The fulfillment of Yahweh's word begins with four lepers outside the gate of the city. According to ritual law, a leper was quarantined outside the settlement (Lev. 13:11, 46; Num. 12:14–16). Caught in a death trap, the four decide to desert to the enemy camp (7:3–4). When they arrive there, they find the enemy has fled in terror, having heard the noise of a mighty army. Risky mercenary alliances were adopted as a last resort—Isaiah disparagingly refers to the disastrous alliance of Israel with Assyria against the Arameans as being shaved with a "hired razor" (Isa. 7:20). During the days of Israel the territory of Syria was controlled by Aramean city-states. Reference to "kings of Egypt" may have been a rhetorical plural, including the Hittites, or the *primus inter pares* (first among equals) status of the pharaoh among other rulers in Egypt.[15] The Aramean soldiers have fled for their lives (7:7).

The divine message comes full circle as the lepers report back. As with Naaman, the good news is almost stifled (cf. 5:11); the king, acting with prudent skepticism, suspects an enemy ploy to dupe his soldiers, draw them out of the city, capture them alive, and take the city. As in the Naaman story, subordinates point out the only real danger—missing an opportunity to for relief from the famine. His army has been defeated (7:13); nothing is lost in taking a few of the remaining horses and confirming the report. The Jordan is some distance through hostile territory, whether it was crossed at the Jabbok or the Yarmuk, adding panic to the fleeing force.

Food prices become exactly as the prophet earlier announced (7:16). The death of the officer takes place when he is appointed to be in charge of the gate and is trampled by the stampeding people. The final verses bring closure to the story by repeating the prophetic word (7:18–20), which determines the course of events. Yahweh gave the Arameans victory, using them as an instrument of punishment for Israel. The panic of the Aramean army is a performance of the divine will, bringing temporary mercy to a people under judgment.

Land Claims at Shunem (8:1–6)

THIS STORY ABOUT the appeal of the woman of Shunem to the justice of the king is a natural sequel to the story of the desperate woman calling out to the king for justice in the famine at Samaria (6:26). There is no link between the famines; the former was temporary caused by a siege, whereas this one lasts seven years. Elisha continues to assist his patroness from Shunem, this time warning her to leave because of a famine that is about to devastate the land of Israel (8:1). The woman takes refuge in the land of the Philistines (v. 2),

---

15. Kitchen, *The Third Intermediate Period in Egypt*, 326–27 (see note 461). The reference to Hittites appears to be a popular anachronism.

somewhere in the southwest coastal plain where rainfall is adequate to support a good agricultural life.[16] When the woman returns, she finds her properties have been taken over. Though Elisha is no longer present, his influence comes to her assistance in getting a hearing with the king.

The legal details for loss of land tenure are not given. The woman of Shunem may have become a widow, since her husband was already old when Elisha first met her (4:14); this is not stated, nor should his death have affected her right to the land. The land may have become crown property in her absence or may have been land leased by the crown on condition certain services were rendered.[17] The text indicates that the problem is one of confiscation; in her absence the properties have been taken over, possibly by another family member or neighbor. Earlier the woman lived securely among her people without need (4:13), but her situation has drastically changed. The property is legally hers, possibly through inheritance, but she has no access to it.

The activities of Elisha are of interest to many during his lifetime, including the king. Gehazi has regained access to the king's court after being struck with leprosy. The king desires an interview with Gehazi because he wishes to know more about Elisha. The arrival of the woman of Shunem to lodge her complaint, accompanied by her son, provides an immediate opportunity to verify the event of his being raised back to life. The king is moved by her story and appoints an officer to be in charge of restoring her property. This king acts much more nobly than his predecessor Ahab, who had no hesitation in confiscating the property of Naboth. The reputation of Elisha and his legacy influence the king to act immediately; the woman of Shunem receives back her properties with all the attendant revenues due to her.

Regime Change at Damascus (8:7−15)

ELISHA IS IN Damascus on the occasion of King Ben-Hadad's being ill. The fame of the prophet is well known in Damascus, so it is only natural that the king should inquire about the outcome of his illness. The king sends Hazael, one of his trusted deputies, with a substantial remuneration to receive a word from the prophet. Though this is the gift of a king, forty camel loads must be read as hyperbole (v. 9); more descriptive is the gift the wife of Jeroboam brought to Ahijah the prophet (1 Kings 14:3).

---

16. Aharoni, *The Land of the Bible*, 25; as far as Gaza rainfall "suffices for growing good crops of grain on the plains."

17. See Roland de Vaux, *Social Institutions* (vol. 1 of *Ancient Israel*; New York: McGraw Hill, 1965), 124; K. H. Henry, "Land Tenure in the Old Testament," *PEQ* 86 (1954): 10−13.

The encounter is not what Hazael expects; Elisha commissions him with the message that the king will live, though in fact the king will die (2 Kings 8:10).[18] The message is mixed; the king will not die of his illness (the subject of his inquiry), but he will die at the hands of an assassin.[19] The news so shocks Hazael that his gaze remains transfixed until he feels embarrassed (v. 11); it is broken only by the weeping of the man of God.[20]

God has already declared that Hazael will be the instrument of punishment to Israel (1 Kings 19:15–17); Hazael will be anointed through Elisha and will bring destruction on Israel. As the incredulous Hazael stares at the prophet, the impact of Elijah's words overcome Elisha's composure. Here stands the man who will crush innocent citizens of Israel. The prophet knows that Hazael will become king of Aram (2 Kings 7:13) and that war against Israel will be the inevitable outcome.

Events transpired as the prophet says (8:14–15); Hazael reports to his master that he will live, but the next day Hazael takes a water soaked mesh and suffocates his lord (cf. Josephus, *Ant.* 9.92).[21] Hazael is well known in history as the usurper who took over the Aramean throne in Damascus. Zakkur, king of Hamath, in the inscription that celebrates the defense of his capital Hazrak (the biblical Hadrak of Zech. 9:1), names Hazael as the father of Ben-Hadad, the king of Damascus who led a coalition against him.[22] Shalmaneser III, in his eighteenth year (841 B.C.) defeats Hazael in his expansions into Assyria and lays siege to Damascus.[23] The "feats" that Hazael will accomplish (8:13) are described from an Aramean point of view. The crushing of children and slashing of pregnant women might be victory to a conquering king, but they are not great feats to the most vulnerable victims of war.

---

18. The Hebrew scribes changed "go, say to him (*lw*), you will live," to "go, say 'you will not (*l'*) live.'" The change was simply the exchange of one letter, made in the interests of protecting the integrity of Elisha. The correct reading is preserved in the *qere* (the word vocalization) as well as all of the versions.

19. As suggested by Wiseman, *1 & 2 Kings*, 214.

20. The subject of the first half of the verse is not specified; Elisha may be the subject of the stare, the shame, and the weeping (NEB), or a change of subject can be indicated by inserting the name Hazael (NIV). The "man of God" is named as the one weeping, an indication of a change of subject for the second half of the verse. This is the interpretation followed by Josephus (*Ant.* 9.90).

21. The word for cloth (*makbēr*) is related to the netted fleece of goat hair (*kābîr*), which Michal used to provide disguise for David in his bed (1 Sam. 19:13, 16).

22. Donner and Röllig, *Kanaanäische und aramäsche Inschriften* #202 (side A line 4); the name Hazael is also found in another Aramean fragment (#232).

23. A translation of the annalistic text is given in Pritchard, *An Anthology of Texts and Pictures*, 191.

GOD AT WORK in human affairs. Naaman, who has been leading raids into Israel, ends up finding healing in the rivers of the Jordan. The role of the Jordan is the link to another story about the sons of the prophets attempting to expand their meeting quarters at the Jordan (6:1–7). At Dothan, Elisha frustrates the Aramean sorties into Israel with divine information as to their location (6:8–23). War with Ben-Hadad brings severe famine during a siege against Samaria (6:24–33); Elisha comes to the aid of the victimized citizens of Samaria (7:1–20). War and famine bring about the exile of the woman of Shunem to the land of the Philistines (8:1–6). Through the testimony of Gehazi, apparently because Elisha is no longer alive, the woman is able to have her property restored. Elisha has sufficiently cordial relations with the royal house of the Arameans that he is able to visit the palace in Damascus and appoint Hazael as the new king (8:7–15). Elisha as the man of God has a role in both alleviating suffering and effecting the sovereign judgment of God.

This collection of stories about Elisha shows that God's will may done on earth even during times of apostasy, political conflict, suffering, and despair. God is at work in human kingdoms; an Aramean army is not only thwarted in its militant border raids but is brought to submission and cessation of hostilities; a prophet of Israel becomes the messenger of political change in a foreign nation. Amidst the horror and anguish of war the mercy of God can be found; a small group of faithful at the Jordan River are assisted in constructing new quarters; starving citizens of the capital city gain relief; a woman whose property has been confiscated receives justice.

The miracle of the floating axhead is a simple act of mercy; no prophetic word is fulfilled, no judgment stated, no promise given, no indictment on the decision to build new facilities. The miracle does not emphasize spectacular powers. Elisha must ask to ascertain the location of the iron. A new handle is cut to bring the iron to the surface. The sense of the word cut (*qṣb*) seems to be fitting to the right size and shape (cf. 1 Kings 6:25; 7:37). A new handle is required, because the miracle signals a kind of new beginning (cf. 2 Kings 2:20). The story shows how Elisha acts promptly and decisively to meet a need, as in the case of the bitter water (2:19–22) or the inedible food (4:38–41). The action itself is similar to the other occasions where Elisha comes to the aid of the prophetic band (cf. 2:21; 4:41). Elisha is shown to be a compassionate leader, but able to provide only through divine assistance in ordinary things.

Nothing is said about the occasion of the Aramean invasions (6:8). The absence of the names of the kings or the political circumstances has an important effect on the impact of the narrative. Elisha is not seen to be on either side of the conflict; he first protects the Israelite army from ambush and then prevents a massacre of the Arameans. The focus of the whole story is on vision, particularly the ability to see beyond usual perception. Elisha is able to know what the Aramean king is planning and can warn the Israelite king accordingly (6:9–10); he is able to show his servant the armies of Yahweh around Dothan, which the Aramean armies cannot see (vv. 16–17). Elisha prays again, and a blinding light overcomes the Aramean armies, so they can be led right into the capital city (vv. 18–19). Elijah prays again, and the normal vision of the Aramean soldiers is restored and they realize they are in Samaria. The story is not about military victory or political developments. It is a story about the difference between sight and vision, about being controlled by the temporal or by the transcendent. Political powers are subordinated to the sovereignty of God; Elisha completely outmaneuvers both military establishments and brings an end to the hostilities.

Covenant consequences. In keeping with Deuteronomistic theology, these stories show that there is no escape from the conditions of the covenant. The apostasy of Israel brings the judgment of war but not the absence of the divine warrior. In the Aramean raids, God is the informant frustrating the schemes of the Aramean king repeatedly, to the point where he becomes completely enraged (6:11). In the siege of Samaria, the army is put to flight because of the plight of starving citizens. In neither case does this result in the actual defeat of the enemy army. The divine warrior is at work in acts of mercy to the victims of war, but the judgment of war is a consequence from which there is no escape. The curses of the covenant are clearly stated and well known.

> Even the most gentle and sensitive man among you will have no compassion on his own brother or the wife he loves or his surviving children, and he will not give to one of them any of the flesh of his children that he is eating. It will be all he has left because of the suffering your enemy will inflict on you during the siege of all your cities. The most gentle and sensitive woman among you—so sensitive and gentle that she would not venture to touch the ground with the sole of her foot—will begrudge the husband she loves and her own son or daughter the afterbirth from her womb and the children she bears. For she intends to eat them secretly during the siege and in the distress that your enemy will inflict on you in your cities. (Deut. 28:54–57)

This gruesome description of the curse of the covenant is not a vengeful punishment of an insulted God. This description is the inescapable reality of war and the dreadful consequences of the anarchy that war perpetuates. Failure to honor the divine order of the covenant leaves the people at the mercy of the nations. They suffer in the ways of all other nations. The vassal treaties of Esarhaddon not only mention eating the flesh of one's children but also adults eating one another and mothers barring their doors to their daughters.[24] The curses of Deuteronomy, exemplified in these stories of Elisha, describe a society outside of the order that God has designed. This is not what God has chosen for his people; the house of Omri chose the ways of the nations for themselves.

Disobedience to the covenant and the experience of the covenant curse does not imply God has abdicated his people or his promises. The divine warrior is still present, as is evident in these stories. At the same time the role of the divine warrior is not the way it was experienced in the days when God acted as the Redeemer of his people to make them a peculiar people. In the ideal, God acting as warrior took place in three stages: preparations for the war, the battle, and the sequel to victory.[25]

Preparation required knowing God's will and being spiritually ready; in the conquest of Jericho the people were required to consecrate themselves for the day of battle (Josh. 3:5) and to renew the covenant commitment through circumcision of the new generation (5:2–8). This obviously was not usual military strategy; the battle itself was won by the power of God. Jericho, a mighty fortified city, was conquered when the Israelites marched around it in ceremony, led by the ark, accompanied with the blowing of horns; the walls came down with a shout (6:20). Since the battle belonged to Yahweh, praise followed victory (e.g., Ps. 144:9–10). The spoils of war belonged to Yahweh; in the case of Jericho, it was everything in the city (Josh. 6:17–19). None of the classic signs of the divine warrior are present in these battles with the Arameans. At the same time God is at work through the prophet Elisha.

The power of the prophetic word. These stories about Elisha and the Arameans are more about the power of the prophetic word than about God as the victor in war. However the power of the prophetic word requires the presence of God as the warrior. Gone is the expectation that Yahweh will provide the incomprehensible ingredient of success. DeVries describes this as a more sophisticated situation, where Israel's faith has grown more supernaturalistic, ascribing victory to mysterious forces of twilight, without human effort.[26] The real difference is the apostasy of the nation; the prophet announces the day of relief, not as a reward of faithfulness but as the transcendent negation of complete despair. The problem is the faithlessness of

---

24. Pritchard, ed., *Ancient Near Eastern Texts Relating to the Old Testament*, 538, lines 448–50.
25. Longman and Reid, *God is a Warrior*, 33–47.
26. Simon J. DeVries, "Temporal Terms as Structural Elements in the Holy War Tradition," *VT* 25 (1975): 103.

Israel, as expressed by the king and his captain, rather than the absence of God from history.

The power of the divine warrior is released in the words of the prophet. When the servant of Elisha awakes to find Dothan surrounded by the Aramean army, he is paralyzed with fear (6:15). The response of Elisha is that one with Yahweh is more than a mighty military (v. 16). Rofé thinks that the phrase "Elisha prayed" begins a parenthetical explanation, much like that of later rabbinic technique, in which the figurative is explained by the literal.[27] Elisha has simply stated that God is more powerful than the Arameans, but the explanation shows visually how the forces of God around Elisha are more numerous than the Aramean army (v. 17). Rofé thinks that the explanation ends with the resumptive phrase when Elisha prays again (v. 18a), after the army descends. This would specify that the army that came down to Elisha is not the enemy Arameans (NIV), but the divine army. The power of God protects Elisha and strikes the Arameans with a blinding light so the prophet is saved and the army led away.

In the siege of Samaria, the apostate king views Elisha as a prophet with unlimited power from God. The woman's cry for justice against the greed of her neighbor over the corpse of a child so shocks the king that he calls for Elisha's head. The rights of the case are so contorted that justice is not even conceivable. Believing it is impossible for God to allow such heinous acts to occur, acts so contrary to human nature, he can only expect that the man of God should have prevented such calamity. Elisha again remains unperturbed at the ranting of the king. He simply requires his servants to block the executioner at the door until the king arrives (6:32). When the king arrives, Elisha calmly announces that there will be sufficient food the next day.

Such a promise is incomprehensible to the king's captain. However, the armies of Yahweh again rout the Arameans (7:6–7), just as the prophet said, abandoning sufficient provisions so that the famine is broken. The work of the divine warrior, through the word of the prophet, is evident both in the provision of food and the trampling of the skeptical captain.

The path of wisdom. The path of wisdom is to follow consistently the right choice of values. In actual life situations this may not be possible. The story of Solomon and the two prostitutes quarreling over the life of a child (1 Kings 3:16–27) is often compared with the account of two women quarreling over the life of a child for food (2 Kings 6:24–31). Conditions of severe famine created by war bring about conditions in which normal values

---

27. Alexander Rofé, "Elisha Dothan (2 Kings 6:8–23): Historico-Literary Criticism Sustained by the Midrash," in *Ki Baruch Hu: Ancient Near Eastern, Biblical, and Judaic Studies in Honor of Baruch A. Levine,* ed. Robert Chazan (Winona Lake, Ind.: Eisenbrauns, 1999), 348, 352.

of motherhood are subordinated to the need for survival. Injustice is created by a refusal to give up the life of a child. War creates an ambiguity about wisdom and justice, folly and wickedness.[28]

In the instance of the two prostitutes, maternal instincts become the means by which Solomon determines the true mother of the living child. However in that story it is also true that one of the women has subordinated those instincts and is willing to sacrifice the life of a child; Solomon, apparently, would have been willing to allow that to take place. In the second story the conflict is over a sense of justice, which is present even in the revolting conditions of war, and the protection of the life of a child, a maternal love, which prevails even in the face of famine. Faced with such a dilemma and the inhumanity of the woman pleading for justice, the wicked king simply admits his impotence and tears his garments, revealing the fact that he is wearing the clothing of a penitent. Only God has the power to bring deliverance in such a situation (6:27). No amount of wisdom can prevail in such a circumstance.

The story of Solomon's receiving divine wisdom is meant to teach us that God honors the right choice of values so that our choices can work out for good. The story of the two women during the Syrian siege is not intended to compromise the significance of the gift of wisdom Solomon received.[29] War is truly a dread in which no amount of wisdom can bring about justice, but this does not undermine the possibility of a good and just king, of goodness and justice in society derived from the benefit of wisdom in learning to live together. This wisdom is a divine gift in that it is revealed to us through instruction that comes from God and is made available to us through his presence in particular circumstances. Wisdom is to trust God in situations beyond the ability of human intelligence to judge or human power to change. God honors choices made in submission to the truths of wisdom.

TOOLS OF OUR WARFARE. The Israelites experience the activity of the divine warrior in many different ways, depending on their situation, but the presence and activity of God is at work through his prophets. The rule of God is demonstrated through Elisha the man of God rather than the king. Protecting the poor, bringing life and

---

28. Hugh S. Pyper, "Judging the Wisdom of Solomon: The Two-Way Effect of Intertextuality," *JSOT* 59 (1993): 25–36, argues that the second story qualifies the first, to say that the wise and the wicked are not readily evident and that the monarchy fails as all human enterprise must fail.

29. Stuart Lasine, "The Ups and Downs of Monarchical Justice: Solomon and Jehoram in an Intertextual World," *JSOT* 59 (1993): 37–53.

justice, leading armies, and acting as a covenant champion are all part of the ideal royal profile.

The apostle Paul reminds the Ephesians that the situation is no different for them (Eph. 6:10–13). They need to be strong in the Lord and in the power of his might; they must put on the whole armor of God so that they can take their stand against the wiles of the devil. They are not struggling with an enemy of flesh and blood, but against rulers, authorities, and mighty forces of this dark world, against spiritual wickedness in the heavenly places. Behind the evil forces at work in the world are transworldly forces that put Paul into prison. Equipped with the spiritual armor of God it is possible for Christians in this world to stand against such forces. This spiritual armor is nothing other than faith in the truth of the gospel (6:14–17); above all it is prayer to the divine warrior (v. 18), and steadfast prayer at all times for all the saints.

In the essentials of spiritual warfare, the present world is no different from the tortured topsy-turvy world of Elisha. Christians in many different places are ravaged by the turbulence of war, just as the faithful in the days of Elisha. Where actual physical warfare is not present, Christians struggle against ideologies and social forces designed to undermine the rule of God in this world, the way of life God has ordained through his Word for those created to represent him as his image. Everywhere the faithful are called to be like Elisha and his followers; they must resist evil and show mercy, as they are able. As with Elisha, their weapon is prayer, and their assurance is that the divine warrior will act on their behalf even as he did in the distressing days of Omride apostasy.

The community in oppressive times. The account of the floating axhead (2 Kings 6:1–7) is an example of the function of community in oppressive times. Of immediate significance is the fact of community and its importance. The faithful are not only in need of each other, but they are in need of adequate facilities so they can meet with the prophet and with each other. Henton Davies observes that the community represents freedom for the followers of Elisha; freedom works through restraint, through consideration of the needs of the group.[30]

Freedom is not uninhibited liberty to follow an individual course of action; such individuals are not free but forced to work within the orbit of their own narrow personality and opinions. Freedom comes with the enablement of the community, the mutual support of others in the faith. Such freedom has a price. The leader of such a community might be regarded as "a very irascible and bald-headed old gentleman who didn't mind delivering children to

---

30. G. Henton Davies, "The Balance of Freedom," *Int* 6 (1952): 417–19.

bears, let alone theological students to their proper place."[31] The result of sharing might be that a valuable item is lost, buried beneath the water. The point of the floating axhead was not simply to show that Elisha is a wonder worker, for Elisha displays many of his own limits in the situation. A new handle is prepared and cast where the iron has fallen, signifying a new beginning for one who has failed and the power for the community to continue.

The brutality of human government. The brutality of governments toward their own people is ever present. In that cruelty it is frequent that famine is used as a murder weapon. As stated recently by Edgar Chen and David Marcus, famine endures only because the international community and governments continue to perceive it as an act of nature and not a human rights disaster.[32] They quote Nobel Prize-winning economist Amartya Sen to say that "famine is, after all, so easy to prevent that it is amazing that it is allowed to occur at all." Histories prove that people often starve because it is politically advantageous.

> Stalin engineered an apocalyptic famine in the 1930s to exterminate millions of politically suspect Ukrainians. Mao pursued the "Great Leap Forward" with deliberate disregard for the misery it wrought, starving at least 20 million Chinese to death. Dubbing his strategy "emptying the sea to catch the fish," Mengistu Haile Mariam targeted the infamous 1984–85 famine in Ethiopia against civil insurgents.[33]

The world continues to perpetuate such atrocities. At the time of writing, Mugabe in Zimbabwe has followed the same policy, bringing the one-time breadbasket of Africa to the precipice of famine. Ironically, Mengistu fled to Zimbabwe to escape indictment for genocide in Ethiopia.

The ancient practice of siege warfare creating temporary famine within a city is a modest crime by modern standards. Whatever the size of the monstrosity of famine, it does not change the horror for the individual victims or the helplessness of individuals who might seek to intervene. In the siege of Samaria, even the king is presented as sympathetic, utterly powerless, and revolted by the plea of his own citizen over the refusal of an agreement to share a corpse. In such desperate situations, the determination of right and wrong can be confused and uncertain.

The king appears as a somewhat ambiguous figure in the famine of Samaria. In the larger theology of the Deuteronomistic History, the Omride

<hr>

31. Ibid., 416.
32. Edgar Chen and David Marcus, "When Famine Becomes a Murder Weapon," *National Post* (July 19, 2003), A19.
33. Ibid.

kings were responsible when the wars of judgment came against Israel. In this story the king appears genuinely remorseful as he surveys the wall, wearing sackcloth under his clothes (6:30). When a woman calls out to him for justice because a cannibalistic agreement has been denied, he is genuinely appalled. The reader identifies with his feeling of outrage; how can there be a concern for the injustice of not sharing such grizzly fare, when the real outrage is the war that has driven these poor victims to such extremes? The king responds by demanding the life of Elisha, since he is seen as responsible for this situation in his pronouncements of judgments against Israel. Before the executioner can carry out the task, the king has come to some sense; there is no use blaming the messenger for the bad news. The question is rather how Yahweh can act in this manner (7:33).

This might lead to the conclusion that this story is told to challenge the justice of God.[34] Though this is a legitimate question, the context presents other concerns. Israel as a nation has come to be as other nations. War is a part of the human condition; war is created entirely by humans, they must accept responsibility for its atrocities. God and the prophet are directly involved only to the extent that this particular war is a judgment against Israel. War creates a perversion of values so that good and evil in particular circumstances become entirely blurred.

It is important that the plight of individuals in circumstances such as these not be lost and that judgment not be passed against them. Hens-Piazza appropriately provides an example of this danger:

> A graphic photo of a dying four-year-old Tutsi child lying in the remains of a deserted refugee camp in Burundi, his grieving mother slumped over him, accompanied the headline "Burundi Steps Up Expulsions of Rwandans." The article reviewed the history of the controversy and offered an update of the battle between leaders and the warring factions of the two ethnic groups. The responses of other nations and the UN's gestures were also sketched. Nowhere did the report refer to the mother and child or describe what happened to them. In fact, the impact of the report served to distract and nullify any feeling that might be evoked in the reader response to the photo.[35]

Powerful governing bodies, stymied by forces outside their control, become the total focus of attention. The miserable victims of these forces of

---

34. Stuart Lasine, "Jehoram and the Cannibal Mothers (2 Kings 6.24–33): Solomon's Judgment in an Inverted World," *JSOT* 50 (1991): 48–49.

35. Gina Hens-Piazza, "Forms of Violence and the Violence of Forms: Two Cannibal Mothers before a King (2 Kings 6:24–33)," *Journal of Feminist Studies in Religion* 14 (1998): 95–96.

evil are only used as decoys to call attention to what is regarded as the real story, the story about political power and the apparent means to address the problem.

Divine intervention. The story about the two cannibal mothers in the siege of Samaria does call attention to divine intervention for suffering individuals. Only God can intervene in such calamity, as the king himself acknowledges in his despair. Divine deliverance is one of the topoi of this story.[36] The "windows of heaven" (7:2) are mentioned in the account of the Flood to restrain or release water (Gen. 7:11; 8:2); the other occurrence is found when the prophet Malachi uses the term to describe divine abundance for those who tithe (Mal. 3:10). The windows of heaven become a metaphor for divine prosperity.

A similar motif is found in the Chronicle of Joshua the Stylite while describing the siege of Amid during the Seleucid era.[37] The report details cannibalism but describes a plentiful state of "blessings sent down abundantly from heaven upon all men ... and the rain was falling and the fruits of the earth were growing in their seasons." A repetition of the prophet's words and those of the captain close the account at Samaria (2 Kings 7:18—19), emphasizing the divine response to human cynicism.

Christians in acts of mercy. Rather than a challenge to the justice of Yahweh, these stories of Elisha are an example of his mercy in outrageous times. Yahweh alone provides relief during the cruelties of the Aramean wars. The intervention of the king for the Shunammite after she lost her land is not coincidence but a divine provision as the king is consulting Gehazi about the death-defying feats of Elisha (8:1—6). Humans are treacherous even to their own masters, as Hazael against Ben-Hadad, perhaps even to their own astonishment (8:11). What they consider to be great things in their own conquests are often great judgment and affliction on innocent victims (v. 13). In all of this the faithful are called to show mercy as they can and to know that the sovereignty of God will prevail over the great powers of the world.

As in the days of Elijah, Christians continue to be known for their acts of humanity in the most horrible of human situations. This was the substance of a convocation address by journalist Brian Stewart.[38] What surprised him

---

36. Greenfield, "Doves' Dung and the Price of Food," 125–26.

37. Ibid.

38. Stewart delivered the convocation at Knox College of the University of Toronto on May 12, 2004. The address was posted on the Knox website: http://www.utoronto.ca/knox/pages/News%20and%20Events/brian_stewart.htm. Stewart has received the Gemini Award as "Best Overall Broadcast Journalist" as well as numerous other awards. As a foreign correspondent he has covered many of the world's conflicts, reporting from nine war zones from El Salvador to Beirut.

in over forty years of journalism was the force of Christianity in the drive to serve and help others, a force present from the beginning of Christianity that mysteriously never seems to weaken or grow weary. From the "ringside" seat of a reporter he has found there is no movement closer to the raw truth of war, famines, or crisis and the vast human predicament than organized Christianity in action. There is no alliance more determined and dogged in action than church workers mobilized for common good. They are involved in a vast front stretching from the most impoverished reaches of the developing world to the hectic struggle to preserve caring values in towns and cities of North America. As a journalist he has never reached these front lines without finding Christians already in the thick of it, mobilizing congregations that care, being a faithful witness to truth, the primary light in the darkness, and often the only light.

Stewart came to this admiring view slowly and reluctantly. At the start of his career he had abandoned religion, regarding the church as a tiresome irrelevance. What ultimately persuaded him otherwise was the reality of Christianity's mission, physically and in spirit, before his very eyes. He was moved by quiet individual moments of character, a courage that seemed anchored to some deep core within Christianity.

Stewart recalled a stairwell in Gdansk, Poland. The first unbelievable crack in the mighty Communist empire, which had so often proclaimed triumph over religion, occurred in Poland in the early 1980s, when the Solidarity Movement, supported by the Roman Catholic Church, rose to challenge tyranny, under the leadership of a most unlikely little shipyard electrician Lech Walensa, who later won the Nobel Peace Prize and become president of Poland. When Stewart met him, Walensa had been jailed and was isolated, and his life was so threatened he seemed to be a "dead man walking." Reporters assumed security forces were arranging one of those convenient "accidents" that so frequently happen in the climate of oppression.

A few reporters met him alone on this stairwell as he slipped out to mass. One of them asked if he was frightened. He stopped and looked surprised at the thought. Then he answered in a voice of steel: "No, I am afraid of no one, nothing, only God." With that he walked out into the night; in that dingy stairwell was the purest courage and conscience backed by Christian faith that no force of empire or terror could ever extinguish. Years later in Poland, East Germany, Czechoslovakia, and Romania, Stewart watched the mighty empire crumble away before civil rights movements that often began in equally dingy little church halls and basements—early gatherings the world knew nothing about and would not have taken seriously if it had.

There have been other movements. Bishop Tutu in Soweto in South Africa in the Apartheid era counseled Christians of all races how to mobilize against injustice without losing their humanity. Martin Luther King Jr. began his movement against segregation in some Birmingham church halls. Stewart testifies to many such efforts: saving children in Mozambique from life on garbage dumps, schools for ex-field hands in the fovea-slums of Brazil, the quiet comforting of runaways and addicts in a thousand asphalt city jungles, and small groups of Christians visiting the lonely and mentally fragile in low-income boarding house flats.

Stewart recalls one particular incident in the murderous civil war in El Salvador in the early 1980s, a war of almost casual massacres, when reporters came to quake before the term "Right Wing Death Squads." These death squads would kill anyone from landless peasants to Archbishop Romero in his own cathedral. The policy of journalists was to be in the capital before dark, as it was suicide to be on the roads at night. One afternoon they misjudged the time when interviewing a small group of landless refugees to the north. As the night began to thicken, jungle sounds seemed to grow heavy with menace. As they were packing, a delegation of refugee elders begged them to spend the night because the death squads were active and the presence of journalists might prevent the abduction of all the men or a massacre.

That day Stewart cursed the day he became a foreign correspondent. They too were targets; they rationalized—a satellite feed was waiting, jobs were on the line, what good would it do if they too were killed. As they debated, an old station wagon raced into the camp in a cloud of dust. Out stepped three Christian aid workers waving a Red Cross flag. They insisted the journalists return; it was critical they get the word out. All over that awful war there were small groups of Christians trying to stave off the killings. The journalists left, in great relief. The protection that night by the good Samaritans worked. What if the station wagon had not come?

Stewart is perhaps best known for his famous picture of "the face of famine" in Ethiopia. He was in a Catholic refugee camp when an infant girl brought by her parents was given up for dead. Her grave had already been dug. The infant was given what treatment was available and miraculously lived. In time her father came and took her back home. Years later Stewart was able to successfully find the young woman, now herself a mother, to complete the story of how relief saves lives. It was 1984 when Stewart, along with Michael Buerk of BBC fame, first carried the story of the Great Ethiopian Famine on television. The world responded to their story, but they were not the first. They went because, for months, church aid groups on the ground had seen famine coming and urged the world to take notice.

When they did get in, against considerable Ethiopian resistance, these groups showed them where to go. Once when flying to a disaster story their twin engine plane had to make an emergency landing at a deserted landing strip in the dense jungle in central Africa. They stepped into the middle of nowhere, only to be greeted by a cheerful Dutch Reformed minister offering tea. A veteran cameraman named Mike Sweeny later sighed in exasperation, "Do you think you could ever get us to a story, somewhere, anywhere where those Christians aren't there first!!" It never happened.

Stewart summarized his experience with the following words:

> I'm often asked if I lost belief in God covering events like Ethiopia, then called "the worst Hell on Earth." Actually, like others before me, it was precisely in such hells that I rediscovered religion. I saw so many countless acts of human love and charity, total respect for the most forsaken, for ALL life. I was confronted by the miracle of our Humanity. And I felt again the "Good Infection" of Christian volunteers ... and heard again those words tolling "Even Here ... Even Here."[39]

The Christian witness, of which Stewart speaks, is no less significant than the great works of Elisha during the terrible days of the Syrian wars. The human disasters and pain are not any different in the contemporary world, nor is the power of God through his people in bringing mercy to desperate situations.

39. Ibid.

2 Kings 8:16–10:36

❧

IN THE FIFTH year of Joram son of Ahab king of Israel, when Jehoshaphat was king of Judah, Jehoram son of Jehoshaphat began his reign as king of Judah. ¹⁷He was thirty-two years old when he became king, and he reigned in Jerusalem eight years. ¹⁸He walked in the ways of the kings of Israel, as the house of Ahab had done, for he married a daughter of Ahab. He did evil in the eyes of the LORD. ¹⁹Nevertheless, for the sake of his servant David, the LORD was not willing to destroy Judah. He had promised to maintain a lamp for David and his descendants forever.

²⁰In the time of Jehoram, Edom rebelled against Judah and set up its own king. ²¹So Jehoram went to Zair with all his chariots. The Edomites surrounded him and his chariot commanders, but he rose up and broke through by night; his army, however, fled back home. ²²To this day Edom has been in rebellion against Judah. Libnah revolted at the same time.

²³As for the other events of Jehoram's reign, and all he did, are they not written in the book of the annals of the kings of Judah? ²⁴Jehoram rested with his fathers and was buried with them in the City of David. And Ahaziah his son succeeded him as king.

²⁵In the twelfth year of Joram son of Ahab king of Israel, Ahaziah son of Jehoram king of Judah began to reign. ²⁶Ahaziah was twenty-two years old when he became king, and he reigned in Jerusalem one year. His mother's name was Athaliah, a granddaughter of Omri king of Israel. ²⁷He walked in the ways of the house of Ahab and did evil in the eyes of the LORD, as the house of Ahab had done, for he was related by marriage to Ahab's family.

²⁸Ahaziah went with Joram son of Ahab to war against Hazael king of Aram at Ramoth Gilead. The Arameans wounded Joram; ²⁹so King Joram returned to Jezreel to recover from the wounds the Arameans had inflicted on him at Ramoth in his battle with Hazael king of Aram.

Then Ahaziah son of Jehoram king of Judah went down to Jezreel to see Joram son of Ahab, because he had been wounded.

9:1The prophet Elisha summoned a man from the company of the prophets and said to him, "Tuck your cloak into your belt, take this flask of oil with you and go to Ramoth Gilead. 2When you get there, look for Jehu son of Jehoshaphat, the son of Nimshi. Go to him, get him away from his companions and take him into an inner room. 3Then take the flask and pour the oil on his head and declare, 'This is what the LORD says: I anoint you king over Israel.' Then open the door and run; don't delay!"

4So the young man, the prophet, went to Ramoth Gilead. 5When he arrived, he found the army officers sitting together. "I have a message for you, commander," he said.

"For which of us?" asked Jehu.

"For you, commander," he replied.

6Jehu got up and went into the house. Then the prophet poured the oil on Jehu's head and declared, "This is what the LORD, the God of Israel, says: 'I anoint you king over the LORD's people Israel. 7You are to destroy the house of Ahab your master, and I will avenge the blood of my servants the prophets and the blood of all the LORD's servants shed by Jezebel. 8The whole house of Ahab will perish. I will cut off from Ahab every last male in Israel—slave or free. 9I will make the house of Ahab like the house of Jeroboam son of Nebat and like the house of Baasha son of Ahijah. 10As for Jezebel, dogs will devour her on the plot of ground at Jezreel, and no one will bury her.'" Then he opened the door and ran.

11When Jehu went out to his fellow officers, one of them asked him, "Is everything all right? Why did this madman come to you?"

"You know the man and the sort of things he says," Jehu replied.

12"That's not true!" they said. "Tell us."

Jehu said, "Here is what he told me: 'This is what the LORD says: I anoint you king over Israel.'"

13They hurried and took their cloaks and spread them under him on the bare steps. Then they blew the trumpet and shouted, "Jehu is king!"

14So Jehu son of Jehoshaphat, the son of Nimshi, conspired against Joram. (Now Joram and all Israel had been defending Ramoth Gilead against Hazael king of Aram, 15but King Joram had returned to Jezreel to recover from the wounds the

Arameans had inflicted on him in the battle with Hazael king of Aram.) Jehu said, "If this is the way you feel, don't let anyone slip out of the city to go and tell the news in Jezreel."

¹⁶Then he got into his chariot and rode to Jezreel, because Joram was resting there and Ahaziah king of Judah had gone down to see him.

¹⁷When the lookout standing on the tower in Jezreel saw Jehu's troops approaching, he called out, "I see some troops coming."

"Get a horseman," Joram ordered. "Send him to meet them and ask, 'Do you come in peace?'"

¹⁸The horseman rode off to meet Jehu and said, "This is what the king says: 'Do you come in peace?'"

"What do you have to do with peace?" Jehu replied. "Fall in behind me."

The lookout reported, "The messenger has reached them, but he isn't coming back."

¹⁹So the king sent out a second horseman. When he came to them he said, "This is what the king says: 'Do you come in peace?'"

Jehu replied, "What do you have to do with peace? Fall in behind me."

²⁰The lookout reported, "He has reached them, but he isn't coming back either. The driving is like that of Jehu son of Nimshi—he drives like a madman."

²¹"Hitch up my chariot," Joram ordered. And when it was hitched up, Joram king of Israel and Ahaziah king of Judah rode out, each in his own chariot, to meet Jehu. They met him at the plot of ground that had belonged to Naboth the Jezreelite. ²²When Joram saw Jehu he asked, "Have you come in peace, Jehu?"

"How can there be peace," Jehu replied, "as long as all the idolatry and witchcraft of your mother Jezebel abound?"

²³Joram turned about and fled, calling out to Ahaziah, "Treachery, Ahaziah!"

²⁴Then Jehu drew his bow and shot Joram between the shoulders. The arrow pierced his heart and he slumped down in his chariot. ²⁵Jehu said to Bidkar, his chariot officer, "Pick him up and throw him on the field that belonged to Naboth the Jezreelite. Remember how you and I were riding together in chariots behind Ahab his father when the LORD made this

prophecy about him: 26'Yesterday I saw the blood of Naboth and the blood of his sons, declares the LORD, and I will surely make you pay for it on this plot of ground, declares the LORD.' Now then, pick him up and throw him on that plot, in accordance with the word of the LORD."

27When Ahaziah king of Judah saw what had happened, he fled up the road to Beth Haggan. Jehu chased him, shouting, "Kill him too!" They wounded him in his chariot on the way up to Gur near Ibleam, but he escaped to Megiddo and died there. 28His servants took him by chariot to Jerusalem and buried him with his fathers in his tomb in the City of David. 29(In the eleventh year of Joram son of Ahab, Ahaziah had become king of Judah.)

30Then Jehu went to Jezreel. When Jezebel heard about it, she painted her eyes, arranged her hair and looked out of a window. 31As Jehu entered the gate, she asked, "Have you come in peace, Zimri, you murderer of your master?"

32He looked up at the window and called out, "Who is on my side? Who?" Two or three eunuchs looked down at him. 33"Throw her down!" Jehu said. So they threw her down, and some of her blood spattered the wall and the horses as they trampled her underfoot.

34Jehu went in and ate and drank. "Take care of that cursed woman," he said, "and bury her, for she was a king's daughter." 35But when they went out to bury her, they found nothing except her skull, her feet and her hands. 36They went back and told Jehu, who said, "This is the word of the LORD that he spoke through his servant Elijah the Tishbite: On the plot of ground at Jezreel dogs will devour Jezebel's flesh. 37Jezebel's body will be like refuse on the ground in the plot at Jezreel, so that no one will be able to say, 'This is Jezebel.'"

10:1Now there were in Samaria seventy sons of the house of Ahab. So Jehu wrote letters and sent them to Samaria: to the officials of Jezreel, to the elders and to the guardians of Ahab's children. He said, 2"As soon as this letter reaches you, since your master's sons are with you and you have chariots and horses, a fortified city and weapons, 3choose the best and most worthy of your master's sons and set him on his father's throne. Then fight for your master's house."

4But they were terrified and said, "If two kings could not resist him, how can we?"

⁵So the palace administrator, the city governor, the elders and the guardians sent this message to Jehu: "We are your servants and we will do anything you say. We will not appoint anyone as king; you do whatever you think best."

⁶Then Jehu wrote them a second letter, saying, "If you are on my side and will obey me, take the heads of your master's sons and come to me in Jezreel by this time tomorrow."

Now the royal princes, seventy of them, were with the leading men of the city, who were rearing them. ⁷When the letter arrived, these men took the princes and slaughtered all seventy of them. They put their heads in baskets and sent them to Jehu in Jezreel. ⁸When the messenger arrived, he told Jehu, "They have brought the heads of the princes."

Then Jehu ordered, "Put them in two piles at the entrance of the city gate until morning."

⁹The next morning Jehu went out. He stood before all the people and said, "You are innocent. It was I who conspired against my master and killed him, but who killed all these? ¹⁰Know then, that not a word the LORD has spoken against the house of Ahab will fail. The LORD has done what he promised through his servant Elijah." ¹¹So Jehu killed everyone in Jezreel who remained of the house of Ahab, as well as all his chief men, his close friends and his priests, leaving him no survivor.

¹²Jehu then set out and went toward Samaria. At Beth Eked of the Shepherds, ¹³he met some relatives of Ahaziah king of Judah and asked, "Who are you?"

They said, "We are relatives of Ahaziah, and we have come down to greet the families of the king and of the queen mother."

¹⁴"Take them alive!" he ordered. So they took them alive and slaughtered them by the well of Beth Eked—forty-two men. He left no survivor.

¹⁵After he left there, he came upon Jehonadab son of Recab, who was on his way to meet him. Jehu greeted him and said, "Are you in accord with me, as I am with you?"

"I am," Jehonadab answered.

"If so," said Jehu, "give me your hand." So he did, and Jehu helped him up into the chariot. ¹⁶Jehu said, "Come with me and see my zeal for the LORD." Then he had him ride along in his chariot.

¹⁷When Jehu came to Samaria, he killed all who were left there of Ahab's family; he destroyed them, according to the word of the LORD spoken to Elijah.

¹⁸Then Jehu brought all the people together and said to them, "Ahab served Baal a little; Jehu will serve him much. ¹⁹Now summon all the prophets of Baal, all his ministers and all his priests. See that no one is missing, because I am going to hold a great sacrifice for Baal. Anyone who fails to come will no longer live." But Jehu was acting deceptively in order to destroy the ministers of Baal.

²⁰Jehu said, "Call an assembly in honor of Baal." So they proclaimed it. ²¹Then he sent word throughout Israel, and all the ministers of Baal came; not one stayed away. They crowded into the temple of Baal until it was full from one end to the other. ²²And Jehu said to the keeper of the wardrobe, "Bring robes for all the ministers of Baal." So he brought out robes for them.

²³Then Jehu and Jehonadab son of Recab went into the temple of Baal. Jehu said to the ministers of Baal, "Look around and see that no servants of the LORD are here with you—only ministers of Baal." ²⁴So they went in to make sacrifices and burnt offerings. Now Jehu had posted eighty men outside with this warning: "If one of you lets any of the men I am placing in your hands escape, it will be your life for his life."

²⁵As soon as Jehu had finished making the burnt offering, he ordered the guards and officers: "Go in and kill them; let no one escape." So they cut them down with the sword. The guards and officers threw the bodies out and then entered the inner shrine of the temple of Baal. ²⁶They brought the sacred stone out of the temple of Baal and burned it. ²⁷They demolished the sacred stone of Baal and tore down the temple of Baal, and people have used it for a latrine to this day.

²⁸So Jehu destroyed Baal worship in Israel. ²⁹However, he did not turn away from the sins of Jeroboam son of Nebat, which he had caused Israel to commit—the worship of the golden calves at Bethel and Dan.

³⁰The LORD said to Jehu, "Because you have done well in accomplishing what is right in my eyes and have done to the house of Ahab all I had in mind to do, your descendants will sit on the throne of Israel to the fourth generation." ³¹Yet Jehu was not careful to keep the law of the LORD, the God of

Israel, with all his heart. He did not turn away from the sins of Jeroboam, which he had caused Israel to commit.

³²In those days the LORD began to reduce the size of Israel. Hazael overpowered the Israelites throughout their territory ³³east of the Jordan in all the land of Gilead (the region of Gad, Reuben and Manasseh), from Aroer by the Arnon Gorge through Gilead to Bashan.

³⁴As for the other events of Jehu's reign, all he did, and all his achievements, are they not written in the book of the annals of the kings of Israel?

³⁵Jehu rested with his fathers and was buried in Samaria. And Jehoahaz his son succeeded him as king. ³⁶The time that Jehu reigned over Israel in Samaria was twenty-eight years.

THE ELISHA STORIES demonstrate the sovereignty of God during the tumultuous times of the Omride dynasty. Following these stories the prophetic historian returns to the political developments in Israel and Judah. After Jehoshaphat's death the sins of Ahab come to dominate Judah just as they had Israel. The political influence of Israel over Judah comes through the marriage of Jehoram, son of Jehoshaphat, to Athaliah, daughter of Ahab (8:18).

Jehoram is succeeded by Ahaziah his son, who follows in the ways of his mother, "a granddaughter of Omri" (8:26–27). Only through God's grace in the promise to David can the "lamp" of David be saved from extinction (8:19); mercy prevents the complete collapse of the covenant. With that brief summary of Judah the historian turns to the fulfillment of the judgment pronounced by Elijah on the house of Omri (cf. 1 Kings 19:15–17). The story of Jehu's overthrow is a sustained narrative told to grip the reader with the same intensity that motivated its protagonists. The Omride dynasty is brought to an end with the kind of violence that characterized its rule.

Apostasy of the Kings of Judah (8:16–29)

THE SYNCHRONISM OF Jehoram with the fifth year of Joram son of Ahab (8:16) marks the end of the twenty-five year reign of Jehoshaphat (cf. 1 Kings 22:42; 2 Kings 1:17).[1] It is not quite correct to say that Jehoram begins to

---

1. See Appendix B for the double synchronisms of Jehoram and Joram and the subsequent textual traditions that arose. A coregency of Jehoram with his father Jehoshaphat best accounts for these synchronisms.

reign in the fifth year of Joram (NIV).[2] Jehoram does become king in the fifth year of Joram, but he began to reign with his father two years before Joram. The summary of Jehoram's reign states that the mercy of God preserves the dynasty of David in spite of the fact that Jehoram follows in the ways of the house of Ahab (2 Kings 8:18–19). The promise to David is a light that continues to shine (cf. 2 Sam. 21:17; 1 Kings 11:36; 15:4); the death of a last surviving heir can be described as extinguishing "the only surviving coal" (2 Sam. 14:7). Zion is the location where God has determined to perpetually keep the lamp of his anointed burning (Ps. 132:17). Though the dynasty is preserved, Judah suffers the loss of territory and influence.

Jehoram tries to bring Edom into submission, but without success (8:20–22). The sequence of events is not clear because of the faulty Hebrew text, which was apparently disturbed before the earliest translations. Jehoram crosses over to Zair, a name not otherwise known. The Greek form of the name suggests the location might be Zoar at the southern tip of the Dead Sea (cf. Gen. 13:10; 19:22).[3] Judging from the context, Jehoram and all his chariot forces conduct a night raid on Edom, but the Edomites surround him and the chariot officers, and the army flees back to its tents (i.e., home).[4] The note that the revolt of Edom continues "until this day" (2 Kings 8:22) occurs in other instances of Judah-Edom relations (14:7; 16:6) and shows a special interest in territorial claims when Judah regains its military strength.

Libnah was a Levitical city (Josh. 21:13), located in the southwestern foothills of Judah (the Shephelah) in the vicinity Lachish and Gezer (15:42). It came under attack when Sennacherib lay siege to Lachish (2 Kings 19:8). This is the only notice of a city breaking with the central rule in Jerusalem. The circumstances are not given; the Chronicler reports distant raids into Judah by Philistines and Arabs (2 Chron. 21:16–17), which may have been related to the revolt of Libnah "at that time" (2 Kings 8:22). Apparently the military weakness of Judah gives an important border fort opportunity to advance its own interests.

Ahaziah, son of Jehoram, begins to rule Israel in the twelfth year of Joram

---

2. Thiele, *Mysterious Numbers of the Hebrew Kings*, 100.

3. The name ṣ'r in Isa. 15:5 is written as ṣ'wr in 1QIsaᵃ, a further indication that ṣ'wr in 2 Kings 8:21 means Zoar.

4. Some translations adopt an emendation; instead of Jehoram attacking the Edomites (*wykh ʾt ʾdwm*), it is the Edomites who attack Jehoram (*wykh ʾtw ʾdwm*). The subject of the night raid is ambiguous; the nearest antecedent is Jehoram, but the context makes evident that Jehoram is surrounded by the Edomites and flees. It may be translated to say that the "Edomites surrounded him and his chariot commanders, but he rose up and broke through by night; his army, however, fled back home" (NIV). This makes Edom the initial aggressor, but involves a more radical emendation of transposing clauses.

(8:25) and rules briefly until his death in Megiddo at the hands of Jehu (9:27). In 9:29 his reign is said to have been in the eleventh year of Joram. The difference may be a textual problem,[5] but the number "twelve" may also belong to the original synchronistic data if Judah switched to the nonaccession year system used in Israel.[6] Eleven years would be the synchronism with accession year reckoning. The alliance of Judah with Israel may have been the occasion for harmonizing the method of recording years of reign.

The mother of Ahaziah is Athaliah, here said to be a "daughter [i.e., descendant] of Omri" (8:26), while in verse 18 she is said to be "a daughter of Ahab." This is the only reference to the ancestral father of the dynasty (Omri), which is otherwise remembered by the name and activities of Ahab.[7] The queen mother could exercise considerable influence in affairs of the court, as we saw in the case of Maacah, who was removed by her son Asa from her position because of her devotion to Asherah (cf. 1 Kings 15:13). The influence of Jezebel in fostering foreign cults in Jerusalem continues through her daughter Athaliah. These are best described in terms of "the house of Ahab" (2 Kings 8:27), who was renowned for his support of the prophets of Baal against Elijah.

The end of Ahaziah's reign does not have the usual burial formula. His death is recorded in the following narrative (9:27–28). A circumstantial statement is adopted from that story (9:14–15a) to provide a transition to that account. It explains the presence of Ahaziah in Jezreel where he is caught in the assassination of Joram.

The Revolt of Jehu (9:1–37)

JEHU IS OF the house of Nimshi (cf. 9:20); the use of the name of his ancestor may be because the latter is better known or because it assists in distinguishing Jehu's father from King Jehoshaphat. The anointing takes place clandestinely and hastily, as is necessary if the revolt were to take place with the army leaders (the "brothers" of Jehu) while they are on active duty seeking to capture Ramoth Gilead from the Arameans. Ahab had failed in his attempt to capture the city (1 Kings 22:29–36).

The betrayal of Jehu enables Hazael to retain Ramoth Gilead and to capture other territories in the Transjordan (10:32–33). The brutality of Jehu's

---

5. Cogan and Tadmor (*II Kings*, 98) suggest the number twelve (*štym ʿśrh*) may have developed from the Aramaic form of eleven (*ʿśty ʿśrh*; cf. 2 Kings 25:2).

6. Thiele, *Mysterious Numbers of the Hebrew Kings*, 97, 101.

7. Customarily the founder's name is commemorated in the dynastic title: "house of Saul (2 Sam. 3:1; 9:1); "house of David" (1 Kings 12:19; 13:2); but in the case of Omri it is "house of Ahab" (2 Kings 9:7–9; 10:10–11; 21:13).

revolt severely weakens Israel. In his first year he submits to Shalmaneser III of Assyria; the Black Obelisk states that he pays tribute with gold, silver, precious vessels, a royal scepter, and javelins. It will be two generations before Israel regains its former influence (under the rule of Jeroboam II, see 14:25–27).

Elisha plays a relatively minor role in the anointing of Jehu, especially given the prominence of the commission of Elijah (1 Kings 19:16). Anointing was a regular feature of coronation, but it is specially noted when a dynasty is founded or succession contested (e.g., 1 Sam. 9:16; 10:1; 2 Sam. 2:4; 5:3; 1 Kings 1:34, 39; 2 Kings 11:12; 23:30). Jehu evidently is known to the prophetic envoy; he identifies him among the officers gathered at Ramoth Gilead (2 Kings 9:5). The prophetic oracle has been regarded as an intruding prophetic speech (9:7–10),[8] but the prophecy against the house of Ahab is certainly exploited by Jehu and his party.

The oracle has the two standard elements:[9] There is a judgment relevant to the immediate situation (v. 7), followed by the stereotyped curse (vv. 8–9).[10] The oracle against Jezebel (v. 10) is specifically a fulfillment of the prophetic word (1 Kings 21:23). The judgment speech brings to a climax the accumulated sins of Israel from Jeroboam to Joram.

Calling the prophet a "madman" (9:11) is a derogatory reference to the eclectic nature of prophets.[11] Prophets were those "crazy preachers"; the description does not refer to their activity in prophesying but to their manner of life and speech. But prophets did have influence, even when their ability to declare the divine will was disregarded. The officers know the prophetic emissary with Jehu, and his announcement is regarded as the occasion to act. The followers of Jehu immediately turn the bare steps into an ascent to a royal dais and declare Jehu as king. Blowing a trumpet was customary in installing a king (cf. 1 Kings 1:34, 39). It served as a public announcement to formally submit to the new monarch. Following the accession ceremony, a proclamation to announce the anointed as king was normal procedure (cf. 1:11, 13, 18). Though the prophetic herald is spoken of disparagingly, his word is effective.

The narrative moves to the scene at Jezreel where the coup actually transpires (9:14–15). Joram retreats from Ramoth Gilead to recover from injuries. Jezreel is a logical place, as it serves as the primary royal fortification protecting

---

8. Montgomery, *The Books of Kings*, 400.

9. Hobbs, *2 Kings*, 111.

10. See comments on 1 Kings 14:10 for the idiom describing the destruction of the royal family (v. 8).

11. The word has a wide range of usage denoting erratic and unusual behavior, such as uncontrolled driving (2 Kings 9:20; Zech. 12:4) or insanity (1 Sam. 21:14–15).

the capital and the major administrative centers.[12] Jehu relies on the element of surprise in returning to Jezreel, demanding that no one betray a coronation that has just taken place. Joram will naturally expect that his chief officer is bringing him news from the battlefront when the watchmen see him approach.

The threefold repetition of the question asking whether all is well shifts attention to the actual disruption of peace (9:18, 19, 22). Though Joram may be worried about peace on the battlefront at Ramoth Gilead, the absence of peace is in his own country. In the first instance Joram still functions in the role of king, as the messenger is sent with an order: The king is asking, "Is all well?" (v. 18). Jehu knows Joram is no longer king, and his reply directs attention to the problem: What does the house of Ahab have to do with peace?[13] King Joram may have been asking whether all is well at Ramoth Gilead, but the question is ambiguous. He may also have been asking about Jehu's intent; there is something abnormal about his chief general speeding toward Jezreel with a whole troop of the army.

Jehu's response brings his mission into focus. The rider is in the service of a king who represents the crime of Ahab against Naboth in spilling innocent blood; he has nothing whatever to do with peace. If the rider is asking about whether Jehu's advance is war, the answer is the same: Jehu is bringing revolution to Jezreel. When the rider joins Jehu's troop, a second messenger is sent with the same question.[14]

The narrative further joins Jehu with the prophetic message by describing his driving as "mad" (šiggāʿôn), the same description given to the crazy prophet who came to anoint Jehu (mᵉšuggāʿ; cf. 9:11, 20). Joram by this time clearly knows something is amiss, but on an impulse rides out to meet Jehu without any supporting troops. He acts in naivety, denial, or desperation; the narrative is ambiguous regarding his state of mind. Joram finds Jehu at Naboth's plot and asks whether the mission is one of peace (v. 22), with the hope that the answer may be positive. Perhaps he thinks his presence can change the course of Jehu's action.

Joram is powerless before Jehu. The original formality and authority of "this is what the king says" (9:18) has dissipated entirely. Joram may have been asking about the Aramean front with his question, but only as a diversion from the issue at hand. Jehu has come unannounced, with a formidable force, and

---

12. Ussishkin, "Jezreel, Samaria and Megiddo," 362. Jezreel is ideally located as a fortification because of its location on a summit near the valley and the major roads, with provisions for water and animal fodder.

13. The expression "what do you have to do with peace" is a way of stating that the two have nothing to do with each other (cf. 2 Sam. 16:10; 19:22).

14. Though the Leningrad text lacks the interrogative, it should be included as indicated by most texts and the versions; *pace* Wiseman, *1 & 2 Kings*, 221.

has not allowed the messengers to return. Joram is at the point of confrontation between justice and restitution. He is portrayed as a figure of great pathos; he is not himself responsible for the sins of his mother that robbed the land of justice (v. 22). He does not perceive the social unrest or the divine demand for justice. There can be no peace for Joram.

Joram wheels about in a desperate attempt to escape his fate (9:23). His cry of "treachery" (*mirmâ*) functions as the opposite of peace (*šālôm*). In poetic contexts it is the corresponding word in antithetic lines (e.g., Ps. 35:20; Prov. 11:1).[15] The reign of Ahab was characterized by lies and deceit. His dynasty ends by means of the same treachery that characterized it. The mission to restore peace to Israel is itself one of violence and deceit.

The callous violence of Jehu is carried out in the sense of fulfilling divine judgment. As Joram slumps in the chariot, Jehu recalls how he and his commander Bidkar were riding side by side when the divine utterance was made against the house of Ahab (9:25–26). Jehu is determined to remove not only the ruling descendant of Ahab but also members of the royal family. Ahaziah was married to Athaliah, daughter of Ahab, and allied with Joram. Thus, Jehu pursues Ahaziah, giving orders to shoot him as well (9:27).

Ahaziah flees south toward Samaria but is overtaken at Beth Haggan ("house of the garden").[16] He is shot and wounded at Gur, a location known as Gina in the El-Amarna tablets,[17] modern Jenin, just a mile north of Ibleam.[18] Knowing that he cannot count on the speed of his chariot in the hills of Samaria, Ahaziah turns west towards Megiddo, perhaps in the hope that it is still loyal to Joram. He finds refuge but dies there from his wounds and is brought back to Jerusalem, where he receives a proper burial.[19] The summary of the reign of Ahaziah is inserted as the conclusion to his burial (9:29).[20]

Jehu returns to Jezreel to deal with Jezebel; her attendants join the revolt and throw her down to be trampled on the ground.[21] Though the versions

---

15. S. Olyan, "*Hᵃšalôm*: Some Literary Considerations of 2 Kings 9," *CBQ* 46 (1984): 666–67.

16. Aharoni et al., *The Carta Bible Atlas*, #131 (p. 99), show the journey from Ramoth-Gilead across the Jordan to Jezreel, then across the valley to Beth Haggan.

17. EA, 250; see Aharoni, *The Land of the Bible*, 175. In the Amarna age, the Egyptians, at the same location, killed Lab'ayu, king of Shechem, as he attempted to flee.

18. Ibleam is named in the roster of Canaanite towns of Thutmose III (ibid., 160).

19. The Chronicler says that Ahaziah was found in Samaria and was killed there (2 Chron. 22:8, 9). Williamson thinks that this is a theological statement on the part of the Chronicler and not an alternate historical source; *1 and 2 Chronicles* (Grand Rapids: Eerdmans, 1982), 311–12.

20. For the ascension notice as the "eleventh year" (9:29), see comments on 8:25.

21. The attendants (*sārîsîm*) are eunuchs, clearly attested in the cuneiform descriptions; Cogan and Tadmor provide a thorough discussion of the term (*II Kings*, 112).

say she is trampled by the horses, the Masoretic text is singular, indicating that she is trampled by Jehu (9:33). Jehu goes on to celebrate (v. 34), possibly a meal in which he secures the support of the leaders at Jezreel and assures them of his goodwill.

The abandonment of the cadaver of Jezebel to the scavenger animals (9:35–37) is a particularly disparaging insult against the woman who was queen. The fate of Jezebel emphasizes the fulfillment of the prophetic word (cf. 1 Kings 21:23). The proverb about her body being as dung (*dōmen;* NIV "refuse") in the field is possibly a further insult to her name, calling attention to a second meaning for *zebel* as "manure."[22] Jezebel is not to have a memorial of any kind in Israel.

The Reign of Jehu (10:1–36)

THE DESTRUCTION OF Ahab's house is described in two episodes. The first episode deals with the purging of the entire royal family while Jehu is still in Jezreel (10:1–11). The second describes two events on the road to Samaria (vv. 12–17); these serve as a literary transition to the elimination of the house of Baal in Samaria. The first event is an encounter with royal members of Judah (vv. 12–14) and provides an opportunity for Jehu to eliminate all opposition from the house of Ahaziah. Jehu then meets an enigmatic Jehonadab, described as a Recabite, who allies with him against Baalism (vv. 15–16). Upon his arrival in Samaria, Jehu executes all who remain of the house of Ahab in order to eliminate all sources of resistance to his rule (v. 17). Both massacres are justified with an appeal to the word of Elijah being fulfilled (vv. 10, 17).

Jehu begins his treacherous ways with letters calculated to inspire terror in any of the leaders that may still be loyal to Joram. His objective is to eliminate all the claimants to the throne, described as seventy sons of Ahab. The number seventy designates totality,[23] and the house of Ahab includes all extended family members of Joram who may have a claim to the throne. It is not clear whether the letters go to the leaders of Jezreel (10:1); if the officials of Jezreel are meant, they must have fled to Samaria where the letters are sent. Other versions say the letters are sent to the governors of Samaria, which is likely.

The letters challenge the members of the former regime to contest the regency of Jehu if they are so inclined (10:2–3). The chief steward of the palace, the governor of the city, the officials, and the guardians of the royal

---

22. So Montgomery, *The Books of Kings,* 291, 407; see comments on 1 Kings 16:31.

23. Compare the seventy sons of Jerub-Baal (Judg. 9:5) or forty sons and thirty daughters of Abdon (12:14). Bar-rakib, king of Sam'al, states that his father Panammu took the throne by killing his father and his "seventy" brothers (Donner and Röllig, *Kanaanäische und Aramäische Inschriften,* #215, 3).

sons concede immediately, refusing to install a rival king (v. 5). Jehu then asks that the heads of the royal descendants be brought to Jezreel. There appears to be a deliberate ambiguity in the request, since it is not clear if the chief leaders (heads) are to be brought or the decapitated skulls. This may have been the ruse Jehu uses to claim innocence in the whole affair (v. 9) and imply the massacre is the result of a popular rebellion against Joram. The officials take the corporeal meaning, dutifully bring the decapitated heads of all the members of Joram's family and, on the orders of Jehu, heap them in two piles at the gates of Jezreel (v. 8). The bloody spectacle is an effective tactic of intimidation, used further as an object lesson for the fulfillment of the prophetic word. Jehu uses the opportunity to finish the job of killing all the remaining nobles, advisers, and priests of Joram's reign still in Jezreel.

Once Jehu has the situation in Jezreel fully in his control, he proceeds to the capital Samaria (v. 12). He comes to an obscure place called Beth Eked, identified since Eusebius as the Arabic Beit Qad, a "shepherd's shelter" (NEB), a few miles northeast of Jenin (Beth Haggan).[24] The narrative does not explain the circumstances of this encounter with the brothers of Ahaziah. If the location is correct, it is not on the road from Jezreel to Samaria but high above it to the east. It is hardly possible that the associates of Ahaziah are unaware of the events in Jezreel, and this is not the road they would use if they are simply going there to greet him. It may be that this is a resistance movement intercepted by Jehu.[25]

The group has chosen an inconspicuous route to get to Jezreel, but Jehu discovers them while doing reconnaissance for such bands on his way to Samaria. The text may be read to say their intent is to avenge (*šallēm*) the deaths of the family members of Joram and Jezebel, the queen mother (10:13), rather than to seek their peace (*šālôm*).[26] If this is the correct link to the narrative, it explains the presence of the force that Jehu has with him that enables him to kill forty-two of them.[27] It is imperative for Jehu to control resistance movements in Judah, as there are undoubtedly loyalties to the house of Ahab there as well.

Jehonadab the Recabite seeks out Jehu on the way in order to join his campaign against the Baal cult. His motivations and the significance of his association with the Recabites are not explained. Jeremiah describes the Recabites

---

24. This interpretation of the name assumes an Arabic meaning of ʿqd (meet together); the Targum also supports this interpretation. The only known Hebrew meaning of ʿqd, also known in Arabic, is "bind" (cf. Gen. 22:9). For the traditional location see Montgomery, *The Books of Kings*, 409; Cogan and Tadmor, *II Kings*, 114.

25. Hobbs, *2 Kings*, 128.

26. Ibid. An ellipsis must be assumed to read the text as it stands.

27. The number may be traditional; cf. Judg. 12:6; 2 Kings 2:24.

as an itinerant group who refused wine and an agricultural way of life until the time of the Exile (Jer. 35:5–11). Jeremiah uses them as examples of fidelity to their word, in contrast to the infidelity of Judah in its covenant with Yahweh. Recabite austerity and rejection of sedentary life in Canaan are in themselves insufficient to explain Jehonadab's resolution to join Jehu in the extermination of the Baal cult.

In genealogical lists, the Recabites seem to be associated with the Kenites (1 Chron. 2:55; 4:11–12).[28] Another possibility is to associate the name (*rēkāb*) with the word for chariot (*rekeb*), making the Recabites a guild of chariot builders as Kenite metal workers or as charioteers in war.[29] This would explain Jehu's interest in Jehonadab, but it does not explain why Jehonadab would seek out Jehu, unless his interests are mercenary. Jehonadab joins Jehu in his chariot to Samaria, where Jehu immediately eliminates all the remnants of the house of Ahab.

The second objective of Jehu in Samaria is to purge the ministers of the Baal cult and raze its temple to the ground (10:18–28). This deed is carried out with the same characteristic violence and treachery. Jehu rallies the citizens of Samaria under the ruse that he will be a patron of their god and his temple. It may be that Jehu makes use of a partial aural homonym in making his proposition. Though Jehu says his intent was to "serve" (ʿābad) Baal as none before him (v. 18), his real objective is to "destroy" (ʾābad) all those who serve Baal (v. 19).

Jehu's demand that all the prophets, ministers, and priests of Baal be present is carried out under threat of death (10:19). The call extends to the whole territory of Israel, so the entire temple is filled (vv. 20–21). Care is taken to be sure all the proper vestments are provided and that none but the Baal ministers are present (v. 23). Once the sacrifices are underway, Jehu assembles a force of eighty military officers, guards, and lieutenants outside the temple. Under pain of death they are to make sure no individual escapes (v. 24); their mission extends to the inmost shrine of the temple, to ensure their purge is thorough (v. 25).[30]

---

28. The Kenites were a southern nomadic tribe linked to Moses (Judg. 4:11), known for their skill with metal (cf. Gen. 4:22). In 1 Chron. 2:55 the genealogy must mean that the Kenites come from a place called Hammath, with which the Recabites were also identified (see Japhet, *I & II Chronicles: A Commentary*, 90).

29. See F. S. Frick, "The Rechabites Reconsidered," *JBL* 90 (1971): 279–87; idem, "Rechab," *ABD*, 5:630–32; Hobbs, *2 Kings*, 128–29.

30. Shrine (*dᵉbîr*) is probably to be read for the enigmatic "city" (ʿîr), which otherwise must have a meaning unknown elsewhere. Wiseman suggests that after purging the temple they go out to "the city of the temple" (*1 & 2 Kings*, 228). The difficulty with the expression may be seen in a main Greek codex (Alexandrinus), which translates "city of the king."

The sacred pillar is then burned and crushed (10:26–27). It is often assumed that two different objects must be meant or that this is a doublet (BHS), but the text may be only describing a sequence of events. When Josiah cleansed the temple, the sacred objects were both burned and crushed (23:6). The whole temple complex is torn to the ground; it is unlikely the whole complex is a latrine (NIV), but more likely a dung heap, a permanent public dump.

The summary of Jehu's reign (10:29–36) gives Jehu credit for the change of religion he has brought about in Samaria. The reign of Ahab and its hated religion are ended, and the dynasty of Jehu continues for four generations (v. 30), enduring for almost a hundred years—by far the longest in Israel. This achievement is not without compromise or cost. It is twice noted that Jehu fails to rectify the fundamental problem of cultic worship at Dan and Bethel (vv. 29, 31). The military is so severely weakened that Israel is subjected to Hazael in the Transjordan (vv. 32–33). Aroer by the wadi Arnon is the southernmost city of Sihon, king of the Amorites (Deut. 2:36), the northern boundary of Moab. Gilead, roughly the entire mountainous region associated with the Jabbok, is mentioned twice (2 Kings 10:33); the second half of this verse expands the initial description to include the Bashan region north of the Yarmuk.

Bridging Contexts

FINDING ŠALOM. The outrageous confiscation of Naboth's vineyard became representative of violence against the innocent during the Omride rule. Avenging Naboth's blood becomes the clarion call of the revolt echoing throughout the narrative (9:10, 25–26, 30–37). This incident must have become a *cause célèbre* in Israel and a rallying point for widespread resentment against Ahab and Joram. Wars with Damascus and other neighboring states such as Moab, costly building projects, and an extravagant royal lifestyle (1 Kings 22:39) created a great burden on the people. The presence of Jezebel and her entourage was a constant reminder of these injustices.

The revolt of Jehu is a continuous narrative around the question of peace in Israel. Additions have been made to the narrative as it was integrated into the larger Deuteronomistic History, but they do not distract from the integrity of the account.[31] The drama of Jehu's massacre of the house of Omri moves in a series of scenes. Elisha commissions a servant to Ramoth Gilead

---

31. A review of the unity of the story is provided by Saul Olyan, "Hăšalôm: Some Literary Considerations of 2 Kings 9," 654–59. The conclusion of the reign of Ahaziah serves the Deuteronomistic purpose (9:28–29), but the repetitions of the transition are less easily explained (8:15–16, 28–29).

to secretly anoint Jehu, the commander of Joram's army, to be king over Israel (9:1–10). The actions of the prophet inspire a mutiny within the army ranks and an agreement that Jehu will be the next king (vv. 11–13).

The question "Is all well?" (*bᵉšalôm*) is natural when an orderly meeting is interrupted by an erratic messenger. However in this narrative it takes on a greater significance, as it will be repeated to Jehu several times, with slightly different nuances (cf. 9:17–18, 22, 31). The word *šalôm* indicates prosperity, health, and wholeness. The purpose of government is to provide stability, order, and good community relations; the rule of the house of Ahab became characterized by injustice and chaos. The massive disruption of the revolt of Jehu violates the order of government but is to be the means of restoring integrity of rule (*šalôm*) within Israel.

Following the anointing of Jehu as king, events move to Jezreel (9:15–28). The threefold pattern of the approach of Jehu to the city is familiar (vv. 16–21). Ahaziah sent three contingents of soldiers to capture Elijah (1:9, 11, 13), and three times Elijah asked Elisha to leave him to go on alone (2:2–3, 4–5, 6). The climax is reached on the third approach and a decisive resolution of the confrontation.[32] Each time Jehu is greeted with the same question: *bᵉšalôm* ("Is all well?"). The oracle concerning Ahab is the critical aspect of Jehu's wild ride to Jezreel (9:25–26). It brings the question into focus.[33] Yahweh has sworn that he will restore well-being at Naboth's vineyard, the very field where Ahab violated it. Peace (*šalôm*) is the result of paying back in full (*šillam*) that which was violated. The mission of Jehu is accomplished by ending the violence of the house of Ahab against the innocent, so that peace and order can again be restored to Israel.

From the assassination scene, Jehu goes to the palace in Jezreel. There Jezebel faces her final destiny. She prepared for the occasion, dressed in full royal regalia, as the queen mother she knows herself to be (9:30–37). She adorns her eyes with kohl, a black powder (usually antimony sulfide) used as makeup in Eastern countries, and she does up her hair. She takes her position in the window, no doubt knowing that Jehu will soon arrive. She is playing the role of the alluring woman, calling out to the foolish passerby, seeking to ensnare him (cf. Prov. 7:6–12).[34]

Jezebel poses the question about peace for the last time. Her disdain for Jehu is felt in her bitterly sarcastic words: "Is this peace [*šalôm*], Zimri, the one who

---

32. Hobbs, *2 Kings*, 113.
33. Olyan, "*Hᵉšalôm*: Some Literary Considerations of 2 Kings 9," 664–68.
34. S. Parker, in "Jezebel's Reception of Jehu," *Maarav* 1 (1978): 67–78, depicts the scene as one of seduction, suggesting that *zmr* (Zimri) is derived from the root meaning strong.

killed his master?" (9:31, lit. trans.). The comparison to Zimri is the ultimate insult. Zimri not only failed in his attempted coup, but also died by his own hand when he set the citadel of Jezreel on fire in order to escape capture (1 Kings 16:15–18). Jezebel's question about peace should be understood as antiphrasis for conspiracy (*mirmâ*). The word "peace" maintains the topos of the narrative. For the reader, the execution of Jezebel is a condition of peace.

The termination of the Omride dynasty and Baalism is a further prerequisite for *šālôm* in Israel. The seventy sons of Ahab (i.e., the whole royal house) are put to death by means of subterfuge (10:1–11). The scene then shifts to the temple of Baal in Samaria (vv. 12–28) and the eradication of the Baal cult. By means of a ruse, Jehu brings together all the prophets of Baal, secures their identification, and then has them all killed by his henchmen stationed outside. The sacred pillar is brought out and burned; the temple is torn down and turned into a latrine.

The end of the house of Ahab and the succession of Jehu is the inevitable outcome of divine purpose (9:1–10). The prophetic declaration of the end of a royal house is familiar (vv. 9–10): Ahijah announced the end of the house of Jeroboam (1 Kings 14:1–11), Jehu son of Hanani the end of the house of Baasha (16:1–4), and Elijah the end of the house of Ahab (21:17–24). The action of Elisha in instructing one of the sons of the prophets to anoint Jehu at Ramoth Gilead completes the commission given to him by Elijah (cf. 19:16). The end of Ahab's house has already been declared at the time of the contest with the prophets of Baal at Mount Carmel.

Jehu also kills the royal family of Judah along with that of Israel (9:27–29). With the death of Jehoshaphat (1 Kings 22:41–47), the political history of Judah temporarily merged with that of Israel. The alliance of Judah with Israel through the marriage of Jehoram, son of Jehoshaphat, to Athaliah, daughter of Ahab and Jezebel (2 Kings 8:26), brought Judah to the same spiritual alienation from God as Israel. A summary of the reign of Jehoram (8:16–24) and the one-year reign of his son Ahaziah (vv. 25–29) conclude this phase of Judean history. Ahaziah is killed in the revolt of Jehu (cf. 9:27) as he attempts to flee the scene of Joram's assassination at Naboth's vineyard in Jezreel. Athaliah in turn will attempt to exterminate the house of David and take over the throne. Her plans are foiled by Jehosheba, sister of Ahaziah; she steals away the infant son of Ahaziah and hides him in the temple for six years (11:1–3). A conspiracy of Jehoiada the high priest ends the reign of Athaliah (11:4–21).

Assessment of Jehu. The account concludes with a prophetic assessment of the reign of Jehu (10:29–36). Approval is expressed for ending the rule of the Omrides and the purging of all the prophets of Baal. Jehu is promised four generations (v. 30); the blessing is depicted in a life long enough to see great

great-grandchildren. However, Jehu does not change the practices of worship; the shrines established by Jeroboam son of Nebat at Bethel and Dan continued to be supported. Though he eradicates the Baal cult, Jehu is not absolved from the Deuteronomistic condemnation of following in the ways of Jeroboam. Jehu is also unsuccessful in protecting Israel from the attacks of the Arameans. The reduction of the state of Israel in the Transjordan is a sign of God's continued judgment against Israel.

In Assyrian records, Jehu retains the distinction of being the son of Omri even though he is the usurper who violently ends the Omride dynasty. This can probably be explained by the events of the time. In the year Jehu begins his reign (841 B.C.), Shalmaneser III reappears in southern Syria and succeeds in confining Hazael to Damascus. He claims to have carried off much booty; among the kings who render tribute to Shalmaneser is Jehu, depicted in submissive posture on the famous Black Obelisk. The abolition of the house of Ahab is an act of appeasement from the Assyrian point of view, ridding them of a despised enemy. Jehu's refusal to cooperate with Hazael facilitates the Assyrian advance; Jehu's payment of tribute puts him in the favorable status of king. While the Assyrians called Hazael the "son of a nobody," Jehu is given legitimate status.[35] Shalmaneser returns a few years later (838 B.C.) to raid towns belonging to Hazael and to collect dues from his vassals.

The judgment against Israel does not end with the Omrides. The reality is that Jehu has no choice but to submit to the Assyrians. Gone are the days of Ahab when Israel could ally with the Aramean states against Assyria. Submission to Assyria grants only a temporary respite from the Arameans. Internal political struggles in Assyria lead to open rebellion against Shalmaneser so he can no longer retain control of the western territories. Assyrian expansion declines during the reign of Shamshi-Adad V (824–811 B.C.) and the opening years of Adad-Nirari III (811–783 B.C.). Throughout this period the Arameans continue their expansions in the territories of the eastern tribes of Israel. Jehu pays tribute to the Assyrians and continues to lose territory to the Arameans (13:1–7). His political fortunes are the converse of those of Omri.

The revulsion of war takes on distinct dimensions in the massacres of Jehu. In the war against Moab and the various wars against the Arameans, there were vestiges of God the divine warrior protecting his people.[36] Though all of these wars were divine judgment against apostate Israel, the judgment was executed by an enemy nation, and God intervened to provide deliverance

---

35. Nadav Naʾaman, "Jehu Son of Omri: Legitimizing a Loyal Vassal by his Overlord," *PEQ* 48 (1998): 236–38.

36. See the Bridging Contexts section of 2 Kings 3:1–27 for a discussion of the stages of the divine warrior theme in the history of Israel.

for the suffering citizens of Israel. The war of Jehu, by contrast, is divine judgment against the house of Ahab and the house of Baal, ruthlessly inflicted in a civil war. The assessment of the prophetic authors of the Deuteronomistic History is positive. The verdict on his horrific acts of vengeance, delivered through the voice of the prophetic narrator, is that Jehu is doing what was right according to the divine will (10:30). This civil war is interpreted as God acting as warrior against Israel for abandoning the covenant in order to worship Baal.

The approval given to Jehu stands emphatically as the strongest endorsement given to any monarch in the history of the northern kingdom. Jehu is the only king in Israel who is commended for doing what is right. Elsewhere the commendation of doing what is right according to Yahweh is used for David as the model king (1 Kings 11:33, 38; 14:8; 15:5; 2 Kings 16:2) or for the commendation of one of his successors: Asa (1 Kings 15:11; 22:43), Joash (2 Kings 12:3), Amaziah (14:3), Azariah (15:3), Jotham (15:34), Hezekiah (18:3), and Josiah (22:2). The phrase is used to condemn Jeroboam I (1 Kings 14:8), because a condition of his reign was to do right as David had done (11:38). The verdict on Jehu is not that he has done right as David, but it is clear that the deeds of purging the Baal cult can be compared to those of David. Jehu has fulfilled the prophetic word of Elijah (2 Kings 10:10, 17). His violent deeds achieve divine ends.

The evaluation of doing right in the eyes of Yahweh is more than just a comparison to David; it is used to justify the dynasty of Jehu. Mullen refers to this as a "royal grant" of the same unconditional type given to David and common in the Ancient Near East.[37] Yahweh established an eternal house for David at the time when David determined to build a house for Yahweh (2 Sam. 7:1–17). The promise given to Jehu is limited to four generations, but it is based on obedience like that of David.

The subsequent rule of Jehu, however, cannot receive commendation. The positive word about the revolution is framed by the formulaic condemnation of his rule with the standard Deuteronomistic evaluation for all the kings of Israel: Jehu does not follow fully in God's teaching for Israel; rather, he follows in the sins of Jeroboam in that he does not end the worship of the two golden calves in Dan and Bethel (10:29, 31). These two verses, however, are not equivalent. Verse 29 refers to the "golden calves," a phrase that occurs elsewhere only at the initial establishment of the shrines

---

37. E. Theodore Mullen Jr., "The Royal Dynastic Grant to Jehu and the Structure of the Books of Kings," *JBL* 107 (1988): 194–99. For the nature and function of the royal grant see M. Weinfeld, "The Covenant of Grant in the Old Testament and in the Ancient Near East," *JAOS* 90 (1970): 184–203.

(1 Kings 12:28). Verse 31 specifies his violation of the covenant in that he does not keep the "law of the LORD." This phrase is unique in Kings, but it does have a parallel in the "law of Moses." Solomon is admonished to keep all the regulations of the law (1 Kings 2:3); Amaziah is praised for keeping the law in the matter of revenge (2 Kings 14:6); Josiah is extolled as being incomparable in his devotion to the law of Moses (23:25). Though Jehu does what is right in his initial commission, he does not bring Israel to the acceptable standard of kingship under God.

Hosea, 2 Kings, and Jehu. Jehu also receives notice in the prophet Hosea. The story of Hosea's marriage to Gomer is the story of the relationship of Israel with Yahweh. Hosea's wife and children were Israelites; Gomer's sin of infidelity was not just against Hosea, for her prostitution in the Baal cult symbolized Israel's apostasy. Hosea was instructed to name the first son born to him "Jezreel," for in a little while Yahweh would punish "the house of Jehu for the massacre at Jezreel" (Hos. 1:3–5).

These words are striking, because they seem to be the opposite of the affirmation given by the prophetic writers of Kings. The reigning king during the days of Hosea was Jeroboam II, the great-grandson of Jehu. Though he is not mentioned by name, he seems to be the person meant, not Jehu himself. "House of Jehu" can also mean the country of Israel as a political entity, the whole realm of Jehu. The house of Jehu did come to a violent end in the reign of Zechariah, son of Jeroboam, who was summarily assassinated by his successor Shallum after six months on the throne. Shallum struck Zechariah in Ibleam (15:10), the same city where Ahaziah of Judah was killed by Jehu (9:27). There was an obvious correlation between the end of the dynasty of Jehu and that of Omri and Ahab.

Though judgment on the dynasty of Jehu is like what he inflicted on Joram and the house of Ahab, it is difficult to understand the statement that it is because of the blood that he shed in Jezreel (Hos. 1:4), when this very act is the occasion for highest praise in Kings.[38] Some argue that Hosea represents a dramatic development in understanding how God deals with his people. Far from approving the bloodbath at Jezreel, Hosea establishes a higher and more sensitive standard of evaluation. Jehu was wrong and his dynasty will pay the price for his brutality.[39]

---

38. Michael Moore provides an alternate reading of the prophetic assessment of Jehu in Kings. He thinks the anointing and coronation of Jehu by unknown persons are a prophetic parody on Jehu, similar to the debate between Kothar-wa-Hasis and Baal over his kingship; he finds further analogies between Anat and the purge of Jehu; see "Jehu's Coronation and Purge of Israel," *VT* 53 (2003): 97–114.

39. Hans Walter Wolff, *Dodekapropheton 1: Hosea*, 2nd ed. (BKAT 14/1; Neukirchen-Vluyn: Neukirchener Verlag, 1965), 19–20.

Generally, however, Hosea views Israel's history in the same way as that of the other historians and prophets. It is hardly conceivable that the tradition of Jehu comes down to Hosea without an awareness of the key roles of Elijah and Elisha. Hosea would have condemned Ahab and his house and acknowledged the necessity for the violent overthrow of that infamous regime.[40] Hosea could approve Jehu's action in overthrowing the house of Ahab, but he could not approve his reign in other matters. The house of Jehu turned out to be no different from the previous kings of Israel.

The prophet Hosea turns the promise that Jehu's dynasty will last for four generations into a threat: The reign of the house of Jehu will end in the fourth generation. Along with an approval of the cleansing effected by Jehu's acts there is a misunderstanding of the anointing he was given. Israel conquered Canaan with God as her warrior, but when that purpose was misunderstood and Israelites assumed the land belonged to them to do as they pleased, the promise was forfeited. The Israelites suffered the same fate as the Canaanites before them. Jehu went beyond the call of his mandate and fell into arrogance and self-righteousness, which previously caused the demise of Ahab and his house. The result was the same judgment coming on the reign of Jeroboam as Jehu inflicted on Joram.

It should not be assumed that the sins of Jehu cause the doom of Zechariah, his great great-grandson. No one is condemned for the sins of their ancestors. The judgments against the later kings of the dynasty are brought on by their own behavior. It is the evil and greed of Jeroboam that bring matters to a conclusion. Judgment comes to those who merit it; that judgment has its beginnings with Jehu and the blood of Jezreel. The main charge of Hosea against the royal house of his day is identical to the sin of the Omrides. God will do to the house of Jehu exactly as he did through Jehu in the elimination of the Omrides—and for the same reasons. They are traitors to their own cause in not maintaining zeal for Yahweh.

For Hosea the name Jezreel contains two opposite ideas. Translated it means "May God sow!" Hosea's son is named for the town Jezreel situated in a luscious valley that richly represented the beneficence of God in the fruitfulness of plants, animals, and people. The name suggests that it is Yahweh, not Baal, who gives seed for sustenance of all life. Yahweh is in no sense a competitor for Baal, for he reveals himself not only through fertility in nature but in his mighty deeds in relationship with his people, fulfilling his covenant promises.

The name of the child is a mystery; it can portend both threat and promise. Though it conveys threat in the demise of the kingdom of Jer-

---

40. Francis I Andersen and David Noel Freedman, *Hosea: A New Translation with Introduction and Commentary* (AB 24; Garden City, N.Y.: Doubleday, 1980), 179.

oboam, it does not lose the sense of promise. Where it is said "not my people," it will yet be said "people of the living God" (Hos. 2:1). The Israelites will yet come up from the land, as at the first exodus (cf. Ex. 1:10), and be gathered together in the future great day of Jezreel (Hos. 2:2–3). The name Jezreel signifies a time of revival in which the land will yet be sown with people and animals. God's purpose for his people, which is not accomplished in the zeal of Jehu, will yet be realized for Jezreel.

RESPONDING TO INJUSTICE. The contemporary world has many examples of a *cause célèbre* equivalent to that of Naboth's vineyard. These can range from local issues, such as the plight of the homeless in any major city, to national issues, such as the loss of land by aboriginals, or to international issues, such as disruptions caused by the phenomena known as "globalization"—labor issues, free trade, debt, and emerging markets. Governments at various levels share culpability and responsibility in these matters and must be accountable. Injustice must be addressed, but not in a manner that creates an equal evil in turn.

Although the necessary changes instituted by Jehu are commended for the necessary change they effect, Hosea condemns Jehu's methods as bringing inevitable judgment. His brutal actions are designed to achieve his personal ambitions as a military leader, under the guise of terminating the injustices of the Omride dynasty. Often attempts to deal with evident injustice are so governed by passion, haste, and personal ambition that other victimization occurs in the process.

As Aquinas observed, the passion most immediately associated with injustice is anger. Anger is often justified, inspired by love and respect for those persons whose rights are perceived as being violated. Anger recoils at injustice; it strikes out at what is wrong. It strains to change unjust structures that deprive the vulnerable of political, social, economic, or personal rights that human dignity demands. A good dose of anger can be helpful; anger is creative energy that can be used for positive action. It is like a fire; in a controlled environment, it is a powerful force for good, but out of control it can do irreparable damage. Anger can lash out in harsh words, biting insults, violence, riots, and even war.

Responses to injustice must be gentle and firm. Robert Maloney reminds the church that the gentle find creative ways to express anger in action on behalf of justice and participation in transformation.[41] The prophets address

---

41. Robert P. Maloney, "On Being Gentle and Firm," *America* 188 (April 2003): 21.

injustice with their words and declare that the promised descendant of David will do the same. The root of Jesse will "strike the earth with the rod of his mouth; with the breath of his lips he will slay the wicked" (Isa. 11:4); the servant will be a light to the nations; his words are as a sharpened sword or a polished arrow (49:2). The fullness of the kingdom of God is to bring about peace through the teaching of the covenant, turning the weapons of war into agricultural tools (Isa. 2:3–4; Mic. 5:2–4). Peacemaking and reconciliation are the goals of the gentle.

Christians must learn more of the power of the gospel in the midst of the great injustices of this world. The Community of Sant'Egidio is a movement of laypeople dedicated to evangelization and charity in more than seventy countries. They began by visiting the slums of Rome, providing education for the poor. They show their solidarity with the poor by living with them in a free and voluntary spirit. Maloney reminds us of the role that the Community of Sant'Egidio played in mediating peace in Mozambique.

> After fifteen years of civil war, "human wisdom" would surely have doubted the ability of a "powerless" Italian lay community to accomplish what other much more powerful groups like the United Nations and the Vatican had failed to bring about. Yet negotiations were successfully completed in 1992, with the community's help, and peace continues to reign in that country. Andrea Riccardi, one of the founders of the Community of Sant'Egidio, describes the means used during the peacemaking process as "the 'weak strength' of the Gospel." Could other "powerless" groups show similar courage in offering their services as ministers of reconciliation in other perennially troubled spots of the world?[42]

Gentleness and suffering love. Conversation and dialogue, accompanied by suffering love, will always be among the principal means for settling conflict in the lives of the gentle. Paul tells the Ephesians that Christ is our peace, the one who has broken down the walls of partition (Eph. 2:14). Peter calls on the followers of Christ to be subject to rulers and to follow his example, being patient in suffering even when doing good (1 Peter 2:20–21). If the community of disciples has a genuine passion for the pursuit of justice and peace, it is a clear sign that the kingdom of God is at hand.

Gentleness cannot be passive; passionate gentleness knows how to direct anger, channeling it so that "justice rolls on like a river and righteousness like a never-failing stream" (Amos 5:24). The work and words of the gentle bring about justice that is like a wadi with a perpetual flow of water that erodes

---

42. Ibid.

oppressive social structures and restores the weary. The prayer of W. E. B. DuBois sums up this gentle but firm passion:

> Give us grace, O God, to dare to do the deed, which we well know cries to be done. Let us not hesitate because of ease, or the words of men's mouths, or our own lives. Mighty causes are calling us—the freeing of women, the training of children, the putting down of hate and murder and poverty—all these and more. But they call with voices that mean work and sacrifice and death. Mercifully, grant us, O God, the spirit of Esther, that we may say: I will go unto the king and if I perish, I perish.[43]

In the New Testament, the divine warrior metaphor shifts to warfare conducted against rulers, authorities, powers, and dominions beyond the temporal sphere (Eph. 1:21). Warfare against these forces is no less real than the war of Jehu against Joram and his promotion of the Baal cult. However, the warfare of the Christian against the greed and materialism of the world is of an entirely different order. In Christian eschatology, wars among nations are only a symptom of a much larger cosmic war played out between Christ and the "powers and principalities." In this war, Christ has triumphed not by amassing a greater arsenal and using it more efficiently with the consequences of "collateral damage," as the modern military calls dead people. Christ triumphs by dying ignominiously, tortured to death on a cross, then peaceably rising again to new life. The kingdom of God is thus already "at hand" (Mark 1:15), but is not yet fully consummated until Christ comes again.

In the meantime, the powers of darkness still stalk the earth and still deal in death.[44] It is not the usual role of Christians to take up armed forces against the society in which they live, however oppressive and intolerant such regimes may be. If the powers of evil extend beyond the political powers that promote it, the defense against such forces must be other than military. Paul urges Christians to take on the armor of faith in order to stand against the wiles of the devil (Eph. 6:10–20). The most important weapon for the apostle in prison is prayer; his greatest concern in battling the forces that imprison him is that he will have the courage to bear witness to his faith.

Christian victory and human government. Though governments imprisoned the apostle Paul, he regarded their function as positive and their purpose to be a benefit to every law-abiding citizen (Rom. 13:1–7). It is the responsibility of the Christian to be subject to such powers because God

---

43. Ibid.

44. William T. Cavanaugh, "Dying for the Eucharist or Being Killed by It? Romero's Challenge to First-World Christians," *Theology Today* 58/2 (2001): 178.

has ordained them for the good of society (v. 4). Law-abiding citizens should have nothing to fear from such an authority; temporal authorities have a fearful power, to be directed against those who do what is wrong. Obedience to temporal authorities is thus necessary not only because of the power they possess but because of conscience (v. 5). Every obligation to civil government ought to be fulfilled, every respect shown (vv. 6–7), because these servants of God are continuously dedicated to the task of the control of evil.

Peter in the same way urges exemplary conduct on behalf of all Christians, urging them to be careful not to be controlled by greed, even if their good conduct is derided (1 Peter 2:11–12). Such conduct will eventually come to the praise of God. The duty of Christians is to be subject to all levels of government, whose responsibility it is to avenge wrongdoing (2:13–17).

Christians have a higher allegiance to the kingdom of God, but such freedom is not a license to disregard government regulation; it is imperative to have exemplary conduct as servants of God. At the same time, these directives of Christian responsibility to be subject to governments that may be hostile to citizens of Christian faith should not be understood as condoning tyranny in the interests of being a good citizen. Totalitarianism that denies justice and morality in the interests of the state must be actively resisted. It is sometimes necessary to obey God rather than human beings.

Such resistance is both necessary and costly, as seen in the extraordinary life of Dietrich Bonhoeffer. "Bonhoeffer was firmly and rightly convinced that it is not only a Christian right but a Christian duty towards God to oppose tyranny, that is, a government which is no longer based on natural law and the law of God."[45] Bonhoeffer's resistance to Hitler became political after 1938, when his brother-in-law, the jurist Hans von Dohnanyi, introduced him to the group seeking Hitler's overthrow. Bonhoeffer continued his work for the resistance movement under cover of employment in the Military Intelligence Department, which was a center of resistance. He was arrested on April 5, 1943, and imprisoned in Berlin. Following the failure of the attempt on Hitler's life on July 20, 1944, the discovery of documents linking Bonhoeffer directly with the conspiracy led to his further interrogation and eventual execution at Flössenberg (Bavaria) on April 9, 1945.[46] He died just a few days before the Allies liberated the city.

Ultimately, it was the allegiance owed to God that forced on Bonhoeffer the terrible decision not merely to take a stand against National Socialism,

---

45. G. Leibholz, "Memoir," in *The Cost of Discipleship*, by Dietrich Bonhoeffer; rev. ed. (New York: Macmillan, 1959), 30.

46. Franklin Sherman, "Bonhoeffer, Dietrich," *Encyclopaedia Britannica Macropaedia*, 15th ed., 3:30–31.

but to work for the defeat of his own country.[47] Nationalism stands under God, and it is a sin against him and his call for fellowship with other nations if it degenerates into national egoism and greed. The guiding force in Bonhoeffer's life, all he worked and suffered for, was his faith and love of God, in whom he found peace and happiness. Freedom belongs to humankind as divine grace, but it is a freedom for the divine ordering of life. If this does not guide human freedom, then sacred responsibilities are denied. A Christian then has no other choice but to act, to suffer, and if need be, to die. Bonhoeffer expressed this thought in "Stations on the Road to Freedom," written when he knew his death was certain. The last verse runs as follows:[48]

Come now, solemnest feast on the road to eternal freedom,
Death, and destroy those fetters that bow, those walls that imprison
this our transient life, these souls that linger in darkness,
so that at last we see what is here withheld from our vision.
Long did we seek you, freedom, in discipline, action and suffering.
Now that we die, in the face of God himself we behold you.

Violence has frequently been directed against Christians who work for peace, sometimes in misguided zeal and sometimes in malevolence. In the early 1980s Archbishop Oscar Romero of El Salvador was celebrating mass when he was assassinated. Just as he finished his homily and was about to turn to the liturgy of the Eucharist, a single shot pierced his chest, and he bled to death within a matter of minutes. His blood-soaked vestments are now on display in San Salvador for pilgrims and tourists to see. His killer has remained free. Cavanaugh interprets his death in terms of a theology of the Eucharist. Witness to the death of Christ gives testimony to the body of Christ entering into his suffering in this world.

Oscar Romero stands now as a link in the long chain of martyrs whose blood has contributed to the fertility of the Christian church through the two thousand years of its earthly pilgrimage. It was no accident that he was killed while celebrating mass ... the eucharist is inextricably linked with martyrdom in the life of the church, as exemplified by the life of Oscar Romero. It is not simply that the eucharist is a commemoration of a past dying, the dying of Christ at the hands of the principalities and powers; it is more radical: the eucharist makes present that dying, incorporating the communicants into a body marked with the signs of death, such that Christians, as Paul says, are "always carrying in the body the death of Jesus, so that the life of Jesus

47. Leibholz, "Memoir," 28.
48. Ibid., 23; translated by J. B. Leishaman.

may also be made visible in our bodies" (2 Cor 4:10). The eucharist, in other words, creates a body of people who by definition stand in the line of fire.[49]

The English word "martyr" derives from the Greek word for "witness"; Antipas gave his life as a faithful witness (*martyr*) to Jesus Christ at Pergamum, where the throne of Satan resided (Rev. 2:13). A martyr makes the truth public by the sacrifice of his body. The powers of darkness obscure the truth; martyrs make it shine through the darkness of violence and death. In El Salvador, the people commonly say that Romero died *por decir la verdad* ("for telling the truth").[50] The life and death of the martyr reveals the truth of Christ's triumph and the transitory nature of the powers and principalities. As the apostle John assured the seven churches of Asia, the hour of trial will soon pass and the kingdom of God will arrive triumphant.

The apostle Paul makes clear that Jesus died at the hands of the principalities and powers. Those who sacrifice themselves in pursuit of the kingdom of God are joined in time to the passion of Jesus. The Eucharist is their confession of being one with Christ in confrontation with the powers of darkness. This is the confession of their power; the death of Jesus is followed by the resurrection. Archbishop Romero made this declaration the day before he was killed:

> Easter is itself now the cry of victory. No one can quench that life that Christ has resurrected. Neither death nor all the banners of death and hatred raised against him and against his church can prevail. He is the victorious one! Just as he will thrive in an unending Easter, so we must accompany him in a Lent and a Holy Week of cross, sacrifice, and martyrdom. As he said, blessed are they who are not scandalized by his cross.[51]

The Christian church is to be characterized by victory as it was achieved by Christ and not by the political force of violence. Archbishop Romero is an example of conquering powers of darkness with the victory of faith.

The kingdom of Jehu will endure four generations as a tribute to his eradicating worship at the Baal temple (2 Kings 10:30). Hosea uses this as a threat to northern Israel; the dynasty of Jehu will not last beyond four generations. Kingdoms built on violence survive by violence and end in vio-

---

49. Cavanaugh, "Dying for the Eucharist," 177.

50. Cavanaugh cites Anna Peterson, *Martyrdom and the Politics of Religion: Progressive Catholicism in El Salvador's Civil War* (Albany: State Univ. of New York Press, 1997), 123.

51. Oscar Romero, *The Violence of Love: The Pastoral Wisdom of Archbishop Oscar Romero*, ed. James R. Brockman (San Francisco: Harper & Row, 1988), 241.

lence. The kingdom of Jehu was immediately reduced because of his massacre of all the leaders of the former regime (10:32–33). The Arameans under Hazael immediately limited the domain of Jehu to the west side of the Jordan. The peacemaker that takes a stand against violence belongs to the kingdom of God, and the gates of hell will never prevail against that kingdom (Matt. 16:18). The cost of discipleship expressed by Bonhoeffer in his writings and in his life continues to inspire a firm and gentle response to injustice. This represents the kingdom of God rather than the violent tactics of force.

The kings of the Deuteronomistic History represent the failure of the covenant and the kingdom, even in those instances when they act in zeal for God. This is universally stated to be the case for the northern kingdom, and Jehu is no exception (2 Kings 10:31). It is also the case for the kings of Judah; all of them fail in terms of the kingdom of God. Though Hezekiah successfully resists the Assyrians in faith, in the end his compromise with the Babylonian Merodach-Baladan brings about the judgment that his descendants will go into exile in Babylon (20:17–18). Though Josiah renews the covenant in a great national ceremony, he dies ignominiously in an intervention against the Egyptian king (23:29–30), and the land he has led in revival shortly devolves into oblivion.

The Deuternomistic History is not an account of victory over evil but one of being caught in a cycle of evil. The old covenant fails; Jehu is further testimony to its failure. The prophet Jeremiah declares that the failure of the old covenant will inaugurate the new covenant (Jer. 31:31). Under this new covenant, victory over evil and the powers of darkness will be achieved by God's power in ways most unlike the motives and tactics of Jehu.

2 Kings 11:1-20

WHEN ATHALIAH THE mother of Ahaziah saw that her son was dead, she proceeded to destroy the whole royal family. ²But Jehosheba, the daughter of King Jehoram and sister of Ahaziah, took Joash son of Ahaziah and stole him away from among the royal princes, who were about to be murdered. She put him and his nurse in a bedroom to hide him from Athaliah; so he was not killed. ³He remained hidden with his nurse at the temple of the LORD for six years while Athaliah ruled the land.

⁴In the seventh year Jehoiada sent for the commanders of units of a hundred, the Carites and the guards and had them brought to him at the temple of the LORD. He made a covenant with them and put them under oath at the temple of the LORD. Then he showed them the king's son. ⁵He commanded them, saying, "This is what you are to do: You who are in the three companies that are going on duty on the Sabbath—a third of you guarding the royal palace, ⁶a third at the Sur Gate, and a third at the gate behind the guard, who take turns guarding the temple—⁷and you who are in the other two companies that normally go off Sabbath duty are all to guard the temple for the king. ⁸Station yourselves around the king, each man with his weapon in his hand. Anyone who approaches your ranks must be put to death. Stay close to the king wherever he goes."

⁹The commanders of units of a hundred did just as Jehoiada the priest ordered. Each one took his men—those who were going on duty on the Sabbath and those who were going off duty—and came to Jehoiada the priest. ¹⁰Then he gave the commanders the spears and shields that had belonged to King David and that were in the temple of the LORD. ¹¹The guards, each with his weapon in his hand, stationed themselves around the king—near the altar and the temple, from the south side to the north side of the temple.

¹²Jehoiada brought out the king's son and put the crown on him; he presented him with a copy of the covenant and proclaimed him king. They anointed him, and the people clapped their hands and shouted, "Long live the king!"

¹³When Athaliah heard the noise made by the guards and the people, she went to the people at the temple of the LORD. ¹⁴She looked and there was the king, standing by the pillar, as the custom was. The officers and the trumpeters were beside the king, and all the people of the land were rejoicing and blowing trumpets. Then Athaliah tore her robes and called out, "Treason! Treason!"

¹⁵Jehoiada the priest ordered the commanders of units of a hundred, who were in charge of the troops: "Bring her out between the ranks and put to the sword anyone who follows her." For the priest had said, "She must not be put to death in the temple of the LORD." ¹⁶So they seized her as she reached the place where the horses enter the palace grounds, and there she was put to death.

¹⁷Jehoiada then made a covenant between the LORD and the king and people that they would be the LORD's people. He also made a covenant between the king and the people. ¹⁸All the people of the land went to the temple of Baal and tore it down. They smashed the altars and idols to pieces and killed Mattan the priest of Baal in front of the altars.

Then Jehoiada the priest posted guards at the temple of the LORD. ¹⁹He took with him the commanders of hundreds, the Carites, the guards and all the people of the land, and together they brought the king down from the temple of the LORD and went into the palace, entering by way of the gate of the guards. The king then took his place on the royal throne, ²⁰and all the people of the land rejoiced. And the city was quiet, because Athaliah had been slain with the sword at the palace.

Original Meaning

THE MERGING OF the monarchies of Israel and Judah that occurs with the death of Jehoshaphat only endures for a short period. Joram king of Israel began his reign with the death of Ahaziah, one year after his father's death in 853 B.C. The sole reign of Jehoram of Judah began in the fifth year of Joram and lasted for eight years (2 Kings 8:16–17). Ahaziah ruled briefly until his death, the year that Jehu became king and subject to Shalmaneser (841 B.C.).

Athaliah now attempts to take over the throne following the death of her son Ahaziah (11:1), showing the callous self-interest that has characterized her ancestry. She is unsuccessful in purging every Davidic claimant to the throne since the sister of the murdered Ahaziah hides his son Joash. When Joash is seven years old, the high priest plots to execute the Queen Mother and install the Davidide heir. With the accession of Joash the lamp is preserved in Judah (cf. 8:19); mercy is shown on Judah because of God's promise to David.

From the Deuteronomistic point of view, Athaliah does not have a legitimate reign. There is no formal statement of the length of her reign or a concluding summary. Her seven years of rule are an interim period and are not counted in the forty years assigned to Joash (12:1).[1] With Athaliah the prophetic history shifts to a focus on Jerusalem and sources that derive from Judea (cf. 12:20). The death of Ahaziah in Megiddo sets off a chain of events that leads to the high priest restoring the monarchy and renewing the covenant in Judah. The narrator of the story focuses on the pivotal role played by Jehoiada the high priest. He is familiar with the details of the conspiracy and knows his way around the temple and the palace compounds. This story is an apology for the unprecedented intervention of a high priest in preserving the Davidic dynasty.

The Conspiracy of Jehoiada (11:1–16)

THE RELATIONSHIP OF Athaliah to the Omride dynasty has been much discussed, as her paternity and the identity of her husband are not clearly stated.[2] She is said to be the daughter of Omri (8:26). Two conclusions are possible: Either she is the granddaughter of Omri and daughter of Ahab and Jezebel, or she is the sister of Ahab, and Ahaziah is her grandson. It has been assumed she was married to Jehoram of Judah, but his Omride wife is never named. Jehoshaphat is said to have intermarried with the house of Ahab, but the identity of this woman is not given (2 Chron. 18:1). It may be that Athaliah is a daughter of Omri and under the jurisdiction of her brother Ahab.[3] Ahab enters a treaty of cooperation and protection with Jehoshaphat. This agreement includes the marriage of Athaliah to the Judean king or to his heir apparent, which gives her extensive authority within the court. Her influence explains why the Judean kings (Jehoram and Ahaziah) have the same names as their Omride counterparts.

---

1. Thiele, *The Mysterious Numbers of the Hebrew Kings*, 104–5.
2. For discussion with bibliography see Ktziah Spanier, "The Northern Israelite Queen Mother in the Judaean Court: Athaliah and Abi," in *Boundaries of the Ancient Near Eastern World: A Tribute to Cyrus H. Gordon*, ed. Meir Lubetski, Claire Gottlieb, and Sharon Keller (JSOTSup 273; Sheffield: Sheffield Academic Press, 1998), 141–43.
3. Tamar was under the protection of her brother Absalom (2 Sam. 13); Tamar is also the name of the daughter of Absalom (2 Sam. 14:27), but in the tradition of Old Greek the daughter of Absalom was Maacah (cf. 1 Kings 15:2).

Athaliah comes into the Judean court as the head of an entourage representing her personal and cultic concerns (cf. 2 Chron. 22:3–4). She was the Queen Mother, either as the wife of Jehoshaphat or as his daughter-in-law. As other great ladies, she keeps her position for several reigns. The wife of Jehoram is referred to as a daughter of Ahab (2 Kings 8:18), a possible indication that Athaliah exercises the real authority over the throne. When Ahaziah dies at the hands of Jehu's forces (9:27), Athaliah attempts to kill all the heirs and assume the throne herself (11:1, 3). Her conduct is consistent with that of Jehoram, who killed all the other sons of Jehoshaphat when he came to the throne (2 Chron. 21:4). The elimination of all rival claimants furthers the goal of retaining Omride power in Judah. Athaliah may have prevented Jehu from entering Judah and reuniting Judah and Israel. She is able to retain control of the army and retain the independence of Judah for six years.

The despotism of Athaliah is unsuccessful. Jehosheba, sister of Ahaziah, is able to hide Joash, son of the king and heir to the throne, in the temple. The Chronicler (2 Chron. 22:11) and Josephus (*Ant.* 9.141) say that Jehosheba is also the wife of Jehoiada the priest, which may explain why the young prince is hidden in the temple. The temple must have remained relatively undisturbed by the Baal cult during Athaliah's reign, as the heir to the throne is not discovered.

Jehoiada is in complete charge of the temple and its guards. He swears the guards to secrecy and shows them the surviving heir to the throne. The Carites are of uncertain identification (11:4); they appear to be related to the Kerethi and Pelethi, elite troops of Aegean origin in David's army (2 Sam. 8:18; 15:18; 20:23).[4] Jehoiada summons all the temple guards, who apparently serve on a rotation of one week out of three (2 Kings 11:5–7). Those on duty he assigns to positions at three locations: one-third are at the palace, one-third at the Sur Gate, and one-third at the gate behind the guards. All those off duty (i.e., two-thirds of the total guard) take up positions at the temple to guard the king. Anyone attempting to break through the ranks of the guards will be put to death (v. 8). Highest care is taken to protect the king.[5]

The Sur Gate is otherwise unknown; the Chronicler calls it the Foundation Gate (2 Chron. 23:4). Some have attempted to relate it to the Horse Gate (*sûsîm*) of the palace mentioned later in the story (2 Kings 11:6). The temple and palace complex had various gates known to the authors of the

---

4. See comments on 1 Kings 1:38. The other guards (lit., "the runners") serve as the official bodyguards (cf. 1:5; 14:27).

5. As is evident from variations in the translations, there are textual problems and ambiguities in the text describing the stationing of the temple guards (vv. 5–7).

original account. The narrative is based on a Judean source; the assignments of the guards are obvious to those familiar with the architectural layout.

All the guards assigned to the palace and the temple take their stations with their weapons as instructed (11:9). No further mention is made of the guards at the palace (cf. v. 5), as the focus of activity shifts to the anointing of the king at the temple on this extraordinary Sabbath day. The officers are all given spears and shields, apparently ceremonial armor appropriate for the anointing of the king (v. 10).[6] David captured gold shields from the officers of Hadadezer and brought them to Jerusalem (2 Sam. 8:7); it is probable Jehoiada uses these ceremonial armaments for the occasion. The guards take up their stations around the temple, from south to north around the altar, in order to protect the king (v. 11). The guards seem to have formed a semicircle around the front of the temple.

Once the officers and guards are stationed, the king is brought out for the ceremony. The anointing with oil, the blowing of the horns, and the shouts of the people are reminiscent of the coronation of Solomon (1 Kings 1:39–40) or Jehu (2 Kings 9:13). Joash receives a crown and a copy of the covenant. A diadem served as a sign of royalty in ancient Israel (Ps. 89:39; 132:18). The king was required to keep with him a testimony of the covenant as a constant reminder that he must rule according to divine order (Deut. 17:18–19). The actual presentation of the covenant copy is probably an engraved amulet, which will serve as a reminder of the written covenant testimony, or it may be an inscription like that on the diadem the priest wore, which had the words "Holy to the LORD" (Ex. 28:36).

The tumult of the coronation rouses the attention of Athaliah, who makes her way to the temple to investigate (11:13). Gathered there are the civic leaders (people of the land) who are part of the coronation ceremony (vv. 14, 18, 20). Their activity at times of dynastic crises is regularly noted (21:23–24; 23:30), and they are listed with other civic leaders (Jer. 1:18; 34:19; 37:2). Their presence is required to confirm the accession of the new king; they represent the residents of the land. When Athaliah sees the king, she recognizes immediately that her time as queen is over; she is seized by force and taken to the entrance of the Horse Gate, a gate that opens directly to the palace (cf. Jer. 31:39–40; Neh. 3:28). She is summarily executed, allowing no time for her supporters to raise resistance to the new king.

---

6. "Shield" (*šeleṭ*) is a comparatively rare word variously translated. The war scroll from Qumran speaks of "darts" launched against the enemy. Synonymous with the blade of the spear is that of the "quiver" (*šlṭ*) used to fell the enemy (1QM 6.3); for a translation see Martin Abegg, "The War Scroll," in *The Dead Sea Scrolls: A New Translation*, ed. M. Abegg, M. Wise, and E. Cook (San Francisco: HarperSanFrancisco, 1996), 56. "Quiver" in that context is probably metonymy for the darts it contained.

The Renewal of the Covenant (11:17–20)

THE ANOINTING OF a new king requires renewal of the covenant. The covenant with Yahweh (11:17) is different from the covenant Jehoiada made with the officers and the guards (v. 4). The definite article indicates the covenant that distinguishes the king and the people in their particular relationship with God. This is the first occasion that the making of the covenant is mentioned during the time of the monarchy.

Some commentators find here three covenants: one between the king and Yahweh, one between the people and Yahweh, and one between the king and the people.[7] There is precedent for such relationships: A covenant relationship existed between David and Yahweh (2 Sam. 7:12–14; 1 Kings 1:17), between the people and God (Josh. 24:25–26), and between the people and their king (2 Sam. 5:3). All three aspects may have been included in a single vow to renew the Deuteronomic covenant.

Both the Chronicler (2 Chron. 23:16, 18) and Josephus emphasize the restoration of the Davidic line.[8] This is primary, since the "lamp" of David has come near to extinction. The coronation includes the covenant obligation of the young king in the presentation of the crown jewels (2 Kings 11:12); these affirm the renewal of the Davidic dynasty and the commitment of the king to lead the people according to the book of the covenant kept at his side. Such a commitment obligates the people to loyalty to the new king.

The leaders then follow the pattern of Jehu in the north by purging the land of Baal influence (11:18). The Baal temple is destroyed and its priest killed, and all the artifacts of the temple thoroughly crushed and burned. This is not the end of Baal cult in Jerusalem, however; Hezekiah again removes altars and shrines of Canaanite religion (18:4), as does Josiah following the days of Manasseh (23:4). But a new beginning is established with Joash. Special custodians are appointed for the security of the temple (11:18b–19), providing protection for acts of revenge that might be taken by those loyal to Athaliah.

The restoration of the Davidic dynasty and the renewal of the covenant are the essence of being God's people. The report of the restoration of the temple and the destruction of the Baal temple is concluded by summarizing statements of the coronation of the king and the death of Athaliah (11:19–20). The repetition joins the making of the covenant with the restoration of the dynasty. The summary provides more details on the crowning of the king. Joash is escorted from the temple to the palace, where he is placed on

7. Gray, *I & II Kings*, 579–80; Jones, *1 and 2 Kings*, 2:485–86.
8. According to Josephus, "Jehoiada called together the people and the soldiers to affirm the king by oath, and to provide for his safety" (*Ant.* 9.153).

the throne. Guards provide security along a route through Guard's Gate. The procession goes south from Temple Mount toward the "City of David." The restoration of a true Davidide king and the death of Athaliah bring an end to the domination of the Baal cult in Judah.

Bridging
Contexts

THE PRIESTLY PEOPLE of God. Restoration of king and covenant are pivotal to God's purpose for Israel. This essential requirement is focused around the high priest. Most critics argue that the narrator has joined two accounts in this story of the plot against Athaliah. This would not be unusual, since Kings regularly acknowledges its reliance on official royal sources. Unique to this section is the sudden appearance of the people, who have not been part of the ceremonies up to this point (11:13), and the double notation of Athaliah's death (vv. 16, 20). One source is termed priestly and official (vv. 1–12, 18b–20), while the second is regarded as more popular (vv. 13–18a). Such observations are not conclusive, and the narrative has cohesion as it stands.[9] The narrator concentrates on particular aspects of the drama so that new aspects seem to appear suddenly.

Jehoiada the high priest is central here; he organizes the rebellion, presides over the coronation ceremonies, and orders the death of the queen and the abolition of her cult. After a brief introduction to the coup of Athaliah (vv. 1–3), the narrative describes the removal of Athaliah (vv. 4–16) and the renewal of the covenant (vv. 17–20).[10] Both sections conclude with the installation of the king (vv. 12–14, 19) and the death of Athaliah (vv. 15–16, 20). The removal of Athaliah makes possible the removal of the Baal temple. The priesthood, the army, and the populace are united in the renewal of a Davidic dynasty under God.

The covenant at Sinai established the distinction between the people of Israel and all the other nations of the world (Ex. 19:5–6). It made them a "treasured possession" (s⁽gullâ) to God, a kingdom of priests, a people distinguished in their role in the world. In their collective role as priests they represented the majesty of the Creator to his world (Ps. 8:1, 9). Through them all the families of the earth can receive the blessing of Abraham (Gen. 12:3). At the same time they were to be the means of the families of the world being represented before God.

At Mount Sinai God fulfilled his promise to Abraham in his revelation to them as Yahweh (Ex. 6:2–4). As part of that promise God granted the

---

9. Hobbs, 2 *Kings*, 136; Cogan and Tadmor, *II Kings*, 132; Long, 2 *Kings*, 146–47.
10. The Hebrew chapter division ends with verse 20.

Israelites the land so that they might be redeemed from Egypt and be a nation of priests. They would be a people to God and he would be a God to them (v. 7). This was the significance of knowing the name "Yahweh." The key phrase of Exodus is, "You will know I am the LORD." This was true for Pharaoh and the Egyptians (7:5, 17; 8:18; 14:4, 18) and for the Israelites (10:2; 16:12; 29:44–46). Yahweh did not simply refer to God as Creator, but God in relationship to his people and the world.

The people of the covenant were to be the means of the world coming into relationship with God. This was already observed in affirming the promise to Abraham. God commanded Isaac to sojourn amongst the Philistines at the time of famine (Gen. 26:1–4). There God would fulfill the blessing he had promised Abraham. The sojourn was one of continuous testing until Isaac found sufficient space to live (v. 22). At that point the Philistines came to him seeking the blessing, for they recognized the special relationship Isaac had with God (vv. 28–29). When the Israelites left Egypt, there was a great mixture of peoples who went with them (Ex. 12:38). All who lived with Israel could join in redemption and be as the native born if they were willing to affirm the covenant (vv. 43–49). The nation of priests was the means of the nations coming to know God and being in relationship with him.

The covenant at Sinai was not a once-for-all historical event in the life of the people. It was the beginning of a continuing relationship between God and Israel, initiated earlier in the promise to Abraham.[11] For this reason the covenant had to be renewed regularly (cf. Deut. 31:9–13), so that love and obedience to Yahweh would continue. The sermons of Moses in Deuteronomy were his call to renew the covenant in the land after the rebellious generation had died in the desert (11:26–32; 27:1–10). Joshua did renew that covenant when the people entered the land (Josh. 8:30–35; 24:21–26). That covenant renewal was evidence of God's fulfilling his promise, so that not one single word could be said to have failed (21:45). The land was God's gracious gift to his people (Deut. 7:6–8). As a nation in the land they were to be a people peculiar in their relationship to God that they might show his glory and reveal him to the nations.

Preserving God's people in apostate times. The dominance of the Baal cult utterly destroyed the purpose of Israel's being in the land. Yahweh was no longer the warrior defending his people in the land. With Baal becoming dominant over Judah, there was a danger that all knowledge of the exclusive covenant relationship might be lost. The hope of this relationship being fulfilled rested in the promise to David. Athaliah's attempt to eliminate all

---

11. Peter Craigie, *The Book of Deuteronomy* (Grand Rapids: Eerdmans, 1976), 37.

Davidic heirs of the promise had the potential to extinguish the light Yahweh had provided for his people and the world. It was this urgency that propelled the radical and violent revolt against the Omride rule.

The purge of Jehoiada the priest is not equivalent to that of Jehu for theological reasons. Jehu attacked the cult of Jezebel but continued to promote worship at the northern shrines. Jehoiada removes the obstacles to covenant renewal and restores the possibility of the blessing. He restores the hope of David and worship at the temple as prescribed in the covenant. It is a critical turning point in the preservation of the promise. According the prophetic viewpoint of Kings, this is nothing other than the work of Yahweh in preserving Judah for the sake of David (cf. 8:19). The deliverance of Judah from Baal worship is not merely political and social change; it means the preservation of the purpose God ordained for the people of Israel, namely, that his will may yet be done on earth as it is in heaven.

The account of Athaliah is part of a pattern found in the Deuteronomistic History. Rebellion repeatedly brought the promise to the brink of extinction, but God's mercy prevailed in preserving the promise. Judges portrays a spiral of decay, each successive leader leaving the nation in a more perilous state, each of them failing in more grievous ways. The book concludes with examples of how the Israelites brought the land given them in the Conquest back to the idolatrous ways of the Canaanites. The Danites founded their own sanctuary in the north with the help of a priesthood, which traced its roots back to Moses (Judg. 18:30). This sanctuary became the permanent establishment of an idolatrous shrine when Jeroboam made it one of two places where a gold calf served as the symbol for worship.

During the period of the judges, the Benjamites proved they were no different than the inhabitants of Sodom and Gomorrah. This is shown in the story of a Levite from Ephraim, who went with his servant to Bethlehem to fetch his concubine, who had run away. On their return, the Levite and his servant deliberately avoided Canaanite cities in their search for a place of lodging (Judg. 19:11−30). The citizens of Benjamin showed them no hospitality, a moral failing of the highest order within that culture, and further treated the man and his concubine exactly as the citizens of Sodom had treated the guests visiting Lot (Gen. 19:1−14).[12] This story was the ultimate condemnation of Israel, for Sodom was the quintessence of the iniquity for which the peoples of Canaan were judged.

The Benjamites had proved themselves to be among the worst and most base of the Canaanites. If Benjamin, a leading tribe in Israel, was perverted

---

12. For the conscious literary repetitions linking the two stories, see Block, "Echo Narrative Technique in Hebrew Literature," 325−41.

to the point of exemplifying Canaanite behavior, then a presence of Israel in the Promised Land was virtually extinguished. Hope was restored by the mercy of God through Elkanah and his wife Hannah, one of the few remaining pious homes in Ephraim (1 Sam. 1:1). Hannah, in making petition for a child, vowed to give this child back to Yahweh. Samuel became the corrective to the wicked priests of the time, eventually anointing David to preserve the hope of the covenant in Israel.

It was not only in ancient Israel that the "lamp of David" is brought to the edge of extinction. Matthew tells a parallel story at the time of the birth of Jesus, the Son of David destined to fulfill all the hopes held in the confession of Psalm 2. Matthew begins his Gospel with a specific objective: to show that Jesus Christ, Son of David, Son of Abraham, is the legitimate heir of promise (Matt. 1:1). Having established that the child born to Joseph and Mary is Emmanuel, the child of prophetic promise for the establishment of the kingdom of God (Isa. 7:14; 9:6–7), Matthew relates the attempt of Herod to kill the newborn king of the Jews (Matt. 2:1–18). The Magi, who inquired about the birthplace of the king, are warned in a dream not to report back to Herod, and Joseph is warned to flee to Egypt until Herod dies. Herod, in fear and rage, has all the children in the region of Bethlehem up to two years old put to death, according to the time that the Magi made their inquiry (v. 16). Though in human terms these events may be thought of as a danger to the dynasty of David, the preservation of the child in each instance is evidence of sovereign control that constantly ensured the safety of the promise.

THE SURVIVAL OF **God's church.** The church of the new covenant is called to be the treasured people in this age. The apostle Peter identifies them with those called apart at Mount Sinai in exhorting them to be distinguished by their speech and conduct (1 Peter 2:1–10). Jehoiada restores the temple as a focal point for covenant renewal and the worship of God. The temple was the palace of the King of kings in the midst of the people; in the time of the kingdom of Israel worship was to be exclusively at the one place Yahweh had chosen (Deut. 12:1–5).

Jesus came as the very presence of God represented by the temple; there was no more need for a physical temple after the Incarnation (Matt. 24:1–3; John 2:18–22).[13] With the ascension of Jesus the church has become his

---

13. For Christ as the fulfillment of the end-time temple in the Gospels, see Beale, *The Temple and the Church's Mission*, 169–200.

visible presence in the world, the living stones, elect and precious, built into a spiritual house with the spiritual sacrifice of praise, well-pleasing to God (1 Peter 2:4–5). Peter describes this spiritual house by quoting the words given by Moses to the people at Mount Sinai: "You are a chosen people, a royal priesthood, a holy nation, a people belonging to God, that you may declare the praises of him who called you out of darkness into his wonderful light" (v. 9).[14] The church's mission to declare God's glory in this world, and to declare his glory to the world continues of the mission of Jehoiada the priest and the people of Jerusalem. The church can be no less zealous in its mission than Jehoiada in his time.

The church in this world may feel threatened, even as the temple seemed to be threatened in the time of Athaliah. At the confession at Caesarea Philippi, Jesus assures Peter that he is the rock on which the church will be built and the gates of death will not prevail against it (Matt. 16:13–18).[15] The light of the church is as secure as the lamp of David (2 Kings 8:19); indeed, it is a lamp shining in its own right. Matthew's Gospel is the account of Jesus Christ, Son of David, Son of Abraham (Matt. 1:1). Both the blessing of Abraham and the promise to David find their fulfillment in the person of Christ.

Though the church is the treasured people and the lamp of David in this world in terms of New Testament fulfillment, the times of the church are not equivalent to those of Jehoiada and Judah in the days of Athaliah. Jehoiada takes drastic and violent measures in order to preserve the lamp of David and the covenant against the threats of Athaliah. Political and armed intervention is not the means by which the church shall be preserved from the gates of death. It is rather true that the blood of the martyrs has been the seed of the church. Stephen (Acts 7:59–60), the apostle James (Acts 12:1–2), Paul (cf. Phil. 2:17), Antipas (Rev. 2:13), and Polycarp bishop of Smyrna are but the first of a vast multitude of every tribe and tongue and nation who are saved out of great tribulation in which they give their lives for their faith (Rev. 7:9–15).[16]

From its beginnings the strength of the church has been the willingness of believers to give up their lives for the truth of the death and resurrection of Christ. This is their calling (1 Peter 2:21); Christ suffered on their behalf and left an example that they should follow in his way. The strength of the

---

14. For the use of the Greek term *peripoiçsis* as a translation of the Hebrew *sᵉgullâ* ("treasured possession"), see Hatch and Redpath, *Concordance to the Septuagint and Other Greek Versions of the Old Testament* (2 vols.; Oxford, 1897; reprint, Grand Rapids: Baker, 1983), 2:1125.

15. For a discussion of the name Peter, see Contemporary Significance section of 2 Kings 2.

16. Polycarp is the Christian martyr whose story is preserved in written documentation in *Martyrdom of Polycarp*, a letter from the Church of Smyrna (see the document in any edition of the Apostolic Fathers).

church is not violent political resistance but a willingness to obey God rather than human beings even to the point of death.

Resistance to the church may be as virulent as that exercised by Athaliah in her determination to extend both her political power and religious influence. Considerable judicial conflict over the concept of the separation of church and state took place in Alabama over a monument inscribed with the Ten Commandments placed in a courthouse in Montgomery County. Columnist Christopher Hitchins recently expressed his hatred against such a testimony to the basis of constitutional law.[17] Hitchens "indulges in a prejudiced and supercilious deconstruction of the divine Decalogue, saying 'the true problem is our failure to recognize that religion is not just incongruent with morality but in essential ways incompatible with it.'"

Hitchens expressed his contempt for the Alabama Chief Justice and Ten Commandments advocate Judge Roy Moore as "a fool and a publicity hound." He was resolutely unwilling to recognize that religion is imbedded in all humanity, including himself, and still less able to consider the value of the Christian faith for moral understanding of human conduct. He resented the impact that it has had in determining the legal values of Western culture.

Moore goes on to quote Malcolm Muggeridge, another journalist and sometime British Intelligence operative who started out in life as an atheist but became one of the twentieth century's most articulate Christian apologists. "Who would not rather be wrong with St. Francis of Asissi, St. Augustine of Hippo, all the saints and mystics for 2,000 years, not to mention Dante, Michelangelo, Shakespeare, Milton, Pascal, than right with Bernard Shaw, H. G. Wells, Karl Marx, Nietzsche, the Huxleys, Bertrand Russell, and such like?" Moore concludes with the provocative words of G. K. Chesterton:

> People have fallen into a foolish habit of speaking of orthodoxy as something heavy, humdrum and safe. There never was anything so perilous or so exciting as orthodoxy. It was sanity; and to be sane is more dramatic than to be mad....
>
> The orthodox Church never took the tame course or accepted the conventions; the orthodox Church was never respectable.... It is easy to be a madman; it is easy to be a heretic.
>
> It is always easy to let the age have its head; the difficult thing is to keep one's own. It is always easy to be a modernist; as it is easy to be a snob.... It is always simple to fall; there are an infinity of angles at which one falls, only one at which one stands.

---

17. Reported by Charles W. Moore, "Is Christianity Incompatible with Morality?" in *Christian Week*, ed. Doug Koop (Fellowship for Print Witness; September 16, 2003), 3.

To have fallen into any one of the fads from Gnosticism to Christian Science would indeed have been obvious and tame. But to avoid them all has been one swirling adventure; and in my vision the heavenly chariot flies thundering through the ages, the dull heresies sprawling and prostrate, the wild truth reeling but erect.[18]

Many times, including the present, political forces have determined to extinguish the church, only to have the church grow in the process. The evangelical church in Ethiopia is a notable example. In 1974, the Mennonite church in Ethiopia consisted of fourteen local congregations and approximately five thousand members.[19] Then came the Communist takeover, known in Ethiopia as the *derg*. Mengistu Haile Mariam, an army officer, participated prominently in the overthrow of Emperor Haile Selassie. Emerging through violence as preeminent military ruler by 1977, he sought Soviet aid, established a socialist People's Republic, and fought off Somali incursions and Eritrean rebels. In 1982 the church was driven underground; all church properties were seized, church leaders were arrested and imprisoned.

Politically and economically things did not go well for the people of Ethiopia. Mengistu was elected president in 1987. Regional rebellions increased while Soviet aid receded amid economic deterioration. Mengistu abandoned socialism, but unable to mobilize military resistance, he was forced to flee to Zimbabwe in 1991. The Meserete Kristos Church by that time had become fifty-three congregations with approximately fifty-one thousand members. In 1994 Meserete Kristos College was established to help meet educational needs. By 2005 there were 335 congregations and 780 outreach centers; in 2004 the Meserete Kristos Church added 13,000 new baptized members, in a total faith community of 246,000.

The Meserete Kristos College has been established to become a full Christian university, offering a broad range of programs that will impact Ethiopian society toward a more honest, just, compassionate, and prosperous future. The current government of Ethiopia has granted the college thirteen acres of land, enabling it to move out of the congested rented facilities in the city. Construction of the first phase of a new campus has begun. The college will be a critical resource to a rapidly growing church.

The specter of an Athaliah determined to eliminate the worship of God will continue to arise in different places and different times. The church must not fear, not even at the prospect great suffering, as has happened so fre-

---

18. Ibid.

19. The story of the Mennonite church was obtained by personal interview with the president of Meserete Kristos College in Addis Ababa, Hailu Cherenet Biru, and the Director of Resource Development, Bedru Hussein Muktar.

quently. The "lamp" of David will not be snuffed out. One of the important lessons of the Deuteronomistic History is the preservation of the promise; that promise will prevail in spite of the eventual failure of the kingdom and the exile of the dynasty. As the history concludes, hope is still to be found in Babylon.

2 Kings 11:21–12:21

✌

JOASH WAS SEVEN years old when he began to reign.
¹²ˑ¹In the seventh year of Jehu, Joash became king, and he
reigned in Jerusalem forty years. His mother's name was
Zibiah; she was from Beersheba. ²Joash did what was right in
the eyes of the LORD all the years Jehoiada the priest
instructed him. ³The high places, however, were not removed;
the people continued to offer sacrifices and burn incense there.

⁴Joash said to the priests, "Collect all the money that is
brought as sacred offerings to the temple of the LORD—the
money collected in the census, the money received from personal vows and the money brought voluntarily to the temple.
⁵Let every priest receive the money from one of the treasurers, and let it be used to repair whatever damage is found in
the temple."

⁶But by the twenty-third year of King Joash the priests still
had not repaired the temple. ⁷Therefore King Joash summoned Jehoiada the priest and the other priests and asked
them, "Why aren't you repairing the damage done to the temple? Take no more money from your treasurers, but hand it
over for repairing the temple." ⁸The priests agreed that they
would not collect any more money from the people and that
they would not repair the temple themselves.

⁹Jehoiada the priest took a chest and bored a hole in its lid.
He placed it beside the altar, on the right side as one enters
the temple of the LORD. The priests who guarded the
entrance put into the chest all the money that was brought to
the temple of the LORD. ¹⁰Whenever they saw that there was a
large amount of money in the chest, the royal secretary and
the high priest came, counted the money that had been
brought into the temple of the LORD and put it into bags.
¹¹When the amount had been determined, they gave the
money to the men appointed to supervise the work on the
temple. With it they paid those who worked on the temple of
the LORD—the carpenters and builders, ¹²the masons and
stonecutters. They purchased timber and dressed stone for
the repair of the temple of the LORD, and met all the other
expenses of restoring the temple.

[13]The money brought into the temple was not spent for making silver basins, wick trimmers, sprinkling bowls, trumpets or any other articles of gold or silver for the temple of the LORD; [14]it was paid to the workmen, who used it to repair the temple. [15]They did not require an accounting from those to whom they gave the money to pay the workers, because they acted with complete honesty. [16]The money from the guilt offerings and sin offerings was not brought into the temple of the LORD; it belonged to the priests.

[17]About this time Hazael king of Aram went up and attacked Gath and captured it. Then he turned to attack Jerusalem. [18]But Joash king of Judah took all the sacred objects dedicated by his fathers—Jehoshaphat, Jehoram and Ahaziah, the kings of Judah—and the gifts he himself had dedicated and all the gold found in the treasuries of the temple of the LORD and of the royal palace, and he sent them to Hazael king of Aram, who then withdrew from Jerusalem.

[19]As for the other events of the reign of Joash, and all he did, are they not written in the book of the annals of the kings of Judah? [20]His officials conspired against him and assassinated him at Beth Millo, on the road down to Silla. [21]The officials who murdered him were Jozabad son of Shimeath and Jehozabad son of Shomer. He died and was buried with his fathers in the City of David. And Amaziah his son succeeded him as king.

JOASH IS INTRODUCED with the usual regnal summary including his age, a synchronism with Jehu, the length of his reign, the name of his mother, and a verdict on the worthiness of his rule.[1] The greatest part of the account is devoted to the efforts of Joash to restore the temple (12:4–16), exceeding the efforts of the priests in accomplishing the task. The account concludes with the attack of Hazael, in which the temple is raided and much of the effort to restore the temple is lost (vv. 17–21). The concluding summary includes the typical formula but has the added details of the plot and assassination of Joash, which bring an abrupt end to his reign. Relatively little is recorded for the lengthy reign of forty years.

---

1. The verse numbering of the English versions follows the Greek, which includes the first element of the summary (the age of Joash) with the previous chapter. Chronicles follows the usual chapter division.

The Repair of the Temple (11:21–12:16)

THE REIGN OF Joash is linked with the preceding narrative by giving his age at the time he begins to reign followed by the synchronism with Jehu (11:21–21:1). This reverses the more usual order (cf. 8:16, 25).[2] The name of his mother, Zibiah ("gazelle"), is likely for a woman from Beersheba. Jehoiada has taught the king well and apparently has considerable influence early in his reign, even choosing his wives (2 Chron. 24:3). The priestly training of Joash influences him to take the initiative in temple restoration, with Jehoiada playing a minor role.

In repairing the temple (12:4–16), Joash is compelled to introduce a new method of financing temple maintenance. This method continues to be used until the Exile and eventually is established as a regulation (Neh. 10:32). The temple restoration under Joash refers to two sources of income for repair: the funds brought to the temple (2 Kings 12:4) and the money in the possession of the priests (v. 5), which never comes to the temple (v. 16).[3]

The money that is the possession of the priests is obtained from the "guilt offerings" (ʾāšām) and "sin offerings" (ḥaṭṭāʾâ).[4] These offerings become the property of the priests and can only be eaten by them (Lev. 6:26, 29; 7:6–7). Though they belong to the officiating priest, it can be eaten by any priest. Since the offerings must be eaten quickly, they are distributed to fellow priests who pay for them.[5] This explains the money of the "treasurers" of the priests (2 Kings 12:5, 7); it is obtained from the sale of the offerings.[6] The refusal of the priests to give up their personal income depletes funds for repairs, forcing Joash to find alternate revenues.

Other sources of income to be used for temple repairs consist of monies brought to the temple (12:4). These include funds that are part of a census tax (cf. Ex. 30:11–16) and any voluntary offerings.[7] In course of time enthu-

---

2. Montgomery (*The Books of Kings*, 426–27) observes that the introduction of Joash at age seven provides a literary connection with the previous account of Jehoiada installing the young king at age seven (11:4).

3. Logan S. Wright, "*MKR* in 2 Kings xii 5–17 and Deuteronomy xviii 8," *VT* 39 (1989): 441–42.

4. For a discussion of the reparation and purgation offerings see Jacob Milgrom, *Cult and Conscience: The Asham and the Priestly Doctrine of Repentance* (Leiden: Brill, 1976), 13–16; idem, *Studies in Cultic Theology and Terminology* (Leiden: Brill, 1983), 70–74.

5. Wright, "*MKR* in 2 Kings xii 5–7 and Deuteronomy xviii 8," 443–44.

6. The rare word *makkār* is to be related to the verb "to sell" (*mkr*) and not to the word "neighbor" (*nkr*) and translated as "acquaintance" (KJV, RSV).

7. The Hebrew text indicates two census taxes, one for entering the register and a second as a "valuation of persons," as was done in the payment of vows (cf. Lev. 27:1–8). The text is not certain and may contain a conflated reading.

siasm for the maintenance of the temple wanes, and the priests no longer contribute personal money. The specific date of the twenty-third year of Joash's reign may have been obtained from a building inscription that also made reference to the sources of money for restoration at the time of the temple's dedication (2 Kings 12:6).[8] Joash reaches a new agreement with the priests (v. 7); they will be absolved of responsibility to repair the temple, but they will no longer be in charge of the offerings brought to the temple. A cash box is installed south of the altar to provide for voluntary donations; when an Israelite enters the temple, the Levitical guards at the entrance will receive offerings and deposit them in the box.

This system of collecting voluntary contributions is effective. Periodically the king's recorder and the high priest collect the money and count it. The suggestion that the metal is smelted makes good sense (NEB), since it was common to melt down miscellaneous objects donated to the temple into standard size ingots. Though this may have been done, only the initial stage of binding the coins in bags (ṣûr) is described, not the further stage of smelting it (yṣr). Once the silver is valued, it is used to pay the workers for repairs (v. 11) and the craftsmen needed to prepare the wood and the stone (v. 12). The refurbishing of the temple artifacts used in worship is temporarily suspended to concentrate on the building itself. The monies are entrusted to the workmen, who apparently are more reliable than the priests in using it responsibly.

The Invasion of Hazael (12:17–21)

THE OCCASION OF Hazael's attack is not given, but the sequence of the narrative correlates with the activities of the Assyrians and Arameans. During the reign of Jehu, Hazael took control of the entire Transjordan to the boundary of Moab at the Arnon River (cf. 10:32–33). When Jehu began to reign (841 B.C.), Shalmaneser III appeared in southern Syria and decimated Hazael, confining him to Damascus. Shalmaneser returned a few years later (838 B.C.) to raid towns belonging to Hazael and to collect dues. Jehu submitted to the Assyrians, and Assyrian dominance provided initial respite from the advances of the Arameans.

Assyrian expansion declined during the reign of Shamshi-Adad V (824–811 B.C.). The reforms of Joash in his twenty-third year (813 B.C.) take place just after the end of the twenty-eight-year reign of Jehu (814 B.C.). His death ends the treaty he had with the Assyrians, and Hazael may have taken that opportunity to extend his control in his war with Assyria.

---

8. Nadav Naʾaman, "Royal Inscriptions and the Histories of Joash and Ahaz, Kings of Judah," *VT* 48 (1998): 337–40.

Biblical Gath ("winepress") is one of five cities of the Philistines as well as several others with that name. Not enough detail is given to know with certainty which city Hazael captures here (12:17).[9] Gath is well known in Samuel as the home of Goliath (1 Sam. 17:4; 2 Sam. 21:20–22) and the place where David took refuge when fleeing from Saul (1 Sam. 27: 2). It was strategically located on the road leading up to Jerusalem through the Elah Valley by way of Bethlehem. Hazael exploits this route as he extends his control southward down the Philistine plain; from there he is able to make threats against the capital city.

Joash successfully buys him off with the sacred vessels and temple treasures. Hazael does not seriously consider a conquest of Judah; his goal is to subjugate and control Joash, providing himself taxation revenues in the process. Hazael may have expected Judah to renew its alliance with Assyria in the event of future battles involving control of the western territories. His main goal is to control trade routes along the coast, as he had in the Transjordan.

The summary of the reign of Joash tells of his assassination by his own court officials. No explanation is given, but his capitulation to Hazael and stripping the temple to meet the demands of the Arameans bring about political discontent. Chronicles further tells of dissention with the priesthood that results in Joash's killing Zachariah, son of Jehoiada (2 Chron. 24:20–21). The location of Joash's murder is given as the Millo House on the road down to Silla. The name Millo suggests a built-up terrace, possibly supporting the steep slopes of the Kidron wall to enlarge the area of the palace fortress. It may be the Ophel of later time (cf. 2 Chron. 27:3).

The names of the assassins are identical in the Hebrew and are not unusual (cf. 2 Chron. 17:18; Ezra 8:33).[10] The Chronicler identifies them as the sons of foreign women, Shimeath from Ammon and Shimrith from Moab (2 Chron. 24:26). The Chronicler himself may have supplied this information, in accordance with his belief that when the people turn to alien gods they will suffer divine judgment from alien intervention.[11] It is gratuitous to assume the Chronicler invented the idea that foreigners came to

9. For a discussion on cities named Gath and their locations see B. Mazar, "Tell Gath," *IEJ* 6 (1956): 258–59. Aharoni, et al., *The Carta Bible Atlas*, #133, suggest that Hazael attacks Gath-rimmon/Gittim to the north of Ekron and Philistine Gath. For Gath as Tell es-Sâfil, see J. P. J. Olivier, "Gath," *NIDOTTE*, 4:651–52. Aren M. Maeir proposes archaeological evidence for an attack of Hazael at Philistine Gath mentioned in Kings: "The Historical Background and Dating of Amos VI 2: An Archaeological Perspective from Tell es-Sâfil/Gath," *VT* 54 (2004): 320–37.

10. The Greek has Jezechar for the first name (cf. RSV).

11. Williamson, *1 and 2 Chronicles*, 326.

power in the Judean court; it may have been information simply omitted by Kings.[12] The assassins are probably professional soldiers hired to do the job, but no details are given as to who is behind the conspiracy.

KING AND PRIEST in cooperation. The main intent of this narrative is to present Joash's reign in an approving light, though there are elements of compromise. Although there is no indication that the altars allowed by Joash are places of pagan worship, they are not regarded as acceptable for worship of Yahweh (12:3). No mention is made of the "other gods" common in the condemnation of unfaithful monarchs.

Joash is one of the few kings given a positive evaluation; his rule is characterized by a convergence of priestly and royal interests. Initially the high priest installs Joash and then also instructs him (v. 2). Joash in turn takes the initiative in restoring the temple, overcoming the reluctance of the priests to raise the necessary funds to make repairs possible.

Kings gives an ideal portrayal of the cooperation between royalty and priesthood during the reign of Joash. The high priest enables the dynasty to continue, and the young king follows the instructions of the high priest (12:3). The mutual support of priest and king are the ideal in terms of the covenant. The king is both subject to the covenant and responsible to ensure that the covenant values determine the law of the land (Deut. 17:14–20). The priests are responsible to provide for worship at the temple and to live from the proceeds of the offerings brought to the temple (18:1–8). The stripping of the temple to satisfy the demands of Hazael is not condemned, and the assassination by members of his own court is not explained.

The Chronicler, however, gives a more qualified portrayal of the faithfulness of Joash. While Kings says Joash does what is right all the days of his life (12:2), Chronicles says he does right only during the time that Jehoiada the priest instructs him (2 Chron. 24:2).[13] The Chronicler divides Joash's reign into the years when Jehoiada is alive and the years after his death. His reign after Jehoiada's death is characterized by covenant failure and the development of hostilities between Joash and the priests (24:17–22). The king comes under the influence of the princes of Judah and is led into idolatry. Zechariah the son of Jehoiada publicly chastises Joash, so the king has him publicly stoned.

---

12. Japhet, *I & II Chronicles*, 854.

13. The Hebrew of 2 Kings 12:2 says that Joash does what is right all his days just as Jehoiada taught him (RSV, NEB, NLT), not all the years while Jehoiada taught him (NIV). The NIV translation requires an emendation of the Kings text (the removal of the suffix that refers to the entire time that Joash ruled).

This act of rebellion leads to defeat at the hands of the Arameans and the assassination of Joash by two of his own courtiers (24:23–25).

As is typical in Chronicles, the apostasy of Joash explains his defeat by the Arameans and his assassination by his own servants. In that version, a small contingent of Arameans is able to penetrate right into Jerusalem and wound the king because of his unfaithfulness (2 Chron. 24:24). The Chronicler seems to have had additional sources about the role of Zechariah son of Jehoiada and the conflict between the king and the priests that eventually lead to his death.[14] This expansion of Joash's reign in Chronicles provides a theological consistency in that work, in which every calamity is viewed as a punishment for sin.

The achievements of a life can always be viewed in more than one way, depending on the perspective of the observer. The presentation of Joash in Kings is a problem for the Chronicler, since it leaves the attack of the Arameans and the assassination of the king without explanation. The Chronicler could have made his presentation quite differently and been consistent with his goals, as in the lives of David and Solomon. All he needed to do was omit or alter the notices of the Aramean war and the king's murder. Instead, the Chronicler provides us with an explanation that reveals a contrasting aspect to the good reign of Joash. This information is found in the "annotations on the book of the kings" (24:27), in which the acts of the king are given in much more detail.

The Deuteronomistic History is concerned to show the legitimacy of Joash's reign as the successor to Athaliah the usurper. As the legitimate king he takes the initiative in temple reform (2 Kings 12:4), then takes charge when the project begins to fail (v. 6). The funds are under the control of his secretary (v. 10), who makes the allotments to the faithful workmen (v. 15). These activities are singled out for attention to set the pattern for the authority and validity of the Judean kings. Joash's failures are a harbinger of the fact that ultimate judgment for the failure of the covenant cannot be avoided. Even so the promise of the "lamp of David" endures.

The relation of king and priest in Israel is an anomaly in the ancient world. In other nations the king mediated the rule of the gods to the nation; in Israel God's will was mediated through the covenant, which made the king subservient to the rule of God as taught and practiced by the priest. This was especially true for Joash, who was spared as an orphan and raised under the instruction of the priest.

Joash naturally has a special interest in the temple and its maintenance. This symbiotic relationship has its tensions; the dominance of royal influence

---

14. Williamson, *1 and 2 Chronicles*, 323–24; Japhet, *I & II Chronicles*, 849.

leads to a reduction of the priestly responsibility, so they no longer receive the offerings of the people, nor are they responsible for repairing the building (v. 9). This breach in the relationship deteriorates to the point of hostility, as seen in Chronicles. Though Joash's reign is remarkable in its achievement, it is equally tragic in its failures; it ends with domination by the Arameans and assassination by court members. Though state and temple are in a mutual interdependent relationship, it is impossible to avoid competing interests between king and priests.

CHURCH AND STATE: **partners or conflict?** The situation is different for the church today; the church is best served when it is not supported by the state. It has the right to be protected by the state, as do all other citizens. Often the church faces the hostility of the state; this should not be surprising. The state represents the world, the powers of this age. Jesus warns his followers to expect the hostility of the world:

> If the world hates you, keep in mind that it hated me first. If you belonged to the world, it would love you as its own. As it is, you do not belong to the world, but I have chosen you out of the world. That is why the world hates you. Remember the words I spoke to you: "No servant is greater than his master." If they persecuted me, they will persecute you also. If they obeyed my teaching, they will obey yours also. (John 15:18–20)

The church cannot expect understanding from the world; it can only hope for tolerance and equal treatment with all other groups in society.

The conflict between the church seeking to be faithful to its calling and the church empowered by the military forces of state is the story of the Reformation. When Martin Luther attempted to reform the church, he came into confrontation with the forces of state. He ended up as a refugee in Wartburg Castle after the Diet of Worms.

Though a victim of the power of state, Luther also used the state to his own ends. He initially survived under the protection of Frederick the Wise, and as the Reformation went on he became involved increasingly with the political maneuvering of the German princes. Luther did not hesitate to use state power against the Jews as well as the Anabaptists (who denied the validity of infant baptism). After Emperor Charles V rejected the Augsburg Confession, Luther was ready to use force against him with the Protestant princes leagued in defense. The year Luther died (1546) Europe was plunged into a century of religious wars.

There was one group at the time of the Reformation who attempted to move the church away from identity with and dependence on the state. A group known as the Swiss Brethren formed their first congregation on January 21, 1525, in the face of imminent persecution for their nonconformity to the demands of the state church led by the Reformation theologian Huldrych Zwingli (1484–1531). The immediate question was over infant baptism, which George Blaurach, Conrad Grebel, Felix Manz, and others questioned on the basis of biblical studies; but the real issue was the nature of the church. According to the Brethren, only those who submitted to the lordship of Christ could be true members of his body. The body of Christ received its guidance through the Scriptures and the Holy Spirit, not from or through the civil magistracy.[15] Persecution scattered the Swiss Brethren across Europe, but the movement grew as these doctrinal views found favor with many people.

The relationship between church and state became a perpetual issue for the Anabaptists, as the radical Reformers came to be known. Baptism was not central to their faith and "Anabaptist" was not a name they chose for themselves. Baptism was important to governments for social and political control, but what was important for Anabaptists was a *regenerated church of believers,* which required instruction and accountability, followed by baptism.[16] They believed the apostolic church had fallen beyond reform with its increasing reliance on the state in the fourth and following centuries. Baptism was required as a sign of a new beginning.

For some Anabaptists a *strict dualism* existed between believers and society, leading to rigorous attempts at living a separated life. The first "Brotherly Union," a union of common affirmation of faith in the Schleitheim Confession (1527), adopted seven articles of belief. Article 4 dealt with living a separated life: "Now there is nothing else in the world and all creation than good and evil . . . darkness and light. . . . God . . . admonishes us therefore to go out from Babylon and from the earthly Egypt."[17] Though the lines between church and state were less sharply drawn in the Netherlands and North Germany, the continuum from strict dualism to accommodation was always present in their understanding of church-state relationships. Government should have no role in the church.

The separation of church and state was carried to the extent that it was questionable whether Christians could even participate in state affairs. Dyck

---

15. Corneluis J. Dyck, "Mennonites," *Encyclopaedia Britannica,* 15th ed. (Macropaedia, 1974), 11:904.

16. Cornelius J. Dyck, *Spiritual Life in Anabaptism* (Scottdale, Pa.: Herald, 1995), 14–15.

17. Ibid., 15.

provides a quote from Menno Simons, a later spiritual leader of the Anabaptists, in his Letter to Micron:

> I agree wholeheartedly that the office of magistrate is of God and his order. But I hate those who are Christian, and want to be one, and then do not follow their prince, head, and leader Christ, but cover and clothe their unrighteousness, wickedness, pomp and pride, avarice, greed, and tyranny with the name of magistrate. For those who are Christian must follow the Spirit, Word, and example of Christ, whether they are emperor, king, or whoever.[18]

These words of Menno Simons are as applicable and true as when they were first written. The involvement of Christians in the affairs of government requires some level of compromise. The demands of government can so contradict Christian values that participation is impossible to maintain with integrity.

Modern societies are agreed on the necessity of the separation of church and state, a complete contrast to the covenant ideal committed to the state support of the temple. Such a separation is impossible to maintain fully, as was the harmony of priest and king in the days of Joash and Jehoiada. The Canadian government, for example, following the lead of the courts, has determined that true equality requires the recognition of homosexual marriages. Marriage has been the dominion of both church and state; it has always been an institution of the church in determining family life and an institution controlled by the state for purposes of taxation and ownership of property. The Canadian government has been unsuccessful in efforts to maintain religious freedom and instead has sought to legislate a marriage law, inclusive of same-sex unions, that is contrary to the beliefs and practices of many Christians.

The necessity of secular government is readily accepted in a pluralistic society. The tension between the secular and the sacred remains as difficult as the cooperation of royalty and priesthood under the covenant in Old Testament times. The story of Joash is a warning of the dangers that can lead to self-destructive conflict. Avenues of compromise will be found on many issues if church is to live in harmony with that state and if Christians are to participate in secular power with ethical integrity.

---

18. Ibid., 114.

2 Kings 13:1–14:29

IN THE TWENTY-THIRD year of Joash son of Ahaziah king of Judah, Jehoahaz son of Jehu became king of Israel in Samaria, and he reigned seventeen years. ²He did evil in the eyes of the LORD by following the sins of Jeroboam son of Nebat, which he had caused Israel to commit, and he did not turn away from them. ³So the LORD's anger burned against Israel, and for a long time he kept them under the power of Hazael king of Aram and Ben-Hadad his son.

⁴Then Jehoahaz sought the LORD's favor, and the LORD listened to him, for he saw how severely the king of Aram was oppressing Israel. ⁵The LORD provided a deliverer for Israel, and they escaped from the power of Aram. So the Israelites lived in their own homes as they had before. ⁶But they did not turn away from the sins of the house of Jeroboam, which he had caused Israel to commit; they continued in them. Also, the Asherah pole remained standing in Samaria.

⁷Nothing had been left of the army of Jehoahaz except fifty horsemen, ten chariots and ten thousand foot soldiers, for the king of Aram had destroyed the rest and made them like the dust at threshing time.

⁸As for the other events of the reign of Jehoahaz, all he did and his achievements, are they not written in the book of the annals of the kings of Israel? ⁹Jehoahaz rested with his fathers and was buried in Samaria. And Jehoash his son succeeded him as king.

¹⁰In the thirty-seventh year of Joash king of Judah, Jehoash son of Jehoahaz became king of Israel in Samaria, and he reigned sixteen years. ¹¹He did evil in the eyes of the LORD and did not turn away from any of the sins of Jeroboam son of Nebat, which he had caused Israel to commit; he continued in them.

¹²As for the other events of the reign of Jehoash, all he did and his achievements, including his war against Amaziah king of Judah, are they not written in the book of the annals of the kings of Israel? ¹³Jehoash rested with his fathers, and Jeroboam succeeded him on the throne. Jehoash was buried in Samaria with the kings of Israel.

¹⁴Now Elisha was suffering from the illness from which he died. Jehoash king of Israel went down to see him and wept over him. "My father! My father!" he cried. "The chariots and horsemen of Israel!"

¹⁵Elisha said, "Get a bow and some arrows," and he did so. ¹⁶"Take the bow in your hands," he said to the king of Israel. When he had taken it, Elisha put his hands on the king's hands.

¹⁷"Open the east window," he said, and he opened it. "Shoot!" Elisha said, and he shot. "The LORD's arrow of victory, the arrow of victory over Aram!" Elisha declared. "You will completely destroy the Arameans at Aphek."

¹⁸Then he said, "Take the arrows," and the king took them. Elisha told him, "Strike the ground." He struck it three times and stopped. ¹⁹The man of God was angry with him and said, "You should have struck the ground five or six times; then you would have defeated Aram and completely destroyed it. But now you will defeat it only three times."

²⁰Elisha died and was buried.

Now Moabite raiders used to enter the country every spring. ²¹Once while some Israelites were burying a man, suddenly they saw a band of raiders; so they threw the man's body into Elisha's tomb. When the body touched Elisha's bones, the man came to life and stood up on his feet.

²²Hazael king of Aram oppressed Israel throughout the reign of Jehoahaz. ²³But the LORD was gracious to them and had compassion and showed concern for them because of his covenant with Abraham, Isaac and Jacob. To this day he has been unwilling to destroy them or banish them from his presence.

²⁴Hazael king of Aram died, and Ben-Hadad his son succeeded him as king. ²⁵Then Jehoash son of Jehoahaz recaptured from Ben-Hadad son of Hazael the towns he had taken in battle from his father Jehoahaz. Three times Jehoash defeated him, and so he recovered the Israelite towns.

^{14:1}In the second year of Jehoash son of Jehoahaz king of Israel, Amaziah son of Joash king of Judah began to reign. ²He was twenty-five years old when he became king, and he reigned in Jerusalem twenty-nine years. His mother's name was Jehoaddin; she was from Jerusalem. ³He did what was right in the eyes of the LORD, but not as his father David had done. In

everything he followed the example of his father Joash. ⁴The high places, however, were not removed; the people continued to offer sacrifices and burn incense there.

⁵After the kingdom was firmly in his grasp, he executed the officials who had murdered his father the king. ⁶Yet he did not put the sons of the assassins to death, in accordance with what is written in the Book of the Law of Moses where the LORD commanded: "Fathers shall not be put to death for their children, nor children put to death for their fathers; each is to die for his own sins."

⁷He was the one who defeated ten thousand Edomites in the Valley of Salt and captured Sela in battle, calling it Joktheel, the name it has to this day.

⁸Then Amaziah sent messengers to Jehoash son of Jehoahaz, the son of Jehu, king of Israel, with the challenge: "Come, meet me face to face."

⁹But Jehoash king of Israel replied to Amaziah king of Judah: "A thistle in Lebanon sent a message to a cedar in Lebanon, 'Give your daughter to my son in marriage.' Then a wild beast in Lebanon came along and trampled the thistle underfoot. ¹⁰You have indeed defeated Edom and now you are arrogant. Glory in your victory, but stay at home! Why ask for trouble and cause your own downfall and that of Judah also?"

¹¹Amaziah, however, would not listen, so Jehoash king of Israel attacked. He and Amaziah king of Judah faced each other at Beth Shemesh in Judah. ¹²Judah was routed by Israel, and every man fled to his home. ¹³Jehoash king of Israel captured Amaziah king of Judah, the son of Joash, the son of Ahaziah, at Beth Shemesh. Then Jehoash went to Jerusalem and broke down the wall of Jerusalem from the Ephraim Gate to the Corner Gate—a section about six hundred feet long. ¹⁴He took all the gold and silver and all the articles found in the temple of the LORD and in the treasuries of the royal palace. He also took hostages and returned to Samaria.

¹⁵As for the other events of the reign of Jehoash, what he did and his achievements, including his war against Amaziah king of Judah, are they not written in the book of the annals of the kings of Israel? ¹⁶Jehoash rested with his fathers and was buried in Samaria with the kings of Israel. And Jeroboam his son succeeded him as king.

¹⁷Amaziah son of Joash king of Judah lived for fifteen years after the death of Jehoash son of Jehoahaz king of Israel. ¹⁸As for the other events of Amaziah's reign, are they not written in the book of the annals of the kings of Judah?

¹⁹They conspired against him in Jerusalem, and he fled to Lachish, but they sent men after him to Lachish and killed him there. ²⁰He was brought back by horse and was buried in Jerusalem with his fathers, in the City of David.

²¹Then all the people of Judah took Azariah, who was sixteen years old, and made him king in place of his father Amaziah. ²²He was the one who rebuilt Elath and restored it to Judah after Amaziah rested with his fathers.

²³In the fifteenth year of Amaziah son of Joash king of Judah, Jeroboam son of Jehoash king of Israel became king in Samaria, and he reigned forty-one years. ²⁴He did evil in the eyes of the LORD and did not turn away from any of the sins of Jeroboam son of Nebat, which he had caused Israel to commit. ²⁵He was the one who restored the boundaries of Israel from Lebo Hamath to the Sea of the Arabah, in accordance with the word of the LORD, the God of Israel, spoken through his servant Jonah son of Amittai, the prophet from Gath Hepher.

²⁶The LORD had seen how bitterly everyone in Israel, whether slave or free, was suffering; there was no one to help them. ²⁷And since the LORD had not said he would blot out the name of Israel from under heaven, he saved them by the hand of Jeroboam son of Jehoash.

²⁸As for the other events of Jeroboam's reign, all he did, and his military achievements, including how he recovered for Israel both Damascus and Hamath, which had belonged to Yaudi, are they not written in the book of the annals of the kings of Israel? ²⁹Jeroboam rested with his fathers, the kings of Israel. And Zechariah his son succeeded him as king.

FOLLOWING THE RESTORATION of the dynasty of Judah and the positive assessment of the reign of Joash, the prophetic history returns to the northern kingdom of Israel. Though this section includes the death of Elisha and the reign of Amaziah king of Judah, it begins and ends with the fortunes of Israel in its struggle against Aramean domination.

The focus on Israel remains even in those sections that deal with Elisha (13:10−21) and Judah (14:1−22). Elisha's last word is to prophesy a partial victory over the Arameans. Most of Amaziah's reign is taken up with the folly of his rash war with Israel and the breach of the defenses of Jerusalem.

These chapters are anomalous in their presentation and summaries of the reigns of the Israelite and Judean kings. The conclusion of Jehoahaz king of Israel (13:8−9) is followed immediately with the introduction of Jehoash king of Israel (vv. 10−11) and his regnal summary (vv. 12−13). Two Elisha stories are introduced (vv. 14−21), followed by a report on partial deliverance from the Arameans (vv. 22−25). Amaziah king of Judah is then introduced (14:1−7); most of his reign deals with the war with Israel (vv. 8−14). Amaziah's reign concludes with a repetition of the regnal summary of Jehoash (vv. 15−16). The conclusion to Amaziah's reign is then given (vv. 18−22), and the unit concludes with the reign of Jeroboam (vv. 23−29).

Reprieve from Aramean Oppression (13:1−25)

ASSYRIAN POWER UNDER Shalmaneser III at the time of Jehu (841 B.C.) confines Hazael to Damascus for a time. But Assyrian expansion declines during the reign of Shamshi-Adad V (824−811 B.C.), and the severely decimated power of Israel after the purge of Jehu allows for Aramean expansion in the Transjordan (10:32−33). Hazael and his successor Ben-Hadad III are able to oppress Jehoahaz king of Israel during most of his seventeen-year reign (13:1−3, 7). Even so, a prophetic word declares that Yahweh will send deliverance to Israel (vv. 3−5), which enables the dynasty to survive.

The prophetic note explains that Jehoahaz prays for deliverance and that Yahweh sends a savior (môšîaᶜ) to help them (13:5). This deliverer may have been a political figure, but historically there is no outstanding king who may be regarded as bringing relief to Israel. Adad-Nirari III, the Assyrian successor to Shamshi-Adad V at the end of the nineth century (810 B.C.) has often been suggested as the deliverer.[1] A campaign to the west near the beginning of his reign (ca. 805 B.C.) is well attested in several inscriptions.[2] In this campaign Adad-Nirari encountered a coalition headed by Ataršumki king of Arpad to the west of the Euphrates, in which he subjugated northern Syria. He then went south to Damascus, which submitted and paid an enormous tribute. Jehoahaz of Israel, if he is the king at the time, and kings from the

---

1. Benjamin Mazar, "The Aramean Empire and Its Relations with Israel," *BA* 25 (1962): 115.

2. The evidence for the first campaign is discussed by William H. Shea, "Adad-Nirari III and Jehoash of Israel," *JCS* 30 (1978): 104−9. These include the Sheik Hammad Stela, a fragmentary stone slab, the Shaba᾽a Stela, and the Rimah Stela.

coast of Phoenicia appear to have sent tribute as well rather than risk Assyrian invasion. This is no real deliverance from the Aramean powers.

Hamath, a northern Aramean city, apparently remained loyal to Assyria and became the target of an Aramean coalition headed by Ben-Hadad III of Damascus. A statue erected by Zakkur king of Hamath celebrates the defense of his capital Hazrak (the biblical Hadrak of Zech. 9:1) against a north Syrian coalition of a dozen or more kings led by Ben-Hadad son of Hazael, king of Aram. Zakkur was the successor of Irhuleni, the king who accompanied Hadadezer of Damascus at the battle of Qarqar. The defensive action of Zakkur recorded on the stela likely temporarily distracted the power of Damascus, but this probably did not provide a political deliverance to Israel. Further, the attack of the coalition against Hazrak was after the reign of Hazael in Damascus (cf. 2 Kings 13:22–24), though not likely much later than the end of the reign of Jehoahaz. Damascus itself was reduced to a powerless state by the Assyrian campaign in 796 B.C. Jehoash was soon able to successfully counter the Arameans (vv. 24–25).

In the context of the Elisha passage (13:14–21), it is more likely that the savior (*môšîaᶜ*) intended by the Deuteronomistic Historians is a prophetic figure. This would fit the pattern of Judges, in which a charismatic figure like Deborah inspires nationalistic revival in time of oppression. Hobbs points out the specific verbal parallels between the deliverance described in 2 Kings 13:4–5 and the summary of the theological significance of the Exodus found in Deuteronomy 26:7–9.[3] Such a direct allusion indicates that the Deuteronomists have in mind a succession of prophets, of which Moses is the prototype.[4] If Elisha were this figure, it would be about forty years after his activity in anointing of Jehu to succeed the Omride dynasty.

Ten thousand foot soldiers of Jehoahaz (2 Kings 13:7) are a marked contrast to the ten chariots left to his forces. This statement still serves as an explanation for his subjugation to the Arameans, because the superiority of power belongs to the number of mobile forces. A large number of infantry does not provide resistance to the speed of chariots.[5] Israel is crushed like dust before the Arameans; Amos describes it as being under the threshing sledge (Amos 1:3). Hazael is vastly superior in both infantry and chariots.

Jehoahaz is succeeded by his son Jehoash (2 Kings 13:10–13), the same name as his counterpart in Judah. The synchronistic data for the reign of

---

3. Hobbs, 2 *Kings*, 167–68.

4. For a defense of this thesis see R. P. Carroll, "Elijah and Elisha Sagas," *VT* 19 (1969): 400–415.

5. It is also possible that the word for "thousand" (*ʾelep*) is used in the sense of contingents, as is often the case in the Deuteronomistic History. In that case the army of Jehoahaz is just a few hundred soldiers; Ahlström, *The History of Ancient Palestine*, 604.

Jehoash is idiosyncratic. The thirty-seventh year of Joash of Judah (v. 10) does not correspond to a seventeen-year reign of Jehoahaz beginning in the twenty-third year of Joash (v. 1), or to the reign of Amaziah his son beginning in the second year of Jehoash of Israel (14:1).[6]

Jehoash also has the distinction of being named in the Assyrian records. The Rimah Stela, which records a campaign of Adad-Nirari III deep into Aramean territory, declares that he received tribute from "Ia'asu the Samaritan," along with the rulers of Tyre and Sidon.[7] The king (*mari'*) of Damascus is not named, so it may have been either Hazael or Ben-Hadad III. Shea proposes that this stela records the first campaign of Adad-Nirari III, which according to the eponym list would have been 805 B.C.[8] He further proposes a revision of the biblical chronology, suggesting that the seven-year reign of Athaliah must not be counted in the regnal years, so the reign of Jehoash actually begins in 805, as suggested by his name in the stela.[9] It is possible, however, that the stela contains summaries of several campaigns, so that the tax paid by Jehoash could have been in a campaign as late as 796 B.C. The interpretation of the stela is not sufficiently conclusive to require an extensive revision of the chronology as given in Kings.

The significant events of the reign of Jehoash are only mentioned within the regnal summary of his reign (13:10–13), indicating that these events have been exerpted from the historical records of Jehoash. His victory over Ben-Hadad III is given with a summary of the domination of the Arameans (vv. 22–25), and his war with Amaziah is given as part of the history of the Judean king (14:8–14). The fortunes of Israel begin to rise significantly during the reign of Jehoash until it beomes a formidable and wealthy country under his son, Jeroboam II.

The reign of Jehoash is followed by a report of his visit to Elisha. The prophet has not been part of the history since his anointing of Jehu about forty years previous (9:1–3). The absence of any reference to his activity in the interim shows that interest in Elisha and the sons of the prophets is limited to their significance for the main theme of the history of Israel and Judah under the covenant. The visit of Jehoash is to bring his last respects as Elisha is dying.

The location of this visit is not given; if Elisha dies in the vicinity of his burial near Moab (13:20), it may be near his home in Abel Meholah (cf.

---

6. A possible reconcilation of this data because of a switch to the accession year system in Judah during Amaziah's reign and in Israel during Jehoash's reign is discussed in appendix B.

7. For translation and comment, see S. Page, "Joash and Samaria in a New Stela Excavated at Tell al Rimah, Iraq," *VT* 19 (1969): 483–84.

8. Shea, "Adad-Nirari III and Jehoash of Israel," 106–8.

9. Ibid., 111–13.

1 Kings 19:16). The encomium of Jehoash is the same as that spoken by Elisha to his master, Elijah (2 Kings 13:14; cf. 2:12). The expression "my father, my father" is an attribution of honor by a leader of the younger generation to the older.[10] "The chariots and horseman of Israel" in the first instance referred to the fiery departure of Elijah in glory. Elisha, unlike Elijah, has had active military leadership in the conflicts of Israel against the Arameans (cf. 3:11–19; 6:13–17); the words of Jehoash acknowledge that role and attribute to Elisha the same distinction that belonged to Elijah.

The last action of Elisha is to give a message of promise to the dynasty of Jehu, not unlike the final blessing of other leaders (Jacob, Gen. 49:1–28; Moses, Deut. 33). The king of Israel is instructed to shoot an arrow east towards Aphek, east of the sea of Tiberias. Ahab successfully defended Aphek from an attack of the Arameans (1 Kings 20:22–30), but it had since come under Aramean control. The arrow represents complete victory in regaining Aphek.

The king is then instructed to strike the ground with his arrows. His three strikes signify only a partial recovery from the dominion of the Arameans. The significance of this action is like that of the prophet Ahijah in the call of Jeroboam (1 Kings 11:29–32). They are best regarded as rhetorical, nonverbal communication, persuasive in nature and intent.[11] They are communicative and interactive, a message with a persuasive dimension. The participation of Elisha in guiding the hands of the king (2 Kings 13:16b) conveys the assurance that God will provide victory over the Arameans irrespective of the decimated state of his armies. The limited strikes of the arrows signify that this will not be a complete triumph. The anger of the prophet is instigated by the king's limited faith and resolve.

The legacy of Elisha is last of all remembered in a story about his burial. Aramean conflict with rising Assyrian power provides relief for Israel and other neighboring countries, such as Moab. Moabite raiding bands can extend their liberties well beyond the Arnon, possibly as far north as the hometown of Elisha. Such a band of raiders surprises a group of mourners in the process of burying a comrade. In haste they temporarily dispose of the body in the grave of Elisha, with the result that the man revives. The ministry of Elisha was inaugurated with the curse of death on those who scorned his prophetic anointing (2 Kings 2:23–25). His prophetic anointing is again attested after his death, as contact with his bones leads to life-giving power.

---

10. See comments on 2:12.

11. For other views see Friebel, "A Hermeneutical Paradigm for Interpreting Prophetic Sign-Actions," 25–45. Though similar practices are known among other cultures as a kind of magical power, magic is contrary to the theology of Deuteronomy.

Like the episode with the arrows, it signifies the life-giving power of the prophet for the nation, through the declaration of the divine will.

A summary of events in the Aramean conflict brings the focus of the narrative to the political fortunes of the dynasty of Jehu. Hazael, whose reign extended to about the end of the ninth century, had attempted to forge an alliance in Palestine that would be sufficient to repel the Assyrian advances.[12] His raids deep into Judah had forced a heavy tribute from Joash, who followed the policy of Assyrian alliance (12:17–18). Jehu in similar manner rejected alliances with the Arameans to resist Assyria. Hazael aggressively pursued a policy of bringing them into subjugation, threshing Gilead with an iron sledge (Amos 1:3).

The aggression of Hazael constituted the greater part of the reign of Jehoahaz, whose seventeen-year sovereignty extended into the eighth century. Hazael controlled the major trade routes, exercising control to the Arnon on the east (2 Kings 10:33) and Gath on the west (12:17). Matters begin to change under the reign of Jehoash, with the death of Hazael and the increased Assyrian pressure under the campaigns of Adad-Nirari III. The delay of the judgment of Israel under Jehu's dynasty is in keeping with the covenant promise according to Deuteronomistic theology (13:23; cf. Deut. 6:10–12). The location of the cities that Jehoash is able to recover for Israel is not given (2 Kings 13:24–25); Aphek must have been counted among them (v. 17), and probably Lo Debar and Karnaim (Amos 6:13).

Rise of Israelite Power (14:1–29)

AFTER THE SUMMARY of Jehoash's reign in Israel and a notation of his successes against the Arameans (13:12–13; 22–25), the narrative turns to Amaziah. The topic does not substantially change, because Amaziah becomes subject to Jehoash. Jehoash does not attempt to bring Judah under his rule, since the time for such a union is past, but Judah may have been a vassal to Israel.[13] The disastrous reign of Amaziah ends with his exile and execution in Lachish (14:18–22). His unsuccessful war against Jehoash demonstrates the dominance of Israel (vv. 8–12). The long twenty-nine year reign of Amaziah (14:2) and the fifty-two year reign of Azariah (14:29; 15:2) undoubtedly involve a significant period of coregency.[14]

---

12. Ahlström, *The History of Ancient Palestine*, 605–6. Aramean control may explain stratum VIII–VII at Hazor, in which the former fortress became a mainly residential city with ordinary houses.

13. Ibid., 614.

14. Details of the coregency are discussed in appendix B. The point that Ahaziah lives (but does not reign) for fifteen years after Azariah is made king indicates that his last years are ones of coregency (14:17–21).

The introductory summary of the reign of Amaziah provides the name of his mother as Jehoaddin, meaning "the one in whom the LORD delights" (the theophoric element *yhw* and the verb *ᶜdn*). Though Amaziah is said to do what is right, the ominous note of his rule is sounded in the observation that his reign is not like that of David but rather like that of his father Joash (14:3–4). The high places, not necessarily those of foreign gods, remain in place until the time of Josiah. These were not to be tolerated once the temple was built and designated as the place Yahweh chose for his name to dwell.

Succession to the throne is not without conflict (14:5–6). Joash, father of Amaziah, was assassinated in a political plot (12:21); Amaziah does not deal with the assassins until he has secured his place on the throne (14:5). The situation is somewhat like the succession of David, where civil war erupts with the supporters of Adonijah before the kingdom is stabilized under Solomon's rule (1 Kings 2:46). Those who assassinated Joash are individuals with status and influence, who now threaten the rule of the new king. Special care is taken to point out that Amaziah follows the covenant regulation in the extent of the executions (2 Kings 14:6; cf. Deut. 24:16). Court plots of this type usually involve extended family members, resulting in whole families being decimated in order to prevent further revolt. Amaziah rightly restrains his revenge to those directly responsible for the rebellion.

The circumstances of the battle with Edom (14:7) are not specified, though Chronicles indicates that Amaziah initiates the attack (2 Chron. 25:11). Chronicles reports the gruesome details of ten thousand Edomites being cast from the top of a cliff (25:12). In Kings Sela (meaning the Rock) is a place name (Joktheel), often identified with Petra, a prominent fortification of the Edomites. Some have regarded its towering mountain, today called el-Habis, as the peak from which the soldiers are cast.[15] The Valley of Salt is the location of battles that David had with the Edomites (2 Sam. 8:13; cf. Ps. 60), the "perennial battlefield south of the Dead Sea."[16] The location of the valley and the rock subsequently named Joktheel cannot be determined, but the general area is most likely northern Edom.

There were two main centers in Edom, Petra in the south and Bozrah (Buseirah) in the north, between Sela and Punon.[17] The initial conquests in

---

15. Philip C. Hammond, "Petra," in *Eerdmans Dictionary of the Bible*, ed. D. N. Freedman (Grand Rapids: Eerdmans, 2000), 1042. In spite of ancient tradition supporting this view, it is unlikely that Amaziah penetrates this far south; the port Elath is not taken until the time of Azariah (14:22). Ancient Petra was known as Reqem; the rock was probably Silaᶜ, 2.5 miles (4 km) northwest of Buseirah (Rainey et al., *The Sacred Bridge*, 216).

16. Aharoni, *The Land of the Bible*, 344.

17. Ibid., 40; Aharoni et al., *The Carta Bible Atlas*, #52.

the north are probably achieved with the assistance of the king of Israel, with the aim of dominating the southern portion of the King's Highway on the east side of the Jordan rift. The conflict with Edom goes back to the days of Joash, when Edom gained independence (cf. 2 Kings 8:20–22). Control over Edom is temporary; by the time of Ahaz, Edom has regained its independence (16:6).

If Amaziah has allied with Jehoash of Israel in his efforts to gain control of lucrative trade routes, the cooperation ends in sharp disagreement. Some type of allied warfare with subsequent hostilities and reprisals is indicated in 2 Chronicles 25:5–10, 13. Israelite soldiers are hired and then dismissed; in retaliation for losing out on the spoils of Edom, they loot Judean border cities. Border warfare may be the occasion for Amaziah seeking some type of negotiation with Jehoash (2 Kings 14:8). Jehoash's response indicates that the negotiation initially carries with it a threat of military force (vv. 9–11). Amaziah seriously overestimates his military capability after his defeat of Edom. Jehoash is not intimidated; his reply is laced with scorn. In a strategic attack, he captures Beth Shemesh, a Judean city on the southwestern border of Judah, near the juncture of the Sorek Valley and the base of the hill country.[18]

In a decisive victory, Jehoash takes Amaziah prisoner, then marches unhindered to Jerusalem, breaks down part of its wall, and plunders it (14:12–14). The Ephraim Gate is likely the entrance to Ephraim on the northern wall of the city, and the Corner Gate is the fortified tower at the northern end of the west wall (cf. 2 Chron. 26:9). As a prominent boundary point the Corner Gate becomes associated with eschatological hopes for Jerusalem (Jer. 31:38). The hostages are likely nobility or members of the royal family, kept under guard or held for ransom. The plundering of the temple is reminiscent of the attack of Hazael against Joash.

Amaziah's death and the succession of Azariah (14:19–22) are unexpected after the closing notice of his reign (v. 18). The narrative sequence may be explained by the unusual circumstances of his sucession. After his death and burial it is stated that the people of Judah install Azariah as king in his place (v. 21). A crown prince normally succeeds at the death of his father. The statement indicates that Azariah begins to rule while his father is still alive; Amaziah continues to be titular king. The instability of his position is indicated by the measures he takes to secure his rule (14:5) and by the fact that he is driven into exile and executed (v. 19). Discontent mounts following this

18. It was located in district II of Solomon's administration (cf. 1 Kings 4:9). Beth Shemesh was situated on the southern side of the valley to control access to the interior of Judah.

humiliation inflicted by Jehoash. The conspirators include highly positioned political and military people, since even fortified Lachish proves to be unsafe.

The fate of Amaziah after his capture by Jehoash (14:13) is not stated. Josephus says Jehoash releases him from captivity after the plunder of Jerusalem (*Ant.* 9.202); Kings states that he outlives his protagonist by fifteen years (2 Kings 14:17). The statement that the port of Elath is restored to Judah does not name the subject (v. 22). It appears in the form of an official record, with the obscure statement that this is after the king slept with his fathers.[19] This unnamed king who dies must be Amaziah (NIV); the one who rebuilds Elath must be Azariah, but it is most unusual to refer to his achievements prior to the introduction of his reign in 15:1. Montgomery considers the archival record to be a misplaced item with a clumsy editorial reflection. It is possible the report is found in official records dealing with both Amaziah and Azariah, an indication of their coregency.[20] Amaziah succeeds in gaining control over northern Edom; after his death Azariah achieves the full objective of providing a southern port city on the Gulf of Aqaba. Though control of the port is short-lived (cf. 16:6), it temporarily provides a trade route with south Arabia.

The political power of Judah is totally eclipsed by Israel under the reign of Jeroboam, the successor to Jehoash (14:23−29). The synchronisms for the reign of Jeroboam indicate that political stability and military strength are achieved through Jeroboam's coming to power while his father is still king.[21] The fortunes of the Jehu dynasty rise to impressive heights during the forty-one year reign of Jeroboam (vv. 23−29). His victories reestablish the territorial limits of the reign of Solomon (v. 25; cf. 1 Kings 5:1; 8:65). Lebo Hamath ("entrance to Hamath") is the general area to the south of Hamath providing access to the Euphrates; it may be the modern Lebweh near the source of the Orontes River. The Sea of the Arabah is the area east of the Dead Sea; Amos refers to Karnaim and the valley of the Arabah (Amos 6:13−14).

With the death of Jehoash and the rule of Azariah in Judah, it seems the royal houses of Samaria and Israel come to a new level of cooperation.[22] Vast areas of productive agricultural land, from the prairies of Bashan (Amos 4:1) to the plantations of Carmel (1:1), produce abundant harvests of grain, wine, and oil (Hos. 7:14). The Transjordan caravan routes are under Israelite control as well as the Jezreel Valley and the Sharon Plain.

---

19. Montgomery, *The Books of Kings*, 442−43. This is indicated by the emphatic pronoun at the start of the sentence (*hw'*).

20. Thiele, *Mysterious Numbers of the Hebrew Kings*, 115.

21. This coregency is discussed in the chronology of appendix B.

22. Aharoni et al., *The Carta Bible Atlas*, 103.

The closing summary of Jeroboam's reign is difficult both textually and historically (14:28–29). The Hebrew text says that Damascus and Hamath are restored "for Judah in Israel" (*lyhwdh bysrʾl*). The phrase may be read as a concession that Judah is subservient to Israel, the result of Jehoash's defeating Amaziah. A state named *yʾdy* is found in an Aramaic inscription from Samʾal in north Syria,[23] leading to the suggestion that Hamath in Yaudi is captured for Israel (NEB, NIV). Cogan and Tadmor assert that the identification of *ywhdh* (Judah) with *yʾdy* "can no longer be maintained," because in Akkadian inscriptions *Iaudi* always refers to Judah, and kings of *yʾdy* are always said to be of Samʾal.[24] The least change of the text is to read "Judah and Israel," with the interpretation that the two countries are allies in receiving tribute from Hamath and Damascus.[25] Ahab had established preferential commercial relations with Damascus (1 Kings 20:34); Jeroboam is able to restore that measure of economic control, and it must be assumed that Judah shares in the prosperity of Israel until Assyria begins to exert pressure on Israel in the middle of the eigth century.

 **FULFILLMENT OF THE prophetic word.** The tension the Deuteronomistic Historians feel in describing the Israelite survival of the Aramean threat and the subordination of Judah illustrates the mystery of God's mercy. Though Jehoash and Jeroboam continued in the apostasy of Jeroboam son of Nebat, they are extremely successful politically. The Judean kings are said to have done what is right in the opinion of Yahweh, but both Joash and Amaziah end in disgrace and are assassinated by members of their own court.

This whole segment is concerned with the fulfillment of the prophetic word. The three strikes of the arrows find their fulfillment in the three attacks against the Arameans (13:18, 25). More important, the promise to Jehu that his descendants will rule for four generations is shown to be true in spite of the idolatry of the northern kings (10:30). Amaziah faces the hostility of his countrymen from the start; though he does exercise constraint in securing his rule (13:5–6), following the directives of the covenant that the innocent not be punished, he can only be said to have done good to the measure of his father Joash. He finally dies by conspiracy in exile in Lachish (14:19), shar-

---

23. Donner and Röllig, *Kanaanäische und Aramäsche Inschriften*, #24, 2.

24. Cogan and Tadmor, *II Kings*, 162.

25. M. Haran, "The Rise and Decline of the Empire of Jeroboam ben Joash," *VT* 17 (1967): 296–97.

ing in the judgment that befell his father. The Israelite kings, by contrast, experience success and the restoration of territory (13:25; 14:25) in spite of their apostasy. The first of these is assured by Elisha, the second by the prophet Jonah. In spite of its disobedience, Israel receives divine mercy—its destiny according to the word of the prophets.

The material and organization of the chapter invites inquiry into the process of composition, which does have different outcomes, as seen in the different text versions. Gray suggests that the account of the attack of Amaziah against Joash belonged to northern sources (14:8–16), resulting in a repetition of the regnal summary of Joash when it was incorporated in the history of Amaziah.[26] This episode appears to have belonged to a northern source, referring to Beth Semesh as belonging to Judah (v. 11), but that does not explain the organization of the narrative. The episode is about Jehoash defending his territory against the hostile challenge of Amaziah. The repetition of the regnal summary of Joash is essential to facilitate the transition back to the life of Amaziah (vv. 15–17) and the usual regnal summary of his reign (vv. 18–22).[27] The narrative returns to the northern kingdom with the usual summary of Jeroboam II (vv. 23, 28–29) and the unusual inclusion of the prophetic word of Jonah (vv. 25–27). The method of the prophetic historians is to demonstrate the fulfillment of the prophetic words of Elisha and Jonah. The report is creatively composed from a variety of sources.

The theological explanation for the restoration of Israel is that God in his freedom shows mercy through the preaching of Jonah, the prophet from Gath Hepher, a town on the border of Zebulun (cf. Josh. 19:13). The bitter affliction of Israel probably recalls the Aramean oppression experienced in the days of Hazael and Ben-Hadad (2 Kings 13:3–4). At that time Israel was left without a leader who could deliver them (14:26).[28] Yahweh extends his mercy to preserve Israel during the days of Jeroboam. The terse presentation of the long and notable reign of Jeroboam is not proportionate to his actual accomplishments in political and military affairs. As with Omri, renowned political achievements are regarded as insignificant because they are compromised by following in the sins of Jeroboam son of Nebat.

The Deuteronomistic prophets are inspired to interpret political events according to the blessings and curses of the covenant. Jehu is blessed for his annihilation of the Baal cult in Israel. An Aramaic inscription found at Tel Dan

---

26. Gray, *I & II Kings*, 602–3.

27. The requirement of the transition is seen in the abbreviated version found in the Old Greek text.

28. For the expression "whether slave or free," see comments on 1 Kings 14:10. The metaphor is a way of referring to qualified leadership.

(Tel el-Qâdī, between Hazor and Damascus) gives testimony to the extensive territorial expansions of the later kings of the Jehu dynasty. The inscription is in two fragments that cannot be related in any conclusive fashion.[29] The inscription makes reference to a king of Israel and the "house of David" (bytdwd). Pottery found at the same level as the fragments date them to the late ninth century or the beginning of the eighth century. Assuming the inscription was made by an Aramean king, the most likely candidate is Hazael; the author claims to have killed a king of Israel and of Judah, described as the "house of David."[30] The only king of Israel who matches the fragment of the name preserved is Joram (son of Ahab), and the likely king of Judah is his ally Ahaziah (son of Jehoram). The candidates capable of later destroying this stele set up by a victorious Aramean king are Jehoash and his son Jeroboam.[31] The broken stele is a testimony to these distant intrusions into the territory of Damascus.

There are difficulties with historical reconstruction for the broken stele. The biblical record makes Jehu, not Hazael, responsible for the deaths of Joram and Ahaziah. But it would not be unusual for an Aramean king to claim responsibility, regarding Jehu as his agent in defeating Israel at Ramoth Gilead. Wesselius has proposed that the author of the stele is actually Jehu, writing in Aramaic as a vassal of Aram Damascus.[32] This hypothesis is also unconvincing. The author of the stele claims that Hadad (an Aramean weather god) made him king; Kings, by contrast, tells us Jehu destroyed the Baal temple under the ruse of serving Baal (10:18). Though Jehu may have served Baal along with Yahweh, the hypothesis that the Tel Dan stele is the first royal inscription of Israel to be discovered is scarcely convincing.[33] The biblical record testifies to Hazael decimating the territory of Jehu (10:32–33), though at other times there was some type of alliance between Aram and Israel.[34] The stele does testify to the expansion of Israel to distant

---

29. The first fragment, apparently a part of a large monumental inscription, was found in July, 1993; the second fragment, in two pieces, was found in June, 1994.

30. For a defense of this expression as an Aramaic territorial expression for Judah see Gary A. Rendsburg, "On the Writing bytdwd in the Aramaic Inscription from Tel Dan," IEJ 45 (1995): 22–25.

31. This is the tentative historical reconstruction of Avraham Biran and Joseph Naveh, "The Tel Dan Inscription: A New Fragment," IEJ 45 (1995): 8–11.

32. Jan-Wim Wesselius, "The First Royal Inscription from Ancient Israel: The Tel Dan Inscription Reconsidered," SJOT 13 (1999): 168–69.

33. For an evaluation of the issues see Bob Becking, "Did Jehu Write the Tel Dan Inscription?" SJOT 13 (1999): 191–201.

34. Anson Rainey proposes a passive form for the word "kill" in Old Aramaic; in his translation the author of the stele does not claim to have personally dispatched the kings of Israel and Judah (The Sacred Bridge, 213).

northern territories during the times of Jehoash and Jeroboam, the blessed descendants of Jehu.

Prophetic perspective on moral violations. Such political influence and power bring with it greed and corruption that come under the vigorous condemnation of the eighth-century prophets. Hosea gives a summary as a preface to a series of judgments proclaimed against Israel:

> Hear the word of Yahweh, Israelites
> Indeed Yahweh has a dispute with the inhabitants of the land
> For there is no integrity and no mercy and no knowledge of God
>   in the land
> Swearing, lying, murdering, stealing, committing adultery
> They break out—blood everywhere—and they strike down.
> Therefore the land dries up and all its inhabitants are enfeebled.
> Along with the wild animals and birds of the sky and even fish of the
>   sea, they are swept away. (Hos. 4:1–3)[35]

The chastisement of the prophet is presented as a lawsuit ("dispute") that Yahweh has against Israel for flagrant violations of the covenant. Though attention is immediately directed toward the priest (Hos. 4:4), the "inhabitants of the land" is general and comprehensive for all sectors of society who appear in the following chapters—priest, prophet, king, prince, people, man, woman, child, and even the animals. The words "integrity," "mercy," and "knowledge of God" all designate elements of the covenant faith. The covenant vow was to be a genuine commitment kept with integrity, kindness, and an understanding of the God of the covenant.

The covenant was conceived as a personal relationship with God that affected all other relationships. Failure to understand God led to crimes against humanity and nature enumerated by the prophet (Hos. 4:2). The first five items are a summary of what are usually called the Ten Commandments. "Swearing" or "breaking the oath" is to use the name of God in vain, denying that he is the only and uncompromising deity (Exod. 20:1–7); "lying" is to make false representation with another person (20:16). "Murdering, stealing, committing adultery" are three fundamental violations of human life and addressed in the covenant law (20:13–15).

Two verbs in Hosea describe such violent activity. They will "break out" in anger, and they "will strike" down in violence; blood is shed everywhere (Hos. 4:2b). The ambiguity of the words makes them inclusive of a variety of actions in destroying the life of others. The prophet is likely talking about

---

35. Translation by Francis I. Andersen and David Noel Freedman, *Hosea: A New Translation with Introduction and Commentary* (AB 24; Garden City, N.Y.: Doubleday, 1980), 331.

the shedding of innocent blood by official action. Shedding of innocent blood is the ultimate crime in the eyes of the prophets, symbolizing the rebellion against God in the destruction of human beings made in his image and representing him on earth.

The violation of the covenant also has implications for the earth (Hos. 4:3). When covenant virtues—integrity, mercy, and knowledge of God—are lacking, the disorder affects all creation. God's covenant with Noah included all of the earth (Gen. 9:12–16); humans and all other creatures were committed to divine providence. Violation of the covenant brings the entire creation under judgment; even animals suffer under the violence. The prophet Isaiah looks forward to the day when there will be no pain or destruction in the entire domain of God (Isa. 11:6–11). The "drying up of the land" and the mourning of its inhabitants is a wordplay often used by the prophets (cf. Joel 1:10–12a). When there is a mourning for drought, the people are said to wail and be disgraced, while plants are said to dry up or whither. Judgment for violence of the covenant resulted in ruination (Hos. 4:3). Land dries up and withers, and the living creatures (animals, birds and fish) "are swept away." The denizens of the three great regions of the earth are specified: land, air, and water. Isaiah looks to the day when the chaos of universe will be reversed and the order of creation restored.

The moral violations of Israel at the end of the Jehu dynasty demand prophetic judgment against its leadership, as pronounced by the Deuteronomistic Historians. Their task is to explain the delay of judgment for these covenant violations. This may explain the inclusion of the name of Judah in the context of the extensive northern expansions of Jeroboam (2 Kings 14:28). Writing from a Judean perspective, the Deuteronomistic Historians include Judah in the experience of divine grace during the most splendid period of power after David and Solomon.[36] At the same time they acknowledge that Judah is within the political influence of Israel.

The coming day of the Lord according to Amos. Prosperity and political success must invariably be regarded as gifts of God. Divine mercy is the only explanation not only for the survival of the dynasty of Jehu, but also for its unrivaled wealth and prosperity. This can be described as the "day of the LORD," the time when God defeats the enemies of the covenant people and grants them the abundance of his great storehouse. Amos also knows that there will come a "day of the LORD" that will bring vengeance on Israel as the enemy of God (Amos 5:18–20). This announcement of an inescapable judgment day is preceded by a proclamation of the funeral of Israel. Though Israel is in a time of great prosperity, the prophet from Tekoah in Judah

---

36. Haran, "The Rise and Decline of the Empire of Jeroboam ben Joash," 296.

makes his way to the shrine at Bethel, where he announces the death of the nation (5:1–17). He called on those gathered to worship at the altar to lament; they are attending their own funeral.

In a pattern of repetitions that calls attention to the divine presence, Amos declares the cause of Israel's death (Amos 5:1–17). He expresses lamentation, exhortation, and accusation as he declares the power of the name of Yahweh. His lament is like that of David for Saul (2 Sam. 1:17); Israel has fallen, just like Saul on the battlefield of Gilboa. Israel refuses to seek Yahweh; instead, in violation of the covenant, they have turned justice to bitterness. The worst sins committed concern the greed of accumulating wealth. The Creator of the galaxies, the Lord of the starfields, the universe maker, will not allow such atrocities to go unnoticed.[37] His name is to be praised in judgment. Note the chiastic construction of this section of Amos:

A Lamentation (Amos 5:1–3)
  B Exhortation (5:4–6)
    C Accusation (5:7)
      D Hymn (5:8a-c)
        E "Yahweh is his name" (5:8d)
      D' Hymn (5:9)
    C' Accusation (5:10–12)
  B' Exhoration (5:14–15)
A' Lamentation (5:16–17)

Divine justice will not leave unpunished the blood that is shed everywhere. The reputation of Yahweh, the majesty of his name, is at stake. The "prosperous" (Amos 5:13),[38] those with skill and success, will be silent in that time. Silence is a euphemism for death.[39] The day of Yahweh for Israel will be one of inevitable extinction. Its delay is like that of flight from the mouth of the lion right into the path of a bear; the fugitive finally reaches home, but instead of home being a refuge, he is bitten by a snake in the wall (5:19–20). "The day of the LORD" for Israel will be nothing but darkness.

In the days of Amos, the rich and prosperous reject the preaching of the prophet. Amaziah, the priest at Bethel, expels him from the territory; the land cannot contain this kind of speech (Amos 7:10–13). Amos does not leave without protest and a proclamation of judgment against Jeroboam. He is not a prophet or the son of a prophet; rather, he is a herdsman and farmer

---

37. These phrases are drawn from the lyrics of Bruce Cockburn.
38. Note that the NIV uses the translation "prudent" here.
39. Gary V. Smith, "Amos 5:13: The Deadly Silence of the Prosperous," *JBL* 107 (1988): 291.

of sycamore figs (7:14–15). He is at Bethel under divine compulsion; the lion of Judah (Yahweh) has roared (3:3–8); he is compelled to pronounce the death of Israel. The wife of the priest will be driven to prostitution, and their children will die in battle (7:17). Amaziah himself will die in exile, while foreigners apportion his land for themselves.

God's mercy as seen through the prophet Jonah. Divine mercy delays judgment against the greedy and corrupt nation. One of the great prophetic ironies is that Jonah proclaims such mercy to a fraudulent and oppressive people. Jonah is named as a nationalist prophet who supports the military ambitions of Israel as the word of Yahweh against the enemies of Israel (2 Kings 14:25). Jonah is the prophet who finds it impossible to rejoice in mercy because of the repentant Assyrians (Jonah 3:6–4:1), but who can proclaim prosperity to wicked Israel. Mercy to repentant Assyria is evil for Jonah, but mercy to unrepentant Israel is his mission, at least as stated in the only historical note he receives in the Deuteronomistic History (2 Kings 14:25).

The author of Jonah plays on the word evil. He is called to warn an evil people (Jonah 1:2); when he finally does announce judgment against Assyria, they repent, even to the point of their animals fasting and wearing coarse clothes (3:7). They turn from their evil in the hope that God will relent in his judgment (v. 8). When God sees their repentance, he turns from the evil of judgment that is destined for Nineveh (v. 10). Nineveh's escaping of judgment is evil for Jonah, the greatest of evils (4:1).[40]

Jonah knows well that the name of Yahweh expresses his primary characteristic as mercy. When the Israelites sinned at the time of the golden calf, the name of Yahweh was revealed as meaning "he will be merciful" (Ex. 33:19; 34:6). This significance of the divine name is celebrated by singing it in praise (Ps. 103:8). Jonah has good reason to flee; he knows from this history of Israel at Mount Sinai, and the history of King Jeroboam, that God is merciful to sinners (Jonah 4:2). Jonah can proclaim mercy to a sinful people, but he finds it a complete travesty of good order when applied to the despotism of Nineveh. Jonah prefers death to the thought that Nineveh might escape divine justice for its brutal treatment of all the victims that have suffered in the advance of its armies.

The lesson of the gourd does nothing to change the sentiments of the prophet (Jonah 4:5–9). The mercy of the gourd is fitting, but when it withers and the hot wind blows, Jonah again would rather choose death. Jonah feels it is justified and right that God should spare a mere gourd that could give him some small comfort; he is unwilling, however, to spare a repentant city of

---

40. It is most unfortunate that most translations paraphrase this verse so the connection of the word "evil" is lost. Judgment is evil for God; mercy is evil for Jonah.

120,000 people, not to speak of the many cows (who also repent!). The author of Jonah expresses how difficult it is to understand the lessons of the mercy and justice of God. God is not a respecter of persons. Ninevites who repent will receive forgiveness. Israelites who do not repent will receive judgment.

The Deuteronomistic prophets have a sound theology of divine mercy. They are true to historical events as they know them, and they interpret them accordingly. Israel suffers under the oppression of the Arameans, particularly after Jehu decimates the entire leadership of the former regime, because of their failure to remove the idolatrous shrines (2 Kings 13:3–4). At the same time, God grants them mercy in spite of their failure to reform their ways (v. 5). This mercy extends to the oppressions of greed and wickedness against their own people. The nation is never more powerful or prosperous than the days of Jeroboam (14:23–27), days in which the prophet Amos is commissioned to proclaim Israel's end because they "turned justice to bitterness" (Amos 5:7). The word of Yahweh to Jehu stands firm (2 Kings 10:30), but not more than four generations (15:11–12).

THE QUALITY AND **risk of mercy in the context of justice.** The tension of mercy and justice is particularly evident in the account of the dynasty of Jehu. This is a time of judgment well deserved, since there can be no pretense that Israel has kept the covenant in exclusive worship of God. At the same time, justice includes deliverance and mercy.

There is a double side to justice in covenant theology. Justice is not only the process of establishing an indictment for offenses; it includes the restoration that should result for the victim as a result of the decision. The judge was a helper or deliverer.[41] Yahweh is just such a deliverer in his judgment against the perpetrators of the Baal cult. Deliverance is experienced as an undeserved mercy by the successors of Jehu, who receive unmerited blessing for several generations under Jehoahaz (2 Kings 13:5), Jehoash (13:25), and Jeroboam (14:25–27). Such deliverance is a mercy received in spite of the continuing idolatrous practices at the Bethel shrine. As taught by Jonah in relation to Israel, the Deuteronomistic Historians show that mercy is the primary characteristic of God. Judgment that God may bring against evil is only that mercy may yet be possible for those who seek to know him as their God.

The message of Jesus is that the primary characteristic of God is his mercy. Secular society has a partial assessment of the function of mercy, or of justice as deliverance and recompense for victims. Human perception of justice

---

41. For a discussion, see G. Liedke, "שׁפט (*richten*)," *THAT*, 1001–3.

takes its usual starting point as some form of equal treatment. Justice is punishment meted out for a debt to society; crimes are not perceived as violence against individuals but as an insult to the good order established by government. The courts must determine a sentence defensible as fair for conviction of a crime, with all due consideration of rights for the offender. Justice as a mercy or deliverance for the victim is not given consideration. This is not justice as understood by biblical covenant; God is just because he brings deliverance to his people when he brings judgment on offenders.

Justice can mean that human life must be taken, by lawful authority, in order to prevent the perpetuation of violence. The Omride dynasty was infamous for its killing of the prophets in the interests of perpetuating the power of the Baal cult and the control of imperial power. The attempt of Athaliah to seize the throne of Judah by killing all eligible heirs to the throne was but another example of her mother's violence exemplified in the seizure of Naboth's vineyard. Jehu was anointed as the deliverer from such violence, and in the process exercised much killing of his own. When a life is taken, it can never be thought that justice is to take life in turn. Life is taken to make peace possible; it is the responsibility of courts and law enforcement to protect the innocent. This is justice in the positive sense of providing safety from offenders.

The problem of law enforcement is that the enforcers may be as guilty of violence and wrong as those they seek to punish. Such was the case with Jehu; worship at the shrines continued to flourish, and the goals of the covenant were not realized. Mercy extended to Jehu and his violent ways, as he did provide deliverance from Baal for which he was ordained. Such exercise of violence in the interests of justice can never be the jurisdiction of the church. The church is never required to be deliverer, the agency responsible for the control of violent actions.

Jesus teaches his followers to love their enemies and pray for those who persecute them (Matt. 5:43—44). The followers of Jesus can be no less generous than their Father in heaven in impartiality (v. 48); they must have the integrity of God himself. He makes his sun to shine on all, both the bad and the good, and he provides rain for the just and the unjust (v. 45). If Christian love is limited to returning the love of others, then Christians cannot be distinguished from the practices of the ungodly (v. 46). Lamech could demand that revenge for him be enacted seventy-seven times (Gen. 4:24), but Jesus requires that his followers grant forgiveness until seventy-seven times (Matt. 18:21—22). The character of God is revealed in mercy shown to his unworthy people, as seen in the preaching of Jonah. Such mercy cannot be limited to one race or group. The mercy of God is available for all, just as the sun and the rain.

Mercy particularly requires care for the needy and dependent. In the society of Jehoash and Jeroboam, poverty and dependency are caused by injustice and a violation of covenant loyalty. In economic terms, justice is a heavenly demand; nothing less than full compensation for losses incurred can be considered justice. Care for the dependent, such as widows and orphans, is a justice issue, not a question of mercy (e.g., Isa. 1:16–17). But instead of justice, the leaders of Israel in their greed demand more at the expense of the poor (e.g., Amos 4:1); the leaders of Judah usurp property through economic power (Isa. 5:8; Mic. 2:1–2) and strip the skin and flesh of the poor (Mic. 3:1–3).

The mystery of mercy. Generations in Israel enjoy God's mercy before the warnings of judgment are fulfilled. The Deuteronomists explain this as God's mercy in time of a failure of leadership and the promise of divine preservation (2 Kings 14:26–27). They do suffer punishment for their sins at the hands of the Arameans (13:3–6), but they receive the promise of deliverance from Elisha (13:18–19, 22–25). Mercy is granted to Israel and Judah, but it does not extend to the lower classes and the needy in the land. Mercy makes the powerful more rich and exacerbates conditions for the poor. While God makes his sun to shine on the just and unjust, unjust leaders turn the mercy of God into oppression against the weak.

Mercy has a risk and a price; mercy allows evil to be perpetuated and puts vulnerable people at risk. How should the Christian church deal with offenders guilty of violent crimes, deemed by many to be at risk of offending again? This pressing question forces its way to the front of the Canadian justice system in the case of the notorious killer known as Karla Homolka. Homolka was convicted of killing her own sister and two other teenage girls as an accomplice in the crimes of her former husband, Paul Bernardo. Bernardo was declared a dangerous offender, with no promise of release, but Homolka served her full term agreed upon in a plea bargain for her testimony to convict Bernardo.

People like Homolka pose a challenge for communities, but especially for churches.[42] God is forgiving and accepting of all who desire change; churches declare that everyone is welcome. What would be sufficiently convincing to invite Homolka to be welcomed in a church? Some believe that the church is the best place for offenders to integrate back into the community. Tim Newell, governor of Grendon Prison in Grendon Underwood, Buckinghamsire, England, says the process "can be greatly helped by partnerships with faith communities, and that society will be safer as a result. The Board of Social Responsibility of the Church of England states that the process of

---

42. The following reflections and quotations are those of John Longhurst, "Welcoming Ex-cons Can Challenge Churches," *Winnipeg Free Press* (June 11, 2005), E9.

restoration, mediated through a congregation, can be a vital part of that change."[43] Reaching out to such offenders demands both vigilance and risk.

In a program created to prepare the church to deal with sex offenders, the Church of England Child Protection Advisory Service has adopted three key principles. The church must establish a contract with the offender, clearly delineating the boundaries to be observed when attending church; the church must work closely with the police and other agencies; there must be professional and ongoing assessment of the individual. Mennonites in Ontario have pioneered a program called Circles of Support and Accountability. Eileen Henderson, a volunteer in the program, said in a BBC interview that "some of these guys aren't very nice characters. But even with them you see small changes, small growth, small miracles. These people have done horrendous things, but you see glimpses of the human."

More difficult is a situation where abuse takes place within the church by church workers. Sue Jackson, herself sexually abused by a church youth worker, says, "There is a profound lack of ability to handle power, manipulation, and abuse in healthy ways in the church. Offenders cleverly put responsibility and guilt onto everyone else. They make other people responsible. Christians, with an overdeveloped sense of duty and responsibility, can get sucked into that too."

Sexual exploitation was part of the violence done in Israel during the days of Jeroboam, when Jonah was preaching mercy and expansion of the empire. Amos cited the violence done to Israel by the nations all around as a means of coming to address the violence within Israel. Among his charges of pursuit of the poor, he says, "father and son use the same girl and so profane my holy name" (Amos 2:7). The nature of the offense need not be further defined. While God showed mercy to Israel, the wealthy drank the wine of fines and exploited the vulnerable. Mercy did not change Israel; mercy was presumed or guilt denied even while the prophetic warning declared the judgment of death on the nation to be inevitable.

Mercy does not nullify the truth of the Deuteronomistic Historians that there is divine retribution, that we reap what we sow, as the friends of Job were at pains to prove (Job 4:8). The intervention of mercy does not permit the principle to be predictable in immediate retribution or particular cases, as the friends of Job presumed. The history of Israel does not demonstrate that mercy comes to those who worship at Jerusalem and judgment to those that worship at Bethel and Dan. Though Joash and Amaziah both support worship at the temple, both suffer humiliating defeat before the armies of

---

43. This statement is made in a paper called "Meeting the Challenge: How Churches Should Respond to Sex Offenders" (July 29, 1999).

Arameans and Israelites, and both end up being assassinated by members of their own court. These events do not support the idea that the reason for defeat is failure to worship at the temple only or that support of the temple brings victory and prosperity. At best it may be possible to infer that blessing comes to Israel in its relationship with Judah (2 Kings 14:28), but the reading of history itself testifies to the truth that right must be done for its own sake, without the expectation of immediate reward.

An example of the mystery of faith and prosperity is the story of Aaron Feuerstein and his textile mill in Lawrence, Massachusetts.[44] When the mill burned down on December 11, 1995, Feuerstein could have taken the $300,000,000 in insurance money and walked away into a comfortable retirement. What happened has been described as incomprehensible in the world of business. At seventy years of age he told his three thousand workers he would rebuild the factory and pay them until they could return to work. The decision cost more than $25,000,000 in wages and benefits. Today the mill is up and running again, manufacturing Polartec, a highly regarded lightweight thermal material. Feuerstein, an observant Jew, rebuilt his mill because of his faith. In an interview he quoted the first-century Talmudic scholar Hillel: "In a situation where there is no righteous person, try to be a righteous person." His workers were depending on him, the community was depending on him, his customers and family were depending on him.

The actions of Feuerstein earned him the sobriquet the "Mensch of Malden Mills" (mensch is a Yiddish word for a man with backbone). The story, however, does not have a fairy tale ending. Malden Mills ended up filing for Chapter Eleven protection, struggling to service debt from rebuilding, suffering from loss of market share after the fire and from a sluggish retail market. There is no real connection between faithfulness and financial success. Fine Christians can lose their shirts while scoundrels have eminent success. God is the author of all good, but how that good is experienced in particular circumstances is part of the mystery of mercy.

A business expert, commenting in the New York Times about the financial woes besetting Feuerstein's company following the fire, suggested that his "desire to take principled action somehow blinded him to thinking long term." According to Rabbi Avi Shafran, writing on the website of Aish HaTorah, an international network of Jewish educational centers commented that "she had it exactly wrong of course. Long term was precisely what he was thinking." Immediate results often make no sense in terms of reward and retribution.

44. This story with pertinent observations is related by John Longhurst, "The Mystery of Religious Beliefs and Financial Success," The Winnipeg Free Press (Nov. 15, 2003), E14.

The long-term thinking of the prophets. The presentation of the reigns of Joash and Amaziah of Israel, and Jehoash and Jeroboam of Israel, are told from the viewpoint of long-term thinking. It is important to do right because of the long term, not because of immediate results. According to the prophetic historians, Joash and Amaziah of Judah have the right goals in mind, even though the immediate results for each of them are disastrous. The kings of Israel, particularly Jehoash and Jeroboam, are eminently successful politically, but their reigns receive no commendation in the Deuteronomistic History. Worship at the temple and the values of the covenant are of much more worth than immediate economic success for a few. For the prophets Amos and Hosea, the violence done to the people through violating the covenant is intolerable; in the long term it will bring about the death of Israel. "As a shepherd saves from the lion's mouth only two leg bones or a piece of an ear, so will the Israelites be saved" (Amos 3:12).

The religious leaders of Israel appear to be scarcely aware of their grievous sin in making God's mercy an occasion for the imposition of injustice to the poor. The response of Amaziah the high priest is that there is no place for Amos in Jeroboam's kingdom (Amos 7:10). It may be possible to drive Amos from Israel, but it is not possible to avert the long-term consequences (7:11, 17). Long term is what the prophets are thinking; immediate and lavish material gains achieved with disregard to the injury done to the powerless will bring death to the nation in just one generation.

The prophetic warnings of judgment against the oppressive rich are continued for the church. In the visions of the last plagues, the apostle John sees the judgment of Babylon, the great representative of wealth and oppression in the world (Rev. 18:2–3). The safety of the church depends on her having no association with this Babylon and its sins (vv. 4–8). Babylon the Great will receive double for all the evil she has afflicted on others. Those who enjoy the wealth of this great harlot will lament when they see her smoke ascending, destroying the vast wealth accumulated.

Individual Christians and congregations by necessity are a part of this great and greedy commercial venture. They must be vigilant in using such wealth to seek first the kingdom of God. This is the only way to dissociate from Babylon, to avoid participating in her sins (Rev. 18:4). Seeking first God's kingdom in the wealth of this world is a daily discipline, a continous and conscious choice to use money and resources to further the values of the kingdom of God and to bring others into that kingdom. The choices are not easy, and they are not without compromise. The mercy of God is to be found for the motives of those who participate in the economy of the great harlot, as they are in this world, but at the same time we must seek always to bring justice and good news to the weak and the needy.

2 Kings 15:1–38

IN THE TWENTY-SEVENTH year of Jeroboam king of Israel, Azariah son of Amaziah king of Judah began to reign. ²He was sixteen years old when he became king, and he reigned in Jerusalem fifty-two years. His mother's name was Jecoliah; she was from Jerusalem. ³He did what was right in the eyes of the LORD, just as his father Amaziah had done. ⁴The high places, however, were not removed; the people continued to offer sacrifices and burn incense there.

⁵The LORD afflicted the king with leprosy until the day he died, and he lived in a separate house. Jotham the king's son had charge of the palace and governed the people of the land.

⁶As for the other events of Azariah's reign, and all he did, are they not written in the book of the annals of the kings of Judah? ⁷Azariah rested with his fathers and was buried near them in the City of David. And Jotham his son succeeded him as king.

⁸In the thirty-eighth year of Azariah king of Judah, Zechariah son of Jeroboam became king of Israel in Samaria, and he reigned six months. ⁹He did evil in the eyes of the LORD, as his fathers had done. He did not turn away from the sins of Jeroboam son of Nebat, which he had caused Israel to commit.

¹⁰Shallum son of Jabesh conspired against Zechariah. He attacked him in front of the people, assassinated him and succeeded him as king. ¹¹The other events of Zechariah's reign are written in the book of the annals of the kings of Israel. ¹²So the word of the LORD spoken to Jehu was fulfilled: "Your descendants will sit on the throne of Israel to the fourth generation."

¹³Shallum son of Jabesh became king in the thirty-ninth year of Uzziah king of Judah, and he reigned in Samaria one month. ¹⁴Then Menahem son of Gadi went from Tirzah up to Samaria. He attacked Shallum son of Jabesh in Samaria, assassinated him and succeeded him as king.

¹⁵The other events of Shallum's reign, and the conspiracy he led, are written in the book of the annals of the kings of Israel.

¹⁶At that time Menahem, starting out from Tirzah, attacked Tiphsah and everyone in the city and its vicinity, because they refused to open their gates. He sacked Tiphsah and ripped open all the pregnant women.

¹⁷In the thirty-ninth year of Azariah king of Judah, Menahem son of Gadi became king of Israel, and he reigned in Samaria ten years. ¹⁸He did evil in the eyes of the LORD. During his entire reign he did not turn away from the sins of Jeroboam son of Nebat, which he had caused Israel to commit.

¹⁹Then Pul king of Assyria invaded the land, and Menahem gave him a thousand talents of silver to gain his support and strengthen his own hold on the kingdom. ²⁰Menahem exacted this money from Israel. Every wealthy man had to contribute fifty shekels of silver to be given to the king of Assyria. So the king of Assyria withdrew and stayed in the land no longer.

²¹As for the other events of Menahem's reign, and all he did, are they not written in the book of the annals of the kings of Israel? ²²Menahem rested with his fathers. And Pekahiah his son succeeded him as king.

²³In the fiftieth year of Azariah king of Judah, Pekahiah son of Menahem became king of Israel in Samaria, and he reigned two years. ²⁴Pekahiah did evil in the eyes of the LORD. He did not turn away from the sins of Jeroboam son of Nebat, which he had caused Israel to commit. ²⁵One of his chief officers, Pekah son of Remaliah, conspired against him. Taking fifty men of Gilead with him, he assassinated Pekahiah, along with Argob and Arieh, in the citadel of the royal palace at Samaria. So Pekah killed Pekahiah and succeeded him as king.

²⁶The other events of Pekahiah's reign, and all he did, are written in the book of the annals of the kings of Israel.

²⁷In the fifty-second year of Azariah king of Judah, Pekah son of Remaliah became king of Israel in Samaria, and he reigned twenty years. ²⁸He did evil in the eyes of the LORD. He did not turn away from the sins of Jeroboam son of Nebat, which he had caused Israel to commit.

²⁹In the time of Pekah king of Israel, Tiglath-Pileser king of Assyria came and took Ijon, Abel Beth Maacah, Janoah, Kedesh and Hazor. He took Gilead and Galilee, including all the land of Naphtali, and deported the people to Assyria. ³⁰Then Hoshea son of Elah conspired against Pekah son of Remaliah. He attacked and assassinated him, and then suc-

ceeded him as king in the twentieth year of Jotham son of Uzziah.

[31]As for the other events of Pekah's reign, and all he did, are they not written in the book of the annals of the kings of Israel?

[32]In the second year of Pekah son of Remaliah king of Israel, Jotham son of Uzziah king of Judah began to reign. [33]He was twenty-five years old when he became king, and he reigned in Jerusalem sixteen years. His mother's name was Jerusha daughter of Zadok. [34]He did what was right in the eyes of the LORD, just as his father Uzziah had done. [35]The high places, however, were not removed; the people continued to offer sacrifices and burn incense there. Jotham rebuilt the Upper Gate of the temple of the LORD.

[36]As for the other events of Jotham's reign, and what he did, are they not written in the book of the annals of the kings of Judah? [37](In those days the LORD began to send Rezin king of Aram and Pekah son of Remaliah against Judah.) [38]Jotham rested with his fathers and was buried with them in the City of David, the city of his father. And Ahaz his son succeeded him as king.

ISRAEL NOT ONLY survives the Aramean decimation that began with Hazael and Jehu, but for a brief period under Jeroboam II achieves an ascendancy that rivals the kingdom of Solomon. This ascendancy is assisted by a coalition with Azariah king of Judah (792–740 B.C.), whose reign overlaps with a substantial portion of the forty-one year rule of Jeroboam (793–753/2 B.C).[1] The defeat of Edom (14:7) and the capture of Elath (14:22) are both achieved with the assistance of Jeroboam, giving Israel and Judah access to trade on the King's Highway east of Jordan (Num. 20:17; 21:22) and a seaport on the Gulf of Aqabah.

The Reign of Azariah (15:1–7)

AZARIAH IS ALSO known as Uzziah (cf. 15:30, 32, 34); outside of Kings he is known by the latter name (2 Chron. 26–27; Isa. 1:1; 6:1). The difference may have had no significance, because both words from which the names are derived

---

1. See appendix B for the chronological discussion. The synchronism of Azariah indicates the beginning of his sole reign in the twenty-seventh year of Jeroboam (15:1).

(ʿzr and ʿzz) can mean victory or strength. The Chronicler seems to have taken advantage of the synonymity by describing Azariah/Uzziah as a king whose fame spread far and wide, for he was helped marvelously (2 Chron. 26:15). The name of his mother (Jecoliah) similarly means "the LORD [*yah*] has power."

Though Azariah has a long and prosperous reign, his achievements are left unrecorded in the Deuteronomistic History. The single detail of his life for which he is remembered was that he has leprosy (2 Kings 15:5) and thus is required to live in a "free house" (*bêt-haḥopšît*). The significance of this term is not known. Both Josephus (*Ant.* 9.227) and the Targum refer to his living outside the city. In Job the word *ḥopšî* refers to freedom from labor or work after death (Job 3:19); both ancient and modern interpreters have suggested that Uzziah was freed from the duties of the monarchy (NEB). The word also refers to the netherworld in the Baal Epic (*bt ḥptt*); De Moor suggests that the "house of freedom" is antiphrasis for a place of total confinement.[2]

Whatever the specifics of Uzziah's residence, he is unable to perform his administrative and official duties to "the people of the land" (cf. 2 Kings 11:14, 18, 20). This privileged group receives particular services from the king in judicial matters and ritual duties (with leprosy Azariah is not permitted to enter sacred space). Jotham is appointed to carry out the responsibilities of the king in place of his father.

According to Chronicles, Azariah is a militant king who reorganizes the army and develops his weaponry (2 Chron. 26:11–14). He improves the fortifications of Jerusalem and halts the expansions of the Philistine tribes to the south and west (vv. 6–7). The actual military achievements of Uzziah are not preserved with enough precision to be ascertained.

The name "Uzziah" is found in the annals of Tiglath-Pileser.[3] This Uzziah is head of a coalition that battles the Assyrians in the area of Hadrack (north of Hamath). The name is Israelite (not Aramean), but unfortunately no geographical identification for this Uzziah has been preserved. An association of this inscription has been made with another fragmentary tablet that contained an account of a war against *Yaudi*, but Naʾaman has argued convincingly that the latter fragment should be joined to another that belonged to the time of Sennacherib.[4] It is improbable that Uzziah of Judah is head of a coalition of Aramean kingdoms against Tiglath-Pileser.[5]

---

2. KTU 1.4 viii 7; DeMoor, *An Anthology of Texts from Ugarit*, 66.

3. K. Lawson Younger Jr., "The Calah Annals," in *The Context of Scripture*, 2.117A.

4. Nadav Naʾaman, "Sennacherib's 'Letter to God' on his Campaign to Judah," *BASOR* 214 (1974): 25–39.

5. As proposed by Haran, "The Rise and Decline of the Empire of Jeroboam ben Joash," 290–97. The Deuteronomists may have had knowledge of Judah's sharing in tribute received from northern Aramean states, described as "Judah in Israel" (14:12).

There is a peaceful coalition between Azariah and Jeroboam; their control extends into the Transjordan in conducting a census (1 Chron. 5:16–17) and in gaining control over the seaport of Elath (2 Kings 14:22). As the Israelite kingdom begins to disintegrate in the latter days of Jeroboam, Uzziah of Judah may have been viewed as the bearer of divine grace in the northern expansions.

Uzziah's burial is variously said to be with his ancestors (15:7), in the burial field that belongs to the kings (2 Chron. 26:23), and by himself in his own garden (Josephus, *Ant.* 9.227). Inscriptional evidence indicates that the grave of Uzziah was moved.[6] An inscribed plaque in Aramaic and dated to the first century B.C. was discovered in Jerusalem. It states: "Here were brought the bones of of Uzziah, king of Judah. Do not open." The inscription indicates that the bones of Uzziah are located in a solitary tomb. Yeivin has argued that the inscription confirms the burial notice of Chronicles as original;[7] more probable is the observation of Albright that the identification of the solitary grave is based on the datum provided in Chronicles. "The garden of Uzza" (2 Kings 21:18, 26) may have been the burial place of Uzziah.

Disintegration of the Israelite Monarchy (15:8−31)

THE DEATH OF Jeroboam brings an end to the dynasty of Jehu, which was prophesied to continue four generations (10:30). The ascension of Zechariah (15:8) fulfills that prophecy, duly noted in the regnal summary (15:12). The brief reign of Zechariah takes place in the thirty-eighth year of Azariah (v. 8), ending the long alliance of Jeroboam and Azariah.

Social and moral decay, vividly chronicled in Amos, has its effect in the political upheavals that come with the death of Jeroboam. Zechariah rules six months (15:8), and Shallum his successor for one month (15:13). Jabesh is a town in Gilead (Judg. 21:8), and "son of Jabesh" most likely refers to Shallum's place of origin in the Transjordan. Indications are that the political rivalries that follow the death of Jeroboam are territorial, between the tribes on the east and west sides of the Jordan. Menahem, son of Gadi, may have been a Gadite from east of Jordan (2 Kings 15:17; cf. 1 Chron. 5:18). Just fourteen years later Pekahiah is assassinated by Pekah, with the assistance of fifty warriors from Gilead (v. 25). Gilead is a strategic and agriculturally rich territory, recovered by Jeroboam II after decades of Aramean domination. It becomes the base for a new Israelite elite that attempt to seize power in Samaria.

---

6. W. F. Albright, "The Discovery of an Aramaic Inscription Relating to King Uzziah," *BASOR* 44 (1931): 8–10.

7. S. Yeivin, "The Sepulchres of the Kings of the House of David," *JNES* 7 (1948): 30–45.

The assassination of Zechariah takes place at Ibleam according to the Old Greek (v. 10; cf. 9:27), which is often taken to be the correct text (cf. RSV, NEB). This is a change of only one letter from the Masoretic text; the translation "before the people" (NIV) is problematic in that it introduces a late Aramaic word (qᵉbāl) into the Hebrew. In the parallel examples of Menahem (v. 14) and Pekah (v. 25) a place name is provided, and one would expect the same here. A place by name of qᵉbālᶜām, as seems to be suggested by the Masoretic text, is unknown.

Menahem launches an attack from Tirzah against Shallum in Samaria (15:14); Tirzah was fortified by Jeroboam I (cf. 1 Kings 14:17) and was the capital city of Baasha (15:33). Menahem is also said to have attacked Tiphsah (2 Kings 15:16); most translations follow the lead of Old Greek in reading Tappuah (RSV, NEB, NLT). The only Tiphsah known was an important ford on the western bend of the Euphrates, the northern point of the vast kingdom of Solomon (1 Kings 4:24). It was situated at the end of the road that led from Damascus through Tadmor toward the Euphrates.[8] Haran thinks that Menahem does conduct a campaign on the Euphrates in the early part of his reign before Tiglath-Pileser reduces the territories of Jeroboam II.[9]

The notation is connected with the assassination of Shallum (15:13–16) rather than the summary of Menahem's reign (vv. 17–22), indicating that this takes place at the time Menahem siezes the throne. Though political circumstances may have permitted Menahem to conduct a war so distant, the verse is difficult. It says that Menahem strikes Tiphsah and secures all its border areas beyond Tirzah. A reference to Tirzah is incongruent with Tiphsah.[10] Tappuach is located on the border of Ephraim (Josh. 16:8) to the south of Tirzah. If the Old Greek text is followed, Menahem is involved in quelling local resistance to his reign with the same brutality that was characteristic of the Arameans.

Menahem can only achieve and maintain his power through alliance with Pul king of Assyria (2 Kings 15:19–20). Pul is the hypocoristicon by which Tiglath-Pileser is known in later historical writings (cf. v. 29).[11] Assyrian political and economic domination of north Syria and the Phoenician coast is initiated by the conquest of the northern Aramean city of Arpad. Mati-ilu, king of Arpad, was forced to swear a vassal oath of allegiance to Ashur-Nirari V, even

---

8. Aharoni et al., *The Carta Bible Atlas*, #105.

9. Haran, "The Rise and Decline of the Empire of Jeroboam ben Joash," 284–90.

10. Haran proposes that the reference to Tirzah be deleted as a duplicate from v. 14 (ibid., 290). The syntax is problematic, but the text does not say that Menahem "started out from Tirzah" (NIV), as it does in verse 14.

11. Cogan and Tadmor, *II Kings*, 171–72. *Pulu* is a well-attested Assyrian name meaning "limestone (block)" and may have been associated with *Pileser* in the adaption of the nickname.

though he retained power.[12] The ascension of Tiglath-Pileser in 745 B.C. ends Assyrian weakness in the territories west of the Euphrates. According to the Calah recension of the Annals of Tiglath-Pileser, in six years (743–740, 738 B.C.) the monarch conquers and annexes north Syria: Arpad, Unqi, Hadrach, Simmira and its environs, reaching as far as the desert east of Damascus.[13]

The defeat of Arpad is a devastation that impresses the territories of Syria and Israel; over forty years later it still serves as a warning to the citizens of Jerusalem (2 Kings 18:33–34; 19:13). Four years later, in a campaign along the Mediterranean coast, Tiglath-Pileser takes possession of cities in the vicinity of Arvad, subdues Philistia, and turns Gaza into an Assyrian port and "custom house." Assyria is renowned for removing borders, plundering rulers, and deposing the mighty (Isa. 10:13).

Menahem submits to the Assyrians in payment of tribute and in return gains their support so he can secure his kingdom (2 Kings 15:19). This may be required compliance with Assyrian policy, but in view of the violent rivalries for the throne (vv. 16, 25–26) it is more likely that Menahem depends on Assyrian assistance in warfare. The Calah Annals name Menahem as bringing tribute to Tiglath-Pileser;[14] Thiele has made a case for this being in the year 743 B.C., as it immediately follows the section dealing with the events of that year.[15] The inference that Tiglath-Pileser invades Israel is unfounded (NIV, NEB); "Pul the king of Assyria had come" (15:19a) is not the language of invasion (cf. 6:24; 12:17–18; 17:3, 5).

A thousand talents of silver compares well with other sums extracted from vassals by the Assyrians.[16] Since there is no mention of plunder, captives, or deportation in connection with this tribute, most likely it is given

---

12. The inscriptions of Sefire (discovered in a village southeast of Aleppo) record treaties of Mati-ilu, king of Arpad, with neighboring kings (Donner and Röllig, *Kanaanäische und Aramäische Inschriften*, #222A, 1, 3, 14; Hallo and Younger, *The Context of Scripture*, 2.82). The treaty of Mati-ilu with Assur-Nirari V is the only extant document of that Assyrian king; see D. D. Luckenbill, *Ancient Records of Assyria and Babylonia* (Chicago: Univ. of Chicago Press), 1.750.

13. H. Tadmor, *The Inscriptions of Tiglath-Pileser III King of Assyria* (Jerusalem: Israel Academy of Sciences and Humanities, 1994), 27–89; H. Tadmor and M. Cogan, "Ahaz and Tiglath-Pileser in the Book of Kings: Historiographic Considerations," *Bib* 60 (1979): 491–92.

14. Hallo and Younger, *The Context of Scripture*, 2.117A.

15. Thiele, *The Mysterious Numbers of the Hebrew Kings*, 142–45. However the circumstances of Menahem paying tribute and the interpretation of the Assyrian records remain inconclusive. Tadmor states that the tribute referred to in 15:19–20 is paid in 740 B.C. or earlier, with other payments made later with the rest of western vassals; see *The Inscriptions of Tiglath-Pilesar III King of Assyria*, 276.

16. According to the Saba'a Stela, the Mari of Damascus brought 100 talents of gold and 1000 talents of silver to Adad Nirari III (Hallo and Younger, *The Context of Scripture*, 2.114E).

in return for Assyrian military support against Pekah. The vocabulary of the verse suggests this is a payment of fifty shekels (over a pound) of silver for each Assyrian soldier.[17] Fifty shekels was the price of a slave in Assyria at that time.[18] At three thousand shekels to a talent (cf. Ex. 38:25–26), the tribute would pay sixty thousand soldiers.

The ten-year reign of Menahem is followed by a two-year reign of his son Pekahiah (742–740 B.C.). He is assassinated by Pekah, his chief officer, in the citadel of the palace in Samaria (2 Kings 15:25).[19] The citadel is apparently a fortification in the palace complex. The fifty soldiers who assist Pekah would form one military unity with its commanding officer. Pekah is assisted by a military unit from Gilead. His reign of twenty years must overlap with that of Menahem; he apparently has a rival rule in Gilead after the death of Jeroboam II. The nine-year reign of Hoshea (17:1) ends in 723 B.C., when Shalmaneser V of Assyria conquers Samaria and exiles the Israelites.[20] The twenty-year reign of Pekah begins at the same time as that of Menahem (752 B.C.) and ends in 732 B.C. when Hoshea, the last king of Israel, succeeds him.

The year of Pekah's ascension to the throne in Samaria is the same year that King Azariah (Uzziah) dies (15:27; cf. Isa. 6:1). From that point on, the politics of both Damascus and Samaria are dominated entirely by the activities of Tiglath-Pileser (v. 29). During the last days of Pekah (734–732 B.C.), Tiglath-Pileser directs a number of campaigns against Israel in the coastal plain, Galilee, and Transjordan, reducing Israel to the rump state of Samaria ruled by Hoshea as a vassal king.[21] The conquest of Gilead is a continuation

---

17. Hobbs, 2 *Kings*, 199–200. The text says he delivers or makes payment of silver on behalf of Israel; the term "every wealthy man" (*gibbôrê haḥayil*) usually means soldier and probably has the same designation here, making them the recipients.

18. D. J. Wiseman, "The Nimrud Tablets, 1953," *Iraq* 14 (1952): 135, n. 1.

19. The reference to Argob and Arieh in the Masoretic text is unclear. Argob is a territory in Gilead (Deut. 3:4, 14); often the two names are regarded as displaced from verse 29, where they would be associated with Gilead and read as Argob and Havvoth-Jair (Montgomery, *The Books of Kings*, 456). The Greek takes them as the names of two outstanding soldiers from Gilead. They may have been portal figures at the gates of Samaria's palace; Rashi says a golden lion stands in that place.

20. The dates followed here are those of Thiele and adopted by Hallo ("From Qarqar to Carchemish," 174–76). The case for a rival rule was made by H. J. Cook, "Pekah," *VT* 14 (1964): 121–35. The twenty-year reign of Pekah cannot be regarded as a scribal error for two years, as it appears consistent in the biblical synchronisms (cf. 15:32; 16:1). No alternate solution can be offered for dealing with the biblical and Assyrian data in this period; alternate chronologies all make emendations to the chronological data.

21. For a detailed description of the campaigns and the deportations of the Israelites during this period, see K. Lawson Younger, "The Deportations of the Israelites," *JBL* 117 (1998):

of the wars against Damascus and is particularly devastating to Pekah, since that is the heartland of his political power. The conspiracy of Hoshea against Pekah is through the military force of Tiglath-Pileser (v. 30). He removes Pekah in order to establish control over the land of Bit-Humria (Israel).

The territories named as taken by Tiglath-Pileser indicate the main course of the campaign against Israel (v. 29). Ijon is a site on the river of the same name in the fertile valley at the foot of Mount Hermon. Abel Beth Maacah is about fifteen kilometers to the south, just west of Dan in upper Galilee, the modern Abil el-Qamḥ. Janoah is preserved in the names of three modern sites; it is likely located in western Galilee on the road called "the way of the sea" (Isa. 9:1).[22] Kedesh must refer to the northern site by that name, about ten kilometers northwest of Hazor in upper Galilee (cf. Josh. 12:22; 20:7). The territory is summarized in the general reference to Gilead, Galilee, and the whole territory of Naphtali. The campaign is apparently launched from the Beqaʿ Valley in Lebanon, first taking Ijon and Abel Beth Maacah; the armies then turn westward to the foothills above Tyre, assuring a connection to the western bases. From there the armies move southeast, conquer Kedesh, and safely lay siege to Hazor. Forces are sent into all the territories to the south and east (Naphtali and Gilead).

The Reign of Jotham (15:32–38)

THE REIGNS OF Azariah and Jotham overlap with those of the last kings of Israel; the fate of Judah is determined by the vicissitudes of Israel. Jotham becomes king when Azariah is smitten with leprosy (15:5), in the second year of Pekah (15:32). He lives beyond his sixteen-year reign into his twentieth year, when Pekah is assassinated (v. 30). The complexity of the synchronistic data betrays the political turbulence of this period; political struggles lead to various alliances vying for power.

Jotham begins to reign in 750 B.C., ten years before the death of Azariah, and lives beyond the time that he actually retains control over the kingdom. Apparently a pro-Assyrian faction raises Ahaz to the throne in the seventeenth year of Pekah in 735 B.C. (16:1).[23] The sentiments in Judah have shifted; powerful officials have come to regard Israel as a threat and Assyria

---

201–14. In Summary Inscription 13 Tiglath-Pileser claims to have spared only Samaria, a transparent allusion to an annexation that takes place at the same time as Damascus (see Younger and Hallo, *The Context of Scripture*, 2.117G). Summary Inscription 4 refers to his exile of Israel, the death of Pekah, and the installation of Hosea (2.117C, lines 15b–19a).

22. Aharoni et al., *The Carta Bible Atlas*, #146.

23. Thiele dates Jotham from 750 B.C. to 732 B.C., allowing for an accession year as is usual for coregencies.

as a potential ally. Rezin of Aramea and Pekah of Israel attempt to coerce Jotham into an alliance against Assyria (15:37), but Ahaz attempts to gain independence from them through the assistance of the Assyrians (16:5–9). The pro-Assyrian policy effectively ends the reign of Jotham, but it does not deliver Judah; within a generation the armies of Assyria surround Jerusalem, and citizens from Judah are exiled as well.

The reign of Jotham is scarcely independent of either his father Azariah or the domination of the pro-Assyrian forces that put Ahaz into power. Aside from the notation that he exercises royal authority in the place of his father (15:5), the only achievement of his reign given in Kings is that he renovates one of the gateways of the temple (v. 35). Temple repair is of special interest to the worship concerns of the historian; nothing is known of the circumstances requiring repair at this gate. The Upper Benjamin Gate is named as the place where Jeremiah was kept in stocks at the temple (Jer. 20:2). Ezekiel in a vision is transported to the upper, inner gate that opens to the north where he observes the schemes of the temple guards (Ezek. 8:3; 9:2).

Chronicles further mentions that Jotham repairs the wall of Ophel, builds cities in the hill country of Judah, and fortifies the hill country of Judah (2 Chron. 27:3–4). The only war named is a campaign against the Ammonites in defense of Judean boundaries (27:5). The Transjordan defenses may be related to the attacks of the Arameans mentioned in Kings.

Bridging Contexts

ASSYRIAN EXPANSION. Assyrian expansion at the beginning of the eighth century provides relief from the Aramean dominion of Hazael and Ben Hadad III (13:5, 25). When Adad-Nirari assumes full control of the Assyrian kingdom (806 B.C.), he leads a military expedition into Philistia with the intention of punishing the countries who refuse to submit their tribute. He lays siege to Damascus, imposing heavy taxes on its ruler (*mariʾ*), probably Ben Hadad III.[24] In his campaigns the Assyrian monarch claims to have subdued all the lands "up to the great Sea," meaning that all recognize his sovereignty and render the necessary tribute.[25]

The Assyrian domination of Damascus and the surrounding territories allows Jeroboam II to continue the restoration of territory that began under Jehoash of Israel (14:25, 28). The extension of his authority well beyond

---

24. For a translation of the inscription see K. Lawson Younger Jr., "Sabaʾa Stela," in *The Context of Scripture*, 2.114E.

25. This claim is found in the Rimah Stela; see Younger, "Tell Al Rimah Stela" in ibid., 2.114F.

Damascus and throughout the Transjordan perhaps takes place in cooperation with the Assyrian kings.[26] The elite in Samaria prosper, with little awareness of the social breakdown they have created.

Alternately, perhaps the domination of Jeroboam II over Damascus takes
place when Assyrian control of the Aramean territories begins to wane.[27]
The initial prophecy of Amos calls for vengeance against Damascus and
Ammon because they have threshed Gilead and ripped open their pregnant
women (Amos 1:3, 13). The time of these cruelties cannot be specifically
determined, but it may have been during the early days of Jeroboam, when
they are fresh enough in everyone's memory to be a matter of charged emotion. Shalmaneser IV (783–773 B.C.), successor to Adad Nirari III, conducts
a campaign as far as Damascus in the last year of his reign. Under Assur-
Dan III (773–755 B.C.) central Assyrian control grows progressively weaker.
The eponym lists of western campaigns indicate military expeditions go no
further south than Hadrach. Under Assur-Nirari V (755–745) an agreement
is reached with the more northerly region of Arpad. Jeroboam may not have
extended his influence toward Hamath until the last years of his reign, when
the Assyrians have withdrawn from that territory. If that is the case, then the
time between the empire of Jeroboam and the disintegration of Israel is only
a few years.

Isaiah. The events of this chapter are the historical background to the call
of the prophet Isaiah. The year that king Uzziah/Azariah dies (Isa. 6:1) is a
momentous event in the life of this prophet. His vision of the exalted Lord,
his own sense of inadequacy, and his mission of futility to the recalcitrant
leaders of Jerusalem all take place within a concrete historical circumstance.
The death of Uzziah marks the end of a prosperous period in Israel's history.
The chaos in the kingdom of Israel will shortly result in its being absorbed
entirely into the empire of Assyria. The death of Uzziah marks a change in
policy in the kingdom of Judah. The pro-Assyrian strategy of Ahaz brings
Judah into conflict with Pekah and Rezin and also leads Judah decisively
into reliance on Assyria rather than on the Holy One of Israel encountered
in the vision of the prophet. They are trusting in the very nation that will
destroy them (Isa. 10:20).

Isaiah's vision plays a critical role in the word of God to Jerusalem. The
mention of Uzziah's death is much more significant than offering conventional dating. It anchors that vision in Israel's history, much like the inclusion
of the name Pontius Pilate in the Apostle's Creed. It marks a decisive turning

---

26. See W. W. Hallo, "From Qarqar to Carchemish," *Biblical Archaeologist Reader* 2 (1964):
166–69.

27. So Haran, "The Rise and Decline of the Empire of Jeroboam ben Joash," 272–80.

point in God's dealing with Israel.[28] As expressed in the parable of the vine-yard (Isa. 5:1–7), the end of Israel has been divinely determined because of its total disregard for justice and righteousness; its leaders despise the Holy One of Israel (v. 24). Human arrogance will end in utter humilation before Yahweh, who alone is exalted (2:9–11; 17–19).

In his vision Isaiah sees a manifestation of that glory. Initially the prophet sees the divine palace manifest on earth, doorposts and the cloud of glory (Isa. 6:4), but quickly these are transformed into a heavenly scene. In a moment the tip of the robe fills the entire temple, where the King of kings is revealed on the throne surrounded by his fiery attendants declaring the great King to be holy (vv. 1b–3). This holiness is not an ethical quality but the essence of the divine nature, separate from all that is common. The vision provides a the-ological grounding for the inevitable judgment that stands over Jerusalem and its kings.

The vision of the majestic King of kings makes the prophet aware of the utter impotence and sinfulness of his own words as well as those of the people (Isa. 6:5). This is not a barrier to the divine commission. As the hot coal from the heavenly altar touches his lips, he hears the divine voice calling: "Whom shall I send? And who will go for us?" (vv. 7–8). The focus shifts immediately to the prophet's mission to Israel and Judah; he is to dull their minds, stop their ears, and plaster over their eyes, lest by seeing, hearing, and comprehending they will actually repent and be saved. The prophet is the guarantor of complete hardening, the executioner of sinful Israel.

The divine mission is not a universal judgment but is directed toward a particular historical circumstance given in Isaiah's vision. The divine intent of election has become one of destruction (cf. Amos 3:2). Isaiah has experi-enced the eternally present rule of God in all its terrifying majesty and his own rebirth through divine purification and forgiveness, in order that he may perform this act of Israel's destruction. Assyria is the blunt instrument of the divine wrath through which the execution will take place (Isa. 8:6–8; 10:5–6). Before the judgment is complete, the land will be bereft of inhab-itants (6:11–12); Israel's end has come (Amos 8:2).

The destruction of Israel does not simply bring an end to the nation. Just as there is life in a stump when a tree is cut down, so in Israel there remains a holy seed (Isa. 6:13). In the stump is the mystery of the remnant that will return (10:20–23). In the stump resides life that will spring forth as a shoot (11:1); the rule of the ideal king will yet be realized for Israel.[29] The promise

---

28. Childs, *Isaiah*, 54.

29. See H. G. M. Williamson, *Variations on a Theme: King, Messiah and Servant in the Book of Isaiah* (Carlisle, UK: Paternoster, 1998), 30–56, for the development of this motif in Isaiah.

of the ideal king is delivered during the terrifying days when Tiglath-Pileser is advancing against Israel, while Rezin and Pekah attempt to bring Judah into an alliance against him (Isa. 7:1; cf. 2 Kings 15:37).[30] Contrary to the prophet Isaiah and the earlier policy of Jotham, Ahaz chooses not to trust in Yahweh; as a result his kingdom is not secure (Isa. 7:9).

Judah will be shaved by the razor that is hired and its citizens led into exile (Isa. 7:20), but the promise of God's kingdom will stand. The advance of Tiglath-Pileser will turn Gilead and Galilee into Assyrian territories (Isa. 9:1; cf. 2 Kings 15:29). Though Zebulun and Naphtali are brought into contempt, the road toward the sea, the land beyond the Jordan, and Galilee of the nations will yet become glorious. This will happen through the fulfillment of the promise to David in the child who will be born (Isa. 9:6–7). The yoke of slavery will be broken and the weapons of battle removed when the miraculous child begins to rule. The times when the land is brought into contempt will be replaced by times when the land is made glorious. The times of deep humiliation will be turned into times of peace.

The birth of the child is due entirely to the activity of God, as expressed in the passive form of the verbs (Isa. 9:6). This is made explicit by the phrase "the zeal of the LORD Almighty will accomplish this" (9:7). The birth of the king is not primarily portrayed as the arrival of a savior figure.[31] This birth is part of the deliverance that God himself will bring into effect for his people. The provision of the royal figure is God's redemption for Israel. God's purpose is to establish and uphold his kingdom with justice and righteousness from this time and for evermore. The king will inaugurate and maintain God's ideal for the society of Israel. Though Assyria is the rod of God's anger, it will also be part of those high and mighty, whom God will bring low (10:5–15, 28–32). This judgment against the mighty Assyrians (10:33–34) will result in deliverance for Israel (11:1–9).[32]

After this a new ruler will emerge as a second David (Isa. 11:1). His primary role will be to bring justice (vv. 3–5). The poor and the meek will receive a fair hearing unprejudiced by the corruption that more privileged members of society formerly impose on the judicial process. His words will bring about righteousness and faithfulness (vv. 4b–5); this is the work of the ideal king, who will establish the just kind of society demanded by the covenant.

---

30. The mention of the attack of Rezin and Pekah during the reigns of Jotham (2 Kings 15:37) and Ahaz (16:5–7) indicates the overlap of the reign of the two kings and the internal conflict within the rule of Judah; see Thiele, *Mysterious Numbers of the Hebrew Kings*, 132–34.

31. Williamson, *Variations on a Theme*, 33.

32. Ibid., 52.

The Deuteronomistic Historians do not dwell on the eschatological purposes of the kingdom any more than on the political achievements of the individual kings of Israel and Judah. Their concerns are focused on the outward manifestation of faith in worship at the one place that God has ordained. The account of the demise of Israel begins and ends with the kings of Judah responsible for the maintenance of the temple (2 Kings 15:1–7, 32–38). In this respect both can be said to have done what is right, though with the qualification that they continue to tolerate other places of worship (vv. 3–4, 34–35). During the reign of these two kings the dynasty of Jehu ends and the kingdom of Israel self-destructs under internal and external conflicts.

The Deuteronomistic Historians tell the story of Israel's disappearance, which in due course includes Judah as well. For them the failure of worship at the temple is symptomatic of the utter failure of faith in the leaders of the nation. This failure does not bring an end to the promise of the lamp of David (1 Kings 11:36; 15:4; 2 Kings 8:19). The writings of other prophets hold out the hope of that promise when the kingdoms of Israel and Judah have disappeared.

 LIGHT FOR THOSE **in darkness.** History is nothing but the story of the rise and fall of nations, mighty and terrifying in their own time but quickly buried in the sands of time. This theme cannot be better expressed than in the words of Percy Bysshe Shelley in the poem "Ozymandias (1817)."

I met a traveler from an antique land,
Who said:—"Two vast and trunkless legs of stone
Stand in the desert. Near them, on the sand,
Half-sunk, a shattered visage lies, whose frown
And wrinkled lip, and sneer of cold command,
Tell that its sculptor well those passions read
Which yet survive, stamped on these lifeless things,
The hand that mocked them and the heart that fed:
And on the pedestal these words appear:
'My name is Ozymandias, king of kings:
Look on my works, ye Mighty, and despair!'
Nothing beside remains. Round the decay
Of that colossal wreck, boundless and bare
The lone and level sands stretch far away."

In the year that king Uzziah dies, Isaiah sees Yahweh. Uzziah and Jotham preside over one of the most powerful eras in the history of Judah, but one in which entanglements with the powers of this age bring it to a state of complete humiliation. During their time Israel sinks into oblivion, never again to be a force as a nation. Isaiah sees divine deliverance coming through a King of another order. The Gospel writers find the fulfillment of this hope in the birth and work of Jesus. Matthew says that the child should be named Jesus because he will save his people from their sins (Matt. 1:21). In this is fulfilled the word of Isaiah given during those dark days when Israel attacks Judah (Isa. 7:14): "'The virgin will be with child and give birth to a son, and they will call him Immanuel,' which means 'God with us'" (Matt. 21:23). The name Immanuel comes to represent the hope of the kingdom and the promise that Yahweh is at work in the redemption of his people.

The promise of Christmas comes at a dark period in the political history of Israel and Judah. Christians in the northern hemisphere choose to celebrate Christmas at the darkest time of the year, with the anticipation of the return of the sun. This comes to be used as an emblem of the light that dawns with the birth of Jesus. Matthew draws on the words of Isaiah to describe the work of Jesus as a dawning light. Immediately following the temptation, Jesus leaves Nazareth and goes into the region of Galilee among the hills of Zebulun and Naphtali, calling the people to repentance because the kingdom of God has drawn near (Matt. 4:13–17). The people dwelling in darkness see the great light; the light rises on those who live in the land of death (cf. Isa. 9:1–2). The promise of Christmas still comes to a world that lives in the darkness of violence and political turmoil. The circumstances of Uzziah and Jotham reflect well the circumstances in which the hope of the kingdom is proclaimed.

Jesus announces a kingdom of another order, quite the opposite of the kind ruled by Ozymandias, by Uzziah and Jotham, or by Jeroboam, Menahem, and Pekah. It is a kingdom in which those of humble spirit rather than the proud are blessed, where the mourners are comforted, and where the meek inherit the earth (Matt. 5:3–5). Those who hunger after righteousness, are merciful, and are pure in heart become the salt of the earth and the light of the world (5:5–16). The followers of Jesus are the peacemakers, even though they themselves may be persecuted for following values contrary to those of the kingdoms of the world. This is not the sort of kindom that comes through political order; rather, it is the means of bringing peace and justice to the world through words and teaching, as Isaiah said (Isa. 11:4–5). Matthew sees in Jesus the shoot of Jesse, the beginning of a just society where the will of God will be done through the endowment of divine power.

The kingdom proclaimed by Jesus is always about service to others. When John and James come seeking a privileged place in the kingdom, Jesus reminds them that the price for being a part of his kingdom is to give up their lives in following him (Matt. 20:20–23). They do not understand what they are asking or what following Jesus in his kingdom means for them. The kingdoms of this world operate through power (vv. 24–25); in the kingdom of Jesus the mighty are those who serve, even as Jesus himself did not come to be served but to serve and to give his life as ransom for all (vv. 27–28).

Jesus describes the coming of his kingdom as a separation of all people the way sheep are separated from goats (Matt. 25:31–46). The sheep are those who have rendered service in the kingdom of Christ, even though they were completely oblivious to it. The sheep have fed the hungry, shown hospitality to the stranger, clothed the naked, visited those sick and in prison. As much as justice is shown in this way to the needy, it is doing the work of God's kingdom. The goats, by contrast, are those occupied in doing their great deeds; they have their systems of justice, and their justice supposedly has the power to rectify all that is wrong in the world. They do not understand that often their well-intentioned systems of justice further alienate family members and communities. They do little to provide for the many victims caught in ugly situations of violence and pain. They have no part in the divine kingdom.

The religion of modern secular societies does not concern itself with service, with forgiveness and reconciliation. Goals for justice have little to do with victims; crimes are deemed to be against society and against its order of rule, not against individuals who suffer. Goats scoff at reconciliation through forgiveness; the sick, the hungry, the homeless struggle while they grope for their just society. These kingdoms all perish, like those of Jeroboam and Uzziah, because they exist through power rather than the provision of justice and mercy to their people.

Ways to serve in God's kingdom. There are many ways in which the service of God's kingdom can be rendered within the kingdoms of this world. It may be in political office; there are prominent examples of those who have impacted their world through political influence and a commitment to kingdom values. One such notable evangelical was William Wilberforce, a prominent member of the House of Commons in the struggle to abolish the slave trade and slavery itself in the British colonies. In 1787 he helped to found the Society for Effecting the Abolition of the Slave Trade. He was an eloquent and indefatigable sponsor of anti-slavery legislation; his first success came in 1807 with a bill to abolish the slave trade in the British West Indies. In 1823 he became a vice-president of the Society for the Mitigation and Gradual Abolition of Slavery throughout the British Dominions. The Slavery Abolition Act he sought was passed one month after his death on July 29, 1833. Wilberforce was driven by his faith to pursue equality and dignity for all people. This pursuit was not found in the kingdoms of Israel and Judah, even though it was demanded by their covenant. They failed to understand what it meant to worship and serve God, and they failed to bring peace to their people.

Often the work of God's kingdom is found in much less dramatic ways than that of Wilberforce. One such story is that of Harold Park, a Vancouver investor who discovered that there is more to life than living off the proceeds of investments.[33] Harold enjoyed a comfortable stress-free life, playing golf and going to the gym. He discovered that this was not satisfying as a Christian and that the fortunes of this world are volatile. A sharp drop in the stock market brought times of stress and the occasion to reflect on what is valuable and enduring. His focus shifted away from earning money to helping at a drop-in center for street youth in downtown Vancouver. Eventually it led to a position in prison chaplaincy for The Salvation Army in Winnipeg. He worked part time in provincial and federal institutions while completing his seminary training. For Harold there is now nothing more important than helping inmates with their fears and struggles, sharing love and hope with those often forgotten by society.

From a political perspective, the kingdoms of Jeroboam and Uzziah can be regarded as a remarkable success. From the perspective of observing the values of God's kingdom, they are failures, a dark period that comes under divine judgment. Though human kingdoms fail, God's kingdom does not fail. It finds fulfillment in the remnant that turns to God; it finds fulfillment in the proclamation of the Savior who came as the child promised by Isaiah in those dark days. The kingdom of God continues to find expression within the great kingdoms of this world. These kingdoms will crumble, just as surely as all the others before them, but Christ will build his church, and the gates of death will not prevail against it (Matt. 16:18).

---

33. See Harold Park, "Journey to Prison," *Eye Witness* (Otterburne, Manitoba: Providence College, Fall 2003), 3.

2 Kings 16:1–20

❧

I N THE SEVENTEENTH year of Pekah son of Remaliah, Ahaz
son of Jotham king of Judah began to reign. ²Ahaz was
twenty years old when he became king, and he reigned in
Jerusalem sixteen years. Unlike David his father, he did not do
what was right in the eyes of the LORD his God. ³He walked
in the ways of the kings of Israel and even sacrificed his son in
the fire, following the detestable ways of the nations the LORD
had driven out before the Israelites. ⁴He offered sacrifices and
burned incense at the high places, on the hilltops and under
every spreading tree.

⁵Then Rezin king of Aram and Pekah son of Remaliah king
of Israel marched up to fight against Jerusalem and besieged
Ahaz, but they could not overpower him. ⁶At that time, Rezin
king of Aram recovered Elath for Aram by driving out the men
of Judah. Edomites then moved into Elath and have lived
there to this day.

⁷Ahaz sent messengers to say to Tiglath-Pileser king of
Assyria, "I am your servant and vassal. Come up and save me
out of the hand of the king of Aram and of the king of Israel,
who are attacking me." ⁸And Ahaz took the silver and gold
found in the temple of the LORD and in the treasuries of the
royal palace and sent it as a gift to the king of Assyria. ⁹The
king of Assyria complied by attacking Damascus and capturing
it. He deported its inhabitants to Kir and put Rezin to death.

¹⁰Then King Ahaz went to Damascus to meet Tiglath-
Pileser king of Assyria. He saw an altar in Damascus and sent
to Uriah the priest a sketch of the altar, with detailed plans for
its construction. ¹¹So Uriah the priest built an altar in accordance with all the plans that King Ahaz had sent from Damascus and finished it before King Ahaz returned. ¹²When the
king came back from Damascus and saw the altar, he
approached it and presented offerings on it. ¹³He offered up
his burnt offering and grain offering, poured out his drink
offering, and sprinkled the blood of his fellowship offerings on
the altar. ¹⁴The bronze altar that stood before the LORD he
brought from the front of the temple—from between the new
altar and the temple of the LORD—and put it on the north
side of the new altar.

¹⁵King Ahaz then gave these orders to Uriah the priest: "On the large new altar, offer the morning burnt offering and the evening grain offering, the king's burnt offering and his grain offering, and the burnt offering of all the people of the land, and their grain offering and their drink offering. Sprinkle on the altar all the blood of the burnt offerings and sacrifices. But I will use the bronze altar for seeking guidance." ¹⁶And Uriah the priest did just as King Ahaz had ordered.

¹⁷King Ahaz took away the side panels and removed the basins from the movable stands. He removed the Sea from the bronze bulls that supported it and set it on a stone base. ¹⁸He took away the Sabbath canopy that had been built at the temple and removed the royal entryway outside the temple of the LORD, in deference to the king of Assyria.

¹⁹As for the other events of the reign of Ahaz, and what he did, are they not written in the book of the annals of the kings of Judah? ²⁰Ahaz rested with his fathers and was buried with them in the City of David. And Hezekiah his son succeeded him as king.

Original Meaning

THE ACCOUNT OF the sixteen-year reign of Ahaz is considerably longer than that of the fifty-two year reign of Azariah. Unlike Azariah, Ahaz has no particular political accomplishments; under his rule Judah shrinks in influence and independence. The space given to Ahaz is a result of the special interests of the Deuteronomistic Historians, particularly the territorial claims of Judah and developments in temple worship.

These two issues are interrelated through the presence of Tiglath-Pileser. Ahaz depends on this king for his own authority and in turn incurs a heavy financial indemnity with the Assyrians. Ahaz, dependent on their assistance to maintain Judah's independence against Rezin and Pekah, is in no position to retain control over the Transjordan territories, especially the important seaport at Elath (16:6). In order to meet his financial obligations to the Assyrians, Ahaz has to strip the temple of its precious metals (v. 8), even to the extent of removing the bronze from the temple artifacts (vv. 17–18). The Deuteronomistic evaluation of these compromises is best summarized in the condemnation that he is following in the practices of the kings of Israel (v. 3). He not only supports worship at the high places (v. 4), but he corrupts worship at the temple itself.

The relationship of Ahaz to Tiglath-Pileser is not obvious, either in the Deuteronomistic reports or in the mutilated Assyrian records pertaining to the initial campaign into Philistia in 734 B.C. On the one hand, if Ahaz appeals to Tiglath-Pileser before the campaign into Philistia as an initial act of submission to the Assyrian king, he is a willing vassal in opposition to Syria and Israel. On the other hand, if his appeal is made after Judah is subjugated in the campaign, he is simply petitioning his master to come to his aid in time of distress. The bribe (*šōḥad*, 16:8) sent to Tiglath-Pileser could be to initiate an alliance with the Assyrians, or it could be the payment required to obtain Assyrian assistance in retaining the throne (v. 8). In either case, reliance on a foreign power is contrary to trusting God and is viewed negatively by the prophetic writers.

Political Compromise (16:1–9)

THE POLITICAL TURBULENCE at the end of Jotham's reign caused by the campaign of Tiglath-Pileser disrupts the regular succession of Judean kings. This has resulted in conflicting synchronisms, possibly the result of the incorporation of various records for the beginning and end of the reigns of Jotham and Ahaz. Jotham lives beyond his sixteen-year reign (15:30, 33); Ahaz becomes king twelve years before Hoshea begins to reign (17:1).[1] Tiglath-Pileser may have accorded him some recognition of authority, which north Israelite records count as his formal accession. His independent rule begins in the sixteenth year of the reign of Jotham, though Jotham lives another four years.

The attack of Rezin and Pekah (16:5) is partly an attempt to force Judah to join an alliance in resisting the Assyrian advance.[2] The result noted here is the same as that indicated in Isaiah 7:1: The aggressors fail to engage the Judean army, or at least fail in their attempt to lay siege to Jerusalem. The Hebrew text says that Rezin is successful in capturing the seaport at Ezion Geber (Tel-el-Kheleifeh) for Aram (16:6). The term "recovered" (*hēšîb*) indicates that Elath is restored to the Edomites, who have the proper claim of ownership;[3] Chronicles also refers to an attack by Edom (2 Chron. 28:17). Aharoni suggests that the Arameans assist the Edomites in regaining control of their territory.[4] The Chronicler further reports that Ahaz loses control of

---

1. The conflicting synchronisms and the age of Ahaz at the birth of Hezekiah are discussed in appendix B.
2. In the Calah annals, Tiglath-Pileser names Rezin as one of the targets for tribute in the Syrian campaign; see Hallo and Younger, *Scripture in Context*, 2.117A.
3. Reading *ʾĕdôm* instead of *ʾărôm* is only a change of one similar letter; a misreading of the archive may have led to the addition of the name Rezin.
4. Aharoni, *The Land of the Bible*, 371.

a number of towns that control passes to Jerusalem (28:18);[5] these included Gimzo and Aijalon in the north, Timnah and Beth Shemesh in the Sorek Valley, and Socoh and Gederoth in the Valley of Elah.

Ahaz's appeal to Tiglath-Pileser for help (2 Kings 16:7–8) is a critique of Ahaz based on sources from the court and temple.[6] The wealth sent to the Assyrians is not a "gift" (NIV) but a "bribe" (*šōḥad*). This word depicts derogatively a "hired razor" who will ravage the land of Judah (Isa. 7:20).[7] This exchange should not be compared with submitting tribute as a vassal. Ahaz appeals as a servant and son; the use of "son" as a qualification of servant tends to soften the expression of subservience and dependence. Tiglath-Pileser responds by killing Rezin and exiling the citizens of Damascus to Kir.[8] The historian portrays Ahaz as voluntarily submitting to the Assyrian yoke, a grievous misdeed in addition to his promoting idolatry in the high places.

Temple Innovations (16:10–20)

THE POLITICAL COMPLIANCE to Tiglath-Pileser requires Ahaz to meet him in Damascus to bring tribute.[9] While there he sees an altar that apparently meets the deficiencies of the altar of Solomon, which is described as too small (1 Kings 8:64). There is no indication that the altar is of Assyrian design or that it represents subordination to Assyria. The Chronicler regards use of the altar as bringing offerings to the gods of Damascus, to whom Ahaz turns for help instead of looking to Yahweh (2 Chron. 28:23). The altar is built by Uriah the faithful high priest (Isa. 8:2), according to the model and design Ahaz has prescribed. When Ahaz returns from Damascus he conducts the inaugural ceremony, just as Solomon did at the dedication of the temple. The new altar is elevated, so the king must mount it in order to make the offerings (2 Kings 16:12).

The offerings include those totally burned, the dry offerings of grains, the libations of liquid produce such as oil and wine, and the peace or fellowship offerings, which are consumed by the worshipers (16:13). The old bronze

---

5. Aharoni et al., *The Carta Bible Atlas*, #145.

6. Cogan and Tadmor, "Ahaz and Tiglath-Pileser in the Book of Kings: Historiographic Considerations," 506.

7. Cogan and Tadmor compare it to the Akkadian term *tatu* used to describe a bribe sent for assistance; ibid., 499–503. Taking of bribes was forbidden under the covenant (Deut. 10:17; 16:19; 27:25).

8. Amos says that Kir is the original home of the Arameans (Amos 9:7), to which they will be forced to return (1:5). The location is not known.

9. Summary inscription 7 names "Jehoahaz [the unabbreviated form of Ahaz] the Judahite" among those bringing tribute; Hallo and Younger, *Scripture in Context*, 2.117D.

altar is moved from its place in front of the sanctuary entrance to the north side. All the regular offerings for the king and his officials ("the people of the land," 16:15) are to be brought to the new altar. The old altar is for the exclusive use of the king, where he will worship and pray. The sense of how Ahaz will seek (*baqqēr*, 16:15) Yahweh is not specified, but no cultic practice is implied. The involvement of Uriah the priest suggests that Ahaz does not intend worship contrary to what has been prescribed.

Ahaz removes the frames from the wheeled stands (cf. 1 Kings 7:27–30) with their elaborate metal work, probably as part of the payments made to Assyria (16:17). He also takes down the large basin from the bronze oxen that support it and places it on a stone bed. The "Sabbath canopy" may have been a metal awning, the word "Sabbath" being a metaphor for an inner temple structure (16:18).[10] Naʾaman suggests that this really is a hall where the temple guards can rest; from here they go to their various assignments (cf. 11:5, 7, 9).[11] The renovation of this hall is part of the reorganization of the private royal passageway to outside the building. The hall is probably located at the junction of the palace and the temple, so the guards can enter it to rest or leave it to go on duty. All these changes are regarded negatively as an accommodation to Assyrian influence.

FAILURE TO TRUST GOD. The regnal summary condemns Ahaz for governing according to the abominable practices of the Canaanites that Yahweh drove out before Israel (16:3). A leading motif in the Deuteronomistic History is that God gave Canaan to Israel because of the iniquity of the Amorites, but that Israel itself became Canaanite in its practices (Judg. 2:1–5). Ahaz carries this to the extent of making his son pass through the fire. It is not certain if this describes child sacrifice; the writer quotes the language of Deuteronomy to typify the sordid conduct of the Canaanites (Deut. 18:9–10), where passing sons through the fire is named with various practices of divination. The same practice may be referred to by the description of "burning sons and daughters in the fire" (Deut. 12:31; Jer. 7:31; 19:5). Mesha king of Moab sacrificed his son (2 Kings 3:27), and offering children to Molek was one of the practices of the high places (Jer. 32:35). Passing children through the fire may have been a dedicatory rite, but apparently child sacrifice was practiced in severe times of distress.

---

10. The structure in the temple is otherwise unknown; the word for awning (*mûsak*) may be derived from *skk*, "to cover."

11. Nadav Naʾaman, "Royal Inscriptions and the Histories of Joash and Ahaz, Kings of Judah," *VT* 48 (1998): 346–47. He suggests *mûsak* is derived from *swk* ("to fence").

The Deuteronomistic Historians find fault with Ahaz because of his promotion of idolatrous worship at the high places and his innovations to the temple. The alliance with the Assyrians delivers Ahaz in his time of crisis, but the cost requires stripping the temple of its precious metals—the gold and silver, and even the bronze that was a part of the water basins of the outer court. The prophet Isaiah finds fault with Ahaz at the fundamental level of his unwillingness to trust God (Isa. 7:1–17). The various compromises of worship, so significant to the Deuteronomists as evidence of covenant failure, are manifestations of one essential problem: failure to trust God. Ahaz figures prominently in Isaiah's message to Jerusalem during the days of the Syrian crisis, but there is no mention of worship at the high places or manipulation of worship at the temple. The Assyrians are not allies but the agents of judgment in exiling the population of Judah.

The crisis for faith comes with the attack of Rezin and Pekah in an attempt to overthrow Ahaz and install Tabeel ("good for nothing") as king to aid them in their cause (Isa. 7:3–6). Isaiah meets the king while he is inspecting his water supply to assure him that there is no cause for fear. The presence of Isaiah's son Shearjashub ("a remnant will return") is an invitation to trust God.[12] Rezin and Pekah have already exhausted their fury; they are nothing more than two smoldering firebrands. Merely human cities such as Damascus and Samaria are no threat to Ahaz's security, because they will themselves shortly disappear (vv. 8–9). The real cause for concern is whether Ahaz can trust God. This is put to the king in a phrase that plays on the Hebrew root commonly used in English as "amen" (ʾmn): If you do not believe (taʾᵃmînû), you will not be secure (tēʾāmēnû, 7:9).

The sign Immanuel. Underlying the assurance to Ahaz is the divine promise for the house of David (Isa. 7:13). Ahaz may weary God in his rejection of the sign (v. 12), but this will not alter God's purpose for his nation. The name "Immanuel" is possibly the best-known symbol of divine faithfulness, but it comes with a double significance.[13] Ahaz's unbelief shatters the solidarity between the king as representative of the house of David and the

---

12. Wildberger (*Jesaja Kapitel 1–12*, 2nd ed. [BKAT 10/1; Neukirchen: Neukirchener Verlag, 1980], 1:277–78) discusses the many possible ways that the name itself might be applied in the historical circumstance. In Isaiah, the remnant refers to the faithful group that turned to God in trust following the Assyrian decimation of Judah (Isa. 10:20–22; 11:11, 16). They represented the eschatological hope of the nation.

13. Childs, *Isaiah*, 66–68. The significance of the sign is understood through the meaning of the name, as emphasized by Wildberger (*Jesaja*, 293–94). For the biblical use of the term "Immanuel," see Rikki E. Watts, "Immanuel: Virgin Birth Proof Text or Programmatic Warning of Things to Come (Isa 7:14 in Matt 1:23)?" in *From Prophecy to Testament: The Function of the Old Testament in the New*, ed. Craig Evans (Peabody, Mass.: Hendrickson, 2004), 92–113.

faithful people of Israel. For those of unbelief (Ahaz and his people), the sign of divine presence is one of destruction (7:17), but for those who believe the sign is a pledge of God's continuing presence in deliverance (7:16). The withdrawal of Israelite and Aramean armies vindicates the prophet's word and shows that the fear of Ahaz and his people is groundless if they will only trust in God.

The prophet Isaiah describes the coming devastation of Judah with the vivid imagery of the prosperous land being reduced to a place of briars and thorns (Isa. 7:18–25). The devastation is such that an inhabitant will struggle for life with a young cow and two sheep (v. 21), but even in such circumstances these few pitiful animals will produce such an abundance that the survivors will feast on curds and honey (v. 22).

The mysterious name "Immanuel" is further clarified in Isaiah's proclamation concerning Judah and Assyria (8:1–10). The figure of a trickle of water depicts the weakness of the divine promise in contrast with the mighty strength of Assyria that Ahaz has appealed to. The meager supply of water is an allusion to the spring of Gihon in the Kidron Valley channeled to pools on the lower east side of the city. Since Judah refuses this divine supply, Yahweh will bring the Assyrians like a flood; the mighty water of the Euphrates will flow over Judah—not to provide deliverance, as Ahaz assumes, but to sweep the country away. The judgment concludes with the name "Immanuel" (8:8). "Immanuel partakes of the judgment enveloping the people and land of Judah, but the divine judgment executed by the Assyrians has its limits explicitly because of the reality of 'God-with-us.'"[14] The unbelief of the king and the people have brought about a double significance of the meaning of the name; the presence of God will bring about judgment, even though it holds out the promise of the redemption of the people.

The judgment against the nations brings assurance of the fulfillment of the divine promise (Isa. 8:9–10). The people from far countries may band together in a plan to destroy God's people. The nations are represented in the concrete presence of Assyria; its plans will be thwarted because of the presence of Immanuel. The people are offered a pledge of salvation because of the divine presence in the midst of judgment. Such optimism is not based in political fortunes or psychological optimism; it is a result of the assurance that God's faithfulness will prevail in spite of the faithlessness of the Davidic king.

The Deuteronomistic Historians look back on all these events, pondering the question of the future of the covenant and of Jerusalem. Their concerns for the temple and the strength of the country are not to be minimized. Their king has betrayed them; the policy of bribing the Assyrians is not only

---

14. Childs, *Isaiah*, 73.

an enormous cost in the short term, but utter loss in the long term. Ahaz has inherited a perilous situation, but his appeal to mighty earthly powers subverts his country. The pro-Assyrian policy that brought him to power results in complete servitude to his master.

Ahaz has inherited an exceedingly difficult political situation. Judah was an independent and wealthy nation for more than two generations under the rule of Uzziah and Jotham. Ahaz's highest priority, as in any society, is to maintain the standard of living and exercise of power established in the previous regimes. In the judgment of the pro-Assyrian group that put Ahaz into power, the only hope of achieving this is to join forces with the Assyrians. In their judgment—and history proves them correct—the coalition of Aramean states will not be able to resist the Assyrians. Their solution is to accept the inevitable in the hope of being granted some independence in vassal status. This is contrary to the way of the covenant, in which reliance on any other nation is forbidden. History also proves the truth of the covenant; within a generation the Assyrians plunder Judah, though it is never made an Assyrian territory as Israel was.

The sign of "God with us" is both a promise and a threat. Matthew interprets the name the same as Isaiah does. It is a promise to those who trust God in accomplishing his redemption; it is a threat if they determine instead to protect their material prosperity by relying on the military powers such as Assyria or Rome. The choice is not whether God will be present; the choice is only in the response to that presence.

When Ahaz declines the offer of a sign, the prophet declares that Yahweh will give him a sign anyway (Isa. 7:13–14). The threat that Ahaz fears will disappear, as the prophet has said, but the result will be a greater judgment—the king of Assyria (v. 17). The fulfillment of the Immanuel promise comes with the birth of Christ (Matt. 1:22–23). God with us in the present time is not different from what it was for Ahaz. It is a promise to those who seek first the kingdom of God and his righteousness. The presence of Christ is a threat for those who seek to protect their material well-being in this world by making it their highest priority. They are in danger of losing everything that is of such value to them.

GOD AND THE use of human wealth. Biblical prophecy has left Ahaz as a paradigm for the choice to trust in God for one's well-being. In seeking to protect his earthly inheritance, he loses it all. Had he been willing to trust God with his kingdom, he and his people could have been secure. Jesus in the same way promises his followers that all the needs of this earthly life will be provided to those who make the kingdom of God their concern (Matt. 6:25–33). By contrast, those who seek treasure on this earth will find it will rust and decay (vv. 19–21), if it is not taken away, as Tiglath-Pileser strips the treasures of the temple.

Today's church includes many who leave everything to follow Christ, live in actual solidarity with poor people, and are insulted, hated and persecuted for this. At the same time, the church depends on the generosity of people of means to further its mission. The rich in the Gospels are by no means hard-working middle or upper-middle class people, but the arrogant and blind super-wealthy of imperial societies, reflected today in the super-rich or in global corporations.[15] It is the mission of corporations to earn money; it is the mission of Christians to use those earnings for the kingdom of God.

It is not easy for individual Christians to separate personal mission from corporate commercial enterprise. The separation is difficult both in the business practices by which money is earned and in the investment of the earnings that are realized. To some measure, commerce in this world must be conducted according to the rules established by government and corporate practice. When these practices contradict Christian ethics, they must be abandoned for the sake of the kingdom, even at the sacrifice of profit. As with Ahaz, the temptation is to follow the powers of political and economic forces rather than to submit to Christ's presence and his work in the world. More often, as with Ahaz, the pursuit of the corporate mission inspires priorities that are contrary to God's work in the world. Such wealth is no longer in service of the kingdom of God, even if token charity continues to be practiced.

A large part of Jesus' teaching concerns the use of wealth. The narrative of the rich man and poor Lazarus is the Lukan culmination of Jesus' teaching about the danger of wealth. Because the good news originates among the ᶜanāwîm (i.e., marginal and humble people who are open to God, such as Zechariah, Mary, the shepherds, Anna, and Simeon), Luke's Gospel is often called the "Gospel for the Poor." Yet there is far more material about the dangers of great wealth and the pitfalls the rich face in responding to the good news, so this Gospel may also be rightly called "Somber News for the Wealthy."[16]

The somber warning of the story about Lazarus and the rich man is that, like Ahaz, the rich man does not recognize his peril until it is too late (Luke 16:19–31). Once the great chasm has been fixed between the rich man in Hades and the poor man in Abraham's bosom, the rich man becomes con-

---

15. John R. Donahue, "Woe or Weal," *America* 184/3 (Feb. 2001): 47.
16. John R. Donahue, "Time for a Vision Check," *America* 185/8 (Sept. 2001): 39.

cerned not only about his own fate but especially that of his five brothers. He assumes that if some great sign could take place, such as Lazarus's returning from the dead to warn them, they will repent. But the deception of wealth is not deterred by such signs. Those unwilling to hear the warnings of Moses and the prophets will not be persuaded by such a miracle. The disaster of trusting in wealth and power is evident only after the judgment is past.

There is much implicit in the parable of the rich man and Lazarus. The reason for the judgment of the rich man and the merit of Lazarus is not made explicit. It is apparent that certain conventions were known and understood in the social context as characteristic of the type of rich man in the story.[17] The rich are characterized as having amassed their wealth by perjury, robbery, and duplicity. Unmistakable in the parable is the hedonism of the rich, particularly the clothing and the sumptuous daily feasting and entertainment. Lazarus is not virtuous merely by being poor; the poor are characterized by self-control and discipline, by their simple way of life that does not rob from others. This story is an attack on the hedonism and the immorality that wealth engenders. These are contrary to the values of the kingdom.

The choices of Ahaz are typical of the values of the wealthy seeking security for their possessions. He chooses to trust political and economic forces rather than God. In so doing he is willing to not only desecrate the temple by robbing it of its valuable metals, but to set up in its precincts foreign altars. In all of this, God is still with Ahaz. During his reign the kingdom of Israel disappears entirely, the nation that he so fears, but his own people come under the domination of the same Assyrians. Wealth is important to life in this world, but not as an end in itself. Pursued as a goal, it brings judgment and is lost. Wealth used in dependence on God and in furthering the kingdom of God enables his presence and blessing. But Ahaz chooses to make the security of his wealth through temporal forces his god, and in so doing he loses the blessing of the sign of Immanuel. Christians, who have experienced the blessing of the fulfillment of Immanuel, must beware of falling into the same condemnation.

---

17. Ronald F. Hock, "Lazarus and Micyllus: Greco-Roman Backgrounds to Luke 16:19–31," *JBL* 106 (1987): 461–62.

2 Kings 17:1–41

❦

IN THE TWELFTH year of Ahaz king of Judah, Hoshea son of
Elah became king of Israel in Samaria, and he reigned nine
years. ²He did evil in the eyes of the LORD, but not like
the kings of Israel who preceded him.

³Shalmaneser king of Assyria came up to attack Hoshea,
who had been Shalmaneser's vassal and had paid him tribute.
⁴But the king of Assyria discovered that Hoshea was a traitor,
for he had sent envoys to So king of Egypt, and he no longer
paid tribute to the king of Assyria, as he had done year by
year. Therefore Shalmaneser seized him and put him in
prison. ⁵The king of Assyria invaded the entire land, marched
against Samaria and laid siege to it for three years. ⁶In the
ninth year of Hoshea, the king of Assyria captured Samaria
and deported the Israelites to Assyria. He settled them in
Halah, in Gozan on the Habor River and in the towns of the
Medes.

⁷All this took place because the Israelites had sinned
against the LORD their God, who had brought them up out of
Egypt from under the power of Pharaoh king of Egypt. They
worshiped other gods ⁸and followed the practices of the
nations the LORD had driven out before them, as well as the
practices that the kings of Israel had introduced. ⁹The
Israelites secretly did things against the LORD their God that
were not right. From watchtower to fortified city they built
themselves high places in all their towns. ¹⁰They set up sacred
stones and Asherah poles on every high hill and under every
spreading tree. ¹¹At every high place they burned incense, as
the nations whom the LORD had driven out before them had
done. They did wicked things that provoked the LORD to
anger. ¹²They worshiped idols, though the LORD had said,
"You shall not do this." ¹³The LORD warned Israel and Judah
through all his prophets and seers: "Turn from your evil ways.
Observe my commands and decrees, in accordance with the
entire Law that I commanded your fathers to obey and that I
delivered to you through my servants the prophets."

¹⁴But they would not listen and were as stiff-necked as their
fathers, who did not trust in the LORD their God. ¹⁵They

rejected his decrees and the covenant he had made with their fathers and the warnings he had given them. They followed worthless idols and themselves became worthless. They imitated the nations around them although the LORD had ordered them, "Do not do as they do," and they did the things the LORD had forbidden them to do.

¹⁶They forsook all the commands of the LORD their God and made for themselves two idols cast in the shape of calves, and an Asherah pole. They bowed down to all the starry hosts, and they worshiped Baal. ¹⁷They sacrificed their sons and daughters in the fire. They practiced divination and sorcery and sold themselves to do evil in the eyes of the LORD, provoking him to anger.

¹⁸So the LORD was very angry with Israel and removed them from his presence. Only the tribe of Judah was left, ¹⁹and even Judah did not keep the commands of the LORD their God. They followed the practices Israel had introduced. ²⁰Therefore the LORD rejected all the people of Israel; he afflicted them and gave them into the hands of plunderers, until he thrust them from his presence.

²¹When he tore Israel away from the house of David, they made Jeroboam son of Nebat their king. Jeroboam enticed Israel away from following the LORD and caused them to commit a great sin. ²²The Israelites persisted in all the sins of Jeroboam and did not turn away from them ²³until the LORD removed them from his presence, as he had warned through all his servants the prophets. So the people of Israel were taken from their homeland into exile in Assyria, and they are still there.

²⁴The king of Assyria brought people from Babylon, Cuthah, Avva, Hamath and Sepharvaim and settled them in the towns of Samaria to replace the Israelites. They took over Samaria and lived in its towns. ²⁵When they first lived there, they did not worship the LORD; so he sent lions among them and they killed some of the people. ²⁶It was reported to the king of Assyria: "The people you deported and resettled in the towns of Samaria do not know what the god of that country requires. He has sent lions among them, which are killing them off, because the people do not know what he requires."

²⁷Then the king of Assyria gave this order: "Have one of the priests you took captive from Samaria go back to live

there and teach the people what the god of the land requires."
²⁸So one of the priests who had been exiled from Samaria
came to live in Bethel and taught them how to worship the
LORD.

²⁹Nevertheless, each national group made its own gods in
the several towns where they settled, and set them up in the
shrines the people of Samaria had made at the high places.
³⁰The men from Babylon made Succoth Benoth, the men from
Cuthah made Nergal, and the men from Hamath made
Ashima; ³¹the Avvites made Nibhaz and Tartak, and the
Sepharvites burned their children in the fire as sacrifices to
Adrammelech and Anammelech, the gods of Sepharvaim.
³²They worshiped the LORD, but they also appointed all sorts
of their own people to officiate for them as priests in the
shrines at the high places. ³³They worshiped the LORD, but
they also served their own gods in accordance with the customs of the nations from which they had been brought.

³⁴To this day they persist in their former practices. They
neither worship the LORD nor adhere to the decrees and ordinances, the laws and commands that the LORD gave the
descendants of Jacob, whom he named Israel. ³⁵When the
LORD made a covenant with the Israelites, he commanded
them: "Do not worship any other gods or bow down to them,
serve them or sacrifice to them. ³⁶But the LORD, who brought
you up out of Egypt with mighty power and outstretched arm,
is the one you must worship. To him you shall bow down and
to him offer sacrifices. ³⁷You must always be careful to keep
the decrees and ordinances, the laws and commands he wrote
for you. Do not worship other gods. ³⁸Do not forget the
covenant I have made with you, and do not worship other
gods. ³⁹Rather, worship the LORD your God; it is he who will
deliver you from the hand of all your enemies."

⁴⁰They would not listen, however, but persisted in their
former practices. ⁴¹Even while these people were worshiping
the LORD, they were serving their idols. To this day their children and grandchildren continue to do as their fathers did.

THE FALL OF Samaria involves a critical correlation between Israelite and Assyrian history. The regnal summary of Hoshea records the final nine years of the nation of Israel, which begins in the twelfth year of Ahaz.[1] The date for the accession of Hoshea can be calculated from the Assyrian records, which show that Shalmaneser conquered Samaria in 723 B.C. According to the Eponym Chronicle, Shalmaneser ascended the throne in Assyria and Babylonia and shattered Samaria; he died in his fifth year (722 B.C.).[2] The mitigation of the usual criticism of Israelite kings in the case of Hoshea is perhaps an acknowledgment of limited independence for his rule (v. 2). His first obligations are to Tiglath-Pileser, who has appointed him, so he has little opportunity for religious matters.[3] His virtue is born out of necessity.

Fall of Samaria (17:1–6)

THE EVENTS THAT lead to the fall of Samaria are only known in general sequence. The Assyrian records are fragmentary for these years; the accounts in Kings (cf. 2 Kings 18:9–12) are ambiguous about the events surrounding the capture of Hoshea and the three-year siege prior to Samaria's fall. Cogan and Tadmor, for example, follow a chronology in which the capture of Hoshea and the subsequent siege are not included in the nine-year reign of Hoshea.[4]

Hobbs stresses the literary structure of this passage about the fall of Samaria (17:3–6).[5] The end of Hoshea's reign is described in two-verse pairs (17:3–4 and 5–6), each of which notes an invasion by Shalmaneser. The report begins with an emphatic irony: Hoshea, who did not sin as did the kings of Israel before him (17:2), is the king whom Shalmaneser attacks (v. 3). In verses 3–4 the author recalls the vivid memory of the attack that ended the nation of Israel and the reason for it. Hoshea rebelled from his servant status and with Egyptian assistance attempted to gain independence; as a result, the Assyrians invaded and imprisoned the king. The author then

---

1. See appendix B for a discussion of the multiple chronologies of Ahaz. If the text is not an error for the second year of Ahaz, Ahaz was coregent with Jotham beginning ten years earlier.

2. For a translation see Alan Millard, "The Babylonian Chronicle," *The Context of Scripture*, 1.137.

3. Summary Inscriptions 9–10 name Hoshea as the appointed king in Samaria; Younger, *The Context of Scripture*, 2.117F.

4. Cogan and Tadmor, *II Kings*, 195.

5. Hobbs, *2 Kings*, 226.

describes the effect of the invasion for the city of Samaria and the population of the country (vv. 5–6); after a three-year struggle, the city fell and large numbers of people were deported.

The identity of So as a king of Egypt is a further problem.[6] Kitchen concludes that So is likely an abbreviation for Pharaoh Osorkon IV (ca. 730–715 B.C.), who ruled over Tanis (Zoan), the eastern part of the Egyptian delta directly adjacent to Palestine. Isaiah condemns the Israelite reliance on Zoan (Isa. 19:11, 13; 30:3–5). There was a longstanding alliance between the rulers of Tanis and Israel, stimulated initially by the campaigns of Shalmaneser III. The weak military of Osorkon IV explains why this alliance is no help to Hoshea.

Israel's deportation takes place in the years following the fall of Samaria after the death of Shalmaneser V. That death delays the consequences for Israel; Sargon II recaptures the city, and the deportations follow.[7] Tiglath-Pileser actually began deporting Israelites in the northern part of Israel years earlier (15:29). Some became part of the Assyrian army; Sargon claims to have captured fifty charioteers from them and taught the rest of the deportees their skills.

Others of the Israelites are deported to Halah and Gozan on the Habur River (17:6). These become skilled workers in building projects or are assigned as farmers to lands owned by state officials in the main part of Assyria.[8] Several years later (after 716 B.C.), other deportees are less fortunate; they suffer the hardships of living in a frontier region described as "towns of the Medes" (i.e., in the Zagros Mountains). These are deported after Sargon has put down a revolt and exiled many people there.[9] The defeat of Samaria was part of an extensive western campaign that extended to the Philistine cities supported by the Egyptians.

Punishment of Idolatry (17:7–23)

A PROPHETIC SERMON details the sins that are responsible for the fall of Israel (and Judah; cf. 17:19). The sermon is typical of others found in the Deuteronomistic History; it recalls the way in which God gave the land of Canaan to Israel and condemned idolatrous worship (cf. Josh. 23; Judg. 2:11–23). Con-

---

6. The possibilities are discussed thoroughly by Kitchen, *The Third Intermediate Period in Egypt*, 372–75.

7. In "The Great 'Summary' Inscription" from ancient Dur-Šarrukin (modern Khorsabad), Sargon claims to have conquered Samaria and taken captive 27,290 people (Hallo and Younger, *The Context of Scripture*, 2.118E).

8. Younger, "The Deportation of the Israelites," 221–22. Dur-Šarrukin, Sargon's new capital, is located in the district of Halah.

9. Ibid., 223.

forming to the ways to the Canaanites causes Israel to be sold into the hands of its enemies and expelled from the land God gave them.

The sermon falls into two main sections (2 Kings 17:7–13 and 14–19), with a conclusion that recapitulates the sins of Jeroboam that started Israel on the path into idolatry (vv. 20–23).[10] These two main sections are well balanced: Each begins with a general statement of the sins of Israel (vv. 7–9a and 14), followed by a detailed list of the misdeeds of the people (vv. 9b–12 and 15–18). The first section concludes with the warning that God gave Israel through the prophets (v. 13), the second with the warning that Judah received through the fall of Israel (v. 19). The warning against Judah is commonly regarded as intrusive, but this fails to take into account the function of the sermon in the Deuteronomistic History as a message to the exiles.

The only mention of Israel's kings here is in the general introduction of the sins of Israel (17:8b). Syntactically it is a difficult clause because it interrupts the sequence in which Israel is the subject (cf. RSV, NRSV; NEB omits the clause as secondary). The translation in verse 9 that the Israelites "secretly did things against the LORD" is also doubtful (cf. RSV, NIV); the Hebrew word translated "secretly" occurs only in this verse, and its meaning must be inferred from context. It more likely means that the Israelites attributed to God things that are not true (cf. NEB),[11] such as worshiping Yahweh under the image of a molten calf. This was the adoption of foreign practices introduced into the worship of Yahweh.

The erection of stone pillars and Asherah are also examples of this (v. 10). The wooden poles or trees of Asherah were symbols of the Canaanite fertility goddess of the same name.[12] Her worship was particularly attractive to women (cf. 1 Kings 15:13; 2 Kings 23:13–14). The term for "idols" (*gillûlîm* in 2 Kings 17:12) is found frequently in Ezekiel, where it is a collective term for all cultically defiling sins.[13] It denotes what is totally foreign to Yahweh, impurities that require cleansing.

Religions of Samaria (17:24–33)

THE EXILED ISRAELITES are replaced with people from other lands. Sargon II's deportations differed from those of Tiglath-Pileser III, which were unidirectional. This apparently had to do with the divergent political goals of the

---

10. Hobbs, *2 Kings*, 226–27.

11. The Greek translation interprets the word as "cloaking one's words"; the Hebrew word (*ḥpʾ*) is sometimes considered a variant of a word that means "to cloak, cover" (*ḥpḥ*).

12. Gideon (the Hacker) was given his name because he cut down and burned the Asherah pole (Judg. 6:28–29); it is possible the Asherah was a stylised pole as it appears on a clay model of a cultic scene (J. C. de Moor, "אֲשֵׁרָה," *TDOT*, 1:441–43).

13. H. D. Preuss, "גִּלּוּלִים," *TDOT*, 3:2–3.

respective kings.[14] Egypt plays an important role in Assyrian strategy; the Assyrians need access to the Philistine coast and Egypt in order to realize their economic goals. Tiglath-Pileser was concerned with controlling the major trading centers on the Levantine coast. Gaza is prominent in the inscriptions and became a commercial center where Arabian tribes were forced to pay dues for its use.

Sargon II continued the policy of securing the Damascus-Megiddo-Egypt route and quick access to the Philistine states, but the rump state of Samaria was not particularly integral to that objective. Samaria was important as a trading center, and thus Sargon populated it with Arabians as well as those from the diverse areas of Assyria.[15] Not only did this divert some of the Arabian trade to that area, in which nomads played an important role, it also repopulated desolate and impoverished areas to reinforce the western border of the Assyrian empire.

The list of peoples transported to the region of Samaria reflects historical reality and must derive from direct knowledge of the situation.[16] The five nationalities noted in 17:24 correspond with Mesopotamian locations conquered by Sargon II in the latter part of the eighth century. The repatriation of a priest to Bethel to teach the newcomers how to fear Yahweh (vv. 27–28) also accords well with known Sargonic policy. The peoples brought to repopulate Israel add Yahweh to the gods from their homelands as another god to worship (v. 33).

The Bethel sanctuary continues to function as the place to worship Yahweh, but other temples at high places are built in various cities for the worship of other gods, led by their priests (17:28–29). The high places are of no single architectural type; worship takes place in "the shrines" on the high places, while sacrifices are offered on the altars, which presumes some type of sanctuary in the various locations.[17] The historical source is remarkably tolerant of the worship practices of the mixed peoples of the region; there is no condemnation such as is common in the exclusive demands of the Deuteronomistic Historians for worship in Jerusalem.

Samaria is the name of the Assyrian province established in the hill country of Ephraim. Its repopulation takes place over several decades from scattered areas of the Assyrian empire. The people from various regions (v. 24) are identified with their particular religious practices (vv. 30–31). Succoth

---

14. Younger, "The Deportations of the Israelites," 225–26.

15. The deportees from Assyria are mentioned in the Nimrud Prism, those from Arabia in annals 120b–123a; ibid., 216, 226; idem, *Context of Scripture* 2.118A; 2.118D.

16. W. Boyd Barrick, "On the Meaning of *bêt-habbamôt* and *batê-habbamôt* and the Composition of the Kings History," *JBL* 115 (1996): 632–36.

17. Ibid., 641–42.

Benoth is not otherwise known as the name of a Babylonian divinity; the chief god was Marduk and his consort Sarpanitu. Banitu (the creatress) is sometimes an epithet of Ishtar; *skwt bnwt* may be translated as "image of Banit(u)."[18] Cuthah in central Babylon is the sacred territory of Nergal, god of the plague and the underworld. Hamath may refer to the city on the Orontes or to Amate on the Uqnu River in Elam; Ashima is an unknown divinity.[19] Avva is likely the Elamite city Ama, and the gods are Ibnahaza and Dirtaq.[20] The territory of Sepharvaim cannot be identified, and the names Adrammelech and Anammelech as given in the Hebrew text do not represent known divinities in the Aramean or Assyro-Babylonian pantheons. Attar-melek, if the equivalent, is another version of Ishtar/Astarte; Anammelech may be the Mesopotamian sun god Anu, but human sacrifice is not normally associated with this deity.

Persistent Covenant Disobedience (17:34–41)

IN THE WORSHIP fostered at Bethel and the other high places before the deportation, the people did not "fear the LORD" (v. 34, NASB). They included unacceptable elements of other religions and, of course, did not accept or use the temple at Jerusalem. The end of Israel becomes the occasion for a concluding exhortation on the failure of the covenant from the time of the Exodus "to this day" (v. 34). This phrase resumes the prophetic sermon describing disobedience that led to the end of Israel "to this day" (v. 23; NIV, "and they are still there"), which was broken off by the description of the repopulation of Samaria (vv. 24–33). The final summary repeats the phrase: "To this day" the people fail to observe the loyalty of the covenant oath they have taken (vv. 40–41). Repetitive phrases are typical in Hebrew narrative to mark the beginning and end of a distinct literary unit within a larger composition.

Bridging Contexts

REASONS FOR THE demise of Israel. This chapter is characterized by the burden of the prophets of the Deuteronomistic History. A regnal summary (vv. 1–2) and records of annalistic sources (vv. 3–6) explain the fall of Samaria. A framing repetition marks an interruption in the main narrative: "carried Israel away into exile" (vv. 6b, 23b). The narrative

---

18. A suggestion of Lipinski (*UF* 5 [1973], 202–4), noted by Cogan and Tadmor, *II Kings*, 211.

19. Amos 8:14 may be another reference to this divinity.

20. Cogan and Tadmor, *II Kings*, 212. For Amate and Ama see Luckenbill, *Ancient Records of Assyria and Babylonia*, 2.32.

resumes with an account of the resettlement of Samaria after the deportation of its citizens and the accompanying syncretistic practices (vv. 24–33). A lengthy prophetic homily in language typical of the Deuteronomistic writers reviews the reasons for the fall of Israel, recalling the practices that were violations of properly worshiping God as king at the temple (vv. 7–23).[21]

Long describes this as "a colossal anachrony," in which the author interrupts the temporal sequence of a narrative. Information is supplied retrospectively (*analepsis*) to provide reasons for the catastrophe.[22] The reach extends far back beyond the parameters of the monarchy (vv. 7–8), but it also extends proleptically to the demise of the southern kingdom (vv. 19–20). The author then reverts to *analepsis* to recall the precise moment when the northern kingdom went astray.

The chapter concludes with a double repetition. An outer frame repeats a connecting motif that ties the conclusion with the main subject of the narrative: "[These nations] feared the LORD" (vv. 33, 41, NASB). The inner frame encloses a proleptic commentary that extends the temporal reach far beyond the exile of the northern kingdom.[23] The story overtakes the narration of the northern exile and its aftermath (vv. 1–6, 24–33). The commentary merges the past into the present of the authors, or at least their sources; the transgressions committed long ago continue "to this day." This phrase occurs three times (vv. 23, 34, 41), at the junctures of the descriptions of cultic practices that characterize Israel. That day is reminiscent of a time like that of Josiah, when efforts are made to centralize worship at Jerusalem, to the extent that the altar at Bethel is destroyed along with other shrines in the high places (23:15–19).[24] In the end Judah is included in this same indictment against Israel (17:19–20); the reforms of Hezekiah and Josiah do not spare Judah from the same judgment. The account of Israel's fall becomes the occasion for summarizing the covenant failure that seals the destiny of both nations.

Two very different points of view are expressed in the main sections of this sermon (17:7–23). The conclusion expresses the standard view stated throughout the history of Israel, that the cause of Israel's sin can be traced back to Jeroboam son of Nebat (vv. 18–22). He caused Israel to be separated from Judah and led Israel to sin in his ways. Special note is made of the warnings of the prophets and their fulfillment.

---

21. A compilation of phrases characteristic of Deuteronomic language is provided by Weinfeld, *Deuteronomy and the Deuteronomic School*, 320–55.

22. Burke O. Long, "Framing Repetitions in Biblical Historiography," *JBL* 106 (1987): 389, 397.

23. Ibid., 398.

24. Geoghegan, "'Until this Day' and the Preexilic Redaction of the Deuteronomistic History," 222–23.

The two main sections of the sermon hold the people rather than the kings responsible for the idolatry (vv. 7–12, 14–17); they built the high places and worshiped there, and they rejected the covenant and its warnings. This is the assessment that is generally given to Judah; the kings are exonerated as following in the ways of David, but the people practiced at the illicit cult sites (1 Kings 22:44; 2 Kings 12:4; 14:4; 15:4, 35). The high places may have served as places of worship until the temple was built (1 Kings 3:2), but the Deuteronomists regarded it as idolatrous from that time forward. This sermon on the exile of Israel applies to Israel the standard of Judah, giving it precedence over the sins of Jeroboam. Not even the mention of the two smelted calves brings a condemnation of their perpetrator (v. 16).

The exhortation on the end of Israel reviews the concepts repeatedly illustrated in the Deuteronomistic History. Though the people fear Yahweh (v. 33a), they serve their own gods according to the rites of the nations that Yahweh drove out of the land (v. 33b). A standard word pair ("fear/serve") is used to express the impropriety of syncretistic religion. Such incongruity—fearing Yahweh but serving other gods—does not begin with the Assyrian importation of foreign peoples. The whole history of Israel has been a failure to observe the covenant according to the exclusive standard required by Deuteronomy (vv. 34–35). The values of that covenant should have been their wisdom in the eyes of all the nations (Deut. 4:6–8); it should have set them apart and made them the envy of all the other nations. The requirement was that the Israelites not neglect (forget) this covenant, but teach it continuously throughout their generations (v. 9). The problem is that they failed to meet the obligation (2 Kings 17:38); they continuously returned to their earlier practices (17:40).

Sectarian Judaism. The lessons of covenant failure are not lost on later generations. The punishment of the Exile becomes the subject of much reflection on the proper observance of the covenant. It results in the development of various sects within Judaism whose goal is to rectify the failures that led to the Exile and to prepare for the advent of the kingdom of God. One such document is the charter of a group of sectarians first discovered in a medieval genizah (storage place for sacred texts) in Cairo that has come to be known as the *Damascus Document*.[25] Ten fragmentary copies of this work are among the documents discovered in the Qumran caves (eight from Cave 4, one in Cave 5, and one in Cave 6). The document contains regulations for the life of a new covenant community formed in exile in the land of Damascus. The community took its name from the prophecy of Amos, which warned of an exile to Damascus (Amos 5:27).

---

25. Solomon Schechter originally published this as *Fragments of a Zadokite Work* (Documents of Jewish Sectaries 1; Cambridge: Cambridge Univ. Press, 1910).

The *Damascus Document* recalls the faithfulness of God to the covenant during the Exile: "For when Israel abandoned Him by being faithless, He turned away from them and from His sanctuary and gave them up to the sword. But when He called to mend the covenant He made with their forefathers, He left a remnant for Israel and did not allow them to be exterminated" (CD A1, 3–5).[26] The community was formed in the second century before Christ, in the "era of wrath," 390 years from the time the Israelites were handed over to the power of Nebuchadnezzar. God then caused to grow from Israel and from Aaron a "root of planting to inherit His land and to grow fat on the good produce of His soil. They considered their iniquity and they knew that they were guilty men" (A1 7–9). God raised up for them a teacher of righteousness to lead them "in the way of His heart. He taught to later generations what God did to the generation deserving wrath, a company of traitors. They are the ones who depart from the proper way. That is the time of which it was written, 'Like a rebellious cow, so rebelled Israel' (Hos. 4:16)" (A1 10–14).

The *Damascus Document* contains two principal parts. (1) The first is an exhortation in which the teacher urges the "sons of light" to separate from the wicked. (2) The legal section lists the rules for the community members. These include regulations for Zadokite priests, skin diseases, and feminine kinds of impurity, and laws connected with crops, purity and impurity, oaths, marriages, business transactions, purification, the Sabbath, the temple, blasphemers, Gentiles, and foods. The community involves men who have families, earn wages, and own property. The location of "Damascus" is not certain; it may refer to Babylon, to Syria, or to the wilderness area around Qumran. Members of the community regard themselves as true followers of the covenant, in opposition to a "Man of Mockery," who "sprayed on Israel lying waters; he led them to wander in the trackless wasteland. He brought down the lofty heights of old, turned aside from paths of righteousness, and shifted the boundary marks that the forefathers had set up to mark their inheritance, so that the curses of the covenant took hold on them" (A1 15–16).

The *Damascus Document* is one of several that provide regulations for a strict covenant community, sometimes called a *yaḥad* ("unity").[27] Documents known as *halakâ* contain regulations for practicing covenant laws, such as prohibitions of carrying an object within a house to the outside, or something outside into a house (cf. Ex. 16:29). One of the first discovered and more

---

26. The translations are those of M. Wise, M. Abegg, and E. Cook, *The Dead Sea Scrolls: A New Translation* (San Francisco: HarperSanFrancisco, 1996).

27. Documents of Jewish sects are discussed by Peter Flint and James VanderKam, *The Meaning of the Dead Sea Scrolls* (San Francisco: HarperSanFrancisco, 2002), 210–19.

extensive documents at Qumran is that known as the *Rule of the Community*. It begins with a statement about the nature and purpose of the community and continues with a ritual for entry into the covenant community, instructions for the yearly renewal of the covenant, a section on sincere repentance, an explanation of the community's dualistic, predestinarian views, rules for meetings, and punishments for breaking community rules. The community is described as a temple, a spiritual sacrifice; the *Rule of the Community* details the duties of the Instructor and the times for praise. It ends with a hymn of praise offered by the Instructor.

Sectarian Judaism did not provide a solution for obedience to the covenant. It did breed a great deal of hostility between different groups and dissension over numerous practices. There was, for example, sectarian division over the function of the temple and its legitimate priesthood. Sects like the one at Qumran considered the temple to be defiled and unacceptable for worship; they retreated into the desert to wait for the wars of the end, which they believed would be soon. They disagreed over matters of *halakâ*, regulations for correct conduct.

An example of such an issue regards the purity of water. A question arose over the purity of water that was poured into an impure container. Did the impurity flow upward to the source of the water to make it impure, or was the impurity limited to the water that was in the container? There were also disagreements over the calendar. Certain groups held to a yearly calendar of 364 days, divided into quarters, with 91 days in each quarter. This provided for a continuous cycle of months of thirty days, with one day added in each quarter, so that festival days always fell on the same day of the week. Other groups followed a more lunar cycle, with six months of twenty-nine days and six months of thirty days, to provide for a year of 354 days. Every third year a month of thirty days was intercalated to restore the seasonal cycle.

True faith and submission to God. The goal of sectarian Judaism was to be true to the covenant in ways that those before them failed. According to Jesus, the various sects failed to understand the essentials of the covenant—true faith and submission before God—and were not better than those that preceded them. Jesus advises his listeners not to think he has come to destroy the teaching of Moses and the Prophets; rather, he has come to assist them to understand them correctly. His warning is essential; his teaching is so different from that of sectarian Judaism that they will conclude he is violating the Word of God.

Sects tended to focus on external rites; faith is a matter of the mind and heart. The tenth commandment warned against sins of the mind; obedience to Yahweh must begin in the mind. The Ten Commandments are summarized in covetousness. One must not, for instance, covet another's wife, for that is the beginning of adultery (Ex. 20:17). Jesus in turn says to his hearers, "Anyone who looks at a woman lustfully has already committed adultery with her in his heart" (Matt. 5:28). Sectarian Judaism managed to reduce the covenant requirements to externals. Jesus calls this hypocrisy. Religious leaders, for instance, would take an oath by the temple, which they regarded as not binding; however, if they took the oath by the gold on the temple, it was binding (Matt. 23:16). In this way they were able to nullify the third commandment; since they did not use the name of God, they believed they were somehow not bound by their word. That is why Jesus says that unless the righteousness (obedience) of his followers is superior to that of "teachers of the law and Pharisees," they will have no part in the kingdom.

The failures of these sects was an unwillingness to trust God in faith as required by the covenant and in so doing to live with a commitment to covenant ethics. Instead, they wanted to follow their own ethics, to subscribe to an obedience of faith that was self-defined. Sectarianism did succeed in avoiding the syncretism so condemned by the Deuteronomistic prophets. But it did not succeed in bringing about the submission of faith; rather, it brought self-righteousness in their own world of truth. The sectarians approached the problem of the prophets much too narrowly. In their concern to avoid false worship, they created division and acrimony, but they did not generate submission and faith in God.

 THE CHURCH, THE new covenant, and a new exodus. The failures of the old covenant lamented by the Deuteronomists could not be corrected by greater resolution to obey precepts as a means to a relationship with God. This fundamental misunderstanding of the covenant relationship continued to distort a true understanding of a genuine relationship with God. The possibility of a relationship with God from the start was a divine initiative that made those of his covenant "his treasured possession" (Deut. 7:6). The apostle John states it correctly: "We love [him] because he first loved us" (1 John 4:19).

God created Israel to be his bride; he voluntarily entered into an oath with them. The fundamental requirement of that relationship is stated in the primary confession of the covenant book: "Love the LORD your God with all your heart and with all your soul and with all your strength" (Deut. 6:5). God never demands perfection in keeping the pledge; his love is perfect and abundant to pardon. At the occasion of the golden calf, God revealed his name to Moses as being gracious, loyal, and slow to anger (Ex. 33:19; 34:6).

Our God is one who will always forgive our sins and heal our diseases (Ps. 103:3). God requires a loyalty to that promise; as with the oath of marriage, the covenant partner must always receive uncompromised fidelity.

The failure of the covenant relationship that resulted in the Exile did not bring an end to the promise of God or his love for his people. The church is that treasured possession established by the covenant oath at Mount Sinai (Ex. 19:5–6). Peter makes this plain in his requirement that we taste and see that the Lord is gracious (1 Peter 2:3). In 2:9 he quotes Exodus 19:5–6 to describe Christians as a temple made of living stones, a kingdom of priests, a treasured possession, proclaiming the praises of the one who called us into his marvelous light. The name Immanuel is the prophetic way of declaring that a remnant will turn to God (Isa. 10:20–21).

Matthew understands this remnant to be fulfilled and to continue in the followers of Jesus; he refers repeatedly to Isaiah's promise of the dawning light that will come for all peoples (Matt. 4:15–16; cf. Isa. 9:1–2; 12:15–20; cf. 42:1–4). The Deuteronomistic speech on the end of Israel is a sober reminder that the conditions of a relationship with God have not changed for the church. Israel's transgression was the failure of the people to love and trust God and instead to follow in the materialistic ways of the nations (2 Kings 17:7, 14). The church is called to be God's faithful remnant.

Jesus self-consciously interprets his death as a fulfillment of the redemption begun at the Exodus, as a renewal of the covenant that was broken. Jeremiah said there would be such a "new covenant" (Jer. 31:31–34); it is a covenant of a new mind, written on our hearts, declaring that God is our God and we are his people. Jesus made his death the implementation of that new covenant and gave his church a perpetual confession of this new covenant. Note that when Jesus made the Passover celebration of redemption a memorial of his death, he said, "This cup is the new covenant in my blood, which is poured out for you" (Luke 22:20). Jesus instituted the new covenant as a confession to the new Exodus.

The Passover celebrated salvation, which began with the Exodus from Egypt (2 Kings 17:7, 36). Isaiah promised redemption to the exiles; there would be another exodus in which the glory of Yahweh is revealed (Isa. 40:3–5). The exodus promised by Isaiah finds its ultimate fulfillment in Jesus Christ: "The beginning of the gospel about Jesus Christ, the Son of God. It is written in Isaiah the prophet . . . a voice of one calling in the desert, 'Prepare the way for the Lord, make his straight paths for him'" (Mark 1:1–3, quoting from Isa. 40:3).

The Exodus was renewed in Jesus' death and resurrection, as declared to Moses and Elijah on the Mount of Transfiguration; Luke uses the word *exodos* to describe the events about to take place in Jerusalem (Luke 9:31).

Christianity is this new exodus, Christians the members of this new covenant. The church continues the work of God, for which the prophets longed.

In this new covenant there is forgiveness of sins; each one teaches the other to know the Lord, as Jeremiah promised. Jesus turns the Passover into a confession of this new covenant. The wine is his blood of the covenant, shed for many for the forgiveness of sins (Matt. 26:28). Paul declares the cup of the Passover is the new covenant in the blood of Christ; eating the bread and drinking the wine must be done in remembrance of Christ until he comes (1 Cor. 11:25–26). The Eucharist is the confession of the new redemption that follows the failures of the old covenant.

Covenant obedience. The church continues to have its own challenge in attempting to exercise faith and obedience under the new covenant. From the beginning, the dangers of syncretism, so condemned by the Deuteronomistic Historians, has threatened the life of the church. Paul warned the Colossians not to let anyone judge them by what they ate or drank, or in regard to festivals, monthly celebrations, or Sabbath days (Col. 2:16). Some in Colosse had a false humility, delighting in the worship of angels (v. 18); they disqualified others from the kingdom, claiming special powers on the basis of the things they had seen. Their pride carried them away into idle speculations.

Sectarianism has been also a grave danger to the church from the beginning. Divisions and strife entered the Corinthian church, not long after Paul was there; certain groups preferred Paul, Apollos, or Cephas, and some claimed the supremacy of Christ (1 Cor. 1:10–13). Each claimed some superior knowledge in living the life of faith.

A covenant requires trust and faithfulness. Where there is trust in God and commitment to his kingdom, there is faithfulness to the relationship established by the covenant obligation. The Deuteronomistic Historians measured trust and faithfulness in specific terms of worship. Failure to reverence God alone according to the regulations of the temple in Jerusalem brought condemnation. This measure of covenant faithfulness was principally pertinent in judging the loyalty of the people collectively and explaining the cause of the Exile. Other measures of covenant faithfulness included individual measures of conduct. With the disappearance of Israel, these measures included the specific requirements of belonging to a particular community.

One of the most notable documents of concerning such covenant obedience at Qumran uses the phrase "works of the law."[28] This phrase should

---

28. Six manuscripts of this sectarian document were found in Qumran cave 4. It is known as 4QMMT, an abbreviation for *miqṣāt maʿáśeh hattôrâ*. For the propsal that this is the

not be interpreted as a works religion, for faith was indeed the fundamental requirement for entering the community. This document (4QMMT) has three sections: The first deals with calendar, the second deals with covenant obligations, and the third is an exhortation to covenant commitment. It is in this third section that the sect's understanding of faith and covenant loyalty is expressed. It uses language like that of the New Testament to urge covenant fidelity.

Paul warns the Galatians against seeking salvation by such obedience to works of the law (Gal. 3:5); the gift of the Spirit is a fulfillment of the covenant promise. Redemption is received by faith, just as Abraham received it when he trusted God (3:6–8). The third section of 4QMMT has language similar to what Paul uses in applying to Christians the covenant trust required of Abraham (Gen. 15:6).[29] "We have (indeed) sent you some of the precepts of the Torah according to our decision, for your welfare and the welfare of your people" (C 27). Observance of these works of the law "will be counted as a virtuous deed of yours, since you will be doing what is righteous and good for the welfare of Israel" (C 31).

The phrase "counted as righteousness" is first used of Abraham (Gen. 15:6); it is also used to describe the action of Phinehas in stopping the plague at Baal Peor (Ps. 106:31). The Qumran writer is probably echoing the Psalms reference. Acting on the promise in faith qualified Abraham to enter into the covenant (Gen. 15:6–21). The action of Phinehas was a similar demonstration of faith counted as righteousness for future generations. The Qumran covenanters believed that following their directives was an obedience of faith that would bring them the benefits of the covenant relationship.

The apostle James quotes the promise to Abraham in the same spirit as is found in the Qumran document:

> Was not our ancestor Abraham considered righteous for what he did when he offered his son Isaac on the altar? You see that his faith and his actions worked together, and faith was made complete by what he did. And the scripture was fulfilled that says, "Abraham believed God, and it was credited to him as righteousness," and he was called God's friend. (James 2:21–23)

Faith is requisite to belonging to the new covenant. The evidence of faith is found in adherence to the oath obligation. In this respect the new covenant

---

equivalent of "some of the works of the law" see Martin G. Abegg, "4QMMT C 27, 31 and 'Works of Righteousness,'" *DSD* 6 (1999): 139–47. The document is fragmentary, even with the complement of all six copies.

29. The official translation of the document is the work of Elisha Qimron and John Strugnell, *Qumran Cave 4 V* (JDJ 10; Oxford: Clarendon, 1994).

is not different from the old covenant as understood by the Deuteronomistic Historians or the later Qumran sectarians.

Paul and James would affirm the covenant concept as expressed in 4QMMT, but they would differ vigorously with the understanding of covenant obligations. Paul does not deal with the postbiblical regulations found in MMT in speaking about the "works of the law," but he does deal with circumcision, Sabbath-keeping, and food laws. This has little to do with discussions of streams of liquids (MMT, B 55–58) or the presence of dogs in the temple precincts (MMT, B 58–62). In speaking of the "works of the law," Paul deals with a different version of ritual obedience, but like the Qumran sectarians, it has to do with the rites and practices peculiar to a faith confession in the context of the temple presence.

Such rites have lost their significance with the absence of the temple and the presence of Jesus as the glory of God revealed among us (John 1:14). The difference of the new covenant is the glory of God revealed in Jesus Christ. With the coming of Jesus, the old symbols and rituals have passed away and can have no role in making confession of faith in God.

James looks for the confession of faith along the lines of that required by the prophets in urging justice and care for the poor: "Suppose a brother or a sister is without clothes and daily food. If one of you says to him, 'Go, I wish you well; keep warm and well fed,' but does nothing about his physical needs, what good is it? In the same way faith by itself, if it is not accompanied by action, is dead" (James 2:15–17). The new covenant expresses nothing new in its requirement for covenant faith. The former covenant always had as its priority respect for all people and care for the needy. These were "works of the law," in the sense that the Torah and the prophets always required justice as the practice of faith. So James can conclude, "You see that a person is justified by what he does and not by faith alone" (2:24). Profession of belief apart from commitment and obedience is not faith.

The ritual requirement of the Deuteronomistic Historians or the regulations of the sectarians that followed them are not relevant under the new covenant. Demanding that such rituals be observed is to fail to understand their symbolic significance for God's presence and to deny the divine presence in Jesus Christ. This is why all such "works of the law" are so resisted and condemned by Paul. The principle of covenant faith, however, has not changed, nor has its essential requirement of care for all people, particularly those of "the family of believers" (Gal. 6:10). Those who neglect this covenant obligation cannot be said to have faith and trust in God.

Facing materialism. Modern Christians face all the perils of the ancient Israelites in the practice of faith. The danger in Israel was a compromise with Baal religion, essentially a materialist cult. Canaanite religions served gods of fertility; the quest of their religion was to serve the gods for the prosperity of their herds and crops. During the days of Jeroboam and Azariah, Israel and Judah did become extremely wealthy. Their materialism expressed itself in a failure of justice to care for the poor, as the prophets emphasized, but also in their neglect of the temple, as stressed by the Deuteronomistic Historians.

The apostle Paul has a similar warning to Christians: We must put away our former conduct corrupted by deceitful desires (Eph. 4:22). Those outside the covenant live in a vain way of thinking, their understanding is darkened; they are alienated from the life of God (vv. 17–18). We as Christians must be renewed in our thinking, for we are a new creation, restored to function as the image of God (vv. 23–24). Modern Christians, as easily as Israel, can be deceived by material desires and thus fail to keep our covenant with God.

Humans have a distinct role in this world. We belong to the material world and have material needs. We have been created to serve as God's image-bearers in this world, to represent his rule and his presence. As the image of God, we participate in the holy—that which is separate from this world. Our lives as humans in the material world are not an end in itself; they are to serve the purpose of the holy, to make known the majestic name of Yahweh in all the earth (Ps. 8). Ancient Israel became caught up with the material in Baal worship and failed the requirement of the covenant. Baal is ever present in the materialism of human society and a threat to the faithful of the new covenant in the same way.

2 Kings 18:1–20:21

I N THE THIRD year of Hoshea son of Elah king of Israel, Hezekiah son of Ahaz king of Judah began to reign. ²He was twenty-five years old when he became king, and he reigned in Jerusalem twenty-nine years. His mother's name was Abijah daughter of Zechariah. ³He did what was right in the eyes of the LORD, just as his father David had done. ⁴He removed the high places, smashed the sacred stones and cut down the Asherah poles. He broke into pieces the bronze snake Moses had made, for up to that time the Israelites had been burning incense to it. (It was called Nehushtan.)

⁵Hezekiah trusted in the LORD, the God of Israel. There was no one like him among all the kings of Judah, either before him or after him. ⁶He held fast to the LORD and did not cease to follow him; he kept the commands the LORD had given Moses. ⁷And the LORD was with him; he was successful in whatever he undertook. He rebelled against the king of Assyria and did not serve him. ⁸From watchtower to fortified city, he defeated the Philistines, as far as Gaza and its territory.

⁹In King Hezekiah's fourth year, which was the seventh year of Hoshea son of Elah king of Israel, Shalmaneser king of Assyria marched against Samaria and laid siege to it. ¹⁰At the end of three years the Assyrians took it. So Samaria was captured in Hezekiah's sixth year, which was the ninth year of Hoshea king of Israel. ¹¹The king of Assyria deported Israel to Assyria and settled them in Halah, in Gozan on the Habor River and in towns of the Medes. ¹²This happened because they had not obeyed the LORD their God, but had violated his covenant—all that Moses the servant of the LORD commanded. They neither listened to the commands nor carried them out.

¹³In the fourteenth year of King Hezekiah's reign, Sennacherib king of Assyria attacked all the fortified cities of Judah and captured them. ¹⁴So Hezekiah king of Judah sent this message to the king of Assyria at Lachish: "I have done wrong. Withdraw from me, and I will pay whatever you demand of me." The king of Assyria exacted from Hezekiah

king of Judah three hundred talents of silver and thirty talents of gold. ¹⁵So Hezekiah gave him all the silver that was found in the temple of the LORD and in the treasuries of the royal palace.

¹⁶At this time Hezekiah king of Judah stripped off the gold with which he had covered the doors and doorposts of the temple of the LORD, and gave it to the king of Assyria.

¹⁷The king of Assyria sent his supreme commander, his chief officer and his field commander with a large army, from Lachish to King Hezekiah at Jerusalem. They came up to Jerusalem and stopped at the aqueduct of the Upper Pool, on the road to the Washerman's Field. ¹⁸They called for the king; and Eliakim son of Hilkiah the palace administrator, Shebna the secretary, and Joah son of Asaph the recorder went out to them.

¹⁹The field commander said to them, "Tell Hezekiah:

"'This is what the great king, the king of Assyria, says: On what are you basing this confidence of yours? ²⁰You say you have strategy and military strength—but you speak only empty words. On whom are you depending, that you rebel against me? ²¹Look now, you are depending on Egypt, that splintered reed of a staff, which pierces a man's hand and wounds him if he leans on it! Such is Pharaoh king of Egypt to all who depend on him. ²²And if you say to me, "We are depending on the LORD our God"—isn't he the one whose high places and altars Hezekiah removed, saying to Judah and Jerusalem, "You must worship before this altar in Jerusalem"?

²³"'Come now, make a bargain with my master, the king of Assyria: I will give you two thousand horses—if you can put riders on them! ²⁴How can you repulse one officer of the least of my master's officials, even though you are depending on Egypt for chariots and horsemen? ²⁵Furthermore, have I come to attack and destroy this place without word from the LORD? The LORD himself told me to march against this country and destroy it.'"

²⁶Then Eliakim son of Hilkiah, and Shebna and Joah said to the field commander, "Please speak to your servants in Aramaic, since we understand it. Don't speak to us in Hebrew in the hearing of the people on the wall."

²⁷But the commander replied, "Was it only to your master and you that my master sent me to say these things, and not to the men sitting on the wall—who, like you, will have to eat their own filth and drink their own urine?"

²⁸Then the commander stood and called out in Hebrew: "Hear the word of the great king, the king of Assyria! ²⁹This is what the king says: Do not let Hezekiah deceive you. He cannot deliver you from my hand. ³⁰Do not let Hezekiah persuade you to trust in the LORD when he says, 'The LORD will surely deliver us; this city will not be given into the hand of the king of Assyria.'

³¹"Do not listen to Hezekiah. This is what the king of Assyria says: Make peace with me and come out to me. Then every one of you will eat from his own vine and fig tree and drink water from his own cistern, ³²until I come and take you to a land like your own, a land of grain and new wine, a land of bread and vineyards, a land of olive trees and honey. Choose life and not death!

"Do not listen to Hezekiah, for he is misleading you when he says, 'The LORD will deliver us.' ³³Has the god of any nation ever delivered his land from the hand of the king of Assyria? ³⁴Where are the gods of Hamath and Arpad? Where are the gods of Sepharvaim, Hena and Ivvah? Have they rescued Samaria from my hand? ³⁵Who of all the gods of these countries has been able to save his land from me? How then can the LORD deliver Jerusalem from my hand?"

³⁶But the people remained silent and said nothing in reply, because the king had commanded, "Do not answer him."

³⁷Then Eliakim son of Hilkiah the palace administrator, Shebna the secretary and Joah son of Asaph the recorder went to Hezekiah, with their clothes torn, and told him what the field commander had said.

¹⁹:¹When King Hezekiah heard this, he tore his clothes and put on sackcloth and went into the temple of the LORD. ²He sent Eliakim the palace administrator, Shebna the secretary and the leading priests, all wearing sackcloth, to the prophet Isaiah son of Amoz. ³They told him, "This is what Hezekiah says: This day is a day of distress and rebuke and disgrace, as when children come to the point of birth and there is no strength to deliver them. ⁴It may be that the LORD your God will hear all the words of the field commander, whom his

master, the king of Assyria, has sent to ridicule the living God, and that he will rebuke him for the words the LORD your God has heard. Therefore pray for the remnant that still survives."

⁵When King Hezekiah's officials came to Isaiah, ⁶Isaiah said to them, "Tell your master, 'This is what the LORD says: Do not be afraid of what you have heard—those words with which the underlings of the king of Assyria have blasphemed me. ⁷Listen! I am going to put such a spirit in him that when he hears a certain report, he will return to his own country, and there I will have him cut down with the sword.'"

⁸When the field commander heard that the king of Assyria had left Lachish, he withdrew and found the king fighting against Libnah.

⁹Now Sennacherib received a report that Tirhakah, the Cushite king of Egypt, was marching out to fight against him. So he again sent messengers to Hezekiah with this word: ¹⁰"Say to Hezekiah king of Judah: Do not let the god you depend on deceive you when he says, 'Jerusalem will not be handed over to the king of Assyria.' ¹¹Surely you have heard what the kings of Assyria have done to all the countries, destroying them completely. And will you be delivered? ¹²Did the gods of the nations that were destroyed by my forefathers deliver them: the gods of Gozan, Haran, Rezeph and the people of Eden who were in Tel Assar? ¹³Where is the king of Hamath, the king of Arpad, the king of the city of Sephar-vaim, or of Hena or Ivvah?"

¹⁴Hezekiah received the letter from the messengers and read it. Then he went up to the temple of the LORD and spread it out before the LORD. ¹⁵And Hezekiah prayed to the LORD: "O LORD, God of Israel, enthroned between the cherubim, you alone are God over all the kingdoms of the earth. You have made heaven and earth. ¹⁶Give ear, O LORD, and hear; open your eyes, O LORD, and see; listen to the words Sennacherib has sent to insult the living God.

¹⁷"It is true, O LORD, that the Assyrian kings have laid waste these nations and their lands. ¹⁸They have thrown their gods into the fire and destroyed them, for they were not gods but only wood and stone, fashioned by men's hands. ¹⁹Now, O LORD our God, deliver us from his hand, so that all kingdoms on earth may know that you alone, O LORD, are God."

²⁰Then Isaiah son of Amoz sent a message to Hezekiah: "This is what the LORD, the God of Israel, says: I have heard

your prayer concerning Sennacherib king of Assyria. ²¹This is
the word that the LORD has spoken against him:

> "'The Virgin Daughter of Zion
>> despises you and mocks you.
> The Daughter of Jerusalem
>> tosses her head as you flee.
> ²²Who is it you have insulted and blasphemed?
>> Against whom have you raised your voice
> and lifted your eyes in pride?
>> Against the Holy One of Israel!
> ²³By your messengers
>> you have heaped insults on the Lord.
> And you have said,
>> "With my many chariots
> I have ascended the heights of the mountains,
>> the utmost heights of Lebanon.
> I have cut down its tallest cedars,
>> the choicest of its pines.
> I have reached its remotest parts,
>> the finest of its forests.
> ²⁴I have dug wells in foreign lands
>> and drunk the water there.
> With the soles of my feet
>> I have dried up all the streams of Egypt."
>
> ²⁵"'Have you not heard?
>> Long ago I ordained it.
> In days of old I planned it;
>> now I have brought it to pass,
> that you have turned fortified cities
>> into piles of stone.
> ²⁶Their people, drained of power,
>> are dismayed and put to shame.
> They are like plants in the field,
>> like tender green shoots,
> like grass sprouting on the roof,
>> scorched before it grows up.
>
> ²⁷"'But I know where you stay
>> and when you come and go
>> and how you rage against me.

²⁸Because you rage against me
      and your insolence has reached my ears,
  I will put my hook in your nose
      and my bit in your mouth,
  and I will make you return
      by the way you came.'

²⁹"This will be the sign for you, O Hezekiah:

  "This year you will eat what grows by itself,
      and the second year what springs from that.
  But in the third year sow and reap,
      plant vineyards and eat their fruit.
  ³⁰Once more a remnant of the house of Judah
      will take root below and bear fruit above.
  ³¹For out of Jerusalem will come a remnant,
      and out of Mount Zion a band of survivors.

The zeal of the LORD Almighty will accomplish this.

³²"Therefore this is what the LORD says concerning the king
of Assyria:

  "He will not enter this city
      or shoot an arrow here.
  He will not come before it with shield
      or build a siege ramp against it.
  ³³By the way that he came he will return;
      he will not enter this city,

                                        declares the LORD.
  ³⁴I will defend this city and save it,
      for my sake and for the sake of David my servant."

³⁵That night the angel of the LORD went out and put to
death a hundred and eighty-five thousand men in the Assyrian
camp. When the people got up the next morning—there were
all the dead bodies! ³⁶So Sennacherib king of Assyria broke
camp and withdrew. He returned to Nineveh and stayed there.

³⁷One day, while he was worshiping in the temple of his
god Nisroch, his sons Adrammelech and Sharezer cut him
down with the sword, and they escaped to the land of Ararat.
And Esarhaddon his son succeeded him as king.

²⁰:¹In those days Hezekiah became ill and was at the point
of death. The prophet Isaiah son of Amoz went to him and

said, "This is what the LORD says: Put your house in order, because you are going to die; you will not recover."

²Hezekiah turned his face to the wall and prayed to the LORD, ³"Remember, O LORD, how I have walked before you faithfully and with wholehearted devotion and have done what is good in your eyes." And Hezekiah wept bitterly.

⁴Before Isaiah had left the middle court, the word of the LORD came to him: ⁵"Go back and tell Hezekiah, the leader of my people, 'This is what the LORD, the God of your father David, says: I have heard your prayer and seen your tears; I will heal you. On the third day from now you will go up to the temple of the LORD. ⁶I will add fifteen years to your life. And I will deliver you and this city from the hand of the king of Assyria. I will defend this city for my sake and for the sake of my servant David.'"

⁷Then Isaiah said, "Prepare a poultice of figs." They did so and applied it to the boil, and he recovered.

⁸Hezekiah had asked Isaiah, "What will be the sign that the LORD will heal me and that I will go up to the temple of the LORD on the third day from now?"

⁹Isaiah answered, "This is the LORD's sign to you that the LORD will do what he has promised: Shall the shadow go forward ten steps, or shall it go back ten steps?"

¹⁰"It is a simple matter for the shadow to go forward ten steps," said Hezekiah. "Rather, have it go back ten steps."

¹¹Then the prophet Isaiah called upon the LORD, and the LORD made the shadow go back the ten steps it had gone down on the stairway of Ahaz.

¹²At that time Merodach-Baladan son of Baladan king of Babylon sent Hezekiah letters and a gift, because he had heard of Hezekiah's illness. ¹³Hezekiah received the messengers and showed them all that was in his storehouses—the silver, the gold, the spices and the fine oil—his armory and everything found among his treasures. There was nothing in his palace or in all his kingdom that Hezekiah did not show them.

¹⁴Then Isaiah the prophet went to King Hezekiah and asked, "What did those men say, and where did they come from?"

"From a distant land," Hezekiah replied. "They came from Babylon."

¹⁵The prophet asked, "What did they see in your palace?"

"They saw everything in my palace," Hezekiah said. "There is nothing among my treasures that I did not show them."

¹⁶Then Isaiah said to Hezekiah, "Hear the word of the LORD: ¹⁷The time will surely come when everything in your palace, and all that your fathers have stored up until this day, will be carried off to Babylon. Nothing will be left, says the LORD. ¹⁸And some of your descendants, your own flesh and blood, that will be born to you, will be taken away, and they will become eunuchs in the palace of the king of Babylon."

¹⁹"The word of the LORD you have spoken is good," Hezekiah replied. For he thought, "Will there not be peace and security in my lifetime?"

²⁰As for the other events of Hezekiah's reign, all his achievements and how he made the pool and the tunnel by which he brought water into the city, are they not written in the book of the annals of the kings of Judah? ²¹Hezekiah rested with his fathers. And Manasseh his son succeeded him as king.

THE END OF the northern kingdom of Israel came during the reign of Hezekiah when Sargon vanquished Samaria (18:9–12; cf. ch. 17). Shalmaneser dealt with a rebellious Hoshea by attacking Samaria; after Shalmaneser's death, Sargon besieged Samaria and deported Israelites during a rapid campaign, which included virtually all the Levant.[1]

The Assyrian advance continues with the devastating attack of Sennacherib king of Assyria against Judah in the fourteenth year of Hezekiah's reign (18:13–16). The importance of the Assyrian siege in Deuteronomistic History is evident in the length of the account (18:17–19:36). Little else is said of Hezekiah; the events associated with the siege demonstrate both his faithfulness and his failure. Jerusalem is delivered because of the faith of Hezekiah, but his faithlessness in allying with Merodach-Baladan of Babylon

---

1. Kings names Shalmaneser as the conquering king; the same claim is made in the Babylonian Chronicle (Millard, *The Context of Scripture*, 1.137). Sargon, in his inscriptions, claims (eight times) to have conquered Samaria. His great "Summary Inscription" is explicit on the conquest of Samaria (Younger, *The Context of Scripture* 2.118E 23–27). For a full discussion of the evidence see K. Lawson Younger, "The Fall of Samaria in Light of Recent Research," *CBQ* 61 (1999): 461–82.

shows that the ultimate destiny of Judah will be the same as that of Israel (20:17–19). Though Hezekiah is more like David than any of other king before him, the failures leading to exile are present in his reign as well.

The Faithful King (18:1–12)

IN CONTRAST TO all the previous kings of Israel and Judah, Hezekiah is introduced as the faithful king, one who reformed Judean worship and moved Judah toward the ideal of the covenant. Hezekiah is not merely similar to David as Asa (1 Kings 15:11) or Jehoshaphat (22:43) were, but is the very model of the Davidic ideal (2 Kings 18:3, 5). His faithfulness results in the preservation of Jerusalem, a stark contrast to the captivity of Israel.

This point is made explicit by recounting again the fall of Israel, which takes place early in Hezekiah's life, while he is coregent with his father, Ahaz.[2] Hezekiah's independent rule begins in 715 B.C., fourteen years before the siege against Jerusalem.[3] He is rewarded for his faithfulness, not only in successfully resisting the Assyrian advances but also in securing his boundaries toward the Philistine territories (18:7–8). Hezekiah's trust is particularly evident when he refuses to yield to the Assyrians, even when the fortified cities of Judah are destroyed and the Assyrian armies have encircled Jerusalem.

The religious reform of Hezekiah is not related to a rebellion against Assyria. During the Assyrian siege the Rabshakeh (NIV "field commander") infers that the destruction of the high places, altars, and Asherah poles is evidence that Hezekiah has actually rebelled against his own God (18:22). This Assyrian leader feels that Hezekiah cannot encourage the people of Jerusalem to trust in their God when their own king has offended him by removing his images.

It is reasonable for the Assyrians to assume that the Israelite God was honored by these images; the Assyrian general makes a point about the removal of Israelite images, but not about the removal of Assyrian images.[4]

---

2. For a summary of the chronological difficulties, see the conclusion of Appendix B.

3. The earliest record of the siege is the Rassam cylinder, which bears the date Iyar 700 B.C., a half year or so after the end of the hostilities. See the translation of Mordechai Cogan, "Sennacherib's Siege of Jerusalem," *The Context of Scripture*, 2.119B.

4. The studies of Mordechai Cogan, *Imperialism and Religion* (Missoula, Mont.: Scholars Press, 1974), and John McKay, *Religion in Judah under the Assyrians* (Naperville, Ill.: Allenson, 1973), have shown that the Assyrians did not impose their religion on subjugated territories. S. Holloway cautions that distinctions between religio-political treatment of client states and provinces as proposed by Cogan and McKay is untenable; *Aššur is King! Aššur is King: Religion in the Exercise of Power in the Neo-Assyrian Empire* (Leiden: Brill, 2002), 198. Forcible introduction of divinized images into palaces and city temples is known only in Mesopotamia; it is impossible to extrapolate the geographical extent of such royal iconography.

Hezekiah's religious reform is political, possibly in anticipation of Assyrian attacks. Removal of the high places not only follows the demands of the covenant, but it centralizes the authority of Hezekiah in Jerusalem. Hezekiah initiates a significant buildup of economic resources and civil power.[5] The relegation of Israel to Assyrian control during Hezekiah's early years (cf. Isa. 8:21–9:1) necessitates preparations for further Assyrian advances.

The high places, pillars, and Asherah poles are familiar cult objects; the bronze serpent, referred to as "the bronze thing," is mentioned only here. The name (*nᵉḥuštān*) is a clever combination of the word snake (*nāḥāš*) and bronze (*nᵉḥōšet*).[6] When the Israelites had been afflicted with venomous snakes in the desert, healing was found by looking at a bronze snake Moses made and elevated on a bronze pole according to God's instruction (Num. 21:4–9).

The image of a dead snake as an agent to bring life fits the logic of the Israelite sacrificial system; though no connection is suggested, the identification of the bronze snake with the desert serpent is entirely credible.[7] Hezekiah rigorously adheres to the covenant requirement; his allegiance to God demonstrates God's wisdom that will be the envy of the nations (18:6; cf. Deut. 4:4–8). His prosperity is not only prudent administration, but also divine blessing.

Devastation of Judah (18:13–16)

THE SUCCESS AND prosperity of Hezekiah come to an abrupt end with Assyria's invasion of Judah. This short description of Judah's devastation has its parallel in Sennacherib's boast of the conquests of his third campaign: "As for Hezekiah the Judean, I besieged forty-six of his fortified walled cities and surrounding smaller towns, which were without number.... He himself, I locked up in Jerusalem, his royal city, like a bird in a cage."[8]

A monumental wall relief from the palace of Sennacherib in Nineveh commemorates the battle over Lachish and the deportation of its inhabitants.[9] This commemoration of that siege demonstrates its strategic importance in Assyria's military advance. Sennacherib records a payment of thirty talents of gold (approximately one ton) and eight hundred talents of silver

---

5. Andrew G. Vaughn, *Theology, History and Archaeology in the Chronicler's Account of Hezekiah* (Atlanta: Scholars Press, 1999), 19–79. Archaeological evidence of the major centers and territories of Judah show that population and economic activity significantly increased during the time of Hezekiah.

6. Hobbs, *2 Kings*, 252.

7. Robert C. Stallman, "נָחָשׁ," *NIDOTTE*, 3:86.

8. M. Cogan, "Sennacherib's Siege of Jerusalem," *The Context of Scripture*, 2.119B.

9. Pritchard, ed., *The Ancient Near East in Pictures*, 371–73.

(approximately thirty tons). The exact correspondence to the amount of gold listed in 18:14 is striking; the greater quantity of silver may be explained by the inclusion of the precious metals stripped from the temple.[10] The Assyrian annals are much more detailed, including a long list of booty items and the captivity of over two hundred thousand Judeans.

The discrepancy between this account and the following story of Jerusalem's deliverance has led to the suggestion that there are two campaigns against Judah. The first campaign in 701 B.C. ends in Assyrian victory and an assertion of its hegemony over Judah. A second campaign after the capture of Babylon in 689 B.C. ends in an Assyrian retreat to Nineveh and the assassination of the Assyrian king a short time later. It is not surprising that the Assyrian records make no mention of such a campaign, since records of defeat are never retained. Yet Assyrian history shows that the conquest of Sennacherib is so devastating that there is no resistance to Assyrian domination in the west even after his assassination and the ascension of Esarhaddon.

The Assyrian records never claim to have taken Jerusalem. The best explanation for leaving Jerusalem unconquered is that Sennacherib abandons the campaign after his army is decimated in his third campaign (19:35). The main problem with postulating a second western campaign is the claim that the biblical account has conflated two different wars into one.[11] But Judaean source material could hardly have confused two separate wars, nor is it likely two wars would have been conflated for the sake of simplification.

Deliverance of Jerusalem (18:17–19:37)

KINGS REPEATEDLY EMPHASIZES the use of various sources in writing the covenant history of Israel and Judah. This section seems to be a separate source from the previous description of the attack. The account of the devastation is usually described as archival, as shown by the date formula and its data on the treasury and temple. The name of Hezekiah has a distinct spelling in the archival account. According to the Assyrian sources, the tribute is sent after Sennacherib sets out for Nineveh; the plundering of the treasuries to send tribute is the end of the event.[12] The narrative then reverts to events as they unfold during the attack. Most likely the two sources are simply joined in order to avoid conjectural resconstructions.

---

10. Cogan and Tadmor, *II Kings*, 299.

11. William R. Gallagher, *Sennacherib's Campaign to Judah: New Studies* (Studies in the History and Culture of the Ancient Near East 18; Leiden: Brill, 1999), 8.

12. The surrender of Hezekiah is unique in royal inscriptions, and some embarrassment is behind it. The view of Judah was quite different (2 Kings 19:21b). Sennacherib's return without taking Jerusalem was probably occasion for derision elsewhere (Gallagher, *Sennacherib's Campaign to Judah*, 140–41).

The narrative alludes to various locations in a sequence of events that are not fully explained. The biblical events are part of a larger Assyrian campaign into Philistia and Judah. Following the annals of Sennacherib, the cities of Timnah, Ekron, Azekah, and Gath first come under siege.[13] Lachish, the largest city conquered, is then attacked; the dirge of Micah over the other towns of the Shephelah suggests the fate of other populations in the area (Mic. 1:8–16). It is probably at this point that Hezekiah sends messengers to offer a conditional surrender, allowing him to keep his throne (18:14).[14] The offer is refused; Sennacherib instead sends his chief officials and a significant military force to Jerusalem (18:17). Lachish falls to the Assyrians, and its inhabitants are deported.

Sennacherib then proceeds to Libnah (19:8), where his officials meet him. He continues his conquest of Judean cities, but is diverted to Eltekeh to deal with an Egyptian force that has arrived there (v. 9). This turn of events has a mitigating effect on the Assyrian negotiations; another delegation is sent to Hezekiah, though the demands are not specified (vv. 10–13). Death in the Assyrian army forces Sennacherib to retreat to Nineveh (vv. 35–36). He reaches an agreement for withdrawal that requires Hezekiah to pay tribute, which is sent to Nineveh.

Jerusalem attracts a heavy military force under the direction of the top generals (18:17). The Tartan (NIV "supreme commander") is the highest official after the king (cf. Isa.20:21); the Rabsaris (NIV "chief officer") is often dispatched on duties at the head of Assyrian forces; the Rabshakeh (NIV "field commander") is the personal attendant of the king. The "aqueduct of the Upper Pool, on the road of the Washerman's Field" (a place for washing garments) is also mentioned in Isaiah 7:3, but its location and the source of the water is not known. Eliakim, the royal steward in charge of the palace (cf. 1 Kings 4:6), is at the head of Hezekiah's delegation (2 Kings 18:18); the "secretary" and the "recorder" are the other chief-ranking officers. In the ensuing speech, Hezekiah is always referred to by his personal name, while the Assyrian king is designated "the great king."

The field commander is the spokesman for the Assyrians, quite possibly because of his fluency in languages (18:26–27). His attack centers on the question of trust (vv. 21–25). Reliance on Egypt is compared to a splintered reed (Egypt had many marshy waters) that will pierce the hand rather than serve as support. Trust in God is undermined, because presumably Hezekiah has insulted Yahweh by removing the high places. Thus, the only reasonable

---

13. Aharoni, *The Carta Bible Atlas*, 117–18 (# 154).

14. Gallagher has thoroughly examined all the sources in suggesting the following sequence of events (*Sennacherib's Campaign to Judah*, 261).

alternative is to enter an agreement with the Assyrians. The Assyrian even claims that his presence at Jerusalem indicates the Judahite God has abandoned his people and joined the Assyrian side.

The shouting to the people on the wall is designed to intimidate. Though the envoys of Sennacherib and the Jerusalem delegates know Aramaic well, the international language of the day, the field commander insists on speaking Judahite (18:28), the Hebrew dialect of the south. He threatens the people with the dire consequences of starvation, which is the typical result of siege warfare (v. 27; cf. 6:24–31).

As is typical of brutal conquerors, his promise is one of prosperity and independence (18:31–32). Sennacherib boasts of conquests of Aramean cities that have been captured much earlier (v. 34); Hamath and Samaria were captured by Sargon, Arpad by Tiglath-Pileser III (cf. 17:24). Hezekiah is duly humbled by this intimidation (19:3); it is a day of distress, rebuke, and contempt. The day is equivalent to a stillbirth, a proverb also quoted by Hosea (Hos. 13:13). Yet in spite of such threats, the prophet Isaiah assures Hezekiah that Sennacherib will soon hear news that will drive him back to his own land.

The message of Isaiah leads to a transition in the narrative. The report of the arrival of the Egyptians causes an Assyrian withdrawal (19:8–9a). There is a certain parallel in the sequence of events that follow (19:9b–34). Since Stade, it has often been proposed that there are two sources for the same series of events.[15] "So he again sent" (19:9b) can also mean "so he returned," since the Hebrew verb *šûb* can be adverbial ("again") or can mean "return." Gallagher has reviewed all the arguments and concludes that evidence of two sources for the same event is unconvincing.[16] The narrative reads sensibly as a sequel; the Egyptians do not effect a withdrawal of the Assyrians, so Hezekiah must go to Isaiah a second time to receive words of assurance.

The repeated boasts of Assyrian conquests are impressive (19:12). Gozan was a provincial capital on the upper Habor River; Rezeph was capital of a large Assyrian province in upper Mesopotamia; the Arameans of Eden on the Euphrates were resettled in far eastern Zagros region of the Diyala River; Lair was in northeastern Babylonia (v. 13). In response to such taunts, Hezekiah prays; he is granted access to the temple, where he prays before the cherubim (v. 15), who represent the throne of the Creator of the universe.

Isaiah delivers an answer to Hezekiah's prayer as a mocking song (19:21–28). The wagging of the head is a sign of scorn (19:21; cf. Ps. 22:7; 109:25).

---

15. B. Stade, "Anmerkungen zu 2 Kö. 15–21," *ZAW* 6 (1886): 173–80. These two sources are customarily labeled B1 (18:17–19:9a) and B2 (19:9b–37), distinguishing them from the annalistic report (18:13–16), which is labeled A.

16. Gallagher, *Sennacherib's Campaign to Judah*, 149–59.

The sentiment of the song is typical of Isaiah; the divine plan has been determined from the beginning of the world (2 Kings 19:25; Isa. 40:21; 46:10). The Assyrian boasts of his conquests; the people are rendered powerless, dismayed, and confounded, and fortifications have been shattered. However, the Assyrians will not escape the destruction of war, which they have executed as part of God's judgment (cf. Isa. 10:5–7). God knows their every action, their every pursuit (2 Kings 19:27).[17] Assyrians led their prisoners by placing rings in their lips and attaching ropes to them; they themselves will be taken captive as wild animals with hooks.

The assurance that Sennacherib will be turned back to the way he came is given twice: in the conclusion to the taunt song (19:28c), and in the pledge that God will be the fortress for Jerusalem (19:33–34). Judah will feel the effects of the foreign presence; it will be two years before a normal agricultural cycle of sowing and harvest can resume (vv. 29–30). Intentional destruction of fields, such as cutting down vineyards, is well attested in Assyrian records.[18]

Though there will be a great deportation of peoples, those who survive will take root as a healthy plant, once again making the country prosperous (19:30). The second oracle makes it clear that there was no actual siege against Jerusalem as at Lachish and the other fortified cities of Judah (vv. 32–34). God protects Jerusalem for the sake of his own name and because of his promise to David (cf. 1 Kings 11:32). The continuation of the Davidic dynasty is confirmed.

A naturalistic explanation of the destruction of the Assyrian armies because of a plague misses the point of the narrative. Traditions arose to explain the miraculous deliverance (cf. Sir. 48:20–21; Josephus, *Ant.* 10.19–21). The account of Herodotus, the fifth-century Greek historian referred to by Josephus, has no relevance for the Bible. His version is that mice chewed up the quivers and bows, disarming the Assyrians. Mice were traditional carriers of plagues, suggesting that Herodotus retold the story in Greek terms.[19] Most likely the Egyptian account that Herodotus relied on had its own origin as

---

17. "Every action" (*qmk*) is restored on the basis of the Isaiah parallel in Qumran; the haplography took place because of similarity with *qdm* (east wind), which was found in the previous verse (in place of *qmh*, translated "grows up").

18. Tiglath-Pileser ravaged the environs of Damascus: "His gardens . . . plantations, which were without number, I cut down, not one escaped" (Luckenbill, *Ancient Records of Assyria and Babylonia*, 1.776); he did the same in Chaldea: "The . . . groves which were (planted) along his (city) walls, I cut down" (1:792).

19. Historians cannot deal with such questions; Gonçalves is typical in regarding the plague as a theological explanation for the deliverance: *L'expédition de Sennachérib en Palestine dans la littérature hébraïque ancienne* (EBib, New series 7; Paris: Gabalda, 1986), 483–84.

an echo of the story from Jerusalem.[20] The Bible properly explains the phenomena as a divine deliverance—with no further explanation.

The Bible ignores the twenty years that elapse before the assassination of Sennacherib. The point is that divine judgment is meted out on the cruel Assyrian invader. Later Babylonians similarly view their destruction of Assyria as just retribution on Sennacherib. The circumstances of his murder are unknown, as is a god by the name of Nisroch (possibly a deliberate corruption). The Babylonian Chronicle confirms the assassination of Sennacherib.[21] Adrammelech is a phonetic reproduction of the Assyrian Arad-Ninlil (pronounced Arda-milissu).

Deliverance from Illness (20:1–11)

HEZEKIAH'S ILLNESS RECEIVES a loose chronological link with the time of the Assyrian invasion. It takes place at almost the same time; the invasion takes place in the fourteenth year of Hezekiah (18:13), and he rules a total of twenty-nine years (18:2). He is given an extra fifteen years of life at the time of his illness (20:6).[22] The message of Isaiah for Jerusalem is affirmative, but initially not so for its king. On receiving the news of his impending death, King Hezekiah turns to God. Isaiah returns with the message that Hezekiah will be delivered, as will Jerusalem, because of God's reputation and the promise made to David (20:6; cf. 19:34).

The healing of Hezekiah from some type of skin disease is facilitated with a fig cake plaster. Jewish and classical sources show that dried figs were widely used for their medicinal qualities.[23] The healing is followed by a request for a sign. Hezekiah seeks assurance that he will live to give praise to God, as expressed so eloquently in the song in Isaiah (Isa. 38:19–20). The prophetic sign is given as an evidence of the significance of the healing.

Josephus interprets a shadow moving ahead as signifying a life that has already passed; Hezekiah requests that it return ten degrees, signifying a return to life and health instead of approaching death (*Ant.* 10.28).[24] Shad-

---

20. Gallagher, *Sennacherib's Campaign to Judah,* 245–51.

21. Millard, "The Babylonian Chronicle," 1.137, iii 34–38.

22. The visit of Merodach-Baladan almost certainly precedes the siege, which takes place in 701 B.C. The last year of his rule is 703 B.C. It is improbable that a visit subsequent to that time would have been possible or sensible; see John Walton, "New Observations on the Date of Isaiah," *JETS* 28 (1985): 129–32.

23. See R. K. Harrison, "Medicine," *IDB,* 3:331–34. The type of skin disorder is related to a root meaning "inflamed" (to be hot); it is used for the plagues in Egypt (Ex. 9) and in Job 2.

24. According to the Hebrew text, "the shadow has moved ahead ten degrees" (*hlk*); most translations turn this into a question to ask if the shadow should move ahead ten degrees (*hylk*) or turn back ten degrees.

ows naturally lengthen, just as people naturally grow old; Hezekiah is asking for a reversal of the normal progression. The steps appear to be a feature within the structure of the building that enable measurement of time.

Failure of Faith (20:12–21)

THE VISIT OF the Babylonian envoys has the same general chronological link to the time of the Assyrian siege. The sequence is arranged to show the threat to Jerusalem and the Davidic dynasty, the basic purpose of the Deuteronomistic History.[25] The Assyrians are constantly at war with the Babylonians. Merodach-Baladan ("Marduk has given a son") ruled twice in Babylon, first during the reign of Sargon until forced into the marshes of Lower Mesopotamia (720–709 B.C.), and again briefly after the reign of Sargon (704–703). No purpose for the visit is stated; it is probably an effort to maintain goodwill between common enemies of the Assyrians.

Hezekiah's display of all his treasures to the Babylonian envoys is the kind of confidence in foreign alliances that the prophet Isaiah so vehemently condemns (Isa 31:1). "Storehouse" ($n^e k\bar{o}t$) is an Akkadian loanword, indicating a repository for booty; it may have had a particular architectural style used by Hezekiah. The Sargonid kings of Assyria also had vast armories for storing and training puposes, which may have been emulated by Hezekiah.

For this perfidy with the Babylonians, Hezekiah receives the ultimate judgment; his dynasty will end with his descendants going into exile. However during Hezekiah's time, the city of Jerusalem is spared judgment. Hezekiah is famous for his defenses of the city, particularly in securing a water supply (20:20). This involved cutting a tunnel under the walls of the city to carry the waters of the Gihon spring to the Siloam Pool. An inscription at the entrance to the tunnel commemorates this feat of ancient engineering.[26] The tunnel is over five hundred meters (over 1,600 feet) long, essentially an enlargement of natural dissolution channels. To save time as the Assyrians advance, it is cut by two groups of workmen working toward each other.

Hezekiah resigns himself to the declaration of judgment he receives (20:20); the word of Yahweh is appropriate. The statement of self-interest, that there will be peace during his days, is drawn into Kings from Isaiah's account.[27]

---

25. Richard S. Hess, "Hezekiah and Sennacherib in 2 Kings 18–20," in *Zion City of our God*, ed. Richard Hess and Gordon Wenham (Grand Rapids: Eerdmans, 1999), 40–41. The pattern of three consecutive actions is a technique in biblical narrative.

26. For a translation see K. Lawson Younger Jr., "The Siloam Tunnel Inscription," *The Context of Scripture*, 2.28.

27. See A. H. Konkel, "The Source of the Story of Hezekiah in the Book of Isaiah," *VT* 43 (1993): 477–78.

The failure of peace is a motif in Isaiah (Isa. 48:22; 57:21). Hezekiah does not fall into the category of the wicked, but his faithlessness in the matter of the Babylonian embassy is one more example of why Judah goes into exile.

Bridging Contexts

YAHWEH AND SENNACHERIB. In later Jewish tradition Hezekiah becomes venerated as a man of faith and success. In Sirach he is remembered for his fortifications and water provision, his obedience like that of David, the sign he received, and his revelation of the future (Sir. 48:17–25). In the Talmud, Hezekiah is the messiah, and Sennacherib is like Gog and Magog (*b. Sanb.* 94a). Rabban Johanan ben Zakkai at his death asked that a throne be prepared for Hezekiah king of Judah, who is coming (*b. Ber.* 28b). The veneration of Hezekiah in later tradition is readily understood as a development from the Deuteronomistic Historians, who portray Hezekiah as a man of faith, both in the narrative (2 Kings 18:5–6) and in the speeches of the field commander (18:17–25, 28–25). Hezekiah is a model of covenant fidelity.

It is notable that Kings gives so little attention to the cultic reforms of Hezekiah, insofar as the measure of covenant fidelity is worship in Jerusalem. The key achievement of his reign as remembered in the prophetic sources is the deliverance of Jerusalem. This is particularly relevant to the central concern of the Deuteronomistic Historians, whose intent is to provide a theological explanation for the Exile. Hezekiah is the supreme example of how exile is averted by faithfulness. The theology of trusting in God is presented in the words of the principal characters. The real protagonists in the story are Sennacherib and Yahweh, though they never actually appear on the scene. They act through their respective representatives, Isaiah and the field commander (Rabshakeh). Their war of words reveals the real issue, as articulated by Fewell:

> The Rabshakeh claims that Hezekiah's words are empty (18:20), offensive to Yahweh (18:22), and deceptive (18:30, 32). The people's words are imprudent (18:22), and Yahweh's words are not simply misleading (19:10), but are out-and-out double-dealing (18:25)! Hezekiah and Yahweh classify the Assyrian's words as mocking (*brp*, 19:4, 16, 22, 23), blasphemous (*gdp*, 19:6, 22), and raging (*rgz*, 19:27, 28).[28]

The speech of the field commander is presented as a counter to that of the prophet Isaiah.[29] The field commander takes his position by the aqueduct

---

28. Dana Fewell, "Sennacherib's Defeat: Words at War in II Kings 18:13–19:37," *JSOT* 34 (1986): 83.
29. Dominic Rudman, "Is the Rabshakeh Also among the Prophets? A Rhetorical Study of 2 Kings XVIII 17–35," *VT* 50 (2000): 101–3.

of the Upper Pool in the highway of the Washerman's Field (18:17); this is the same location where Isaiah earlier encountered Ahaz (Isa. 7:5).

The words of the field commander are introduced like the oracles of a prophet (2 Kings 18:19, 29, 31; cf. 19:6). His claim that Egypt cannot be trusted is the virtual equivalent of the prophet (18:21, 24; Isa. 31:1). He promises to grant peace to the people so that everyone may "eat from their vine and fig tree and drink water from their own cistern" (2 Kings 18:31). This was the experience of the people in the days of Solomon (1 Kings 5:5) and was the hope held out for those vanquished (Mic. 4:4). In effect, Sennacherib offers a new covenant to supersede the one in force between Yahweh and Israel. This is the point of offering the Israelites a "blessing" (2 Kings 18:31).[30] Sennacherib promises the benefits of the covenant with God if the people will only surrender to him.

Yahweh's response through Isaiah is not so much a reply to Hezekiah as it is to Assyrian arrogance (19:21–31). The taunting oracle asks whom the Assyrian has scorned (v. 22); this is a direct response to the question about whom Hezekiah has trusted (18:22; 19:10). The Assyrian demands to know who has escaped from his power (18:33–35; 19:12–13). God rehearses his claim (19:23–24) and then declares his plans made long ago (vv. 25–28): The Assyrians themselves will be led away as captives. The promise of sowing and harvesting is particularly fitting to a besieged city (19:29–30). God makes plain that he is the One to offer terms of life and death (vv. 32–34); Sennacherib cannot usurp that role.

Hezekiah in Kings and Isaiah. In the book of Isaiah, the faith of Hezekiah is set in deliberate contrast to the perfidy of Ahaz. Both Ahaz and Hezekiah are threatened with the destruction of Jerusalem (cf. Isa. 7:1–2). Ahaz is given the assurance of the prophet, who meets him on the road by the pool; mere human forces, represented by the capital cities of Samaria and Damascus and their respective kings Pekah and Rezin, can be no threat to the Holy One of Israel (17:7–9a). Ahaz is offered a sign but refuses it (7:11–13). By contrast, when Hezekiah is confronted with the words of the field commander, he seeks out Isaiah with a word from Yahweh. When confronted with a threat to his life, he turns in prayer to Yahweh and receives a sign that will assure his recovery (38:1–8). In contrast to faithless Ahaz, Hezekiah is a model king, one who exemplifies trust and dependence on God on behalf of his people.

In Isaiah, the healing becomes an example for the restoration of Jerusalem. The sign is an immediate sequel to the promise of healing (Isa. 38:7–8) rather

---

30. The word $b^e r\bar{a}k\hat{a}$ is the standard formulation for expressing the benefit derived from covenant fidelity. "Make peace with me" (NIV) has the sense of "earn benefits from me (by making a covenant)."

than a separate section assuring the king that he will yet worship at the temple (2 Kings 20:8–11). Following the promise of the sign, Isaiah introduces a psalm of Hezekiah celebrating his restoration to life and worship (Isa. 38:10–20). The text in Isaiah is subtly adjusted so the focus is no longer on the king but on the restoration of the city.[31] In Isaiah there is no mention of healing in response to the prayer of Hezekiah; the prophet promises an addition of fifteen years to the life of Hezekiah and assures him that God will deliver him and Jerusalem from the power of the Assyrians.

The sign follows, as an assurance God will deliver the king and the city from the threat of Sennacherib. The poem serves as a message of hope for the city. As Ackroyd has shown, the psalm of Hezekiah concentrates on his experience as a restoration back to life, typical of metaphors used in Lamentations and Jeremiah for the experience of exile.[32] The climax is reached with the individual joining the community in worship at the temple. The illness and death of Hezekiah become a kind of judgment and exile; the song points to the possibility of the restoration of the people of Zion.

The texts of Isaiah do not refer to Hezekiah personally going up to the house of Yahweh, as in 2 Kings 20:5, 8. Whereas in Kings attention focuses entirely on Hezekiah as an individual, in Isaiah he typifies the restoration of the community, and the royal line in particular, as continuing to worship in the Lord's house. In this new context, reference to a single visit to the temple is inappropriate.[33] The climax of the poetic account of Hezekiah's restoration comes with the celebration that he and his children give praise to God throughout their lives in the house of Yahweh:

> The living, the living—they praise you,
>   as I am doing today;
> fathers tell their children
>   about your faithfulness.
> The LORD will save me,
>   and we will sing with stringed instruments
> all the days of our lives,
>   in the temple of the LORD. (Isa. 38:19–20)

In Isaiah, the Hezekiah story provides a transition to a message of hope and restoration (Isa. 40–55). The Hezekiah story ends as it does in Kings, with the prophecy that the descendants of Hezekiah will go to captivity in

---

31. Konkel, "The Sources of the Story of Hezekiah in the Book of Isaiah," 478–81.

32. P. R. Ackroyd, "The Death of Hezekiah—A Pointer to the Future?" in *De la tôrah au messie: mélanges H. Cazelles*, ed. M. Carrez, J. Doré, and P. Grelot (Paris: Cerf, 1981), 344–46.

33. H. G. M. Williamson, "Hezekiah and the Temple," in *Texts, Temples and Traditions*, ed. Michael V. Fox et al. (Winona Lake, Ind.: Eisenbrauns, 1996), 52.

Babylon. A bridge to the message of hope antecedes the Hezekiah story (esp. Isa. 35), with the themes of divine judgment on the nations and the return of the redeemed to Zion. Numerous literary motifs of the second half of Isaiah are introduced. The narrative of Hezekiah, adopted and adapted from the book of Kings, becomes a demonstration of God's defeat of the nations and hope for the return to Zion and worship at the temple.[34]

The faithfulness of Hezekiah does not receive the same emphasis in Isaiah as it does in 2 Kings, since Isaiah lacks the introduction 2 Kings 18:1–12; the threat to Judah is minimized, because Isaiah does not include the report on the Assyrian devastation of all the fortified cities (vv. 13–16). The healing of Hezekiah becomes less central, as Isaiah does not have two distinct sections concerning the healing (20:1–7) and the sign for the healing (vv. 8–11). Instead, the prayer and the sign emphasize restoration to life; the restoration of the king also holds promise for the community of faith. The loss of the nation can be sustained as long as there is the promise of continued worship of God at the temple, which symbolizes God's presence in the world.

Hezekiah in Chronicles. In Chronicles Hezekiah becomes the ideal king. Though the textual similarity is more limited, the dependence of the Chronicler on 2 Kings is obvious. The introduction (2 Chron. 29:1–2) and conclusion (32:33–34) have been adopted from his source. The three main events of Kings are treated in the same order: the siege of Sennacherib (32:1–21), Hezekiah's illness (vv. 24–26), and the visit of the Babylonian envoys (v. 31).

The account of Hezekiah is among the longest in Chronicles (2 Chron. 29–31), describing at length his restoration of the temple, Passover celebration, appointment of temple personnel, and provisions for the temple. The Passover includes an invitation to the people of Israel, who have already been exiled by the Assyrians; they respond in great numbers (30:10–13), even though they are not consecrated (30:18–20). The prayer of Hezekiah heals the people, according to the formula given by Solomon (7:14). This extensive development of Hezekiah's reign gives a different significance to the material that has been carefully followed from the Kings source.

After all the magnificent reform Hezekiah has undertaken, the attack of Sennacherib comes as an assault against the city of God. The Chronicler does not concern himself with multiple appearances of emissaries before the city. Sennacherib's efforts at intimidation are combined into a single event;

---

34. For detailed analysis of the textual history of these Hezekiah accounts, see Konkel, "The Sources of the Story of Hezekiah in the Book of Isaiah," 462–82; for additional literary analysis, see H. G. M. Williamson, *The Book Called Isaiah* (Oxford: Clarendon, 1994), 184–239.

the letters occur between the threats of the field commander and shouting to the people on the wall (32:15–18). Hezekiah has thoroughly prepared for the attack, and the city of Jerusalem is invincible under divine protection.

The Chronicler portrays Hezekiah as a second Solomon.[35] The days of Solomon are described as days of blessing; the hope of Israel is to return to such a time. During the time of Ahaz, Israel comes to be in a state of virtual exile. South and north have become apostate. Hezekiah's renewal provides for restoration and unification, a time that can be compared with Solomon's. The king begins to restore the temple as soon as he begins to reign (2 Chron. 29:3). Solomon built a house dedicated for the burning of sweet spices, continual showbread, and regular offerings. Hezekiah refers to these items in his confession (29:7) and makes provision for their restoration (v. 18). He appoints the priests and the Levites (31:2) and makes provision for the restoration of the sacrifices (31:3).

At the time of the celebration of the Passover under Hezekiah there is "great joy in Jerusalem, for since the days of Solomon son of David king of Israel there had been nothing like this in Jerusalem" (30:26). One distinctive of Hezekiah's celebration, similar to the dedication of the temple under Solomon, is its duration; it lasts an extra seven days (30:23; cf. 7:8–9).

A second indication of renewal in Chronciles is Hezekiah's success in inviting the northern remnant to participate in the feast; as in the days of Solomon, all Israel is united in worship at the temple. The Passover is observed with all the people (30:5), including the resident aliens from Israel (30:25). The reunion of Israel in the celebration of worship at the temple reverses the times of unfaithfulness in the days of Ahaz. Repentance and restoration bring about the ideal of the kingdom of God, as it was known in the days of Solomon.

The Chronicler portrays Hezekiah according to his central theological concerns. A king who has acted faithfully will know God's blessing through victory in war (32:1), building programs, wealth, fame among the Gentiles, healing in times of illness, and the regard of his people at death.[36] The Chronicler is much concerned about exile and restoration. Hezekiah is a model for avoiding exile and enjoying restoration. He shows the path to recovery after foreign domination under Ahaz. His faithfulness avoids exile for Judah in his days (32:26).

In both Kings and Isaiah the visit of the Babylonians becomes the portent of exile; in Chronicles this is depicted differently. In the earlier accounts the visitors from Babylon come in response to the miraculous recovery from ill-

35. Dillard, 2 *Chronicles*, 237.
36. Ibid., 260–61.

ness; in Chronicles they come in response to the well-known Babylonian interest in astrology, inquiring about the reversal of the shadow (2 Chron. 32:31). The suggestion of political intrigue found in Kings is absent, and Hezekiah's display of wealth is regarded positively (32:27–29). The visit of the envoys is seen as a test from God (v. 31), which is necessary after Hezekiah's prior deviation and repentance. The account of Hezekiah in Chronicles concludes on a positive note. The Chronicler becomes the first to treat Hezekiah, along with David and Solomon, as a messianic figure. In his faithfulness he embodies the hopes of Israel for the restoration of a united people enjoying peace, victory, and prosperity.

Hezekiah and Babylonians. In the final analysis, the Deuteronomistic History is about the Exile. Babylon as a place of exile appears for the first time at the conclusion of the Hezekiah story. This appearance demonstrates the blindness of the king to historical reality. The Babylonians' "seeing" the complete stock of the treasuries of temple and palace point toward a threatening future (2 Kings 20:13).

The most probable reason for the visit of Merodach-Baladan and his emissaries is to seek cooperation against the Assyrians. With an alliance in the west, Merodach-Baladan can engage the Assyrians on two fronts at the time of the ascension of Sennacherib. Hezekiah fails to appreciate his own vulnerability to Babylonian power. The Babylonian inspection of the Judean resources, even in the interests of an alliance, is an initial stage in taking possession of them. This event apparently takes place just before the fifteen years are added to his life, and possibly before the Assyrian attack, which occurs in his fourteenth year. The exposure of all military and economic resources to those from "a foreign land" (2 Kings 20:14–15) is an ominous portent of the future (Deut. 29:22–23). Inspection of the Promised Land by foreigners is a sign of judgment like that of Sodom and Gomorrah.

Hezekiah's response to the prophetic word of judgment appears to be that of resignation and cynicism: "The word of the LORD you have spoken is good. . . . Will there not be peace and security in my lifetime?" Though many attempts have been made to explain the severity of the judgment against Hezekiah, the narrative gives no indication that the threat of exile is a direct consequence of his actions. The judgment that will shortly occur is not by accident, nor is it evoked directly by the misdeeds of the king. Events are unfolding according to the divine plan: "The word of God is fulfilled in history; it has not failed."[37]

The final words about "peace and security" in the lifetime of Hezekiah are derived from Isaiah. They are not found in the earliest texts of Kings, and they

---

37. Von Rad, *Studies in Deuteronomy*, 78.

are a characteristic marker in Isaiah (Isa. 48:22; 57:21).[38] In Isaiah, they are particularly appropriate following the theology of the poem of Hezekiah, which points to the possibility of life and hope in spite of judgment. The response of Hezekiah is to be regarded as acceptance of the divine will and, with the final phrase, emphasizes the divine grace extended during the lifetime of the faithful king.[39]

Whatever the failure of Hezekiah in his willingness to entertain the Babylonians, his loyalty and faithfulness are not without an enduring benefit. Prophetic words of judgment can be regarded as salvific for the lifetime of the king, as is the case with Micah the prophet in the days of Hezekiah (Jer. 26:16–19). Hezekiah is credited with the appropriate response to the words of Micah, with the result that judgment is delayed. The positive assessment given to Hezekiah in the days of Jeremiah seems to be present in Kings as well.

FAITHFULNESS. Faithfulness is primary in any relationship and is the most fundamental requirement in a relationship with God. A covenant is the highest commitment of faithfulness; for Hezekiah, the covenant is both collective and personal. He represents the people who have entered into a divine covenant and leads them to faithfully observe it. This is possible only because of his own faithfulness, seen in both his response to the Assyrian threat and his illness.

Christians in the same way are called to faithfulness, both collectively and individually. In writing to the Corinthians, Paul exhorts the believers to be faithful to Christ, because all things are theirs in Christ (1 Cor. 3:21–23). He uses the metaphor of a steward to describe the calling of Christians to represent God in his world. All things belong to Christ, and by extension to his followers. When Paul refers to "stewards of the mysteries of God" (4:1, NASB), he means that Christians fulfill the work of God's kingdom in this world until such time as it is consumated in the second coming of Christ. As stewards responsible for the work of the kingdom in this world, faithfulness is the one fundamental requirement (v. 2).

Such stewardship is much more than just giving money or being prudent with material possessions. It means to use every moment of time as a gift from God in a way that honors God. In this respect Christians must not become

---

38. Konkel, "The Sources of the Story of Hezekiah in the Book of Isaiah," 477.

39. P. R. Ackroyd, "An Interpretation of the Babylonian Exile: A Study of II Kings 20, Isaiah 38–39," *SJT* 27 (1974): 340–41.

unduly introspective; Paul himself notes that he does not spend time on self-examination (1 Cor. 4:3–5). He knows of nothing that will compromise his faithfulness, but that judgment belongs to the Lord. When the Lord comes, he will make manifest our intentions more clearly than we can know them now.

Hezekiah is a model of the exhortation the apostle leaves Christians. The motives of Hezekiah can be questioned in the way he dealt with the Assyrians, in his prayer during the time of his illness, and particularly in his culpability in exposing his wealth and military capabilities to the Babylonian emissaries. In all of these matters Hezekiah is simply presented as a king in pursuit of faithfulness, doing the best he can within his own circumstances.

In the case of the Assyrian siege, Hezekiah brings his case to God through the mediation of the prophet Isaiah in quiet confidence: "It may be that the LORD your God will hear all the words of the field commander, whom his master, the king of Assyria, has sent to ridicule the living God, and that he will rebuke him for the words the LORD your God has heard. Therefore pray for the remnant that still survives" (2 Kings 19:4). In the announcement of his impending death, Hezekiah seeks solitude and leaves his request for healing unspoken; in prayer he recalls his loyalty, dedication, and integrity before God (20:2–3). With the announcement of inevitable exile, Hezekiah accepts the fate of his people as God's will fulfilled, with gratitude for his grace extended in the present (v. 19). Hezekiah is not flawless, but he always pursues faithfulness.

A faithful life inspires faithfulness in others. Hezekiah inspires faithfulness in his time, with the result that Jerusalem is spared and a time of peace comes. Faithfulness, however, is not abandonment to commitment; it requires careful thought concerning the optimum way to serve the kingdom with the resources available and the challenges of the circumstances.

Sometimes faithfulness requires the ultimate commitment of dying for the truth. Antipas, from the church of Pergamum, was a faithful witness (*martys*) to the point of death (Rev. 2:13). Polycarp, the second-century bishop of Smyrna, when called on to revile Christ, replied: "Eighty and six years have I served Him and He hath done me no wrong. How can I revile my Lord and Savior?" (*Mart. Pol.* 9.3). Unfortunately, in the course of Christian history, martyrdom has been desired as a way of demonstrating the ultimate commitment. Willingness to die can be a failure to be willing to live for the purpose to which God has called us. Life is a gift to be used as a steward, unless it is simply impossible to do so.

Since the time of the martyrs, who were the seed of the church, many have suffered and given their lives in faithfulness to the gospel. *Voice of the Martyrs*, the worldwide organization begun by Richard Wurmbrand, daily gathers scores of reports of Christians being faithful under circumstance of severe persecution and death.[40] The writer to the Hebrews exhorts Christians to be faithful in time of suffering (Heb. 10:32–39). They suffered public humiliation and identified with those who so suffered; they suffered the plundering of their possessions. Endurance of suffering for the sake of the kingdom is the mark of faithfulness, which will bring a great reward.

Faithfulness and holy war. Zeal for a cause is not to be regarded as the faithfulness demanded of God's children. Our zeal may not be God's cause or God's way. An interview with a suicide bomber reveals something of zeal for a goal, where the end justifies the means, but which has nothing to do with being faithful to more important values. Marwan Abu Ubeida (a generic Iraqi name) prepared for months to climb into a bomb-laden vehicle or to strap on an explosives-filled vest.[41] He spent much time rehearsing his last prayer: "May Allah bless my mission with a high rate of casualties among the Americans. May he purify my soul so I am fit to see him, and may I see my *mujahedin* brothers who are already with him."

At age twenty, Marwan was a battle-hardened insurgent, a jihadi foot soldier. His oversize hands were heavily calloused from use of his favorite weapon, the Russian-made PKC machine gun. His journey to become a suicide bomber began when American soldiers fired on a crowd of demonstrators at a school, killing twelve and wounding many more. Marwan was part of the protest, but escaped unharmed. A few days later he and friends collected arms from a military site abandoned by the Iraqi army and attacked a building occupied by U.S. soldiers. Marwan was part of a long list of volunteers; when he was finally accepted, it was the happiest day of his life. He could hardly wait for the time of his opportunity; he was ready to die.

Patience and discipline are certainly critical to the mission of a suicide bomber. Waiting is the hardest part; volunteers need to undergo a program to discipline the mind and cleanse the soul. The training is done by field commanders and clerics sympathetic to the insurgency. The training is mainly psychological and spiritual. Marwan spent his time reading the Koran, the history of the jihad, and the great martyrs who had gone on before. Suicide bombers immerse themselves in spiritual contemplation and prayer, seeking to free their minds of negative thoughts toward their fellow humans, except for Americans and their infidel Iraqi supporters. They share their final hours with fellow suicide bombers, with expectations that they will meet again in heaven.

---

40. Examples of persecution in dozens of countries may be found at www.persecution. net and www.persecution.org.

41. Aparisim Ghosh, "Inside the Mind of an Iraqi Suicide Bomber," *Time* (July 4, 2005), 10–15.

Marwan was certain that he was on a pure path. "Yes," he said, "I am a terrorist. Write that down; I admit I am a terrorist. The Koran says it is the duty of Muslims to bring terror to the enemy, so being a terrorist makes me a good Muslim." Marwan quoted lines from the surah (section of the Koran) known as Al-Anfal (The Spoils of War): "Against them make ready your strength to the utmost of your power, including steeds of war, to strike terror into the enemy." Marwan's only regret was that innocent fellow Iraqis might be killed. If some did die, when they got to heaven, Allah would ask them to forgive him. Marwan would not be a hero; unlike Palestinian martyrs, his identity would not be known. That did not matter to him; the only person who matters is Allah, and the only question he asks is how many infidels were killed.

Jihad (struggle or battle) is a religious duty imposed on Muslims to wage war in the spread of Islam. Jihad can be fulfilled through the heart, the tongue, the hand, and the sword. "Jihad of the heart" consists of spiritual battle against evil in one's own life; "jihad of tongue and hand" is largely accomplished by supporting what is right and correcting what is wrong. "Jihad of the sword" is physical warfare against unbelievers and enemies of the Islamic faith. This is often translated as "holy war," the same phrase scholars use for divine warfare in the Bible. But we must maintain a sharp distinction between the two. Divine warfare in the Bible occurs when God fights on behalf of his people. Jihad in Islam is when people go to war on behalf of God. This inspires the mind of a suicide bomber like Marwan, making him believe he is on a pure path to an exalted eternal state.

The distinction between "holy war" in Christianity and Islam has not been well maintained. The ideal of biblical "holy war" is exemplified in the Hezekiah story; Hezekiah, helpless before his enemies, turns to Isaiah for direction and turns in prayer to the Holy One seated in his royal throne above the cherubim (2 Kings 19:15). "Holy war" takes place when 185,000 Assyrian soldiers die in the camp in one night (v. 35) and Sennacherib returns in defeat to his own country, where he is killed by his own sons (vv. 36–37). This is the occasion of Hezekiah being faithful and trusting God, so inadvertently and elegantly expressed in the words of the field commander.

Such "holy war" is most easily enacted when there is no alternative. Hezekiah has already stripped the royal treasury, and the land has been plundered (18:14–16). Egypt has already proved to be of no help. His is fully a war of defense. Divine warfare is not always defensive, and human participation can be a part of divine warfare, as the stories in Joshua attest. Warfare has often been carried on in the name of God, not unlike the jihad of the sword.

Among the most infamous of wars for God are the Crusades. It is ironic that the Crusades should have begun with a council that both officially sanctioned war and promulgated peace. The Council of Clermont convoked by Urban II in 1095 included a canon that granted a plenary indulgence (the remission of all penance for sin) to those who undertook to aid Christians in the East. This peace movement was designed to protect those in distress, such as those Christians who lived in the oppression of Muslim lands.

Precisely what the pope said when he addressed a large crowd of representatives will never be known, since surviving accounts were written years later.[42] He apparently stressed the plight of Eastern Christians, the molestation of the Christian pilgrims, and the desecration of the holy places. He urged those of his hearers guilty of disturbing the peace to turn their energies toward a holy cause. Cries of *Deus volt* ("God wills it") were heard everywhere; it was also decided that those who agreed to go should wear a cross. A large popular element joined the warrior knights. The result was less than the desired end of undertaking a pilgrimage with the most exalted of motives and an acceptance of suffering.

Faithfulness and prayer. A contrast to the Crusades is the legacy of Pope John Paul II. His legacy for the church is likely to be mixed, but his influence as a spiritual leader has been demonstrated in the enormous response to his death, especially by the young. Irish novelist Colm Toibin describes the effect of John Paul's dramatic gesture of holding his head in his hands for twenty minutes before a crowd of one million pilgrims in Poland. What he did ceased to be a public gesture, but became instead intensely private. "He was offering the young who had come here in the infant years of Eastern European democracy not a lesson in doctrine of faith or morals but some mysterious example of what a spiritual life might look like."[43]

Prayer was a fundamental aspect of the way Karol Wojtyla lived and the way he died. Any attempt to evaluate the enormous response to his death has to consider his prayer life. *National Geographic* photographer Jim Stanfield spoke of being alone with John Paul in the Garden of Our Lady at Castel Gandolfo, the pope's summer residence. The Holy Father went to a kneeler and started to pray; then they walked for about a mile. Stanfield says, "That was probably the most significant and the most rewarding experience of my life, bar none."[44] Faithfulness in prayer is one of the most challenging disciplines of the Christian life.

A second concern characteristic of John Paul II was his pastoral concern for young people. Journalist Vittorio Messori writes of John Paul's discovery

---

42. Marshall W. Baldwin, "Crusades," *Encyclopaedia Britannica Macropaedia*, 15th edition, 5:299.

43. Quoted by Robert Proctor, *Commonweal* 132 (June 3, 2005): 19.

44. Ibid.

of the essential importance of youth as a young priest in Poland.[45] Youth is a time given by providence to each person and given as a task: to answer the fundamental questions concerning not only the meaning and purpose of life, but also the concrete project or direction life will take. Youth is the period of the personalization of human life. It is also the period of communion; a human being has a vocation to love. Young people know that they have to live for and with others; they know that their life has meaning when it becomes a free gift to one's neighbor.

Faithfulness and endurance of pain. Another area of faithfulness is the endurance of pain. In the case of Hezekiah, prayer was rewarded with an extension of health, but loss of strength is the inevitable experience of human life in this world. John Paul was a model in his public persona, but also in the suffering he endured. Death and pain in the body are two of our greatest fears as human beings. John Paul II lived and died publicly. He believed he was being led by the Holy Spirit; he believed there were no coincidences in life. His natural talents and habits enabled him to make what can be called a good death. More people followed the death of John Paul than any other major news media event. The reaction to his death was occasioned in large measure by the way he triumphed over sickness and death.

Faithfulness and disappointment. A most difficult circumstance for faithfulness is disappointment and failure to reach a goal. This was the case for Hezekiah in the message he received concerning the future of his people. Irrespective of his life of reform and dedication to the true worship of God, the end for his people would be the judgment of exile. Hezekiah determined to pursue peace in his time. It did not change his commitment or his faithfulness.

The disappointment of failure was also expressed in the prayer of Moses. On the very edge of the Promised Land, Moses asked that he be allowed to just step over the river to at least symbolically represent the achievement of his life desire (Deut. 3:23—29). This was not just his own failure; Moses suffered because of the rebellion of others, and he died with them. His only fulfillment was to observe the land from the peaks of Mount Pisgah. Joshua was delegated to go on to fulfill the mission.

This is remembered in Psalm 90, a psalm designated as a "prayer of Moses." The psalm reflects on life in the presence of a God who is eternal (vv. 1—6), holy (vv. 7—12), and merciful (vv. 13—17). His eternal nature is a reminder of the relative duration of required faithfulness; the length of time in life is not nearly as significant as faithfulness. The struggle in life is because we belong

---

45. Proctor refers to the Italian version (ibid., 20), translated as *Crossing the Threshold of Hope.*

to the world of the common, a world of suffering, a world separated from the holiness of God. The prayer of Moses is that we may experience both joy and fulfillment because of God's mercy. Joy is that experience of peace that is equal to the troubles of the day (vv. 14–15); fulfillment is to know that God has taken our work and made it part of his kingdom (vv. 16–17).

Moses is not remembered for his disappointment in not crossing the Jordan; it is seldom recalled that he spent the majority of his life in the desert and the early part of it in alienation from his people. Moses is remembered as the leader of Israel, the mediator of the covenant relationship. Hezekiah is not remembered for being the first to receive the announcement of exile. Rather, he is remembered for his faithfulness, for being a king who symbolized hope in time of death, for being a king who was a type of messianic significance.

There are times when faithfulness in the Christian life seems as futile as Moses in the desert or Hezekiah sparing Jerusalem. There may be long and agonizing illness, years of constant caregiving. There may be years of labor, where work seems nothing more than drudgery in order to make a living. Faithfulness in this world is not always rational. Often its value can only be recognized in looking back at how God has used it. Faithfulness is the one thing God requires of stewards. The consequences of failure to be faithful are certain. The end of the book of Kings is one testimony of the results of unfaithfulness.

2 Kings 21:1–26

MANASSEH WAS TWELVE years old when he became
king, and he reigned in Jerusalem fifty-five years.
His mother's name was Hephzibah. ²He did evil in
the eyes of the LORD, following the detestable practices of the
nations the LORD had driven out before the Israelites. ³He
rebuilt the high places his father Hezekiah had destroyed; he
also erected altars to Baal and made an Asherah pole, as Ahab
king of Israel had done. He bowed down to all the starry hosts
and worshiped them. ⁴He built altars in the temple of the
LORD, of which the LORD had said, "In Jerusalem I will put my
Name." ⁵In both courts of the temple of the LORD, he built
altars to all the starry hosts. ⁶He sacrificed his own son in the
fire, practiced sorcery and divination, and consulted mediums
and spiritists. He did much evil in the eyes of the LORD, provoking him to anger.

⁷He took the carved Asherah pole he had made and put it in
the temple, of which the LORD had said to David and to his son
Solomon, "In this temple and in Jerusalem, which I have chosen
out of all the tribes of Israel, I will put my Name forever. ⁸I will
not again make the feet of the Israelites wander from the land I
gave their forefathers, if only they will be careful to do everything I commanded them and will keep the whole Law that my
servant Moses gave them." ⁹But the people did not listen. Manasseh led them astray, so that they did more evil than the
nations the LORD had destroyed before the Israelites.

¹⁰The LORD said through his servants the prophets:
¹¹"Manasseh king of Judah has committed these detestable
sins. He has done more evil than the Amorites who preceded
him and has led Judah into sin with his idols. ¹²Therefore this
is what the LORD, the God of Israel, says: I am going to bring
such disaster on Jerusalem and Judah that the ears of everyone
who hears of it will tingle. ¹³I will stretch out over Jerusalem
the measuring line used against Samaria and the plumb line
used against the house of Ahab. I will wipe out Jerusalem as
one wipes a dish, wiping it and turning it upside down. ¹⁴I will
forsake the remnant of my inheritance and hand them over to
their enemies. They will be looted and plundered by all their

foes, [15]because they have done evil in my eyes and have provoked me to anger from the day their forefathers came out of
Egypt until this day."

[16]Moreover, Manasseh also shed so much innocent blood
that he filled Jerusalem from end to end—besides the sin that
he had caused Judah to commit, so that they did evil in the
eyes of the LORD.

[17]As for the other events of Manasseh's reign, and all he
did, including the sin he committed, are they not written in
the book of the annals of the kings of Judah? [18]Manasseh
rested with his fathers and was buried in his palace garden, the
garden of Uzza. And Amon his son succeeded him as king.

[19]Amon was twenty-two years old when he became king,
and he reigned in Jerusalem two years. His mother's name was
Meshullemeth daughter of Haruz; she was from Jotbah. [20]He
did evil in the eyes of the LORD, as his father Manasseh had
done. [21]He walked in all the ways of his father; he worshiped
the idols his father had worshiped, and bowed down to them.
[22]He forsook the LORD, the God of his fathers, and did not
walk in the way of the LORD.

[23]Amon's officials conspired against him and assassinated
the king in his palace. [24]Then the people of the land killed all
who had plotted against King Amon, and they made Josiah his
son king in his place.

[25]As for the other events of Amon's reign, and what he did,
are they not written in the book of the annals of the kings of
Judah? [26]He was buried in his grave in the garden of Uzza.
And Josiah his son succeeded him as king.

Original Meaning

MANASSEH BECOMES THE "Jeroboam I "of Judah, the
figure who personified all the sins of the subsequent
kings of Israel (1 Kings 16:6, 19, 26, 31, etc.). Manasseh's fifty-five year reign of apostasy between
good kings Hezekiah and Josiah makes his evil worse by contrast. He begins
by restoring all the cult places destroyed by Hezekiah, his father (2 Kings 21:3).

Manasseh goes beyond any previous king of Judah in multiplying idolatries (21:6). His reign is oppressive and violent (v. 16); Josephus reports that
prophets are slaughtered daily until Jerusalem overflows with blood (*Ant.*
10.38). According to tradition, Isaiah is among them (*Martyrdom and Ascen-*

sion of Isaiah, 5.1).[1] The sins of Manasseh are not his alone; he seduces the people of Judah to become idolatrous, with abominations worse than the Amorites who had lived there before (2 Kings 21:9, 11). The short two-year reign of Amon continues the age of idolatry fostered by Manasseh. His reign is brought to an abrupt end by a palace coup.

Abominations of Manasseh (21:1–18)

WITH THE DISAPPEARANCE of the northern kingdom, there are no more synchronisms for the ascension of each king. Manasseh is born in the forty-second year of Hezekiah (who lived a total of fifty-four years); according to Josephus, the prayer of Hezekiah for recovery from his illness is only in order that there will be an heir for the throne (*Ant.* 10.25–27). It may be that Manasseh is the only surviving son, or else older brothers are bypassed for reasons unknown.

The dates of Manasseh's reign must be calculated from the time of the captivity. The Babylonian Chronicle gives the exact date when Nebuchadnezzar captures Jerusalem and takes Jehoiachin prisoner to Babylon[2]—on the second of Adar in the seventh year of Nebuchanezzar (i.e., March 15, 597 B.C.). The twenty-nine years of Hezekiah end in 686 B.C.; Manasseh, Amon, Josiah, and Jehoiakim reign for a total of ninety-nine years. The reign of Manasseh must have begun in 596 B.C., giving him a ten-year coregency with Hezekiah.[3] Manasseh reigns the longest of all the Judean kings.

Assur is at the height of its power after the conquest of Egypt (671 B.C.); any attempt to break away, as Hezekiah did, is out of the question. Though Manasseh is loyal to Assur, there is no evidence that Assyria ever demanded adherence to its own religious practices or interfered in any way with the native practices of conquered countries.[4] No Assyrian vassal treaty contains clauses that relate to practice of religion; it is not even certain that a loyalty oath, such as the one imposed by Esarhaddon on his eastern vassals, is ever

---

1. For a translation and commentary see M. A. Knibb in *The Old Testament Pseudepigrapha*, ed. James H. Charlesworth (Garden City, N.Y.: Doubleday, 1985), 2:147–49, 163. Both Justin Martyr and Tertullian repeat the tradition that Isaiah was sawed in half, probably the same tradition alluded to by the author of Hebrews (Heb. 11:37).

2. Millard, "The Babylonian Chronicle," 1.137 (Chronicle 5, rev. 11–13).

3. Thiele, *The Mysterious Numbers of the Hebrew Kings*, 173–74. The coregency cannot have occurred with the kings who follow Amon, since none of them are placed on the throne by their predecessor.

4. The establishment of a new province by definition entailed the installation of a governor, with the imposition of the "symbol of Aššur." This description in the inscriptions was narrative shorthand for the administration of loyalty oaths, probably in the presence of Assyrian battle standards. Two different classes of priests were involved in this exercise; Holloway, *Aššur is King*, 331–32.

imposed on Manasseh.[5] In other words, the abominable foreign practices of Manasseh are apparently totally voluntary. There is nothing to suggest this facilitates favor with his Assyrian masters.

Manasseh must have had the support of the leaders of Judah in his practice of foreign worship. Assyria has not yet met the disaster declared by Isaiah (Isa. 10:12–19). There may have been a reaction to the reforms of Hezekiah, especially by those who worshiped at the various shrines in the countryside before Hezekiah dismantled them. Manasseh reverses the policies of his father, both in the practice of faith and in the submission to Assyria.

Manasseh advances foreign worship in a number of ways. The host of heaven is worshiped in the two temple courts (21:3, 5) and on the roof of his palace (23:12). Jeremiah witnesses family worship of the Queen of Heaven in Jerusalem (Jer. 7:18). Worship of astral deities also occurs—a Canaanite practice that Israel was warned about before their entry into the land (Deut. 4:19; cf. 17:3).

Passing the sons through the fire is named along with sorcery and consultation of mediums. This again is a specific violation of the covenant (Deut. 18:10–11). Passing one's sons through the fire probably concerns funeral rites, as may be suggested by its association with consultation of ghosts and spirits of the dead.[6] Rituals that involved children do not indicate that the children were slaughtered for these rites (cf. Jer. 7:32; 19:5; 32:35). Incineration of bodies took place at a dedicated location called a *tophet* by archaeologists (based on the Hebrew references). Such a place had a low enclosure wall and was used for generations. Those buried were primarily premature, stillborn, and young infants, buried with a special ceremony.

Necromancy was practiced through a ritual pit through which mortals communicated with the chthonic deities of the underworld (cf. 1 Sam. 28:7). The carved image of the Asherah implies something even worse than the standard Asherah pole (2 Kings 21:7).[7] Setting the image in the temple is a desecration of the one place that represented divine ownership and fulfillment of the promise to David.

The narrative leads into divine speech with the citation of the promise to David and the condition to rest in the land (21:7b–10). The words of the prophets to the violation of the covenant announce the ultimate judgment against Jerusalem. The fate of Samaria, within the living memory of many of the citizens of Judah under the reign of Manasseh, should have caused ring-

5. Cogan and Tadmor, *II Kings*, 272.

6. Zevit, *The Religions of Ancient Israel*, 550–52.

7. Popular religion involving Asherah is attested by blessing formulas saying, "I bless you by YHWH and his Asherah." This formula is found at Kuntillet ʿAjrud (southwest of Kadesh Barnea), and Khirbet el-Kom (eight miles west of Hebron). For a full discussion see Zevit, *The Religions of Ancient Israel*, 359–405.

ing in the ears of those who heard the warning. The "plumb line" of Samaria (21:13) is a graphic image used by the earlier prophets (cf. Amos 7:7–8). Ordinary tools of construction become God's standard of destruction. Jerusalem's being wiped clean as a washed pan turned upside down is an equally graphic proverb. God has had his fill of Judah's sinning; the city will be emptied out, its social order turned completely upside down.

The good remnant found in the reforms of Hezekiah will be uprooted and cast out. The nation is no longer God's inheritance, unique among the other nations (2 Kings 21:14; cf. Ex. 19:5; 1 Kings 8:51, 53). The shedding of innocent blood is also a metaphor for injustice against the poor, one of the greatest offenses committed by those who had themselves once been slaves (Isa. 1:15–17). Manasseh is the only king to have misdeeds noted in the concluding formula (2 Kings 21:17). The "garden" (enclosure) of Uzza in which Manasseh is buried may have been an enclosed space constructed in honor of a Canaanite astral deity. The cult of Attar-melek, the Venus star, in Arabic is known as Uzza.

The Assassination of Amon (21:19–26)

AMON IS BORN when his father is forty-five, making it unlikely that he is the oldest son. Another example of a young son succeeding after a long reign is Ramesses II of Egypt (thirteenth century); his twelve oldest sons died before he was succeeded by Merneptah, who was himself nearly sixty at his accession. The location of Jotbah (21:19) is uncertain, but most probably to be identified with a location in lower Galilee found in the annals of Tiglath-Pileser III. There may have been a policy of southern kings marrying women from the north in order to strengthen relations with the former Israelite state.

The reign of Amon is brought to an abrupt end by conspirators from his own court. No details are given concerning the uprising. Perhaps this is an anti-Assyrian uprising, possibly in connection with disturbances during the reign of Ashurbanipal (640 B.C.). Whatever the case, the plot fails. Representative civic leaders dispatch the conspirators and make Amon's son Josiah king. The "people of the land" are those loyal to David during times of dynastic crisis (cf. 11:14, 18, 20), ensuring the continuity of the dynasty.

MANASSEH IN CHRONICLES. Manasseh is an example of how the consequences of sin are not confined to the sinner. The consequences of his sin results in the eventual exile of the entire nation; God decides "to remove [Judah] from his presence because of the sins of Manasseh and all he had done, including the shedding of innocent blood . . .

the LORD was not willing to forgive" (24:3b–4). The effects of Manasseh's deeds are irreversible; the announcement of exile made to Hezekiah becomes a pronouncement of irreversible judgment against the nation (21:10–15). Manasseh, uniformly and unambiguously, is the worst king of Judah in the valuation of the Deuteronomistic Historians.

In Chronicles, the life of Manasseh divides into two eras: sin and repentance (2 Chron. 33:1–20). The period of transgression is anchored in the Deuteronomistic History (vv. 1–8). The pattern of faithfulness and then failure, where 2 Kings has a uniform portrayal, is found with other kings in Chronicles (Rehoboam, Joash, Amaziah, and Uzziah). These four earlier kings go from righteousness to sin; only Manasseh transforms from wickedness to righteousness.

The prophetic speech announcing judgment in 2 Kings 21:10–15 is reduced to just one verse in 2 Chronicles 33:10. The Chronicler makes no mention of the one distinguishing sin of Manasseh, that he filled Jerusalem with blood from end to end (2 Kings 21:16). Instead, the Chronicler tells of the exile and repentance of Manasseh (2 Chron. 33:11–13) and his subsequent work of restoration (vv. 14–17). The conclusion of his reign is again adapted from Kings (2 Kings 21:18–20); Chronicles notes his prayer of repentance in contrast to the sins he committed. The dissimilar portrayal of Chronicles creates a greater dissonance than that of other kings because of his central position as being responsible for the Exile according to 1–2 Kings.

Since the days of Wellhausen, the account of Chronicles has been regarded as a theologically slanted creation to explain why the worst king of Judah should have reigned the longest. This argument is undermined by the fact that the Deuteronomistic Historians had a theological perspective that is no less pronounced in their portrayal of the lives of each king.[8] The Chronicler does not make any direct correlation between the length of a king's reign and his piety, nor does he confine the consequences of guilt to one generation.

The absence of an exile of Manasseh in Assyrian records is not significant; those records are fragmentary, so it is impossible to know what was never recorded or has been lost. It is notable that the Chronicler makes Babylon the place of exile (2 Chron. 33:11), when he knew full well that Nineveh was the capital of Assyria. Attempts have been made to correlate Chronicles with the turbulent international politics of the seventh century and the revolt of Shamash-shuma-ukin, ruler of Babylon, against his younger brother Ashur-

---

8. For a discussion of the historical issues, see Brian Kelly, "Manasseh in the Books of Kings and Chronicles," in *Windows into Old Testament History: Evidence, Argument, and the Crisis of "Biblical Israel,"* ed. V. Philips Long, David W. Baker, and Gordon J. Wenham (Grand Rapids: Eerdmans, 2002), 133–46.

banipal. After a number of campaigns, Elam was decimated and much of its population deported; it is not known how long Ashurbanipal resided in Babylon or whether Manasseh was involved in the rebellion.

Manasseh's exile cannot be regarded as a creation of the Chronicler for the punishment of the king, for the sin encompasses the people as well as the king (2 Chron. 33:9–10), whereas the exile of the king does not affect the land, the people, or Jerusalem.[9] The Chronicler chooses to appropriate historical information for his theological purpose;[10] the extraordinary transgression of Manasseh is worthy of a much more severe punishment than arrest and exile.

The account of Manasseh in Chronicles demonstrates that no matter how grievous the transgression and its influence, opportunity for repentance is ever present. As Dillard explains, both the judgments of Kings and Chronicles are the Word of God:

> At a theological level this tension can be reconciled in the awareness that all that we do is touched both by sin and by the grace of God. The best deeds of human beings are never devoid of the taint of sinfulness; conversely, men at their most evil are never utterly bereft of the restraining grace of God. Either view—that focusing on evil or on grace—provides a coherent picture. The biblical historians in this sense are not reductionistic, but taken together display life in its complexity.[11]

The Chronicler is interested in showing that the consequences of sin can be mitigated. He is not concerned to show the reasons for the Exile but to show that Israel, like Manasseh, can turn to Yahweh and experience restoration. Manasseh becomes the example to the believing community of the necessity and possibility of repentance. Kings is about realizing the reasons for the Exile and its consequences; it has its focus on Manasseh's effect on the people: "The people did not listen. Manasseh led them astray, so that they did more evil than the nations the LORD had destroyed before the Israelites" (2 Kings 21:9). The Chronicler provides a subtle but significant variation on this verse: "Manasseh led Judah and the people of Jerusalem astray, so that they did even more evil than the nations the LORD had destroyed before the

---

9. Japhet, *I & II Chronicles*, 1,009.

10. An examination of the source citation of the Chronicler (33:18–19) is provided by W. Schniedewind, "The Source Citations of Manasseh: King Manasseh in History and Homily," *VT* 51 (1991): 455–60. The peculiar form of the citation indicates that the Chronicler has added his own interpretation to an original source. The citation indicates that the apocryphal "Prayer of Manasseh" is based on an earlier record.

11. Dillard, *2 Chronicles*, 270.

Israelites" (2 Chron. 33:9).[12] Chronicles emphasizes the immediate consequences of Manasseh's deeds rather than the rebellion of the people spurred on by the sins of Manasseh.

Contributions and consequences of Manasseh. Manasseh is able to retain control over the land of Judah for a lifetime. During his long reign he ruthlessly silences his opponents, likely supported by the presence of the Assyrian army in the land. He leaves the kingdom in a state of unrest, which results in the assassination of his son Amon, who succeeds him (2 Kings 21:23). Amon's short reign is depicted as nothing more than a continuation of the idolatrous ways of his father. Perhaps the violent action taken in relation to Amon's religious policies is an attempt to regain influence for the Jerusalem priesthood. The assassins in turn are unable to achieve their ends and die for their efforts; Josiah the son of Amon is made king.

In this whole period, the stabilizing factor is the presence of the civic leaders ("the people of the land"), who remain loyal to the Davidic dynasty. They are not supporters of the religiopolitical policies of Manasseh and Amon; they are loyal to their own traditions, as is seen in their influence during Josiah's kingship.

Whatever reforms Manasseh manages to effect after his repentance, they are not of lasting consequence. His military undertakings include the building of a high outer wall around the city of David (2 Chron. 33:14) and manning the fortified cities with army commanders. His spiritual reforms involve the reversal of his earlier cultic innovations and renewal of worship to Yahweh (vv. 15–16), though this does not include the abolition of worship at the high places outside Jerusalem (v. 17).

Amon is remembered as doing evil just like his father (v. 22), a memory shared by the prophet Jeremiah (Jer. 15:4). It may be that Manasseh removes symbols of Phoenician worship under pressure from the Assyrians, as part of the condition of restoration to his throne.[13] The evils engendered by self-serving interests are not readily reversed, and for the authors of Kings, the changes executed by Manasseh are not even worth mentioning.

One consequence of Manasseh's idolatrous reign is a focus on "the day of the LORD," as is evident in the prophecy of Zephaniah. His condemnation of idolatry (Zeph. 1:4–5) and his pronouncement of judgment on foreign enemies (2:4–15) take place following the reigns of Manasseh and Amon. Judgment will come because of the evils of idolatry, violence, and oppression (3:1–2). Yahweh will prove wrong those who think that nothing will hap

---

12. The Chronicler replaces "them" in the Kings account with "Judah and the people of Jerusalem," thus drawing attention to the effect of the king on the entire people.
13. Williamson, *1 & 2 Chronicles*, 394–95.

pen to them (1:12); he will search Jerusalem with lamps to make sure that not a single evildoer escapes. The arrogant of Judah have built houses, but they will not live in them (1:13). Those helplessly caught in evils like those of Manasseh's reign can do nothing other than turn to the divine warrior. The day of Yahweh is a summons to repentance and humility (2:1–3); only in repentance is there any hope.

The judgment of the day of Yahweh is not an end in itself; it holds out promise and hope for the land of Judah, where there has been exile and desolation. That day will become a source of blessing for the remnant of Judah (Zeph. 2:6–7, 9). They will spread out from their own land and occupy territory formerly held by their enemies. The possibility of survival (v. 3) becomes a promise for the future. Judgment will be worldwide (3:8), but Yahweh will save and transform people from the nations, engendering their worship of him (vv. 9–10). The day of Yahweh is fundamentally one of hope; humble and truthful people of the covenant will follow in its ways (vv. 11–13), and they are promised restoration and worldwide renown because of God's love (vv. 15–20).

The pronouncement of Kings concerning inevitable exile must be heard; such a fulfillment is a reminder that God's word does not fail. In the days of Manasseh and following are those who look forward to the great consummation of the kingdom, just like the Christians in Revelation. They also know that the Word of God cannot fail but will be fulfilled.

THE CONSEQUENCES OF one person's sins. The effects of the sins of one person can extend to many others. Other individuals are drawn into errant ways, and many victims suffer the results of evil. This is particularly true when transgressions are committed by persons in political power. Most often oppressive actions are exercised under the rubric of peace and liberty. Commonly, the results are irreversible for generations, and many pay a terrible price, as is the case with Manasseh. Religion and race are often a part of malevolence exercised against others.

Zimbabwe is one of the most tragic modern stories of havoc brought on a country through a long process of political manipulation. When Robert Mugabe came to power in 1980, he brought the promise of peace and cooperation after decades of colonial rule and a bitter civil war.[14] As head of the renamed nation of Zimbabwe, he quickly became recognized as an international statesman.

---

14. The following information was provided by BBC News, Africa, Feb. 15, 2000, posted at http://news.bbc.co.uk/1/hi/world/africa/643737.stm.

Mugabe was raised as a Roman Catholic and educated in missionary schools; he received the first of his seven degrees from South Africa's Fort Hare University. Once he achieved popular support, his promises of reconciliation and democracy were overtaken by an inflexible authoritarianism and a deep distrust of opposition. Initially he built a coalition government with fellow guerilla leader Joshua Nkomo, but suspicion of the arms resources of Nkomo led to a brutal crackdown on his followers. Mugabe became an ardent nationalist, blaming white Zimbabweans and their alleged foreign backers for the economic collapse of his country.

Mugabe has made much of his devout Christianity, but it has not been evident in his personal or public conduct. He ended his marriage to marry a former private secretary forty-one years his junior. At the same time he pursued a moral campaign against homosexuality, making such "unnatural acts" punishable with up to ten years in prison. He committed his armed forces to a wasteful colonial type of intervention in the Congolese civil war. There were many accusations of officials growing rich from Congo's rich mineral reserves, while Zimbabwe's own economy plummeted out of control. A land that had been the breadbasket of Africa became impoverished, completely unable to provide food or shelter for its own citizens.

Mugabe not only impoverished his own people, but he also took aggressive action to change the image of his country by demolishing illegal shantytowns. The rationalization was that this was necessary to rid the country of settlements that became hives of illegal trade in scarce hard currency and food.[15] Rights groups claimed the operation left at least 300,000 people homeless. Some were killed in the process; thousands were forced into camps on the outskirts of Harare, the capital city. The opposition Movement for Democratic Change estimated that well over one and a half million people were displaced. They claimed that the crackdown was meant to punish its supporters in the urban strongholds where it kept most of its parliamentary seats.

As the faithful like Isaiah suffered to the point of death under the reign of Manasseh, so many in Zimbabwe have died under the regime of Mugabe. Their hope must be as those who waited for the day of Yahweh in the times of Manasseh. This is the only response possible for modern-day Christians caught in a spiral of evil like that of Zimbabwe. As political solutions elude them, they must turn in humility to the Lord. The rule of God seems elusive in such situations. The lament of the psalmists becomes poignantly real (e.g., Ps. 74; 89). The story of Manasseh serves both as warning and as hope for those in similar political distress.

---

15. Details published by Reuters, Sunday July 3, 2005.

2 Kings 22:1–23:30

OSIAH WAS EIGHT years old when he became king, and he reigned in Jerusalem thirty-one years. His mother's name was Jedidah daughter of Adaiah; she was from Bozkath. ²He did what was right in the eyes of the LORD and walked in all the ways of his father David, not turning aside to the right or to the left.

³In the eighteenth year of his reign, King Josiah sent the secretary, Shaphan son of Azaliah, the son of Meshullam, to the temple of the LORD. He said: ⁴"Go up to Hilkiah the high priest and have him get ready the money that has been brought into the temple of the LORD, which the doorkeepers have collected from the people. ⁵Have them entrust it to the men appointed to supervise the work on the temple. And have these men pay the workers who repair the temple of the LORD—⁶the carpenters, the builders and the masons. Also have them purchase timber and dressed stone to repair the temple. ⁷But they need not account for the money entrusted to them, because they are acting faithfully."

⁸Hilkiah the high priest said to Shaphan the secretary, "I have found the Book of the Law in the temple of the LORD." He gave it to Shaphan, who read it. ⁹Then Shaphan the secretary went to the king and reported to him: "Your officials have paid out the money that was in the temple of the LORD and have entrusted it to the workers and supervisors at the temple." ¹⁰Then Shaphan the secretary informed the king, "Hilkiah the priest has given me a book." And Shaphan read from it in the presence of the king.

¹¹When the king heard the words of the Book of the Law, he tore his robes. ¹²He gave these orders to Hilkiah the priest, Ahikam son of Shaphan, Acbor son of Micaiah, Shaphan the secretary and Asaiah the king's attendant: ¹³"Go and inquire of the LORD for me and for the people and for all Judah about what is written in this book that has been found. Great is the LORD's anger that burns against us because our fathers have not obeyed the words of this book; they have not acted in accordance with all that is written there concerning us."

¹⁴Hilkiah the priest, Ahikam, Acbor, Shaphan and Asaiah went to speak to the prophetess Huldah, who was the wife of

Shallum son of Tikvah, the son of Harhas, keeper of the
wardrobe. She lived in Jerusalem, in the Second District.

¹⁵She said to them, "This is what the LORD, the God of
Israel, says: Tell the man who sent you to me, ¹⁶'This is what
the LORD says: I am going to bring disaster on this place and
its people, according to everything written in the book the
king of Judah has read. ¹⁷Because they have forsaken me and
burned incense to other gods and provoked me to anger by all
the idols their hands have made, my anger will burn against
this place and will not be quenched.' ¹⁸Tell the king of Judah,
who sent you to inquire of the LORD, 'This is what the LORD,
the God of Israel, says concerning the words you heard:
¹⁹Because your heart was responsive and you humbled yourself before the LORD when you heard what I have spoken
against this place and its people, that they would become
accursed and laid waste, and because you tore your robes and
wept in my presence, I have heard you, declares the LORD.
²⁰Therefore I will gather you to your fathers, and you will be
buried in peace. Your eyes will not see all the disaster I am
going to bring on this place.'"

So they took her answer back to the king.

²³:¹Then the king called together all the elders of Judah and
Jerusalem. ²He went up to the temple of the LORD with the
men of Judah, the people of Jerusalem, the priests and the
prophets—all the people from the least to the greatest. He
read in their hearing all the words of the Book of the
Covenant, which had been found in the temple of the LORD.
³The king stood by the pillar and renewed the covenant in the
presence of the LORD—to follow the LORD and keep his commands, regulations and decrees with all his heart and all his
soul, thus confirming the words of the covenant written in this
book. Then all the people pledged themselves to the
covenant.

⁴The king ordered Hilkiah the high priest, the priests next
in rank and the doorkeepers to remove from the temple of the
LORD all the articles made for Baal and Asherah and all the
starry hosts. He burned them outside Jerusalem in the fields of
the Kidron Valley and took the ashes to Bethel. ⁵He did away
with the pagan priests appointed by the kings of Judah to
burn incense on the high places of the towns of Judah and on
those around Jerusalem—those who burned incense to Baal,

to the sun and moon, to the constellations and to all the starry hosts. ⁶He took the Asherah pole from the temple of the LORD to the Kidron Valley outside Jerusalem and burned it there. He ground it to powder and scattered the dust over the graves of the common people. ⁷He also tore down the quarters of the male shrine prostitutes, which were in the temple of the LORD and where women did weaving for Asherah.

⁸Josiah brought all the priests from the towns of Judah and desecrated the high places, from Geba to Beersheba, where the priests had burned incense. He broke down the shrines at the gates—at the entrance to the Gate of Joshua, the city governor, which is on the left of the city gate. ⁹Although the priests of the high places did not serve at the altar of the LORD in Jerusalem, they ate unleavened bread with their fellow priests.

¹⁰He desecrated Topheth, which was in the Valley of Ben Hinnom, so no one could use it to sacrifice his son or daughter in the fire to Molech. ¹¹He removed from the entrance to the temple of the LORD the horses that the kings of Judah had dedicated to the sun. They were in the court near the room of an official named Nathan-Melech. Josiah then burned the chariots dedicated to the sun.

¹²He pulled down the altars the kings of Judah had erected on the roof near the upper room of Ahaz, and the altars Manasseh had built in the two courts of the temple of the LORD. He removed them from there, smashed them to pieces and threw the rubble into the Kidron Valley. ¹³The king also desecrated the high places that were east of Jerusalem on the south of the Hill of Corruption—the ones Solomon king of Israel had built for Ashtoreth the vile goddess of the Sidonians, for Chemosh the vile god of Moab, and for Molech the detestable god of the people of Ammon. ¹⁴Josiah smashed the sacred stones and cut down the Asherah poles and covered the sites with human bones.

¹⁵Even the altar at Bethel, the high place made by Jeroboam son of Nebat, who had caused Israel to sin—even that altar and high place he demolished. He burned the high place and ground it to powder, and burned the Asherah pole also. ¹⁶Then Josiah looked around, and when he saw the tombs that were there on the hillside, he had the bones removed from them and burned on the altar to defile it, in accordance with

the word of the LORD proclaimed by the man of God who foretold these things.

[17]The king asked, "What is that tombstone I see?"

The men of the city said, "It marks the tomb of the man of God who came from Judah and pronounced against the altar of Bethel the very things you have done to it."

[18]"Leave it alone," he said. "Don't let anyone disturb his bones." So they spared his bones and those of the prophet who had come from Samaria.

[19]Just as he had done at Bethel, Josiah removed and defiled all the shrines at the high places that the kings of Israel had built in the towns of Samaria that had provoked the LORD to anger. [20]Josiah slaughtered all the priests of those high places on the altars and burned human bones on them. Then he went back to Jerusalem.

[21]The king gave this order to all the people: "Celebrate the Passover to the LORD your God, as it is written in this Book of the Covenant." [22]Not since the days of the judges who led Israel, nor throughout the days of the kings of Israel and the kings of Judah, had any such Passover been observed. [23]But in the eighteenth year of King Josiah, this Passover was celebrated to the LORD in Jerusalem.

[24]Furthermore, Josiah got rid of the mediums and spiritists, the household gods, the idols and all the other detestable things seen in Judah and Jerusalem. This he did to fulfill the requirements of the law written in the book that Hilkiah the priest had discovered in the temple of the LORD. [25]Neither before nor after Josiah was there a king like him who turned to the LORD as he did—with all his heart and with all his soul and with all his strength, in accordance with all the Law of Moses.

[26]Nevertheless, the LORD did not turn away from the heat of his fierce anger, which burned against Judah because of all that Manasseh had done to provoke him to anger. [27]So the LORD said, "I will remove Judah also from my presence as I removed Israel, and I will reject Jerusalem, the city I chose, and this temple, about which I said, 'There shall my Name be.'"

[28]As for the other events of Josiah's reign, and all he did, are they not written in the book of the annals of the kings of Judah?

²⁹While Josiah was king, Pharaoh Neco king of Egypt went up to the Euphrates River to help the king of Assyria. King Josiah marched out to meet him in battle, but Neco faced him and killed him at Megiddo. ³⁰Josiah's servants brought his body in a chariot from Megiddo to Jerusalem and buried him in his own tomb. And the people of the land took Jehoahaz son of Josiah and anointed him and made him king in place of his father.

JUDGMENT AGAINST JERUSALEM is delayed but cannot be averted, not even by one of the noblest kings to reign on the throne of Judah. Josiah is the long-awaited king promised by the prophet of Judah to reverse the cursed idolatry introduced by Jeroboam (1 Kings 13:2). He is described as following in the ways of David (2 Kings 22:2), but he is also described in the same terms as the ideal king of Deuteronomy (Deut. 17:20). Josiah does not turn from the teaching of the covenant to the right or to the left (2 Kings 22:2). There is no king like him; he exceeds even Hezekiah in his devotion to the teaching of Moses, from which he does not deviate (23:25). Josiah is a second Moses to complement King Hezekiah, who had been the ideal second David.

One might expect that the expansive reforms of Josiah, instituting the centrality of the temple in worship, and his renewal of the covenant as directed by the Law of Moses (Deut. 31:9–13) would bring about at least a temporary change in the fortunes of Judah. Instead, Josiah dies at the hands of a foreign king (2 Kings 23:29), and the reforms he instituted perish immediately with the succession of his son Jehoahaz. Manasseh is responsible for the death of Josiah; his sin dooms the reform to futility. Josiah's reign is the first stage on the way to exile.

Discovery of the Book of the Covenant (22:1–20)

THE THIRTY-ONE YEAR reign of Josiah ends in 609 B.C., when he dies fighting the Egyptians in their campaign to the Euphrates against Haran (23:29–30). The Babylonian Chronicle provides a fixed date for the Egyptian campaign.[1]

---

1. A series of cuneiform tablets covers the years from 745 B.C. into the late Seleucid period (second century B.C.). Entries follow a chronological order, introduced by the year of reign of the king of Babylon, though not every year is included. Nabopolassar, perhaps a descendant of Merodach-Baladan, wrested control of Babylon from the Assyrians in 626 B.C. The famous Nebuchadnezzar ruled for forty-three years (605–562 B.C.), but only the first eleven years are covered by the surviving tablets (Millard, "The Babylonian Chronicle," 1.137).

Josiah's reign begins in 640, and he reigns during the declining years of the Assyrian empire, which begins with the death of Ashurbanipal (ca. 631 B.C.). Assyria loses control of Babylon when Nabopolassar comes to power (626 B.C.); Nineveh itself is captured in 612 B.C. The final attempt to retain independence with the help of Egypt fails at the battle of Carchemish in 605 B.C. The reign of Josiah takes place during massive transitions of power in international affairs.

The conspirators of Amon are themselves killed by certain civic leaders referred to as "the people of the land" (21:24), who then place Josiah on the throne at age eight. Regents from this group must have been responsible for the king during the years of his minority. His mother is from the Shephelah, the hilly region between the southern coastal plain and the Judean mountains; Bozkath is part of the same administrative district as Lachish, Eglon, and Makkedah (Josh. 15:39). The account of Josiah's reign is introduced (2 Kings 22:2) and concluded (23:25) with the standard formulas for keeping the covenant: He does not turn to the right or to the left (Deut. 5:32; 17:20), but loves God with all his heart, soul, and strength (6:4).

The disastrous state of the temple must have taken place during the apostate reign of Manasseh. In that time the book of the covenant seems to have been entirely forgotten. The Chronicler provides a variant description of the reform; according to him, Josiah begins to seek the God of David in the eighth year of his reign and to remove the idolatrous high places from Judah and Jerusalem in the twelfth (2 Chron. 34:3). The temple purification begins in his eighteenth year, at which time the book of the covenant is discovered (34:8, 14). Reforms thus begin before the discovery of that book when Josiah turns twenty, the age of majority (34:3).[2]

The Deuteronomistic History has a particular focus on the book of the covenant; thus, the events are associated with it during the reign of Josiah. It is not difficult to understand why the book may have been moved from its proper place beside the ark of the covenant (Deut. 31:26); Manasseh would not have wanted it there, nor would the priests have wanted to provoke him by leaving it there.

Throughout Judah's history, repairs to the temple were a continuous necessity. Joash had initiated a policy for financing temple maintenance (2 Kings 12:9–15), and the procedures initiated by Josiah follow that same procedure. Hilkiah, the priest responsible to refurbish the temple, was not likely present during the reigns of either Manasseh or Amon. The families of both Hilkiah and his colleague Shaphan are recoverable through a combination

2. Williamson, *1 and 2 Chronicles*, 398.

of biblical and epigraphic data.[3] Hilkiah is the son of Shallum (Meshullam), who served as high priest during the reign of Manasseh (1 Chron. 9:11; Ezra 7:1–2). Shaphan is son of Azaliahu (2 Kings 22:3), who is also a son of Shallum/Meshullam, quite possibly the same person as Hilkiah's father; if so, Shaphan is Hilkiah's nephew. Hilkiah probably receives his position early in the reign of Josiah and initiates a change in the state-sponsored religion present in the temple.

The book found in the temple is readily identified as "the Book of the Law" (22:8; probably Deuteroomy; cf. Deut. 4:44–45; 31:9–13). It was in the custody of the priests along with the ark and was to be read to all Israel at the Feast of Booths every seventh year. Josiah becomes profoundly repentant when he learns about the neglect of the covenant and takes immediate action. In order to learn God's will (cf. Deut. 18:1–8), he dispatches a delegation to the court prophetess, who lives in the newly expanded area of the city.[4] Huldah is the only woman prophet during the kingdom period; she belongs to priestly circles, and her husband is likely the uncle of Jeremiah, instrumental in the reforms of Josiah (Jer. 32:7).[5] The message of the prophetess is an unequivocal application of the book's message to the inhabitants of Judah and Jerusalem. The curse of the covenant rests on them (e.g., Deut. 28:58–68).

The only mitigation to be found in the words of Huldah is a personal application to the king. His penitence will prevent the disaster of the Exile from taking place during his lifetime. The "desolation and curse" on the inhabitants of the kingdom cannot be averted (2 Kings 22:19, NASB; cf. Deut. 28:37), but Josiah will die in peace. In all other circumstances this would signify a natural death, not a death in war as befalls Josiah (2 Kings 23:29–30). Only in such a circumstance of disaster can Josiah's burial in Jerusalem be described as peaceful.[6] Peace for Josiah means he will be buried in his own grave with other distinguished kings of Judah.

Renewal of the Covenant (23:1–20)

THE INEVITABILITY OF judgment on Jerusalem announced by Huldah is a call for Josiah to take immediate action to renew the vow of the covenant collectively,

---

3. See Fox, "Royal Officials and Court Families" 225–28; W. Boyd Barrick, "Dynastic Politics, Priestly Succession, and Josiah's Eighth Year," *ZAW* 112 (2000): 572–78.

4. This was probably located on the western hill; see Nahman Avigad, *Discovering Jerusalem* (Nashville: Nelson, 1983), 23–60.

5. See R. R. Wilson, *Prophecy and Society in Ancient Israel* (Philadelphia: Fortress, 1980), 219–23.

6. Richard D. Nelson, *First and Second Kings* (Interpretation; Louisville: John Knox, 1987), 257.

as prescribed in the book that was found (e.g., Deut. 31:9–13). The inclusion of both civil and religious leaders as representatives makes the covenant effective in both civil and religious jurisdictions. This is a high point in the history of the nation; the people not only enter into a covenant with God, but the covenant becomes the legal foundation of the political order.[7] Renewal of the covenant is enacted with the purification of worship at the orders of King Josiah.

Purification begins in Jerusalem and focuses on the temple (23:4–14). The cult practices are those of Canaanite religion, which apparently flourished under Assyrian domination during the days of Manasseh. Cult objects of Baal and Asherah, male and female fertility deities, and the "host of heaven" (cf. Deut. 4:19) are burned in the terraces of the Kidron Valley.[8] These slopes descend directly from the temple and are a convenient dumping place. Bethel is the northern border of Judah, next to the Assyrian province of Samaria. The dispersion of ashes there symbolizes the defilement of foreign altars to the borders of Judah.

Purification extends to idolatrous objects and to those who led in such practices. A wooden cult statue of Asherah is removed from the temple and burned, the image installed there by Manasseh (cf. 21:7). The "quarters of the male shrine prostitutes" are probably rooms connected to the cult of Asherah. These "sacred persons" have been interpreted in terms of the prohibition of Deuteronomy against sacred prostitution (Deut. 23:18–19), though there is no evidence for ritual prostitution of a fertility cult. "Sacred prostitution" may be a term for any licentious behavior of such consecrated persons.[9] As was customary, cult statues were clothed and fed; a group of women were responsible to weave garments for the Asherah idol.

Nothing is known of cultic installations at the city gates. "The gates" (*haššᵉᶜārîm*, 23:8) has been read as "goat demon" (*haššᵉᶜîrîm*), a cult mentioned elsewhere (cf. Lev. 17:7; 2 Chron. 11:15).[10] A gate named Joshua Gate in Jerusalem is not known.[11] The purification "from Geba to Beersheba" defines

---

7. Volkmar Fritz, *1 & 2 Kings* (CC; Minneapolis: Fortress, 2003), 403.

8. "Fields" (NIV) interprets the Hebrew word *šᵉdēmâ* to be related to *śādeh* ("field"), but the etymology is unknown. The word *šᵉdēmâ* is found in the context of vines and may suggest a trellis (Isa. 16:8; Hab. 3:17). The terrain of the Kidron Valley was terraced, on which vines were cultivated (*HALAT*, 4:1322).

9. Cogan, *1 Kings*, 387.

10. Gray, *I & II Kings*, 730; NEB "satyr." Goat demons were regarded as guardian deities of the threshold of the gates. Gray prefers emendation to "gate-keeper," perhaps an allusion to the bull-colossi at the entrance of Assyrian palaces.

11. Cogan and Tadmor, *II Kings*, 287.

the extent of the kingdom from north to south.[12] The rural priests who come into Jerusalem do not have the same status in Jerusalem, but they do have provision of food (2 Kings 23:9). Their restrictions are similar to physically blemished priests (Lev. 21:22–23); their limited rank is likely dictated by the nature of the reform in the allocation of priests.

Manasseh and Amon, the "kings of Judah" (2 Kings 23:11), were responsible for altars and images of other cults in different parts of the outer temple courts and the upper levels and the roof over the stairway or ascending ramp of Ahaz. Ahaz renovated an exterior entranceway (16:18), and some feature of the structure served as a sundial (20:11), erected by Ahaz for the worship of astral deities. Manasseh also built fire pits (*tōpet*) for various rituals in the burial of children (23:10).[13] It is likely there were legitimate uses for such fire pits, but they came to be identified with other gods (*mōlek*). Idolatrous gods functioned as a king (*melek*), and children are burned to various gods such as Adrammelek and Anammelek (17:31).

Horses were used in the worship of the sun god (Shamash); in Mesopotamia the emblem of the sun god rode a horse-drawn chariot on festal days. The small decorated cult stand from Taʿanach (in the southern corner of the Jezreel Valley) features a flying sun as one of the depictions of deity. Beneath the sun is an animal identified as a horse.[14] One of the registers is an empty space between two sphinxes, which may indicate that this stand depicts the invisible Yahweh. Josiah's purifications involve the removal of shrines that go back to the time of Solomon (1 Kings 11:5–7). The "Hill of Corruption" (2 Kings 23:13) is a wordplay on the Mount of Olives; instead of the "mount of anointing" (*har hammišḥâ*) it is the "mount of destruction" (*har hammašḥît*). Filling the idolatrous places with human bones renders them untouchable (cf. Num. 19:16).

Josiah has a special interest in Bethel as a territory that once belonged to Judah (2 Chron. 11:12). Jeroboam set up a border shrine there in establishing his kingdom. Josiah's desecration of the altar by burning the bones of the graves on it fulfills the words of the prophet from Judah in the time of Jeroboam (1 Kings 13:1–2). The bones of the prophet are spared, along with those of the old prophet from Bethel, described here as from the territory of Samaria. The purging of the shrines in the cities of Samaria also fulfills

---

12. On the basis of Samarian ostraca, the Geba in question is located to the north of Samaria; Aharoni et al., *The Carta Bible Atlas*, #139.

13. See comments at 21:6 for the practice of child immolation in Israel.

14. The horse interpretation is defended by Glen Taylor; he connects it with sun worship, in *Yahweh and the Sun: Biblical and Archaeological Evidence for Sun Worship in Ancient Israel* (JSOT 111; Sheffield Academic Press: Sheffield, 1993), 30–31. The animal, however, lacks a mane and does not have the hairy tail of a horse.

prophecy (13:32). Josiah shows no tolerance for the priests of those high places, but punishes them according to the instructions found for the treatment of idolatrous cities (Deut. 13:13–19).

Celebration of the Passover (23:21–25)

CELEBRATION OF THE Passover is an essential aspect of covenant renewal. Its introduction resumes the account of the renewal ceremony (23:1–3), which is interrupted by the lengthy description of Josiah's reforms, and concludes the account of Josiah's bringing Judah into conformity with the covenant requirements. With the removal of all the rural shrines, Jerusalem is established as the central place for the Passover celebration, according to the requirement of the covenant (Deut. 16:5–6). The last reported covenant renewal was in the days of Joshua (Josh. 8:30–35, repeated in 24:1–26); the covenant of Josiah is the first occasion since that time when the Passover was celebrated as a national festival with official leaders. The Passover began as a family festival celebrated in each home (Ex. 12:1–20). A central celebration is a monarchic innovation.

The renewal also involves purging all false prophecy in Israel, as also required by the covenant (Deut. 18:9–14). Consultation with the dead was a usual method for receiving a divine oracle. "Mediums and spiritists" refer to some type of necromancy; the ʾôb (2 Kings 23:24; NIV "mediums") is a ritual pit through which communication can be established with the deities of the underworld. It is an ancient term attested in most Near Eastern languages. The use of "household gods" (tᵉrāpîm) also goes back to ancient practice (Gen. 31:19; Judg.17:5; 1 Sam. 19:13). These images are of various sizes, always associated with communication with a deity.

Death of Josiah (23:26–30)

THE END OF the reign of Josiah confirms the words of Huldah the prophetess. Nothing can reverse the curse that has come on Judah, which begins with the death of the dedicated king. Egypt becomes an ally of Assyria in the crucial days of its collapsing power. When Ashuruballit II, the last Assyrian king, forms a rump state around Haran after the fall of Nineveh (612 B.C.), Egypt supports him with troops. The march of Neco's army toward the Euphrates three years later is directly related to this support of Assur.

Megiddo is the capital of an Assyrian province and the seat of a governor. It occupies a strategic position and is likely the base of an Egyptian camp. The inner motives of Josiah in going to Megiddo are not obvious. Perhaps with his reforms extending into the territory of Samaria he is attempting to obtain political influence as well. With the collapse of the

Assyrian empire, there may be an opportunity to integrate a key defensive city into his empire. The Egyptians resist such ambitions; their goal is to regain sovereignty over Canaan that they lost at the end of the New Kingdom period (1070 B.C.).

Neco's ambition is to assume control in the former Assyrian provinces. Egyptian forces previously supported weak Assyrian armies in their battles against the Bablyonians. Josiah's encounter with the Egyptians at Megiddo meets with disaster. His tragic death is a calamity. According to the Chronicler, Jeremiah composes a long lament song for his funeral, which remains to his time (2 Chron. 35:25). As at other times, certain civic officials assume leadership and appoint one of Josiah's younger sons to the throne.

Bridging Contexts

JOSIAH'S LEGACY. It is God's nature to extend mercy for the most abominable unfaithfulness (cf. Ex. 33:19; 34:6), but there is a limit to his long-suffering nature. Moses received assurance of the divine presence at the abomination of the golden calf (33:12–14), but such mercy is no longer available for Judah. In thematic terms, Josiah's reign is climactic in the books of Kings. It is the high point of the Deuteronomistic History, which began with the renewal of the covenant at the time of the entrance to the Promised Land. The discovery of the book of covenant renewal inspires the effort of reform and centralization of worship at the temple (2 Kings 23:4–20).

Josiah is the only king to turn to God "in accordance with all the Law of Moses" (23:25). Josiah is the converse of Manasseh, who followed the abominations of the nations (21:2); Josiah does not deviate in any matter (22:2). Manasseh extended worship at the high places (21:3–5, 7); Josiah terminates the foreign priests and purges their places of worship (23:5).

Josiah rectifies three alienations that developed in the history of the kingdom. The first is that created by Manasseh; the second is the division caused by Solomon that left only Judah as the kingdom where the descendants of David ruled; in the last, Josiah destroys all the foreign worship introduced by Solomon and, for good measure, ensures their disuse (23:13–14). Removal of barriers with the north is further achieved by the incineration of the high place at Bethel (v. 15). As much as possible, Josiah rectifies the causes of the Assyrian exile of Israel.

The oracle of Huldah is the impetus for Josiah to undertake these great reforms. The warnings of the Book of the Law require immediate action (22:15–17). The second part of her oracle addresses the future of the king (vv. 19–21). Like Hezekiah, his humility and repentance assure him of peace in his time, including a peaceful death. Both aspects of the oracle are the word of God in ways the hearers of the prophetess cannot fully comprehend.

At the time of her oracle, the full extent of the judgment for the nation is not yet apparent. Contrary to the implication of the message, rending of garments and taking an oath will not change the enormity of the calamity in store for the people. The promise of a peaceful death for the king gives no indication that he will die violently at the hands of a foreign king. Josiah has done all the right things in response to God's Word. His repentance and reform cannot rescue the nation. The words of Huldah confirm the irrevocable judgment of God. The reign and death of Josiah begin the execution of the sentence that rests on the land.

The problem of Josiah's death. The violent death of Josiah is a critical question for the prophetic word. The prophetic authors of Kings suggest their own answer concerning the peaceful death of Josiah. In their version of the encounter at Megiddo, Pharaoh Neco goes up to battle against the king of Assyria (23:29).[15] This suggests that Josiah dies at the hands of an ally.[16] Such a death is to die "in peace." Peace (šālôm) is the quintessence of covenant; this word expresses communal relations between friends, parties, and nations.[17]

David instructed Solomon to kill Joab because he had put to death two men who were in alliance with him: Abner (2 Sam. 3:21) and Amasa (19:14). David required the life of Joab because he had spilled war-blood in peace (bᵉšā-lôm); Joab therefore could not be allowed to die in peace (1 Kings 2:5). If this is the intent of the description in Kings of the death of Josiah, it is a fulfillment of the prophetic word in a way that is not anticipated. It drives home more forcefully the point that the Exile cannot be avoided; King Josiah's dying in peace does not indicate deliverance from judgment but is another indication of its inevitability.

The Chronicler portrays Josiah on friendly terms with the Egyptians (2 Chron. 35:20–23); Neco is on his way to Carchemish, and Josiah goes to meet him. Neco does not want to fight Josiah but intends to engage his "house of war." The converse to be inferred is that Josiah represents for him a "house of peace"; that is, Neco regards Josiah as an ally. He counsels Josiah not to oppose God, lest he die; Neco, from a Judean point of view, is con-

---

15. The Hebrew of this verse indicates a hostile intent (ˁlh ˁl), as is evident in other contexts (e.g., Judg. 18:9). The paraphrase "to help the king of Assyria" (NIV) must either assume an emendation of the text (so BHS) or an unusual use of the preposition.

16. Baruch Halpern, "Why Manasseh Is Blamed for the Babylonian Exile: The Evolution of a Biblical Tradition," VT 48 (1998): 501–2.

17. Philip J. Nel, "שלם," NIDOTTE, 4:131.

sidered to be on a mission for God on his way to Carchemish.[18] Josiah refuses to heed this word of God through Neco; he is mortally wounded in a confrontation with the Egyptians and dies in Jerusalem.

According to the Babylonian Chronicle, Pharaoh Neco is not going to Carchemish to battle the Assyrians, but to ally with them in their war with Nebuchadnezzar. The motives of Josiah in his attempted intervention at Megiddo do not appear evident in the historical sources, or they are not relevant to the historians in their prophetic declaration of God's word. Given Josiah's commitment to cultural and religious reform, the implication is that in an irrational move he somehow intends to further his reforms and increase his influence in the region.[19]

The author of Kings does not indicate that Josiah goes to Megiddo to engage the Egyptians in war. Ahaz had been summoned by the Assyrian king to confirm his responsibilities as a vassal to the imperial power (2 Kings 16:7–10); a similar intent may be inferred for Josiah's going to Megiddo. Yet the book of Kings gives no reason for Josiah's death, though it is not described as the result of battle (23:29).

There is no doubt about Josiah's intent in Chronicles; Josiah intends to intervene against the Egyptians and ignores their warnings against his rash action (2 Chron. 35:21). This is evident in the Chronicler's sources; Assyria is not mentioned in Chronicles, since the mission of Neco was regarded as divinely inspired.[20] The Chronicler makes Josiah culpable for his actions; Josiah has deliberately disguised himself going into battle in the hopes that he will escape the word of God that has come through his servant Neco.[21] This disobedience serves to explain Josiah's death at the hands of the Egyptians. Kings does not explain Josiah's death other than to use it as an indication that God has begun to act in his removal of Judah from the land.

---

18. The Rab-shaqeh proposes to have the same kind of divine mission for Jerusalem: "Moreover, is it without the LORD that I have come up against this place to destroy it? The LORD said to me, Go up against this land, and destroy it" (2 Kings 18:25 NRSV; Isa. 37:10).

19. Zipora Talshir discusses the text of Kings and the historical situation in "The Three Deaths of Josiah and the Strata of Biblical Historiography (2 Kings XXIII 29–30; 2 Chronicles XXXV 20–5; 1 Esdras I 23–31)," *VT* 46 (1996): 213–20.

20. The ambiguity of political motivation makes the account more correct, in that it does not infer that Neco was going to attack Assyria (Halpern, "Blaming Manasseh," 503–4). Talshir's suggestion that the Chronicler creates a fictitious war to serve his own theological ends only indicates a predisposition to the historical priority of Kings ("The Three Deaths of Josiah," 219). Kings and Chronicles are equally concerned with a correct theological interpretion of the events.

21. There may be a deliberate allusion here to Ahab, who similarly disguised himself in going into battle against the Arameans (1 Kings 22:30).

The story of Josiah highlights the different historical explanations for the Exile. In Chronicles there is no foreordination of the Exile; it is a result of the collective sin of the people (2 Chron. 36:14–16). Since it is the people who are punished in the Exile, it is the people who are responsible for such a judgment. They have profaned the temple and rejected repeated prophetic warnings, making a mockery of them. The judgment announced by Huldah is postponed because the people repent during the extensive reforms of Josiah (2 Chron. 34:24–28). Chronicles presents the Exile as an interruption in nationhood rather than a final rupture of the covenant (36:22–23).[22] While Kings holds Manasseh accountable for the Exile (2 Kings 21:10–14), it also recognizes that this is the final verdict in a long history of offending Yahweh, beginning from the Exodus (v. 15). It is this second explanation that is developed in Chronicles.

The announcement of the Exile because of the sins of Manasseh conditions the understanding of the oracle of Huldah. Her words anticipate a total exile, and they serve to explain the peaceful death of Josiah. The medievals "addressed this conundrum with aplomb."[23] Rashi comments on the announcement that Josiah will die in peace: "And what is this 'peace'? 'Your eyes will not see' the destruction of the temple." Qimhi explicitly poses the question of peace in relation to Josiah's death in battle: "That the temple was not destroyed in his days, and thus (the Chronicler) explains and goes on: 'Your eyes will not see all the evil that I am bringing to this place.'"

The usual understanding of Huldah's words indicate a peaceful and natural death: Josiah will be "gathered to his fathers." The Chronicler reports that Josiah is brought back to Jerusalem, where he dies and is buried (2 Chron. 35:24). There he reports the usual lamentations, making special mention of the lamentation of Jeremiah, which becomes an ordinance continuously practiced in Israel (v. 25).

Josiah, Solomon, and Hezekiah. Josiah is described as an incomparable king (2 Kings 23:25); in this respect he joins Solomon (1 Kings 3:12) and Hezekiah (2 Kings 18:5) in being like no other king before him. Each of these three kings excels in different ways. Solomon is praised for his wisdom and wealth, Hezekiah for his unparalleled trust, and Josiah for his reforms.[24] If the wicked deeds of Manasseh are responsible for the demise of the nation, then one must also set the regression of most kings over against the positive standards set by a few.

---

22. Halpern, "Blaming Manasseh," 485.

23. Ibid., 497.

24. A discussion of how the attributes of these kings are developed in the books of Kings is provided by Gary N. Knoppers, "'There Was None Like Him': Incomparability in the Books of Kings," *CBQ* 54 (1992): 411–31.

The greatness of Solomon's reign was legitimated by his dream at the Gibeon sanctuary. There, Solomon as an inexperienced king requested "a discerning heart to govern your people and to distinguish between right and wrong" (1 Kings 3:8–9). God also granted that which he did not ask, "riches and honor—so that in your lifetime you will have not equal among kings" (v. 13). The wisdom of Solomon was encyclopedic; it not only included the ability to discern right in difficult situations, as in the case with the two prostitutes (3:28), but it enabled great building projects and a "breadth of understanding as measureless as the sand on the seashore" (4:29).

Solomon's administration was renowned as none other, enabling each person to dwell under his own vine and fig tree (1 Kings 4:25). Foreigners were astonished at his wealth; the Queen of Sheba realized she had not heard the half (10:4–6), and Hiram pronounced a benediction on him (5:7). The summary of Solomon's reign confirms his incomparability (10:23–24); he was greater than all the other kings of the earth in riches and wisdom. Solomon secured two of the Davidic promises: the nation of Israel and the building of the temple.

The reign of Hezekiah is introduced with the theme of trust (2 Kings 18:5). The speech of the field commander repeatedly challenged the trust of Hezekiah (vv. 19–24). He warned against trusting in God, since the God of Israel could not be more successful than any other gods of the lands (vv. 29–30). All of this had the effect of confirming to the hearers this noble quality of Hezekiah, providing assurance that the Assyrians would not be able to defeat Jerusalem. In the end the field commander himself had to concede that Hezekiah had not been dissuaded (19:10).

Hezekiah shows the importance of prayer at critical moments, like the prayer of David (2 Sam. 7:18–29) and Solomon (1 Kings 8:22–53).[25] David prayed for the promise of the kingdom, and Solomon prayed for restoration in time of failure. Hezekiah affirmed the supremacy of Yahweh (2 Kings 19:15), like David (2 Sam. 7:22) and Solomon (1 Kings 8:23). Hezekiah offered his prayer in the temple, in accordance with the prayer of Solomon, who enjoined that prayers be made from the house of Yahweh (8:27–30, 33, 35, 38–40, 42, 44, 48). Like Solomon, Hezekiah requested that God's eyes would be open to his temple (2 Kings 19:16) in order that he might hear the blasphemy spoken against him. Though the trust of Hezekiah would not prevent the exile of his sons, he is the noble example of how trust is effectual against the military forces of imperial powers.

Josiah is the king who comes closest to fulfilling the requirements of the Book of the Law. He is the king who turns to God with all his heart, soul,

---

25. Knoppers, with reference to Richard Pratt (ibid., 421).

and strength (2 Kings 23:25; cf. Deut. 6:4–5). Love for God is demonstrated in loyalty to the covenant requirements; in this regard Josiah excels as no other king. The covenant requires repentance and obedience (Deut. 30:1–2); Josiah's reaction to finding the Book of the Law inspires an immediate rending of garments and a resolve to discover his full obligations through consulation with a prophet (2 Kings 22:11–13). His repentance is the merit on which his eyes will be spared the ultimate judgment that must come upon the city (vv. 19–20). Josiah leads the people in an unprecedented renewal of the covenant (23:1–3) and celebration of the Passover (vv. 22–23). Like no other king, Josiah reverses the failures of the nation. His Passover celebration marks a return to a time before the united kingdom.

Understanding the mystery of evil. Though the guilt of Manasseh and the collective guilt of the Exile explain the death of Josiah, his story leaves a legacy for understanding the mystery of evil. As has been observed, Kings and Chronicles each deal with this problem differently. Chronicles increases the culpability of Josiah for his own demise because of his failure to heed the words of Neco. The question continues to be raised in succeeding literature.[26] The two explanations of the encounter at Megiddo are repeatedly contemplated in understanding the lessons of Josiah's death.

The Greek version of Chronicles has additional verses, which add the guilt of Manasseh as a reason for the death of Josiah. The work in the Apocrypha known as 1 Esdras has a paraphrase of Kings and Chronicles, which explains how the sins of the previous generations provoke the anger of Yahweh, without specific reference to Manasseh. Josiah dies in the battle at Megiddo, but the question of agency is left ambiguous; the implication seems to be that Josiah dies at the hand of God. In Sirach Josiah is remembered in completely positive terms (Sir. 49:1–7). David, Hezekiah, and Josiah are singled out as the only kings who do not commit grave sin.

Jeremiah is singled out as the mistreated prophet, the one who spoke of both the demise and the restoration of the nation. Josephus modifies Huldah's prophecy to say only that calamity will be delayed until after the death of Josiah (*Ant.* 10.60–61). Josephus follows the account of Chronicles in detailing the death of Josiah (10.74–78) but makes Neco the bearer of a message from God. Depending on the text followed, it is fate alone, or a fated boastfulness, that is responsible for Josiah's death. As summarized by Begg, the main lesson of Josephus is that those who conform to the excellent laws of God receive the felicity of God.[27]

---

26. An examination of the various treatments of Josiah is provided by Steve Delamarter, "The Death of Josiah in Scripture and Tradition: Wrestling with the Problem of Evil," *VT* 54 (2004): 29–60.

27. C. Begg, "The Death of Josiah: Josephus and the Bible," *ETL* 64 (1988): 161.

Josephus somewhat evades the dilemma, providing some sort of higher explanation. In the *Apocalypse of Baruch,* an alternate interpretation of the Exile is provided (2 *Bar.* 1.1–5). The people force their kings to commit evil, but the result of their exile is a blessing to the nations. This seems to be an interpretation of Kings (2 Kings 23:16–17), along with hope like that promised to Abraham (Gen. 12:3). Baruch elevates the righteousness of Josiah, making him the only one in his generation who acts with faithfulness. The Talmud, in the context of the blowing of the *shofar* (*b. Taan.* 22b) has divergent explanations: Josiah presumes to prevail over Neco, because Neco trusts in idols; Josiah is punished because he should have consulted Jeremiah but did not; on his deathbed Josiah acknowledges that his actions were in rebellion against God.

In the traditions of Josiah, various attempts are made to deal with his death. The explanation of Kings, that Josiah's death is the beginning of the fate of the Exile, and of Chronicles, that Josiah fails to heed the Word of God, are variously developed. In a mixture of ways, later authors shift or diminish guilt, elevate character, or introduce new historiographic understandings. All are obliged to wrestle with the question of culpability and victimization in the death of Josiah. If he is culpable, is it through willful defiance, ignorance, or something else? His death demands reflection on the divine administration of justice in the world. No explanation becomes dominant, nor is there an effort to harmonize them. The work of God in the lives of his people can never be reduced to one formula.

JOSIAH'S SUCCESS. IN the Dallas Museum of Fine Arts hangs a painting by Thomas Hart Benton, a twentieth-century Missouri artist.[28] The late afternoon sun casts harsh shadows across a twisted landscape. A man stands at the side of an empty road with a suitcase tied together with pieces of rope. He stares across the road to an abandoned farmhouse, wooden walls weathered gray, roof falling in. In one corner of the painting is a bleached skeleton of a steer. As the man looks across the rutted road, he scratches his greying beard as if pondering something. The painting seems poised to tell a story; the tile on the wall reads: "The Prodigal Son."

As Benton tells that parable, the prodigal has waited too long. The home that would have welcomed him has become a ramshackle ruin; the

---

28. As told by Patrick J. Wilson, "Between Text and Sermon: 2 Kings 22:1–23:3," *Interpretation* 54 (2000): 413.

fatted calf that once would have fed a homecoming feast is now only bones drying under a tortured, unforgiving sky. The viewer may protest; this is not the way to tell the story. That is the story of Josiah measured by the fate of the nation.

Josiah reads like a story of too little too late. This would not have been his own assessment of his life's work. The oracle of Huldah leaves some ambiguity as to the extent of the exile that threatens, but the Book of the Law that was found is clear enough about its possibility. The king knows that it is possible in his lifetime. Even if he knew exile would happen in his lifetime, he would likely have done exactly as he did; the Book of the Law instructed him as to his course of action. His reforms are right, irrespective of the eventual outcome for Judah. His action is to the glory of God—which is always the ultimate goal, and a goal that is achievable. If Josiah had as his only goal the preservation of Judah, it is too little too late.

Success in leadership must be measured by the impact it has on people. It has been said that leadership is getting people to go where they want to go by getting them to do what they do not want to do. The success of such a task is a matter of perspective. Within his time, Josiah is immensely successful, more so than any other king who preceded him in the matter of reform. He leads the nation in an unprecedented revival, going back to times before the monarchy even began (23:22). Though the fate of the nation is sealed, Josiah is instrumental in preserving the covenant. This is especially evident in the life of Jeremiah.

Jeremiah and the new covenant. Jeremiah's call comes in the thirteenth year of King Josiah (Jer. 1:1–2), just five years before the discovery of the Book of the Law in the temple (2 Kings 22:3; 23:23). Jeremiah was an impressionable young man during the reforms of Josiah. The memory of the renewal of the covenant oath (23:1–3) with its concomitant celebration of the Passover (vv. 21–23) and purification of the religion of Judah (vv. 4–22) must have been indelibly etched in the memory of the young prophet.

Jeremiah's call comes through a blossoming almond. The Hebrew name of the almond is "the watcher" (*šāqēd*); it teaches Jeremiah that God is ever alert to the fulfillment of his Word, and that God is about to act (Jer. 1:11–12). No word is more solemn than a vow witnessed by God. A vow has the potential of blessing and curse, as is manifest when Huldah read from the Book of the Law. The renewal of the covenant as the people were about to enter the Promised Land held out to them the option of blessing and curse, life or death (Deut. 30:19–20). It demanded loyalty to God: to love the Lord God and to "cling" to him. The heavens and the earth gave witness to this vow, indicating that its endurance was eternal. The great Passover celebration was at the same time a solemn commitment to faithfulness.

Jeremiah is called to watch over the nation (Jer. 1:10); his work is to uproot and tear down, to destroy and to overturn, to build and to plant. These terms are a series of alliterated poetic pairs, ready to roll off the tongue:

lintôš	*wᵉlintôṣ*
ûlᵉhaᵃᵇîd	*wᵉlahᵃrôs*
libnôt	*wᵉlintôaᶜ*

It may be that the first two pairs of his calling are not so clear until the death of Josiah, but there is no question of the loyalty of the prophet to his mission. He suffers much in his vocation. Five years after Josiah's death, the scroll he writes is systematically burned while it is being read to King Jehoiakim (Jer. 36:9–26). In the last days of the kingdom, Jeremiah is accused of deserting to the Babylonians and is imprisoned (37:13–15), though Zedekiah continues to consult him seeking a word from Yahweh (vv. 16–17). Later he is thrown into a miry pit where he is in danger of starvation (38:1–13). The prophet refuses to compromise the oath he took in the days of Josiah.

Jeremiah is not only the prophet of doom, but also the prophet of the new covenant. The covenant he took in the days of Josiah will not die, even though he and the nation are to go into exile. His task is also watching to plant and to build (1:10; 31:28). The new covenant will be that of a transformed mind in which the relationship with God will remain secure (31:33–34). Jeremiah lives by his words. Two years before the final invasion of the city, he goes out to claim a property in Anathoth that is his to inherit (32:1–15); his action signifies a time of restoration to the land. The commitment of the prophet is more than words; Jeremiah stakes his life's work on the promise that the Exile is not the end of the covenant.

The equivalent oath is no less decisive under the new covenant than it was in the days of Josiah. The vow of the new covenant is observed in baptism and in communion. Baptism is the declaration of belonging to Christ, of being immersed with him in his death and raised to a new life (Rom. 6:3–11). It is what Jeremiah means when he says that God's instruction will be in the minds of those of the new covenant, that God will be their God and they will be his people (Jer. 31:33–34). The Eucharist is the transformation of the Passover to become a memorial to the death of Christ (1 Cor. 11:23–26). These two sacraments must be as significant in the life of the Christian as the renewal of the covenant and the Passover that initiated the revival of Josiah.

Expressing Christian values. In a society increasingly hostile to any public expression of the values of the Christian faith, Christians must stand by their own covenant confessions as resolutely as Jeremiah. This must be done judiciously, being sure that it is the gospel that is the offense; it must be done articulately, being sure that the values are properly understood. Christians must recognize that they do not have jurisdiction over state policy in a democracy; at best they can have influence in its formulation. However, in whatever role in life they may find themselves, they must be true to their faith.

This can be costly. A federal politician in Canada, prominent as minister of health, was elected on a platform that was firmly opposed to abortion. His party initiated a law that left virtually no restrictions on abortion.[29] The result was the immediate demise of a political career that had spanned a large part of this man's life. Supporting Christian values in a society bent on individual rights has its price, no less than that suffered by Jeremiah in the last days of Judah.

The critical role of written revelation. The story of Josiah illustrates the critical role of written revelation to establish practice of faith. Josiah began the work of purification in Jerusalem some ten years before the discovery of the Book of the Law in the temple (2 Chron. 34:3). It was the written Word that was the impetus to renewing the vow and centralizing worship at the temple. Though tradition and symbol are critical to faith, the written Word provides a foundation to endurance and faithfulness.

The power of the written Word of God in the English language is well illustrated in the life of William Tyndale. An Oxford scholar and lecturer at Cambridge, he became convinced that the Bible alone should determine the practices and doctrines of the church, and that every believer should be able to read the Bible in his or her own language. Church authorities were well aware of the power of the written Word in the hands of the faithful. Barred from continuing his work in England, Tyndale went to Germany, where he received support from wealthy London merchants. His New Testament was printed at Cologne in 1525.

Tyndale began work on the Old Testament, but was captured in Antwerp and executed at Vilvoorde in 1536. Tyndale's version is the first vernacular English text to be published and became the basis for most English transla-

---

29. During 1988, the Canadian Supreme Court declared the Federal law regulating abortion (Section 287 of the Criminal Code) was in conflict with the Canadian Charter of Rights and Freedoms—the Canadian constitution. Regulating abortion was thus viewed as unconstitutional. Parliament tried to pass a replacement law, but was unable to compromise on a suitable wording. The country has remained to this day without a law regulating abortions. Decisions are left up to the women, their doctors, and medical associations. Section 223 of the Criminal Code states that "a person commits homicide when he causes injury to a child before or during its birth as a result of which the child dies after becoming a human being." That is, for a person to be charged with murder with respect to the death of a fetus, the fetus must be intentionally injured before or during birth, and would have to be born alive and later die. See www.religioustolerance.org/abo_supr.htm (March 6, 2006).

tions, including the King James Version of 1611. The influence of Tyndale to the present demonstrates the power of the written Word.

Interpreting Scripture in a faith community. While the written Word is of critical importance, it functions in a larger context that is no less essential. When the scroll was found in the temple, Josiah immediately consulted a prophet to determine its significance and a proper response to it. The written Word of itself is not adequate for understanding and practice of the Christian faith. The scroll discovered in the temple was in the language of the people and essentially of their culture. Even in that context, its significance was not self-evident.

A contemporary translation, done so that it is accessible to every believer, can and must accomplish many more tasks than the book found by Josiah. The modern world is far removed from the world of the Scriptures. There are enormous differences of culture and custom and economic and social systems; symbols and metaphors of the ancient world are enigmatic to a modern individual. The profound language and thought of many parts of Scripture cannot be captured at the average reading level of a translation. The hermeneutical methods by which Christ is interpreted as a fulfillment of the Old Testament are sometimes elusive to the most diligent and well-informed student of the Scriptures.

Certain critical questions are answered in the creeds. The church in the first centuries determined the ontological definitions concerning the person of Christ in the formulation of the Nicean creed. Modern technology and changing cultural practice continue to bring difficult ethical questions to a Christian worldview. The practice of faith is a collective exercise, as in the days of Josiah. Christians must be part of a congregation, and congregations a part of the larger faith community. Within the Christian community, the Word of God is the foundation of faith, and every believer must be familiar with it.

The problem of evil. The life of Josiah remains an example of the problem of evil. Trouble and suffering may be the result of natural calamity or human activity. War is one of the worst of evils and is entirely the product of human aggression. The Scriptures testify that God is sovereign over all human activity; the prophetic task is to interpret relations between nations. The explanation for the Babylonian attack was to be found in the book found in the temple.

It is problematic that the beginning of judgment begins with the best of all kings, particularly when he has received the assurance that he will die in peace. The answer to this conundrum comes in various voices, and to some measure they are in tension with each other in the assignment of personal responsibility. One lesson from the Josiah story concerning the problem of evil is that answers must not be readily given, but at the same time the implications of events such as the violent death of a good king are to be seriously considered.

In wrestling with the problem of evil, John Stackhouse asks the question: "Can God be trusted?" He begins with a reminder of our theological limitations:

> Some things that we think we want to know will always remain unknown to us, whether in the nature of the case it is impossible for us to comprehend them, or because in God's kind wisdom they are kept from us. We can seek knowledge where it may be found. And then we can consider whether we have adequate ground for holding on to our belief in God.[30]

The German philosopher Leibniz held that "all is for the best in this best of all possible worlds." Explanations for the world as mortals know it do not prove satisfying, since full explanations are not available. Part of the problem is in the very definition of evil. Beyond this are the moral questions: How is innocence determined? Why is the experience of evil so inconsistent?

Questions of innocence and evil are paramount in the Josiah story. What culpability did the great king share in his own death? In what way did he die in peace? Similar questions have plagued Christians. In 1755 at 9:30 a.m. on a Sunday morning an earthquake struck Lisbon. Much of the Catholic city was at mass. In six minutes thirty churches and twelve thousand homes were destroyed. As thousands raced from the rubble, a series of tsunamis carried many more to their deaths. A series of fires raged throughout the city. Fifteen thousand died in the earthquake; the final death toll was as high as sixty thousand.

This terrible tragedy was the inspiration for Voltaire to write *Candide*, a satire on faith in God. Dr. Pangloss, the object of his parody of faith, is generally thought to be modeled on Leibniz. What made Voltaire so angry was that certain believers at the time thought that the earthquake was God's anger at Lisbon's "sinful" ways. That theory must maneuver around some troubling questions. Why should judgment come on the faithful at worship? Why pious Lisbon rather than licentious Paris?

The prophets of the Deuteronomistic History do not attempt to answer the question of justice in the death of Josiah. This tragic event is explained in terms of the larger circumstance of the nation. They understand God's Word to be fulfilled in history, as the curse of the covenant comes on them.

---

30. John G. Stackhouse Jr., *Can God Be Trusted? Faith and the Challenge of Evil* (New York: Oxford Univ. Press, 1988), 3.

The Chronicler, as is customary in his writing, finds explanation for Josiah's death in terms of his own personal culpability: He willfully refuses the message of Yahweh that came through the unorthodox channel of a foreign king. Such explanations are possible only under the privilege of divine inspiration. For the Deuteronomists and the Chronicler, the answer to the question of trust is the same: History informs them that God alone is trustworthy.

The trustworthiness of God is their assurance that the covenant relationship will continue for those who trust God. The promised fulfillment of the new covenant is his response to the problem of evil. As a servant of the new covenant, Jesus Christ is humiliated by the taunts of soldiers in an agonizing crucifixion. His identification with the worst of human suffering is heard in his words from the cross: "My God, my God, why have you forsaken me?" (Matt. 27:46). Those words are so poignant that the Gospel writers remember them and repeat them in Aramaic, just as they heard them. Jesus uses this quotation from the most painful of the lament psalms (Ps. 22:1) to identify with the deepest of human suffering. He voluntarily chooses the way of human suffering in order to gain victory over it. The crucifixion of Jesus is not just another man dying on a cross; his voluntary choice of suffering qualifies him to be the Messiah, the One who fulfills the hope of the new covenant. Christians believe that on the cross things change.[31] That cross does not just show us things; it does something once for all.

Christianity provides hope. The voluntary suffering of Christ demonstrates that commitment to the covenant in the fateful days of Josiah was justified. No other faith offers hope the same way. If God cannot or will not do something about suffering, there is no hope. Then mortals suffer evil alone. God's loyalty to his covenant in the days of Josiah, Jeremiah, and Jesus reminds us that God both can respond and has responded to evil. The story of Josiah is to help believers grasp faith and hope. God our Redeemer will be sufficient in the time of suffering.

---

31. Ibid., 115.

❦

JEHOAHAZ WAS TWENTY-THREE years old when he became king, and he reigned in Jerusalem three months. His mother's name was Hamutal daughter of Jeremiah; she was from Libnah. ³²He did evil in the eyes of the LORD, just as his fathers had done. ³³Pharaoh Neco put him in chains at Riblah in the land of Hamath so that he might not reign in Jerusalem, and he imposed on Judah a levy of a hundred talents of silver and a talent of gold. ³⁴Pharaoh Neco made Eliakim son of Josiah king in place of his father Josiah and changed Eliakim's name to Jehoiakim. But he took Jehoahaz and carried him off to Egypt, and there he died. ³⁵Jehoiakim paid Pharaoh Neco the silver and gold he demanded. In order to do so, he taxed the land and exacted the silver and gold from the people of the land according to their assessments.

³⁶Jehoiakim was twenty-five years old when he became king, and he reigned in Jerusalem eleven years. His mother's name was Zebidah daughter of Pedaiah; she was from Rumah. ³⁷And he did evil in the eyes of the LORD, just as his fathers had done.

²⁴:¹During Jehoiakim's reign, Nebuchadnezzar king of Babylon invaded the land, and Jehoiakim became his vassal for three years. But then he changed his mind and rebelled against Nebuchadnezzar. ²The LORD sent Babylonian, Aramean, Moabite and Ammonite raiders against him. He sent them to destroy Judah, in accordance with the word of the LORD proclaimed by his servants the prophets. ³Surely these things happened to Judah according to the LORD's command, in order to remove them from his presence because of the sins of Manasseh and all he had done, ⁴including the shedding of innocent blood. For he had filled Jerusalem with innocent blood, and the LORD was not willing to forgive.

⁵As for the other events of Jehoiakim's reign, and all he did, are they not written in the book of the annals of the kings of Judah? ⁶Jehoiakim rested with his fathers. And Jehoiachin his son succeeded him as king.

⁷The king of Egypt did not march out from his own country again, because the king of Babylon had taken all his territory, from the Wadi of Egypt to the Euphrates River.

[8]Jehoiachin was eighteen years old when he became king, and he reigned in Jerusalem three months. His mother's name was Nehushta daughter of Elnathan; she was from Jerusalem. [9]He did evil in the eyes of the LORD, just as his father had done.

[10]At that time the officers of Nebuchadnezzar king of Babylon advanced on Jerusalem and laid siege to it, [11]and Nebuchadnezzar himself came up to the city while his officers were besieging it. [12]Jehoiachin king of Judah, his mother, his attendants, his nobles and his officials all surrendered to him.

In the eighth year of the reign of the king of Babylon, he took Jehoiachin prisoner. [13]As the LORD had declared, Nebuchadnezzar removed all the treasures from the temple of the LORD and from the royal palace, and took away all the gold articles that Solomon king of Israel had made for the temple of the LORD. [14]He carried into exile all Jerusalem: all the officers and fighting men, and all the craftsmen and artisans—a total of ten thousand. Only the poorest people of the land were left.

[15]Nebuchadnezzar took Jehoiachin captive to Babylon. He also took from Jerusalem to Babylon the king's mother, his wives, his officials and the leading men of the land. [16]The king of Babylon also deported to Babylon the entire force of seven thousand fighting men, strong and fit for war, and a thousand craftsmen and artisans. [17]He made Mattaniah, Jehoiachin's uncle, king in his place and changed his name to Zedekiah.

THE DEATH OF Josiah is the beginning of the last days of Judah. Within four years Nebuchadnezzar invades Judah, and the first exiles (with Daniel among them) are taken to Babylon (Jer. 46:2). Egyptian control begins with the death of Josiah in 609 B.C.[1] The campaign of Neco lasts for three months; upon his return, Neco deposes Jehoahaz and installs Eliakim (Jehoiakim) as king. During that time the Babylonian king Nebuchadnezzar campaigns against Judah, taking the first of the captives to Babylon (2 Kings 24:1); in the eleventh year of Jehoiakim, Nebuchadnezzar

---

1. From the details of the Babylonian Chronicle, this event can be fixed to early summer (Tammuz=June/July) of 609; A. K. Grayson, *Assyrian and Babylonian Chronicles* (Locust Valley, N.Y.: Augustin, 1975), 19, 96.

puts Jerusalem under siege and installs Mattaniah (Zedekiah) as king (24:15–17), putting an end to Egyptian hegemony over Judah (24:7). Just eleven years after the appointment of Zedekiah, the final siege against Jerusalem will end the rule of the descendants of David in Jerusalem.

Egyptian Intervention (23:31–35)

THE CIVIC LEADERS of Israel appoint Shallum to succeed Josiah (2 Kings 23:30; Jer. 22:11–12). Shallum is the fourth son of Josiah according to the Davidide genealogy (1 Chron. 3:15); he receives the throne name Jehoahaz when he is anointed king. His mother comes from the countryside of the Shephelah. Jehoahaz is appointed by the same leaders who made Josiah king (2 Kings 21:24), in the hopes that he will continue the policies of his father. Neco imprisons him in Riblah, an Assyrian administrative center on the Orontos River in the north Lebanon Valley. The site later serves as headquarters for Nebuchadnezzar during his campaigns in the west (25:6, 20). Neco levies an indemnity against Judah, making it a vassal of Egypt. The number of talents of gold appears to have been lost in the Masoretic text; old Greek says ten talents of gold, which is proportionate in relation to the amount of silver. There is no concluding regnal summary for Jehoahaz, since he dies in Egypt; the place of his tomb is not known.

Neco makes Eliakim the king of Judah on his successful return from Haran. The name Eliakim is changed in minimal fashion, simply replacing the divine element (*ʾel*) with the covenant name (*yhw*). This name change may have been connected with an oath of loyalty. Neco demands a special tax, which is levied from the civic leaders who have influence over the throne. Menahem used the same procedure to pay Tiglath-Pileser (15:20). The tribute in silver is only one-tenth of what was required by the Assyrians.

Babylonian Control (23:36–24:17)

JEHOIAKIM, JOSIAH'S SECOND son, is twenty-five when Josiah dies; he must have been born when Josiah was only fourteen. His mother is from Rumah, identified with Aruma near Merom in upper Galilee. This northern location indicates Josiah took wives from the north to strengthen his associations there, much as Manasseh did in marrying a woman from Jotbah (21:19).

Political forces change during Jehoiakim's reign. Pharoah Neco fails to restrict the power of the Babylonians at Haran. Egypt controls the Levant for about four years, until the Babylonians conquer Carchemish in 605 B.C. Jeremiah tells us that Neco marches north against Nebuchadnezzar, meeting him at Carchemish in the fourth year of Jehoiakim (Jer. 46:2). Nebuchadnezzar is victorious, but that same year he must return to Babylon to take control of the throne after his father's death. In his accession year, Nebuchadnezzar follows up this victory with a campaign to the borders of Egypt.[2] Another campaign to the west is conducted in his first full regnal year, resulting in the capture of Ashkelon and arousing such fear in Judah that a fast is proclaimed (Jer. 36:9). Jehoiakim, enthroned by the Egyptians, soon comes under the domination of the Babylonians, the successors of the Neo-Assyrian empire.

Nebuchadnezzar marches to Egypt in his fourth year but fails to gain a victory.[3] Neco followed up his victory by invading the southern coast and taking Gaza (cf. Jer. 47:1). This is the time of Jehoiakim's rebellion against Babylon (2 Kings 24:1). Jehoiakim is caught in the power struggle; Nebuchanezzar stays in Babylon rebuilding his army in his fifth year, which gives Neco the opportunity to rebuild his position in encouraging a coalition against Babylonia.[4]

In his sixth year Nebuchadnezzar again goes west (599 B.C.), his engagements including an attack against the Arabs in the desert (Jer. 49:28–33). The main entry for his seventh year is the capture of Jerusalem.[5] Nebuchadnezzar also uses detachments from Aram, Ammon, and Moab in the attack against Jerusalem (2 Kings 24:2).[6] The expedition against Judah is a punitive action, because Jehoiakim has broken his vassal oath.

Jehoiakim dies before the city surrenders and is followed by his eighteen-year-old son, Jehoiachin. He reigns only three months (24:8). Nebuchadnezzar himself arrives to join the army besieging Jerusalem, and Jehoiachin surrenders, sparing the city from destruction (vv. 11–12).[7] Jehoiachin pays for the policy of his father with exile, not only of himself but also of his harem, high officials, and upper classes of society, including all skilled workers. The temple and the palace are emptied of their treasures, as was common practice (vv. 13–16).

The total of the exiles is given in round numbers, either ten thousand (v. 14) or eight thousand (vv. 15–16). Another tally of exiles in the seventh

---

2. Ibid., 20, 99–100.

3. The Babylonian text says "the king of Akkad and his army turned and (went back) to Babylon" (ibid., 101).

4. Ahlström, *The History of Ancient Palestine*, 782–83.

5. According to the chronicle, he "encamped against the city of Judah, and on the second day of the month of Adar he captured the city and seized its king. A king of his own choice he appointed in the city" (Grayson, *Assyrian and Babylonian Chronicles*, 102).

6. It is possible the text should read Edom instead of Aram, because there is no kingdom in Aram at this point in time.

7. The writer of Kings calls this the eighth year of Nebuchadnezzar, while Jeremiah calls it the seventh (Jer. 52:28), as does the Babylonian Chronicle. The discrepancy may be accounted for by accession year reckoning used in Babylon, or it may have been a year later when the exiles actually leave for Babylon.

year of Nebuchadnezzar is 3,023 (Jer. 52:28), but this may refer to the deportees from the countryside. Before leaving Jerusalem, Nebuchadnezzar installs Mattaniah as his vassal king, the youngest son of Josiah; he has the same mother as Jehoahaz (2 Kings 24:17–18; cf. 23:31).[8] His throne name is Zedekiah; he rules until the fate of the kingdom of Judah is sealed.

Bridging Contexts

EZEKIEL. Ezekiel the priest is among the leaders exiled to Babylon in the siege of Nebuchadnezzar against Jerusalem in his eighth year of his reign (2 Kings 24:8–12). The importance of this historical situation can be seen by the dates provided in Ezekiel. All sections in the prophecy are dated according to the time of the Exile.[9] The book begins with the fifth year of the captivity of Jehoiachin (i.e., 593 B.C.; Ezek. 1:2). The last date given is the twenty-fifth year of the captivity (573 B.C.), which introduces the vision of the new temple (40:1).

The dates of Ezekiel follow a chronological arrangement that corresponds to the divisions of the book. Ezekiel 1–24 deals with events before the final destruction of Jerusalem (586 B.C.). Chapters 25–32 are oracles against the nations dated at the time of the fall of Jerusalem, except for the notation of the failure of the siege of Tyre (29:17) in the seventeenth year (571 B.C.), which is linked to a judgment against Egypt. Chapters 33–39 are oracles dealing with restoration hopes and conditions after the destruction of Jerusalem (33:21). The book closes with a description of the ideal future of the people (chs. 40–48), a vision dated to the fourteenth year after the city was conquered (573 B.C.). The five dated sections in chapters 1–24 are in chronological order. The second section against the nations is arranged topically into a collection of oracles against Tyre (26:28:19) and Egypt (29–32). The last two sections are dated generally.

Though the fortunes of the temple are critically important to Ezekiel as a priest, he presents the Exile in terms of God's being true to his name. Though his message is stubbornly resisted (Ezek. 3:4–9), Ezekiel stoutly declares the reversal of the Exodus (7:1–6). The Exodus involved a revelation of God's name, beginning with Moses at the burning bush (Ex. 3:12–14).

---

8. Chronicles presents an alternate view of the relationships. Jehoiachin and Zedekiah are both sons of Jehoiakim (2 Chron. 3:16); only two sons of Josiah are king: Jehoiakim and Shallum (Jehoahaz). Japhet provides a full discussion (*I & II Chronicles*, 97–99); the earlier tradition of Kings is to be preferred, but the Chronicler is consistent in his genealogical presentation (cf. 2 Chron. 36:10).

9. Ezekiel provides sixteen dates in total; for a tabulation see M. Greenberg, *Ezekiel 1–20* (AB 22; New York: Doubleday, 1983), 8.

The divine name was understood in ways previously unknown (6:2–8). Pharaoh needed to receive an answer to his question: "Who is the LORD, that I should obey to him?" (5:2). Pharoah received an answer ten times; the plagues made known God's name to the Egyptians (7:5, 17; 8:18; 14:4, 18). Divine redemption made God's name known to Israel for future generations (10:2; 16:6, 12; 29:45–46; 31:13). Conversely, Ezekiel announces that the end of Israel, experienced without mercy, will teach Israel the same lesson: "Then you will know that I am the LORD" (Ezek. 7:1–9). This time the day of Yahweh is not the beginning but the end of Israel.

The revelation of Yahweh's name is also an oath whereby God affirms the choice of his people and the fulfillment of his promise to them. This is the force of what it means to hear the words "I am the LORD." Ezekiel understands the time of God's election of the nation to be that of the revelation of his name.[10] He paraphrases the self-revelation of God given at the time of the Exodus as an oath to Israel (Ezek. 20:5–6; cf. Ex. 6:4–5):

> On the day I chose Israel,
>> *a* I swore with uplifted hand to the descendants of . . . Jacob
>>> *b* and revealed myself to them in Egypt
>> *a'* With uplifted hand I said to them,
>>> *b'* "I am the LORD your God"—
> On that day I swore to them that I would bring them out of Egypt into a land I had searched out for them, a land flowing with milk and honey.

The leaders of Judah have come to Ezekiel in exile in order to seek the God who took the oath of the covenant. The message of the prophet is that he can do nothing other than pass judgment on them (Ezek. 20:4). The declaration of the name when God made his covenant with Israel requires uncompromising allegiance (vv. 7–8). Israel has never left the idolatries of Egypt. The fate of Jerusalem is sealed; there will be no pity.

The time of exile is to bring the Israelites to know their God just as much as the times of redemption and promise. God is not a person to show favorites to any nation (Deut. 10:12–20); idolatrous Israel will not receive mercy any more than any other nation. There is always a tendency to misunderstand God's promise; that promise never pertains to those who turn from God. Perhaps because of deliverance in the days of Hezekiah, there was a tendency to think that the temple as the place of divine residence would be spared (Jer. 7:4). Such thinking is utterly errant; Ezekiel the priest observes the glory of God leave the temple toward the east (Ezek. 10:18–19). The name of God will not be compromised.

---

10. M. Greenberg, *Understanding Exodus* (New York: Behrman House, 1969), 134–35.

LESSONS IN THE **midst of pain.** The tumultuous last days of Judah are an opportunity to learn faithfulness and trust in God. The Deuterono-mistic Historians understand it this way; Egyptian and Babylonian interventions are not a sign of God's absence but confirmation of his presence. Life in a vassal province is not evidence of the failure of the covenant, but assurance that God will honor his name, as Ezekiel said (Ezek. 20:39—44). These events are part of God's work in history; the faithful will become stronger in faith.

Times like those of Jehoiakim continue to be experienced. One of the most powerful examples of such a *danse macabre*[11] for people of faith took place in Ukraine at the end of World War I. The traumatic upheaval of the Russian Revolution and Civil War was particularly devasting in Ukraine. Living in the rich heartland of Ukraine, devout, hardworking, and self-sufficient German colonists could not anticipate the violence and chaos that would come with revolution and counterrevolution.

The first tremors were felt with land liquidation laws, which called for all colonists to sell off their land holdings within eight months. This threat had grave implications for the future, but the government was so busy with the war that the laws were only sporadically enforced and few were affected. The German colonists were patriotic citizens, who were conscientious about non-combatant military service in forestry or medicine. When the revolution came, many colonists welcomed it. It meant their military duties would end and that they did not need to worry about czarist property liquidation laws.

The positive developments were quickly superseded by ominous developments. The time-honored system of autonomous village and district government was abruptly replaced by hastily organized revolutionary councils made up of peasants, workers, ex-servicemen, and assorted riff-raff. They seldom answered to any higher authority, and to advance their own powers they "requisitioned" huge supplies of grain, livestock, food, clothing, and currency from the colonies. Total anarchy was delayed by the Whites, a volunteer army that represented various anti-Bolshevik groups and favored the old czarist regime. By fall of 1919, the Whites were defeated by an anarchist group led by Nestor Makhno.

The months that followed were most horrific. Under the black flag of anarchy, the Makhnovites went on a prolonged orgy of plunder, rape, and murder. Over a period of three months about seven hundred colonists died; many more were left destitute, wounded, and homeless. Ironically their pros-

---

11. "Dance of death."

perity provided Makhno with the means to maintain his brutal oppression. By late December the Red Army began taking control, but disease and starvation killed several times as many people as the invasions. In the summer of 1920, the Whites thrust north from Crimea and engaged the Red Army in a summer-long, see-saw battle. Some villages changed hands several times. By November Makhno was on the run and the Red colossus held in its iron grip the fractious Ukraine.

Testimony to these dreadful events has been preserved in the diary of a survivor named Dietrich Navall (Dietrich Neufeld).[12] Navall records the following of one of the many home invasions he endured:

> "Hey, there's a piano here," came the shout. "Who plays it? Come on, gals, play something for us."
>
> The middle daughter [Liese], a spirited girl, stepped forward bravely. With a defiant glance, she sat down at the piano. She opened the book and began to play a Bach air while the wild, travel-stained brutes sprawled around ... uttering filthy mother-of-God oaths, they leaped to their feet and demanded dance music. The poor girl protested that she didn't know any. She retreated from the piano, frightened and confused. The coarse brutality of these wretches was enough to sicken us all.
>
> The bandits' greed for valuables was insatiable. They were all trying to get ahead of each other. When evening came they demanded a light. They then attacked the china cabinet, taking out glasses and smashing them.... They amused themselves by tearing books out of their bindings.

Such horrendous stories have been repeated many times. The Mennonite experience has been enacted in a docudrama entitled "... and When They Shall Ask."[13] I grew up hearing of these stories from my grandparents, who also survived that era. My mother was not yet born when the revolution happened, but she grew up in a home that lived with the legacy. I made a copy of the docudrama available to her, but she was never able to watch it. The emotional impact of warfare cannot be understood by those without such an experience.

As a young teenager I remember visits with my maternal grandparents. I remember the poverty and the struggles of those bereft of everything coming

---

12. These diaries have been translated and edited by Al Reimer as *Dietrich Neufeld's A Russian Dance of Death: Revolution and Civil War in the Ukraine* (Winnipeg, Man.: Windflower Communications, 1997).

13. A David Dueck Film Production, 1984.

to a foreign land and struggling with language as they tried to find a way to earn a living on the farm. What I have come to appreciate more than ever is their unwavering faith. It is said that God is all you need, but you do not know that until God is all you have. That was the faith story of my mother and her parents.

The same story is true for the Israelites in Exile. They suffered the same alienation and ignominy. The story preserved in Kings is testimony to the strength and resolution of their faith.

2 Kings 24:18–25:30

ZEDEKIAH WAS TWENTY-ONE years old when he became king, and he reigned in Jerusalem eleven years. His mother's name was Hamutal daughter of Jeremiah; she was from Libnah. ¹⁹He did evil in the eyes of the LORD, just as Jehoiakim had done. ²⁰It was because of the LORD's anger that all this happened to Jerusalem and Judah, and in the end he thrust them from his presence.

Now Zedekiah rebelled against the king of Babylon.

¹So in the ninth year of Zedekiah's reign, on the tenth day of the tenth month, Nebuchadnezzar king of Babylon marched against Jerusalem with his whole army. He encamped outside the city and built siege works all around it. ²The city was kept under siege until the eleventh year of King Zedekiah. ³By the ninth day of the fourth month the famine in the city had become so severe that there was no food for the people to eat. ⁴Then the city wall was broken through, and the whole army fled at night through the gate between the two walls near the king's garden, though the Babylonians were surrounding the city. They fled toward the Arabah, ⁵but the Babylonian army pursued the king and overtook him in the plains of Jericho. All his soldiers were separated from him and scattered, ⁶and he was captured. He was taken to the king of Babylon at Riblah, where sentence was pronounced on him. ⁷They killed the sons of Zedekiah before his eyes. Then they put out his eyes, bound him with bronze shackles and took him to Babylon.

⁸On the seventh day of the fifth month, in the nineteenth year of Nebuchadnezzar king of Babylon, Nebuzaradan commander of the imperial guard, an official of the king of Babylon, came to Jerusalem. ⁹He set fire to the temple of the LORD, the royal palace and all the houses of Jerusalem. Every important building he burned down. ¹⁰The whole Babylonian army, under the commander of the imperial guard, broke down the walls around Jerusalem. ¹¹Nebuzaradan the commander of the guard carried into exile the people who remained in the city, along with the rest of the populace and those who had gone over to the king of Babylon. ¹²But the

commander left behind some of the poorest people of the land to work the vineyards and fields.

[13]The Babylonians broke up the bronze pillars, the movable stands and the bronze Sea that were at the temple of the LORD and they carried the bronze to Babylon. [14]They also took away the pots, shovels, wick trimmers, dishes and all the bronze articles used in the temple service. [15]The commander of the imperial guard took away the censers and sprinkling bowls—all that were made of pure gold or silver.

[16]The bronze from the two pillars, the Sea and the movable stands, which Solomon had made for the temple of the LORD, was more than could be weighed. [17]Each pillar was twenty-seven feet high. The bronze capital on top of one pillar was four and a half feet high and was decorated with a network and pomegranates of bronze all around. The other pillar, with its network, was similar.

[18]The commander of the guard took as prisoners Seraiah the chief priest, Zephaniah the priest next in rank and the three doorkeepers. [19]Of those still in the city, he took the officer in charge of the fighting men and five royal advisers. He also took the secretary who was chief officer in charge of conscripting the people of the land and sixty of his men who were found in the city. [20]Nebuzaradan the commander took them all and brought them to the king of Babylon at Riblah. [21]There at Riblah, in the land of Hamath, the king had them executed.

So Judah went into captivity, away from her land.

[22]Nebuchadnezzar king of Babylon appointed Gedaliah son of Ahikam, the son of Shaphan, to be over the people he had left behind in Judah. [23]When all the army officers and their men heard that the king of Babylon had appointed Gedaliah as governor, they came to Gedaliah at Mizpah—Ishmael son of Nethaniah, Johanan son of Kareah, Seraiah son of Tanhumeth the Netophathite, Jaazaniah the son of the Maacathite, and their men. [24]Gedaliah took an oath to reassure them and their men. "Do not be afraid of the Babylonian officials," he said. "Settle down in the land and serve the king of Babylon, and it will go well with you."

[25]In the seventh month, however, Ishmael son of Nethaniah, the son of Elishama, who was of royal blood, came with ten men and assassinated Gedaliah and also the men of Judah and the Babylonians who were with him at Mizpah. [26]At this,

all the people from the least to the greatest, together with the army officers, fled to Egypt for fear of the Babylonians.

²⁷In the thirty-seventh year of the exile of Jehoiachin king of Judah, in the year Evil-Merodach became king of Babylon, he released Jehoiachin from prison on the twenty-seventh day of the twelfth month. ²⁸He spoke kindly to him and gave him a seat of honor higher than those of the other kings who were with him in Babylon. ²⁹So Jehoiachin put aside his prison clothes and for the rest of his life ate regularly at the king's table. ³⁰Day by day the king gave Jehoiachin a regular allowance as long as he lived.

THE DEUTERONOMISTIC HISTORY ends with six vignettes about the end of the state of Judah. After a brief record of the reign of Zedekiah (24:18–20), the fates of several elements in Jerusalem are recorded. These include the doom of the king (25:1–7), the city itself (25: 8–12), the temple (25:13–17), religious, military, and civil personnel (25:18–21), the chaos of the inhabitants after the collapse (25:22–26), and finally the clemency shown to a previously exiled king (25:27–30). Every element of life in Judah is destroyed. Sacred and symbolic buildings are desecrated and ruined, holy vessels are carried away, and the king is maimed and exiled. Even the puppet administration of Gedaliah fails, and those responsible flee to Egypt.

Breach and Plunder of Jerusalem (24:18–25:21)

ZEDEKIAH BEGINS HIS eleven-year reign "in the spring" when Nebuchadnezzar takes Jehoiachin captive to Babylon (2 Chron. 36:10). The accession year of Zedekiah begins in the spring of Nebuchanezzar's eighth year (597 B.C.).[1]

The tenth year of Zedekiah is the eighteenth year of Nebuchadnezzar according to Jeremiah (Jer. 32:1). The siege of Jerusalem begins in the tenth month of the ninth year of Zedekiah (2 Kings 25:1; Jer. 39:1). Jeremiah is imprisoned the next year (587 B.C.). Famine prevails, the city is eventually broken, and the king flees on the ninth day of the fourth month of the eleventh year (2 Kings 25:2–3), the nineteenth year of Nebuchanezzar (586 B.C.). The Babylonian Chronicles end with Nebuchadnezzar's eleventh year

---

1. Following the chronology of Thiele, *Mysterious Numbers of the Hebrew Kings*, 190–91. Cogan and Tadmor begin Zedekiah's reign in spring of 596 B.C., making the eleventh year 586/85 (*II Kings*, 317).

(594 B.C.), so the historical reconstruction of the destruction of Jerusalem depends entirely on biblical data, supplemented by indirect references in Egyptian sources.

Zedekiah takes the throne as a sworn vassal of Nebuchadnezzar. The Babylonians expect little resistance from Judah; the deportation of military personnel and high officials requires that a new administration must be restructured. Zedekiah has a difficult time maneuvering among the various factions; some hope for the return of Jehoiachin (alternately Jeconiah), hoping for a more vigorous resistance to the Babylonians (Jer. 28:1–4).

It is not clear what inspires Zedekiah's rebellion (2 Kings 25:1). The march of Pharaoh Psammetichus II (595–589 B.C.) to Phoenicia in 591 B.C. may have been interpreted as a revival of Egyptian strength. As a representative of the Palestinian region, Zedekiah would look to Egypt for help. Thus, Zedekiah breaks his treaty with Babylon by sending messengers to Egypt to ask for horses and troops (Ezek. 17:15). The Egyptian pharaoh is succeeded by his son Hophra, who increases Egypt's political activities in Palestine.[2] The Babylonians encounter no resistance to their advance through Palestine. Nebuchadnezzar chooses to attack Jerusalem first, besieging it in 588 B.C. Earthen ramps are thrown around the city to prevent anyone from escaping.

The siege of Jerusalem lasts for about a year and a half. Once the wall is breached, King Zedekiah and his entourage flee toward Jericho, perhaps in an effort to escape to Ammon, an ally of Jerusalem. The royal party is captured in the level area at Jericho. The group is taken to the military headquarters in Riblah, where the king witnesses the death of his sons before being blinded and led to Babylon.

The destruction of Jerusalem is thorough. Temple, palaces, and houses are burned, the temple vessels including the enormous bronze Sea and the wheeled bronze stands are broken and taken as booty—all those items described in the account of Solomon's construction of the temple. The temple is of chief concern, since it served as a symbol of the legitimacy of the monarchy. With the capture and destruction of Jerusalem, the kingdom of Judah ceases to exist.

Reign of Gedaliah (25:22–26)

THE BABYLONIAN POLICY for conquered territory did not involve rebuilding destroyed cities. Under a Babylonian official, the rural population was expected to carry on with their lives; de-centralization made a national upris-

---

2. An ostraca from Tell ed-Duweir reports that a son of Elnathan had gone to Egypt; a top military emissary in Egypt indicates some type of alliance (Ahlström, *History of Ancient Palestine*, 794).

ing hard to organize. Gedaliah belongs to a prominent noble family; his grandfather was a scribe during the days of Josiah (2 Kings 22:3); his father was a member of the mission sent to Huldah (22:12), and he also intervened to save Jeremiah from the mob (Jer. 26:24). Jeremiah supports Gedaliah, appointed by the Babylonians as governor at Mizpah (Jer. 39:14). The army officers enter into oath with Gedaliah (2 Kings 25:24); they need assurance there will be no reprisals for their having fought against the Babylonians. They are granted amnesty to now serve the Babylonians.

After a short time, Gedaliah and the Babylonians at Mizpah are murdered by a band led by Ishmael son of Nethaniah, a member of the royal family. He and a number of other Judahites were able to escape before the siege of Jerusalem began. Ishmael kills a number of others, including eighty men coming from Shechem and Shiloh to bring offerings and incense at the temple place as a rite of mourning (Jer. 41:5–6). It is not certain if Ishmael is contesting Gedaliah's position as a leader of Judah. The murder is hardly an act of rebellion against the Babylonians; it is a vendetta against those who are viewed as collaborating with the Babylonians.

The people of Judah, fearful of Babylonian revenge, flee to Egypt, forcing Jeremiah and Baruch to go with them (Jer. 43:4–7). The report of their flight indicates that the judgment of exile is carried out in totality. Gedaliah's death is the extinction of all national existence.

Release of Jehoiachin (25:27–30)

AMEL-MARDUK, SON AND successor of Nebuchadnezzar, reigns for two years (561–560 B.C.). His accession year becomes the occasion to grant amnesty to prisoners. Jehoiachin was apparently charged with some act of treason and was thrown into prison until the death of Nebuchadnezzar. Jehoiachin is then granted a favored status in relation to other captive kings; it is not specified what these privileges actually mean. He is confined to the court of the Babylonian king, with his family. Seven sons are born to him in exile (1 Chron. 3:17–18).

Bridging Contexts

FAITH AND HOPE. Jeremiah preserves an almost verbatim copy of the fate of Jerusalem (Jer. 52:1–27). A shorter version of the fall of Jerusalem and Zedekiah's tragic end is found earlier in Jeremiah's prophecy (39:1–14). The evaluation of Jehoiakim (Jer. 52:2) and the punishment of the Exile (vv. 3, 27) are both characteristic of Kings. Jeremiah 52 functions as an appendix; it follows after the words of the prophet are concluded (51:64b). A comparison of the various texts of Jeremiah and Kings indicates that an account of the fall of Jerusalem as preserved in Kings serves as the conclusion of Jeremiah, and a second account of Jeremiah's fate is merged with portions of this in his memoirs (Jer. 39).[3] The traumatic experience of exile and the destruction of Jerusalem and the temple create a crisis of faith. More than one record of the events is preserved, and these records are variously integrated into prophetic compositions.

The crisis of faith is not the end of hope in the covenant promise. The full force of the covenant curse brings an end to the kingdom and the loss of the land of promise. Hope is to be found only in the Babylonian exile and among the exiles in Babylon.[4] The Deuteronomistic History ends with the desolation of Judah; symbols of faith and hope continue beyond Judah. The Deuteronomistic view concerning the future of Judah as a nation is more enigmatic. The release of Jehoiachin may be viewed as an expression of hope for the Davidic dynasty (2 Kings 25:27–30). There appear to be significant resonances with Solomon's prayer for restoration (cf. 1 Kings 8:46–53).[5] This may be nothing more than hope for a good life in exile.

There are also a number of comparisons that can be made with Mephibosheth.[6] Both have a place at the king's table (cf. 2 Sam. 9:7, 11, 13) and both suffer a disability (cf. 4:4; 9:3, 13). The fate of Saul's house seems to be recalled at the end of the Davidic dynasty in the tearing apart of the kingdom (1 Sam. 15:28; 28:17; 1 Kings 14:8; 2 Kings 17:21). Both Mephibosheth and Jehoiachin seem to represent a dynasty that survives, though incapable of functioning as a royal order. The parallels to Mephibosheth suggest that Jehoiachin is testimony to the survival of Israel, even in exile.

Mention of Jehoaichin's release at the end of the Deuteronomistic History introduces a glimmer of hope in that the Davidic dynasty does survive. Just as Joash survived the virtual extinction of the Davidic dynasty, so does Jehoiachin. The influence of that hope takes effect when Zerubbabel, Jehoiachin's grandson, is made governor of Judah by the Persians (cf. Hag. 1:1). Faith and promise are preserved among the exiles in Babylon, where the temple vessels, the king, the priests, and other leaders are located. Hope is found among those whose trust is in the God of the covenant; the One who redeemed them from Egypt can also bring them back from Babylon.

---

3. Cogan and Tadmor, *II Kings*, 321.

4. Robert P. Carroll, *Chaos to Covenant: Prophecy in the Book of Jeremiah* (New York: Crossroad, 1981), 248.

5. For a full discussion see Donald Murray, "Of All the Years the Hopes—or Fears? Jehoiachin in Babylon (2 Kings 25: 27–30)," *JBL* 120 (2001): 245–65.

6. Jeremy Schipper, "'Significant Resonances' with Mephibosheth in 2 Kings 25:27–30," *JBL* 124 (2005): 521–29.

Righteousness and hope. The name Zedekiah, the last king of Judah, becomes the basis of a sermon in prophetic preaching. That name means "Yahweh is righteous." To know Yahweh as a righteous God is to know him as judge. Jeremiah anticipates a future day when righteousness will have the salvific sense that is inherent in the word. Righteousness is a deed that God will perform, a deliverance that he will bring.[7]

Isaiah spoke about the righteousness that would come quickly, the salvation that God would bring, not only for Israel but for all nations to the farthest coastlands (Isa. 51:4–5). The ultimate work of God's justice is that there will be deliverance and salvation for all. Jeremiah anticipates the day when another son of David, a righteous Branch, will rule; the name by which he will be called is "the LORD Our Righteousness." Jeremiah refers to this time as "the days are coming" (Jer. 23:5–6). Then the people will no longer remember the Exodus as the great deliverance, but they will remember the Exodus from the land of the north and from all the other lands to which they have been driven.

Later on the prophet Jeremiah repeats the promise; in the coming days the righteous Branch will lead Israel to live in security (33:15–16). God will never abandon his kingdom or the promise that there will be a descendant of the King David on the throne of Israel. The temple and its officials will be revived and its symbolic offerings reinstated (33:17–18). To know Yahweh is to know that he is merciful and compassionate (see Ex. 33:19; 34:6). God's work never ends in punishment, but in the victory of his grace.

The prophetic promise did not result in the revival of the nation. Covenant expressed in national terms failed miserably. But there will be a restoration and a return to the land. The Chronicler ends on that hope (2 Chron. 36:22–23); God's anointed will include a Persian king who will order the rebuilding of Jerusalem. The punishment is of limited duration; the land must be relieved of its disobedient people for the number of years they failed to keep the Sabbath (vv. 20–21).

The Sabbath was the preeminent sign of the covenant (Ex. 31:12–18), the symbol that these people belonged to God, the Holy One, to a realm that is more than just the common realm of this earth. The Sabbath is expressed in terms of a day, a seventh year, or a fiftieth year. The Chronicler counts the number of seventh-year Sabbaths in which the covenant has not been confessed and makes that the time of punishment. After that comes restoration, a second exodus.

The Second Temple period never results in the salvation anticipated in prophetic preaching. It results instead in a rigidity of rules applied to the

---

7. In modern Hebrew ṣᵉdāqâ is used for prosperity and charity.

covenant and in continual conflict with the surrounding peoples. Instead of peace there is conflict within and without. The Gospel writers find the fulfillment of the righteous Branch in the son born to Joseph and Mary; this one is the Son of David (Matt. 1:1). In him righteousness will flourish. Paul describes him as the one who makes peace between the nations (Eph. 2:14–18). The covenant fulfilled in him will offer access for all to the Father in heaven. This is the Redeemer promised to Zion, who will remove all their iniquity; this one is the fulfillment of the new covenant (Rom. 11:26–27). In this righteous Branch all Israel will be saved.

LIFE GOES ON. Life goes on. In whatever manner death takes place, life continues, and the living must adjust to new circumstances. Death is the end of an individual life in this world; the death of an individual may also be the end of a marriage or the end of any number of other relationships. Sometimes death takes place without the death of an individual. The death of a marriage may take place because of divorce; the death of a community may take place because of political fiat, because of war, or simply because there are no longer sufficient cultural supports for it to continue. Whenever death takes places, those affected must learn a new way of life.

Death is a process. The process itself can be long and agonizing, or it can be swift and unexpected, whether it be the death of an individual, a marriage, or any other relationship. Depending on the process and the circumstances, the pain is experienced in different ways and at different levels. In many respects, the death of a marriage in divorce or the death of a community is more painful than physical death. In physical death there is an absolute termination; the death of a marriage or community is like a death that does not die. If children are involved in the death of a marriage, something of continuity with the former relationship is unavoidable. In the death of a community, like that of Judah, there is much continuity with the past, but also much alienation, in which highly valued relationships and customs end.

Expressing the pain of death. The pain of death must be expressed. In the death of an individual, a specific ceremony is involved, in which the memory of a life is shared and there is disposal of the body. In the Jewish community especially, the disposal of the body is an important part for the grieving to take place and hope to be expressed. Throughout the millennia, particularly after the Holocaust when the word "crematoria" took on a horror all its own, Jews shuddered at the idea of reducing a body to ashes. There is a ritual process involving washing, purifying, and dressing the body in shrouds.

In interpreting the Torah, the rabbis prohibited a body from being cremated, autopsied, or cosmetically altered. Such practices, they claimed, desecrate the holiness of the deceased as well as allow the mourners to continue living in denial of their loss. In contrast, the traditional Jewish burial demonstrates respect for the dead and comfort for mourners. As mourners witness the kindness shown by the *chevra kadisha*,[8] they recognize that when their time comes, they too will be cared for by concerned community members. Their own fear of dying is thereby allayed.[9]

The equivalent of the funeral service for the exiles of Israel is found in Lamentations. This sequence of five poems was composed sometime after the destruction of Jerusalem, quite possibly for ceremonies commemorating the event. Lamentations does not report or narrate the tragic events of its subject matter. Rather, it expresses a complex cluster of emotions—sorrow, anger, guilt, hope, despair, fear, self-loathing, revenge, compassion, forgiveness, uncertainty, and disorientation.[10] The Exile evoked all of these feelings, which are subjected to scrutiny, deliberation, and argumentation. Images are superimposed over each other like a film montage.

The poetry of Lamentations moves from one emotional high to the next. Conflicting emotions are held simultaneously. Zion confesses that Yahweh is right and that she has rebelled (Lam. 1:18), but immediately the people are called to inspect Zion's wounds, to observe that her young men and women have been led into captivity. Zion's confession of rebellion is softened in light of the punishment she receives, but the Exile is justified by the conduct of the rebel.

The function of a lament is not to resolve a problem or come to a conclusion. It surveys, articulates, and probes the variegated tapestry of emotions provoked. It included the various groups of the community: children (4:1–4), rich and privileged (vv. 5, 7–8), mothers (v. 10), prophets, priests, and elders (vv. 13, 16), and even the king (v. 20). Emotions must be controlled by reason, but they must not be unreasonably suppressed. Expression of emotions is one mechanism by which orientation is made to life that goes on.

The exile leads to customs of fasting in remembering the tragedy that took place (Zech. 7:3). In modern Judaism these have evolved into the *Bein Hametzarim* (Between the Straits), a period of mourning that runs from the seventeenth day of Tammuz, the fourth month of the Jewish religious year, to the

---

8. Lit., "sacred community," a term used to describe a Jewish burial society.

9. Barry Freundel comments on Jewish burial customs in "Cremation Obliterates Ritual," *Moment* 26/4 (August 2001): 61.

10. F. W. Dobb-Allsopp, "Lamentations, Book of," in *Eerdmans Dictionary of the Bible*, ed. D. N. Freedman (Grand Rapids: Eerdmans, 2000), 785.

nineth day of Av (Tisha be-Av), the fifth month (variously, about June to August). This observance commemorates the days between the first breaching of the walls of Jerusalem in 586 B.C. to the subsequent destruction of the temple. Marriages and haircuts are forbidden during these three weeks. The nine days of Av are observed with special intensity: meat and wine are forbidden except on the Sabbath, the blessing of the New Moon is omitted, and prophecies of doom from Jeremiah and Isaiah are read in the synagogue on the three Sabbaths that fall within this period. The period ends with a twenty-four-hour fast.

Lament and memory of the past in the celebration of anniversaries are a way of honoring those who have gone before, who have enabled life to be what it is in the present. It is a way of dealing with the continuous change in life, with death that relentlessly confronts the living. It is one aspect of expressing the hope that lies before us, the knowledge that whatever are the losses of the past, life goes on.

It is said that those who lose all their possessions lose a lot, those who lose their friends lose a lot more, and those who lose hope have lost everything. The exiles have lost their possessions and were separated from many of their friends, but they never lose hope. Their memory of the Exile is one expression of the faithfulness of God—and implicitly therefore hope in the faithfulness of God for the future.

Appendix A:

The Greek Text of Kings

THE GREEK TRANSLATION OF KINGS has a different compositional arrangement than that known in the Masoretic text (Hebrew) used in English translation. In Old Greek versions of Kings, the division between Samuel and Kings was made after the summary of David's reign (1 Kings 2:11). This observation was first made by H. St. John Thackeray in his study of the Greek text of Kings.[1] He demonstrated that 2 Samuel 11:2 to 1 Kings 2:11 are a distinct translation from the rest of Samuel and Kings. The second section in which this distinct translation is taken up with the same thoroughness is 1 Kings 22 through 2 Kings. The chapter sequence of the Greek translation has 1 Kings 21 preceding chapter 20; the story of Naboth's vineyard follows immediately the account of Elijah in his struggle against Baal (1 Kings 17–19). The account of the Aramean wars follows (1 Kings 20), and the account of the oracle of Micaiah (1 Kings 22) is a transition to events that involve Jehoshaphat and the descendants of Ahab.

With the discovery of the Dead Sea Scrolls, Dominique Barthélemy was able to show that these sections of Samuel and Kings were a revision of the Old Greek done in the first century before Christ.[2] The first section was a logical choice for the revision (currently referred to as *kaige*-Theodotion), as it began with the account of the house of David and ended with a summary of his reign. The second revision dealt with the demise of the nations of Israel and Judah following the corrupting influence of Baal worship in Israel, which nearly came to be the state religion of Judah as well under the power of Athaliah, daughter of Ahab.

A second peculiarity of the Greek translation of Kings is the presence of two lengthy miscellanies in the introduction to the reign of Solomon. The first is found after 1 Kings 2:35 (enumerated 35[a-k]), the second after 2:46 (enumerated 46[a-l]). Each miscellany begins with a statement of Solomon's wisdom, and each uses the sands of the seashore as a simile: the first for Solomon's wisdom, and the second to describe the numbers of Israel. This seems to imply that the wisdom of Solomon equaled that of all Israel.

---

1. See H. St. John Thackeray, "The Greek Translators of the Four Books of Kings," *JTS* 8 (1907): 262–78.

2. See *Les devanciers d'Aquila: Première publication intégrale du texte des fragments du dodécaprophéton* (VTSup 10; Leiden: Brill, 1963), 141.

The first miscellany deals with Solomon in his building activities, the second with his government, administration, and supplies. They are incorporated into the main text of Kings as part of the ordering and interpretation of the book. They are collections of alternative translations, variant readings, glosses, doublets, and the like, gathered and arranged to present the wisdom of Solomon. In a number of instances the miscellanies contain information known in the Masoretic text of Kings, but otherwise unknown in the Greek text of Kings. The main goal of these miscellanies seems to be a systematic attempt to make midrashic capital out of textual variants and in so doing to present Solomon as a pious and good king.[3] They appear to be the product of an alternate school of thought on certain leading figures in Kings.

---

3. For a full study of the miscellanies see D. W. Gooding, *Relics of Ancient Exegesis: A Study of the Miscellanies in 3 Reigns 2* (Cambridge: Cambridge Univ. Press, 1976).

Appendix B:

The Chronology of Kings

ONE OF THE IMPORTANT ISSUES in understanding the state of Israel and Judah in relation to international affairs is chronology. Historical relationships can only be understood in the framework of correlating sequences of events. Horn refers to chronology as the "skeleton of history."[1] The complicated synchronisms given in the regnal records of Kings cannot be understood apart from an absolute chronology that correlates events. The purpose of this appendix is not to provide a complete chronology of Kings; many have been attempted, with little consensus on acceptable methods of dealing with conflicting data. This appendix provides an outline of the issues and the means by which fixed dates can be obtained. With some exceptions, the commentary follows the dating system of Edwin Thiele as a useful means of dealing with the data of Kings. This appendix uses the end of the Omride dynasty as the means for correlating events in Kings with other historical records.

An absolute chronology for Assyria and Egypt can be established by correlating recorded events with astrological data.[2] Mesopotamian chronology in Julian years is established on the basis of lists of officials, royal annals, and king lists that can be corroborated with astronomical information. An eclipse of the sun noted in the month of Simanu during the year of an official named Pur-Sagale in the ninth year of King Assurdan III has been astronomically calculated as being June 15, 763 B.C. This provides a chronological scheme for Assyrian history to the year 648 B.C. This is corroborated and supplemented by the Alexandrian scholar Ptolemy (A.D. 70–161), who used annals and astronomical observations to provide a chronology from 747 B.C. to the Roman imperial period. His *Almagest* provides over eighty solar, lunar, and planetary positions that have been verified by modern astronomers. The dates of the Neo-Babylonian kings have been established on the basis of business documents.[3] This provides an absolute chronology within which known events may be put in context.

There is considerable difficulty in knowing how to relate the confusing dates of Kings to this chronology. Many historians simply abandon any

---

1. Siegfried H. Horn, "From Bishop Ussher to Edwin R. Thiele," *AUSS* 18 (1980): 37.

2. Edwin R. Thiele, *The Mysterious Numbers of the Hebrew Kings* (Grand Rapids: Zondervan, 1983), 67–72.

3. R. A. Parker and W. H. Dubberstein, *Babylonian Chronology 626 B.C.–A.D. 45*, 2nd ed. (Studies in Ancient Oriental Civilization 24; Chicago: Univ. of Chicago Press, 1946), 9–10.

---

attempt to understand the Kings numbers and work out an approximate scheme. Bright follows the chronology of Albright,[4] Hayes and Miller adopt a similar approximate system.[5] There are many problems understanding a relative chronology within Kings, as there are many inconsistencies readily observable (e.g., 1 Kings 16:23, 29). Thiele has worked out a system that seeks to correlate all the internal data of Kings, but is also compatible with known events.[6] This system accounts for the data in a manner sufficient to suggest that certain basic presuppositions are correct and is probably the best way to correlate Assyrian and biblical history.[7] Ahlström accepts the fundamental premises of Thiele but is much more cautious in assigning exact dates in the absence of correlating evidence.[8] The system of Thiele has the advantage of taking the biblical numbers seriously as preserved from ancient sources. The complication of the system is scarcely a valid criticism, since chronology is by nature a complicated matter.

The system of Thiele involves a number of inferences about the chronological records preserved in Kings. Some historians find these unacceptable, but they make perfectly good sense in the chronological system of Kings. One of the most important is that of coregencies, in which rulership was temporarily shared between two kings. In some cases a king, because of war or illness, appointed his son to rule while he was still on the throne. Without coregencies the total lengths of reigns in Kings become much too high.

Another related inference is that of dual dating. Beginning at 1 Kings 15:1 the accession of each king of Israel or Judah is given as a synchronism with the regnal years of the other kingdom. In dual dating the date of accession is given as the beginning of the sole reign, but the total years include both the coregency and the sole kingship.

There are two further complications. The first is the month of the new year when the reign of a king officially began. This could be either in the spring (the month of Nisan) or the fall (the month of Tishri). The second complication is how to count the portion of the year in which a king came to rule before the beginning of the official year. This may be counted as a full year in the total (nonaccession system), so a single year is actually counted in the total reigns of both kings. If the partial year is distinguished as an accession year, the total includes only the complete years of reign. Both systems were used at different times.

---

4. John Bright, *A History of Israel*, 3rd ed. (Philadelphia: Westminster, 1981), 229.

5. J. Maxwell Miller and John H. Hayes, *A History of Ancient Israel and Judah* (Philadelphia: Westminster, 1986), 220–21, 226–27.

6. Thiele, *Mysterious Numbers of the Hebrew Kings*, 43–65.

7. William W. Hallo, "From Qarqar to Carchemish: Assyria and Israel in the Light of New Discoveries," *Biblical Archaeologist Reader* 2 (1964): 153.

8. Ahlström, *The History of Ancient Palestine*, 562–63.

The reign of Ahab is a critical starting point for establishing the dates of the kings in Israel and Judah. The Assyrian Monolith Inscription places Ahab at the Assyrian battle against the coalition of Aramaean kings at Qarqar in 853.[9] The usurper Jehu, who annihilated the Omride dynasty (2 Kings 10:11), is named on the Black Obelisk, which can be dated to 841.[10] The two-year reign of Ahaziah son of Ahab (1 Kings 22:52) and the twelve-year reign of Joram son of Ahab (2 Kings 3:1) fit in this period, indicating that the twenty-two year reign of Ahab (1 Kings 16:29) must have ended in 853. Part of the twelve-year reign of Omri (v. 23) was shared with Tibni, because Israel was temporarily divided into two parts, half following Tibni and half following Omri (vv. 21–22). Following the principle of dual dating, the sole rule of Omri began in the thirty-first year of Asa (v. 23), but the total rule began in the twenty-seventh year of Asa at the revolt of Zimri (v. 15). The two-year reign of Elah (v. 8) began in the twenty-sixth year of Asa. Baasha reigned twenty-four years beginning in the third year of Asa (15:33). The two-year reign of Nadab (v. 25) began in the second year of Asa. The reign of Jeroboam lasted twenty-two years (14:20). This chronological data places the division of the kingdom in 930. This "skeleton of history" is critical to provide a correct historical context for the events narrated in Kings.

Following the principle of non-accession year dating in Israelite records, in which each king is assigned an extra year, the following chart shows the chronology of Israel calculated from the absolute dates of the Omride dynasty and going back to Jeroboam.

Joram	852–841	(12 years)[11]
Ahaziah	853–852	(2 years)
Ahab	874–853	(22 years)
Omri	885–874	(12 years)
Tibni	885–880	(5 years)
Elah	886–885	(2 years)
Baasha	908–886	(24 years)[12]
Nadab	909–908	(2 years)
Jeroboam	930–908	(22 years)

9. Pritchard, *An Anthology of Texts and Pictures*, 188–92.

10. Ibid., plates 100A, 100B. For a description or the Black Obelisk and a translation of the Jehu portion, see Mitchell, *The Bible in the British Museum*, 46–49.

11. Beginning with the fixed dates of the sons of Ahab, the date of the division of the kingdom can be established with a fair degree of accuracy.

12. Baasha appears to have one year too many because the beginning of the years of the ancient calendars do not correlate to the Julian calendar. A solution is to indicate both

The synchronisms of Kings make possible an absolute dating of the kings of Judah as well. Since Judah used the accession year method of dating, the years of a reign given in Kings are the actual totals. Rehoboam reigned seventeen years after the division of the kingdom (14:21). Abijah reigned three years with his first official year beginning in the eighteenth year of Jeroboam (15:1–2). The accession year of the long reign of Asa began in the twentieth year of Jeroboam (15:9), his first official year in the twenty-first year of Jeroboam. The following is the chronology of Judah from Rehoboam to Asa.

Rehoboam	930–913	(17 years)
Abijah	913–910	(3 years)
Asa	910–869	(41 years)

The synchronisms for the end of the Omride dynasty (Ahaziah and Joram) with Jehoshaphat, king of Judah and successor to Asa, are complicated by double synchronisms for the beginning of the reign of Jehoram son of Jehoshaphat. According to the Masoretic text, Jehoshaphat came to reign in the fourth year of Ahab (1 Kings 22:41), so that his twenty-five year reign extended into the fifth year of Joram, son of Ahab (2 Kings 8:16).[13] This chronology accounts for Jehoshaphat being present in the battle against Moab during the time of Joram son of Ahab (2 Kings 3:1–27). However, Jehoram was already in the second year of his reign when Ahaziah son of Ahab died (2 Kings 1:17). A second synchronism states that Jehoram son of Jehoshaphat began to reign in the fifth year of Joram son of Ahab when Jehoshapat was still king (2 Kings 8:16). According to the Masoretic text, Jehoshaphat appointed his son Jehoram as king during the reign of Ahab and before the battle against Moab. The sole rule of Jehoram began only in the fifth year of the reign of Joram son of Ahab. The reign of Jehoshaphat did extend into the reign of Joram son of Ahab, which explains his presence at the battle of Moab.

The Old Greek (Lucian) follows a different chronological scheme with the dating of Jehoshaphat, beginning his twenty-five year reign earlier, in the eleventh year of Omri, so his reign ends during the time of Ahaziah. The Old Greek chronology excludes Jehoshaphat from involvement with Joram in the battle against Moab (2 Kings 3). In the Old Greek account, all refer-

---

years involved in the Julian calendar (e.g., 909/908), but for the sake of simplicity only one year is given for each reference. Thiele shows the pattern in detailed charts: *Mysterious Numbers of the Hebrew Kings*, 82.

13. Ahab reigned twenty-two years (1 Kings 16:29) and his son Ahaziah just over one in non-accession year reckoning (22:52), so the twenty-five year reign of Jehoshaphat extended to the fifth year of Ahab's son Joram.

ences to the king of Judah in the battle against Moab are rendered anonymously. In the regnal summary (3:1), the Old Greek says only that Joram son of Ahab reigned in Israel twelve years. However, the chronology of the Masoretic text with its assumption of coregency of Jehoram with Jehoshaphat is consistent.

There are several difficulties with the synchronisms between the dynasty of Jehu and the kings of Judah. The synchronisms for the reign of Jehoash are bad arithmetic; the thirty-seventh year of Joash of Judah (2 Kings 13:10) does not correspond to a seventeen-year reign of Jehoahaz beginning in the twenty-third year of Joash (13:1), or to the reign of Amaziah his son beginning in the second year of Jehoash of Israel (14:1). The Greek manuscripts variously provide the accession synchronism as the fortieth, thirty-sixth, or thirty-ninth year of Joash. This shows evidence of attempts to provide corrections. Gray accepts the Masoretic text but proposes a two-year coregency of Jehoash with Jehoahaz.[14] Thiele, in a more complex scheme, says that with Jehoash in Israel and with Amaziah of Judah, the records of the kings of Israel and Judah adopted an accession year system of reckoning.[15] Jehoahaz had only sixteen actual years (under the non-accession year numbers), and with Israel beginning its year earlier than Judah in the month of Nisan, the beginning of the sixteenth year of Jehoahaz was in the thirty-seventh year of Joash, as the Hebrew text has it. The death of Jehoahaz according to the biblical chronology occurred in 798 B.C. This allows twenty-seven actual years for Jehu and sixteen actual years for Jehoahaz, beginning from the coup of Jehu in 841 B.C.

A twenty-nine year reign of Amaziah beginning in the second year of Jehoash of Israel (2 Kings 14:2) followed by a fifty-two year reign of his successor Azariah (14:21; 15:2) cannot be reconciled with the political events of Assyrian history. The second year of Jehoash of Israel would have been 796 B.C., if a switch to accession year reckoning is assumed.[16] The accession year of Jehoash began in 798 B.C., so his second year coincided with the end of the actual thirty-nine year reign of Joash of Judah (835–796 B.C.). The advancements of Tiglath-Pileser III into Israel took place from 743–738 B.C., at the very end of the life of Azariah, when Pekah of Israel was already on the throne (15:19, 27, 29; cf. Isa. 6:1; 7:1).

Only two solutions are possible; the number of years assigned to Amaziah must be significantly reduced, or a coregency with Azariah must be allowed. Assuming the text is correct, the total of fifty-two years for Azariah includes

---

14. Gray, *I & II Kings*, 597.
15. Thiele, *The Mysterious Numbers of the Hebrew Kings*, 105–6.
16. For the calculation see ibid., 106–9.

the time of his coregency with Amaziah; his accession synchronism (2 Kings 15:1) indicates the beginning of his sole rule (an example of dual dating). It appears that Azariah was placed on the throne as regent after Amaziah's defeat at Beth Shemesh and the raid by Jehoash on Jerusalem (14:13), with Amaziah remaining as a titular king. This would further explain the notice that Azariah lived (but did not reign) for fifteen years after the death of Jehoash (v. 17). The sixteen-year reign of Jehoash of Israel ended in 781 B.C., and the twenty-nine years of Amaziah ended in 767 B.C. Amaziah continued to live in Jerusalem until a conspiracy forced him to flee to Lachish, where he was assassinated.

The data for the northern kingdom would indicate a lengthy coregency between Jehoash and Jeroboam. The synchronisms leave a gap of twelve or thirteen years between Amaziah and Azariah of Judah if there is no coregency. Jeroboam came to reign in the fifteenth year of Amaziah (14:23), who reigned for fourteen more years (14:2). The reign of Azariah, successor to Amaziah, did not begin until the twenty-seventh year of Jeroboam (15:1). Since there is no mention of such an "interregnum," it can only be concluded that the Deuteronomistic Historians did not understand there to be one. The synchronism for Jeroboam marks the year of his accession as sole ruler. Amaziah came to rule in the second year of Jehoash of Israel (14:1), calculated above to be 796 B.C.; the fifteenth year of Amaziah was 782/781 B.C. The sole reign of Azariah began with the end of the reign of Amaziah fifteen years later (767 B.C.). That was the twenty-seventh year of the total reign of Jeroboam (15:1), so the beginning of his coregency can be calculated to be 793 B.C.[17] Jeroboam was on the throne for twelve years before the death of his father (782 B.C.), and his forty-one year reign (14:23) continued for fourteen years after the sole reign of Azariah began (767 B.C.). Amos began to prophesy near the end of his reign (Amos 1:1). Jeroboam was succeeded by Zechariah in 753 B.C. (2 Kings 15:8); that was the thirty-eighth year of Azariah. Azariah reigned fifty-two years (15:2), from 792 B.C. to 740 B.C.

The synchronisms for Ahaz are not easy to reconcile. Ahaz is said to have begun to reign in the seventeenth year of Pekah (16:1), a correlation that indicates Pekah had a rival reign in the Transjordan during the twelve-year reign of Menahem.[18] However, the synchronism that begins the reign of Hoshea in the twelfth year of Ahaz (2 Kings 17:1) cannot be reconciled with the state-

---

17. The chronological data of this period is extremely difficult, but allowing for coregency these biblical data "are actually amazingly accurate and constitute and extremely valuable source for bringing to light many interesting and important details of Hebrew history" (ibid., 114). For detailed calculations of this period see 105–18.

18. The reign of Pekah began in 752 B.C., just after the death of Jeroboam II; Ahaz began to reign in 735 B.C.

ment that Hoshea assassinated Pekah and began to reign in the twentieth year of Jotham (15:30).[19] The nine-year reign of Hoshea came to an end with the fall of Samaria in 723 B.C., so he must have begun in the year 732 B.C.

Various proposals have been made to resolve these conflicting data.[20] One solution is to emend the text, as proposed by Gray; Hoshea came to rule in the second year of Ahaz rather than the twelfth (17:1).[21] A textual error of ten years may have occurred when the number was indicated by a cipher. Alternately, Ahaz may have been adopted as coregent with Jotham during those unsettled times; Tiglath-Pileser may have accorded him some recognition of authority, which north Israelite records counted as his formal accession.[22] This served as the synchronism for the reign of Hoshea; Ahaz began to reign as coregent in 743 B.C.

A second issue in the data of Ahaz is that he was twenty years old when he began to reign, that he reigned for sixteen years (16:2), and his son Hezekiah was twenty-five years old when he began to reign (18:2). This would mean that Hezekiah was born when Ahaz was eleven, an unlikely age to become a father. If a coregency of Ahaz began ten years before his sixteen-year reign, then Ahaz was about thirty when his sixteen-year reign began; in that case he became a father at a more realistic age of twenty-one. While this may explain the chronological data, the statement of the text would suggest that Ahaz was twenty when his sixteen-year rule began. There appear to be several chronologies for the reign of Ahaz, a likely result of Assyrian interference and the political conflicts of the times.

Particularly difficult problems are associated with the end of Israel and the reign of Hezekiah. According to Kings, the Assyrians destroyed Samaria

---

19. Jotham reigned from 750–735 B.C., though he continued to live to his twentieth year (732 B.C.).

20. Thiele thinks that the editors of kings made a twelve-year error in calculation, because they did not realize the reign of Pekah overlapped that of Menahem and Pekahiah (*Mysterious Numbers of the Hebrew Kings*, 134–37). For a review of various chronological proposals see Konkel, "Hezekiah in Biblical Tradition," 30–43. Complex revisions of synchronistic data have been proposed: John McHugh, "The Date of Hezekiah's Birth," *VT* 14 (1964): 446–53; C. Shedl, "Textkritische Bemerkungen zu den Synchronismen de Könige von Israel und Juda," *VT* 12 (1962): 90–93; Antti Laato, "New Viewpoints on the Chronology of the Kings of Judah and Israel," *ZAW* 98 (1986): 210–21.

21. Gray, *I & II Kings*, 68, 641.

22. Harold Steigers: "The Interphased Chronology of Jotham, Ahaz, Hezekiah, and Hoshea," *Bulletin of the Evangelical Theological Society* 9 (1966): 86–87. The sole rule of Ahaz then began after the death of Jotham. Roger Young thinks that two different viewpoints were represented in the chronologies of 2 Kings 15–18, that both were present in the court records and both were preserved by the historians of Kings; "When Was Samaria Captured? The Need for Precision in Biblical Chronologies," *JETS* 47 (2004): 577–95.

---

during the sixth year of Hezekiah (2 Kings 18:10). Based on Assyrian records, the destruction of Samaria took place in 723 B.C., placing the ascension of Hezekiah in 727/726 B.C. This is in accordance with the statement that Hezekiah began to rule in the third year of Hoshea (2 Kings 18:1), the last king of Israel, who ruled for nine years (cf. 17:1). A second synchronism states that Sennacherib attacked Jerusalem in the fourteenth year of Hezekiah (18:13); on the basis of specific Assyrian records, this siege must be dated to 701 B.C. According to this second synchronism, Hezekiah ascended to the throne in 715 B.C. The clarity of the data in relation to the reign of Hezekiah and the Assyrian attacks against Samaria and Jerusalem is a compelling reason to accept a coregency for Hezekiah that began during the reign of Hoshea; his sole rule began in 715 B.C., a well-established anchor point in establishing the chronology for the last kings of Judah. Other approaches to the problem are to dismiss the synchronism with the Israelite kingdom, to emend those synchronisms, or to regard the datum of the siege in the fourteenth year as an errant calculation.[23] All of these proposals are more problematic than coregency.

The problems of chronology in the Hebrew Bible continue to be examined. A number of studies have appeared in the last fifteen years that may be noted for further reference:

Barnes, W. H. *Studies in the Chronology of the Divided Monarchy of Israel.* HSM 48; Atlanta: Scholars Press, 1991.

Becking, B. "Chronology: A Skeleton without Flesh? Sennacherib's Campaign as a Case Study." Pages 46–72 in *'Like a Bird in a Cage': The Invasion of Sennacherib in 701 B.C.E.* Ed. L. L. Grabbe. JSOTSup 363. Sheffield: Sheffield Academic Press/Continuum, 2003.

Galil, G. *The Chronology of the Kings of Israel and Judah.* Studies in the History and Culture of the Ancient Near East 9. Leiden: Brill, 1996.

Goldberg, J. "Two Assyrian Campaigns against Hezekiah and Later Eighth Century Biblical Chronology." *Bib* 80 (1999): 315–36.

Hayes, J. H. "The Beginning of the Regnal Year in Israel and Judah." In *The Land That I Will Show You: Essays on the History and Archaeology of the Ancient Near East in Honor of J. Maxwell Miller.* Ed. J. A. Dearman and M. P. Graham. JSOTSup 343. Sheffield: Sheffield Academic Press, 2001.

Hooker, P. K. "The Year of Josiah's Death: 609 or 610 B.C.E.?" Pages 96–103 in *The Land That I Will Show You: Essays on the History and Archaeology of the Ancient Near East in Honor of J. Maxwell Miller.* Ed. J. A. Dearman and M. P. Graham. JSOTSup 343. Sheffield: Sheffield Academic Press, 2001.

---

23. For a summary discussion see Andrew G. Vaughn, *Theology, History, and Archaeology in the Chronicler's Account of Hezekiah* (Atlanta: Scholar's Press, 1999), 7–14.

Hughes, J. R. A. *Secrets of the Times: Myth and History in Biblical Chronology*. JSOT-Sup 115. Sheffield: Sheffield Academic Press, 1990.

Kelle, B. E. "'Hoshea, Sargon and the Final Destruction of Samaria: A Response to M. Christine Tetley with a View towards Method." *SJOT* 17 (2003): 226–44.

McFall, L. "A Translation Guide to the Chronological Data in Kings and Chronicles." *BSac* 148 (1991): 3–45.

Naʾaman, N. "The Historical Background to the Conquest of Samaria (720 B.C.)." *Bib* 71 (1990): 206–25.

Tetley, M. C. *The Reconstructed Chronology of the Divided Kingdom*. Winona Lake, Ind.: Eisenbrauns, 2004.

Scripture Index

Subject Index

Subject Index

Josephus, 19, 97, 120, 267, 317, 383–85, 397, 412, 454, 501, 603, 604, 620–21, 644–45
Joshua, 103
Josiah, 35–36, 633–46
Judaism, 309–10, 581–84, 669–70
judgment, 331–36
justice, 190–93, 287, 346, 539–41

kingdom of God, 559–61
kings, and God's will, 357–60

Lacau, Pierre, 204
Leibniz, G. W., 650
Lewis, C. S., 312–13
liberalism, 364–65
Lisbon earthquake of 1755, 650
Luther, Martin, 283, 374–75, 389, 517
LXX, *see* Septuagint

market (stock market), 313–14
Marx, Karl, 214
mammon, 314–15
Manasseh, 620–27
materialism, 306–8, 312–17, 588–89; philosophical materialism, 312–13
martyrdom, 494, 506, 613
Mengistu Haile Mariam, 508
Menno Simons, 519
Mephibosheth, 666
mercy, 336, 435, 538–39, 541–42
Meserete Kristos Church (Ethiopia), 508
Mesha, 392–94
Micaiah, 351–54
miracles, 419, 421–23, 455
missions (Christian), 463–66
Moab, 392–94, 396–99, 402
Moore, Michael, 357
Moses, 103, 302–3, 308–9, 311–12, 617–18
Mount Carmel, 299
Mugabe, Robert, 627–28
Müntzer, Thomas, 71–73
mysticism, 361

Naaman, 427–36, 441
Naboth, 339–42
name theology, 180–83, 329–31, 399–400, 656–57
Naram-Sin, 254–55
Nathan, 53–55, 61–62

National Prayer Breakfast, 89
Ncube, Pius (Archbishop of Matabeleland, Zimbabwe), 437
Nebuchadnezzar, 653–56, 663–65
Neufeld, Dietrich, 659
New Yorker, 259
number schemes, 136–37, 220, 302, 304

Obadiah, 298–99
Old Greek (translation of the Old Testament), 55, 58, 77, 95, 355, 368, 370, 644, 671–72, 676–77
Omri, 21, 271–73, 278–80
Origen, 20
Ortberg, John, 228–29

Park, Harold, 561
Passover, 638, 647
pastoral work, 256–57
Peasant's Revolt, 71–72
Peter, 386–88
politics; the church and political power, 281–84; political activism, 71–74
postmodernism, 256–57
Potok, Chaim, 152
prayer, 361–62
priesthood; priests in ancient Israel, 358
"promise to David," 60–67, 103–5, 182–83, 203, 223, 503–5, 557–58, 567–68, 667–68
prophecy, 27–29, 222–23, 244–46, 249, 251–52, 257, 326–27, 351–54, 357–59, 382–85, 395–96, 476, 527, 536–37, 568–69, 639–40
prosperity gospel, 107–8, 149, 210
prostitution, 81–83, 90–91; shrine prostitutes, 247

Queen of Sheba, 201–4
Qumran, 581–83, 586–88

Recabites, 480–81
reconciliation, 287
Rehoboam, 240–42, 247
religion, 288; religion and government (religious freedom), 363–65, 375–76
rest theology, 183–85
Riley, Bob, 109
rituals, 159–61, 185, 300
Romero, Oscar, 493–94
Russian revolution, 344–45, 658–59

Author Index

Author Index